Considerations of Territorial Planning, Space, and Economic Activity in the Global Economy

Helmuth Yesid Arias Gomez
Masaryk Institute of Advanced Studies (MIAS), Czech Technical University in Prague, Czech Republic

Gabriela Antošová
Institute of Education and Communication, Czech University of Life Sciences in Prague, Czech Republic

A volume in the Advances in Finance, Accounting, and Economics (AFAE) Book Series

Published in the United States of America by
    IGI Global
    Business Science Reference (an imprint of IGI Global)
    701 E. Chocolate Avenue
    Hershey PA, USA 17033
    Tel: 717-533-8845
    Fax: 717-533-8661
    E-mail: cust@igi-global.com
    Web site: http://www.igi-global.com

Library of Congress Cataloging-in-Publication Data

Names: Arias Gomez, Helmuth Yesid, 1972- editor. | Antošová, Gabriela,
  1983- editor.
Title: Considerations of territorial planning, space, and economic activity
  in the global economy / Helmuth Yesid Arias Gomez, and Gabriela
  Antosova, editors.
Description: Hershey, PA : Business Science Reference, [2023] | Includes
  bibliographical references and index. | Summary: "This book studies the
  intersectionality of territory and economy that requires an analysis to
  propose a set of solutions in terms of sustainability and feasible
  strategies of public policy presenting a diversity of approaches,
  theories, and experiences amid an international and multicultural
  effort"-- Provided by publisher.
Identifiers: LCCN 2022039766 (print) | LCCN 2022039767 (ebook) | ISBN
  9781668459768 (hardcover) | ISBN 9781668459775 (paperback) | ISBN
  9781668459782 (ebook)
Subjects: LCSH: Sustainable development. | International economic
  relations. | Interregionalism.
Classification: LCC HC79.E5 C6176 2023 (print) | LCC HC79.E5 (ebook) |
  DDC 338.9/27--dc23/eng/20221207
LC record available at https://lccn.loc.gov/2022039766
LC ebook record available at https://lccn.loc.gov/2022039767

This book is published in the IGI Global book series Advances in Finance, Accounting, and Economics (AFAE) (ISSN: 2327-5677; eISSN: 2327-5685)

British Cataloguing in Publication Data
A Cataloguing in Publication record for this book is available from the British Library.

For electronic access to this publication, please contact: eresources@igi-global.com.

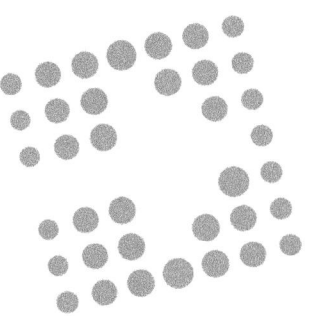

Advances in Finance, Accounting, and Economics (AFAE) Book Series

Ahmed Driouchi
Al Akhawayn University, Morocco

ISSN:2327-5677
EISSN:2327-5685

MISSION

In our changing economic and business environment, it is important to consider the financial changes occurring internationally as well as within individual organizations and business environments. Understanding these changes as well as the factors that influence them is crucial in preparing for our financial future and ensuring economic sustainability and growth.

The **Advances in Finance, Accounting, and Economics (AFAE)** book series aims to publish comprehensive and informative titles in all areas of economics and economic theory, finance, and accounting to assist in advancing the available knowledge and providing for further research development in these dynamic fields.

COVERAGE

- Economic Indices and Quantitative Economic Methods
- Economics of Agriculture and Biotechnology
- Wages and Employment
- Corporate Finance
- Comparative Accounting Systems
- Economic Theory
- Ethics in Accounting and Finance
- Statistical Analysis
- Economics of Innovation and Knowledge
- Taxes

IGI Global is currently accepting manuscripts for publication within this series. To submit a proposal for a volume in this series, please contact our Acquisition Editors at Acquisitions@igi-global.com or visit: http://www.igi-global.com/publish/.

Titles in this Series

For a list of additional titles in this series, please visit: www.igi-global.com/book-series

Advanced Machine Learning Algorithms for Complex Financial Applications
Mohammad Irfan (CMR Institute of Technology, India) Mohamed Elhoseny (American University in the Emirates, UAE) Salina Kassim (International Islamic University of Malaysia, Malaysia) and Noura Metawa (University of Sharjah, UAE)
Engineering Science Reference • © 2023 • 292pp • H/C (ISBN: 9781668444832) • US $270.00

Exploring the Dark Side of FinTech and Implications of Monetary Policy
Sheraz Ahmed (LUT University, Finland) John Agyekum Addae (LUT University, Finland & Ghana Communication Technology University, Ghana) and Kwame Simpe Ofori (International University of Grand-Bassam, Côte d'Ivoire & University of Electronic Science and Technology of China, China)
Business Science Reference • © 2023 • 300pp • H/C (ISBN: 9781668463819) • US $250.00

Blockchain Applications in Cryptocurrency for Technological Evolution
Atour Taghipour (Normandy University, France)
Business Science Reference • © 2023 • 308pp • H/C (ISBN: 9781668462478) • US $250.00

The Past, Present, and Future of Accountancy Education and Professions
Nina T. Dorata (St. John's University, USA) Richard C. Jones (Hofstra University, USA) Jennifer Mensche (St. Joseph's College, USA) and Mark M. Ulrich (CUNY Queensborough Community College, USA)
Business Science Reference • © 2023 • 300pp • H/C (ISBN: 9781668454831) • US $215.00

Handbook of Research on Changing World Economic Order in the Post-Pandemic Period
Sushanta Kumar Mahapatra (IBS Hyderabad, The ICFAI Foundation for Higher Education, India) and Vishal Sarin (Lovely Professional University, India)
Business Science Reference • © 2023 • 470pp • H/C (ISBN: 9781799868965) • US $325.00

Handbook of Research on Artificial Intelligence and Knowledge Management in Asia's Digital Economy
Patricia Ordóñez de Pablos (The University of Oviedo, Spain) Xi Zhang (Tianjin University, China) and Mohammad Nabil Almunawar (Universiti Brunei Darussalam, Brunei)
Business Science Reference • © 2023 • 531pp • H/C (ISBN: 9781668458495) • US $295.00

Future Outlooks on Corporate Finance and Opportunities for Robust Economic Planning
Siraj Kariyilaparambu Kunjumuhammed (Modern College of Business and Science, Oman) and Nithya Ramachandran (University of Technology and Applied Science, Oman)
Business Science Reference • © 2023 • 335pp • H/C (ISBN: 9781668453421) • US $240.00

701 East Chocolate Avenue, Hershey, PA 17033, USA
Tel: 717-533-8845 x100 • Fax: 717-533-8661
E-Mail: cust@igi-global.com • www.igi-global.com

Table of Contents

Foreword xvi

Preface xviii

Acknowledgment xxii

Section 1
Introduction

Chapter 1
Space and Production Specialization 1
Helmuth Yesid Arias-Gomez, Masaryk Institute of Advanced Studies (MIAS), Czech
Technical University in Prague, Czech Republic

Section 2
Ukraine: Looking at the Future

Chapter 2
Startup Ecosystem as the Basis of Enterpreneurship Development: Regional Aspects 18
Olena Dymchenko, O.M. Beketov National University of Urban Economy in Kharkiv, Ukraine
Valentyna Smachylo, O.M. Beketov National University of Urban Economy in Kharkiv, Ukraine
Olha Rudachenko, O.M. Beketov National University of Urban Economy in Kharkiv, Ukraine
Natalia Dril, O.M. Beketov National University of Urban Economy in Kharkiv, Ukraine

Chapter 3
Educating Competitive Professionals: A Requirement of the Modern Urban Economy 47
Olena Lvivna Ilienko, O.M. Beketov National University of Urban Economy in Kharkiv, Ukraine
Oksana Oleksiivna Rezvan, O.M. Beketov National University of Urban Economy in Kharkiv,
Ukraine

Section 3
Europe: The Strength of Economic Integration

Chapter 4

Towards Places and Ecosystems: The Integrated Management of Locations, Destinations, and the Living Space 70

Julian Philipp, Catholic University of Eichstätt-Ingolstadt, Germany
Harald Pechlaner, Catholic University of Eichstätt-Ingolstadt, Germany

Chapter 5

Project Management and Changes in Inbound Tourism to the Czech Republic: A Case Study of Germans Incoming During the Coronavirus Crisis 94

Gabriela Antošová, Institute of Education and Communication, Czech University of Life Sciences in Prague, Czech Republic
Karel Němejc, Institute of Education and Communication, Czech University of Life Sciences in Prague, Czech Republic

Chapter 6

Rural Districts: Application of the Core-Periphery Model to Rural Development 107

Juan Sebastián Castillo-Valero, University of Castilla-La Mancha, Spain
Maria Carmen García-Cortijo, University of Castilla-La Mancha, Spain

Chapter 7

Cultural Heritage and Its Impact on Territorial Development: The Case of Spain 116

Jesús Heredia-Carroza, University of Seville, Spain
Ignacio Martínez-Fernández, University of Seville, Spain
Luis Antonio Palma-Martos, University of Seville, Spain

Chapter 8

Geographical Preconditions of the International Controversies Around the Turów Mine 126

Artur Boháč, Technical University of Liberec, Czech Republic
Ewa Łaźniewska, Poznań University of Economics and Business, Poland
Joanna Kurowska-Pysz, WSB University in Dąbrowa Górnicza, Poland

Chapter 9

Innovative Potential of Regions: Accelerator of Sustainability and Development 147

Vojtech Kollár, Bratislava University of Economics and Management, Slovakia
Silvia Matúšová, Bratislava University of Economics and Management, Slovakia

Chapter 10

Common Assessment Framework in the Czech Republic Public Sector: Main Issues for the Czech Republic Regions and Municipalities 168

Jan Procházka, Czech Technical University in Prague, Czech Republic

Section 4
Turkey: The Door to Europe and Asia

Chapter 11
Regional Growth Model With Spatial Externalities 183
Merve Baysoy, Istanbul Bilgi University, Turkey

Chapter 12
Evaluating Different Growth Strategies: The Case of Turkey 205
Adem Gök, Kirklareli University, Turkey
Deniz Güvercin, University of Lincoln, UK

Chapter 13
Analysis of System Marginal Price in the Turkish Electricity Market 225
Aslı Boru İpek, Kütahya Dumlupınar University, Turkey

Section 5
India: The Potential of a Giant

Chapter 14
Territorial Planning Models in Homestays: An Indian Context 242
Saumya Kapil, Christ University, India
Bindi Varghese, Christ University, India

Section 6
USA: Laying Out Smart Cities

Chapter 15
Smart City in the Global Economy: Information and Organization Support Development 257
Tetiana Momot, Coggin College of Business, USA
Russell Triplett, Coggin College of Business, USA
Angelo Cristian Azueta, Coggin College of Business, USA
Olena Filonych, The Educational and Scientific Institute of Economics and Management,
*   Kharkiv, Ukraine*

Section 7
Latin America: Territory and Natural Resource Abundance

Chapter 16
Analyzing the Spatial Configuration of Agriculture: The Colombian Case 280
Helmuth Yesid Arias-Gomez, Masaryk Institute of Advanced Studies (MIAS), Czech
*   Technical University in Prague, Czech Republic*
Juan Pablo Cely, Pedagogical and Technological University of Colombia, Colombia

Chapter 17
Economic Deglobalization, Regionalism, and Localism Processes Driven by Populism and
Nationalism 298
    José G. Vargas-Hernandez, Instituto Tecnológico Mario Molina, Mexico
    Omar C. Vargas-González, Tecnológico Nacional de México, Ciudad Guzmán, Mexico

Compilation of References 313

About the Contributors 347

Index 354

Detailed Table of Contents

Foreword xvi

Preface xviii

Acknowledgment xxii

Section 1
Introduction

Chapter 1

Space and Production Specialization 1
> *Helmuth Yesid Arias-Gomez, Masaryk Institute of Advanced Studies (MIAS), Czech*
> *Technical University in Prague, Czech Republic*

This chapter overhauls some fundamental theoretical principles commonly consulted when tackling a territorial analysis, and the implications that arise when the economic activity alters the genuine territorial status quo. The discussion will focus on the economic vein of this subject, although this perspective can also incorporate geographical, environmental, and urban approaches, inter alia. The emphasis will be put on the stubborn and ever-present phenomenon of agglomeration of economic activities, in some cases triggered by the exploitation of resources geographically pinpointed, or motivated by the exploitation of economies of scale, pecuniary externalities, or technological spillovers.

Section 2
Ukraine: Looking at the Future

Chapter 2

Startup Ecosystem as the Basis of Enterpreneurship Development: Regional Aspects 18
> *Olena Dymchenko, O.M. Beketov National University of Urban Economy in Kharkiv, Ukraine*
> *Valentyna Smachylo, O.M. Beketov National University of Urban Economy in Kharkiv, Ukraine*
> *Olha Rudachenko, O.M. Beketov National University of Urban Economy in Kharkiv, Ukraine*
> *Natalia Dril, O.M. Beketov National University of Urban Economy in Kharkiv, Ukraine*

StartupBlink displays a map of the startup ecosystem and a research center that works to identify the dynamics of startup ecosystems around the world and help accelerate their growth. For a detailed investigation of the best practices for developing generalized recommendations for the development of the startup ecosystem, it is proposed to group countries, taking into account their rating and the changes that occurred in 2021 compared to 2020. Thus, the section groups countries by 5 clusters of startup ecosystems, which in the future may become the basis for the development of recommendations for business development and the formation of startup ecosystem strategies.

Chapter 3

Educating Competitive Professionals: A Requirement of the Modern Urban Economy......................47

Olena Lvivna Ilienko, O.M. Beketov National University of Urban Economy in Kharkiv, Ukraine
Oksana Oleksiivna Rezvan, O.M. Beketov National University of Urban Economy in Kharkiv, Ukraine

In the chapter the authors proceed from the fact that the processes of economic globalization mainstream the problem of educating and shaping a competitive professional for the urban economy having completely new competencies, skills, and knowledge. The authors have suggested a scientific and methodical system based on understanding "competitiveness" as an integrated concept, and focused on the formation of specific components included in its content, namely: needs-motivational, cognitive-operational, and reflective-evaluative components. It is advocated that the development of these components requires a technological approach associated with a gradual introduction into the training program a number of disciplines with an intensive focus on competitiveness formation. Additionally, the impact of the extracurricular activities such as participating in local and international projects, as well as cooperating with career centers, consultants on the students' competitiveness development has been considered.

Section 3
Europe: The Strength of Economic Integration

Chapter 4

Towards Places and Ecosystems: The Integrated Management of Locations, Destinations, and the Living Space 70

Julian Philipp, Catholic University of Eichstätt-Ingolstadt, Germany
Harald Pechlaner, Catholic University of Eichstätt-Ingolstadt, Germany

Traditionally, locations, destinations, and living spaces have been managed, developed, and marketed separately. However, various global megatrends such as digitalization, globalization, or climate change—as well as changing needs of workers, tourists, or residents—have put these spatial layers in a state of transformation. In the course of this transformation, integrated spatial development and management concepts have emerged over the past two decades, as modern cities need to manage their neighborhoods and living spaces, business locations, leisure and culture offers, and their tourism attractions holistically. Two main development paths are elaborated: place management, and the ecosystem approach.

Chapter 5

Project Management and Changes in Inbound Tourism to the Czech Republic: A Case Study of Germans Incoming During the Coronavirus Crisis 94

Gabriela Antošová, Institute of Education and Communication, Czech University of Life Sciences in Prague, Czech Republic
Karel Němejc, Institute of Education and Communication, Czech University of Life Sciences in Prague, Czech Republic

The aim of this chapter is to introduce current German clientele with regards to inbound tourism to the Czech Republic, and to uncover concrete forms of support of inbound tourism from Germany to the Czech Republic. Content analysis was provided for the quantitative and qualitative secondary data about the inbound German tourism to the Czech Republic for the years 2012-2019. Furthermore, the analysis compares the turnout of separate quarters of the period from 2015 to 2020 with an emphasis on seasonal trends and changes in inbound tourism due to the COVID-19 pandemic and related restrictions. Good results of this source market in the Czech Republic's inbound tourism are usually taken for granted due to its size and geographical proximity; however, the implications of the pandemic are reflected not only on tourist arrivals from Germany but also on their support, which is implemented in relation to the German market by selected entities at all levels of tourism management in the Czech Republic, and also some private entities.

Chapter 6
Rural Districts: Application of the Core-Periphery Model to Rural Development 107
Juan Sebastián Castillo-Valero, University of Castilla-La Mancha, Spain
Maria Carmen García-Cortijo, University of Castilla-La Mancha, Spain

This work introduces an original methodology for analysing the role of intra-rural population movements in the formation or consolidation of rural districts. For this purpose, the authors adapted Rosen's hedonic models, developed in other areas of the economy, to explain individual decisions in rural migration dynamics. The methodology was drawn up to explain population movements in rural areas, on a sub-regional scale, as a new centre-periphery dynamic. Empirical application of this methodology in the future might be useful for better explaining sub-regional dynamics and for the design of territorial development policies.

Chapter 7
Cultural Heritage and Its Impact on Territorial Development: The Case of Spain 116
Jesús Heredia-Carroza, University of Seville, Spain
Ignacio Martínez-Fernández, University of Seville, Spain
Luis Antonio Palma-Martos, University of Seville, Spain

Within the cultural sector, cultural heritage presents a series of interesting features for the territorial development of the local and regional Economy. This sector presents a prevalence of wage employment and a larger size of business establishments than the rest of the services sector. While small companies and micro-companies predominate in the services sector with 99,4% in 2019, for companies related to cultural heritage, the weight of companies with less than 50 employees does not reach 97.3% for this year. Also, it is essential to highlight the legacy value that makes cultural heritage endure over time for future generations to enjoy it; it also creates awareness and territorial roots of the populations, and, finally, is a fundamental asset for tourism and branding of the territories.

Chapter 8
Geographical Preconditions of the International Controversies Around the Turów Mine 126
Artur Boháč, Technical University of Liberec, Czech Republic
Ewa Łaźniewska, Poznań University of Economics and Business, Poland
Joanna Kurowska-Pysz, WSB University in Dąbrowa Górnicza, Poland

The chapter examines the physical-geographical and human-geographical characteristics of the Czech-Polish-German Three-border region, particularly the Turoszów Spur in Poland and its surroundings behind the borders. These characteristics differ within the region and influence socioeconomic settings and cross-border flows. Resulting asymmetries became more visible in connection with the controversies around the Turów Mine located in the Turoszów Spur. The arguments took place mainly between the Czech Republic and Poland. However, Germany cannot be overlooked due to its importance in the region.

Countries neighboring the mine are not satisfied with its long-term effects on their border areas, and their attitudes were shared by the EU. The analysis is interdisciplinary and mainly grounded in geography, specifically neo-environmental determinism, and border studies, predominantly examining the effects of market forces and cross-border flows. The text aims to illustrate the significance of geographical factors in the small region without extreme geographical barriers or differences.

Chapter 9

Innovative Potential of Regions: Accelerator of Sustainability and Development............................ 147
Vojtech Kollár, Bratislava University of Economics and Management, Slovakia
Silvia Matúšová, Bratislava University of Economics and Management, Slovakia

The concepts of innovation and innovation potential have become crucial in the implementation of conceptual changes and strategic plans leading to changes in competitiveness. Innovation consists of the realization of new ideas projected into products, services, processes, systems, and social relations. Quantitative growth of innovations in the country and its regions as innovative capital is reflected in the innovativeness of products and the quality of services provided, affecting the behaviour of employees, the culture of companies, and the perception of the value of innovative products by consumers. The aim of the research is to compare the results of Slovakia and its regions with the results of European and V4 countries in terms of innovation potential. Based on analysis and comparison, the authors identified the strengths and weaknesses in the innovation potential of Slovakia and Slovak regions and the gaps that need to be overcome regarding the increase of the innovation potential and sustainable development.

Chapter 10

Common Assessment Framework in the Czech Republic Public Sector: Main Issues for the Czech Republic Regions and Municipalities 168
Jan Procházka, Czech Technical University in Prague, Czech Republic

This chapter deals with the common assessment framework (CAF) and its application in the local and regional administration in the Czech Republic before the summer of 2022. After a background about how CAF works and should be applied, there are two parts about how the quality policies and CAF are used for the public administration and public sector in the country. The discussion and the solutions and recommendations parts discuss the most important issues found for the topic and for the (future) research itself. A short part about possible future research directions follows up on these issues.

Section 4
Turkey: The Door to Europe and Asia

Chapter 11

Regional Growth Model With Spatial Externalities 183
Merve Baysoy, Istanbul Bilgi University, Turkey

This chapter presents a spatially augmented growth model that includes technological interdependence among regions to consider locational and neighbourhood effects on growth. The role of space, which can be defined in several ways, plays an important role in economic growth processes. The different types of tests allow the authors to determine the spatial dependence in regional data and specify an appropriate model. The characteristics of neighbours may stimulate or hamper the economic growth rate of a country. The spillover effects of a country are a substantial issue for a regional perspective in the economic growth process. The economic growth of a country is affected by the performance of growth rate of its neighbours. The economic growth rates depend on both region and neighbouring region characteristics, the weight matrix, which shows the spatial connectivity structure of regions and the strength of spatial dependence based on model specification.

Chapter 12

Evaluating Different Growth Strategies: The Case of Turkey 205
Adem Gök, Kirklareli University, Turkey
Deniz Güvercin, University of Lincoln, UK

Analyzing Turkey over 2005: Q1-2017: Q4 period by ARDL approach, the study examines the growth performance of export-led, FDI-led, consumption-led, FPI-led, and investment-led strategies. The study also examines the impact of these growth strategies on various macroeconomic indicators including inflation, unemployment, and exchange rates. Results indicate that consumption-led growth strategy increases growth and unemployment without exerting statistically significant effects on any other indicators. FDI-led growth strategy positively contributes to economic growth, employment, inflation, and trade deficit. Export-led growth strategy positively contributes to economic growth, employment, external debt, and inflation. Investment-led growth strategy does not affect economic growth and employment but positively affects trade deficit and external debt. FPI-led growth strategy decreases economic growth, does not generate employment, and decreases inflation, external debt, and trade deficit.

Chapter 13

Analysis of System Marginal Price in the Turkish Electricity Market 225
Aslı Boru İpek, Kütahya Dumlupınar University, Turkey

Due to climate change, growing energy prices, and increasing energy consumption, energy efficiency has become a key topic in recent years. Most energy market traders also want to be able to foresee the energy market in the future so that they can take the appropriate actions to optimize their trading profits. As a result, energy market evaluation models are required. Energy markets, on the other hand, are location-dependent, as each market has its auctions and procedures. As a result, specific models for each energy market should be developed. The primary aim of this study is to provide a comprehensive comparison of various machine learning methods in the Turkish electricity market. A comparative analysis is provided on support vector machines (SVM)-based methods, k-nearest neighbors (KNN)-based methods, and ensemble-based method to analyze system marginal price (SMP). According to the accuracy value, the ensemble-based method gives better results.

Section 5
India: The Potential of a Giant

Chapter 14

Territorial Planning Models in Homestays: An Indian Context 242
Saumya Kapil, Christ University, India
Bindi Varghese, Christ University, India

Homestays have become a sustainable accommodation option in the tourism industry. With roots in the ancient period, the revival of homestays brings an eco-friendly alternative to visitors and the local community. The agglomeration of the fringed existence of this business will result in a more significant profit and focused policymaking opportunity for governmental and non-governmental organizations. The observations in the study indicated a need for analysis of homestay clusters. This study systematically reviews the existing literature aiming to provide specifications needed for management of homestay clusters in India. This chapter identifies guidelines and has indicated external and internal determinants for an organized homestay business. The factors in the formation of agglomeration are an integrated effort driven by local community participation and appropriate government intervention for regional sustainable growth and development.

Section 6
USA: Laying Out Smart Cities

Chapter 15

Smart City in the Global Economy: Information and Organization Support Development.............. 257
    Tetiana Momot, Coggin College of Business, USA
    Russell Triplett, Coggin College of Business, USA
    Angelo Cristian Azueta, Coggin College of Business, USA
    Olena Filonych, The Educational and Scientific Institute of Economics and Management,
        Kharkiv, Ukraine

The research is devoted to developing a smart city information and organization support model based on the most prominent international smart city ranking practices of systematization. The concepts are summarized. The smart cities in the global economy in the context of leading international rankings were analyzed. Special attention is given to the variations in measurement methodologies to capture the impact of smart cities, including the Smart City Index and the Strategy Index. The top 10 smartest cities in the global economy were analyzed in terms of international rankings. The emphasis is given to American cities. The proposed smart city information and organization support model is based on the concept of the Smart City Balanced Scorecard (SCBS), which allows systematically identifying and organizing priority areas for the development of a smart city and specify strategic directions in each priority area. An approach to calculating the ranking of the integrated indicator of sustainable development of a smart city (R-SCBS) according to the Balanced Scorecard is developed.

Section 7
Latin America: Territory and Natural Resource Abundance

Chapter 16

Analyzing the Spatial Configuration of Agriculture: The Colombian Case 280
    Helmuth Yesid Arias-Gomez, Masaryk Institute of Advanced Studies (MIAS), Czech
        Technical University in Prague, Czech Republic
    Juan Pablo Cely, Pedagogical and Technological University of Colombia, Colombia

The authors deploy a descriptive approach for recognizing recent trends in the Colombian agricultural output. They combine the production analysis and the spatial perspective, streamlining the data and the spatial positioning. Using the agricultural Census 2014, they identified the territorial trends in flourishing commodities pushed by forceful changes in the international demand, and by the pressing tightening in the international food markets. In contrast, the Colombian competing imported products were demoted by the foreign imported production. The Colombian agriculture has been influenced by subsequent frameworks of economic policy, spanning from the protectionist stage through the liberalization era, until the current predominance of bilateral trade agreements. The spatial analysis bears out a random distribution of agricultural output across the territory, demonstrating the diversity of production and a scattered spatial pattern. In spite of the disparate production diversity, the agricultural export supply shows scarce diversification.

Chapter 17
Economic Deglobalization, Regionalism, and Localism Processes Driven by Populism and
Nationalism 298
José G. Vargas-Hernandez, Instituto Tecnológico Mario Molina, Mexico
Omar C. Vargas-González, Tecnológico Nacional de México, Ciudad Guzmán, Mexico

The aim of this chapter is to analyze the nationalism and populism as the driving forces of economic deglobalization processes and regionalism. The analysis departs from the assumption that the economic deglobalization processes responds to more complex dynamic forces created by the economic, financial, and the most recent health crisis that blocks the continuity of the economic globalization. Moreover, at the center of the analysis is the conceptualization that both globalization and deglobalization are two faces of the same coin, but with opposite driving forces. Nationalism and populism are the driving forces of deglobalization leading to find regional and more local solutions to economic growth and social and environmental problems.

Compilation of References 313

About the Contributors 347

Index 354

Foreword

As an educator for over forty years, I have witnessed considerable changes in global activities: political power structures, economic policies, technological advances, infrastructure developments, and of course how we educate individuals to meet the needs of the 21st century.

In November of 2019, I presented a paper at The 26th Nordic Intercultural Communication (NIC) Conference held at Vidzeme University in Latvia. During the conference I was introduced to Gabriela Antošová from the Institute of Education and Communication, Czech University of Life Sciences in Prague and later met, Helmuth Yesid Arias Gomez, from the Masaryk Institute of Advanced Studies, Czech Technical University in Prague (MUVS-CVUT). As a team of dedicated scholars, they have pursued their academic goals for creating a more indepth understanding of international economic developments from a global perspective. I have reviewed chapter proposals and have co-authored a chapter for their first publication, Innovative Strategic Planning and International Collaboration for the Mitigation of Global Crisis, with IGI Global publishers.

Research on teaching and learning has provided better understanding of how students learn and what tools are best used for their learning. However, what we teach is key to innovations and advancements that are made in creating new and improved possibilities as our global regions become more connected and interdependent for resources and prosperity. The notion of educating individuals for economic growth and competition is not novel. In terms of economic objectives, human capital theory argues that by investing in education, the quality of workers will be improved, and consequently, the wealth of the community will be increased. In the mid 19th century, Horace Mann, an American educator and reformer, often referred to as the father of American schools, used human capital theory to justify community support of public schools. A century later, in his 1964 book, Human Capital, Gary Becker maintained that the economic growth depends on the knowledge, information, ideas, and general health of the workforce.

As we move into the 21st century, the information age is upon us; educating individuals for the needs for production require more technological and analytical skills to be competitive. Digitization is used more widely than ever before. The book addresses the growing use of tools such as GIS (Geographic Information Systems), CAF (Common Assessment Framework), DMO (Destination Management Organizations), and systems such as regional management, which integrates different stakeholder groups and societal, natural, technological, and economic aspects related to entrepreneurial activities.

During the 1990s, American economist Robert Reich claimed that inequality between people and nations was the result of differences in knowledge and skills. This book addresses the notion of disparity among regions over the past century; global economic development following decades of political turmoil, changing geographic boundaries, war-torn nations, pandemics, and climate changes, creating poverty and disparity for those individuals from those regions. Several chapters focus on the current atrocities in Ukraine, with scholars optimistic for not only repairing the damages done to the territories, but addressing ways to improve the economic developments and collaboration with other nations in a more competitive and productive manner. The editors combined the most disparate cases of economic deployment on specific territories, using a solid foundation relying on both economics and geography. This comprehensive approach provides the framework for interpreting such compelling processes.

As communication and transportation become increasingly available for more people around the globe, individual lifestyles have changed and tourism has become an even more significant, viable industry for international investment.

Those individuals who are curious and want to travel might find a multitude of ways to learn about other cultures and people today through tourism. The chapter on agritourism (chapter 14) caught my attention because a colleague spent time Working on Organic Farms (WOOF-ing). There are creative ways that tourists might help rural economies while learning more about new regions.

There is much to be learned from reading this book, as it focuses is on the future of regional development and innovative ideas for the improvement of living standards. Topics discussed include economic geography, sustainability, tourism, territorial planning, public policy, economic history and social sciences among others. It is intended to illustrate international experiences in the analysis of economic localization and to describe how both space and human activity resonate with each other. This set of experiences is strongly compelling for scholars, lawmakers, policymakers, students, and the general informed public.

Susan E. Seigel
Independent Researcher, USA

Preface

The territory articulates the nature and actions of people, and frames the constraint for the development of economic undertakings and human activities in general. In every corner of the world, regardless of the local challenges, there has been a reflection about the role of territory in the development of each society. Among the topics covered in this book are the environment, urban expansion, economic activity, the clustering of firms and people. This collective work makes an effort to globally resonate, local answers to the territorial and spatial challenges that emerge from idiosyncratic discussions, and their solutions.

This book offers an overarching approach in terms of the diversity of countries, the motley methodological proposals and the comprehensive set of scientific fields. We can learn much about the global solutions proposed when the territorial challenges emerge, by taking into account the constrains within the natural surroundings, and by promoting urgent environmentally friendly development.

The book is arranged in six geographic and thematic sections: Ukraine, Europe, Turkey, India, USA, and Latin America in order to stress the necessity of a common coherence, as these territories face problems and when formulating solutions. Likewise, this geographical approach emphasizes the disparate sort of resources and endowments, natural conditions, and potentialities that must be managed everywhere, in order to implement a strategy of sustainable development.

Moreover, this book contains 17 chapters of timely contributions coming from 11 countries: Ukraine, Germany, Czech Republic, Spain, Slovakia, Poland, Turkey, India, USA, Colombia, and Mexico. This interdisciplinary collection of approaches addresses the challenges of managing the territory in a sustainable way.

Beginning with a theoretical introduction, the first chapter, "Space and Production Specialization," initiates the context for understanding the exposition of subsequent chapters. It surveys some theoretical interpretations of the spatial concentration around the urban agglomerations. Two theoretical approaches predominate for understanding the territorial production specialization: (1) the comparative advantage principle and (2) the exploitation of economies of scale.

The second geographic section, "Ukraine: Looking at the Future," is devoted to Ukraine for obvious reasons, and invites the local society to share their perspectives to resume the task of building the future, with the idiosyncratic resources and the most valuable asset: its people.

The second chapter, "Startup Ecosystem as the Basis of Entrepreneurship Development: Regional Aspect," explores the field of innovation and points out the local experience in the Kharkiv region, which strives to foster entrepreneurship, startups, and new projects. The region has been proposed as a local robust techno-environment, that is based on private efforts and government support for encompassing initiatives by individuals who are eager to launch startups. The chapter reminds us the Marshallian agglomeration process or the technological spillover process, forcefully emphasized by Krugman and the researchers of location theory.

The third chapter, "Educating Competitive Professionals: A Requirement of the Modern Urban Economy," describes the recognizable effects on the territory of two relevant aspects of the society and the economy, stressing the local necessities of Ukrainian society. The emphasis is posited on: (1) the changing requirements for the labor factor meeting the necessities of the urban contexts in the modern sectors, and (2) the technologically advanced activities. This idiosyncratic Ukrainian reflection intends to mold a more competitive labor force demanded by the predominant urban activities.

The third geographical section, "Europe: The Strength of Economic Integration," is intended to address the continental experiences, taking into account that the European development strategy is foremost designed to be implemented from the regions.

The fourth chapter from Germany, "Towards Places and Ecosystems: The Integrated Management of Locations, Destinations, and the Living Space," proposes to design a more comprehensive model of exploitation of tourism. It integrates the urban topics, the locations and the tourism activity as a holistic effort combining the spatial planning, the public policy, and the role of local stakeholders. However, commonly the tourism has been exploited in a disintegrated way conveying a myriad of unanticipated negative effects.

From the Czech Republic, the fifth chapter, "German Inbound Tourism to the Czech Republic: Support and Changes," focused on the role of tourism as the trigger of regional development in border regions. The chapter consults the results of a survey conducted amid German tourist, monitoring their preferences and likes. The processing of the data, provides elements for designing strategies intended to enhance the attractiveness of the Czech Republic, as a relevant destination for German Tourists.

The sixth chapter, "Rural Districts: Application of Core Periphery Model to the Rural Development," develops a model of "Rural Districts", as a spatial and territorial deployment of regional cores of activity and provision of services, which are surrounded by small towns. This chapter proposes the definition of territorial arrangements guided by demographic movements of population, which are motivated by economic and familiar necessities. The migration from the rural milieu towards the urban cores enticed by the urban utilities and by prosperity, explains the depopulation in the rural areas.

The seventh chapter, "Cultural Heritage and Its Impact on Territorial Development: The Case of Spain," tackles the territorial implications of the development of cultural industries based on unexhausted cultural assets. The European Union development policy, is fully based on a clear "bottom up" regional perspective. In light of European guidelines, the sustainable exploitation of the cultural heritage is a multilevel commitment. This includes spanning the local identification of location, the regional promotion of common localized attractions, the national implementation of public policies, and the European role for stimulating and funding of this cultural and economic strategy.

The next chapter in this section, "Innovative Potential of Regions: Accelerator of Sustainability and Development," points out that the role of regions as innovative milieus. The authors appraise several standards of innovation measurements at the European level. Subsequently, a comparison is made between Slovakian regions. Regarding regional inequalities, there is a forceful mobilization of private resources towards the most attractive territories, meanwhile the government must reinvigorate the lagged regions by making them more attractive.

The ninth chapter, "Geographical Preconditions of the International Controversies Around the Turów Mine," presents a threefold dimension in a long lasting dispute between three European countries, which originated by the exploitation of the Turów coal mine. This is one example of a conflictive economic exploitation at a common national border. Here the economic outcomes benefit only one participant, but the negative externalities are spread extensively throughout the region. Some solutions are implied when facing similar conflicts.

The tenth chapter, "Common Assessment Framework in the Czech Republic Public Sector: Main Issues for the Czech Republic Regions and Municipalities," presents a set of quality system standards to be implemented at a regional and local level for the improvement of the public sector services. This approach termed as CAF, is based on specific principles to be successful. It first must be intended to the people development and with their involvement, it must purport the efficiency as a "Result-oriented" system and it must comply patterns of Social responsibility.

The fifth geographical section, "Turkey: The Door to Europe and Asia," emphasizes the role that Turkey might play in bridging cultural and economic gaps.

The eleventh chapter titled "Regional Growth Models With Spatial Effects/Externalities" is a technical chapter exposing the application of spatial econometrics into the estimation of growth, taking into account the effect of neighbor regions on local economic performance. The principles of spatial analysis and spatial econometrics explain the strong interdependence across spatial unities.

The author of the twelfth chapter, "Evaluating Different Growth Strategies: The Case of Turkey," investigates the macroeconomic implications of different growth strategies, combining the estimation of a set of equations, and calibrating the estimates of macro variables, assuming an open economy. The Auto Regressive Distributed Lag is applied for better understand the long-term relationships between the set of time series. The choice of determined growth strategy is troublesome, because the strategy itself sets in motion undesirable effects on the equilibrium of partial markets (mainly the exchange rate and goods markets).

The final chapter in this section, "Analysis of System Marginal Price in Turkish Power Market," explores a breaking problem that predominates amid the European concerns for the power supply. This chapter contributes to answer the question: in what ways has the market improved after the liberalization? The recent wave of liberalization had a market-oriented inspiration and reduced the state sectorial intervention. The outmoded energy system was rooted on the reduction of production and operating costs, whereas the new scheme tends to be more profit oriented.

Another geographical section, "India: The Potential of a Giant," is devoted to a large country in terms of territory and demography. India represents an emerging country whose economic experiences can be replicated elsewhere in the developing world.

The fourteenth chapter, "Territorial Planning Models in Homestays: An Indian Context," tackles the territorial implications of the homestay tourism model as an alternative for earning an income in the Indian countryside. The regions of Rawla Kaneriya, Hodka, Gujarat, Uttarakhand, West Bengal and Kerala, loom as inspiring cases for the implementation of a regional policy of economic development and a territorial planning strategy. Subsequently, it provides an opportunity for the farmers to function as a tourist host, harnessing the linkages between tourism, agriculture, and the rural sector.

The geographical section "USA: Laying Out Smart Cities" stresses the American potential to generate urban technological environments based on cutting-edge technological sectors, the accumulation of skilled human capital and the profuse mobilization of investment and capitals. The chapter in this section, "Smart City in the Global Economy: Information and Organization Support Development," applies a methodology which relies on the identification of priority areas, and the implementation of strategies intended to spur the development in each one. It inspires plans of urban development laying out more functional and sustainable cities, and also more competitive nodes of global production.

The book's last geographical section, "Latin America: Territory and Natural Resources Abundance," exposes the continent's ample endowments of natural resources, as well as its human potentialities. However, this section also reveals severe pitfalls in terms of macroeconomic management, access to available financing, the rigid external constraint and the unsurmountable social inequality.

The sixteenth chapter, "Spatial Configuration of Colombian Agriculture," focuses on the spatial disposition of agriculture in Colombia, resorting to the cartographic tools for deploying the municipalities which predominantly contribute to the agricultural output. This chapter describes ways that production specialization harnesses the comparative advantages, stemming from idiosyncratic conditions such as territory's sun exposure, tropical climate, territory's altitude and water availability. The scattered spatial pattern of production illustrates the diversity in climate and natural conditions, the natural richness and the national potential for ensuring food security. However, the authors also point out the scarce diversification of agricultural exports demonstrates evident pitfalls in terms of competitiveness.

The final chapter, "Nationalism and Populism as the Driving Forces of Economic Deglobalization, Regionalism, and Localism Processes," is focused on the role of the regions after meaningful global transformations. Recent trends demonstrate some inward moves and the predominance of reshoring process which are currently at its peak. The "de-globalization" process, motivated by nationalist interests, restricts the flows of goods, people, and capital, and strives for a rearrangement which brings back home, the worldwide scattered production phases. In conclusion, the authors propose an argument amid such global disruptions: the role of regions and territories should be redefined.

Hopefully, the book will become an obligated source of inspiration for the formulation of public policies, for the implementation of empirical research and analysis and for improving the public awareness about these territorial problems. This book is based on the rigor of science; however, it is accessible and can be constructive to a vast widespread public as well. The proposed solutions in the book, can be tackled at a staggered territorial level: the local context, the regional level, the national domain, and the supranational perspective.

Perhaps, the ultimate goal of this common effort is to generate a discussion for improving the real situation of citizens, for reinforcing the territorial efficiency and to promote a more equitable regional development. The solutions must come from the empowerment of local stakeholders, who are able to take control of their own process of development by using all available technology and their idiosyncratic resources.

Helmuth Yesid Arias Gomez
Masaryk Institute of Advanced Studies (MIAS), Czech Technical University in Prague, Czech Republic

Gabriela Antošová
Institute of Education and Communication, Czech University of Life Sciences in Prague, Czech Republic

CZECH TECHNICAL UNIVERSITY IN PRAGUE
MASARYK INSTITUTE OF ADVANCED STUDIES

Acknowledgment

We express our deepest gratitude to each author of the chapter and reviewer for their unwavering engagement with the project, and their efforts for improving progressively the quality of work. We thank specially the astonishing efforts of the Ukrainian contributors working amid such disturbing and dangerous conditions.

The editors are also thankful to the Masaryk Institute of Advanced Studies at the Czech Technical University in Prague, and to Institute of Education and Communication at Czech University of Life Sciences in Prague, for their stimulating academic support.

We thank specially the role of Susan Seigel, Ed.D. as an advisor providing initiatives and watching for the quality of English texts and the coherence of ideas. Thanks to the co-editor Ing. Gabriela Antosová Ph.D., for her ingenuity and the enthusiastic role in inviting some of the groups of researchers included in the chapters. We appreciate specially her experience in previous editing projects.

We acknowledge the ingenuity and the creativity of the Editorial Advisory board.

Editorial Advisory Board

Juan Sebastian Castillo Valero, *Institute of Local Development, University of Castilla la Mancha, Spain*
Jefferson Enrique Arias Gómez, *Universidad el Minuto de Dios, Bogotá, Colombia*
Pavel Krpálek, *College of International and Public Relations Prague, Czech Republic*
Renáta Machová, *J. Selye University, Komárno, Slovakia*
Karel Němejc, *Institute of Education and Communication. Czech University of Life Sciences, Czech Republic*
Susan E. Seigel, *Independent Researcher, USA*

Helmuth Yesid Arias Gomez
Masaryk Institute of Advanced Studies (MIAS), Czech Technical University in Prague, Czech Republic

Gabriela Antošová
Institute of Education and Communication, Czech University of Life Sciences in Prague, Czech Republic

CZECH TECHNICAL UNIVERSITY IN PRAGUE
MASARYK INSTITUTE OF ADVANCED STUDIES

Section 1
Introduction

Chapter 1
Space and Production Specialization

Helmuth Yesid Arias-Gomez
 https://orcid.org/0000-0003-0107-8611
Masaryk Institute of Advanced Studies (MIAS), Czech Technical University in Prague, Czech Republic

ABSTRACT

This chapter overhauls some fundamental theoretical principles commonly consulted when tackling a territorial analysis, and the implications that arise when the economic activity alters the genuine territorial status quo. The discussion will focus on the economic vein of this subject, although this perspective can also incorporate geographical, environmental, and urban approaches, inter alia. The emphasis will be put on the stubborn and ever-present phenomenon of agglomeration of economic activities, in some cases triggered by the exploitation of resources geographically pinpointed, or motivated by the exploitation of economies of scale, pecuniary externalities, or technological spillovers.

INTRODUCTION

The geographical space measured in distances and transport costs is a recognizable category in the trade, in spite of the abstraction made by the mainstream theories. The inclusion of transport costs in the New Economic Geography (NEG) models incorporated a notion about geographical proximity between trade partners, and weakened the traditional seamless either in the trade theory and location theory. In other domains, there is a clear disruption in the NEG regarding the consolidated field of Urban Economics. Brakmannn et al. (2009b) settle a fundamental difference between the two approaches to the extent that later assumes the cities as isolated entities with no mutual interaction, whereas the former emphasizes the spatial influences that reverberate each other, when analyzing the regions.

Hereon the spatial dimension will be clearly asserted as one crucial determinant in the production specialization, in the economic geography and in the trade theory. However, recent efforts strive to understand the principle of trade and comparative advantages, based on the definition of a space product dimension (Hausmann & Klinger, 2007), with a subsequent empirical applications (Cicerone et al., 2020). However, this product space approach to specialization, relies on the relatedness of products when the

DOI: 10.4018/978-1-6684-5976-8.ch001

countries redefine their specialization pattern establishing a production and sectoral dimension, but not a geographical one.

Crevoisier (1996) points out that in economic models the concept of space belongs strictly to an abstract and unreal idea, which is unable to match the "metric" space as a concrete reference with specific dimensions. However, he proposes a dimension of space dealing with proximity and mainly with interactions and economic transactions. Some models fruitlessly, intended to explain the spatial behavior but have been relegated to simple descriptive efforts. In the German tradition, the proposed geometry as appears in Christaller and Losch, is rooted in a description which lacks any explicit market framework required for building an economic structure of localization (Krugman, 1991; and Krugman, 1993). Without any microeconomic root, the observation of graphical set of triangles of Weber or hexagons of Losch gives the impression that spatial economics is merely a deployment of geometry (Scotchmer & Thisee, 1992). The analysis of space in economics requires the forceful inclusion of one specific market structure, with a forceful microeconomic bedrock.

The trade theory and the location theory had divergent predecessors in the field of economics. The first one descends from the Ricardian tradition, and the second one is related to the von Thunen's work on land rents. The first one assumes discrete and internally seamless nations (Krugman, 1993) and in spite of his lack of realism, this has been the dominant paradigm for 200 years.

The easier way to connect space and economic activity is pointing where production thrives. In doing so, the spatial outcome is the relevant role of specific areas where the output, the employment or the producers set on. One stubborn trait of production is the spatial concentration in particular spots, due to various reasons. In some cases, the production shows stunning concentration because of geographical and climate endowments (agriculture, tourism), but also because of economies of scale, and because firms try to harness the spillovers and pecuniary externalities (manufacturing and urban economics).

The reasons for the predominance of one placement instead of the other lie in the alternated influence of primary forces related with natural conditions, and then, in the appearance of a sort of increasing returns process. Krugman (1993) modelled the emergence of one particular city: (Chicago), which advantages were fully determined by its location. This made up a "First Nature" advantage, nearby the canal connecting the Mississippi and the Great Lakes. However, the advent of railroad weakened the river transportation, and the natural benefit plummeted. But once the importance of Chicago as a core market was consolidated, a self-sustaining process of "Second Nature" was launched. These 'First Nature' and 'Second Nature' phases represent the sequential process of alternation between an initial expansion, fully relying on natural determinants, and a second stage propelled by the strength of increasing returns.

Paraphrasing Krugman's asseveration, the production is more clustered than the resources, which emphasizes that just a fraction of production concentration is explained by the access to resources (Fujita & Krugman, 2004). The remaining fraction of concentration corresponds to pecuniary externalities and spillovers.

The next step is to interpret the stylized facts. In the case of agricultural production, the cause is unambiguously and immediately related to the natural conditions which propitiate the expansion of specific crops matching the climate, the territory's altitude, etc. This idea is coherent with the Ricardian theory which designates the differences in cost and productivity, as the explanation of the flourishing of specific production anywhere. Some activities as tourism can follow the same logic. Already at the end of the 19th century, Marshall (1890) attributed the original explanation for industrial localization to the access to natural resources.

Accordingly, with the NEG the strength of increasing returns spurs the spatial concentration. It is possible that some historic accidents or local advantages launched a productive undertaking, but such subsequent forces make pervasive the predominance of the original spots. Ultimately, the causation set in motion by the increasing returns is the relevant force, and not the original natural advantage itself (Krugman, 1991). In fact, when looking at the differentiation of economic landscape, some sort of cumulative causation appears and explains the blatant agglomerations (Krugman, 1993).

However, the inclusion of space into economic modelling was troublesome, while the predominant paradigm relied on the constant returns. But upon surviving along the non-competitive schemes and the spatial processes of concentration, the spatial categories leaked into the economic models (Scotchmer & Thisse, 1992; Krugman, 2008).

In most cases the industrial activity appears concentrated in some points of space and the productive profile of agglomerations tends to be specialized, because the firms detect unusual advantages derived from setting on in the proximity to other firms. The analysis of this stunning regularity has been tackled by Marshall, Krugman and other theorists, whose works cleared the way for envisioning other aspects such as increasing returns, specialization, self-sustaining concentration, and so on.

The stubborn spatial concentration of the activity can be unleashed by random factors, which are described by Krugman as accidents of history. Next, the ulterior mechanism of accumulative causation is triggered by the exploitation of economies of scale, unleashing a reinforcing process which in turn, enhances the original advantages of localization (Krugman, 1991).

The regional divergence analysis points the role of advanced regions, and the backwardness or underdevelopment of the other lagging territories. In the light of this contrast, the core areas radiate a dazzling economic success and entice more and more firms, leading to a pervasive agglomerative process. Using the Krugman's metaphoric language, the intensive concentration of people and firms bends the space surrounding the city, and once the curvature is made, the self-sustaining process can last a long time (Krugman, 1993).

When analyzing the spatial distribution of economic activity, the framework must be matched to the sectorial distribution on territory.

In the Ricardian and neo classical theoretical vein, the production profile matches the endowments and the geographical conditions, in such a way that the spatial pattern of production ends up fully determined by cost advantages. Sectors as tourism and agriculture respond to natural determinants as can be appreciated on Figure 1. The economic theory shows that a more long-lasting explanation for the production specialization is rooted in the differentials in productivity due to the classical comparative advantage.

For more than 200 years in economic science, the Ricardian pattern has been the predominant framework for the interpretation of trade and production specialization. In such sort of models, the source of trade relies on the unequal natural condition and geographical determinants, in such a way that, in the absence of these differences, the exchanges and the trade become irrelevant. In the Ricardian paradigm, there is no room for trade when two countries with similar natural conditions are producing similar commodities. The typical textbook includes the exercise comparing the ratio of factorial requirements and accordingly, the trade makes sense only when the two countries show a different ratio of requirements of factors for each commodity (Blaug, 1990).

Some variants of such intellectual structure appear in the Heckscher-Ohlin's model, which concludes that economic specialization in each country is induced by the exclusive production of commodities that are intensive in the own most abundant factor. The factor abundance model relies on a few assumptions: perfect competition, homogeneous goods, constant returns to scale, inexistence of transport costs and international immobility of factors. However, such theoretical assumptions cannot be reconciled with spatial approach principles (Brackmann et al., 2009).

Figure 1. Europe: Agricultural Output by Regions (2016).
Source: Own elaboration based on EUROSTAT data.

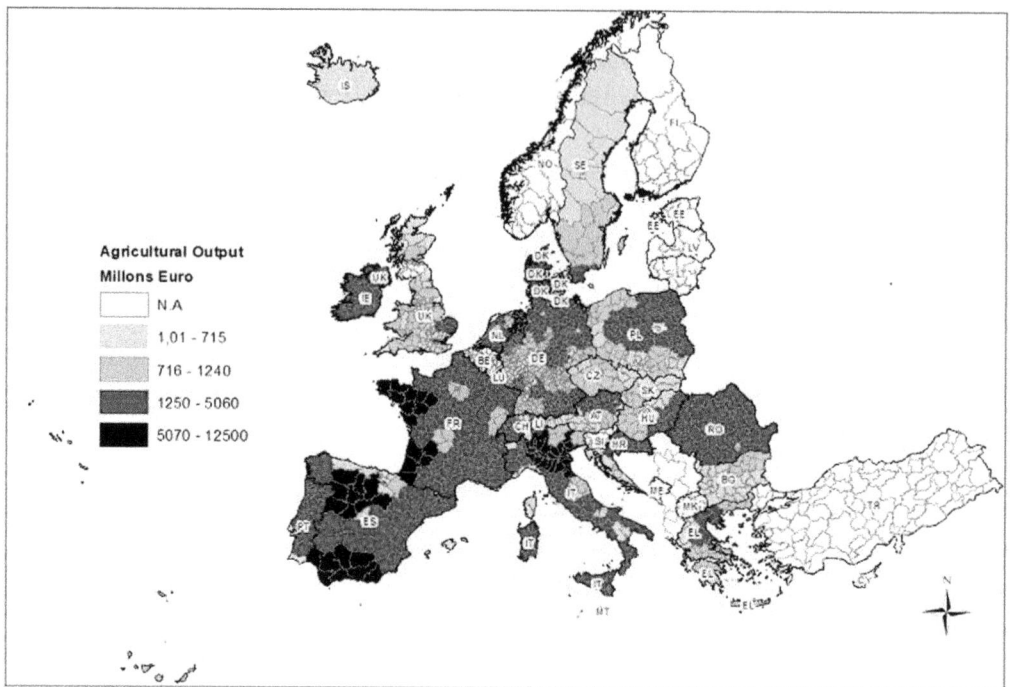

BACKGROUND

The von Thunen model nowadays is used for determining the urban land rents, assuming a diminishing gradient, going away from the central city towards the hinterlands. The original 1826 version was intended to analyze the spatial distribution of crops around the central city, assuming a relevant influence of transport costs. The spatial outcome is an optimal arrangement that deploys the commodities having the most expensive haulage, close to the city (in this way the transport cost is minimized). This pioneering version imparts how the land can be allocated according to diverse competing uses, and how the agricultural production can be distributed spatially. Each commodity can bid for the scarce land taking into account the price of the commodity and the level of profitability, upon paying the land rent. The model assumes that all the plots exhibit similar quality, and there is free entry of competitors, which are enticed by the profit. Therefore, if the differences are dismissed, the distances and the spatial criterion are the sole criteria for setting up the production. Likewise, having differential transport costs across commodities, the profit must be adjusted and along the spatial arrangement each crop sets on according the correspondent profitability criterion (McCann, 2013).

The final outcome of von Thunen's model represents a set of concentric rings deployed around the central placement: the city. The juxtaposition of rings makes up the space where to allocate the crops, and the model demonstrates a declining trend in the rent of land as long as the distance to the central placement increases. Assuming the city as the vertex in the geometrical arrangement, the production of vegetables, a hard-to-transport commodity, lies along the closer ring. Immediately, grain crops will be deployed in the next ring, due to the easiness to haul this commodity or, put in another way, due to the lower transport costs. By economic reasons, no crops will set on beyond the external frontier of the spatial arrangement because, it is impossible to cover full transport costs and rent costs upon pricing the production.

In this way, the model contributes to predict a non-negative rent gradient, which represents the prices of land dropping monotonically along with a haulage distance. Consistent with the Ricardian tradition, the von Thunen model considers the determination of rent of land as a residual category of costs, after paying for the supplementary production factors (McCann, 2013).

In the light of the 1826 von Thunen's contribution, Samuelson (1983) recognizes in such a preliminary work the inception of an incipient neoclassical argument fully applied subsequently in the core of economic theory. The ancient von Thunen model assumed a clear Ricardian influence when describing the determination of land rent. By the way, this Von Thunen model pioneered the concept of marginality, defined as the marginal increments conveyed by additional changes in the model variables, a general concept so extensively used in the framework of the neoclassical stream of thought. In fact, using a beautiful archaic vocabulary, in the context of a narrative intended to describe the nowadays applied concept of marginal productivity, von Thunen refers to the "*significance*" of the factor as the rise in the output derived from the increase of further units of the production factor, maintaining the other factors equal.

For illustrating the validity of von Thunen's insights, commonly touted in the analysis of the urban economy and the behavior of land rents, two recent examples appear in the figures 2 and 3.

In the figure 2, the descriptive illustration for Granada (Spain) imparts the stubborn concentration of higher land prices around the city center and the business core. The most peripheral areas demonstrate lower prices, mainly in the northern fringe and in the outskirts. The drop in land prices is less noticeable in the southern part, but the decreasing trend remains.

Figure 3 highlights the pattern of prices in a central area of Bogotá. The distribution of land prices is unequal, with the high price levels depending on the proximity to important avenues and to the central Bolívar square as well.

DISCUSSION

In the 19th century, Marshall designated three forces spurring the spatial agglomeration of firms. In his *Principles* (1890) he stressed the outright influence of access to natural resources which motivates the decision of firms for setting up their factories. The book language is descriptive and actually the type of manufacturing activities leaned to be agglomerated, appears at odds with the current cutting-edge technological sectors. However, the ever-lasting three Marshallian agglomerative forces are fully operative nowadays.

Figure 2. Granada (Spain). Urban distribution of the price of land
Source: Chica et al. (2007).

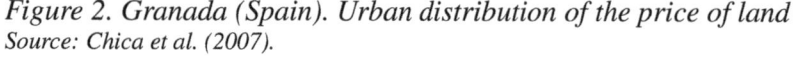

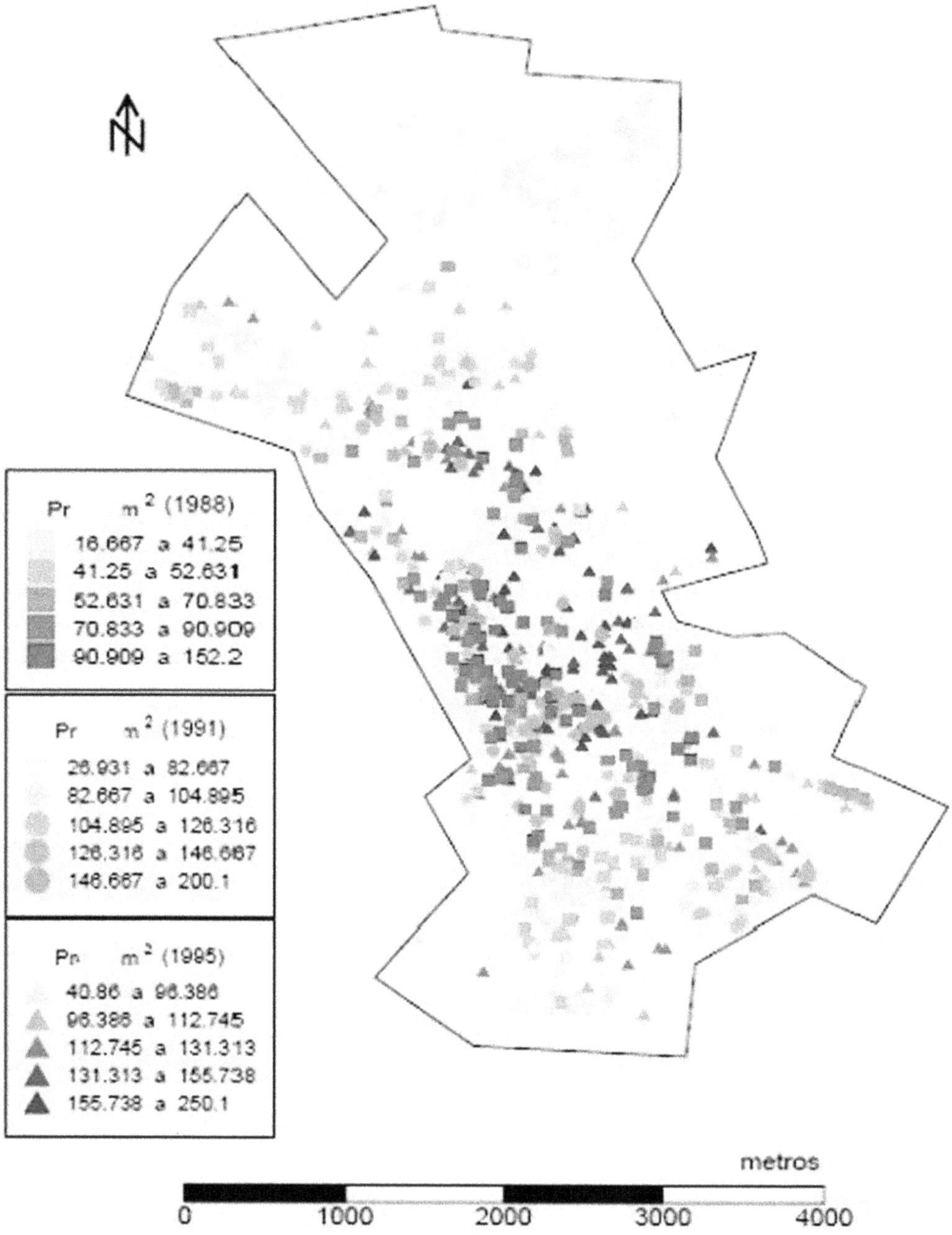

In a descriptive paragraph, Marshall recognizes the close link between iron, pottery and straw plating and the strategic position of natural resources. Next, he proceeds to deploy the advantages of the three agglomerative forces and mentions the famous quotation describing the *"mysteries on the air"* which can be internalized by all producers standing nearby. This mention of Marshallian externalities was the inception of the theoretical stream which emphasizes the relevance of the technological interaction, and the knowledge transmission as sources of growth and spatial agglomeration.

Figure 3. Bogotá: Borough of Candelaria. Urban distribution of the price of land
Source: Own elaboration. Based on IDECA data.

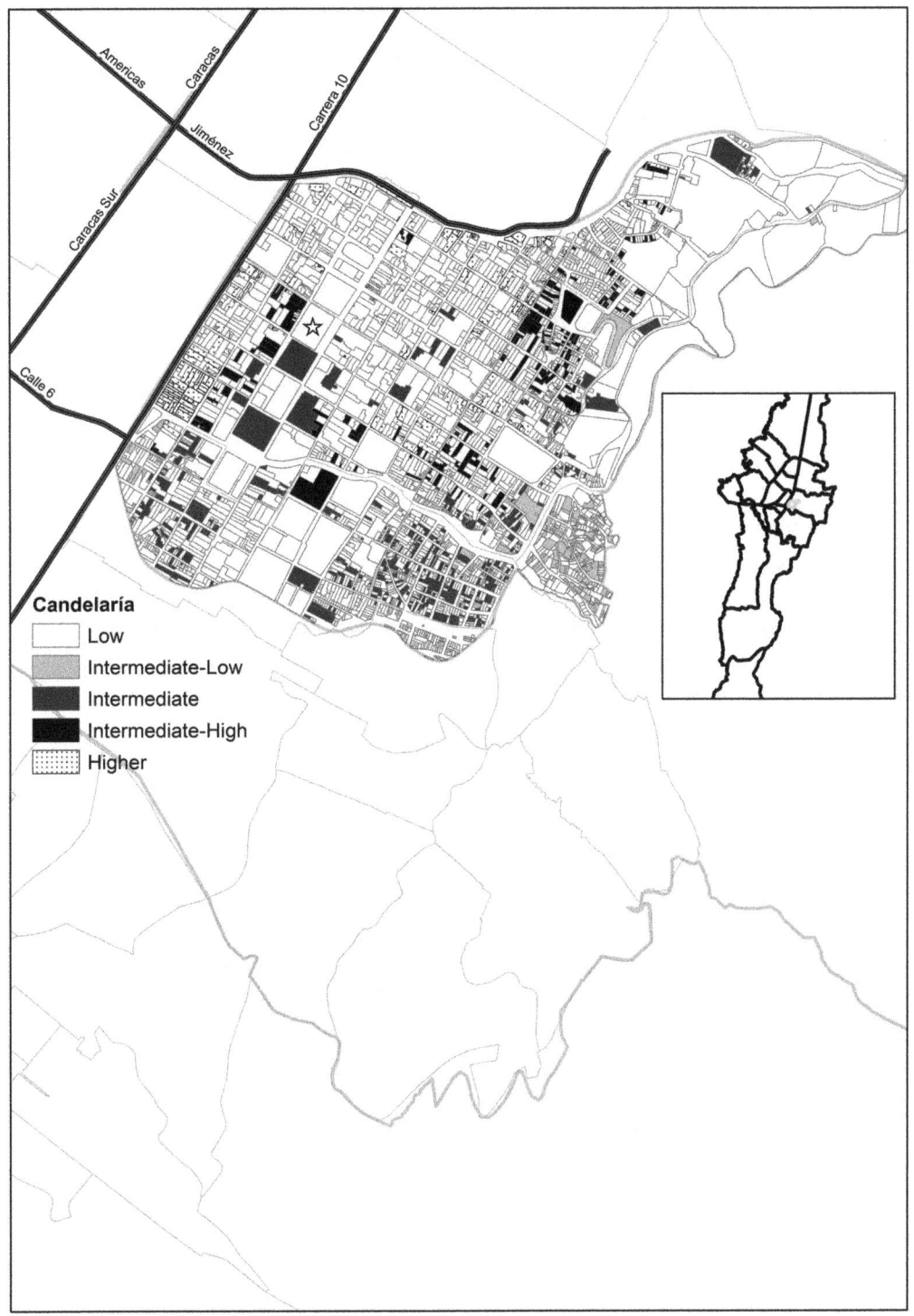

Later, the spillovers demonstrated to be hard to track and to measure. The flaws conveyed by the theoretical tractability of the purely Marshallian technological spillovers have been ubiquitously pointed out by Krugman (1991), Brakmann, Garretsen & van Marrewijk, (2009a, 2009b) and Fujita and Krugman (2004). They all argue the pitfalls laying in the intangibility of spillovers for measurement purposes. Instead, Krugman prefers to introduce the "pecuniary" externalities unleashed by the firms' strategic interaction, which come about fully by market interactions.

In such theoretical vein, the most recent relevant disruption in terms of trade and location theory, has been the Krugman analysis on New Economic Geography (NEG) focused in the agglomerative phenomena and the spatial economic concentration. The Krugman's role is the most prominent, but the set of Marshallian sources of agglomeration have been embraced by modern economists, just adding a more formal shape and mathematical tractability. Such a list of Marshallian sources of agglomeration appears in Krugman and Fujita (2004) and Krugman (1991) as follows:

- Linkages
- Labor Density
- Pure Technological Externalities.

In analyzing the blatant trends in the spatial concentration, the core - periphery model incorporates the transport costs (implicitly involving a spatial category) and the mobility of productive factors (specifically the labor factor). Accordingly, Krugman (2008) presents a light version of the core periphery model.

As explained before, the basic parameters are transport costs (τ), the weight of industrial workers (μ) and the influence of economies of scale (F/S). This basic framework typically appears in the first generation of NEG Models.

$$F/S > \tau * (1 - \mu)/2 \text{ [1]}.$$

the agglomeration forces can reinvigorate the dominant role of the cores of agglomeration if τ becomes lower, F/S is reinforced and industrial workers grasp a higher share in the labor force.

Under specific values of parameters, NEG models predict a pervasive process of concentration, which ends up in an unambiguous core – periphery scheme. This spatial equilibrium and this unequal distribution of manufacturing is reinforced by a forceful cumulative causation mechanism, which perpetuates the predominant role of manufacturing cores and on the other hand, the peripheries which end up relegated and deprived from any manufacturing activity.

The dynamics of models and the final spatial equilibrium depends on slight changes in parameters that can induce radical modification in the outcomes. Furthermore, NEG models predict an abysmal regional divergences as long as manufacturing concentration is perpetuated. In the seminal contribution of Krugman (1991), the initial condition starts from an even spatial landscape and ultimately, after the interaction of forces of the model, the final result is a core periphery equilibrium consistent with a regional divergence process (Brakmann et al., 2009b).

The NEG doesn't identify basic causes explaining the emergence of a concrete core of activity, assigning a high degree of randomness to the choice of specific places. In other cases, in addition to the emergence of manufacturing seeds in specific spots by chance, some kind of self-fulfilling prophecy intervenes when all firms convene to set on in some space, activating an agglomerative movement due to the shared expectation of localization (Krugman, 1992).

Therefore, if the manufacturing plants are established somewhere from the scratch, an increasing returns process perpetuates the industrial agglomeration over there (Krugman, 1995), leading to an outcome characterized by deep regional divergences, as predicted in the core – periphery model. In other words, the core–periphery frames do not explain why the division between regions arises, or why originally akin countries can make up such unlike economic structures (Ottaviano & Puga, 2004). In analyzing the spatial concentration, the unequal spatial distribution of economic activities is set in motion by the influence of the increasing returns, embedded in a microeconomic framework of non-competitive equilibria (typically monopolistic competition). In fact, as long as other rivals threaten the spatial power of the incumbent firm by entering the market, the monopolist requires the spatial isolation for harnessing the full advantages of its market power (Scotchmer & Thise, 1992).

When interpreting the trade and the production specialization, the Ricardian and the NEG – NTT (New Trade Theory) divert in the theoretical frameworks and the model's assumptions. However, in spite of such opposite positions of their theoretical models, there have been endeavors to gather such theoretical streams and to bridge the gaps between paradigms. Recent empirical analyses, use both theoretical approaches to understand manufacturing specialization (Pflüger & Tabuchi 2016; Ricci, 1999).

Figure 4. Europe: Number of Manufacturing Workers (2018).
Source: Own elaboration based on EUROSTAT data.

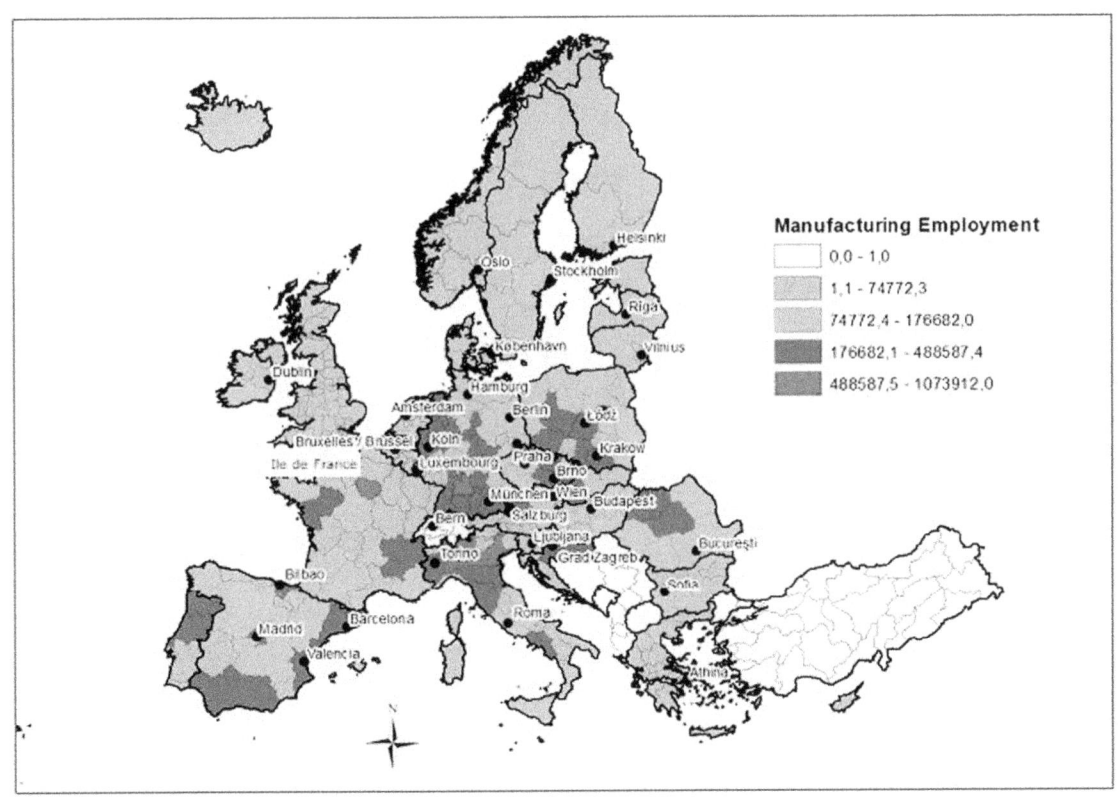

In the end, some first nature aspects and historical accidents explain the irruption of manufacturing activities at specific spots. However, the further pervasive process is set in motion by the forces of increasing returns which spur a self–reinforcing process of spatial concentration, and the perpetuation of manufacturing activities (see Figure 4). In any case, the is the cumulative causation unleashed the relevant process, instead of the anecdotal original conditions and the eventual historical accidents.

Figure 5. Italy: The Industrial Districts (2005).
Source: ISTAT.

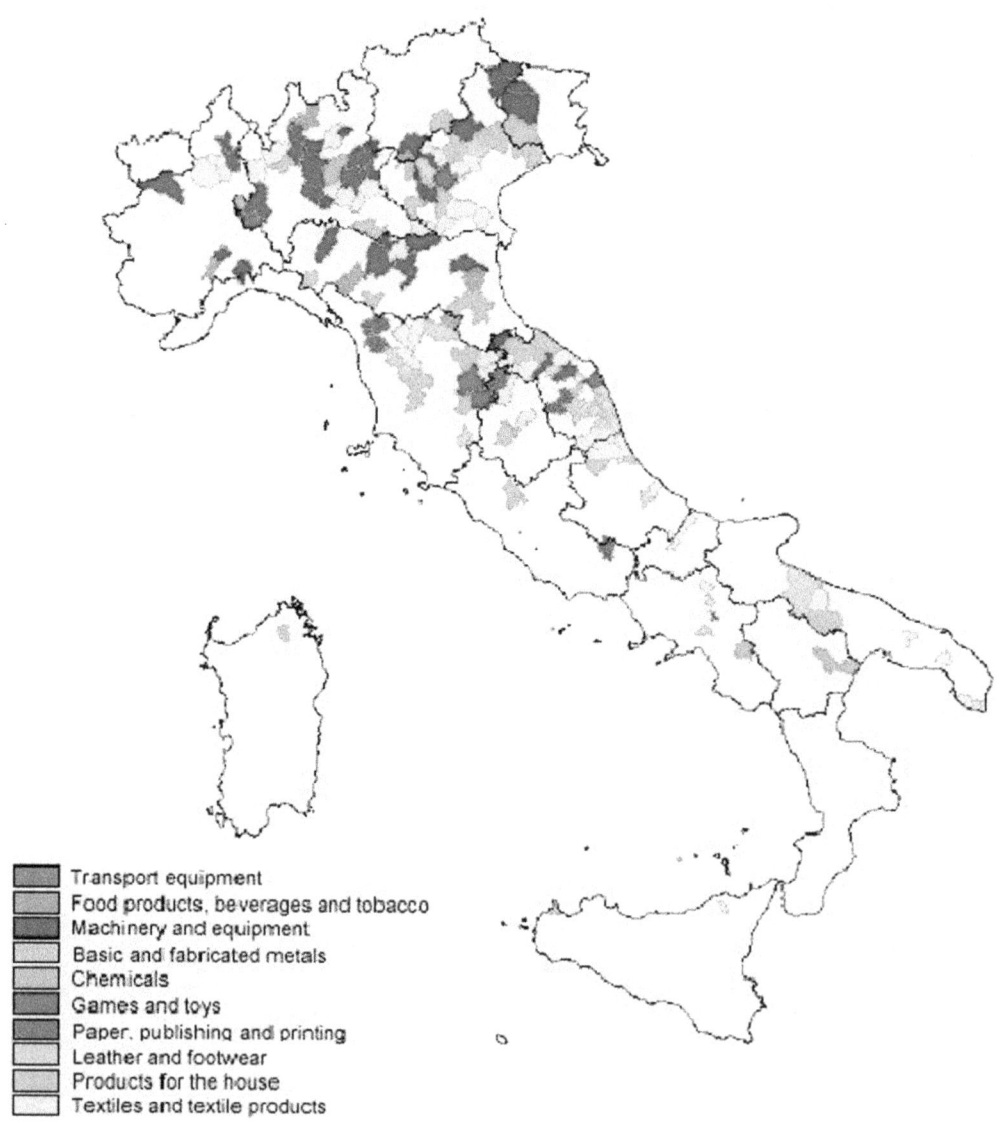

▨	Transport equipment
▨	Food products, beverages and tobacco
▨	Machinery and equipment
▨	Basic and fabricated metals
▨	Chemicals
▨	Games and toys
▨	Paper, publishing and printing
▨	Leather and footwear
▨	Products for the house
▨	Textiles and textile products

Now, in the purest Marshallian tradition came up the Industrial Districts methodology intended to deploy areas of agglomeration spatially identified at a local scope, applying a predominant criterion of mobility by labor reasons. The final result is the arrangement of maps pointing out the proximity of cores of economic activity and a set of associated towns gravitating around a such core of activity, deploying cartographies in which the production specialization is stressed and pinpointed. The Industrial District is defined as a socioeconomic entity embedded in a local-territorial base, supported by the interaction between communities of people and small and medium firms, both integrated in the same productive process (ISTAT, 1996). This analysis has been developed from the individual firm into a system of spatial interactions, involving the clustering of small firms gravitating around a big company or a set of medium firms, and extending a network based on collaboration or competition (Sforzi, 2007).

An excerpt from the Statistical Report is presented on Figure 5 (ISTAT, 2005). The empirical evidence supports the positive effect on productivity and innovation, derived from the geographical and organizational proximity between firms belonging to similar sectors. It excels the plausibility of the Industrial Districts approach, based on the evidence that higher productivity is present either in traditional sectors or in more technologically advanced activities (Sforzi, 2007).

The analysis of Industrial Districts is regularly conducted by the Italian office ISTAT and is commonly used as an input for the formulation of public policy. The result imparts that the analysis made in this way involves one third of the Italian employment and the geographical scope of the areas included in the maps corresponds to the 22% of Italian population. As long as the Industrial District analysis demarcates a concrete set of municipalities (comune) depending on the regularity and representativeness of commuter movements, some general observations can be highlighted. On average, the representative district is made up of 15 local units (comune), with an average population of 94.5 thousand people (ISTAT, 2015).

FUTURE RESEARCH DIRECTIONS

With the Ohlin's and Krugman's works, one fascinating way opens in the integration between the international trade theory and the regional specialization (Krugman, 1993, 2008). The most remote link between international trade and regional specialization dates back to the Ohlin's contribution in the 60s. It's not surprising that the Ohlin's approach, inspired by a neoclassic view of equalization in the price of factors, involves the economies of scale during the production of a few specific goods. (Krugman, 1999).

Therefore, the conclusions derived from the analysis of trade between countries are also suitable for assessing the exchanges between regions and their specialization. According to scientists, this kind of intellectual effort can be applied on different spatial scales. Ricci (1999) uses the same categories of specialization regardless of the scope of analysis: country, region or municipality. Moreover, in another paper, Ricci developed a combined analysis applying Ricardian and NEG categories, assuming the intervention of regions or location, indistinctly as they can be perceived as countries for analytical purposes (Ricci 1997). On the other hand, Krugman (1992) argues that the same forces explaining the international specialization can be used for understanding the regional distribution of manufacturing inside countries, an approach that gives rise to the interpretation of the specialization within countries.

In a such integrated framework, the combination of the comparative advantage and the economies of scale approaches, leads to surprising outcomes in terms of the spatial equilibria and the results of the model. Even more, some results have reversed the NEG's conclusions as well, for instance, the reduction in transport cost does not necessarily convey a reinforcement of the larger region as the core of activity.

It's possible that new firm sets up in a small region, if the productivity is larger over there, under the condition that the productivity effect is stronger than the size effect (Ricci, 1999). According to gravitational principles, the more intensive economic interactions, the shorter the distances are. It means that the proximity between economic agents can usually enhance the exchanges in the trade analysis, and closer countries become strategic partners in terms of exports and imports.

As explained previously, the NEG - New Trade Theory (NTT) stream emphasizes the role of increasing returns and transport costs that involve spatial decisions which leads to the existence of few plants to exploit unexhausted economies of scale, intended to serve the whole market in a centralized way. Obviously, the predominant criterion for setting on is the proximity to huge markets in order to minimize transport costs. In fact, when spatial models introduce the transport costs, give rise to the notion of distances and remoteness or proximity, expanding the scope of analysis and breaking the classical assumption of inexistence of transport costs in the shipments of goods. Definitively, the new incorporation of such notion determines the location decisions taking into account the level of transport costs.

This change of perspective involved the integration of trade theory (NTT) into the NEG developments. In fact, before the advent of the New Trade Theory, the traditional trade theories were encompassed in a set of assumptions as free shipments of goods and the immobility of factors, a clear context defining the typically comparative advantage-based specialization.

Likewise, in the vein of the New Economic Geography, the implementation of models based on increasing returns makes up a plausible explanation of spatial concentration and specialization because by enhancing the scale of production, the firms can specialize in a concrete variety amid a diversity of them, curtailing simultaneously the average cost. In the opposite, the traditional constant return paradigm (Ricardian) shows a typical landscape of "courtyard" capitalism, with individual spatial units producing everything with no specific specialization (Krugman 1991; Ottaviano & Puga, 1997).

However, the incorporation of the spatial category in economic models has been troublesome due to the common confusion between the abstract concept of space and the measurable territory. In the mainstream of economics, the behavior of agents across space is assumed to be an exercise of propelling a set of functional categories which were originally conceived at the most abstract level of the models, for instance the concept of a market, which from the scratch is not embedded in spatial categories (Crevoisier, 1996).

In contrast, the Krugman's research path is rooted in a theoretical framework based on the full mobility of factors and the introduction of transport costs, a scenario more consistent with the realm of Economic Geography than with the Trade Theory's (Krugman, 2008, 1991). In spite of seemingly opposite positions of theoretical models, there have been endeavors to gather the two theoretical streams and bridge the gaps between paradigms (The Ricardian paradigm and the New Trade Theory-New Economic Geography). Recent empirical analyses use both theoretical approaches to understand manufacturing specialization and the distribution of firms.

Currently, the new generation of NEG models interprets the specialization as a process combining the comparative advantages and the economies of scale, giving rise to an ample range of spatial equilibria. Some outcomes convey results which are at odds with the traditional core - periphery conclusions, because the peripheries are also endowed with specific resources that under specific conditions, can unleash concentration dynamics seemingly favorable for the bloom of lagging regions.

Accordingly, Krugman (1991), Ottaviano & Puga (1997), Ricci (1999) and Pfluger & Tabuchi (2016) pledge for a blended interpretation, combining the comparative advantages and increasing returns for explaining the localization and the specialization. This theoretical stunt clears the way for interpreting the current manufacturing expansion around the world, either in developed or developing countries. The behavior of model's parameters determines the final result in terms of spatial equilibrium.

In some models as the Ricci's (1999), agglomeration can come about not in a larger region (as NEG would expect), but in the region where productivity is higher and the absolute advantage more forceful. Bringing the conclusion to the real world, there is a theoretical opportunity for spurring the economic development in lagging regions. When a competitive advantage is strong enough and transport costs are low, the full specialization proclaimed by the Ricardian tradition will predominate in the end.

The "path dependence" regarding the past trend and the preponderance of historical accidents pave the way for launching an accumulative and self-sustaining process of spatial concentration (Krugman, 1992). However, the process of concentration can take place through the action of expectation accomplishment. In the words of Ottaviano & Puga (1997), common beliefs confirm the cumulative causation expected by everyone, and finally all plants end up standing closely. If the origin of economic activity is expected by all agents, the following process will be unleashed: the pervasive reproduction of spatial concentration. Once one spot is favored and attracts firms, the manufacturing growth over there will feed on itself. In fact, the advantages of each country stem from diverse sources, but the productive vocation of regions or countries relies on their respective attributes and natural traits (Krugman, 1994).

CONCLUSION

When observing the spatial unequal distribution of production and the uneven spatial intensity portrayed on economic maps, the first question to be resolved is how the local production specialization can be figured out. For 200 years the mainstream theories focused on Ricardian categories emphasizing differences in costs and productivities. However, after the NEG came along, new models based on non-perfect competition and fully based on increasing returns frameworks, contributed to understand the new bulk of trade exchanges performed between similar countries, with akin factorial endowments. But in the end, the last generation of models provides a combination of comparative advantages, economies of scale and the New Economic Geography to explain the production specialization.

Another fascinating field of research is the proposed Krugman's and Ohlin's integration of interregional trade and international trade. Assuming free mobility of factors and transport costs, similar analytical framework and conceptual tenants can be applied in the interpretation of productive specialization between countries, but also within a domestic context, in order to understand the disparate production profiles of the regions. Accordingly, the regions and economic agents can ascertain the local endowments and comparative advantages for shipping the local output abroad or domestically as well.

Analyzing the regional backwardness and the pervasive territorial underdevelopment, the promotion of 'First Nature' conditions can trigger an initial process of expansion in peripheral regions, but the subsequent 'Second Nature' influence of the increasing returns can bolster a process of regional convergence. The new generation models of NEG combining comparative advantages and increasing returns principles, can point the way to run the approaches of regional development.

The analysis of location required an explicit microeconomic context. After the geometric effort of the German school lacking any microeconomic backdrop, the set of models based on monopolistic competition contributed to insert the increasing return paradigm into the interpretation of the unequal spatial distribution of the economic activity. Specific manufacturing undertakings or clusters are set in motion by random accidents or local comparative advantages, but the ulterior cumulative process, based on the exploitation of economies of scale, takes over as the more powerful force during the manufacturing consolidation. The von Thunen's land rent model, interestingly, combines the transport costs and the rent, but lacks an explicit description of the conditions for the appearance of the central placement.

The three Marshallian sources of agglomeration are the fruitful contributions, that have inspired most of the subsequent research intended to interpret the overwhelming expansion of technological sectors. However, the pure Marshallian externalities (spillovers) are harder to model, and the pecuniary externalities turned out to be very relevant. The set of externalities and strategic moves that firms perform in the market, reverberate the firm behavior. To the extent that this "pecuniary externalities" become more tractable, they have been incorporated into economic models.

Echoing the Krugman's analysis, the increasing returns forces also lie in the pervasive expansion of cities, and in the growth of the service sector that came about simultaneously with population growth. Accordingly, the urban economics is explained, at least partially, by the full influence of increasing returns and economies of scale.

The expansion of technological sectors, the digitalization, the generalization of networks, the heyday of China's role in the international trade as a labor abundant country, and the recent re-shoring trend in international chains of production, pose a challenge for the interpretation of new trends in production specialization and in the analysis of the hard core of the trade theory. In addition, the interaction of economics, spatial econometrics, Geographic Information Systems and other ancillary fields, shed light on the new empirical facts, and furnish a different vision of the present world and challenging future trends.

REFERENCES

Blaug, M. (1990). *Economic Theory in Retrospect*. Cambridge University Press.

Brakmannn, S., Garretsen, H., & van Marrewijk, Ch. (2009a). *The new Introduction to Geographical Economics* (2nd ed.). Cambridge University Press. doi:10.1017/CBO9780511818745

Brakmannn, S., Garretsen, H., & van Marrewijk, Ch. (2009b). Economic Geography Within and Between European Nations: The Role of Market Potential and Density Across Space and Time. *Journal of Regional Science*, *49*(4), 777–800. doi:10.1111/j.1467-9787.2009.00633.x

Chica, J., Cano, R., & Chica, M. (2007). Modelo hedónico espacio-temporal y análisis variográfico del precio de la vivienda. [Spatio-temporal hedonic model and variographic analysis of house prices.]. *GeoFocus*, *7*, 56–72.

Cicerone, G., McCann, P., & Venhorst, V. (2020). Promoting regional growth and innovation: Relatedness, revealed comparative advantage and the product space. *Journal of Economic Geography*, (20), 293–316.

Crevoisier, O. (1996). Proximity and Territory versus space in regional science. *Environment & Planning*, *28*(9), 1683–1697. doi:10.1068/a281683

Fujita, M., & Krugman, P. (2004). La nueva geografía económica: pasado, presente y futuro. [The new economic geography: past, present and future.] Investigaciones Regionales, 4, Asociación Española de Ciencia Regional Madrid, 177-206

Hausmann, R., & Klinger, B. (2007). The Structure of the Product Space and the Evolution of Comparative Advantage. *CID Working Paper,* 146. Center for International Development at Harvard University.

ISTAT. (1996). *Rapporto Annuale. La situazione del paese nel 1995* [Annual Report. The situation in the country in 1995.]. Istituto Nazionale di Statistica.

ISTAT. (2005) I Sistemi Locali del Lavoro. Censimento 2001. [Local Labour Systems. 2001 Census.] Dati definitivi. Istituto Nazionale di Statistica. Roma.

ISTAT. (2015). Statistiche Report. I distretti Industriali. [Statistics Report. Industrial districts.] Istituto Nazionale di Statistica. https://www.istat.it/it/files//2015/02/Distretti-industriali.pdf

Krugman, P. (1980). Scale economies, product differentiation, and the pattern of trade. *The American Economic Review, 70*(5), 950–959.

Krugman, P. (1991). Increasing return and economic geography. *Journal of Political Economy, 99*(3), 483–499. doi:10.1086/261763

Krugman, P. (1991). *Geography and trade.* MIT Press.

Krugman, P. (1993a). On the relationship between trade theory and location theory. *Review of International Economics, 1*(2), 110–122. doi:10.1111/j.1467-9396.1993.tb00009.x

Krugman, P. (1993b) First nature, second nature and metropolitan location. *Journal of Regional Science, 33*(2). 129-144.

Krugman P., (1998). Space: the final frontier. *Journal of economic perspectives, 12*(2), 161 – 174.

Krugman, P. (1999) Was It All In Ohlin? MIT. https://web.mit.edu/krugman/www/ohlin.html

Krugman, P. (2008). *The increasing returns revolution in trade and geography.* Nobel Prize Lecture. Stockholm. www.nobelprize.org

Krugman, P. (2008). *New trade, new geography, and the troubles of manufacturing.* Nobel Price Slides Lecture. www.nobelprize.org

Marshall, A. (1890). *Principles of economics* (8th ed.).

McCann, P. (2013). *Modern urban and regional economics.* Oxford University Press.

Ottaviano, G., & Puga, D. (1997). Agglomeration in the global economy: a survey of the new economic geography. Center for Economic Performance. *Discussion Paper 356,* 1 – 32.

Pflüger, M., & Tabuchi, T. (2016) Comparative advantage and agglomeration of economic activity. Institute for the Study of Labor. *Discussion Paper 10273.* Bonn.

Ricci, L. (1997). A Ricardian Model of New Trade and Location Theory. *Journal of Economic Integration, 12*(1), 47–61. doi:10.11130/jei.1997.12.1.47

Ricci, L. (1999). Economic geography and comparative advantage: Agglomeration versus specialization. *European Economic Review, 43*(2), 357–377. doi:10.1016/S0014-2921(98)00065-8

Samuelson, P. (1983) Thünen at two hundred. [Thünen at two hundred.] *Journal of Economic Literature*, *21*(4), 1468-1488

Scotchmer, S., & Thisee, J. (1992). Space and competition a puzzle. *The Annals of Regional Science*, *26*, 269–286.

Sforzi, F. (2007). Il contributo dei distretti industriali al cambiamento dell'economia italiana. [The contribution of industrial districts to the change of the Italian economy.] *Economía italiana, 1*, 79-104.

KEY TERMS AND DEFINITIONS

Commuters: The population used to realize daily or periodical movements between towns for labor purposes. In some countries, this information can be drawn from Population Census information.

Increasing returns: It happens when the quantitative increase in the output is proportionally higher than the quantitative increase in the variable input and it is consistent with the enlargement of the scale of production. When the firm operates in the increasing return segment, the average cost tends to drop by the increase of the output.

Marshallian Industrial Districts: in the ISTAT (the Italian statistical office) methodology corresponds to the spatial deployment of small and median size firms agglomerated around local manufacturing profiles. With the information about labor commutation, a particular local core can be singled out as focal point of relevant economic activity, irradiating employment opportunities to conterminous municipalities.

New Economic Geography (NEG) and New Trade Theory (NTT): the fields of research opened by the Nobel Prize for Economics 2008 Paul Krugman based fully on the exploitation of economies of scale. The bedrock for the original models is rooted in the microeconomic assumption of monopolistic competition, with firms exerting market power, and taking advantage of unexhausted economies of scale. The Krugman contribution provides a framework for interpreting the trade pattern, the international specialization and the spatial concentration of production.

Pecuniary Externalities: In the Krugman theory, it means the effects that fims can receive by the strategic interaction with other firms through the market. Empirically, the pecuniary externalities are more tractable and easier to track than the Pure Externalities.

Pure Externalities: Theoretically it corresponds to the benefits for the firms derived from setting up close to each other. It deals with the technological knowhow which can be transmitted by the spatial proximity.

Section 2
Ukraine:
Looking at the Future

Chapter 2
Startup Ecosystem as the Basis of Enterpreneurship Development:
Regional Aspects

Olena Dymchenko

O.M. Beketov National University of Urban Economy in Kharkiv, Ukraine

Valentyna Smachylo

O.M. Beketov National University of Urban Economy in Kharkiv, Ukraine

Olha Rudachenko

O.M. Beketov National University of Urban Economy in Kharkiv, Ukraine

Natalia Dril

O.M. Beketov National University of Urban Economy in Kharkiv, Ukraine

ABSTRACT

StartupBlink displays a map of the startup ecosystem and a research center that works to identify the dynamics of startup ecosystems around the world and help accelerate their growth. For a detailed investigation of the best practices for developing generalized recommendations for the development of the startup ecosystem, it is proposed to group countries, taking into account their rating and the changes that occurred in 2021 compared to 2020. Thus, the section groups countries by 5 clusters of startup ecosystems, which in the future may become the basis for the development of recommendations for business development and the formation of startup ecosystem strategies.

DOI: 10.4018/978-1-6684-5976-8.ch002

INTRODUCTION

StartupBlink displays a map of the startup ecosystem and a research center that works to identify the dynamics of startup ecosystems around the world and help accelerate their growth.The Global Startup Ecosystem Index consists of hundreds of thousands of data points that are processed using an algorithm that considers several dozen parameters. The methodology for calculating the StartupBlink ecosystem index includes 3 components: quantitative, qualitative indicators, and an assessment of the business environment. The research methodology is based on the analysis of the dynamics of countries ' ranks of changes in the Global Startup Ecosystem Index rating from StartupBlink, which allows to determine dynamic changes by year (2021-2020), as well as structural changes that led to such changes in the context of index components. For a detailed investigation of the best practices for developing generalized recommendations for the development of the startup ecosystem, it is proposed to group countries taking into account their rating and the changes that occurred in 2021 compared to 2020. For this purpose, these methods are enhanced by cluster analysis, which forms the homogeneous groups of countries and determines common characteristics. The purpose of cluster analysis is to form relatively homogeneous groups (clusters) in the variable space based on a set of models and methods for aggregating rows in the data matrix. Thus, the section groups countries by 5 clusters of startup ecosystems, which in the future may become the basis for the development of recommendations for business development and the formation of startup ecosystem strategies.

StartupBlink is of the particular interest, it displays a map of the startup ecosystem and a research center that works to identify the dynamics of startup ecosystems around the world and help accelerate their growth. For a detailed investigation of the best practices for developing generalized recommendations for the development of the startup ecosystem, it is proposed to group countries taking into account their rating and the changes that occurred in 2021 compared to 2020. Thus, the section groups countries by 5 clusters of startup ecosystems, which in the future may become the basis for the development of recommendations for business development and the formation of startup ecosystem strategies.

Most of the venture capital and innovations are concentrated in only a few regions of the world, studying the experience of startup development in these countries and regions is very important. The startup ecosystem permeates all walks of life. The regional level plays an important role in the overall development.

The Global Startup Ecosystem Index consists of hundreds of thousands of data points that are processed using an algorithm that considers several dozen parameters. The methodology for calculating the StartupBlink ecosystem index includes 3 components: quantitative, qualitative indicators, and an assessment of the business environment.

Global Startup Ecosystem Index 2021 presents a rating of countries with a total number of 100, where total Score (corresponds to the position in the rating) and Rank Change (from 2020) are marked (shows the change in the rating in 2021 relative to 2020). The research methodology is based on the analysis of the dynamics of countries ' ranks of changes in the Global Startup Ecosystem Index rating from StartupBlink, which allows to determine dynamic changes by year (2021-2020), as well as structural changes that led to such changes in the context of index components. For a detailed investigation of the best practices for developing generalized recommendations for the development of the startup ecosystem, it is proposed to group countries taking into account their rating and the changes that occurred in 2021 compared to

2020. For this purpose, these methods are enhanced by cluster analysis, which forms the homogeneous groups of countries and determines common characteristics. The purpose of cluster analysis is to form relatively homogeneous groups (clusters) in the variable space based on a set of models and methods for aggregating rows in the data matrix.

Clustering, or cluster analysis, is a statistical procedure which task is to divide a sample of objects into non - overlapping subsets called clusters. Each cluster must consist of similar objects, and objects from different clusters must differ significantly from each other. The cluster analysis method is the formation of relatively homogeneous groups (clusters) in the space of variables based on a set of models and methods for aggregating rows of a data matrix. The use of cluster analysis has a certain sequence of actions and involves the use of several methods.

Thus, the section groups countries by 5 clusters of startup ecosystems, which in the future may become the basis for the development of recommendations for business development and the formation of startup ecosystem strategies.

A comparative analysis of the definition of the essence of the startup was carried out and established The characteristic distinguishing features of the startup, the author's definition of the concept of "startup" is provided. The essence of the ecosystem and the start-up of the ecosystem are considered. The levels of the startup ecosystem are defined. An example of a local startup ecosystem is O.M. Beketov National University of Urban Economy in Kharkiv. The legal framework for supporting the development of entrepreneurship and startups at the international, national, and regional levels has been studied. Other types of support for entrepreneurship and the startup movement in Ukraine were analyzed. Based on the cluster analysis of startup ecosystems of 100 countries based on the Global Startup Ecosystem Index, 5 clusters were selected. The goal of the author's team is to determine the impact of the qualitative and quantitative economic and business environment on the country's place in the ranking and to summarize standard features for the countries of each cluster.

BACKGROUND

Beginning the investigation, there is a need to decide on the basic category – startup. For this purpose, the team of authors investigated a set of definitions of scientists and opinions of entrepreneurs, which are summarized in table 1.

Obviously, there is no single agreed vision of the essence of startups. Each of them focuses on certain specific features of startup activities. In the previous investigations, the authors also considered the definition of a startup and its characteristic features, emphasizing the differences between startups and conventional, traditional entrepreneurship (Dymchenko, Smachilo, Rudachenko, & Drill, 2022; Smachilo, Halina, & Chaika, 2021). The characteristic distinguishing features of the startup are:

- innovation, a startup is based on a new idea, a way to solve a problem or meet a need, a new product, a new business model, something that will distinguish it from others;
- high risk – since it is based on innovation, risks in all areas are growing;
- rapid growth – startups are more growth-oriented than traditional businesses;
- scalability – the new business model can be extended to other regions, countries, or areas;
- small number of employees, team approach to formation.

Table 1. Approaches of defining a startup

Definition	Author
a project organization or company in various business areas that commercializes a new business model by combining innovative ideas and improving technology in an uncertain environment	Eric, 2011
	Lee and Kim, 2019
individual businesses or corporations that have been operating for less than seven years since the start	Han and Park, 2019
«A startup is a company with fewer than 100 employees that is still not publicly traded»	Caprio, n.d. in McGowan, 2022
startups are looking for a specific business model that is profitable and can be scalable in the future, while the company uses the existing model	Blank & Dorf, 2013
A startup is a new, newly created company that builds business on the basis of innovation or innovative technologies, has a limited number of resources (both human and financial) and plans to enter the market. The innovative technologies it implements can be global (i.e., this innovation will be an innovation for the whole world) or local (i.e., this technology and idea are borrowed, but will be an innovation in a particular region or country)	Chazov, 2013
a new type of business activity based on innovative technologies and minimization of capital investment when starting it.	Fedorov, 2021

Source: Own Elaboration

Thus, under the startup in terms of the investigation, our team will understand the initial stage of entrepreneurship, which is based on solving the problem in innovative ways and tools, the implementation of which involves the formation of economic and social value in a high-risk environment and the creation of a scalable business model.

The "ecosystem" term was first applied by botanist Arthur Roy Klapham in 1930. This concept is formed by the prefix exo-, which comes from the Greek οῖκος (oíkos), which means "house", and was understood as "environment" or "place where life develops", and the word system.

The term "system" comes from the Greek word systema (whole, interconnected, made up of parts), that is, it is a set of elements that are in relations and connections with each other and form a certain integrity, unity. But a system is not just a set of interconnected elements, but also the ability to perform a certain given function.

In biology, an ecosystem is understood as a community of living organisms combined with non-living components of their environment that interact as a system of biotic and abiotic components that are considered to be connected to each other through nutrient cycles and energy flows.

The application of the "ecosystem" concept in the economic context is first mentioned in the investigation of Moore (1993), which coined the term "entrepreneurial ecosystem". In his opinion, the company's ecosystem includes not only owners and employees, but also government agencies, existing and potential competitors, suppliers, and so on. In other words, the entrepreneurial ecosystem covers not only the internal environment of the enterprise, but also the external one. The main feature of the entrepreneurial ecosystem is the optimal combination of competition and interaction, and business should be aimed at developing the entrepreneurial community.

Also, the ecosystem in the business context is mentioned in the report of Deloitte Consulting "Business ecosystems reach adulthood", which offers the following definition: "Ecosystems are communities consisting of various subjects that dynamically develop, create and acquire new content in the process of both interaction and *competition*" (*Business ecosystems come of age,* n.d.).

Nachira (2002) considers the business ecosystem as a digital business ecosystem, based on the use of information and computer technologies, and provides the sharing of resources for the purpose of creating and developing business, knowledge, and infrastructure. In his opinion, the main subjects of the digital business ecosystem are:

- research, educational, and innovation centers;
- enterprises and their associations;
- local self-government and state administrations.

Isenberg (2010) developed recommendations for creating effective national ecosystems in his paper "How to start an Entrepreneurial Revolution", in particular:

- no need to copy Silicon Valley;
- the ecosystem should be built according to local conditions;
- involve private businesses;
- support high potential projects;
- spread successful practices (projects);
- change business culture;
- use resources responsibly;
- do not create clusters administratively, but help them grow organically;
- regulate the bureaucracy and regulatory framework.

A generally accepted definition of the "ecosystem" concept has not been formulated in the literature yet. Jacobides, Kenamo, and Haver (2018) do mark two approaches in the literature for its understanding. Within the first approach, the ecosystem is perceived as a group of organizations that are largely interdependent in terms of factors of production and output; in the second approach, it is perceived as a system of interdependent technologies. These approaches define two directions of research related to ecosystem analysis: 1) in the strategic management area; 2) in the technology management area.

Thus, within the framework of research in the field of strategic management, the following definitions of an ecosystem are presented. In the paper (Adner, 2017). Innovation ecosystems are considered as mechanisms of cooperation, through which firms combine their individual proposals into a kind of coherent and customer-oriented one. The authors of (Iansiti & Levien, 2004) believe that business ecosystems are free networks of suppliers, distributors, outsourcing firms, manufacturers of related products or services, technologies, providers, and many other organizations that influence the company and are under its influence by creating and delivering their own offers.

The authors of (Kapoor & Lee, 2013) consider the business ecosystem as interdependent actions performed by the firm, customers, companies that create additional products, and suppliers. And in (Autio & Thomas, 2014), an ecosystem is defined as a network of interconnected organizations associated with a local firm, or a platform that includes both the manufacturer and third-party participants, which creates and assigns new value through innovation. Also, this helps to produce the products, technologies, and services that customers need.

So, it can be noted that an ecosystem is a set of institutions and organizations that interact and enter into relationships of interdependence, create conditions for the successful functioning of enterprises, and also help to produce products, technologies, and services that customers need.

Next, let's look at the concept of "ecosystem" in the context of application to startups. Different authors and scientists have different approaches to defining the "startup ecosystem" concept. Scientists' views on this concept are shown in table 2. The terms "innovation ecosystem" and "startup ecosystem" are related.

Table 2. Definition of the concept of "startup ecosystem" by various scientists

Author	Definition of the concept of "startup ecosystem"
Jackson, 2011	Innovation ecosystems combine two important and largely separated economies – the knowledge economy, which develops on the basis of basic research, and the commercial economy, which is driven by the market
Bramwell, Hepburn, and Wolfe, 2012	The innovation ecosystem is formed due to the presence of not only a dynamic set of economic agents and institutions engaged in innovation activities, but also a dynamic set of their multidimensional internal connections
Fedulova and Marchenko, 2015	"a set of organizational, structural and functional components (institutions) and their relationships involved in the process of creating and applying scientific knowledge and technologies that determine the legal, economic, organizational and social conditions of the innovation process and ensure the development of innovation activities both at the enterprise level and at the level of the region and the country as a whole according to the principles of self-organization"
Consulting company Startup Commons	The startup ecosystem is formed by people, startups at different stages of the life cycle, and various local organizations (physical or virtual) that interact with each other as a system for creating and scaling new start-up companies. These organizations can be classified into categories such as universities, company investors (business angels, venture funds, crowdfunding platforms, etc.), supporting organizations (incubators, accelerators, collaboration platforms, etc.), research organizations, service companies (in particular legal ones), and large corporations
Caleb, 2014	The main role is assigned to entrepreneurs, as their leadership is a key to the success of the startup economy. Entrepreneurship support is provided from seven main sources (ecosystem feeders): local (state) authorities, universities, mentors, service companies, corporations, investors, and community events. Each of the sources, in turn, is divided into subgroups, the number and qualitative composition of which affects the degree of development of the startup economy.

Source: Own Elaboration

Thus, the startup ecosystem will be understood as a network that unites various subjects of the innovation process (universities, venture companies, marketers, entrepreneurs, audit, and consulting agencies, etc.), which interact with each other on the basis of certain agreed rules of the game.

It is also important to define and describe the components of the startup ecosystem. The overall ecosystem of a startup can be represented in fig.1.

So, the startup ecosystem is represented by 4 levels, each creating conditions for the development and successful functioning of startups.

The review of literature sources made it possible to identify the main components of innovation ecosystems: higher educational institutions (HEIs), scientific institutions that supply innovations for commercialization; the venture capital market that provides financial resources for the process of creating innovations, developing innovative ecosystems and implementing them in business structures (venture funds, asset management companies, business angel networks); innovative infrastructure to support entrepreneurship (material: technoparks, business incubators and accelerators, development institutions, and intangible: service companies to meet the needs in accordance with the specifics of the work of innovative companies); small and medium-sized businesses, demand for high-tech products, technologies and startups; a regulatory framework that creates conditions for the emergence and development of innovators.

Figure 1. Startup ecosystem by levels

In conditions when the country does not have a sufficiently developed innovative infrastructure at the national level, universities take the initiative to create individual elements of the ecosystem at the local level. so, in the conditions of the Ukrainian economy, it is relevant to study the best world experience in forming the ecosystem of startups at universities, as a place of generation, accumulation of innovative scientific and technological knowledge and development of creative entrepreneurship.

Universities play a fairly large role in the formation of innovative ecosystems. The model of the innovation ecosystem of the university is represented by research units, such as the research part, the research institute, the research sector, which include both departments in which research is conducted (scientific departments, laboratories, centers), and scientific support structures (departments of scientific and technical information, research support, financial planning and personnel). During the formation of the university's innovation ecosystem, it is important to implement the process of commercialization of innovative ideas. The practice of the development of the startup ecosystem at O.M. Beketov National University of Urban Economy in Kharkiv contains the elements presented in Fig. 2.

Beketov Startup School Junior and Beketov Startup School are aimed at teaching schoolchildren and students the basics of startup activity and creating their own startups. The activities of Beketov Business Incubator, Beketov Science Park, and the "Megapolis" Technology Transfer Center are aimed at providing infrastructure and consulting for youth entrepreneurship. The business incubator is focused specifically on the successful implementation of startups and business ideas and is a logical part of supporting promising startups that have become graduates of the Beketov Startup School.

The Technology Transfer Center "Megapolis" carries out university-wide, national, and international coordination support for technology transfer for all representatives of the local startup ecosystem of O.M. Beketov National University of Urban Economy in Kharkiv.

The university ecosystem is based on the concept of SMART-of specializations (figure 3), coordinated with the Development Strategy of the Kharkiv region until 2025 and focused on the SMART-city direction.

Figure 2. Startup ecosystem O.M. Beketov National University of Urban Economy in Kharkiv

STARTUP ECOSYSTEM
O.M. Beketov National University of Urban Economy in Kharkiv

Beketov startup School junior

development school, which is intended for schoolchildren of the Kharkiv region and provides training and development of their own startup project

Beketov   Business Incubator

to create infrastructural and consulting support for youth entrepreneurship

Beketov startup school

for students, young scientists who have their own idea or development for startup projects. They are provided training, mentoring and expert support, pitching startup projects and business plans

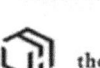 **the «Megapolis» Technology Transfer Center**

provides university-wide, national and international coordination support for technology transfer for all representatives of the local startup ecosystem of O.M. Beketov National University of Urban Economy in Kharkiv

Beketov Science Park

is designed for the development of highly scientific developments and further commercialization of scientific and startup projects developed in the previous stagest

Figure 3. Directions of SMART-specializations O.M. Beketov National University of Urban Economy in Kharkiv

SMART-city

SMART-house

SMART-transport

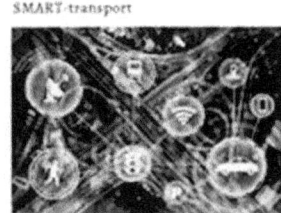

BEKETOV STARTUP SCHOOL

SMART-water

SMART-grind

DIRECTIONS OF SMART-SPECIALIZATIONS
BEKETOV STARTUP SCHOOL

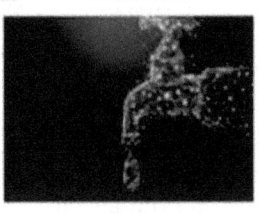

SMART-care

SMART-ecology

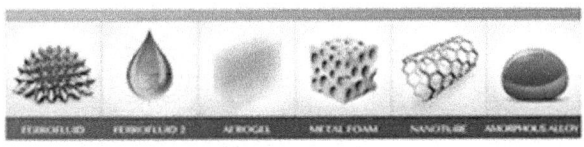

SMART-composite

The European Commission has developed an Entrepreneurship Action Plan 2020 that will contribute to strengthening Europe's entrepreneurial capacity. It aims to support start-ups and small businesses as around 50% of these companies fail in the first five years. This plan will help create an environment for the development of entrepreneurship, given that it is these small and medium enterprises (SMEs) that create the majority of jobs in Europe (Commission sets out Entrepreneurship Action Plan, 2013).

The priorities for the development of the Plan are lifelong education with an emphasis on the new generation of entrepreneurs and a focus on youth, women, the elderly, migrants and the unemployed. The plan also includes measures to promote the creation of start-ups and new businesses, to make transfer of business more efficient and to improve access to finance. In addition, the plan aims to introduce new insolvency rules to help entrepreneurs start a new business after bankruptcy (*Entrepreneurship 2020 Action Plan*, 2020).

According to these rules, businesses hit by the economic crisis will receive a possibility under a new European commission proposal to modernize European rules on cross-border business insolvency.

"Business is essential to creating jobs, but creating it and sustaining its work is difficult, especially in today's economic climate," said Vice President Vivian Reading, EU Commissioner for Justice. "Our current insolvency rules need to be updated to make it easier for viable businesses in financial difficulty to stay stable rather than liquidate. Every year, 1.7 million jobs are lost due to insolvency. We want to give companies and the people they hire a "second chance."" It is supposed to be the first step towards the system approach to the EU's "rescue and recovery" culture.

Antonio Tajani, Vice President of the Commission for Industry and Entrepreneurship added: "Research shows that 'second-starters start-ups' are more successful and last longer than other start-ups; they are growing faster and hiring more workers. Thus, failure in entrepreneurship should not lead to a "life sentence" prohibiting any future entrepreneurial activity but should be seen as an opportunity for learning and improvement – a view that we already fully accept today as the basis for progress in scientific research".

Insolvency is a fact of life in a dynamic modern economy. About half of the businesses have been in existence for less than five years, and around 200,000 firms go bankrupt in the EU every year. This means that about 600 companies in Europe go bankrupt every day. A quarter of these bankruptcies have a cross-border element. But the evidence suggests that failed entrepreneurs learn from their mistakes and tend to do better the second time. Up to 18% of all successful entrepreneurs have failed in their first venture. Therefore, it is extremely important to have modern laws and effective procedures to help enterprises with sufficient economic content to overcome financial difficulties and get a "second chance."

The revision of the EU Insolvency Regulation aims to amend existing rules in order to create a favorable environment for business in times of financial difficulty.

The changes should also help lenders get insurance to recover their money, which might have been lost in liquidation.

The main task is to solve the financial difficulties of the debtor, while protecting the interests of the creditor (*Civil justice,* n.d.).

The results of the Eurobarometer survey showed that the desire to be self-employed fell from 45% to 37% among European citizens as a result of the lack of financial security guarantees during financial crises (Commission sets out Entrepreneurship Action Plan, 2013).

Entrepreneurship and small and medium-sized enterprises (SMEs) support by EU and European commission includes SME definition and SME strategy. SME definition as a small and medium-sized enterprises (SMEs) is important for access to finance and EU support programs targeted specifically at these enterprises. SME strategy includes European SME week; SMEs' access to markets; Late Payment Directive; SME Test; Taxation and SMEs; Accounting and SMEs; SME envoys network; SME Assembly; SME Performance Review; Start-up procedures; Supporting entrepreneurship; Entrepreneurship education; Women entrepreneurs; Transfer of businesses; Family business; Insolvency prevention and second chance; Erasmus for Young Entrepreneurs; European Enterprise Promotion Awards; Migrant entrepreneurs.

According to Entrepreneurship education, as one of the main parts of entrepreneurship development and supporting policy, the European Commission is supporting projects to help improve, promote, and assess the impact of entrepreneurship education in Europe.

Teachers play an important role in entrepreneurship education. It is important that they are trained in the right teaching methods, that they can improve their knowledge and skills, and that they share best practices with colleagues across all EU countries (Projects and studies on entrepreneurship education).

As a part of this educational system, The Virtual Guide to Entrepreneurial Learning like a part of The Entrepreneurial School (TES) was developed (The Entrepreneurial School).

TES is one of the largest entrepreneurship education initiatives in Europe, co-funded by the European Commission through the Competitiveness and Innovation Program (CIP). It aims at supporting teachers' professional development in applying entrepreneurial learning in several subjects and learning environments (primary, secondary, upper secondary and vocational schools).

This objective is achieved primarily by developing the Virtual Guide to Entrepreneurial Learning with entrepreneurial tools and methods organized in teacher-friendly packages and by training over 4,000 teachers in 18 countries in Europe who will be the first beneficiaries of the Virtual Guide and teacher training scheme.

The project's activities have been developed thanks to the National Focus Groups that were established at a local level in Denmark, Finland, Italy, Norway, Poland, Portugal, Slovakia, and UK. These National Focus Groups include individuals from a variety of institutions/partners and stakeholders from education, business, government and civil society. They have a connection to national work on entrepreneurship education and play a key role in promoting a pan-European development of entrepreneurial learning.

Throughout TES, the National Focus Groups are involved in the following activities: help to kick off the project at a national level, participate in the scope, search and testing activities, coordinate teacher training phase in the countries, give input on the quality framework, provide support as teachers begin to use the Virtual Guide.

Emphasis is placed on making European education and training systems more socially inclusive and the six priorities include improving people's skills and employment prospects and creating open, innovative and digital learning environments, while at the same time cultivating fundamental values of equality, non-discrimination and active citizenship (Joint Report under the ET 2020 strategic framework for European cooperation in education and training, 2020).

The European Economic And Social Committee:

- believes that society should not look upon entrepreneurship as a cure-all, but rather as an aid to achieving a return to growth;
- is concerned however that the Multiannual Financial Framework approved by the European Council will undermine the implementation of the action plan, which will end up as little more than a financially unsustainable set of good intentions;

- reiterates the need to give the various stakeholders on the ground the means to disseminate and promote best practices in entrepreneurship, irrespective of their origin (public or private) or area of activity;
- calls for the Commission and Member States to implement the action plan in close cooperation with the various SME representative organizations;
- agrees that policies promoting entrepreneurship have to be coordinated with education policies, at both national and European levels;
- believes that the Commission should declare one of the two coming years to be the "European Year of Entrepreneurship", along the lines of other similar campaigns;
- calls on the Commission to establish a fourth area for intervention to strengthen the mentoring, coaching and support activities provided for enterprises, especially the smallest businesses, through intermediary organizations;
- lastly, calls on the European institutions to establish support systems for people who want to begin self-employed work during their retirement (Entrepreneurship 2020 Action Plan, 2020).
- The direction of social entrepreneurship increases its relevance in the modern entrepreneurial ecosystem.

Every day some 2.8 million social economy entities in Europe (Monzon and Chaves, 2017) offer concrete and innovative solutions to key challenges we are facing. They create and retain quality jobs, contribute to social and labor-market inclusion of disadvantaged groups and equal opportunities for all, drive sustainable economic and industrial development, promote the active participation of citizens in our societies, play an important role in Europe's welfare systems, and revitalize Europe's rural (Long-Term Vision for Rural Areas, COM, 2021) and depopulated areas (Krlev, Pasi, Wruk, and Bernhard, 2021).

"Building an economy that works for people: an action plan for the social economy" (The European Commission is not liable for any consequence stemming from the reuse of this publication, 2021) seeks to enhance social innovation, support the development of the social economy and boost its social and economic transformative power. It proposes a series of actions for the period 2021-2030. It builds on the Social Business Initiative (COM,2011) (SBI) and the Start-up and Scale-up initiative14 (COM, 2016). It has been prepared through an open and inclusive process over a two-year period (SWD, (2021).

Startups and businesses are ahead of modern trends in the development of society. Therefore, socially responsible, environmental business, green entrepreneurship and circular economy do not lose their relevance. "Greenovative Europe" is the slogan of the systemic development of Europe. This is what we are talking about By Yannis Fallas, CluBE on the example of Kozani.

"EU Missions and the importance of Climate Neutral and Smart Cities: the case of Kozani" (Fallas, 2022).

EU Missions are a new way to bring concrete solutions to some of our greatest challenges. They have ambitious goals and will deliver concrete results by 2030. The EU Missions are part of the Horizon Europe research and innovation program for the years 2021-2027, tackling five major challenges: Adaptation to Climate Change, Cancer, Ocean and Waters, Soil and Climate Neutral and Smart Cities. We are hereby focusing on the latter, taking into consideration the following: 75% of EU citizens live in urban areas; Global urban areas consume more than 65% of the world's energy; 70% of CO_2 worldwide emissions are due to urban areas. European cities can play a substantial role in contributing to the EU Green Deal target of reducing emissions by 55% by 2030; this practically means that they can offer a *better environment for their citizens. Since climate mitigation is heavily dependent on urban action, the EU will support cities to accelerate their green and digital transformation (Fallas, 2022).*

The main focus of the Kozani Climate Neutrality Plan will center around the following fields: Urban transformation; Energy generation; Management of resources; Circular economy; Digital Transformation.

Accompanied by the transversal themes of Sustainable entrepreneurship; Agriculture; Financing opportunities; Social resilience; Startup Europe.

Startup Europe is an initiative of the European Commission to connect high-tech startups, scaleups, investors, accelerators, corporate networks, universities and the media. It is supported by a portfolio of EU funded projects and policy actions such as the EU Startup Nation Standard, Innovation Radar and the Digital Innovation and Scale-up Initiative (DISC). It is fully aligned with the small and medium-sized enterprise (SME) strategy of the European Commission. Startup Europe strengthens networking opportunities for deep tech scaleups and ecosystem builders to accelerate the growth of the European startup scene (Startup Europe).

The EU Startup Nation Standard is a new initiative announced in the European Commission's new SME Strategy.

European SMEs and startups face several challenges as they pursue ambitions of securing market opportunities and growing their revenues. Many EU countries are already following best practices to help startups address challenges such as venture creation and attracting and retaining talent.

The European Commission in 2020 will establish EU Startup Nation Standard to multiply such practices across the EU to make Europe the most attractive startup and scaleup continent.

In particular, this will include the launch of a political initiative calling for commitments from EU countries to implement such practices at local, regional and national levels. The initiative will focus on making it easier to launch a startup and expand across borders. It will also streamline visa and residency applications for third-country talent, make granting of employee stock options more attractive, promote venture-building and tech transfer from universities, and increase access to finance for scaling up.

The Innovation Radar is the European Commission's data-driven initiative to identify high-potential innovations and innovators in EU-funded research and innovation projects. Its goal is to allow every citizen, public official, professional and businessperson to discover the outputs of EU innovation funding.

Digital startups in the central, eastern and south-eastern Europe (CESEE) region face an investment gap compared to innovators in other European regions. To address this gap in a geographically targeted way the digital innovation and scaleup initiative (DISC) was launched in 2019 by the European Commission in cooperation with several other international institutions. DISC pursues these aims by addressing the existing market gap, enhancing investments and strengthening technical assistance programs focused on digital innovations and the scale-up of digital startups in the CESEE region.

As an initial and specific stage of entrepreneurial activity, a startup needs special methods, tools and support mechanisms. Such support can be implemented at various levels: global (international); national; regional (local); local.

Research (Lee and Kim, 2019) show that the presence of a support system for entrepreneurship by the government at any level already has a positive impact on the intentions of potential entrepreneurs to start a business in any form. The existence of such a system makes sense, this has been proven in various studies. Thus, in (Kim, 2008) it was established that the existence of companies that received support is longer than that of those that did not receive same support. If the support program is effective and newly created business entities are satisfied with it, then this leads to greater efficiency of startups (Lee and Yang, 2018). Accordingly, the formation of the startup ecosystem of a city, region, or state requires a comprehensive combination of the most effective support tools. The authors of the investigation (Lee and Kim, 2019) rely on the conclusions made in (Solomon et al., 2013), where it was established that obtaining management or technological support, supporting the main business functions (marketing, financial management and operational activities), is more effective for low-productive startups, while support in functions such as human resources and capital raising had a great impact on high-performance startups (Seo et al., 2014).

Investigating the realities of Ukraine, it is necessary to pay attention to the need of improving support for the startup movement, which, according to (Fedorov, 2021) is as follows: the creation of investment insurance and a guarantee system; the creation of a state register of structures that work in the field of venture investment; ensuring guarantees of companies ' intellectual property rights; the formation of a mechanism for the formation and use of venture fund funds; the creation of an up-to-date regulatory framework that would regulate legal relations in the field of investing in innovations. The authors, agreeing with the above, note the need to promote the creation of transparent and simple mechanisms for obtaining financial support and its control.

Therefore, entrepreneurship needs support at all levels, including the regional one. Investigations show that since the late 60s of the last century, there has been a tendency to transfer resources and decision-making powers to the regional and local levels (Storey, 1994). This trend has been realized in the OECD countries through a set of support programs that are differentiated by goals and target groups and are focused on improving the dynamics of enterprises, in particular startups, by using hidden entrepreneurial ability, improving the regional business climate and promoting joint behavior (Storey, 1994). According to (*A startup guide and toolkit for local government,* 2017), usage of local support programs has a number of advantages, which should include: a better level of adaptation to the needs of the territory and business; involvement of a wider range of actors, which can provide a wider range of competencies on this issue to the authorities. Accordingly, to optimize local support, you should take into account the factors that will affect the formation of a local startup ecosystem. Thus, in Lesáková (2012), 6 factors that were determined by Storey in 1994 are given: demographics, unemployment, wealth, educational and professional profile of the labor force, the prevalence of small businesses, level of security with their own housing.

These factors will definitely affect the development of the territory, with different impacts though, which will depend on the country, historical, national, and cultural background. So, in the context of domestic realities, such a factor as the prevalence of small firms will not be a determining factor for starting a business, as well as the availability of the own housing, in conditions of distrust of the financial and credit system and existing credit conditions, will not determine it as a start for entrepreneurship. In addition to the above, the authors can add obstacles caused by the mentality – people are afraid of failure and are not ready to take risks; low business culture, which causes problems of agreement between founders; distrust of traditional investors and businessmen to invest in startups and distrust of government institutions and the credit sector in general. *The Guidelines for Local and State Governments to Promote Entrepreneurship* (Motoyama and Wiens, 2019) indicate that venture funds and incubation centers are often tools for promoting entrepreneurship development by local governments. At the same time, these tools are not always combined effectively. The standard model is one that combines government, venture funds and business incubators, but, according to Motoyama and Wiens (2019), it is more expedient to focus it on the entrepreneur and attract existing entrepreneurs. This recommendation is based on a study (Jackson D. J.) that proves the effectiveness of local connections compared to national or global ones for the success of entrepreneurs. This is because both new and existing entrepreneurs move in a single business environment, so successful local businessmen can become sources of useful information, knowledge, and motivation for those who start a new business. That is why the local startup ecosystem should create communication between startups, scientific institutions, investors who find it difficult to identify local entrepreneurs, and other entrepreneurs who already operate in this area in this territory. The role of local self-government bodies is to promote interaction between entrepreneurs and institutions that support entrepreneurship (Motoyama and Wiens, 2019). This allows creation an environment that catalyzes and provides synergy through training, interaction, establishing relationships and discussing problems and receiving feedback from existing entrepreneurs, experts, consultants, trainers (Motoyama and Wiens, 2019). Good examples of promoting the development of the startup movement at the city level are the creation of municipal startup centers in Mariupol (Startup development center opened in Mariupol, 1991) and Kharkiv (*Municipal IT-Startup Center To Be Opened In Kharkiv,* 2019).

It is important to provide investments to as many future entrepreneurs as possible during the formation of the ecosystem, which requires competitive selection of the best start-up projects and their initial financial support from the investment fund. According to the authors (Motoyama and Wiens, 2019), it is better to provide a smaller amount of investment to a larger number of startups than one large investment, which will create a certain network and group of startups that will be able to support each other and integrate into the local business environment.

Various examples of institutions (organizational structures) to support startups, including incubators, startup schools (centers) and accelerators, venture and other funds that were created with the participation of private investors, foreign grant programs or organizations, local authorities and the state are presented in the table. 3.

Thus, we can present a set of participants in the local startap ecosystem, which includes local authorities, as well as structures belonging to the territorial community; consultative and controlling bodies that relate to the functioning of business; educational and scientific institutions that, among other things, have their own formations promoting innovation; business promotion institutions (business incubators, accelerators); associations of employers, business and the public, whose activities are aimed at mutual sustainable development (clusters, public organizations, contractual and legal associations); operating business; investors, venture funds, and financial and credit institutions.

The problem of entrepreneurship development should be considered at the level of a national security problem, since such a problem is based on acute issues such as employment, job creation, tax revenues, social and political stability in the state and region.

One of the core issues related to the government and local authorities' operation should be the result of the development of entrepreneurship in general and, in particular, the real material sector. Governmental agencies are required to support and encourage the development of entrepreneurship both in the country and in the region. Therefore, issues related to the promotion of entrepreneurial activity are becoming particularly relevant.

Promotion of entrepreneurial activity refers to a set of actions on the part of government structures (state, regional and local authorities), as well as public organizations that ensure the development and effective functioning of business structures.

Support for business activities at the state level can be carried out through:

- transfer of state property and land plots to entrepreneurs for business activities;

Table 3. Analysis of startup support institutions (based on data from sites and (Babiachok & Kulchytskyy, 2018)

Name	Site	Characteristics
UNIT.CITY	https://unit.city/	The largest innovative technology park in Eastern Europe. An ecosystem that promotes innovative entrepreneurship and research. As well as creating companies that are successful in the global market. UNIT.City is a friendly community of people who help each other create new companies and products. It offers international networking and business strengthening, including grant and mentoring programs, from among others Amazon and Berkeley University; attracting investment and financing at various stages of the startup.
IN Venture	https://inventure.ua/	it attracts financing for investment projects, sells companies from various sectors of the economy, searches and selects assets for investment, as well as builds and implements a strategy for investing and managing private capital.
GrowthUp	http://growthup.com	it focuses on helping tech startups on the early stages and creating a product for the western market
Startup Depot Startup School University Edition	http://startupdepot.lviv.ua	co-working space in Lviv and its training program for young people who want to develop their innovative business
Radar Tech	https://radartech.com.ua/	a technology cluster that combines industry-specific corporate accelerators to create an ecosystem that promotes the implementation of ideas, growth and development of economic sectors. In cooperation with large companies, it conducts acceleration programs
iHUB	http://ihub.world/ua	the project, which is supported by the Ministry of foreign affairs of the Kingdom of Norway, develops the ecosystem of innovative enterprises in Ukraine and Eastern Europe, and increases the level of education of young innovators in order to strengthen the social and economic development of this part of the world. Currently in Ukraine, iHUB centers are located in Kyiv, Lviv, Chernihiv, Vinnytsia.
StartupUkraine	https://startupukraine.com/	co-working space in Kyiv and training events on entrepreneurship development. Helps developing entrepreneurship among young people through intensive camps and other training programs, the benefits of which are highly appreciated by their participants.
1991 Open Data Incubator	https://1991.vc/	A space for training and developing local IT initiatives and companies. The project was created by civic tech organization SocialBoost with the assistance of the Mariupol City Council and the USAID Project "Economic support for Eastern Ukraine".
Ukrainian startup Foundation	https://usf.com.ua/	The Mission of the Ukrainian Startup Fund (USF) is to promote the creation and growth of early-stage technology startups in Ukraine, with a view to enhancing their global competitiveness. USF provides capital for early-stage startups, and in pursuit of its Mission, seeks to facilitate efforts to incubate, accelerate, and otherwise promote those startups, and promote Ukraine's technology startup ecosystem. Support for startups in the early stages of development in the form of grants without participation in capital; financing startup training in national and international accelerators; offering new financial and non-financial opportunities for startups
AgroHub	https://agrohub.org	it was created to ensure Ukrainian agricultural companies to implement more innovations from Ukrainian developers of technological solutions.
StartUp Kharkiv	http://startup.create.kharkiv.ua/	Municipal institution. The first municipal startup center that provides advisory, educational and informational support to startups.
YEP incubator	https://www.yepworld.org/ua/	academic startup incubators network. An opportunity to try your hand at entrepreneurship without risks and launch your own startup in 3 months.
Feelgoodlabs	https://startup.network/ua	an incubator for social and urban projects that works mainly with municipalities and united territorial communities. At the moment, a project from Chortkiv is being implemented

Source: Own Elaboration

- assistance in the organization of material and technical support and information services, training and retraining of personnel, arrangement of undeveloped territories with industrial and social infrastructure facilities;
- incentives with the help of economic levers (targeted subsidies, tax incentives) for technology modernization, innovation, and the development of new types of goods and services;
- providing targeted loans to entrepreneurs.

The government is constantly implementing a number of issues aimed at supporting entrepreneurship in crisis times. For example, during the quarantine period caused by the SARS-CoV-2 virus, the government introduced a business support system helping to remove the financial burden on entrepreneurs as much as possible. These restrictions include (*Ministry of Health and Protection of Ukraine,* n.d.):

1. credit holidays: banks have several options for loan restructuring: full or partial exemption from payment of the loan body during quarantine with appropriate loan extension; capitalization of interest payments.
2. tax preferences: exemption from accrual and payment of fees for land used in economic activities, real estate tax for residential premises for March; restriction of the application of most fines for violation of tax legislation; moratorium on documentary and factual inspections (exceptions – VAT refund checks); permission for individual entrepreneurs temporarily not to fill out the income book, etc.;
3. support for small and medium-sized businesses: micro, small and medium-sized enterprises have the opportunity to participate in programs financed from the state and local budgets, receive assistance for business development in both financial and non-financial form;
4. support for agrarian business: cheaper purchase of agricultural machinery and equipment; cheaper loans; development of farms; development of animal husbandry; development of gardening, viticulture and hop growing; continued support through the program 5-7-9% (about 60% of loans within the program); support and development of private land reclamation systems, as well as the provision of state grants for the development of state land reclamation systems;
5. business information support: to conduct business in quarantine conditions, businesses are invited to use public services and online information resources, which are also presented within the framework of the program Diya.Business.

In the war time, the government also provides a number of programs that are aimed at promoting and supporting business activities. These programs include (Action. Business):

- compensation for IDP (Internally displaced person) employment;
- temporary relocation of enterprises from war-affected regions;
- a single digital interaction platform to help relocate business;
- complete overview of enterprise relocation initiatives;
- government grant program for business from the state – eRobota;
- credit programs. Microfinance for business;
- lending to enterprises under the "5-7-9%" program;
- microfinance of veteran businesses;
- financing of Ukrainian exporters, etc.

It was a large-scale national project "Diya.Business" (Action. Business) gaining a huge popularity that is for the development of entrepreneurship and export initiated by the Ministry of digital transformation of Ukraine together with the office for the development of entrepreneurship and export – a state institution that is responsible for the development and support of Ukrainian entrepreneurship in the domestic and foreign markets, which provides a number of projects and programs aimed at the development of entrepreneurship in Ukraine. The government also provides for a number of laws, bylaws and other regulatory documents that ensure the stability, support and development of entrepreneurship (table. 4).

Table 4. A list of laws, bylaws, and other regulatory documents that provide support for entrepreneurship by the authorities. Compiled on the basis of (Verkhovna Rada of Ukraine. Government portal).

Document name	Date and number
Economic code of Ukraine, Article 48	Records of the Verkhovna Rada of Ukraine (RVR), 2003, № 18, № 19-20, № 21-22, p.144
Law of Ukraine «On development and state support of small and medium-sized businesses in Ukraine»	Records of the Verkhovna Rada of Ukraine (RVR), 2013, № 3, p.23 … № 2290-IX as of 31.05.2022
Law of Ukraine «On local self-government in Ukraine»	Records of the Verkhovna Rada of Ukraine (RVR), 1997, № 24, p.170…№ 2321-IX as of 20.06.2022
Law of Ukraine «On the national program for promoting the development of small businesses in Ukraine»	Records of the Verkhovna Rada of Ukraine (RVR), 2001, № 7, p.35… № 4731-VI as of 17.05.2012
Law of Ukraine «On development and state support of small and medium-sized businesses in Ukraine»	Records of the Verkhovna Rada of Ukraine (RVR), 2013, № 3, p.23… № 2290-IX as of 31.05.2022
Law of Ukraine «On investment activity»	Records of the Verkhovna Rada of Ukraine (RVR), 1991, № 47, p.646… № 2254-IX as of 12.05.2022
Law of Ukraine «On the basics of state regulatory policy in the area of economic activity»	Records of the Verkhovna Rada of Ukraine (RVR), 1997, № 24, p.170… № 2321-IX as of 20.06.2022
Decree of the President of Ukraine «On liberalization of entrepreneurial activity and state support for entrepreneurship»	№ 779/2005 as of 12.05.2005
Decree «On approval of the concept of the national program for the development of small and medium-sized businesses for 2014-2024»	№ 641-p as of 28.08.2013

Source: Own Elaboration

However, this list includes only the main laws with their latest amendments and revisions. It is worth noting that legislation is constantly being updated and stabilized in all areas of business activity.

Special attention should be paid to the Kharkiv region, since among the presented values of gross regional product (GRP) (State Statistics Service of Ukraine), the Kharkiv region belongs to the top three regions in terms of GRP indicators.

The Kharkiv region is home to a large number of small and medium-sized businesses in the service, wholesale and retail sectors, which are an integral part of the region.

Thus, the local self-government authorities of the Kharkiv region have developed a number of projects and programs that determine the main ways to implement the state policy of development and support of entrepreneurship at the city level, in close connection with active regional policy, employment policy and investment and innovation directions of the city's development. Such programs are also aimed at strengthening the role of local self-government bodies in the process of supporting entrepreneurship, increasing its importance in the socio-economic development of the city and are an effective tool for solving topical issues of entrepreneurship.

One of these programs is the one «On approval of the Program to support the development of entrepreneurship in Kharkiv for 2018-2022» dated 08.11.2017 No. 834/17 (Register of acts of the Kharkiv City Council), the main divisions of which include:

1. Improvement of the regulatory framework in the field of entrepreneurial activity.
2. Financial, credit and investment support.
3. Resource and information support of entrepreneurship.
4. Development of entrepreneurship support infrastructure.

Interaction of government authorities with the business community is represented precisely by resource and information support for the development of small and medium-sized businesses. This is confirmed by a large number of enterprises, organizations and institutions located in the Kharkiv region (table.5) who are now actively cooperating with businesses.

Table 5. Resource and information support in the Kharkiv region

Institution`s name	Legal status	Main functions
Department of Innovative development and image projects management	Local government administration	Strengthening the positive image of Kharkiv both in Ukraine and the international community by consolidating and concentrating the financial, scientific and industrial potential of the city to create and implement large-scale image, innovation and investment projects, creating appropriate legal, social, economic and organizational conditions for this
Association of industrialists and entrepreneurs of Kharkiv - regional branch of the All-Ukrainian public organization Ukrainian Union of industrialists and entrepreneurs	Public organization	Support of small and medium-sized businesses, promotion of business development and attracting investment in the Kharkiv region
Youth Council under the Kharkiv mayor	Public organization	Support and development of youth in Kharkiv region
YEP - network of academic startup incubators	Network of academic startup incubators	Creating an ecosystem of youth entrepreneurship that provides opportunities for young people for personal and professional development

Source: Own Elaboration

So, support for entrepreneurship in Ukraine, by creating a favorable environment for the development of entrepreneurship, identifying all the components that stimulate the formation, attraction of new and expansion of existing small and medium-sized businesses is one of the main directions of implementing the policy of state and regional economic development. Entrepreneurship influences the structural adjustment of the economy of both the country and the region, contributes to the economical use of resources and plays a number of important functions in the economic development of the region.

DISCUSSION

The authors in (Dymchenko et al., 2022) conducted a cluster analysis of startup ecosystems in 100 countries based on the Global Startup Ecosystem Index (StartupBlink: Global Startup Ecosystem Index, 2021), which made it possible to summarize the ratings of countries in 5 clusters. This allowed to identify the features of the development of startup ecosystems, provide characteristics of each group of countries, and in the future to become the basis for developing recommendations and forming strategies for the development of the startup ecosystem.

So, only one country belongs to cluster 1 – USA – which has been leading with a large gap in this rating for several years and has a maximum total score of 124.42 points. The largest part of this rating is taken by qualitative indicators, their value is 101.17, which is almost 6 times higher than the next country in the rating, Great Britain. The quantitative component of the United States is 19.45 points of the rating, which is also 2.4 times higher than in the United Kingdom, which occupies the next place in the Global Startup Ecosystem Index rating. The business component of the United States also has the highest value, 3.8 points of the rating, but there are a number of countries that are close to the United States in this component (Sweden 3.78, Great Britain 3.7, New Zealand 3.69, Norway 3.66, etc.).

The second cluster includes countries that are representatives of the top 20 (a total of 17 countries from 2nd to 18th place; Total Score: 28,719 – 9,633) and are characterized by a high level of the index, as well as moderate changes within the limits of falling by a maximum of -6 positions (Spain) and growing by a maximum of 7 (China). Despite the change in position in the rating, the countries of this cluster are the leaders of the startup movement in the world.

The third cluster is represented by the largest number of countries (45) that are in the range from 19 to 98 positions of the rating and have minor changes in rank in this interval both in the direction of decline (maximum – 4 positions: Brazil, Italy) and in the direction of growth (maximum 5 positions: Turkey, Nigeria, Bangladesh), or have no changes in the rating (South Korea, Japan, Denmark, Austria, Thailand, Vietnam, Lebanon, Qatar).

The fourth cluster is represented by countries that have achieved rapid growth in the rating in 2021 compared to 2020 (minimum – 7, maximum – 18 positions): a total of 11 countries, among which the maximum growth in the rating is shown by the United Arab Emirates (+18 positions), Saudi Arabia (+17 positions), Uruguay (+15 positions), New Zealand (+14 positions).

The last, fifth cluster is represented by 22 countries, including Ukraine, which occupies the 34th position in 2021 (Total Score 5,705) and has a drop of 5 points. The countries of this cluster are characterized by a negative rating change in 2021 (from -4 to -19 positions): Azerbaijan (-19 positions), Dominican Republic (-18 positions), Ecuador (-15 positions), Moldova (-13 positions), Hungary, Bosnia and Herzegovina, Morocco (-12 positions), Slovenia, Serbia, Paraguay (-11 positions), Greece (-10 positions).

To determine the strength of the influence of each component (quantitative, qualitative and business environment) on the formation of the overall result and place in the rating and in the cluster, an analysis of the dynamics of their changes was carried out. The results for clusters are presented in Tables 1-5.

So let us analyze in more detail cluster 1, which includes only one country that is the absolute leader in this group of clusters – United States (Table 6).

Next, we will analyze cluster 2, which is shown in Table 7.

To assess the impact of changes in each component (x1 - Quantitative component; x2 - Qualitative component; x3 - Business environment) on changes in the rating for each cluster, a regression analysis was performed, the results of which are summarized in table.

Table 6. Dynamics of changes in cluster 1

Country	Change ranking	Quantitative component	Qualitative component	Business environment	Total score
United States	0	-0,33	1,29	0,3	1,253

Source: Own Elaboration

Table 7. Dynamics of changes in cluster 2

Country	Change ranking	Quantitative component	Qualitative component	Business environment	Total score
United Kingdom	0	0,99	2,95	0,37	4,313
Israel	0	1,56	6,81	0	8,333
Canada	0	0,25	1,8	0,11	2,156
Germany	0	0,62	2,57	0,09	3,283
Australia	-2	-0,16	2	0,01	1,855
Sweden	4	-0,41	4,41	0,1	4,1
China	7	0,8	5,13	0,23	6,156
Switzerland	0	1,01	2,75	-0,14	3,62
Singapor	6	1,5	3,97	-0,28	5,176
The Netherlands	-5	0,69	-0,04	-0,01	0,648
France	0	0,83	2,62	0,22	3,67
Estonia	-2	0,39	1,46	0,48	2,325
Finland	-1	0,43	1,6	0,24	2,278
Spain	**-6**	**0,54**	**-0,49**	**0,27**	**0,325**
Lithuania	-1	0,49	0,38	0,52	1,376
Russia	0	0,23	0,8	0,27	1,288
Ireland	0	0,32	2,35	0,33	-2,997

Source: Own Elaboration

Table 8. Dynamics of changes in cluster 3

Country	Change ranking	Quantitative component	Qualitative component	Business environment	Total score
South Korea	0	0,33	1,87	0,12	2,325
India	3	0,25	2,24	0,66	3,135
Japan	0	0,66	2,04	-0,19	2,508
Denmark	0	0,69	1,76	-0,14	2,299
Belgium	1	0,82	0,95	-0,04	1,727
Brazil	-4	-0,03	0,97	0,04	0,968
Taiwan	4	0,59	0,58	0,73	1,902
Portugal	4	-0,07	1,93	0,04	1,898

continues on following page

Table 8. Continued

Country	Change ranking	Quantitative component	Qualitative component	Business environment	Total score
Austria	0	0,47	1,08	0,31	1,856
Italy	-4	0,17	0,67	0,21	1,045
Poland	-3	0,21	0,81	0,34	1,346
Norway	2	0,27	1,35	0,09	1,719
Bulgaria	-3	-0,11	0,05	0,37	0,31
Chile	-2	-0,27	0,48	0,3	0,503
Croatia	2	-0,16	0,86	0,29	0,984
Mexico	3	0,1	0,58	0,34	1,018
Argentina	-1	0,14	0,23	0,19	0,558
Romania	4	-0,16	0,7	0,18	0,723
Luxembourg	-3	0,27	0,23	-0,41	0,09
Turkey	5	-0,04	0,5	0,1	0,557
Colombia	-1	-0,03	0,39	-0,07	0,284
South Africa	4	0,16	0,52	-0,04	0,622
Thailand	0	0	0,15	-0,01	0,133
Philippine	1	0,1	0,09	-0,12	0,063
Iceland	3	0,2	0,27	-0,01	0,47
Cyprus	-2	-0,03	0,13	-0,63	-0,543
North Macedonia	2	-0,08	0,52	0,11	0,553
Vietnam	0	0,09	0,15	-0,06	0,177
Malta	1	0,28	0,09	0,05	0,411
Kenya	1	-0,02	0,33	0,08	0,384
Nigeria	5	0,03	0,48	0,17	0,674
Jordan	3	0,02	0,21	0,02	0,258
Liechtenstein	1	0,13	0,06	-0,02	0,165
Lebanon	0	0,09	0,02	-0,11	0,006
Jamaic	-3	0	0,06	-0,09	-0,029
Georgia	-1	0,01	0,05	-0,06	0,001
Ghana	4	0,02	0,09	0,05	0,166
Panama	4	0,04	0,05	0,05	0,138
Qatar	0	0,04	0,05	0,03	0,119
Cape Verde	4	0,1	0,03	0	0,136
Mongolia	5	0,06	0,03	0,04	0,143
Kuwait	2	0	0,06	0,02	0,08
Bangladesh	5	0,04	0,06	0,04	0,132
Somalia	1	0,05	0,03	-0,03	0,059
Nepal	2	0,03	0,02	0,02	0,071

Source: Own Elaboration

Table 9. Dynamics of changes in cluster 4

Country	Change ranking	Quantitative component	Qualitative component	Business environment	Total score
United Arab Emirates	**-18**	0,38	2,24	0,72	3,338
New Zeland	-14	0,46	0,96	1,21	2,622
Malaysia	-8	0,31	0,59	0,31	1,216
Indonesia	-9	0,1	0,67	0,4	1,172
Uruguay	-15	0,07	1,08	0,99	2,141
Bahrain	-9	0,14	0,09	0,22	0,458
Egypt	-11	0,1	0,22	0,21	0,535
Saudi Arabia	-17	0,18	0,15	0,33	0,655
Pakistan	-7	0,01	0,07	0,05	0,136
Kazakhstan	-10	0,08	0,06	0,1	0,235
Sri Lanka	-7	0,07	0,02	0,06	0,141

Source: Own Elaboration

Table 10. Dynamics of changes in cluster 5

Country	Change ranking	Quantitative component	Qualitative component	Business environment	Total score
Czechia	-6	0,08	0,54	0,14	*0,806*
Ukraine	**-5**	**0,17**	**-0,09**	**0,46**	*0,648*
Latvi	-6	0	0,17	-0,23	-0,063
Slovenia	-11	-0,12	0,09	-0,76	-0,797
Hungary	-12	0,06	0,03	-0,76	-0,659
Serbia	-11	-0,2	0,1	-0,83	-0,934
Greece	-10	-0,18	0,09	-0,94	-1,023
Slovakia	-5	-0,05	0,08	-0,9	-0,876
Peru	-6	0,09	-0,04	-0,47	-0,409
Armenia	-8	-0,15	0,07	-0,67	-0,751
Belarus	-4	-0,02	0,03	-0,11	-0,102
Rwanda	-4	0,01	0,1	-0,08	*0,046*
Moldova	-13	-0,09	0,04	-0,4	-0,444
Albania	-6	-0,01	0,05	-0,1	-0,059
Tunisia	-5	0,02	0,04	-0,1	-0,043
Bosnia and Herzegovina	-12	-0,04	0,04	-0,15	-0,149
Ecuador	-15	-0,03	0,01	-0,16	-0,183
Azerbaijan	**-19**	**-0,05**	**0,02**	**-0,2**	**-0,23**
Paraguay	-11	-0,03	0,04	-0,1	-0,107
Morocco	-12	0	0,03	-0,05	-0,036
Dominican Republic	-18	-0,09	0,02	-0,15	-0,211
Uganda	-8	0	0,02	-0,05	-0,027

Source: Own Elaboration

In order to assess the influence of the change in each component (x1 - Quantitative component; x2 - Qualitative component; x3 - Business environment) on the change in the rating (y -**Change ranking**) of the country's ecosystem for each cluster, a regression analysis was conducted, the results of which are summarized in the table.

Table 11. Results of regression analysis for clusters 2-5 (calculated and developed by the authors)

Cluster	Model	Multiple R	R Square	F
2	y=1,73 - 1,41X1 - 0,34X2+4,67X3	0,762754484	0,581794402	20,86752564
3	y= 40,58-9,83X1-14,83X2+10,16X3	0,368343923	0,135677246	6,749934034
4	y= - 8,41-0,14X1- 2,31X2-3,89X3	0,717234	0,514425	2,471962
5	y= - 10,04+28,43X1+7,89X2-3,04X3	0,48585268	0,236052827	1,853946204

Source: Own Elaboration

SOLUTIONS AND RECOMMENDATIONS

Cluster 1 analysis showed that for the period from 2020 to 2021, United States still dominates the global startup ecosystem. In 2021, the United States maintained a significant gap between itself and the rest of the world. At the same time, the gap in the overall score slightly narrowed between the United States and lower-ranked countries. If analyzing each component in more detail, table 1.1 clearly shows that the quantitative component characterizes the downward trend by -0.33, but the other components show their growth. Thus, the growth of the absolute indicator in 2021 was 1,253.

It is also important to note that 12 cities in the US are in the top 30 cities in this ranking, and the top 1000 includes 267 US cities (in 2021, 28 new cities appeared in the world ranking). San Francisco remains the world leader in innovation (first place in the rating, 328.996 points), where the world's largest innovation center, Silicon Valley, is located. The US dominates several industries: e-commerce and retail technology, marketing and sales technology, healthcare, as well as social and leisure activities. The Global Open Internet, the dominance of the English language in the world, opportunities for funding and support from both private and public structures, and immediate access to global markets allow the United States to remain a leading country (Dymchenko et al., 2022).

Thus, cluster 1 analysis shows that the United States is still the country of opportunity that most clearly represents innovative and breakthrough technological opportunities in the world.

Cluster 2 includes 17 leading countries that have moderate both positive and negative changes in rank, including no changes in rank. Cluster 2 analysis showed that in 2021, it was Spain that had significant negative changes, which flew out of the top 10 and took 15th place in the world, that is, it has a drop in rank by 6 positions. Such negative changes occurred due to a drop in the qualitative component (-0.49), while other components have a slight increase. It is worth noting that Spain currently ranks 9th in the world in terms of quantitative indicators and its rating for business. The Netherlands also has a negative trend, where their rank fell by 5 positions, which was negatively affected by the qualitative component (-0.04) and business environment (-0.01). At the same time, quantitative component and total score the Netherlands have improvements.

A positive trend of +7 positions is observed in China, where all components have significant advantages. So, the total score of China increased by as much as 6,156. such a sharp jump indicates the transition of China from a low-tech developing country to an advanced powerful technological one, which should inspire any other country with the same aspirations.

Singapore also has a positive trend. This country has risen 6 steps from 16th place in the world in 2020 to 10th in 2021. Such a significant increase in rank demonstrates how fast the Singapore startup ecosystem is developing. Singapore has a high level of qualitative component and quantitative component, but Singapore's business environment is low and has a drop (-0.28) compared to most other countries in the top ten (with the exception of China).

Most countries of the world (United Kingdom, Israel, Canada, Germany, Switzerland, France, Russia, Ireland) remained in the same place as they occupied in 2020, but their components have some negative and positive trends. So, for example, Ireland consistently remained on the 18th place, its quantitative component, qualitative component and business environment has improved, however, with such positive changes, its total score has a drop of (-2.997).

Cluster 3 countries are almost fully characterized by an increase in the absolute value, except for Cyprus (-0.543) and Jamaica (-0.029); as well as a positive shift in the qualitative component. Downward changes occur in the quantitative component and in the business environment. At the same time, we should mention countries that had an increase in all components and, accordingly, an increase in the Total Score, but at the same time had a negative change in the rating (Argentina, Italy, Poland).

The growth of the 4th cluster countries in 2021 was mainly due to the improvement of quality indicators and indicators of the business environment in the country, but in some cases also due to quantitative indicators compared to 2020 (in the United Arab Emirates there was an increase in quality indicators by 13 times; in Saudi Arabia, quantitative indicators increased by 4.6 times, qualitative indicators by 3.53 times and business environment by 4.13 times; in Uruguay, the values of quantitative indicators increased by 22.6 times, qualitative indicators by 2.67 times and business-environment by 3.49 times; in New Zealand, the quantitative indicators of the index increased 7 times).

If one separately considers each of the countries where rapid growth has taken place, it should be noted that today, for example, the UAE ranks 2nd in terms of innovation development in the Middle East, and its city, such as Dubai, has entered the top 50 in the world in terms of software and data and a high concentration of technological innovations. There was also a significant increase in Abu Dhabi, which rose by 146 positions in the ranking of 1000 cities of the world ecosystem index, and took 169th place. Among the UAE's successful startups there is a Middle East's first unicorn, Careem, which was sold to Uber for almost 3 billion dollars. Also positive is the constant reform of business by the government and the adoption of laws that promote entrepreneurs and the banking system that promotes innovation (Dymchenko et al., 2022).

The analysis of countries in cluster 5 shows some ambiguity, despite the only general trend – a significant drop in the overall rating of countries (from -5 to -19). First of all, we should highlight the Czech Republic separately, which, having fallen by 6 positions in the overall rating, shows an increase in the absolute indicator by 0.806, which is due to the growth of all three components. A similar situation is observed in two other countries of the cluster - Ukraine and Rwanda, which have an increase in the absolute indicator, which is due to the growth of two of the three components. Ukraine has an absolute growth rate of 0.648 due to the growth of the quality component (+0.17) and the improvement of the business environment (+0.46) and a slight reduction in the quality component (-0.09). All countries in the cluster, except Czechia and Ukraine, show a deterioration in the business environment. Only 5 countries in the cluster have a quantitative component growth (Czechia, Ukraine, Peru, Rwanda, Tunisia) and 3 countries have no changes in this component (Latvia, Morocco, Uganda). Only two countries in the cluster have a decrease in the qualitative component - Ukraine and Peru. Everyone else shows an increase behind it.

From the table 10 it is clear that each cluster has a different value of Multiple R and R Square, which show a fairly low level of correlation (an R Square below 0.4 is characterized as low). Coefficients near X demonstrate different strength and direction of influence on Change ranking.

The second cluster is the most closely related (R Square = 0.58179), and X1 and X2 are inversely related and have a weak influence on y. In the fourth cluster, R Square = 0.5144, and all coefficients have an inverse effect on Change ranking.

FUTURE RESEARCH DIRECTIONS

Further research will be devoted to conducting a detailed regression-correlation analysis of all countries in the rating, which will allow determining the impact and significance of each component both on the place in the rating and within individual clusters.

CONCLUSION

Thus, as a result of the investigation, the following conclusions were obtained:

1. Modern approaches of defining the category of "startup" concept were analyzed, which made it possible to form the author's vision of a startup as an initial stage of entrepreneurship, which is based on solving the problem by innovative ways and tools, which implementation involves the formation of economic and social value in high-risk conditions and the creation of a scalable business model.
2. The modern startup ecosystem was investigated, and a level demarcation of entrepreneurship support was conducted.
3. Modern international funds, grants, and documents to support entrepreneurship and startups were reviewed.
4. Support for entrepreneurship by state and local authorities was given, both in Ukraine and in other countries. It is proved that support for entrepreneurship is necessary at all levels of management, including at the regional level.
5. The models of startup ecosystem constructed via cluster analysis formation processes made it possible to summarize the ratings of countries by 5 clusters. This made it possible to highlight the features of the development of startup ecosystems, provide characteristics of each group of countries, and in the future will become the basis for developing recommendations and forming strategies for the development of the startup ecosystem.

REFERENCES

Adner, R. (2017, January). Ecosystem as Structure: An Actionable Construct for Strategy. *Journal of Management, 43*(1), 39–58. doi:10.1177/0149206316678451

Autio, E., & Thomas, L. D. W. (2014). Innovation ecosystems: implications for innovation management. In M. Dodgson, D. M. Gann, & N. Phillips (Eds.), *The Oxford Handbook of Innovation Management*. Oxford University Press.

Babiachok, R. I., & Kulchytskyy, I. I. (2018). Main trends in the development of startups in ukraine - problems, obstacles and opportunities. EU. https://www.civic-synergy.org.ua/wp-content/uploads/2018/04/Osnovni-tendentsiyi-rozvytku-startapiv-v-Ukrayini-1-1.pdf

Blank, S., & Dorf, B. (2013). *The Startup Owner's Manual Startup: The Founder's Handbook*. Alpina Publisher.

Bramwell, A., Hepburn, N., & Wolfe, D. A. (2012). *Growing innovation ecosystems: university-industry knowledge transfer and regional economic development in Canada, Final Report*, p. 62. University of Toronto.

Business Center. (1991). Startup development center opened in Mariupol. *Business Center.* https://cutt.ly/1kcTYx3

Caleb, H. (2014). *Savannah's startup ecosystem.* HiimCaleb. http://www.hiimcaleb.me/savannahs-startup-ecosystem/

Chazov, E. (2013). Startup as a new form of business. *Scientific works of the National University of Food Technologies, 52*, 122-128

COM. (2011). Communication From The Commission To The European Parliament, The Council, The European Economic And Social Committee And The Committee Of The Regions. European Comission. https://eur-lex.europa.eu/LexUriServ/LexUriServ.do?uri=COM:2011:0681:FIN:EN:PDF

COM. (2016). Communication From The Commission To The European Parliament, The Council, The European Economic And Social Committee And The Committee Of The Regions: A European agenda for the collaborative economy. European Comission. https://ec.europa.eu/transparency/documents-register/detail?ref=COM(2016)356&lang=ru

Deloitte. (n.d.). *Business ecosystems come of age.* Deloitte. https://www2.deloitte.com/za/en/pages/strategy-operations/articles/business-ecosystems-come-of-age.html

Dymchenko O.V., Smachilo V.V., Rudachenko O.O., & Drill N.V. (2022). Modeling the processes of formation of startup ecosystems on the basis of cluster analysis: entrepreneurial aspect. *Communal management of cities, 2*(169), 71–78.

EESC. (2020). Entrepreneurship 2020 Action Plan. EESC. https://www.eesc.europa.eu/en/our-work/opinions-information-reports/opinions/entrepreneurship-2020-action-plan#downloads

Eric, R. (2011). *The Lean Startup: How Today's Entrepreneurs Use Continuous Innovationto Create Radically Successful Businesses*. Crown Books.

European Comission. (2021). *Long-Term Vision for Rural Areas.* European Comission. https://knowl-edge4policy.ec.europa.eu/publication/communication-com2021345-long-term-vision-eus-rural-areas-towards-stronger-connected_en

European Comission. (n.d.). *Civil justice.* Europa. https://ec.europa.eu/justice/civil/commercial/insol-vency/index_en.htm

European Comission. (n.d.). *Projects and studies on entrepreneurship education.* European Comission. https://ec.europa.eu/growth/smes/supporting-entrepreneurship/entrepreneurship-education/projects-and-studies-entrepreneurship-education_en

European Comission. (n.d.). *Startup Europe.* European Comission. https://digital-strategy.ec.europa.eu/en/policies/startup-europe

Fallas, Y. (2022 July 1). Opinion: EU Missions and the importance of Climate Neutral and Smart Cities: the case of Kozani. *Greenovate!* https://greenovate-europe.eu/opinion-eu-missions-and-the-importance-of-climate-neutral-and-smart-cities-the-case-of-kozani/

Fedorov, R. K. (2021). The state and main directions of development of startups in Ukraine. *Electronic professional edition: Effective economy, 4.* http://www.economy.nayka.com.ua/pdf/4_2021/202.pdf

Fedulova, L. I., & Marchenko, O. S. (2015). Innovative ecosystems: essence and methodological prin-ciples of formation. *Economic theory and law, 2*(21), 21–33.

Giving honest businesses a second chance: Commission proposes modern insolvency rules. (2012) European Commission. https://ec.europa.eu/commission/presscorner/detail/en/IP_12_1354

Greenovate. (2013). *Commission sets out Entrepreneurship Action Plan.* Greenovate! https://greenovate-europe.eu/commission-sets-out-entrepreneurship-action-plan/

Han, J. H., & Park, H. Y. (2019). Sustaining Small Exporters' Performance: Capturing Heterogeneous. *Effects of Government Export Assistance Programs on Global Value Chain Informedness. Sustainability, 11*(8), 2380. doi:10.3390u11082380

Iansiti, M., & Levien, R. (2004). *The Keystone Advantage: What the New Dynamics of Business Eco-systems Mean for Strategy, Innovation, and Sustainability.* Harvard Business School, Press.

Isenberg, D. J. (2010). How to start an entrepreneurial revolution. Harvard business review, 88(6), 40-50.

Jackson, D. J. (2011). *What is an innovation ecosystem?* National Science Foundation. http://erc-assoc.org/sites/default/files/topics/policy_studies/ DJackson_Innovation%20Ecosystem_03-15-11.pdf

Jacobides, M., Cennamo, C., & Gawer, A. (2018). Towards a Theory of Ecosystems. *Strategic Manage-ment Journal, 39*(8), 2255–2276. doi:10.1002mj.2904

Joint Report under the ET 2020 strategic framework for European cooperation in education and training. (2020). Retrieved from https://www.tesguide.eu/policy-strategy/itemid/41941/

Kapoor, R., & Lee, J. M. (2013). Coordinating and Competing in Ecosystems: How Organizational forms Shape New Technology Investments. *Strategic Management Journal, 34*(3), 274–296. doi:10.1002mj.2010

Kharkiv. (2019 April 14). *Municipal It-Startup Center To Be Opened In Kharkiv.* Kharkiv IT Cluster. https://it-kharkiv.com/en/municipal-it-startup-center-to-be-opened-in-kharkiv-2/

Kharkiv. (n.d.). *Register of acts of the Kharkiv City Council.* Kharkiv. http://kharkiv.rocks/reestr/663864

Kim, H. A. (2008). *Study of the Inñuences of Public Support Programs on the Technology Innovation and Survival in the IT Small Enterprises.* Science and Technology Policy Institute.

KPMG. (2017). *A startup guide and toolkit for local government.* KPMG. https://citiespowerpartnership. org.au/wp-content/uploads/2021/02/AustraliaLocal-Government-StartupGuide.pdf

Krlev, G., Pasi, G., Wruk, D., & Bernhard, M. (2021). Reconceptualizing the Social Economy. *Stanford Social Innovation Review.*

Lee, W., & Kim, B. (2019). Business sustainability of start-ups based on government support: An empirical study of Korean start-ups. *Sustainability, 11*(18), 4851. doi:10.3390u11184851

Lee, Y. J., & Yang, Y. (2018). An impact of startup business performance by entrepreneurs' perceived importance, satisfaction, and level of meeting to expectation over government startup business aid programs. *Asia-Pac. J. Bus. Ventur. Entrep,* (13), 31–41.

Lesáková, L. (2012). The role of business incubators in supporting the SME start-up. *Acta Polytechnica Hungarica, 9*(3), 85–95.

McGowan, E. (2022 April 7). What Is a Startup Company, Anyway? *StartUps.* https://www.startups. com/library/expert-advice/what-is-a-startup-company

Monzon, J. L., & Chaves, R. (2017). European Economic and Social Committee, Recent evolutions of the Social Economy in the European Union, p. 66.

Moore, J. F. (1993). Predators and prey: A new ecology of competition. *Harvard Business Review, 71*(3), 75–86. PMID:10126156

Motoyama, Y., & Wiens, J. (2019). *Guidelines for Local and State Governments to Promote Entrepreneurship.* Ewing Marion Kauffman Foundation. https://cutt.ly/FkcTPlr

Nachira, F. (2002). Towards a network of digital business ecosystems fostering the local development. *European Commission Discussion Paper. Bruxelles,* p. 23.

Seo, J. H., Perry, V. G., Tomczyk, D., & Solomon, G. T. (2014). Who benefits most? *The effects of managerial assistance on high-versus low-performing small businesses. Journal of Business Research, 67*(1), 2845–2852. doi:10.1016/j.jbusres.2012.07.003

Smachilo, V., Halina, V., & Chaika, D. (2021). Formation of a local startup ecosystem. *Economy and Society, 2021*(23). doi:10.32782/2524-0072/2021-23-9

Solomon, G. T., Bryant, A., May, K., & Perry, V. (2013). Survival of the fittest: Technical assistance, survival and growth of small businesses and implications for public policy. *Technovation, 33*(8-9), 292–301. doi:10.1016/j.technovation.2013.06.002

Startup Blink. (2021). *StartupBlink: Global Startup Ecosystem Index.* Startup Blink. https://www.startupblink.com/startupecosystemreport202

Startup Commons. (n.d.). *What Is Startup Ecosystem?* Startup Commons. www.startupcommons.org/what-is-startup-ecosystem

Storey, D. J. (1994). *Understanding the Small Business Sector. The Birth of Firms. London.* International Thomson Business Press.

SWD. (2021). *Annual Single Market Report 2021.* European Union. https://eur-lex.europa.eu/legal-content/en/TXT/?uri=CELEX%3A52021SC0351

The Entrepreneurial School. (n.d.). *The Entrepreneurial School.* TES Guide. https://www.tesguide.eu/

UA Gov. (n.d.). *Verkhovna Rada of Ukraine.* Government portal. https://zakon.rada.gov.ua/

UA Government. (n.d.). *Ministry of Health and Protection of Ukraine.* Covid19.gov. https://covid19.gov.ua/prohramy-pidtrymky-biznesu

UKR Stat. (n.d.). *State Statistics Service of Ukraine.* UKR Stat. https://www.ukrstat.gov.ua/

KEY TERM AND DEFINITION

GRP: Gross regional product

Chapter 3
Educating Competitive Professionals:
A Requirement of the Modern Urban Economy

Olena Lvivna Ilienko

O.M. Beketov National University of Urban Economy in Kharkiv, Ukraine

Oksana Oleksiivna Rezvan

O.M. Beketov National University of Urban Economy in Kharkiv, Ukraine

ABSTRACT

In the chapter the authors proceed from the fact that the processes of economic globalization mainstream the problem of educating and shaping a competitive professional for the urban economy having completely new competencies, skills, and knowledge. The authors have suggested a scientific and methodical system based on understanding "competitiveness" as an integrated concept, and focused on the formation of specific components included in its content, namely: needs-motivational, cognitive-operational, and reflective-evaluative components. It is advocated that the development of these components requires a technological approach associated with a gradual introduction into the training program a number of disciplines with an intensive focus on competitiveness formation. Additionally, the impact of the extra-curricular activities such as participating in local and international projects, as well as cooperating with career centers, consultants on the students' competitiveness development has been considered.

INTRODUCTION

The problem of educating a competitive professional becomes especially relevant for employees working in the domain of the urban economy. In a situation of economic instability, a decline in production and a disappearance of many jobs, the role of the professionals within the urban economy able to demonstrate effective activities and guarantee not only functioning of municipal enterprises and organizations but also to increase their competitiveness becomes important.

DOI: 10.4018/978-1-6684-5976-8.ch003

Researchers (Kubanov, 2014; Posylkina and Bratishko, 2016; Romanovskyi et al., 2014; Zadorozhna, 2013) believe that to overcome the crisis in urban economy, it is necessary to involve the employees with completely new competences, skills and knowledge that are targeted not only at implementation of the general production processes, but also a systemic reformation and management of the sector. These professionals should be highly competitive, as only such managers are able, to ensure the competitiveness of the industry. Therefore, it is necessary to understand that educating of professionals for municipal organizations, institutions and local government entities should reflect not only the needs of the present, but also cater to the challenges of the future.

The authors hypothesize that the development of competitiveness components of a professional of the urban economy requires designing a scientific and methodical system as well as methods for its implementation in the process of educating students at the university level.

The objectives of this chapter are to: (1) substantiate competitiveness forming of future professionals of the urban economy as a response to the demands of potential employers; and (2) develop a set of competitiveness components and a scientific and methodical system for formation of the competitiveness components as well as methods of this training implementation.

BACKGROUND OF THE STUDY

The Origins of the Term "Competitiveness"

The analysis of the scientific literature focused on the topic gives grounds for asserting that the term "competitiveness" is considered recently as a scientific concept in various fields of knowledge: economic, managerial, psychological, pedagogical, sociological, philosophical, highlighting certain features and definitions within each sphere.

Foremost, it should be noted that the concept of "competitiveness" comes from the concept of "competition". In scientific literature, the concept of "competition" appeared in the 19th century, which was primarily due to its appearance in the everyday language of the Western European states. The concept was designated by a word taken from the Latin language (con + currere - "to coincide, collide"). A similar word is used in Italian, French, Portuguese, Norwegian, Danish, Swedish, German and Dutch languages. At the same time, the term "competition" (competencia) is characteristic of the English and Spanish languages, which comes from the Latin "competition" (com + petition - "aspiration to achieve, achieve something").

Academic Contributions within the Concept of "Competition" in the Economic, Psychological and Philosophical Sciences

A number of outstanding economists have made a significant contribution to the development of the concept of "competition" in the economic science (Porter, 1980; Ricardo, 2001; Smith, 1997, 2007). Porter (1980) proposes the first typology of competition strategies, proves that the competitiveness of a company depends on the competitiveness of its environment in the cluster, develops a methodology for analyzing competitiveness, describes the stages of growth in the competitiveness of the national economy. J. Mill (1980) notes that competition is a law that establishes regulatory rules on the labour market. He points out that free competition should be promoted especially in the field of production, calling it the best feature of capitalism. F. Hayek (2001) believes that competition promotes a better use of people's knowledge and abilities, stimulates rationality, thus promotes personality development.

Also, there are a number of scholars who initiated the study of *personality competitiveness*, in particular, researching the personality of a professional. For example, Bandura (1984), asserts that within the concept of self-efficacy, competitiveness is the ability of people to realize and think through their behavioral features in such a way that they correspond to certain specific tasks or situations. The researchers Greison & O'Dell (1991) point out that the characteristic features of competitiveness are needed to achieve success and self-confidence, which is based on one's awareness of their personality's own abilities and capabilities.

Martens (1976) claims that the goal of the society is to form a competent and competitive personality through the process of socialization. According to Martens, being competitive means performing many social roles, which contributes to the effectiveness of the socialization process. Therefore, competitiveness consists in the successful performance of a social role in accordance with needs. Moreover, Allport (1998, 2002) asserts that the competitiveness of an individual develops through the analysis of the phenomenon of a mature personality, while noting that this state of mind continues throughout a person's life. Maslow (2003, 2006) considers the concept of self-actualization important for personality development, i.e. development of human abilities, the realization of his/her needs throughout life. According to Maslow, a person capable of self-actualization adequately and effectively perceives information, centralizes the efforts on the task, and not on himself/herself. Following Maslow, Rogers (1984, 2000) indicates the need for self-actualization of the individual. Only in this case it can be called a fully functioning personality, i.e., capable of self-realization, awareness of their purpose in life. Such a person is able to be flexible, adaptable, self-confident, and creative. Openness to new experiences in a person's life is an important factor in the formation of the self-esteem.

Drawing from the work of Freud's studies (2016) in ego-psychology, competitiveness is a psychosocial quality, which means strength and confidence and comes from a sense of the person's own success and usefulness, bringing awareness of his/her abilities to effectively interact with environment and withstand competition. Erikson (1996) advocates that a person becomes more and more competitive while interacting with the environment in the process of the development.

Actually, the standard of competitiveness is determined by the social norms and cultural traditions accepted in a certain social group, a specific type of each society. Therefore, competitiveness is characterized by timeliness and a peculiar social order for the formation of a certain standard for the individual. For example, in the Soviet society the negative attitude toward competition and individual competitiveness might be explained by the fact that competition was quite often confused with conflict, and sometimes these concepts were even used as synonyms.

Considering the philosophical foundations of the concept of competitiveness of an individual at the present stage, it is necessary, in the authors' opinion, to turn to the philosophy of American pragmatism (Ilienko, 2018a). James (1997, 2000) is inclined to explore the conditions in which an individual, when interacting with the surrounding social environment, achieves the best results, fully realizes himself/herself. According to J. Dewey (1999, 2003), an individual is an extremely flexible, mobile social subject; therefore, the main task of the social philosophy, as well as philosophy in general, is to help an individual to find the best ways to adapt to the existing state of the affairs, to the social environment. An individual lives and develops in this environment, therefore, he/she has to interact with it, making sure that this interaction is constructive in nature.

The Concept of Competitiveness Studies Applied to Pedagogical Science

In modern pedagogy the problem of developing a successful instruction for educating a competitive professional with varying degrees of completeness and a certain set of characteristics is investigated in connection with the problem of continuous professional training of qualified specialists in various types of educational institutions at various levels, as well as in connection with the problem of formation of the professionalism of a specialist.

Recently, the interest and, accordingly, the number of scientific works (Andriiako, 2010; Rezvan, 2014; Romanovskyi, et al., 2014; Romanovskyi, et al., 2018; Shapovalov, 2017; Zakharova, et al., 2017; Zavalevskyi, 2013) focused on various approaches, mechanisms, aspects of competitiveness formation of a future professional in the process of training at the university have increased.

Competitiveness is revealed in studies mainly through the priority, core qualities of an individual: clarity of goals and value orientations, diligence, creative attitude to work, ability to take risks, independence, leadership, stress resistance, striving for continuous self-development and production of a high-quality product (Andriiako, 2010).

Researching the role of communicative competence of future teachers, Zavalevskyi (2013) observes that employers are interested in the professionals who possess "emotional stability, an ability to choose an optimal style of communication in different situations, reasonably argue their own point of view and manage their behavior" (Zavalevskyi, 2013, p.76). Taking into account this point of view, the authors consider it important to introduce into the content of the disciplines of psychological and linguistic orientation the information about specific features of professional communication and develop communicative techniques and technologies. In addition, researchers focus on monitoring the requirements of employers for job applicants, which determine specific competences needed for a certain position (Rezvan, 2014; Zavalevskyi, 2013).

The competitiveness of a specialist does not end with employment - the employee can continue to use this quality in the process of performing production functions and career growth. Considering the difference between a competitive product and a competitive person, O. Romanovskyi, et al., (2014) identifies the following features of the competitiveness of a professional:

1. An active life position: any consumer product passively "waits" for someone to choose it for purchase, a professional in the labor market can take an active part in this choice, i.e. can choose a certain option from those employers who would like to hire him/her, to employ, that is, in fact, to "buy";
2. A dominant role of quality, not price: today every employer needs to hire professionals, therefore, the criterion "price - quality" cannot be used here in the sense that the low "price" of a specialist becomes an advantage and a certain compensation for the insufficient quality; and
3. The possibility of quality growth: as a rule, even a fairly competitive product purchased by a buyer gradually loses one or another of its qualities in the process of a regular use, and therefore, looses its competitiveness, while a truly competitive professional, capable of self-education and self-improvement, can increase the level of competence in the process of the professional activities. (Romanovskyi, 2014, p. 67).

The Requirements of Potential Employers to the Professional of the Economic Profile

Discussing the requirements of potential employers to the professionals of the economic profile R. Kubanov (2014) suggests two levels of the professional requirements for economists: first, the requirements presented in various types of job descriptions for the employees of the economic profile (they actually reflect requirements for the professional activities of an economist) and, secondly, the requirements of the employers. According to Kubanov (2014), employers demonstrate great interest to the ability of an economist to think strategically and make fast, correct decisions; constantly evolve; be able to organize information and statistics; work with the computer and its devices; have knowledge of different operating systems; know the laws and normative regulations governing economic activities as well as the basics of the information security; be able to work in the conditions of information charged environment and an organized local network; be able to provide information in verbal, graphical, numerical forms.

Semichenko (2004) advocates the effectiveness of the professional training of a competitive economist based on the improvement of the university curriculum and the content of the disciplines. She emphasizes that the transformation of the content of professional training into the content of the discipline is a complicated process, since a qualitatively new, special system of knowledge appear integrating the elements, which have been still unknown.

Researching the requirements for professionals in the field of economics in preparation for -activities in the agrarian sector, Viter (2012) focuses on the fact that a future economist should be prepared for a rapid adaptation to the conditions of scientific and technological progress; for business activities in the sector of private property, etc. It is also specified the instructor should master teaching the discipline in accordance with the modern developments in the science, "providing knowledge and skills of the methods and means of successful life-sustaining activities in those conditions that will be formed in Ukraine and Europe in the nearest future" (Viter, 2012, p. 142).

Moreover, Zavalevskyi (2013) defines the personal component of employability that allows a professional to be competitive in the labor market and involves formation of moral and ethical, intellectual and volitional personality qualities.

The authors have benefited from the ideas of Vachevskyi et al. (2007) who advocates that the students will realize the flexibility and interconnection of the process of professional education with restructuring of the economy and the employment of population, development of various forms of ownership and management in the process of production of competitive products or material goods with an orientation on the buyer's market.

The authors also find it useful for the competitiveness of future economists to emphasize both the regional needs of the labor market (specific vacancies for economists in specific regions depending on the specialization of the enterprises of this region) and the requirements of consumers regarding the final product of the production (competitiveness of the goods). Generally, the professional competence of an economist should be manifested in the analysis of these requirements and the effect on the restructuring of the production. In addition, a modern professional of urban economy greatly benefits when he or she is involved in socially significant projects, possibly, voluntary activities of an economic orientation. As for the correspondence of a professional economic training to the requirements of the labor market, the use of a competent approach becomes important, particularly, in cases when the future employer engages the training of the professional and training becomes an especially significant activity for an individual.

DISCUSSION

Competences of the Professional Required by the Employers in Modern Urban Economy

At the modern stage of the urban economy development, higher educational establishments require a more substantiated list of the competences needed by the professionals in the workplace to incorporate them into the programs of training for the Bachelor and master's degree levels. Traditionally, the requirements for the managers of the sector are registered in the job descriptions, which are considered as a basis for defining the competences needed. Most recently, urban economy has a large number of different positions and professions. Job descriptions regulate the organizational and legal status of the employees and determine their specific tasks and responsibilities, rights, powers, competences, knowledge and qualifications needed to ensure the effective work of the employees. Since university graduates, often claim to occupy leadership positions, the authors focused on the descriptions of these positions in the urban economy personnel system and identification of the core competencies that are required.

Having analyzed the approved job descriptions of the local governments of different regions of Ukraine, starting from the job description of the local mayor and the entire administrative apparatus to the job description of the heads of various branch departments, the authors have come to a conclusion that the instructions only state the basic:

1. rights, duties and tasks of an official (for example, contributes to drafting of budgets in the areas of housing and communal services and construction, architectural and urban planning, rational use of allocated funds; controls the transparency of management decisions, etc.);
2. qualification requirements (full higher education at the educational qualification level of the master's degree);
3. knowledge, including knowledge of the laws of Ukraine and the state language. For some positions, the requirements are expanded to special knowledge (foundations of regional management, personnel management, foundations of law, forms and methods of work with mass media, case management, etc.); and
4. the criteria of subordination and responsibility.

Therefore, in the analyzed material, there is a lack of clearly defined requirements for the competences that a candidate or an official must possess. These competences should be developed for each individual institution, which belongs to the urban economy or the local government. In order to expand the list of competences, the requirements for selecting candidates have been reviewed for the vacancies of experts/advisers/specialists of the municipal sector reform programs and government bodies of different levels, funded by international funds and institutions. In this research, the following flagship projects and programs have been used: Municipal Energy Reform in Ukraine" (USAID Project); "Urban Heating Reform in Ukraine" (USAID Project); DESPRO - Swiss-Ukrainian project "Support for decentralization in Ukraine" (funded by the Swiss Confederation); "Urban Infrastructure Development - 2" and "Increasing the Energy Efficiency in the District Heating System of Ukraine" (both projects were funded by the World Bank).

As the result of studying and analyzing the requirements for experts from these international programs, the authors find it expedient to use these groups of the requirements as a guide for the university programs developers. It is suggested that the proposed competences should include the basic requirements needed to meet the challenges of the current state of the industry development and be divided into four groups: (1) General qualification requirements for professional knowledge; (2) General qualification requirements for professional skills (abilities); (3) Special qualification requirements for professional knowledge; and (4) Special qualification requirements for professional skills/abilities (Ilienko, 2018b).

1. *General qualification requirements for professional knowledge* include: knowledge of normative legal acts (the Constitution of Ukraine, the laws of Ukraine "On Local Self-Government in Ukraine", "On Service in Local Self-Government Bodies", "On Civil Service", "On the Principles of Prevention and Counteraction to Corruption" and other laws of Ukraine on the organization and activities of local self-government bodies, decrees and orders of the President of Ukraine, resolutions of the Verkhovna Rada of Ukraine, resolutions and orders of the Cabinet of Ministers of Ukraine, other subordinate norms and legal acts regulating the development of appropriate management areas, etc.); the principles of public service; requirements for official behavior of a public officer; fundamental rights, obligations and restrictions of a public officer; the availability of specific professional knowledge required to perform professional duties.

2. *General qualification requirements for professional skills (abilities)* include: work in a specific area of activity; organization and implementation of tasks; realization of managerial decisions; effective planning of the working time; work planning; conducting business negotiations; analysis and forecasting using new software products; effective cooperation with the colleagues; constructive criticism; assessment and use of international experience in certain spheres of activities; use of modern office equipment and software products; systematic qualification improvement; preparation of business correspondence; communication in a foreign language.

3. *Special qualification requirements for the professional knowledge* necessary for the performance of official duties include: availability of special qualification, confirmed by a document of higher education of the state standard corresponding to the directions of activities of the structural unit; availability of professional knowledge (depending on the directions of activities of the institution or department); knowledge of the basics of project management; knowledge of the methods of analysis, planning and forecasting of economic processes; knowledge of socio-economic, investment opportunities of the economy of the territorial entity; knowledge of the methods for assessing the effectiveness of activities in the field of investment attraction and interaction with investors; knowledge of the forms of public-private partnership.

4. *Special qualification requirements for professional skills (abilities)* include: organizational work; critical thinking and system approach to problem solving; making managerial decisions; analytical work; exercising control; conducting business negotiations; conflict resolution and using mediation tools; using the methods of building interpersonal relations; determining motivation of the subordinates' behavior; making public speeches; maintaining interaction with the media.

At the present stage, educating professionals in the field of urban economy takes place in the direction of its modernization and introduction of the European standards of education. At the same time, it is suggested to take into account both national peculiarities and the current state of the Ukrainian economy as well as possible trends for its development. Accordingly, the preparation of professionals for urban economy should be based on the urgent needs of its modernization and management improvement.

Apart from studying the job descriptions for the leading positions, fifteen human resources managers of enterprises in the economic sector were involved in conducting a pilot study (March-April 2016) on the requirements for the professionals in urban economy. Thus, according to the employers, a competitive economist is one who shows a high level of professional competences, in particular, is able to conduct a financial analysis of the company's activities (82%), calculate and control the cost of goods (63%), plan the economic activities of the company (54%), keep track of payables and receivables (44%), effectively carry out contractual activities (79%), while showing accuracy and responsibility in working with primary documentation, management reporting (57%), interacting with external auditors (38%).

Furthermore, the respondents noted that they also set additional requirements for potential employees, which to a greater extent relate to personal qualities that determine the ability and desire for self-improvement. Thus, orientation in the modern legislative framework (62%), updating of professional knowledge through constant review of economic literature and specialized websites (33%), as well as participation in various seminars, webinars and professional trainings (55%) were identified as personal assets important for employment.

The analysis of the requirements for the professional qualities of the employees in the field of urban economy, as well as surveys of potential employers were taken into account when developing a scientific and methodological system for the formation of a competitive professional of urban economy. Sixty-two students of the Educational and Research Institute of Economics and Management of O.M. Beketov National University of Urban Economy in Kharkiv participated in the experimental work in 2016-2020. The reliability of the experimental data was ensured by the organization and conduct of an experimental study in the real conditions of educating professionals of urban economy at the university.

Therefore, in the research, the authors proceed from the fact that the development of the necessary set of competences for the formation of a future competitive professional in the field of urban economy should be based on using the best practices of urban enterprises in the world practice and the requirements that apply to managers at various levels, as well as requirements for personnel by local potential employers for organizations that are at the stage of the industry reformation.

On the basis of the analysis of the scientific literature and the requirements of employers, a structural model of the professional's competitiveness was designed, consisting of three components - need-motivational, cognitive-operational, and evaluation and reflexive, and a scientific and methodological system was developed, the application of which is aimed at the formation of all components of competitiveness of the professional of urban economy. The technology for implementation of the scientific and methodological system for the formation of the professional's competitiveness of urban economy is presented in the next subsection.

Competitiveness Components of the Professional of Urban Economy

To form the competitiveness of the future professional managers of urban economy, the authors distinguish such structural components of the specialist's competitiveness as *need-motivational, cognitive-operational* and *evaluation and reflexive.*

It is proved in the research that the need-motivational component of the competitiveness of the future professional of urban economy is determined by the motivation of the students regarding their professional activity, in particular, with a focus on achievement, success and career development; provides the need for self-regulation of behavior and performance. The desire for self-affirmation and self-expression is determined by the awareness of the need for self-development and mastery of the profession, as well as a continuous professional self-improvement.

As for the cognitive-operational component, it is concluded that the content of this component includes professionally and socially significant personal qualities; professional knowledge, abilities and skills that form an integrity of the perception of the profession; ensure effective decision-making in professional activities, determine the success of the professional's competitive behavior.

The evaluation and reflexive component is determined by the reflection of the quality of the process and the result of professional activity from the standpoint of the requirements of the labor market; implementation of self-assessment, self-control, self-analysis, management of self-development and professional growth, self-regulation of behavior; formation of self-knowledge and self-assessment of the professional potential, the level of competitiveness, as well as the reasons that impede its development.

However, the authors believe that the formation of the competitiveness components can not be completed within the limits of the educational environment. By activating the development of the future professional's competitiveness within the university environment, the educators launch the mechanism of their self-development within the professional environment in which this ability will be implemented. Therefore, the maximum results of the competitiveness formation and development can be primarily expected from the self-expression of the individual as a competitive professional in the professional environment.

Thus, competitiveness formation of the professional, in particular for urban economy, can be considered as a first stage of its development in the process of professional education. At this stage, the authors believe, the principle of complementarity is applied, that is, the mutual influence of the educational and socio-professional environment on the development of the individual as a competitive professional. In this process, each environment contributes its own component, resulting in a constant synergy that leads to the improvement of the environment and the methods of training. This principle provides for a constant feedback with the professional environment (stakeholders), contact with potential employers in this field, which determines their participation in all stages of the process of forming the future competitive professional (pilot questionnaire, participation in the preparation of educational and professional programs, evaluation of the results of the familiarization, educational and production practices etc.).

Therefore, the design and implementation of a scientific and methodological system for the formation of the competitiveness of the professional of urban economy should be carried out taking into consideration the suggested competitiveness components.

The Scientific and Methodological System of Forming the Competitiveness Components of the Future Professional of Urban Economy

As the result of the research, it was determined that the need-motivational and reflexive-evaluative components of competitiveness can be formed during the full cycle of implementation of the scientific and methodological system, while the cognitive-operational component requires a technological approach to its formation, which is connected with a gradual introduction into the training program of future specialists a set of educational disciplines, the content of which should be adjusted in accordance with the actualization of the problem of competitiveness.

It was noted that the need-motivational and reflexive-evaluative components of the competitiveness of future professionals of urban economy cannot be considered in isolation from the process of formation of the cognitive-operational component due to the fact that the level and content of motivation and reflection change according to the characteristics of the individual's orientation and interest in the professional activities.

Methods of Forming Need-Motivational and Evaluational and Reflexive Components of the Competitiveness of the Professional of Urban Economy

To form the *need-motivational* component of the competitiveness of the professional of urban economy, the authors identified the tasks providing for its development: 1) high motivation of professional activity, achievement motivation, high level of aspirations; 2) need for a successful activity and recognition of achievements; 3) need for self-regulation of behavior and activity, self-assertion, self-expression, need for self-development and mastering the profession; 4) need for continuous professional self-improvement.

The formation of the need-motivational component of the competitiveness of future professionals of urban economy takes place both in the process of teaching the disciplines of the humanitarian and professional cycles as well as within the scope of targeted trainings of the students.

Practical tasks on activation of the motivational potential of the individual, work with a motivational dictionary, trainings on setting goals and their successful achievement borrowed from the experience of Semichenko (2004) and adapted for the professionals of urban economy, are defined as effective ways of forming the need-motivational component of the competitiveness. The positive experience of successful entrepreneurs who are famous patrons and are involved in charity can be discussed in the English language class. Students study and analyze the professional achievements and philanthropic activities of five outstanding entrepreneurs; make comparative and summary tables; determine the personal traits that are characteristic of these people; develop definitions of these characteristics while working in small groups and give examples from the proposed texts or their own experience; work with motivational quotes.

Therefore, the implementation of the above-mentioned methods and ways of influencing the students in the educational process, made it possible to actualize their motivation regarding activities of professional realization, focus on self-expression in a competitive professional environment.

The tasks of forming the *evaluation and reflexive* component include the formation of skills of reflection of the quality of the process and result of the professional activity; development of self-assessment, self-control, self-analysis, management of self-development and professional growth, self-regulatory of behavior in the activity of the professional of urban economy; self-understanding and self-assessment of professional potential, implementation and evaluation of one's own competitiveness level, identification of reasons, which hamper its development, etc.

The formation of reflexive skills of future professionals of urban economy is carried out both in the process of teaching disciplines in class and within the scope of independent activities of students. According to the results of real or simulative interviews with the employers, students analyze their own achievements and shortcomings. Reflective self-assessment of readiness for professional activities is revealed through evaluation of resume effectiveness: students analyze the reasons for the employer's negative decision by correlating the level of their demands with the achieved result. In addition, future professionals have the opportunity to find out the opinion of the peer students about the content of the resume.

In order to orient future professionals of urban economy in awareness of their active resources and real opportunities relevant for getting a job, students are suggested to create intelligence maps "My Future Profession". The authors consider it important to focus students' attention on mental maps as a method of recording information in a concentric form that is logically connected in personal perception. In the process of the mentioned activity, future professionals develop the ability of a perspective reflection, which allows them to determine goals and resources for their achievement.

As a result of the implementation of reflexive methods, future professionals of urban economy learn to realize their own goals, assess the level of readiness for professional implementation, identify personal resources that can help in finding and obtaining a job, and achieve the adequacy of self-assessment regarding the level of personal competitiveness.

Pedagogical Technology of Forming the Cognitive-Operational Component of Competitiveness of the Professional in Urban Economy

The formation of the *cognitive-operational* component of competitiveness of future specialists of urban economy requires, in the authors' opinion, the introduction of a special pedagogical technology associated with a gradual introduction of academic disciplines into the curricula of future specialists, whose content should be adjusted according to the actualization of the competitiveness problem.

In particular, in the first year of educating within the framework of the academic disciplines of the general academic cycle ("Ukrainian Language for Professional Purposes", "Psychology", "English language") it is considered expedient to present the role of communication in competitive relations; to provide information on competitive relations in society and in professional environments; to actualize personality qualities positive for competitiveness (adequate self-esteem, confidence, leadership, etc.).

In the second year, the specialist educating program must be supplemented with professional disciplines; therefore, the mentioned stage of forming the cognitive-operational component of competitiveness should be focused on the formation of general and professional competence of the future professionals of urban economy.

In the third year, students have to learn to implement the acquired competences in practice; consequently, the task of this stage of competitiveness formation is the actualization of general and personal competences as necessary for professional recognition. At this stage, students have to understand the requirements of potential employers to applicants for vacancies.

The fourth year of educating is marked by the organization of students' work in the framework of bachelor's degree program aimed at implementation and presentation of graduate qualification work, so it is considered necessary to actualize the formation of skills of interaction and teamwork as important for the future competitive professional.

Thus, the stages of the technology of forming the cognitive and operational component of the future professional's competitiveness of urban economy are determined as follows:

- formation of the system of knowledge about competitiveness and communicative skills (1st year);
- formation of general professional and personal competences (2nd year);
- actualization of general professional and personal competences (3rd year);
- formation of teamwork skills (4th year).

However, as it has been mentioned earlier, the formation of a particular personal ability, especially competitiveness, is not completed within the same environment. Therefore, the implementation of the scientific and methodological system within the framework of the professional training at the university, especially in the field of urban economy, can be considered as an initial stage of forming competitiveness which should be continued in professional environment.

The authors believe that the formation of a complex of professional competences, enabling students to perceive the professional sphere of activity holistically, objectively and dynamically, occurs through a modular and supplementary model of introduction into the educational process of the information about the competitiveness of the modern professional in urban economy. The modular model implies inclusion of special topics and modules into the academic disciplines, and the supplementary model includes work on formation of competitiveness of a future professional outside the academic classes.

It should be noted that the use of the modular model is focused on the formation of competitiveness of the professional, i.e., thematic representation of the concept of competitiveness in the content of the defined academic disciplines.

For instance, one of the purposes of the discipline "Ukrainian Language for Professional Purposes" is formation of skills of effective business communication that is considered to be important in the aspect of professionals' competitiveness formation. In this case, the first step, which determines the level of communication efficiency in the business community, is the presentation of oneself as a practitioner in the resume form, and therefore, it is important to teach students how to create this communicative product, the content and form of which can become an effective introduction for the future collaboration with the employer. It should be noted that the motivation for students when creating a resume is to become aware of the high competition in the labor market among the economists of the economic field of training, and thus the applicant must make every effort to present positively their professional and personal qualities to the prospective employer.

The tasks of analyzing and creating a resume are intended to familiarize students with the structure and basic rules of creating a resume to obtain employment. Comparison of the examples of properly executed resumes and those that contain mistakes makes it possible to acquaint students with writing and formatting a resume in such a way as to successfully beat the competition and land a desired position. In the analysis, students are encouraged to give their suggestions for improving the suggested resumes, to explain which mistakes should be avoided. The next task is to create one's own resume, discuss it with partners and introduce the necessary changes.

Within the framework of the discipline *"English Language"* students continue to shape the skills of creating an effective resume in an international context. They have an opportunity to analyze English business documentation, advertisements for vacant positions and take part in simulation interviews in English. The results of the research show, for instance, that stressful interviews are a good way to demonstrate the skills of a job applicant, such as the ability to think quickly, stay focused, make decisions, and react to conflicts. In today's globalized world, organizations and companies demand a creative, dynamic work from their staff, which can be composed of people representing different cultures and possess different levels of proficiency in English. It should be noted that among the reasons why applicants failed to get an employment, the inability to communicate clearly, poor pronunciation and grammar are second in importance (Job Interview, 2022).

The stages of training students in English interview skills in the international context are: the preparatory stage, participation in interviews, the evaluation stage and feedback implementation. During the preparatory stage, students encounter the following tasks: 1) to prepare and tell about the positive and negative experience of participating in job interviews or other interviews; 2) search the Internet for professional skills and competencies tested during the interview; 3) search for websites with questions of the interviewer and think about possible responses; 4) prepare documents necessary for participation in the simulation interview (resume, cover letter, acknowledgement sheet).

At the next stage, students are shown films that contain footage of how candidates participate in competency-based interviews. During the discussion of these interviews with students, the instructors identify the problem areas of communication (in particular, nonverbal and intercultural aspects) and propose ways to solve the problem. The sampling includes an interview, where certain problems can be explained by cultural misunderstandings. At this stage, students likewise focus their attention on discussing the application documents of the applicants for the vacant position and their structure according to the standards of English-speaking countries. Later, the standard interview procedure, the importance of self-knowledge and the ability to demonstrate their strengths are discussed. It should be noted that Western interviewers give preference to self-confident candidates. For representatives of Western countries, this implies skills such as proactivity, motivation, independent thinking, autonomy and responsibility. It is likewise important to focus students' attention on nonverbal communication, since many details may vary in different cultural contexts, such as gestures, eye contact, physical distance, etc. Moreover, it is necessary to reinforce and discuss such items as punctuality, clothing, duration of answers and questions, time to think through complex issues. It is important to emphasize that personal impressions, such as physical distance, body language, laugh, accent, pronunciation, tone and the pitch of voice or use of humor can be as relevant as the professional skills and experience of the applicant for the vacant position.

During the evaluation and feedback phase, students review videos from the websites of international career counselling companies and discuss interviews made by career consultants, human resource managers and professionals, to hear their arguments and comments. Additionally, it is advisable to focus on the differences in communication procedures in the English and Ukrainian environments. For example, in English-speaking countries, as opposed to Ukraine, the questioning of the interviewer is accepted. This is often taken as a sign of candidate's detailed orientation and pro-activity in filling the vacant position. Specific features of different types of interviews are likewise discussed with the students, such as group interviews, pro-active interviews, stressful interviews, etc.

In order to give students an opportunity to gain hands-on experience in managerial activities and implementation of professional communication in the English classroom, case studies are designed which highlight the problem of professional's competitiveness. The problem of competitiveness is mainstreamed in the cases in several directions: students analyze and discuss, for example, the company's competitive advantages, the company's strategies in dealing with staff members, the competitive advantages of an individual specialist, and the documents required to access employment. Through such work students likewise become aware of the essence of their competitiveness as a professional.

An example of a creative task on development of competitiveness of a future professional used for the hands-on training exercises on the discipline "Fundamentals of Business Communication" is the task on the topic "Formation and Analysis of the Organizational Culture Level". The purpose of the creative work is to teach students to analyze the process of organizational culture formation, determine its types and components, the sequence of manager's actions during its development; to discuss the competitive advantages of organizational culture of companies and organizations. Students are tasked with reading examples of the organizational culture of well-known companies and identifying the components that, in their opinion, are most important for the formation of a strong corporate culture of an organization. The next step is to provide suggestions for improving corporate culture and justify them. To benefit from students' personal experience in assessing the type of corporate culture, they are tasked to evaluate the organizational culture of the university they study at, namely to determine, which of the components of the organizational culture are most pronounced in the university, what functions the existing organizational culture performs and fails to perform, whether the organizational culture of the university is strong and what methods would be advisable for the organizational culture of the university to be developed. Proceeding from the fact that a strong organizational culture is a sign of the organization's competitiveness, in particular the university, in performing the task students are given the opportunity to make a reflection on how they perceive their higher education, understand its competitive advantages and assess their personal competitiveness.

Within the discipline "Psychology", the students' knowledge about the role of manipulation in professional activity is updated. In particular, after updating the knowledge of verbal and nonverbal manipulation for future specialists instructors provide a training to resist this phenomenon in modern management and marketing. The training consists of three parts: the introductory part providing information on its objectives and guidelines on the forms of activity; the main part in which students are involved in the interaction according to a certain task; the final part in which the results of the training are discussed. In particular, first, students gain knowledge about assertiveness as a quality that makes it possible for them to express self-esteem and respect for their communication partner; second, they perform the exercise "polite refusal" aimed at developing the skills of refusing a person's request (Morhunova & Rezvan, 2017, p. 28); third, they discuss their own emotional state felt by each communicant (both the asker and the refuser) during the refusal process.

Conducting "Team Building" training in classes in the discipline "Psychology" was likewise found to be a coherent task of shaping the future professional's competitiveness. The aim of the training consists in developing the students' ability to work successfully in a team, namely the creation of an effective team model, the formation and strengthening of a common team spirit, appreciation each other's differences, team building, acquiring the skills of working together and learning the way of developing a common strategy. Psychological drills "We are one team!" and "My contribution to the team" train teamwork skills, actualize each participant's awareness of his or her role in the team, the contribution he or she makes to the teamwork and to the development of respect for other team members, recognizing the importance of their roles.

The updating of information about the competitiveness of both the enterprise and the professional within the discipline "Economics of the Enterprise" is facilitated by the work on the topic "Assessment of the Meso Environment of the Enterprise. Analysis of Competitors." The analytical task is aimed at developing students' skills to analyze such element of inter-enterprise environment as competitors and the ability to analyze both competitive advantages and disadvantages, to determine the competitiveness of enterprises of urban economy and other enterprises using comparative tables. Students are guided that the more an enterprise (professional) knows about its competitors, the more it (he) will be able to do so as to provide higher quality services and make them more attractive to customers. While performing the work, students identify advantages/disadvantages of their competitors and make up comparison tables, compare advantages of enterprises of urban economy and their competitors. Moreover, an attempt should be made to identify the enterprise-alone characteristics (professional's characteristics), thus enabling to achieve clear competitive advantages in a certain market sector. When discussing competitive advantages, students work in small groups, which makes it possible for them to apply their skills in teamwork and joint decision-making.

The humanistic aspect of competitiveness issues is mainstreamed in the process of studying the discipline "The City as a Social System" (2nd year). The purpose of teaching the discipline is to familiarize students with the city concept, the typology and evolution of cities, the current state of urban development (post-industrial city) and the opportunities that the city as a social structure provides a person with as its part and as an individual. Consciousness of the future specialists of urban economy is directed to the fact that each citizen is included, on the one hand – in the city social networks (i.e. is a user of each of these networks), and on the other hand – in the development of a particular social structure (as he/she is a representative of one of them) - an employee of a particular organization that creates a product for other users of the city social networks. In this respect, important for each urbanite as a representative of the social system is his/her demand for other representatives of society, which means that social responsibility of each future specialist is referred to.

In classes on the discipline "The City as a Social System", students implement a course project on the social organization of the city. They need to conduct an analysis of a particular city in terms of the presence or absence of a comfortable urban environment in it. The competitiveness of the future professional is formed in this task by developing a critical sociological point of view and the ability to apply sociological theories to the analysis of urban society, creating an effective competitive project and its presentation, as well as developing the professional's creative potential.

In completing the project, students consider the varieties of social connections and patterns of social life inherent in cities and their different cultural contexts. Analysis of urban communities makes it possible for them to focus on the social life of citizens, territorial associations (networks of interactions), to study the socio-cultural processes of urban community life, public and private in their living space, referring to the research of urban everyday life. The creative task involves providing suggestions for the development of one's own hometown. It is noted that the social targeting of the projects is important, i.e., the use of the theory of generations. Urban projects should be linked to specific generations of the city rather than focusing on the average citizen.

For students to consolidate the skills to respond to the needs of the society and be successful social partners it is necessary to create conditions for implementation in volunteer organizations, which gives one the flexibility to join a socially oriented activity. In particular, students get the opportunity to be realized creatively within the centers operating on the basis of O.M. Beketov National University of Urban Economy in Kharkiv (KhNUUE). Such activities are carried out within the framework of a supplementary model for the formation of the competitiveness of the professional of urban economy.

Participation in the project "Gender Audit of Urban Space" conducted in Kharkiv, Chuhuiv (Kharkiv region) and Komsomolsk (Poltava region) made it possible to orient future professionals of urban economy on the importance of taking into account the social needs of the population to ensure effective use of urban recreational areas. The students conducted a survey on meeting the needs of children of different ages and genders within playgrounds; safety of being in recreation areas; equipment for people with low mobility (mothers with baby carriages), etc. After conducting the audit, the heads of territorial administrations were provided with proposals for improving the conditions of certain areas for the users.

So, in the process of studying, students get the opportunity to both learn the specifics of the content of the concept of "competitiveness" in relation to the organization and professional, and to join diversified activities so as to acquire competitiveness within the professional environment.

In the framework of the discipline "Management" in the third year of training, educators note the need to develop the competitiveness of the future professional, in particular, when performing creative tasks on the topic "Diagnosis of the Stages of the Enterprise's Life Cycle". The task objective is to develop students' skills in creating a graph of the company's life cycle, highlighting the competitive advantages of each cycle; analyzing the manager's actions and their sequence, which resulted in a competitive advantage for the company in the industry market at a certain stage, as well as creating a plan for company's successful development for the near future and conducting its presentation.

According to the task, students should get acquainted with the provided information about well-known domestic and foreign companies, for example, AUDI and PRADA companies, identify the main stages of the life cycle of the above companies, completing the table. Additionally, it is necessary to determine the current stage of the company's life cycle, what level of competitiveness it possesses and to propose recommendations for extending the company's life cycle. The proposed development plan of the company is presented in the form of written assignments produced or an oral presentation.

In the fourth year of educating students, the formation of future professional's competitiveness in the field of urban economy is implemented within the study of the discipline "Project Analysis". Assessment of projects efficiency and competitive advantages contributing to the priority of their financing are discussed in the classes on "Models and Mechanisms of Projects Financing". As a result of the analysis associated with the construction of graphs and filling out tables, the student is assigned the task of selecting the most efficient projects among all the available in the company, using the "cost-effect" relationship. When discussing competitive advantages, it is considered appropriate to concentrate resources on those projects that provide the main contribution to the overall results. Students are likewise encouraged to join in evaluating the effectiveness of real student business projects submitted to the startup competitions at the university Business Incubator.

Consequently, the formation of specific skills and qualities contributing to the improvement of the professional's competitiveness occur in the process of students' educational and cognitive activities within certain disciplines and opportunities to implement the acquired competencies, during extracurricular activities conducted in the university's student centers.

At the control stage of the experimental work, a positive dynamics of the competitiveness formation of the professional of urban economy was revealed by all indicators, in particular, a high level of competitiveness was registered in 26.98% of the participants of the experimental group and 56% of the participants demonstrated an average level of competitiveness.

SOLUTIONS AND RECOMMENDATIONS

The results of the study have demonstrated that the formation of a competitive professional of urban economy is expedient to carry out using the scientific and methodological system developed by the authors. The suggested scientific and methodical system has been developed and tested at the Educational and Research Institute of Economics and Management of O.M. Beketov National University of Urban Economy in Kharkiv in 2016-2020. The proposed system, which has been implemented in the educational process, provides for the supplement of the content of the academic disciplines separate modules and topics that reflect the content of the concept of "competitiveness", its essence and importance in professional activities. The pedagogical technology of introducing modules that focus on the formation and development of competitiveness skills is shown in Table 1.

The main task of the first year of educating is to form students' professional and communicative competences, in particular, foreign language competence, as well as basic knowledge about competition as a factor of development of the society and personality. In the second year of educating, both *general competences* such as: ability to locate, analyze and apply information obtained from various sources, solve problems and make decisions; to demonstrate ethical responsibility for professional decisions; as well as *professional* ones: identification of company's types of competitive advantages; performance of calculations related to the evaluation of the level of competition in the industry; providing economic substantiation and concretization of the functions of company competitiveness management are formed. The task of introducing the module model in the third year of training is to form students' general competencies related to the skills of team interaction and personnel management (organizational, leadership) and professional competencies related to HR-management (recruiting new personnel): developing job profiles; creating requirements for candidates to the position; developing professional staff selection procedures; etc. In the fourth year of educating students within the discipline "Project Analysis" the following professional competencies are formed: development of the structure and organization of the project work; planning the implementation of the project in time; definition of project costs and resources; development of a risk response plan.

When determining the complex of disciplines necessary for the formation of the competitiveness of the future professional, it was assumed that students will be able to use the previously received information about competitiveness to solve the tasks of the following disciplines. The authors believe that the future professional cannot be realized as a "synthesizer" of knowledge in various fields of science unless intersystem associations are formed in his/her consciousness, covering various systems and disciplines, forming generalized concepts, interrelation of theories. Therefore, a competitive professional begins where there is an opportunity to solve the problem of building a holistic picture from the fragments acquired by studying various sciences or different approaches within the same science.

Table 1. Introduction of information on competitiveness within the framework of academic training in the specialty "Economics of the Enterprise of Urban Economy" at O. M. Beketov National University of Urban Economy in Kharkiv

Course	Discipline	Learning Objectives of the Students
1 course	Ukrainian Language for Professional Purposes	To prepare a resume or curriculum vitae that contains updated information of competitive elements of one's experience.
	English language	To prepare professional resumes and other supporting documents for positions within an international business environment.To prepare for potential positions through simulated interviews.
	Fundamentals of Business Communication	To understand the benefits and individual roles of successfully working in a team; organization and maintenance of business relationships.
	Psychology	To learn the rules for resisting manipulation in business environment.To master the effective methods of argumentation, conviction, denial, recognition of psychological states for effective communication at job interviews.
2 course	Economics of the Enterprise	To understand the system of ensuring product competitiveness (Module "Company's Products". Competitiveness of Products".) Module "Company's Competitiveness").
	City as a Social System	To understand the role of corporate social responsibility as a competitiveness factor
	Competitiveness of the Enterprise	To learn the theoretical foundations of competitive relations at the enterprise.
3 course	Management	To develop individual projects in the field of personnel management;
4 course	Project Analysis	To evaluate the project implementation rate by key success criteria (compared to other projects).

FUTURE RESEARCH DIRECTIONS

The conducted research does not cover all aspects of the problem of forming a future competitive professional of urban economy. In further research, it is suggested to solve the problem of supplementing educational programs for the majority of the core disciplines with methods and means of forming the competitiveness of the future professional, taking into account the international best practices and the needs of potential employers in the country and the region.

Rapidly changing requirements of the industry representatives for educating professionals in the field of urban economy should be taken into account through a close cooperation of the both parties concerned: by conducting regular surveys among local and all-country potential employers, involving them in the creation and evaluation of the university educational programs, opening research laboratories on the basis of production sites, expanding and diversifying the system of production trainings, attracting industry representatives to participate in Job Fairs, etc.

CONCLUSION

As the results of the research indicate, the degree of development of the problem of professional training of the competitive professional in philosophical, psychological, and pedagogical aspects is revealed. The dependence of the competitiveness of the enterprises of urban economy on the competitiveness of the personnel, the professionals capable of intellectual and professional development and implementation of innovations according to the world standards, creation of competitive products is emphasized.

When developing methods and means of educating competitive professionals in the field of urban economy, the qualification requirements for specialists in this industry, which are presented to participants in international projects, as well as the results of a survey of a group of human resources managers in the industry, are used.

The structural components of the competitiveness of the professional of urban economy are distinguished: need-motivational (motivation for professional realization, focus on achievement, success and career development), cognitive-operational (professionally significant, socially significant personal qualities; professional competences, professional mobility and activity in professional self-expression), evaluation and reflexive (reflection of the quality of the process and the result of professional activity from the standpoint of market requirements; self-assessment, management of self-development and professional growth, etc.).

On the basis of the characteristics of the competitiveness components, a scientific and methodical system for the formation of the competitive professional of urban economy is developed. The formation of a complex of professional competencies for competitiveness components, which enables students to perceive the professional activities holistically, objectively and dynamically, takes place according to the modular (adding special topics, modules to educational disciplines) and supplementary (extracurricular activities) models of introduction to the training process the information on the competitiveness of the modern professional of urban economy.

The main academic disciplines are specified, within which the system of forming the competitiveness of the professional of urban economy is implemented, provided an opportunity to consistently influence the student's personality in order to orient them to competitiveness in the profession. In the first year of studies, the task is to acquire basic knowledge about competition as a factor in the development of the society and the place of the individual in competitive world. Later, attention is focused on the formation of general and professional competences of the professional of urban economy such as ability to work in a team, adaptability, ethical responsibility for professional decisions, assessment of competition on the market, economic justification and specification of the functions of managing the competitiveness of the enterprise. recruiting new staff, developing a structure and organizing project work; determination of project costs and resources, etc.

Within the supplementary model of the system of formation of the competitive professional of urban economy the students have the opportunity to implement the acquired competencies within and outside the university environment.

As the result of the experimental work, the dynamics of shifts in the formation of each of the criteria of competitiveness of the future professionals were tracked and measured. The control testing conducted at the end of the experiment, showed significant positive changes in all controlled criteria which indicates the effectiveness of the proposed method of competitiveness forming of the professional of urban economy.

REFERENCES

Allport, G. (1998). Lichnost v psihologii [Personality in psychology]. KMP+; Yuventa.

Allport, G. (2002). *Stanovlenie lichnosti. Izbrannye trudy [Becoming a Personality. Selected Works]*. (L. V. Trubicynoy & D. A. Leonteva, Trans. in Eng.). Smysl.

Andriiako, T. Yu. (2010). Pedahohichna sutnist i struktura konkurentospromozhnosti [Pedagogical essence and structure of competitiveness]. *Pedahohichna nauka: istoriia, teoriia, praktyka, tendentsii rozvytku [Pedagogical science: History, theory, Practice, development trends], 1*(3). http://intellect-invest.org.ua/pedagog_editions_e-magazine_pedagogical_science_vypuski_n3_2010_st_6/.

Bandura, A. (1984). Regulation of cognitive process through perceived self efficacy. *Developmental Psychology, 25*(5), 729–735. doi:10.1037/0012-1649.25.5.729

Dewey, J. (1999). *Psykhologiya i pedagogika myshleniya [Psychology and pedagogics of thinking]*. (N. M. Nykolskaya, Trans. in Eng.). Labirint.

Dewey, J. (2003). Problema cheloveka [Problem of a human]. *Rekonstruktsyia v filosofii [Reconstruction in philosophy]*. (L. E. Pavlova, Trans. in Eng.). Moskva, 133–450.

Erikson, E (1996). *Identichnost: yunost i krizis [Identity: youth and crisis]*. (A. V. Tolstyh, Trans. in Eng.). Progress.

Freud, A. (2016). *Psihologiya YA i zashchitnye mekhanizmy [Psychology of I and defensive mechanisms]*. Piter.

Greison, J., & O'Dell, K. (1991). *Amerykanskiy menedzhment na poroge XXI veka [American management on the threshold of the XXI century]*. Ekonomika..

Hayek, F. A. (2001). Individualizm i ekonomicheskiy poryadok [Individualism and economical order]. Moskva: Izograf; Nachala-Fond..

Ilienko, O. (2018a). Philosophical foundation of the concept of competitiveness of an individual. *Imperatives of civil society development in promoting national competitiveness: Proceedings of the 1st International Scientific and Practical Conference*, Batumi, Georgia, *1,* 270–272.

Ilienko, O. (2018b). Specific features of training competitive professionals of municipal economy. *European Humanities Studies: State and Society, 3,* 33–45.

James, W. (1997). *Prahmatizm. Volia k vere [Pragmatism. Will to believe].* (L. V. Blinnikova, & A. P. Poliakov, Trans. in Eng.). Respublika.

James, W. (2000). *Psikhologiya lichnosti [Psychology of a personality].* Moskva: Teksty..

Job. Interview. *Career Studies.* Retrieved from https://www.fehb.org/Classes/AEC/AECCulArts/pdfFiles/Job%20Interviewing%20Skills%20Lesson%20Plan.pdf

Kubanov, R. (2014). Vymohy do profesiinoi pidhotovky fakhivtsiv ekonomichnykh spetsialnostei ta yikh realizatsiia v osvitnomu protsesi vyshchoho navchalnoho zakladu [Requirements for professional training of economic specialists and their implementation in the main process of a higher educational institution]. *Naukovyi visnyk Melitopolskoho derzhavnoho pedahohichnoho universytetu [Scientific Bulletin of the Melitopol State Pedagogoical University], 2*(13), 294–301 (in Ukr.).

Martens, R. (1976). *Sotsialnaya psikhologiya i sport [Social psychology and sport].* Fyzkultura y sport [Physial Education and sports].

Maslow, A. (2003). Samoaktualizaciya [Self-actualization]. *Prosveshchennyy menedzhment, Organizacionnaya teoriya [Enlightened Management, Organizational Theory]* (N. Levkinoy, A. C. Hekha, Trans. in Eng.). Piter, 41-147..

Maslow, A. (2006). *Motivatsiya i lichnost [Motivation and personality].* Piter..

Mill, J. (1980). *Osnovy politicheskoy ekonomiki [Basics of political economy]* (Trans. in Eng.). (Vol. 1). Progress..

Morhunova, S. O., & Rezvan, O. O. (2017). *Treninh sotsialnoi vzaiemodii: navch.-metod. posibnyk [Social interaction training, educational and methodological manual].* Miskdruk.

Porter, M. (1980). *Competitive strategy: techniques for analyzing industries and competitors.* The Free Press.

Posylkina, O. V., & Bratishko, Yu. S. (2016). Doslidzhennia vymoh robotodavtsiv do kandydativ na posadu menedzhera iz sotsialnoi vidpovidalnosti suchasnykh farmatsevtychnykh pidpryiemstv [Study of employers' requirements for candidates for the position of social responsibility manager of modern pharmaceutical enterprises]. *Upravlinnia, ekonomika ta zabezpechennia yakosti v farmatsii [Management, economics, and quality assurance in pharmacy], 3*(47), 38-44 (in Ukr.).

Rezvan, O. O. (2014). *Formuvannia profesiino-refleksyvnoi pozytsii maibutnikh fakhivtsiv avtomobilno-dorozhnoi haluzi [Formation of a professional and reflexive position of future specialists in the automobile and road industry].* Tochka.

Ricardo, D. (2001). *The principles of political economy and taxation.* EconLib. https://www.econlib.org/library/Ricardo/ricPCover.html

Rogers, K. R. (1984). *Empatiya. Psihologiya emociy [Empathy. Psychology of emotions]* (Trans. in Eng.). MGU.

Rogers, K. R. (2000). *Stanovlenie lichnosti: vzglyad na psihoterapiyu [Becoming a personality: a look at the psychotherapy]* (Trans. in Eng.). EKSMO-Press..

Romanovskiy, A. G., Mihaylichenko, V. E., & Gren, L. N. (2018). *Pedagogika liderstva: monografiya [Pedagogics of Leadership: a monography].* FLP Brovin A. V.

Romanovskyi, O. H., Ponomarov, O. S., & Reznik, S. M. (2014). *Otsinka konkurentospromozhnosti fakhivtsia i yakosti yoho profesiinoi pidhotovky: navch.-metod. posib [Evaluation of the competitiveness of a specialist and the quality of his professional training: educational and methodological manual].* NTU, KhPI.

Semichenko, V. A. (2004). *Problemy motivacii povedeniya i deyatelnosti cheloveka. Modulnyy kurs psihologii. Modul,, Napravlenost": lekcii, prakticheskie zanyatiya, zadaniya dlya samostoyatelnoy raboty [Problems of motivation of behavior and human activity. Modular psychology course. "Direction" module: lectures, practical exercises, tasks for independent work].* Millenium.

Shapovalov, V. I. (2017). *Konkurentosposobnost lichnosti v paradigme innovacionnogo pedagogicheskogo menedzhmenta [Competitiveness of the individual in the paradigm of innovative pedagogical management].* Uchil. http://uchil.net/?cm=83719...

Smith, A. (1997). *Teoriya nravstvennyh chuvstv [Moral sentiment theory].* Respublika..

Smith, A. (2007). *Issledovanie o prirode i prichinah bogatstva narodov [Research on the nature and causes of the wealth of nations].* Eksmo..

Vachevskyi, M. V., Madzihon, V. M., & Prymachenko, N. M. (2007). *Osnovy ekonomiky: navch. posibnyk [Basics of economy: a tutorial].* Ped. dumka.

Viter, S. (2012) Vymohy do maibutnikh fakhivtsiv ekonomichnoho profiliu u konteksti pidhotovky dlia ahrarnoi sfery [Requirements for future specialists of the economic profile in the context of training for the agrarian sphere]. *Molod i rynok, 6 (89),*140-145.

Zadorozhna, N. V. (2013). Formuvannia komunikatyvnoi kompetentnosti u profesiinii pidhotovtsi ekonomistiv [Formation of communicative competence in professional training of economists]. *Neperervna profesiina osvita: teoriia i praktyka [Continuous Professional Education: Theory and Practice], 3-4,* 75-78. http://nbuv.gov.ua/UJRN/NPO_2013_3-4_13 (in Ukr.).

Zakharova, M. A., Mezynov, V. N., & Karpacheva, Y. A. (2017). *Teoriya i praktika formirovaniya konkurentosposobnosti uchitelya v vuze: monografiya [Theory and practice of the teacher competitiveness formation at the university: a monograph].* EHU ym. Y. A. Bunyna.

Zavalevskyi, Yu. I. (2014) *Teoretyko-metodychni zasady formuvannia vchytelia yak konkurentospromozhnoho fakhivtsia: monohrafiia [Theoretical and methodological principles of the formation of a teacher as a competitive professional: a monograph].* Bukrek.

KEY TERMS AND DEFINITIONS

Competitiveness of the Professional of Urban Economy: This consists of such structural components as *need-motivational, cognitive-operational* and *evaluation and reflexive* defined by the motivation of the students regarding their professional activity, availability of professionally and socially significant personal qualities; professional knowledge, abilities and skills that form an integrity of the perception of the profession, the reflection of the quality of the process and the result of professional activity from the standpoint of the requirements of the labor market.

Principle of Complementarity: This is reflected in the mutual influence of the educational and socio-professional environment on the development of the individual as a competitive professional. This principle provides for a constant feedback with the professional environment (stakeholders), contact with potential employers in this field, which determines their participation in all stages of the process of forming the future competitive professional.

Process of Competitiveness Development: This combines formation of competitiveness during the professional education with the subsequent use of this quality in the process of performing production functions and career growth.

Professional Requirements by the Employers in Modern Urban Economy: These include: (1) General qualification requirements for professional knowledge; (2) General qualification requirements for professional skills (abilities); (3) Special qualification requirements for professional knowledge; and (4) Special qualification requirements for professional skills/abilities. The professionals should be capable of intellectual and professional development and implementation of innovations according to the world standards, creation of competitive products.

Technology of Competitiveness Forming of the Professional: An introduction into the educational process a set of techniques of forming and developing competitiveness of the professional of urban economy using modular and supplementary models. The modular model implies inclusion of special topics and modules into the academic disciplines, and the supplementary model includes work on formation of competitiveness of a future professional outside the academic classes.

Section 3

Europe:
The Strength of Economic Integration

Chapter 4
Towards Places and Ecosystems:
The Integrated Management of Locations, Destinations, and the Living Space

Julian Philipp
Catholic University of Eichstätt-Ingolstadt, Germany

Harald Pechlaner
Catholic University of Eichstätt-Ingolstadt, Germany

ABSTRACT

Traditionally, locations, destinations, and living spaces have been managed, developed, and marketed separately. However, various global megatrends such as digitalization, globalization, or climate change—as well as changing needs of workers, tourists, or residents—have put these spatial layers in a state of transformation. In the course of this transformation, integrated spatial development and management concepts have emerged over the past two decades, as modern cities need to manage their neighborhoods and living spaces, business locations, leisure and culture offers, and their tourism attractions holistically. Two main development paths are elaborated: place management, and the ecosystem approach.

INTRODUCTION

The Management of Locations, Living Spaces, and Destinations

Traditionally, the different spatial layers of cities and regions – mainly the location, the living space and the destination – are perceived, managed and developed separately. The term location refers to the economic layer of a city or region and the various businesses and firms settled in it. Economic development is often the main responsibility of local or regional business development agencies, or economic development agencies that focus on attracting businesses and fostering the economic development by creating and maintaining industrial districts or clusters, offering incentives or providing infrastructural support (Nie,

DOI: 10.4018/978-1-6684-5976-8.ch004

1993). The main tasks of location management or economic development are 1) the protection of existing and creation of new jobs, 2) securing and optimizing the local economy and financial power, and 3) creation of a balanced economic structure (Markert, 2018). Hence, there is usually a close cooperation and exchange between the administration of a location and the local businesses. There are three layers of economic development: local economic development including businesses, founders, employees or politics; regional economic development including chambers, associations, banks, the public, educational institutions or citizens; and the trans-regional economic development including governments, investment funds, national associations or labor unions. Therefore, the tasks and responsibilities of location management and economic development are quite diverse, ranging from technological funding to regional marketing to simple building permissions or sales of industrial areas (Vogelgesang & Stember, 2021).

The living space is "the inhabited or occupied space of a social group and [...] the sum of people, infrastructures, [...] culture and identity" (Döll-König & Pechlaner, 2022, p. 6) that people encounter in their daily life. Its management is often within the responsibilities of city and rural developers, resident bureaus, as well as urban and rural planning or development departments that focus on the use and development of land and aim at "address[ing] the basic human needs of communities" (Cobbinah, 2017, p.223). Key tasks of the management of cities or urban and rural living spaces include the development of concepts for the design, organization and leadership of urban development processes and projects, the communication and cooperation with participating actors, and the implementation of these concepts and plans (Sinning, 2011). Following new trends and developments of the past decades, relatively new tasks of living space management are the culturalization of urban and rural politics, the development and implementation of project for improving socially underprivileged areas, attraction building through events and projects, and local participation (Ostergren & Rice, 2004). According to Sinning (2011), urban and rural living space management includes neighborhood management, infrastructure management, housing management, facility management, floor management, brownfield management, mobility management or sustainability management. Despite similar management and development intentions and approaches, there are some significant differences between urban and rural spaces as well, such as the population density, the relationship among residents, public and transport infrastructure, economies, or costs for housing or other essential goods (cf. Mair, 2010).

Then again, local and regional tourism management and marketing is often the role of the respective destination management organization (DMO) that coordinates public and private stakeholders to further develop the local tourism process by providing tourism products and services and attracting visitors to the destination (Reinhold et al., 2019). Historically speaking, destination management started with a focus in information and infrastructure provision as well as industry representation. When the markets became more demand-driven, new forms of marketing, financing and organization emerged that, in the age of digitalization, further developed into a management of customer journeys and destination networks focusing on specific target groups and processes (Bieger & Klumbies, 2022) and often drawing upon the routes and attraction points that initially attract visitors to a destination and influence their movement patterns (Beritelli et al., 2015). Depending on its transaction costs, power asymmetries, interdependencies, control mechanisms, knowledge base and informal connections, destinations can be dominated either by a community or a corporate model (cf. Beritelli et al., 2007). DMOs can have different structures – they can be governmental departments, divisions within such departments, government-like corporations, public-private agencies, private corporations or even non-for-profit organizations – and usually focus their work around external marketing, internal management, and strategic development (Presenza et al., 2005). Primary tasks of DMOs are the production and supply of services, the development of new, distinctive and competitive products, and both internal and external communication (Sainaghi, 2006). Beyond that, modern DMOs are also involved in activities such as research, resource stewardship, risk management, relationship building, human resource training, lobbying, information provision, business support, or various additional tasks that come up in terms of branding, visitor experiences, leadership or crisis management (Pearce, 2015).

BACKGROUND

The Need for Integrated Location, City and Destination Management

These separated approaches have lately been challenged in numerous ways: First of all, the traditional separation between location management, living space management and destination management has had numerous implications for the respective cities and regions. It has resulted in the emergence of "self-reliant organizations and process flows that run independently from one another and [...] make integration more difficult" (Döll-König & Pechlaner, 2022, p. 6), aiming at addressing the increasing number of target groups within the sectoral constraints and rules of these organizations to develop suitable strategies and policies. As different institutions and actors are responsible for each of these layers, additional stakeholders or target groups that are affected are often not considered in decision-making processes (Wiesner, 2021). Yet, various components of these layers are already linked to other layers; from a tourism perspective, Postma et al. (2017) claim that the industry cannot anymore be separated from its spatial surroundings. A tourism management and development approach that is separated from the respective city or regional management and mainly focuses on attracting guests and increasing tourism revenue or, for example, leaves too much power, responsibility and decision-making in the hands of growth-oriented and often transnational corporations (cf. Benedikter, 2020) can lead to overcrowding or overtourism, exceeded capacities of places and attractions, noise or waste pollution or negative effects on the natural and built environment (Dodds & Butler, 2019). On the same time, many destinations around the world suffer from 'undertourism', hardly profit from global tourism revenues and, hence, lack opportunities for developing their economy and living space (cf. Butcher, 2017). As these consequences mainly relate to the quality of life within a destination, this aspect has become a major determinator of the overall perception residents and locals have of tourism (Kachniewska, 2015). Ultimately, this can lead to anti-tourism protests of the local population that is increasingly looking for a satisfactory quality of life and, hence, values cultural and leisure offers, an attractive environment and surroundings, smart mobility and infrastructures, affordable housing, and diverse gastronomy and events (Pechlaner et al., 2018; Thees et al., 2020). Even businesses and firms are in an increasingly competitive global search for talents and highly skilled workers and cannot rely solely on financial benefits anymore; an attractive living space and leisure environments play an increasingly important role for potential future employees (Sycheva et al., 2019). Following separated approaches, different interests within one place – such as the protection of a natural area vs. the creation of a new industrial site – may collide. On an international level, the spatial separation together with the organizational separation – that is, the separated organization per city, region or nation – has led to various spatial disparities, either to a positive or a negative side (Kilper, 2009). To sum this up, "the vision of an economically thriving region that offers a high quality of life and a fabulous visitor experience is fulfilled by the city of the future" – that is, where different target groups and spatial layers meet (Hedorfer, 2022, p. 8).

Secondly, global external effects are becoming increasingly important. Digitalization, artificial intelligence, globalization as well as re-globalization, demographic change, climate change, geopolitical issues or pandemics – developments, trends and crises like these, affecting spatial management on a local, regional, national and international scale, are referred to as global megatrends and have become influential and inevitable over the past decades. Many of these megatrends vary across different cities or regions and, in some cases, may reveal their vulnerability and sensibility, further accelerating their global competition (Petersen, 2022) or the independence of the place of work and the actual place where one resides or currently stays (Bieger & Klumbies, 2022). It is particularly since the beginning of the 21st century that spatial development and planning is facing these challenges (Hill & Prossek, 2012).

Thirdly, changes on the demand side are challenging locations, living spaces and destinations as well. The era of unquestioned mass production and mass consumption of both products and services appears to come to an end as consumers tend to consume more ethically, sustainably and considerably (Khalil et al., 2021). More and more people – workers, entrepreneurs, residents and travelers alike – are searching for quality of life, authenticity, personal encounters, individuality, sustainability or various forms of coexistence (Bichler, 2018). Similarly, the traditional physical separation between the workplace and one's home is becoming less and less applicable due to new forms of work and increasingly flexible work and life patterns, eventually leading to a mixture of target groups that a single person can identify with (Bieger & Klumbies, 2022).

While economic development and the quality of life of residents have traditionally been considered in urban and rural planning concepts and strategies, tourism development is often the responsibility of the respective destination management organization. Accordingly, traditional destination marketing includes a representation of the respective city or region as well, thereby leaving residents and other local stakeholders out of the marketing, branding and decision-making process (Kerr, 2005). However, tourism, as stated above, cannot be perceived, managed and developed separately from its spatial context and surroundings anymore as it is already connected to numerous fields of everyday life such as leisure, housing, mobility or wellbeing (Postma et al., 2017). This (exemplary and very limited) list illustrates how the tourism space and other surrounding spaces such as the living space influence each other and result in fuzzy and overlapping boundaries between tourist and non-tourist products, services and concepts. Much rather than that, tourism is "an important force of urban change that requires long-term policy, planning and good governance in which tourism in which tourism is integrated" (Terzibasoglu, 2016, cited in Postma et al., 2017, P. 97). As tourism is an inter- and multidisciplinary field with touchpoints to academic fields such as economy, sociology, geography, politics, information sciences, anthropology, psychology or architecture, it is vital to consider it when in the development of integrated location, living space and destination concepts (cf. Philipp, Thees & Olbrich, 2022).

Furthermore, a holistic and integrated management may also make it easier for the respective places and regions to act based on the United Nations Sustainable Development Goals (SDGs) that were developed in 2015 in order to "recognize that ending poverty and other deprivations must go hand in hand with strategies that improve health and education, reduce inequality, and spur economic growth [...] while tackling climate change and working to preserve our oceans and forests" (United Nations, 2022). An integrated spatial management may contribute to these 17 SDGs by following a triple bottom line approach of economic, ecological and social goals: 1) economic sustainability by contributing to added value, fostering the regional economy and creating employment, 2) ecological sustainability by avoiding negative impacts on biodiversity, reducing the usage of resources and reducing pollution and emissions, and 3) social sustainability by satisfying guests and hosts alike, fostering intercultural exchange and enabling participation of residents (cf. Schmied et al., 2009).

For clarification purposes, if not already made clear within these first sections: in this contribution, the term "integrated" refers to the holistic consideration and implementation of different layers of cities and regions, such as the economic location, the tourist destination or the living space of locals; it does not refer to an integration in terms of physical development or policies, that others researchers or publications may refer to (see, for example, "policy integration" or "integrated area development", as mentioned in Stead & Meijers, 2009). Neither does the term in this paper refer to integrative, that is inclusive, elements within any of the single layers of a city or region, as for example in "integrated destination management" as proposed by Persic and Magas (2005).

SOLUTIONS

The Increasing Discourse on Holistic, Integrated Spatial Management

Following these challenges and trends, the discussions on a holistic and integrated management of locations, living spaces and destinations are not new, but have already started in the early 1990s. One fundamental and widely recognized early work is *Marketing Places* by Kotler et al. (1993). They are among the first to refer to cities, living spaces and destinations as "places" and advise them to focus on an improved communication, good infrastructure, skilled workforce, support of local entrepreneurship and businesses, public-private partnerships and distinctive attractions, among others, in order to a) better face challenges, crises and unexpected developments and b) holistically meet the needs of whom they see as core customers of places – tourists, residents, businesses and investors. This approach is in line with the central place theory by Christaller (1933) that highlights the importance of the tertiary sector and the infrastructure and accessibility of services in a spatial context. The term place management has been picked up by various scholars ever since, including Walsh (2001), Kerr (2006), Innerhofer et al. (2016) or Wiesner (2021). According to Walsh (2001), place management is defined by addressing the disadvantages particular target groups and stakeholders experience, achieving community well-being through responsibility and accountability, solving interdependent issues through coordinated and integrated policies, and redesigning basic processes of governance and administration. Kerr (2006) confirms that a holistic perception of locations and destinations is becoming increasingly important as both traditionally focus on their own target groups and thereby exclude others; consequently, both a product perspective and a corporate perspective are equally important when developing holistic spatial concepts.

Apart from the works of Walsh (2001), Kerr (2005) and others, it was mainly in the 2010s that the discussions on place management, often still in the context of place branding, increased. From a territorial perspective, Basile et al. (2016) summarize place management as "a result of its capacity, its social actors and governance, and the analysis, creation and maintenance of relationships [...] between the [tangible and intangible] territory components [...] and its many and varied stakeholders" (p. 469). These relationships may happen within and in between a micro level (key actors and people), a meso level (city governance) and a macro level (social issues and external stakeholders). Hence, they conclude that awareness not only of the number but also the diversity of stakeholders is crucial for any spatial or territorial planning and decision-making process and that the usage of existing knowledge of these stakeholders can enhance the production of new results and solutions. Wiesner (2021) highlighted the importance of considering diverse stakeholder expectations and self-organized stakeholder networks and, as a conclusion, calls for a joint management of location, destination, culture, trade fairs, city and living space.

A differentiation needs to be made between "place" as a) a term for actual integrated and holistic management of different spatial layers of cities and regions, b) a term used for a holistic but marketing-focused branding of cities, and c) a term used for inner urban spaces. The latter has been discussed for an even longer period of time. Among the most prominent researchers in this direction are O'Leary and Iredale (1976), Burgess (1982) or Ashworth and Voogd (1990). Even though the aforementioned book by Kotler et al. (1993) has a marketing focus and title as well, it is derived from an integrated perception and management perspective of these places. As described by O'Leary and Iredale (1976, p. 156), the marketing focus of this term aims at "creat[ing] favorable dispositions and behavior towards geographic locations", focusing on the external promotion of the respective city. Additional sources, obviously, do exist but would exceed the scope and focus of this chapter as they usually focus on marketing and promotion instead of a holistic, integrated place management and will therefore not be considered or discussed. In addition, place often refers to urban spaces, squares and design (cf. Carmona, 2021), which is not a focus of this chapter either, but will be briefly grasped with the concept of atmospheric design. Nevertheless–as the place term is of high importance in this chapter, its origin and context need to be understood first. According to Smith (2018), by referring to cities, destinations, or locations as "places" we aim at understanding and developing them beyond their surface level that we encounter as temporary visitors or as residents that are not connected or involved. Creating places is about making the familiarity, complacency, freedom, unknown and the spectacle of cities and destinations accessible and experienceable to all its stakeholders and target groups.

However, before moving over to management-focused considerations, a few thoughts on holistic city marketing may be of interest in the context of this chapter. In their recap of 25 years of city marketing and its objectives, fields of action, actors and organizational structures, Block and Icks (2010) date the origins of this development back to the 1970s when some cities in the United States of America as well as in the United Kingdom initiated a switch from their traditional "city development policy" towards an entrepreneurial city. They define city marketing as a target group-oriented design and marketing of cities with the overall goal of increasing the quality of life of residents and the attractiveness of the city in the international competition in a sustainable way. The focus of this approach, in the area of public-private partnerships, is on location marketing (for businesses and entrepreneurs), tourism marketing (for tourists and business travelers), event marketing, city marketing (for the local and, if applicable, regional population) and, only in the public arena, administrative marketing (for citizens and politics), which altogether require a definition of the target groups and customers a city wants to attract and, accordingly, the goals and processes of its city management and marketing. Hence, the tasks of city marketing are diverse – from increasing the city's attractiveness to enabling participation of locals and keeping them informed, to fostering economic development, among others (Block & Icks, 2010).

It was already in 1999 when Thierstein noted that a modern location management is more than just a business approach that is has often been up until that time, but much rather "an art that needs to be addressed with engagement, brain and heart" (Thierstein, 1999, p. 12) and that its- stakeholder groups require an integrated management that depends on the cooperation between all its actors, fosters mutual exchange and learning within the region, moderates conflicts that appear in the regional development process, and needs decentralization. From an academic and management-oriented perspective, Bieger (2001) describes the reciprocal synergy effects of the tourism industry, the local population and the companies and businesses located there (see Figure 1). He describes four development stages of traditional destination management: 1) and 2) and 3) and 4) a closer cooperation between the marketing and management of the destination, location and living space. Thorns (2002) speaks of urban tourism as a tool that may foster the transformation of cities as it helps to redevelop historical sites, preserve local culture and provide new attractions, yet needs to be managed carefully and holistically in terms of, for example, commercialization.

Figure 1. Synergies between tourism, the population and the economy.
Source: Bieger & Klumbies, 2022.

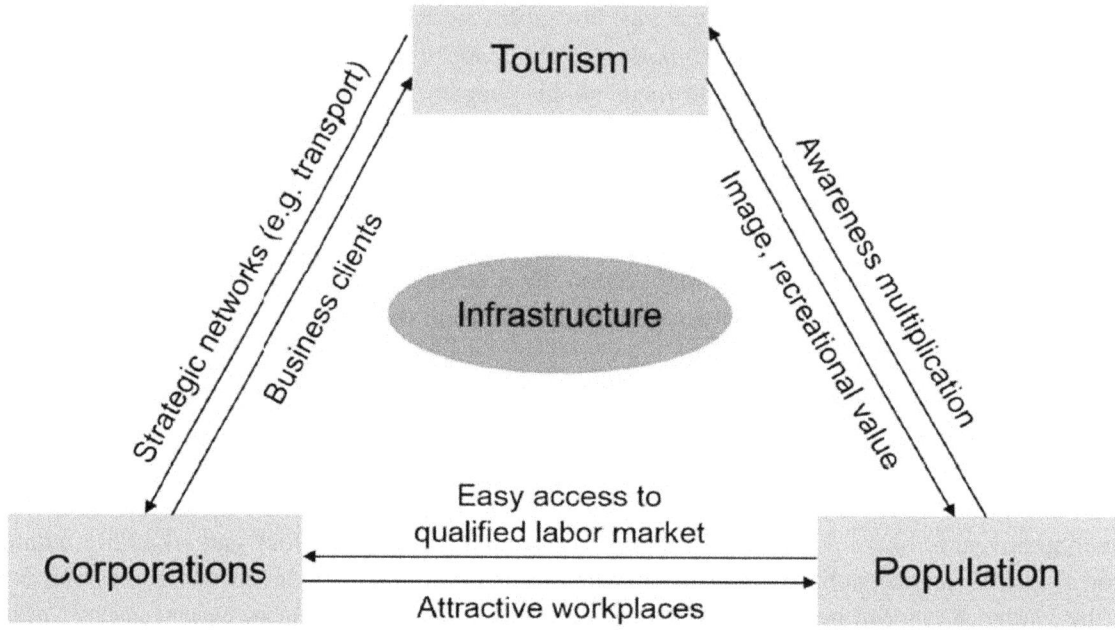

In 2002, Thierstein summarized a number of developments and trends that have, at that time, caused a change of spatial planning from the mainly state- and policy-controlled traditional approach towards a new approach that focused on regional, territorial and spatial development. According to him, the origins of this switch lie in the expanded spatial reach of local authorities, in the emergence of new actors and players that co-shape territories and places, and in the application and implementation of a new perception and understanding of space "as a production factors of socio-economic realities" (Thierstein, 2002, p. 11). The consideration of regional development has been taken up by other scholars as well. Pike et al. (2007) argue that the first step of regional development is to understand and conceptualize "what it is, what it is for, and [...] what it should be" (p. 1265). According to them, the definition of this term has changed over time as additional political, economic, social, cultural and ecological aspects across different scales have been added and may include different themes and values that have determined its historical and geographical differentiation.

Stead and Meijers (2009) refer to the so-called European Spatial Development Perspective (ESDP) of 1999 as a fundamental step forward in the understanding and scope of spatial planning. Accordingly, spatial planning approaches need to consider both sectoral and spatial issues, hence integrating both a horizontal and a vertical consideration and cooperation. In this way, various authorities and actors are included, creating new forms of public-private partnerships, increasing the interdependence between government and societal actors and, thereby, increasing the decentralization of governmental agencies and the complexity of spatial planning or development at large. Holistically managed cities and regions of the future need to "provide high-paying, service-sector jobs at tend to the welfare of the underprivileged, […] guarantee a healthy environment, […] invest in infrastructure to facilitate transportation and communication, […] assure housing markets respond to both public and private sector demands, […] look after public safety[,] affirm personal freedoms and […] realize the role of education, recreation, culture, and the arts" (Johnson & Shultz, 2016, p. 566). Accordingly, Hall (2020) describes modern urban and town planning as "thinking about where people will live, work, play, study, shop[, making planning] a complex web stretching way beyond the planning office" (p. 3). Holistic approaches, therefore, need to close the gap between the grand idea and the actual processes and procedures in councils, agencies and consultancies.

Integrated approaches have also been discussed in different contexts or variations: Pechlaner et al. (2008) speak of innovative location development and management in terms of an integration and cooperation between tourism and the traditional industry to foster synergies in the design of products and services that can be successful in the long run; Pechlaner et al. (2006) refer to attraction management as cross-sector concept for the integrated management of experience-oriented attractions in destinations and locations; in the context of strategic product development, the ongoing development of a location can be realized through constant innovations and the development of tourist products and attractions to increase the attractiveness of said location (Pechlaner & Fischer, 2009; Eckert & Pechlaner, 2019); Pechlaner and Schön (2010) have also used the regional building culture to highlight the importance of local identity and identification and, hence, the role of architecture in terms of the attractiveness of destinations and regions; even art and culture can be perceived as integrative elements as they have the potential to transform and revitalize unattractive neighborhoods into diverse and vibrant attraction points for both locals and visitors (Innerhofer et al., 2016).

From tourism perspective, tourism development needs to be addressed in broader context of community or regional development goals, entailing assessment of economic social environmental impacts of tourism. In integrative allows for collaborative planning with affected stakeholders and assessment of planning issues that foster integration of tourism with overall regional development (Marcouiller, 1997). Urban destination competitiveness comes down to the ability and capacity of the city to provide rich tourism offers, infrastructure and overall urban attractiveness benefitting visitors, businesses, and citizens alike (Paskaleva-Shapira, 2007). Pechlaner (2019) affirms that even the overall perspective of tourism has already changed from a destination focus to a more integrative view of regional networks with consideration of societal, political, and economic phenomena in non-tourism contexts as well. Networks are defined as a set of actors and their relationships between each other (cf. Jansen, 2006). These regional networks can be used to explain and illustrate the increasing perception of integrated concepts: in a global competition that requires flexibility, adaptability and an ability to react, networks allow an application of these characteristics much better than hierarchical structures and long decision-making processes (Bachinger & Pechlaner, 2011) as they are not necessarily restricted to organizational, societal or geographic boundaries (Renz, 1998) and consist of various individuals, groups and companies (Mack, 2003). Meijers (2007) confirms that a network model may help to counteract the deficiencies of the classic central place theory by Christaller (1933), especially in polycentric regions. Hence, focusing on networks can help to establish a particular spatial network quality that, further enhanced, can lead to a higher quality of encounters and relationships (see Figure 2), which are both becoming increasingly important in terms of an integrated location and destination management, by focusing on culture and values as drivers for a new quality approach (Pechlaner et al., 2017).

Figure 2. Hospitality Qualities.
Source: adopted from Pechlaner et al., 2017.

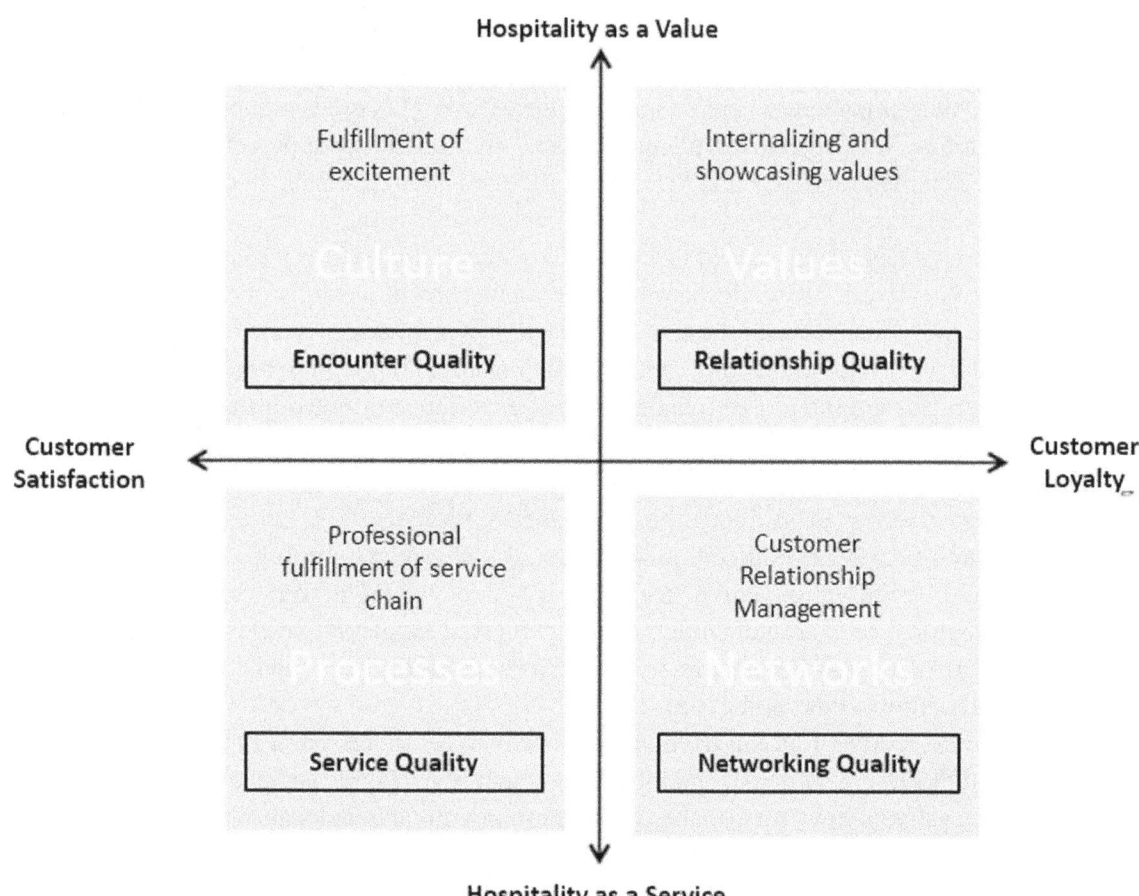

City and regions as well as their reputation are becoming more important in the global competition of cities, regions, countries, are becoming location factors and drivers. Reputation can be influenced by focusing on strengths and fostering identification, positive perception and memorability (Schneider-Sliwa et al., 2009). Modern foci are family-friendly housing, the housing environment, offers for kids, affordable housing, education, cultural offers for all groups not only high culture, central leisure and nature. Hence, pivotal fields of action are housing/living, family, education and work, culture, tourism, economy. In both a living space and a tourism perspective, the design of the atmosphere is becoming increasingly important for residents and visitors and in terms of international competition. Atmospheric design refers to the perceptions that different target groups have of particular places or elements and areas within these places, hence, "atmospheres are always and everywhere [and] are characterized by emotional and mood-related properties" (Rauh, 2022, p. 183). The atmosphere is perceived through peoples' senses and connects them with their present natural, cultural, or built environment (Volgger & Pfister, 2020).

In order to achieve such an integrated place management, the management and governing systems need to be adapted as well, and even beforehand. Early on, Reddel (2002) has proposed a further development from public management towards a new governance that further empowers citizens and local actors by adapting five major aspects: the problem focus (from focusing on outcomes and outputs towards focusing on a shared ownership), culture (from a public interest owned by executives and bureaucracy towards ad hoc coalitions for change complexity and open processes), the implementation (from contract-based agreement and compromise towards coalition building), the skills (from technical expertise based on monitoring and assessment towards stakeholder dialogue, deliberation and association), and the infrastructure (from bureaucratic structures with representation of directly affected interests towards centralized involvement and coalitions).

There are several ways which may facilitate the involvement and participation of broad stakeholder groups in a spatial context, two of which will be discussed in more detail in the following paragraphs: destination governance as an example of spatial or territorial governance, and smart cities (as well as their adaptation to tourism, which is referred to as smart destinations). In recent years, the term governance has received increasing attention from both scholars and practitioners as an approach that allows for a more customer- and stakeholder-centered development and management. It is derived from corporate governance that "offers organizations a set of instruments to govern, control and monitor themselves, and enables the implementation of previously defined structures and standards" (Pechlaner et al., 2011). Applied to the spatial context, the destination governance approach, as an example, stands out (Pechlaner & Raich, 2005; Beritelli et al., 2007; Volgger et al., 2017). Volgger et al. (2017) differentiate between three perspectives on destination governance: a descriptive one, referring to a collective, strategic management, marketing and planning; an instrumental one that refers to its different coordination options, and a normative-prescriptive one that requires an understanding of the blurred nature of tourism destinations in order to guarantee responsible, sustainable and efficient coordination. In the light of recent megatrends as outlined earlier, or the influence of the COVID-19 pandemic, Pechlaner et al. (2022) suggest destination governance to put a stronger focus on stakeholder networks as a foundation for the future destination to be resilient, transformative and sustainable. Despite its tourism focus, these understandings of spatial governance may be applied to other spatial contexts as well. Implementing a participative governance shared among various stakeholders can help to integrate a spatial network approach (cf. Raeymaeckers & Kenis, 2015).

The smart city approach, too, has potential to foster the convergence of tourists and residents as Romao et al. (2018) state. They claim that the smart city is a prerequisite for the sustainable city of the future as a place for all that also helps improving a city's attractiveness for both residents and tourists, its livability and economic development as well as its environment and culture. This is supported by Gretzel and Koo (2021). They argue that "smart technologies blur the lines between residential areas and tourism precincts" (p. 352), which is accelerated by the rapid growth of urbanization and metropolitan cities all around the world. In this context, the integrated perception of cities and destinations may further enhance their spatial development as they bring in a number of relevant trends and developments: while smart cities focus on sustainability, quality of life and smart governance, smart destinations have the potential to enhance service-related aspects such as smart experiences, smart business ecosystems or smart value creation. Hence, the concept of a smart tourism city could be a holistic approach towards the integrated management and development of locations, cities and destinations as it is directed towards a holistic well-being and the creation and use of synergies among all stakeholders. The authors build their findings on a study by KPMG that considers smart tourism cities as being "more connected, efficient, transparent, and interactive" (Gretzel & Koo, 2021, p. 356). A few such examples can be: London, where the "Smart London Plan" provides information on traffic, Wi-Fi or rental stations and thereby increases both the visiting experience as well as the daily life of residents; Berlin, where real places are linked to virtual content about their history, engaging and educating both tourists and residents; Hong Kong, where initiatives such as Smart Travel or Smart Life aim at providing data on weather, parking or traffic via mobile apps or smart kiosks.

Examples of Modern Place Management

Despite the discussions on place management that have been around for about three decades by now, a broad and wide implementation still appears to be vague and pending. However, a few exemplary cases exist and will be illustrated below.

- In 2004, as one of the first German cities, **Hamburg** recognized the interdependencies between skilled workers, investors, businesses, tourists and residents and, accordingly, established a brand strategy in order to "bring together humans and businesses, support economic prosperity, increase the touristic attractiveness and work together for a metropolitan area worth living in" (Hamburg Marketing GmbH, 2019, n. p.). The long-term goal was to differentiate itself and its values and characteristics from hundreds of similar destinations and locations around the world. To achieve this, the brand 'Hamburg' is built on 12 principles covering various aspects of the economic, residential and cultural layer of the city, namely: waterfront metropolis; metropolitan area; funfairs and events; shopping; athletic Hamburg; attractive cultural offer; Reeperbahn (Hamburg's entertainment district); metropolis worth living; vibrant scene; attractive business environment; growth and sustainability.

- In 2011, **Eindhoven** in the Netherlands founded its new city marketing organization Eindhoven365 with the overall goal of branding and promoting itself as a technological and designer city. Their strategy focuses on "activating residents, making tourism more sustainable, connecting talents, integrating newcomers and involving design professionals", acting as a "connector within the local system". Accordingly, the vision and narrative for the city and its future development is "The most human innovative city", allowing everyone to participate in and benefit from the city's progress. The results of such a branding and marketing are easi8ly recognizable: despite being a rather small city and community, Eindhoven is among the world's leading places in terms of technology, design and knowledge transfer. Cooperation and networks, as outlined before, are one of the success factors, taking the Brainport as an example: a regional ecosystem of companies, governments and educational institutions that work together for a brighter future.

- Not only cities, even entire regions can become places and brand themselves accordingly. In **South Tyrol** in Italy, an identity model was created in order to identify characteristics, values and competencies that make the region unique and help it transform from a destination or business location towards a living space with a focus on the overall quality of life while respecting both tradition and future. The responsible agency, "IDM Südtirol – Alto Adige AG" ("ADM South Tyrol – Alto Adige AG") defined the region's vision as "South Tyrol, Europe's most desired sustainable living space", which they aim to achieve through their seven priorities: the South Tyrol brand, innovation, internationalization, tourism, agriculture, digitalization, and regionality – altogether building upon the fundamental goal of a sustainable economic development of South Tyrol.

- Another exemplary region is **Tyrol** in the west of Austria. It names itself the "epitome of Alpine sense of life" and "the heart of the Alps". When thinking about a place brand, the created the short and promising vision "Tyrol is the most coveted power place of the Alps". Under this vision, they aim to unite tourism, businesses, agricultural regions, culture, sports and science in order to continuously develop Tyrol towards a "successful place for economy, science, work, culture and tourism". This aim is even represented in the agency's name: Living Space Tyrol Holding (Lebensraum Tirol Holding).

RECOMMENDATIONS

Using the Ecosystem Logic for Spatial Development

In recent years, an alternative conceptual approach has been developed; instead of thinking about places and place management, the different spatial layers may also be considered as a holistic, integrated eco-system. This term originates in natural sciences and refers to a group of living beings, their respective environment and all possible interactions within (Tansley, 1935). This term has later on been applied to various other disciplines such as entrepreneurial ecosystems, business ecosystems, supply chain ecosystems, or smart ecosystems. In the context of entrepreneurial ecosystems, it has been added to il-lustrate the "set of independent actors and factors coordinated in such a way that they enable productive entrepreneurship within a particular territory" (Stam & Spigel, 2017, p. 1), encompassing diverse formal, physical, market, cultural and systemic elements. In this context, an ecosystem has both a spatial and an organizational dimension. As entrepreneurial ecosystems are seen as a driver of local and regional development (Bachinger et al., 2020), this approach can be seen as another spatial development path, either following upon place management or as an alternative path. The ecosystem logic with its focus on actors, elements, interactions and relationships allows for an enhanced consideration of the network approach that helps to achieve a particular quality of encounters and relationships through values, as described above. It may help to connect the various spatial, social and economic networks and, in par-ticular, the location network, regional network and destination network, in a larger, holistic and integrated spatial ecosystem. It is assumed in this context that the four qualities – service quality, network quality, encounter quality and relationship quality – as described by Pechlaner et al. (2017) are an essential driver for the ecosystem development and, hence, require a network analysis or similar approaches to be measured and transformed into recommendations and fields of action.

An early adaptation is the Entrepreneurial Destination (Pechlaner et al., 2018; Thees et al., 2020) that the ongoing discussions on an integrated location and destination management by the aforementioned entrepreneurial ecosystem approach. It considers numerous stakeholders such as entrepreneurs, residents and visitors alike and "adds the perspective of living and leisure[, thus] defin[ing] economic roles and activities by highlighting urban attractiveness" (Thees et al., 2020, p. 171). Modern-day approaches such as co-working or co-experiences or a stronger focus on cross-stakeholder dialogue and exchange, the layers of work, life and leisure are perceived and managed in a more integrated way which may increase local attractiveness for residents, guests and entrepreneurs alike. In turn, a vibrant and active startup environment can have an influence on a city's or region's appearance and attract talents and tourists.

According to Thees et al. (2020), focusing on Munich as an exemplary case study, it is co-creation in particular that can enhance the implementation of spatial management approaches, while co-working can provide the necessary platforms, spaces and tools for networking, exchange and idea generation. The entrepreneurship focus of the entrepreneurial ecosystem approach can help to boost the creative potential of cities and foster the understanding of soft location factors that are becoming more and more important to different stakeholder groups. Hence, this consideration may foster regional resilience as well.

A similar approach is the Entrepreneurial Destination Ecosystem (EDE, see Figure 3) that considers the destination and regional quality of life simultaneously (Bachinger & Pechlaner, 2022). It is a conceptual framework that uses the destination and tourism infrastructure as a basis to explain the contribution of the tourism industry to the entrepreneurial activity of the respective region. The EDE does not focus on the destination or a spatial level but instead on the interactions between tourism and the larger ecosystem as well as the emerging relationships and movement patterns of individuals and ecosystem actors in the network context. Its core hypothesis is that through tourism, the infrastructure and, hence, the attractiveness and quality of life of a destination increase and attract young talent, which enhances the exchange between different local stakeholder groups and contributes to the local entrepreneurship, which may in the end foster regional entrepreneurial activity. The tourist destination, that serves as a foundation and basis of this model, contributes factors such as local and regional contacts and their networking competencies, social capital, local cultural or natural resources or sustainability thinking to the surrounding entrepreneurial ecosystem.

Figure 3. Entrepreneurial Destination Ecosystem.
Source: Bachinger & Pechlaner, 2022.

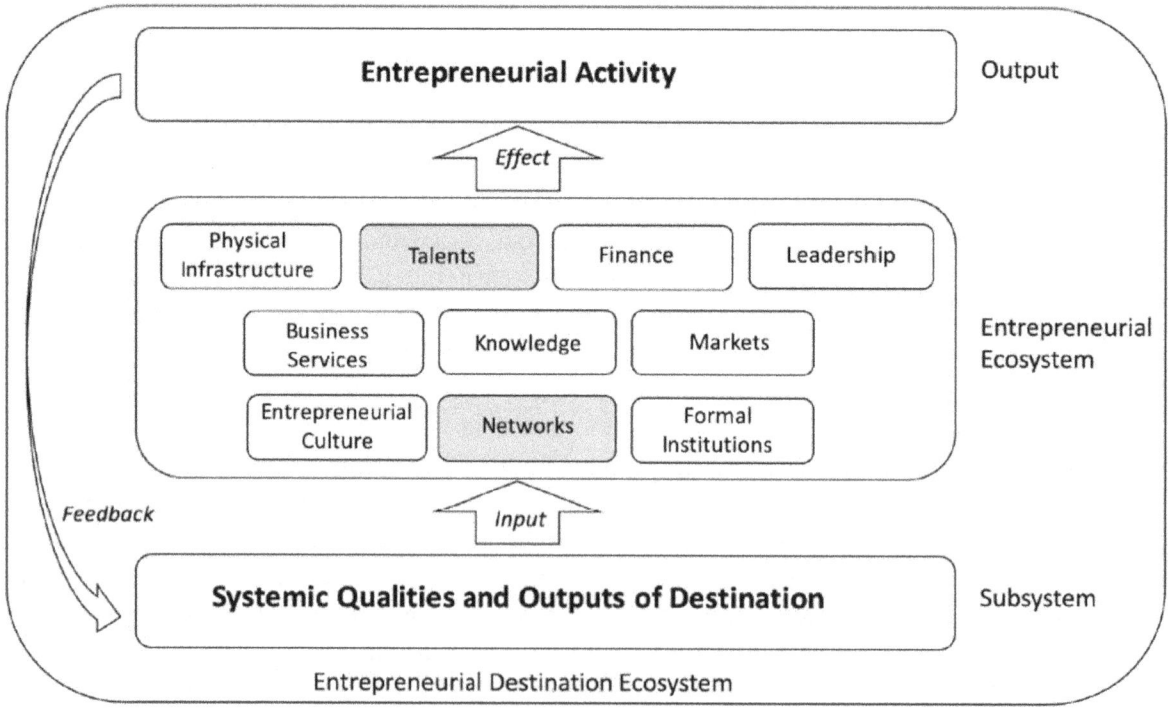

The latest proposition in the ecosystem direction is the Ecosystem of Hospitality (EoH, see Figure 4) – an approach to integrate (economic) locations, (tourist) destinations and cities (living space of locals) into a holistic ecosystem (Pechlaner et al., 2022; Philipp et al., 2022). The EoH allows for rethinking of traditional and common tourism and destination structures by expanding stakeholder networks and develop cultural tourism to a more sustainable tourism culture. Hence, instead of focusing on organizations, it focuses on "the individual and the opportunity for encounters between individuals [as well as] on issues surrounding quality of life, resilience, culture, mobility and connectivity" (Pechlaner et al., 2022, p. 12). It perceives the boundaries between urban and rural as dissolving, which allows for a utilization of the potentials of digitalization in a socially responsible and compatible way. In this way, hospitality may be created – a term used to describe the atmosphere of places (Philipp et al., 2022). A fundamental assumption of the EoH is that both guests and visitors alike increasingly realize that urban development is not only a governmental or strategic task but can lie within the responsibility of its stakeholder groups as well. It shows that by integrating location, living space and destination, new and alternative concepts or fields of action arise that suit the requirements for a broad spatial and holistic transformation based on more individualistic and target group-oriented aspects such as lifestyle orientation, work-life blending or cross-stakeholder dynamics.

Figure 4. Ecosystem of Hospitality.
Source: Pechlaner et al., 2022.

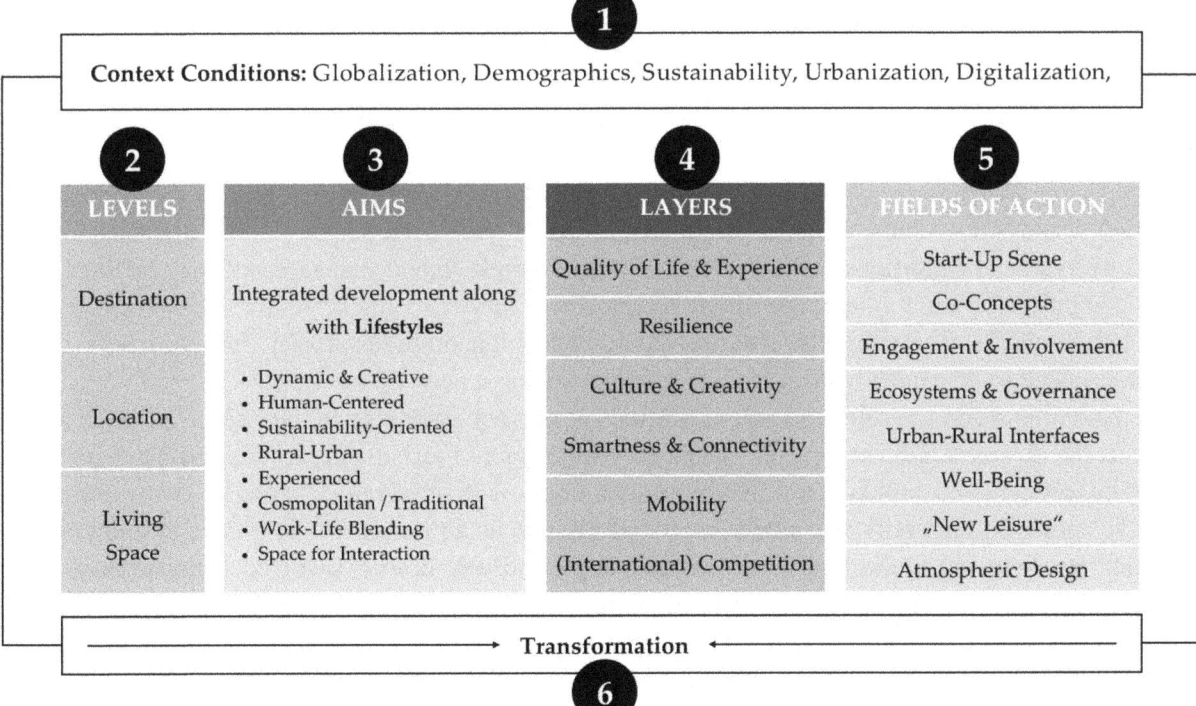

While entrepreneurial ecosystems in general focus on the creation of growth-oriented or even high-growth startups as an economic output (see, for example, the entrepreneurial ecosystems in Silicon Valley or Israel), the adaptation or application of the entrepreneurial ecosystem concept in the tourism or hospitality sector would add additional framework elements such as the culture or landscape of a place or region, thus enable the actors and stakeholders of the ecosystem to focus on sustainable and collaborative entrepreneurship first and foremost (Bachinger et al., 2022).

Practical Implications for Place or Ecosystem Management

Moving towards new forms of spatial management and development – whether this refers to place management, ecosystem management or another integrated and holistic management form of locations, living spaces and destinations – requires an understanding of the roles of change and continuity first and foremost. Change and transformation have always been part of human and urban experiences, and so have places and factors of everyday life (Thorns, 2002). Given this understanding, a reform of the organizational structure is needed as well. According to Bieger and Klumbies (2022), two alternatives to traditional and common independent organizations would either be a) organizations that are still independent but coordinated by a performance contract or mandate as shown with the "Lebensraum Tirol Holding" of Tyrol earlier in this chapter, or b) a merger of these organizations into an integrated organization, as it was done in Hamburg. Regardless of the final organizational form, public interest and the long-term development of the place need to be prioritized over short-term interests or lucrative business models (Ferguson, 2019).

Applying the ecosystem logic to the spatial context would require the provision of a number of factors to make it work, namely systemic conditions (networks, finance, leadership, talent, knowledge, support services) and framework conditions (culture, physical infrastructure, demand, formal institutions), based on the entrepreneurial ecosystem approach of Stam. As hospitality is perceived as a core characteristic of spatial ecosystem approaches such as the Ecosystem of Hospitality (and, in this case, even constitutes its name), it plays a fundamental role. According to Peters and Eichelberger (2022), it is affected and shaped by systemic conditions and vice versa. As an example, talent management may influence the local hospitality culture, while in return the voluntariness or well-being affect the relationships of the ecosystem networks. Therefore, the different qualities that constitute hospitality (both as a service and as a value) need to be carefully measured, for example using a network analysis.

To make this work, the roles and responsibilities of current governing bodies of the different layers – such as the destination management organization in terms of tourism and destination management – need to be reconsidered. Fundamental assumptions about growth or success factors need to be rethought, taking sustainability not only as a side activity but instead, as an umbrella that guides all policies and activities, and focusing on the quality of life of all people and stakeholders involved. Innovation needs to be understood as interlinked and mutually reinforcing with sustainability. Current governing bodies need to become agencies of sustainability governance and sustainable development (cf. Pechlaner & Philipp, 2022). Taking the DMO as a basis for adaptation in this direction, two possible future scenarios would be the transition from a Destination Management Organization towards a Sustainable Tourism Organization (STO) or, moving beyond the focus on tourism, a Sustainable Management Organization (SMO).

Apart from these rather organizational thoughts, additional adaptations need to be considered as well when aiming for holistic and integrated solutions. Regardless of whether the focus is on branding, marketing, or management, or on the place or ecosystem approaches, the "four Rs" as defined by Aitken and Campelo (2011) can be taken as a basis for implementing a cross-stakeholder approach: rights, roles, relationships, and responsibilities. Without going into detailed definitions, the interplay of these terms serves "as an open-ended series of interactions that occur in all directions[,] with a variety of density and/or intensity […] and [that is] based on the social capital of the community" (Aitken & Campelo, 2011, p. 926). It helps to understand the sense of a place, the structure and relationships of the local community, and the complex but dynamic ownership that such approaches require.

One way of enabling the organizational change and allowing for a new ownership structure with broad involvement and participation to be implemented would be the so-called living lab. Living labs are governance tools that promote participation of all relevant stakeholder groups in an innovative and open environment (Thees et al., 2020). One goal of living labs is "the development and implementation of concrete innovation projects through a process of experimentation and evaluation" (Budweg et al., 2011, p. 595) by sharing resources, enabling collaboration networks, delivering knowledge and providing different opportunities for stakeholders to gather and communicate – all while being in real life contexts (Leminen et al., 2017). Ultimately, in order to foster holistic, integrated spatial management approaches, living labs need to follow six principles: 1) openness, 2) users in key roles, 3) meaningful and sustainable interaction, 4) human-centric setting, 5) space for observation, and 6) technological infrastructure (Thees et al., 2020).

CONCLUSION

The present chapter has shown that a variety of trends, developments, challenges and crises of the past decades and, even more, in recent years require new spatial management and development approaches that are resilient, adaptable, sustainable, and oriented at stakeholders and multifaceted networks. Instead of different and independent authorities and institutions managing, for example, the economic location, the living space of residents and locals, or the tourist destination, new and innovative approaches are needed that consider all spatial layers of a city in an integrated and holistic way. Thoughts on place management are not new, but lack a broad implementation. However, examples such as Hamburg or Tyrol demonstrate that place management is not just a theoretical consideration, but a promising way forward in spatial management discussions. The increasing discussions on ecosystems, as of yet primarily in an entrepreneurial and business ecosystem context, may pave the way for an alternative future development of spaces and places. Both approaches – place management or ecosystems – require the respective cities to redefine their governmental and governance structures, considering sustainability as an umbrella for all their future activities and enabling the involvement and participation of all relevant stakeholders.

REFERENCES

Aitken, R., & Campelo, A. (2011). The four Rs of place branding. *Journal of Marketing Management*, *27*(9-10), 913–933. doi:10.1080/0267257X.2011.560718

Ashworth, G. J., & Voogd, H. (1990). *Selling the city: Marketing approaches in public sector urban planning*. Belhaven.

Bachinger, M., Kofler, I., & Pechlaner, H. (2020). Sustainable instead of high-growth? Entrepreneurial Ecosystems in Tourism. *Journal of Hospitality and Tourism Management*, *44*, 238–244. doi:10.1016/j.jhtm.2020.07.001

Bachinger, M., Kofler, I., & Pechlaner, H. (2022). Entrepreneurial ecosystems in tourism: An analysis of characteristics from a systems perspective. *European Journal of Tourism Research*, *31*, 3113. doi:10.54055/ejtr.v31i.2490

Bachinger, M., & Pechlaner, H. (2011). Netzwerke und regionale Kernkompetenzen: der Einfluss von Kooperationen auf die Wettbewerbsfähigkeit von Regionen [Networks and Regional Core Competencies: The Impact of Cooperations on the Competitiveness of Regions]. In M. Bachinger, H. Pechlaner, & W. Widuckel (Eds.), Regionen und Netzwerke: Kooperationsmodelle zur branchenübergreifenden Kompetenzentwicklung [Regions and Networks: Models of Cooperation for a. Intersectoral Development of Competencies] (pp. 3–28). Gabler. doi:10.1007/978-3-8349-6846-3_1

Bachinger, M., & Pechlaner, H. (2022). Entrepreneurial Destination Ecosystem. In D. Buhalis (Ed.), *Encyclopedia of Tourism Management and Marketing* (pp. 93–96). Edward Elgar.

Basile, G., Dominici, G., & Tani, M. (2016). Place marketing and management: A complex adaptive systems view. The strategic planning of the city of Avellino, Italy. *Systemic Practice and Action Research*, *29*(5), 469–484. doi:10.100711213-016-9372-9

Benedikter, R. (2020). Foreword by Roland Benedikter. In H. Pechlaner, E. Innerhofer, & G. Erschbamer (Eds.), *Overtourism: Tourism Management and Solutions* (pp. xiii–xviii). Routledge.

Beritelli, P., Bieger, T., & Laesser, C. (2007). Destination governance: Corporate governance theories as a foundation for effective destination management. *Journal of Travel Research*, *46*(1), 96–107. doi:10.1177/0047287507302385

Bichler, B. (2018). Trends in tourism: A media analysis from 2011 – 2016. In C. Maurer & B. Neuhofer (Eds.), *Iscontour 2018: Tourism Research Perspectives* (pp. 274–285).

Bieger, T. (2001). Kompetenzorientierte kommunale Standortstrategie [Competence-oriented municipal location strategy]. In C. Lengwiler (Ed.) Luzerner Beiträge zur Betriebs- und Regionalökonomie: Vol. 8. Gemeindemanagement in Theorie und Praxis [Lucerne contributes to business and regional economy: vol. 8, Community management in theory and practice, (pp. 445-466). Rüegger.

Bieger, T., & Beritelli, P. (2013). *Management von Destinationen [Management of Destinations]*. Oldenbourg. doi:10.1524/9783486721188

Bieger, T., & Klumbies, A. (2022). From destination management to integrated development of places – enabling personal networks instead of management and control. In H. Pechlaner, N. Olbrich, J. Philipp, & H. Thees (Eds.), *Towards an Ecosystem of Hospitality – Location:City:Destination* (pp. 50–59). Graffeg Publishing.

Block, J., & Icks, S. (2010). *Stadtmarketing [City marketing]*. Bundesvereinigung City- und Stadtmarketing Deutschland.

Budweg, S., Schaffers, H., Ruland, R., Kristensen, K., & Prinz, W. (2011). Enhancing collaboration in communities of professionals using a Living Lab approach. *Production Planning and Control, 22*(5-6), 594–609. doi:10.1080/09537287.2010.536630

Burgess, J. A. (1982). Selling places: Environmental images for the executive. *Regional Studies, 16*(1), 1–17. doi:10.1080/09595238200185471

Butcher, J. (2017). In praise of the holiday revolution. *Spiked.* https://www.spiked-online.com/2017/10/23/in-praise-of-the-holiday-revolution/

Carmona, M. (2021). *Public Spaces, Urban Places: The Dimensions of Urban Design* (3rd ed.). Routledge. doi:10.4324/9781315158457

Christaller, W. (1933). *Die zentralen Orte in Süddeutschland. Eine ökonomisch-geographische Untersuchung der Gesetzmäßigkeit, Verbreitung, und Entwicklung der Siedlungen mit städtischen Funktionen [The central places in southern Germany: An economic-geographical study of the regularity, distribution, and development of settlements with Urban functions]*. Gustav Fischer.

Cobbinah, P. B. (2017). Managing cities and resolving conflicts: Local people's attitudes towards urban planning in Kumasi, Ghana. *Land Use Policy, 68*, 223–231. doi:10.1016/j.landusepol.2017.07.050

Dodds, R., & Butler, R. (2019). *Overtourism: Issues, Realities, and Solutions*. De Gruyter. doi:10.1515/9783110607369

Döll-König, H., & Pechlaner, H. (2022). Foreword. In H. Pechlaner, N. Olbrich, J. Philipp, & H. Thees (Eds.), *Towards an Ecosystem of Hospitality – Location:City:Destination* (pp. 6–7). Graffeg Publishing.

Eckert, C., & Pechlaner, H. (2019). Alternative Product Development as Strategy Towards Sustainability in Tourism: The Case of Lanzarote. In U. Martini & F. Buffa (Eds.), *Marketing for Sustainable Tourism* (pp. 105–122). MDPI.

Ferguson, F. (2019). *Make City: A compendium of urban alternatives*. Jovis.

Gretzel, U., & Koo, C. (2021). Smart tourism cities: A duality of place where technology supports the convergence of touristic and residential experiences. *Asia Pacific Journal of Tourism Research, 26*(4), 352–364. doi:10.1080/10941665.2021.1897636

Hall, T. (2020). *Town planning – the basics*. Routledge.

Hamburg Marketing Gmb. (2019). *Strategischer Marketingplan für das Hamburg-Marketing 2019-2024 [Strategic Marketing plan for Hamburg marketing, 2019-2024]*. Hamberg marketing. https://marketing.hamburg.de/strat-marketingplan.html

Hedorfer, P. (2022). A message from Petra Hedorfer, Chief Executive Officer of the German National Tourist Board (GNTB). In H. Pechlaner, N. Olbrich, J. Philipp, & H. Thees (Eds.), *Towards an Ecosystem of Hospitality – Location:City:Destination* (pp. 8–9). Graffeg Publishing.

Hill, A., & Prossek, A. (Eds.). (2012). *Metropolis und Region: Aktuelle Herausforderungen für Stadtforschung und Raumplanung [Metropolis and Region: Current Challenges for Urban Research and Spatial Planning]*. Verlag Dorothea Rohn.

Innerhofer, E., Pechlaner, H., & Glüher, G. (Eds.). (2016). *Orte und Räume: Perspektiven für Kunst und Kultur [Places and spaces: perspectives for art and culture]*. Athesia.

Jansen, D. (2006). *Einführung in die Netzwerkanalyse – Grundlagen, Methoden, Forschungsbeispiele [Introduction to network analysis—basics, methods, research examples]*. Springer.

Johnson, B. E., & Shultz, B. (2016). Cities of the future. In S. D. Brunn, M. Hays-Mitchell, D. J. Zeigler, & J. K. Graybill (Eds.), *Cities of the World: Regional Patterns and Urban Environment* (pp. 537–570). Rowman & Littlefield.

Kachniewska, M. A. (2015). Tourism development as a determinant of quality of life in rural areas. *Worldwide Hospitality and Tourism Themes*, *7*(5), 500–515. doi:10.1108/WHATT-06-2015-0028

Kerr, G. (2005). From destination brand to location brand. *Journal of Brand Management*, *13*(4/5), 276–283.

Khalil, S., Ismail, A., & Ghalwash, S. (2021). The Rise of Sustainable Consumerism: Evidence from the Egyptian Generation Z. *Sustainability*, *13*(24), 13804. doi:10.3390u132413804

Kilper, H. (Ed.). (2009). *German annual of spatial research and policy 2009: New disparities in spatial development in Europe*. Springer-Verlag. doi:10.1007/978-3-642-03402-2

Kotler, P., Haider, D. H., & Rein, I. (1993). *Marketing Places*. The Free Press.

Leminen, S., Rajahonka, M., & Westerlund, M. (2017). Towards third-generation living lab networks in cities. *Technology Innovation Management Review*, *7*(11), 21–35. doi:10.22215/timreview/1118

Mack, O. (2003). *Konfiguration und Koordination von Unternehmensnetzwerken. Ein allgemeines Netzwerkmodell [Configuration and coordination of corporate network, a General Network model]*. Springer Gabler. doi:10.1007/978-3-322-81488-3

Mair, C. A., & Thivierge-Rikard, R. V. (2019). The Strength of Strong Ties for Older Rural Adults: Regional Distinctions in the Relationship Between Social Interaction and Subjective Well-Being. *International Journal of Aging & Human Development*, *70*(2), 119–143. doi:10.2190/AG.70.2.b PMID:20405586

Marcouiller, D. W. (1997). Toward Integrative Tourism Planning in Rural America. *Journal of Planning Literature*, *11*(3), 337–357. doi:10.1177/088541229701100306

Markert, P. (2018). Wirtschaftsförderung und Standortmarketing [Business promotion and location marketing]. In H. Meffert, B. Spinnen, & J. Block (Eds.), *Praxishandbuch City- und Stadtmarketing [Practical Handbook of City and Town Marketing]* (pp. 205–223). Springer Gabler.

Meijers, E. (2007). From central place to network model: Theory and evidence on paradigm change. *Tijdschrift voor Economische en Sociale Geografie*, *98*(2), 245–259. doi:10.1111/j.1467-9663.2007.00394.x

Nie, L. (1993). *Die Bedeutung der Wirtschaftsförderungsgesellschaft für die regionale ökonomische Entwicklung im Land Nordrhein-Westfalen [The Importance of the Economic Development Agency for Regional Economic Development in the State of North Rhine-Westphalia]* [Unpublished doctoral dissertation, University of Bonn, Germany].

O'Leary, R., & Iredale, I. (1976). The marketing concept: Quo vadis? *European Journal of Marketing*, *10*(3), 146–157. doi:10.1108/EUM0000000005043

Ostergren, R. C., & Rice, J. G. (2004). *The Europeans. A Geography of People, Culture and Environment*. The Guilford Press.

Paskaleva-Shapira, K. A. (2007). New paradigms in city tourism management: Redefining destination promotion. *Journal of Travel Research*, *46*(1), 108–114. doi:10.1177/0047287507302394

Pearce, D. G. (2015). Destination management in New Zealand: Structures and functions. *Journal of Destination Marketing & Management*, *4*(1), 1–12. doi:10.1016/j.jdmm.2014.12.001

Pechlaner, H. (Ed.). (2019). *Destination und Lebensraum: Perspektiven touristischer Entwicklung [Destination and living space: Prospects for tourism development]*. Springer Gabler. doi:10.1007/978-3-658-28110-6

Pechlaner, H., Bieger, T., & Weiermair, K. (Eds.). (2006). *Attraktionsmanagement: Führung und Steuerung von Attraktionspunkten [Attraction Management: Management and Control of Attraction Points]*. Linde.

Pechlaner, H., & Fischer, E. (Eds.). (2009). Strategische Produktentwicklung im Standortmanagement: Wettbewerbsvorteile für den Tourismus [Strategic Product Development in Location Management: Competitive Advantages for the Tourism Industry]. Erich Schmidt Verlag.

Pechlaner, H., Hamann, E.-M., & Fischer, E. (Eds.). (2008). *Industrie und Tourismus: Innovatives Standortmanagement für Produkte und Dienstleistungen [Industry and tourism: Innovative location management for products and services]*. Erich Schmidt Verlag.

Pechlaner, H., Olbrich, N., Philipp, J., & Thees, H. (Eds.). (2022). *Towards an Ecosystem of Hospitality – Location:City:Destination*. Graffeg Publishing.

Pechlaner, H. & Philipp, J. (2022). *Moving from Traditional Destination Understanding Towards a Holistic 'Ecosystem of Hospitality* [Paper presentation]. Rethinking Tourism, Hospitality and Events for a Better Future, Ukulhas, Maledives.

Pechlaner, H., Philipp, J., & Bachinger, M. (2022). *The Entrepreneurial Destination Ecosystem – On the pathway to resilient destinations* [Paper presentation]. 5th Advances in Destination Management Forum, Kalmar, Sweden.

Pechlaner, H., Philipp, J., & Olbrich, N. (2022). Destination Governance: The New Role of Destination Management, Stakeholder Networks and Sustainability. In J. Saarinen & C.M. Hall (Eds.) The Handbook of Tourism Governance. Edward Elgar.

Pechlaner, H., & Raich, F. (2005). Vom Destination Management zur Destination Governance [From destination management to destination governance]. In T. Bieger, C. Laesser, & P. Beritelli (Eds.), *Jahrbuch der Schweizerischen Tourismuswissenschaft 2004/2005 [Yearbook of Swiss Tourism Studies]* (pp. 221–234). IDT-HSG Institut für Öffentliche Dienstleistungen und Tourismus.

Pechlaner, H., Raich, F., & Kofink, L. (2011). Elements of Corporate Governance in Tourism Organizations. *Tourismos: An International Multidisciplinary Journal of Tourism*, *6*(3), 57–76.

Pechlaner, H., & Schön, S. (Eds.). (2010). *Regionale Baukultur als Erfolgsfaktor im Tourismus: Nachhaltige Vermarktung von Destinationen [Regional building culture as a success factor in tourism: Sustainable marketing of destinations]*. Erich Schmidt Verlag.

Pechlaner, H., Thees, H., Eckert, C., & Zacher, D. (2018). Vom Entrepreneurship Ecosystem zur Entrepreneurial Destination – Perspektiven einer Standortentwicklung am Beispiel der Freizeitszene München [From entrepreneurship ecosystem to entrepreneurial destination- Perspectives of location development using the example of the leisure scene in Munich]. In M. Bruhn & K. Hartwig (Eds.), Service Business Development, Band 2: Methoden – Erlösmodelle, Marketinginstrumente [Methods—revenue models, marketing instruments], (pp. 477-508). Springer.

Pechlaner, H., Volgger, M., & Nordhorn, C. (2017). Hospitality Management ist mehr als Service Management: Skizzen eines umfassenden Qualitätsansatzes [Hospitality management is more than a service management: outlines of a comprehensive approach to quality]. In H. Pechlaner & M. Volgger (Eds.), *Die Gesellschaft auf Reisen – Eine Reise in die Gesellschaft [Traveling Society—A Journey into Society]*, (pp. 139–162). Springer Fachmedien. doi:10.1007/978-3-658-14114-1_8

Persic, M., & Magas, D. (2005). *Integrated Destination Management* [Paper presentation]. *4th International Scientific Conference on Kinesiology*, Optija, Croatia.

Peters, M., & Eichelberger, S. (2022). Framework conditions of entrepreneurial ecosystems in destinations. In H. Pechlaner, N. Olbrich, J. Philipp, & H. Thees (Eds.), *Towards an Ecosystem of Hospitality – Location:City:Destination* (pp. 60–67). Graffeg Publishing.

Petersen, T. (2022). Demographic change, decarbonization and digitalization – megatrends changing the outlook for tourism. In H. Pechlaner, N. Olbrich, J. Philipp, & H. Thees (Eds.), *Towards an Ecosystem of Hospitality – Location:City:Destination* (pp. 24–31). Graffeg Publishing.

Philipp, J., Thees, H., & Olbrich, N. (2022). Towards common ground: Integrating destination, location and living space. In H. Pechlaner, N. Olbrich, J. Philipp, & H. Thees (Eds.), *Towards an Ecosystem of Hospitality – Location:City:Destination* (pp. 32–41). Graffeg Publishing.

Philipp, J., Thees, H., Olbrich, N., & Pechlaner, H. (2022). Towards an Ecosystem of Hospitality: The Dynamic Future of Destinations. *Sustainability*, *14*(2), 821. doi:10.3390u14020821

Pike, A., Rodríguez-Pose, A., & Tomaney, J. (2007). What kind of local and regional development and for whom? *Regional Studies*, *41*(9), 1253–1269. doi:10.1080/00343400701543355

Postma, A., Buda, D.-M., & Gugerell, K. (2017). The future of city tourism. *Journal of Tourism Futures*, *3*(2), 95–101. doi:10.1108/JTF-09-2017-067

Presenza, A., Sheehan, L., & Ritchie, J. B. (2005). Towards a model of the roles and activities of destination management organizations. *Journal of Hospitality. Tourism and Leisure Science*, *3*(1), 1–16.

Raeymaeckers, P., & Kenis, P. (2015). The influence of shared participant governance on the integration of service networks: A comparative social network analysis. *International Public Management Journal*, *19*(3), 397–426. doi:10.1080/10967494.2015.1062443

Reddel, T. (2002). Beyond participation, hierarchies, management and markets: 'New' governance and place policies. *Australian Journal of Place Administration, 61*(1), 50–63. doi:10.1111/1467-8500.00258

Reinhold, S., Beritelli, P., & Grünig, R. (2019). A business model typology for destination management organizations. *Tourism Review, 74*(6), 1135–1152. doi:10.1108/TR-03-2017-0065

Renz, T. (1998). *Management in internationalen Unternehmensnetzwerken [Management in international corporate networks]*. Springer Gabler. doi:10.1007/978-3-322-89492-2

Romao, J., Kourtit, K., Neuts, B., & Nijkamp, P. (2018). The smart city as a common place for tourists and residents: A structural analysis of the determinants of urban attractiveness. *Cities (London, England), 78*, 67–75. doi:10.1016/j.cities.2017.11.007

Sainaghi, R. (2006). From contents to processes: Versus a dynamic destination management model (DDMM). *Tourism Management, 27*(5), 1053–1063. doi:10.1016/j.tourman.2005.09.010

Schmied, M., Götz, K., Kreilkamp, E., Buchert, M., Hellwig, T., & Otten, S. (2009). *Traumziel Nachhaltigkeit: Innovative Vermarktungskonzepte nachhaltiger Tourismuskonzepte für den Massenmarkt [Dream goal of sustainabiltity: Innovative marketing concepts for sustainable tourism concepts for the mass market]*. Physica-Verlag.

Schneider-Sliwa, R., Erismann, C., & Saalfrank, C. (2009). *Das Image von Basel: Wohnort, Arbeitsort, Touristendestination und Unternehmensstandort [The image of Basel: place of residence, place of work, tourist destination, and business location]*. Schwabe Verlag.

Sinning, H. (2011). Europäische Stadt und Stadtmanagement: 29 Korrelationen, Widersprüche, Perspektiven [European city and urban management: 29 correlations, contradictions, perspectives]. In O. Frey & F. Koch (Eds.), *Die Zukunft der Europäischen Stadt: Stadtpolitik, Stadtplanung und Stadtgesellschaft im Wandel [The future of the European city: urban politics, urban planning, and urban society in transition]* (pp. 208–228). VS Verlag für Sozialwissenschaften. doi:10.1007/978-3-531-92653-7_13

Smith, J. M. C. (2018). Transforming Places. In J. Smith (Ed.), *Transforming Travel: Realising the Potential of Sustinable Tourism* (pp. 63–78). CABI. doi:10.1079/9781786394194.0063

Stam, E., & Spigel, B. (2017). Entrepreneural Ecosystems. In R. Blackburn, D. De Clercq, J. Heinonen, & Z. Wang (Eds.), *Handbook of Entrepreneurship and Small Business*. SAGE.

Stead, D., & Meijers, E. (2009). Spatial Planning and Policy Integration: Concepts, Facilitators and Inhibitors. *Planning Theory & Practice, 10*(3), 317–332. doi:10.1080/14649350903229752

Sycheva, I. N., Chernyshova, O. V., Panteleeva, T. A., Moiseeva, O. A., Chernyavskaya, S. A., & Khout, S. Y. (2019). Human capital as a base for regional development: A case study. *International Journal of Economics & Business Administration, 7*(1), 595–606. doi:10.35808/ijeba/304

Tansley, A. G. (1935). The use and abuse of vegetational concepts and terms. *Ecology, 16*(3), 284–307. doi:10.2307/1930070

Thees, H., Pechlaner, H., Olbrich, N., & Schuhbert, A. (2020). The Living Lab as a Tool to Promote Residents' Participation in Destination Governance. *Sustainability, 12*(3), 1120. doi:10.3390u12031120

Thees, H., Zacher, D., & Eckert, C. (2020). Work, life and leisure in an urban ecosystem – co-creating Munich as an Entrepreneurial Destination. *Journal of Hospitality and Tourism Management, 44*, 171–183. doi:10.1016/j.jhtm.2020.06.010

Thierstein, A. (1999). Standortmanagement – Alter Wein in neuen Schläuchen oder wie macht man aus einem Gürtel einen Hosenträger? [Site management—old wine in new bottles or how do you turn a belt into braces?] *Anforderungen an ein zeitgemässes Standortmanagement [Requirements for a modern site management].* https://www.alexandria.unisg.ch/13651/1/idt-stmg.pdf

Thierstein, A. (2002). Von der Raumordnung zur Raumentwicklung [From spatial planning to spatial development]. *disP – The Planning Review, 38*(148), 10-18.

Thorns, D. C. (2002). *The Transformation of Cities: Urban Theory and Urban Life.* Palgrave Macmillan. doi:10.1007/978-1-4039-9031-0

United Nations. (2022). The 17 Goals – Sustainable Development Goals. UN. https://sdgs.un.org/goals

Vogelgesang, M., & Stember, J. (2021). Netzwerke, Ebenen und Organisationen der Wirtschaftsförderung [Networks, levels, and organizations of economic development]. In Stember, J., Vogelgesang, M., Pongratz, P. & Fink. A. (Eds.), Handbuch Innovative Wirtschaftsförderung [Handbook for Innovative Business Development] (pp. 97-119). Springer Gabler.

Volgger, M., Pechlaner, H., & Pichler, S. (2017). The practice of destination governance: A comparative analysis of key dimensions and underlying concepts. *Journal of Tourism. Heritage and Services Marketing, 3*(1), 18–24.

Volgger, M., & Pfister, D. (Eds.). (2020). *Atmospheric Turn in Culture and Tourism: Place, Design and Process Impacts on Customer Behaviour, Marketing and Branding.* Emerald Publishing.

Walsh, P. (2001). Improving Governments' Response to Local Communities – is Place Management an Answer? *Australian Journal of Public Administration, 60*(2), 3–12. doi:10.1111/1467-8500.00204

Wiesner, K. A. (2021). *Professionelles Standort- und Destinationsmanagement: Instrumentarien und Praxisbeispiele für erfolgreiches Place-Management und –Marketing [Professional location and destination management: instruments and practical examples for successful place management and marketing].* Erich Schmidt Verlag.

KEY TERMS AND DEFINITIONS

Destination: In tourism, a destination is where tourists and visitors travel to, regardless of whether it is a leisure or business journey. A destination can be a city, a region, a landscape or an entire country. A destination consists of attraction points, tourist infrastructure, tourism-related businesses, and a destination management organization, among others.

Ecosystem: This term is derived from natural sciences and refers to a group of living and non-living components, their environment and all the interactions within. It has been adopted in various scientific disciplines, including business, entrepreneurship or regional development.

Living Space: The living space is the inhabited or occupied space of social groups and the sum of people, infrastructures, culture and identity of the everyday life.

Location: The location is the economic and business-related layer of a city or region and usually managed by an economic development agency with the goal of attracting businesses and fostering the economic development.

Network: Networks are sets of actors and all their relationships and interactions with each other. They can appear within organizations, stakeholder groups, neighborhoods, cities, regions, or beyond. Networks are characterized by low hierarchies and quick decision-making, making them flexible and adaptable.

Place Management: Place management refers to the holistic perception of locations, destinations and living spaces as a whole.

Regional Development: In regional development, spatial management goes beyond the boundaries of cities and considers their geographical surrounding, particularly the rural area, as well.

Space: Derived from physics, where space refers to the three-dimensional extent, in geography the term refers to territorial dimensions. Geographical space is often land in either public or private ownership.

Chapter 5

Project Management and Changes in Inbound Tourism to the Czech Republic:
A Case Study of Germans Incoming During the Coronavirus Crisis

Gabriela Antošová

(iD) https://orcid.org/0000-0001-5330-679X

Institute of Education and Communication, Czech University of Life Sciences in Prague, Czech Republic

Karel Němejc

(iD) https://orcid.org/0000-0003-0368-4228

Institute of Education and Communication, Czech University of Life Sciences in Prague, Czech Republic

ABSTRACT

The aim of this chapter is to introduce current German clientele with regards to inbound tourism to the Czech Republic, and to uncover concrete forms of support of inbound tourism from Germany to the Czech Republic. Content analysis was provided for the quantitative and qualitative secondary data about the inbound German tourism to the Czech Republic for the years 2012-2019. Furthermore, the analysis compares the turnout of separate quarters of the period from 2015 to 2020 with an emphasis on seasonal trends and changes in inbound tourism due to the COVID-19 pandemic and related restrictions. Good results of this source market in the Czech Republic's inbound tourism are usually taken for granted due to its size and geographical proximity; however, the implications of the pandemic are reflected not only on tourist arrivals from Germany but also on their support, which is implemented in relation to the German market by selected entities at all levels of tourism management in the Czech Republic, and also some private entities.

DOI: 10.4018/978-1-6684-5976-8.ch005

INTRODUCTION

The main initiative for this chapter is to emphasize the importance of the German source market, which was amplified in 2020 in the absence of foreign tourist clients in the Czech Republic due to the pandemic of COVID-19. The content analysis based on a study of German current sources of media data.

Due to its size, population and high spending on tourism, Germany is an important resource market for many destinations in the world. For the Czech Republic, it is the most important foreign source market. High numbers of arrivals are taken for granted - the German source market is not systematically given attention in professional articles or publications. This chapter fills these gaps and deals with both the actual traffic from Germany and the support of this traffic. The results of this chapter place Germany in the context of inbound tourism in the Czech Republic and provide a comprehensive view of the activities of individual entities that support this resource market. A comprehensive view of the support of arrivals from Germany is also prepared on the basis of responses from semi-structured interviews conducted in 2020 with representatives of individual entities directly in Germany. Another secondary source was internet data sources from 2012 to the present, partly due to their availability, but also with the aim of the current context of the coronavirus situation with inbound tourism of German clients to the Czech Republic.

The aim of this chapter is to present the current German clientele in the context of inbound tourism in the Czech Republic, and to reveal specific forms of support for inbound tourism from Germany to the Czech Republic. The secondary intention is to reflect in relation to the German source market the changes that tourism and with it inbound tourism from Germany to the Czech Republic will go through due to the pandemic of the COVID-19 disease.

The practical results are findings on German clientele in inbound tourism in the Czech Republic, support for this source market and changes in tourism due to the COVID-19 pandemic. In conclusion, there are suggestions for practice that could complement the identified forms of support for inbound tourism, and thus increase the benefits that the number of visitors to German tourists represents for the Czech Republic.

LITERATURE REVIEW

In 2018, tourism accounted for 2.9% of the Czech Republic's GDP, which corresponds to EUR 6.12 billion. In the tourism sector were employed 241,000 people - accounting for 4.4% of total employment. Consumption in tourism (domestic and foreign visitors) amounted to EUR 11.8 billion, of which domestic tourism accounted for EUR 50.48 billion (43%) and inbound tourism for EUR 67.4 billion (57%). This value was generated by 32.27 million foreign visitors. Czechs spent a total of EUR 3.32 billion on foreign trips, while revenues from tourism exceeded expenditures by EUR 3.4 billion (ČSÚ, 2020).

The map shows up the GDP per capita in EURO in 2019 for the Czech regions and the neighboring countries. Several conclusions:

- The potential markets with highest levels of income are the German and the Austrian Regions.
- Some advertising campaigns can be focused on the German regions, provided the strength in the consume capacity of this regions and the proximity to Czech regions of Karlovy Vary, Liberec and Ústí and Labem.

- In the Czech territory at the German border, several attractions can excel: cultural heritage, snow and sky activities, historical spots, natural surroundings and cultural assets.
- The cheaper cost of living in the CR and the exchange rate effect make more attractive the Czech destinations.

Figure 1. GDP per capita in EURO in 2019 for the Czech regions
Source: Helmuth Yesid Arias Gomez, GIS own elaboration according to data Eurostat, 2019 (unpublished)

Precisely the most lagged Czech regions belong to the border fringe with the German neighbors. Over there a higher international integration can improve the economic conditions in the Czech territories.

More dynamic interactions in the framework of the regional European strategies can be harnessed for integrating the Czech territories with the German regions.

Individual destinations act as competing units that need to be managed for their prosperity and development. However, managing the destination in the way that is known today, with a comprehensive marketing approach, is relatively new. Destination marketing management began to develop in the 1990s in the Alpine countries, the United Kingdom, Canada, and Australia (Palatková, 2011). Back in the 1970s and 1980s, destination management organizations were more commercially oriented in relation to the destination, focusing primarily on promotion, with the aim of quantitative growth of tourism. However, with the advent of globalization and modern technology, there has been a growing awareness of the importance of partnerships between private and public stakeholders to keep the destination competitive (Buhalis, 2000). This partnership is the cornerstone of the current concept of destination management (Pike, 2012).

At the end of 2019, the first persons infected with a new type of coronavirus was identified in central China. A few months later, on March 11, 2020, a COVID-19 pandemic was declared by the World Health Organization (WHO, 2020). Tourism, as an activity related to the movement of people and their encounters, is undesirable during the spread of a contagious disease. Therefore, this sector of the economy was hit first and travel as a non-priority leisure activity (compared to the importance of slowing down the spread of the disease) was restored as one of the latest with strict adherence to hygiene measures.

RESEARCH METHODOLOGY

The main purpose of this chapter is to introduce the current German clientele in the context of inbound tourism in the Czech Republic and to reveal specific forms of support for inbound tourism from Germany to the Czech Republic. The secondary intention is then to reflect in relation to the German resource market the changes that tourism will go through due to the COVID-19 pandemic.

Based on the need for findings, research questions were identified:

VO1: What is the position and characteristics of visitors from Germany within the inbound tourism of the Czech Republic?

VO2: How does the support of inbound tourism from Germany work in the Czech Republic? VO3: What changes will occur as a result of the COVID-19 pandemic in the German source market and in its support?

Content analysis of secondary data on German clientele coming to the Czech Republic is a basic step to answer the above questions. Specifically, an analysis of quantitative indicators is performed, such as the annual number of arrivals and overnight stays of German tourists in the Czech Republic and in the regions for the years 2012-2019. Furthermore, the number of visitors in the individual quarters of 2015–2020 is compared with an emphasis on finding out the effects of seasonality and changes in arrivals due to the COVID-19 pandemic and the associated travel restrictions. We supplement this analysis with a qualitative view of the composition of visitors from Germany, the representation of individual visitor segments broken down, for example, by source federal state, age group, the motive of visit, mode of transport and more.

Another methodological step is the analysis of the current support of inbound tourism from Germany. First, using knowledge from literary research, further study of professional literature and conceptual documents, the entities that participate in the support to varying degrees are defined. Then their role is presented, including a specific activity to support arrivals from Germany and finally yet importantly, the cooperation between individual entities is outlined. The information obtained from secondary sources is enriched with primary data obtained from participatory observation and from semi-standardized interviews. The observations took place from July to November 2020 in the Czech Center Berlin and the CzechTourism branch in Berlin. Interviews were conducted during October and November 2020 in person, by phone, via the Zoom platform or by sending questions by e-mail with representatives of entities involved in supporting inbound tourism from Germany to the Czech Republic, specifically with representatives of the German CzechTourism, Regional Development Department at the Ústí nad Labem Regional Office, Czech Railways, Deutsche Bahn, and the German tour operator Frankenland Travel Group.

Given that the tourism industry is facing major changes related to the COVID-19 pandemic, these changes must also ultimately be reflected in and related to the German source market. Secondary data from current studies and surveys are used for this purpose, as well as primary data obtained from semi-standardized interviews.

This chapter provides a comprehensive view of the current German tourist clientele and ways to support the German resource market. Based on the analysis of the German clientele and the support of inbound tourism from Germany, the proposal part presents proposals to support inbound tourism from Germany, which would complement current support and could lead to increased economic benefits of

German tourist visits to the Czech Republic, or help to gain new visitors, in view of the "restart" of tourism (Antošová, 2022), which occurs due to its temporary suspension due to the pandemic of COVID-19 in 2020-2021.

Figure 2. German inbound tourism to the CR quarterly comparison 2015-2020
Source: own elaboration according to the CSU, 2021

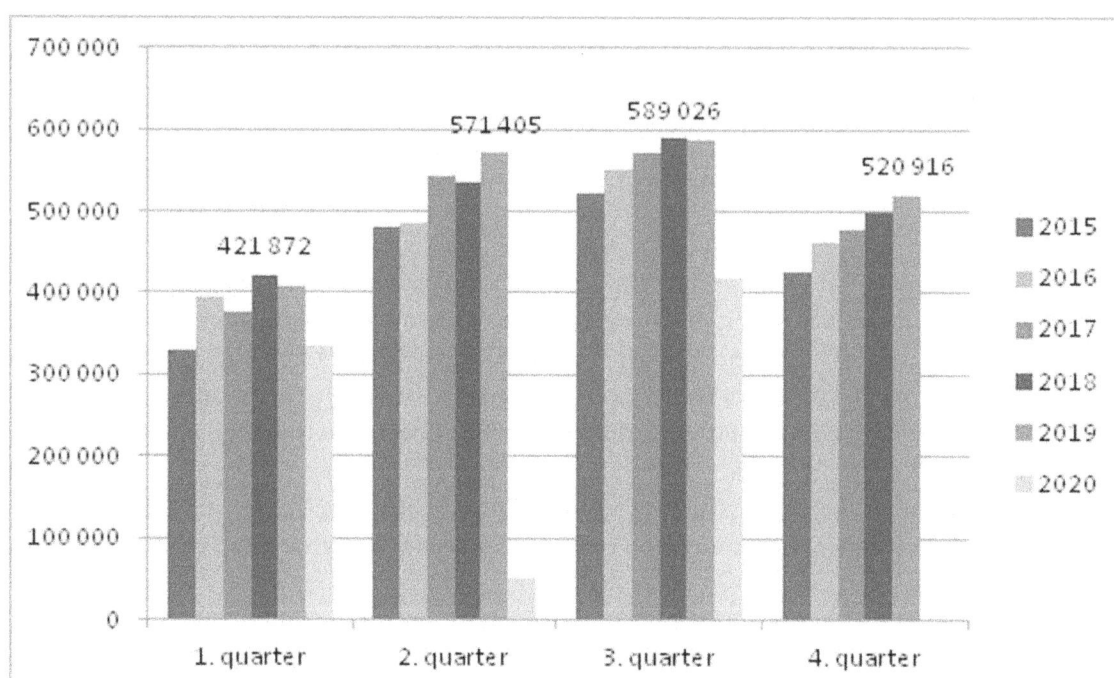

FINDINGS AND ANALYSIS

As a result of the pandemic, the number of arrivals in international tourism fell by 93% year-on-year in 2020 (as of June), a decline unparalleled in modern history. Between January and June 2020, some 440 million international arrivals and associated export revenues of $ 460 billion were lost (UNWTO, 2020).

Numerical estimates of the effects of restrictions related to the coronavirus pandemic on tourism in the Czech Republic were also published by the Confederation of Trade and Tourism in June 2020. Overall, the expected decline was 50% compared to 2019, estimating the total consumption of domestic and foreign visitors at EUR 5.72 billion (SOCR CR, 2020). In order for the loss of income from inbound tourism from abroad to be compensated by domestic tourists, Czechs would have to have about 6-8 weeks of vacation in 2020 and spend thousands of crowns more than usual during the vacation in the Czech Republic (Pancíř, 2020). The estimates at the time, however, did not yet anticipate a worsening of the epidemiological situation in autumn 2020.

The analytical study (McKinsey, 2020) on the effects of the tourism pandemic does not envisage a return to the original numbers of foreign arrivals (globally in 2019) before 2024. The original volume of arrivals in domestic tourism is expected to recover in 2023 (Trimble et al., 2020). The greatest potential for the Czech Republic should be in inbound tourism source countries, from which it is possible to arrive by car due to the distance, which was reflected in the number of arrivals in the summer season 2020, when tourists from neighbouring countries - Germany, Slovakia and Poland were visiting Prague (ČSÚ, 2020b).

This was already confirmed in the summer of 2020, when tourist demand in the European region began to pick up after the release of travel conditions, especially in the case of shorter trips over shorter distances. According to the already mentioned study, the renewed increase in travel to more distant destinations will come later (Trimble et al., 2020). Another reason that adds to shorter journeys is to emphasize the emphasis of the given impact of tourism / mode of transport on the environment. It is expected that even in the long run there will be a decline in air traffic, both on private and business trips - tourism will be more often realized within the region or the European continent (Jiricka-Pürrer, Brandenburg, & Probstl-Haider, 2020).

On the one hand, the pandemic crisis is liquidating for a large part of tourism service providers, on the other hand, it is undoubtedly an opportunity to reconsider the current approach to tourism at all levels, its future development, reflect changes in tourist behaviour, and refocus on new forms of tourism or other tourist segments.

The arrival of changes related to the new conditions for travel was confirmed by a survey (Travel Consul, 2020) conducted in September 2020, which consisted of interviewing 1,021 respondents from twenty different countries (including 27 respondents from the Czech Republic), tourism workers (travel agencies, etc.). More than half of the organizations surveyed, which did not close down during the measures, said that they had responded to the situation caused by the COVID-19 pandemic by changing their product. Half of the respondents adjusted their business model and a third of them used the time to invest in new technologies. A large part of the respondents is also considering a change in the offer of destinations and the establishment of cooperation with new providers of accommodation or other services in the future. Another point that respondents described as crucial was the increase in cooperation with destination management organizations. Activities, whose importance has increased as a result of the pandemic, are joint campaigns to promote the destination and provide destination safety certificates, which, in addition to the price, have become one of the decisive factors for potential tourists in choosing a destination. From the point of view of consumer protection, the temporary urgency of the change in the approach to cancelling tours and stays was also confirmed by the interviewed tour operators.

In addition to the external barriers to tourism, such as travel restrictions when crossing borders (the need for a negative virus test, health, subjective perceptions of the risk of infection, and economic barriers such as income constraints, uncertainty and thus greater willingness to make savings) (Stoffelen et al., 2017), the internal obstacles can be named as well including fear of infection and uncertainty about the course of the journey within the disruption of transport connections. In the short term, during the pandemic, for example, there was a trend of more conscious travel - in smaller groups, to nature, with a greater emphasis on safety. Based on the results of semi-standardized interviews in this regard, the director of the German representation of the CzechTourism emphasized, in particular, the need for flexibility in marketing the destination. The circumstances, which new forms of tourism will emerge from a long-term perspective, will disappear completely, and whether efforts will be made to eliminate some phenomena will depend on the duration of the pandemic and its other effects that have not yet been uncovered (Bieger, 2020). In any case, according to the Czech Association of Small and Medium-sized Enterprises, the tourism sector is "trying to fight for survival" by reaching out to existing clients and gaining new ones, and faces greater pressure on the quality of services - with emphasis on sustainability, digitization and automation of related administration (reservations, orders, payments) (AMSP CR, 2020).

The UNWTO approaches the changes similarly and considers the recommendations for the renewal of tourism such as contactless payments in local transport, contactless check-in for a pre-allocated seat, contactless check-in in accommodation facilities, electronic tickets, creation of new jobs with higher added value through the introduction of new technologies and the understanding of innovation and sustainability as essential building blocks of the "new" tourism as a priority (UNWTO, 2020b).

DISCUSSION AND CONCLUSION

Germany produces the highest numbers of international arrivals to the Czech Republic in long term (over 2 million arrivals and over 5 million stay-overs from 2020). The German interest in the Czech Republic has its roots from before the Velvet Revolution in 1989. The Czech Republic belongs to a top three destinations from the German short-distance countries. Even though the travel restrictions imposed by governments in reaction to COVID-19 pandemic significantly lowered (by almost 30%) the number of arrivals to the Czech Republic in the third quarter of 2020 compared to the previous year, German, Polish and Slovak languages were the most heard foreign languages in the Czech Republic during summer 2020.

This research concluded that Germany, with more than 240 million trips, is Europe's most important source of tourism. Expenditure on tourism, Germany after China and the US the third highest consumption in the world, and moreover since 2007 with the decision of 2009 is constantly growing. The most popular destinations are the direct ones, especially Spain, Italy and Turkey. From the distillation of loved ones, German tourists are simultaneously visited by Austria, the Netherlands, and France. The Czech Republic has a sufficiently good position among nearby destinations in Western and Central Europe - behind the aforementioned trio and Poland, the Czech Republic is the fifth most visited country.

Figure 3. Inbound tourism to the Czech Republic in total
Source: fvw Destination Ranking, 2019

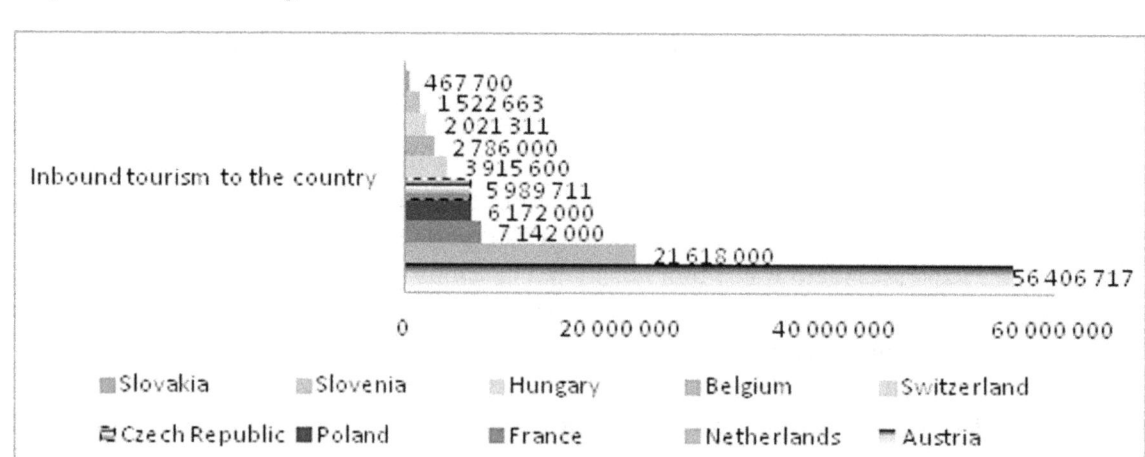

The contribution is considered to be beneficial for the very choice of the topic - good results of this source market in the Czech Republic's inbound tourism are usually taken for granted due to its size and geographical proximity, however, the implications of the pandemic are reflected not only on tourist arrivals from Germany but also on their support, which is implemented in relation to the German market by selected entities at all levels of tourism management in the Czech Republic and also some private entities. Results reflect the effects of the COVID-19 pandemic, which erupted in 2020 and fundamentally affected the tourism industry, including arrivals from Germany.

A closer look at current surveys (Ad Alliance GmbH, 2020), examining the behaviour of Germans during a pandemic, reveals aspects, the uncovering of which can help in further planning the development of inbound tourism from Germany. These surveys conducted in four stages from 20 March to 15 September 2020 in the field of tourism found that 48% of respondents had realized at least one multi-day trip in 2020, with about a third more travelling between German regions than abroad. In terms of trip planning for 2021, 4% fewer respondents plan an individual trip compared to the previous year. Another indicator for the future is the planned categories of accommodation - hotels that plan to use 9% fewer respondents, on the contrary, an increase of 6% was found in the category of private accommodation - cottages and 2% more respondents plan to stay in the camp. With respect to the mode of transport, 12% fewer respondents plan to travel by plane in 2021 than in 2020. 2% more respondents plan to spend their holidays in Germany in 2021, while 7% fewer respondents want to travel to non-European destination. The sensitivity of German consumers to their protection has also changed - for 71% of respondents is important to guarantee a refund in case of non-travel, fair cancellation conditions just before departure and the certainty that in case of flight cancellation, other transport connections or possible closure of state borders they will be able to get home. This phenomenon is also confirmed by the results of semi-standardized interviews conducted in this chapter with tourism service providers for Czech Railways and Frankenland Travel Group. The German representation of CzechTourism added to the issue of consumer protection that this predominance of the end customer is not sustainable, and that the consumer of tourist services will have to take some risks.

Looking at the German interest in travelling, examined in a qualitative survey by the independent non-commercial company Forschungsgemeinschaft Urlaub und Reisen in September 2020, it was shown that the Germans' willingness to travel is the same as in 2019, in all criteria: time, money and interest. They would prefer to travel as usual, only more often in their own car and to already known, trusted destinations (FvW, 2020). The sales manager of the tour operator Frankenland Travelgroup, representing the abundant offer of the Czech Republic, commented that the consequence of the pandemic expected the diversion of German urban tourism to the countryside, where, according to him, there is no such large concentration of tourists. In addition, according to McKinsey study, Germany was of the first markets to return to the intensity of domestic tourism in 2019, combining a strong economy (Beránek, 2013), health care system and a wide range of rural tourism (McKinsey, 2020).

Changes in the Support of Inbound Tourism from Germany

The suspension of foreign tourism has led to an understanding of the importance of nearby markets by all entities (Allex et al., 2013), and according to the statements of individual actors with the same goal - the acquisition of a German tourist - the cooperation will be further deepened. One of the fundamental changes in the support of inbound tourism from Germany is the loss of some of the classic tools of promotion, which were tourism fairs. According to the director of the German representation of CzechTourism, the fairs play a particularly important role in supporting the German source market, which was weakened through the COVID-19 pandemic and the associated cancellation of mass events and the fairs are likely to be replaced by new ways of promotion. The German market can be expected to be more oriented especially to online activities, which have not been as much used due to its relative conservatism. The inexhaustibility of online promotion in relation to the German source market was also mentioned by representatives of the regions, such as the representative for the Department of Regional Development at the Regional Office of the Ústí Region. At a time when, in addition to trade fairs, journalistic journeys have disappeared from possible support tools, online communication with the German market will become more relevant than ever.

Another change is the accent of some topics related to tourism, which to some extent appeared in the past, but the pandemic of COVID-19 deepened their importance in relation to Germany even more. These are mainly digitization and sustainability.

Digitization due to the growing importance of the Internet in planning and purchasing holidays and the growing openness of the German clientele to payments on the Internet; sustainability in the sense of highlighting some regions of the Czech Republic as destinations with an offer of environmentally friendly forms of tourism, or in terms of promoting more environmentally friendly modes of transport, such as rail transport. As also stated by the Director of the German Representation of CzechTourism Germany, the changes in the promotion of the Czech Republic as a whole are already reflected in the forthcoming CzechTourism Strategy for 2021–2025:

"Sustainability is the common denominator of the new marketing strategy of CzechTourism 2021-25 and we will work with it specifically in the framework of promotion of trips by train or public transport in the destination in general, with an emphasis on regional products (Weigl and Zöhrer, 2005), slow tourism, and we want to further strengthen our online presentation."

In conclusion, it is possible to present five proposals to supplement the current model of support for inbound tourism from Germany. The first of them is based on a critical view of current sources of information about German clients, which are available to individual entities involved in the support of incoming from Germany. The recommendation was to create a new way of monitoring traffic from Germany, which would allow to get a better view of visitor profiles, and thus better identify the segments that visit the Czech Republic. During this monitoring, their satisfaction with the specific destination visited in the Czech Republic would also be monitored. The results could become a solid basis for decisions made by destination representatives on the further development of the destination and in planning the promotion of specific tourist products on the German market.

The second proposal concerns new segments, which in the analysis manifested themselves as communication campaigns designed to target groups according to age segmentation. This segmentation can be supplemented by a more elaborate psychographic segmentation, which would not focus on age groups, but on interest groups. Another possible suitable step can be considered communicating the offer of selected border destinations for stays of German schoolchildren, which could lead to an increase in interest in the Czech Republic in the future.

The third proposal reflects the fact that much of the communication associated with holiday planning is being moved to the Internet, even in the German market, which used to be conservative towards new tools. Specifically, it was a proposal to connect the web reservation portals of accommodation facilities with the websites of destination agencies, the implementation of which would make it easier for potential German visitors to plan a trip to the Czech Republic. Another specific recommendation leads to an improvement of the presentation on social networks operated by the CzechTourism for communication on the German source market.

The last two proposals concerned the deepening of cooperation among the German representation of CzechTourism and other entities - especially with the Czech Centers. Although some important aspects were found in the agendas of the Czech Centers and CzechTourism during the analysis, the participating observations showed that their practical use is rare. Therefore, this proposal intends to start the cooperation first by connecting the communication on the Internet to the audience of both organizations and to start using a unified visual presentation. In the post-covid situation, their cooperation should grow into joint promotional projects, in which the experience of the Czech Centers in organizing cultural events would be used to support inbound tourism to the Czech Republic. Joint projects will operate not only outside but also within organizations and will thus lead to the motivation of the representatives of both of them and to more ambitious cooperation in the future.

The last proposal also concerns the cooperation of several entities - namely CzechTourism, Prague City Tourism, Deutsche Bahn and variably regions or DMOs in the Ústí Region. Taking into account the identified opinions of individual entities in support of the German market, the solution is a joint campaign aimed at the starting cities served by Deutsche Bahn on the route to Ústí nad Labem and Prague.

This chapter provided an overview of the German clientele of today, which can be placed in the context of inbound tourism in the Czech Republic. It provides readers with a more detailed look at both the German source market and its support, which should become a crucial topic in the post-covid era when German tourists will be attracted by many destinations. In this context, several proposals have been addressed which may be the subject of further discussion.

REFERENCES

Ad Alliance GmbH. (2020). Studie Die Corona-Pandemie und ihr Einfluss auf den Alltag – 4. [Study The corona pandemic and its impact on everyday life – 4.] *Welle.* https://www.ad-alliance.de/cms/unternehmen/presse/corona-und-ihr-einfluss.html

Allex, B., Brandenburg, B., Liebl, U., Gerersdorfer, T., & Czachs, C. (2013) Hot town, summer in the city – entwicklung von hitzerelevanten Anpassungsstrategien im Städtetourismus [Development of heat-related adaptation strategies in city tourism]. Regional Development and Information Society: 393-398.

AMSP ČR. (2020). *Online conference "Nové trendy v podnikání MSP".* [*New trends in SME* entrepreneurship".] [Video]. Youtube.https://www.youtube.com/watch?v=TDXjfcuFvKQ&list=PLRV-VoSMvlATvlELqO0yMgGlz-wuGLSM8

Antošová, G. (Ed.). (2022). *Innovative Strategic Planning and International Collaboration for the Mitigation of Global Crises.* IGI Global. doi:10.4018/978-1-7998-8339-5

Beránek, J. (2013). *Ekonomika cestovního ruchu [Tourism economics.].* Mag Consulting.

Bieger, T. (2020) *Future of tourism in the wake of relaxing SARS-CoV-2 shutdowns Small steps to a temporary new "normal".* AIEST. https://www.aiest.org/fileadmin/ablage/dokumente/Covid-Reports/Report_20200510_Tourism_Future.pdf

Binggeli, U., Constantin, M., & Pollack, E. (2020. *COVID-19 tourism spend recovery in numbers.* McKinsey. https://www.mckinsey.com/industries/travel-logistics-and-transport-infrastructure/our-insights/covid-19-tourism-spend-recovery-in-numbers?cid=other-eml-alt-mip-mck&hdpid=e3159b12-26b1-4f41-87c3-a48e24932630&hctky=12250927&hlkid=03ea3268d42442ca8b40146eec3c8990

Buhalis, D. (2000). Marketing the competitive destination of the future. *Tourism Management, 21*(1), 97–116. doi:10.1016/S0261-5177(99)00095-3

ČSÚ. (2020). *Nerezidenti v HUZ v Praze v 2Q 2020.* [*Non-residents in HUZ in Prague in Q2 2020.*]. CSU. https://vdb.czso.cz/vdbvo2/faces/cs/index.jsf?page=vystup

ČSÚ. (2020-2021). *Satelitní účet cestovního ruchu.* [*Tourism Satellite Account.*]. CSU. https://www.czso.cz/csu/czso/satelitni_ucet_cestovniho_ruchu

FVW. (2020). *Reiselust der Kunden bleibt ungebrochen.* [*Customers' desire to travel remains unbroken.*]. FVW. https://www.fvw.de/reisevertrieb/datenanalyse/reiseanalyse-september-umfrage-macht-hoffnung-212547

Jiricka-Pürrer, A., Brandenburg, Ch., & Probstl-Haider, U. (2020). City tourism pre- and post-covid-19 pandemic – Messages to take home for climate change adaptation and mitigation? *Journal of Outdoor Recreation and Tourism, 31*, 31. doi:10.1016/j.jort.2020.100329

Palatková, M. (2011). *Marketingový management destinací: strategický a taktický marketing destinace turismu, systém marketingového řízení destinace a jeho financování, řízení kvality v destinaci a informační systém destinace.* [*Marketing management of destinations: strategic and tactical marketing of the destination tourism, system of marketing management of the destination and its financing, quality management in the destination and information system of the destination.*] Grada.

Pancíř, T. (2020). *"K věci": Dopady koronaviru. Rozhovor s ředitelkou Středočeské centrály cestovního ruchu Zuzanou Vojtovou.* [*"To the point": The effects of the coronavirus. Interview with Zuzana Vojtová, Director of the Central Bohemian Tourist Board.*]. Podmailer. https://podmailer.com/podcast/k-v-ci/dopady-koronaviru-ve-st-ednich-echach-neotev-ely-d

Pike, S. (2012). *Destination Marketing. An Integrated Marketing Communication Approach.* Elsevier.

SOCR ČR. (2020). *Dopady na cestovní ruch způsobené pandemií koronaviru.* [*Impacts on tourism caused by the coronavirus pandemic.*]. SOCR CR. http://www.socr.cz/clanek/dopady-na-cestovni-ruch-zpusobene-pandemii-koronaviru/

Stoffelen, A., Ioannides, D., & Vanneste, D. (2017). Obstacles to achieving cross-border tourism governance: A multi-scalar approach focusing on the German-Czech borderlands. *Annals of Tourism Research, 64*, 126–138. doi:10.1016/j.annals.2017.03.003

Travel Consul. (2020) *The Impact and Outlook of The COVID-19 Outbreak to Travel Distribution Partners.* Travel Consul. https://rsvp.theworldsbest.events/o7npp.

Trimble, S.J., Ferran, K., & McDermott, H. (2020). *COVID-19: Pandemic impacts on European city tourism.* https://s3.amazonaws.com/tourism-economics/craft/Latest-Research-Docs/Summary-GCT_corona_regional_RB_EUR-final-TE-PDF.pdf

UNWTO. (2020). *International tourist numbers down 65% in first half of 2020.* UNWTO reports. https://www.unwto.org/news/international-tourist-numbers-down-65-in-first-half-of-2020-unwto-reports

UNWTO. (2020). *Global guidelines to restart tourism.* UNWTO reports. https://webunwto.s3.eu-west-1.amazonaws.com/s3fs-public/2020-05/UNWTO-Global-Guidelines-to-Restart-Tourism.pdf

Weigl, M., & Zöhrer, M. (2005). Regionale Selbstverständnisse und gegenseitige Wahrnehmung von Deutschen und Tschechen. [Regional self-conceptions and mutual perception of Germans and Czechs.]. CAP.

World Health Organisation. (2020). *Coronavirus.* WHO. https://www.who.int/health-topics/coronavirus#tab=tab_1

KEY TERMS AND DEFINITIONS

Changes in the Support of German Inbound Tourism to the Czech Republic: Suggestions for practice that could complement the identified forms of support for inbound tourism and thus increase the benefits that the number of visitors to German tourists represents for the Czech Republic

Digitization and Tourism Sustainability During the Crisis: The tourism sector is "trying to fight for survival" by reaching out to existing clients and gaining new ones, and faces greater pressure on the quality of services - with emphasis on sustainability, digitization and automation of related administration (reservations, orders, payments).

German Interest in Travelling: Examined in a qualitative survey by the independent non-commercial company Forschungsgemeinschaft Urlaub und Reisen in September 2020, it was shown that the Germans' willingness to travel is the same as in 2019, in all criteria: time, money and interest. They would prefer to travel as usual, only more often in their own car and to already known, trusted destinations.

Important Resource Market: Germany is an important resource market for many destinations in the world. For the Czech Republic, it is the most important foreign source market. High numbers of arrivals are taken for granted - the German source market is not systematically given attention in professional articles or publications.

Inbound Tourism: Comprehensive view of the tourism activities of individual entities that support tourism resource market in the selected country. A movement of foreign tourists to the selected country of interest.

New Tourism Segments After Coronavirus Crisis: Analysis manifested themselves as communication campaigns designed to target groups according to age segmentation. This segmentation can be supplemented by a more elaborate psychographic segmentation, which would not focus on age groups, but on interest groups.

Renewal of Tourism: Contactless payments in local transport, contactless check-in for a pre-allocated seat, contactless check-in in accommodation facilities, electronic tickets, creation of new jobs with higher added value through the introduction of new technologies and the understanding of innovation and sustainability as essential building blocks of the "new" tourism as a priority.

The Sensitivity of German Consumers: To their protection has also changed - for 71% of respondents is important to guarantee a refund in case of non-travel, fair cancellation conditions just before departure and the certainty that in case of flight cancellation, other transport connections or possible closure of state borders they will be able to get home.

Chapter 6
Rural Districts:
Application of the Core–Periphery Model to Rural Development

Juan Sebastián Castillo-Valero

 https://orcid.org/0000-0003-0107-8611
University of Castilla-La Mancha, Spain

Maria Carmen García-Cortijo
University of Castilla-La Mancha, Spain

ABSTRACT

This work introduces an original methodology for analysing the role of intra-rural population movements in the formation or consolidation of rural districts. For this purpose, the authors adapted Rosen's hedonic models, developed in other areas of the economy, to explain individual decisions in rural migration dynamics. The methodology was drawn up to explain population movements in rural areas, on a sub-regional scale, as a new centre-periphery dynamic. Empirical application of this methodology in the future might be useful for better explaining sub-regional dynamics and for the design of territorial development policies.

INTRODUCTION

Although the dichotomy between the urban and rural concepts is becoming blurred (Obeso, 2019), traditional theories on population movements are based on this distinction: migration processes from the rural environment to urban areas for economic reasons, to which is added the dynamic of returns from urban areas to peri-urban rings (Brown, 1991; Gedik, 2005; Docampo & Otero, 2012) as a symptom of the exhaustion of urban growth processes (Lewis & Maund, 1976; Wardwell, 1977; De Vries, 1990). Also to be considered is urban-rural migration, an emerging phenomenon in developed countries that accelerated with the COVID-19 pandemic, as part of a broader movement of relocation outside densely-populated areas and in response to the renewed appeal of rural lifestyles (Selod & Shilpi, 2021).

DOI: 10.4018/978-1-6684-5976-8.ch006

However, the existing rural-rural flows, which may even be greater than rural-urban flows (Selod & Shilpi, 2021), are much less documented. Some reasons for this are: a) greater importance is placed on urban considerations; b) urban heterogeneity as opposed to rural homogeneity; and c) intra-rural migration has properties that are common to those of rural-urban movements, which have already been studied (Lucas, 1997, Ahluwalia, 1978; Kikuchi & Hayami, 1983; Rosenzweig and Stark, 1989). The literature does, however, offer some studies on these dynamics (Zimmerbauer & Paasi, 2012, Hamin & Marcucci, 2008, Ray; 2006), which are frequent in southern Europe and function differently, for reasons that are not exclusively economic and are difficult to tie in with the classic theories behind population movements (Haas, 2008).

This complex situation that is uncertain and challenging for the rural world stems from the need to consider new concepts and models to help explain its dynamic and demographic structure and thus facilitate processes of territorial reactivation with endogenous resources. This is the goal of this paper, which is organised as follows. Section 2 describes the need to move towards another dimension in population theories. Section 3 introduces the notion of rural district and develops a hedonic population model. Finally, Section 4 concludes.

BACKGROUND

Population tends towards a type of settlement that changes with time (García & Otero, 2012), and one of the main traditional causes of migratory phenomena is economic (Pissarides & Wadsworth, 1989; Layard et al., 1992; Jennissen, 2003; Márquez et al 2004). Along this line, we find the following theories, among others: a) the Neoclassic Theory, with workers moving to places where labour is short and wages high; b) the Greenwood model (1997) and its disequilibrium variables; c) Myrdal's Theory (1957) and the correlation between population accumulation and concentration of economic activity.

However, population movements are not caused exclusively by economic factors. Other variables may also change decisions to move (Selod and Shilpi, 2021, Massey et al., 1998; Silvestre Rodriguez, 2000, Graves and Greenwood, 1987, Roback, 1988; Treyz et al., 1993; Evans, 1990). The following are some theoretical approaches to this: a) Dual Labour Markets by Michael Piore (1979) connecting migration with diversity in destination regions; b) Gravity Models introducing the distance variable (Ravestein, 1885; Poulain, 1981; Millinton, 1994; Karemera et al. (2000), Pellegrini & Fotheringham, 2002); c) the Network Theory and a migratory phenomenon that is subject to feedback from transmission of the migration experience (Gurak & Caces, 1992).

These theoretical contributions, which undoubtedly help to explain the causes of migrations, must consider and be adapted to a changing population dynamic. Back in 1970, in the United States, a change was noted in the urban growth trend, more so in non-metropolitan areas than in urban areas. For the first time, the central hubs started to be less attractive with a slow decrease in their inhabitants, while residential peripheries continued to grow. In parallel, other rural areas began to see substantial demographic growth with definitive population displacement (Berry, 1976).

These changes did not have economic causes nor did they follow the rural-urban direction of classic models (Arroyo, 2001). It was initially believed that the crisis of the 1970s was affecting the economic structure of the system and causing the loss of population in metropolitan centres, but it was also observed that other minor urban centres did not seem to be affected. This same process was repeated subsequently in Japan, Switzerland, Norway, Italy, Denmark, New Zealand, Belgium France, Germany, Netherlands, and Spain.

It was a fact that urban areas were losing population towards different areas, apparently consolidating rural-rural movements and, more specifically, movements from smaller rural areas to other larger ones. The driving forces behind this change were related to the *new economic geography* described by Krugman (1991) and the principles of the social construction of territories described by *new regionalism* (Söderbaum & Shaw, 2004; Pecqueur, 2001).

The reality is that there is a different, and relevant, scenario for population movements for which a different approach is needed. It has, however, received little attention. The declining rural units on the European map are a symptom of serious structural problems that may lead to their disappearance, holding back personal projects and erasing communities that have a long history and even great potential for the future (Pinilla & Sáez, 2020).

This aspect is what makes it necessary to devise a new theoretical dimension, with a more appropriate and opportune information system to assist in the process of management and decision-making and to support and develop the territory in a rural society in which depopulation is not only a pressing and worrying matter but also engenders other problems. Depopulation exists everywhere, from large cities to densely populated spaces, but when it affects low-density areas—which anyway are very sensitive to change—small variations in their conditions can result in very negative prospects for the future. These authors therefore pose a new term, rural district, and an associated model which is introduced in the next section.

MAIN FOCUS OF THE CHAPTER

A rural district can be defined as an agglomeration of rural territories that are close to each other, have similar geographical characteristics and similarities in their lifestyles, endogenous resources, and a network of relations. Basically, it is a homogeneous entity of a medium size that is similar to the European Union concept of Local Action Groups (LAG).

As a system, a rural district is made up of a set of parts/municipalities among which relations are established that articulate the unit, bringing the whole together as one. Some of these parts/municipalities, usually the larger ones, serve as central or main towns while the remainder are the periphery.

The essence of the rural district is to try to overcome the limitations of the second maxim of Descartes' discourse on method whereby a problem should be divided up into as many simple, separate elements as possible and moving towards the conceptual paradigm of the Gestalt school whereby the whole is more than the sum of its parts, and the general theory of the Bertalanffy system in which a system, in this case the rural district, is a consolidating, dynamic and active entity, full of circular relations and in constant feedback with the changing environment.

But this way of seeing the district needs to be materialised and one way of doing so is by using models. From the many alternatives, we opted for quantitative models because decisions can sometimes only be made in a comprehensive, neutral, rational, and scientific way adopting a mathematical approach. So, using an algorithm we take aspects that seem to build the most appropriate model for our purpose, that is, to explain rural-rural movements.

Our starting point was the assumption that a territorial unit is a heterogeneous and divisible good that has a set of individual attributes, each of which helps to concentrate the population. This approach is similar to the hedonic price theory, which explains the value of a good in terms of its attributes, thus determining implicit demand. Its origin is controversial; some attribute it to Haas (1922) and others to Court (1939). What is clear is that the hedonic model theory has been refined over time. Lancaster (1966) developed the foundations to estimate the utility value generated by the characteristics of a good, and Rosen (1974) established the theoretical support for the hedonic price model.

Very briefly, the Rosen theory establishes that goods i comprise a number k of attributes Q, $Q= (Q_1, Q_2, ..., Q_k)$ and that, to maximise utility, a consumer's decision depends on them. The hedonic model establishes the relation between the value P of a good i and its respective characteristics Q, $P= f(Q)$, with f being the functional relation between P and Q. Therefore, an individual considering its utility function, $U= U(P,Q)$, which depends on value P and on characteristics Q, will consume the product that gives them the greatest satisfaction. So they will decide to consume I_A as opposed to I_B, if the utility generated by the characteristics of the former, I_A, are greater than those of the latter, I_B, $\frac{\partial U / \partial Q_A}{\partial U / \partial IA} > \frac{\partial U / \partial Q_{IB}}{\partial U / \partial IB}$.

If this concept is extrapolated to the level of territory and rural districts, the model to study population movements, P, in a rural district, DR, would be $P= f(Q)$. Therefore, the utility of residing in a municipality, $U= U(P,Q)$, depends on its attributes, Q. So an individual will decide to live in a municipality A as opposed to another municipality B, if the utility provided by the characteristics of the former (A) are greater than those of the latter (B), $\frac{\partial U / \partial Q_A}{\partial U / \partial A} > \frac{\partial U / \partial Q_B}{\partial U / \partial B}$, with A and B belonging to the same DR, A,B $\in$ DR.

Model $P= f(Q)$ is a mathematical representation of a generic reality that does not take individualities into account, has no precise functional form and unknown parameters. A solution for this is econometric specification, which for $P= f(Q)$ would be as follows:

$$P_i = f(Q_{ji}, \varepsilon_i)$$

$$Q_{j,i} = (Q_{1i}, Q_{2i}, ..., Q_{ki})$$

$$\varepsilon_i \sim N(0, \sigma_\varepsilon)$$

$$i=1,2,3, ... h, \ i=\{s, r\}, j=1,2,3, ...k$$

where i represents a municipality in the DR. Some of these are municipalities in the periphery s, and others are municipalities in the centre r, $i=\{s, r\}$, P_i is the populational dynamic of a municipality i within DR, Q_{ji} are the attributes of i, f is the functional relation between P_i and $Q_{j,i}$ and ε_i is the random disturbance normally distributed with mean zero and constant variance $\varepsilon_i \sim N(0, \sigma_\varepsilon)$.

To identify the functional form, f, we apply the technique developed by Box-Cox to obtain the estimations by the method of maximum similarity based on four structures: a) theta model, b) lambda model, c) left-hand-side-only model, d) right-hand-side-only model. These are expressed as follows:

a) Theta model: $P_i^{(\theta)} = \beta_0 + \beta_1 Q_{1i}^{(\lambda)} + \beta_2 Q_{2i}^{(\lambda)} + \ldots + \beta_k Q_{ki}^{(\lambda)} + \varepsilon_i$, con $\theta \neq \lambda$

$\varepsilon_i \sim N(0, \sigma_\varepsilon)$

The variable P is subject to transformation θ and the non-discrete variables Q, to the power λ.

b) Lambda model: $P_i^{(\lambda)} = \beta_0 + \beta_1 Q_{1i}^{(\lambda)} + \beta_2 Q_{2i}^{(\lambda)} + \ldots + \beta_k Q_{ki}^{(\lambda)} + \varepsilon_i$,

$\varepsilon_i \sim N(0, \sigma_\varepsilon)$

The variable P and the (non-discrete) variables Q are subject to transformation λ.

c) Left-hand-side-only model: $P_i^{(\theta)} = \beta_0 + \beta_1 Q_{1i} + \beta_2 Q_{2i} + \ldots + \beta_k Q_{ki} + \varepsilon_i$

$\varepsilon_i \sim N(0, \sigma_\varepsilon)$

Only the dependent variable is transformed.

d) Right-hand-side-only model: $P_i = \beta_0 + \beta_1 Q_{1i}^{(\lambda)} + \beta_2 Q_{2i}^{(\lambda)} + \ldots + \beta_k Q_{ki}^{(\lambda)} + \varepsilon_i$

$\varepsilon_i \sim N(0, \sigma_\varepsilon)$

Only the dependent variables are transformed.

We select the one with the best econometric results.

The model $P_i = f(Q_{ji}, \varepsilon_i)$ is subject to a set of conditions. The first is that if the attributes Q work as centripetal forces attracting population, then the partial derivative of $P_i = f(Q_{ji}, \varepsilon_i)$ is greater than zero, $\frac{\partial P_i}{\partial Q_{j,i}} > 0$. Conversely, the partial derivative of $P_i = f(Q_{ji}, \varepsilon_i)$ is less than zero, $\frac{\partial P_i}{\partial Q_{j,i}} < 0$, if Q, working as centrifugal forces, expel population.

The second condition is that the District must have at least one municipality working as the axis of the system, as the central or main town, that is, a municipality r. To identify it, we apply the ISTAT methodology defined by the Italian National Statistics Institute (1966), based on the algorithms of *Local Protosystems (PSL)*. A municipality is considered the central or main town of the District if *PSL>0.75*, and therefore exercises a force of attraction. The algorithm *PSL* for a municipality A is defined mathematically as

$$PSL_A = \min\left[\frac{MC(A)}{0.75}, 1\right] * \min\left[\frac{W(A)}{1,000}, 1\right]$$

where A is a municipality, $W(A)$ are the employed persons working in A, $MC(A)$ is an indicator of self-containment

$$MC(A) = \min\left[\frac{RW(A)}{W(A)}, \frac{RW(A)}{R(A)}\right]$$

with *RW(A)* being the employed persons who live and work in A.

FUTURE RESEARCH DIRECTIONS

In a scenario of depopulation, the concept of *rural district,* its representative model, and its explanatory variables, complemented with the ISTAT methodology of *local protosystems* would be of interest for public policymaking. Although depopulation of the rural environment is one of the key aspects of public agendas, the process of depopulation continues (Andrés, 2022). In view of these considerations, the method proposed aims to generate empirical evidence to answer questions such as:

- Which factors best explain *intra*-rural dynamics – economic factors or those relating to amenities and public services?
- Does the pattern of *intra*-rural population movement differ in periods of expansion and crisis? If so, to what extent?
- How does the degree of socio-economic development of each rural district affect individual decisions behind *intra*-rural population movements?
- Do public policy actions have any strategic meaning?

CONCLUSION

It is necessary to describe, understand, explain and predict any events, facts, phenomena or situations arising in different areas, and population movements are no exception. In this chapter, we have tried to consider the rural-rural dynamic, which exists but is wrongly relegated to second place.

Theoretically, it is difficult to consider this dimension; the rural district and hedonic population models are representations that might be appropriate. The purpose is to explore the dynamics of territories in which depopulation is reaching a point of no return, with the consequent decline from the socio-economic and environmental points of view. Alarm bells are ringing and we therefore need to establish measures to hold back this phenomenon, which not only affects the rural population but also directly affects urban areas.

REFERENCES

Arroyo, M. (2001). *La contraurbanización: un debate metodológico y conceptual sobre la dinámica de las áreas metropolitanas.* [*Counterurbanization: a methodological and conceptual debate on the dynamics of metropolitan areas.*] Geo Critica. https://www.ub.edu/geocrit/sn-97.htm

Berry, B. J. L. (1976). *Urbanization and Counterurbanization.* Sage.

Brown, L. (1991). *Place, Migration and Development in the Third World*. Routledge. doi:10.4324/9780203321263

Court, A. T. (1939). *The dynamics of automobile demand*. General Motors.

De Vries, J. (1990). Problems in the measurement, description, and analysis of historical urbanization. *Urbanization in history*, 43-60.

Docampo, M., & Otero, R. (2012). Territorial Transition: Theoretical Model and Contrast with the Spanish Case. *Reis*, *139*, 133–162.

Evans, A. W. (1990). The assumption of equilibrium in the analysis of migration and interregional differences: A review of some recent research. *Journal of Regional Science*, *30*(4), 515–531. doi:10.1111/j.1467-9787.1990.tb00119.x PMID:12316475

García, M., & Otero, R. (2012). Transición territorial: Modelo teórico y contraste con el caso español. [Territorial transition: theoretical model and contrast with the Spanish case.]. *Reis*, *139*, 133–162.

Gedik, A. (2005). *Toward a Theory of Mobility Transition: Test of Zelinsky's Theory with the Japanese and Turkish Data, 1955-2000*. Princeton.

Graves, P. E., & Greenwood, M. J. (1987). *Two views of recent regional location patterns in the United States: competing models with noncompeting implications*. Paper presented al the International Conference on Migration and Labor Market Efficiency, Knoxville, TN.

Greenwood, M. J. (1997). Internal Migration in developed countries. Handbook of Population and Family Economics, (vol. 1B). Netherlands.

Gurak, D. T., & Cases, (1992). Migration networks and the shaping of migration systems. en Mary Kritz, Lin Lean Lim and Hania Zlotnik (eds.), *International Migration Systems: A Global Approach*. Clarendon Press, pp.: 150-176.

Haas, G. C. (1922). *Sale Prices as a Basis for Farm Land Appraisal. Technical Bulletin, 9, Agricultural Experiment Station*. University of Minnesota.

Haas, H. (2008). *Migration and development A theoretical perspective. Working papers, Paper 9*. International Migration Institute. University of Oxford. Pp:57

Hamin, E. M., & Marcucci, D. J. (2008). Ad Hoc Rural Regionalism. *Journal of Rural Studies*, *24*(77), 467–477. doi:10.1016/j.jrurstud.2008.03.009

Jennissen, R. P. W. (2003). Economic Determinants of Net International Migration in Western Europe. *European Journal of Population*, *19*(2), 171–198. doi:10.1023/A:1023390917557

Karemera, D., Oguledo, V. I., & Davis, B. (2000). A gravity model analysis of international migration to North America. *Applied Economics*, *32*(13), 1745–1755. doi:10.1080/000368400421093

Krugman, P. (1991). Increasing returns and Economic Geography. *Journal of Political Economy*, *99*(3), 183–199. doi:10.1086/261763

Lancaster, K. J. (1966). A new approach to consumer theory. *Journal of Political Economy, 74*(2), 132–157. doi:10.1086/259131

Layard, R., Balnchard, O., Dornbusch, R., & Krugman, P. (1992). *East-West Migration. The Alternatives*. MIT Press.

Lewis, G. J., & Maund, D. L. (1976). The Urbanization of the Countryside: A Framework for Analysis. *Geografiska Annaler, 58*(1), 17–27. doi:10.1080/04353684.1976.11879409

Lucas, R. (1997). Internal migration in developing countries. Handbook of Population and Family Economics, (vol. 1, pp. 721-798). Elsevier.

Maruri, I., Arboleda, L., & Barrachina, M. (2004). Un modelo de gravedad ampliado para la inmigración internacional en España. [An expanded gravity model for international immigration in Spain.] *RVEH, 12*(3), 149-169

Massey, D., Arango, J., Hugo, G., Kouaouci, A., Pellegrino, A., & Taylor, J. E. (1998). *Worlds in Motion. Understanding International Migration at the End of the Millenium*. Oxford University Press.

Millinton, J. (1994). Migration, Wages, Unenployment and the Housing Market. A Literature Review. *International Journal of Manpower, 15*(9/10), 89–133. doi:10.1108/01437729410074227

Myrdal, G. (1957). *Rich Lands and Poor*. Harper and Row.

Obeso, I. (2019). Definir la urbanización periférica: Conceptos y terminología. [Defining peripheral urbanization: concepts and terminology.]. *Eria, 2*(2), 183–206. doi:10.17811/er.2.2019.183-206

Pecqueur, B. (2001). Qualité et développement territorial: L'hypothèse du panier de biens et de services territorialisés. [Quality and territorial development: the hypothesis of the basket of territorialized goods and services.]. *Économie Rurale (Paris), 261*(1), 37–49. doi:10.3406/ecoru.2001.5217

Pellegrini, P.A. & Fotheringham, A.S., (2002). Modelling Spatial Choice: A Review and Synthesis in a Migration Context. *Progress in Human Geography, 26* (4), 487-510.

Pinilla, V., & Sáez, L. A. (2020). La despoblación rural en España: génesis de un problema y políticas innovadoras. [Rural depopulation in Spain: genesis of a problem and innovative policies.] SSPA. http://sspa-network.eu/wp-content/uploads/Informe-CEDDAR-def-logo.pdf

Piore, M. J. (1979). *Birds of Passage: Migrant Labor in Industrial Societies*. Cambridge University Press. doi:10.1017/CBO9780511572210

Pissarides, C. A., & Wadsworth, J. (1989). Unemployment and the inter-regional mobility of labour. *Economic Journal (London), 99*(397), 739–755. doi:10.2307/2233768

Poulain, M. (1981). Contribution à l'analyse spatiale dúne matrice de migratin interne. [Contribution to the spatial analysis of the internal migration matrix.] Louvaine-La-Neuve, ed. Cabay.

Ravenstein, E. G. (1885). *The laws of migration*. Royal Statistical Society. doi:10.2307/2979181

Ray, C. (2006). Neo-endogenous rural development in the EU. In P. Cloke, T. Marsden, & P. Mooney (Eds.), *Handbook of Rural Studies*. Sage. doi:10.4135/9781848608016.n19

Roback, J. (1988). Wages, rents, and amenities: Differences among workers and regions. *Economic Inquiry*, *26*(1), 23–41. doi:10.1111/j.1465-7295.1988.tb01667.x

Rosen, S. (1974). Hedonic prices and implicit markets: Product differentiation in pure competition. *Journal of Political Economy*, *82*(1), 34–55. doi:10.1086/260169

Selod, H., & Shilpi, F. (2021). Rural-urban migration in developing countries: Lessons from the literatura. *Regional Science and Urban Economics*, 91.

Silvestre Rodríguez, J. (2000). Aproximaciones teóricas a los movimientos migratorios contemporáneos: Un estado de la cuestión. [Theoretical approaches to contemporary migratory movements: A state of the art.]

Söderbaum, F., & Shaw, T. M. (2004). *Theories of New Regionalism*. Palgrave Macmillan.

Treyz, G. I., Rickman, D. S., Hunt, G. L., & Greenwood, M. J. (1993). The dynamics of US internal migration. *The Review of Economics and Statistics*, *75*(2), 209–214. doi:10.2307/2109425

Wardwell, J. M. (1977). Equilibrium and Change in Nonmetropolitan Growth. *Rural Sociology*, *42*(2), 156–178.

Zimmerbauer, K., & Paasi, A. (2013). When old and new regionalism collide: Deinstitutionalization of regions and resistance identity in municipality amalgamations. *Journal of Rural Studies*, (30), 31–40.

KEY TERMS AND DEFINITIONS

Hedonic Population Model: A model that explains population movements in terms of the qualities or attributes of a municipality.

Intra-Rural Movement: The displacement of individuals from one rural area to another.

ISTAT: A methodology drawn up by the Italian National Statistics Institute to identify the municipality that has the largest number of workers.

Main Town: The most important municipality in the rural district, that is, the one with the largest population and most services.

Periphery: The municipalities in a rural district that are not the main towns.

Rural District: A set of rural municipalities with endogenous resources, which are close to each other, have geographical and lifestyle similarities, and have a network of relations.

Chapter 7
Cultural Heritage and Its Impact on Territorial Development:
The Case of Spain

Jesús Heredia-Carroza
https://orcid.org/0000-0003-0107-8611
University of Seville, Spain

Ignacio Martínez-Fernández
University of Seville, Spain

Luis Antonio Palma-Martos
University of Seville, Spain

ABSTRACT

Within the cultural sector, cultural heritage presents a series of interesting features for the territorial development of the local and regional Economy. This sector presents a prevalence of wage employment and a larger size of business establishments than the rest of the services sector. While small companies and micro-companies predominate in the services sector with 99,4% in 2019, for companies related to cultural heritage, the weight of companies with less than 50 employees does not reach 97.3% for this year. Also, it is essential to highlight the legacy value that makes cultural heritage endure over time for future generations to enjoy it; it also creates awareness and territorial roots of the populations, and, finally, is a fundamental asset for tourism and branding of the territories.

INTRODUCTION

Cultural heritage constitutes an important asset in the social and economic development of a territory, representing ways in which its community is expressed (UNESCO, 2015). Cultural heritage is defined as "artefacts, monuments, a group of buildings and sites, museums that have a diversity of values including symbolic, historic, artistic, aesthetic, ethnological or anthropological, scientific, and social significance.

DOI: 10.4018/978-1-6684-5976-8.ch007

It includes tangible heritage (movable, immobile, and underwater), intangible cultural heritage (ICH) embedded into cultural, and natural heritage artefacts, sites, or monuments. It covers industrial heritage and cave paintings" (UNESCO, 2009).

According to Timothy and Boyd (2006) cultural tourism and specifically heritage tourism is the largest and fastest growing global tourism market. In fact, before the pandemic situation, the World Tourism Organization (2018) estimated that four out ten tourists choose their destination depending on its cultural heritage. Following this report of the World Tourism Organization, the annual growth rate in cultural trips will be 15% by the end of the century. So, heritage is an important asset for cultural tourism and, thus, for the development of the territories. Oppio & Dell'Ovo (2021) explored the role of investment in cultural heritage as a development tool to improve the returns of tourism for Italy, showcasing the importance for local communities and a rational use of the local and regional resources.

Due to its huge and diverse cultural heritage Spain is one of the important destinations (Parga-Dans, Gonzales, and Enriquez, 2020). For this reason, after a very complicated stage for the cultural and creative sector with the pandemic situation, a series of measures must be taken regarding its recovery. For this, it is fundamental to analyse the impacts on the territory of the cultural heritage and design cultural and creative territorial development plans.

The results of this chapter contribute to the empirical literature of the economic impacts of the cultural heritage on the territories. Specifically, it analyses the employment of this sector and shows how small companies and micro-companies predominate in the services sector with 99,4% in 2019, for companies related to Cultural Heritage, the weight of companies with less than 50 employees does not reach 97,3% for this year.

The chapter is organized like this, after this introduction, in the second section, the background is presented. Then the empirical strategy followed to estimate the impacts evaluation and its discussion are shown. In the fourth and fifth sections we present solutions and recommendations and future research directions and, finally, conclusions are explained.

BACKGROUND

The development of territories through culture and creativity activities requires the understanding and active participation of all relevant agents, as well as political leadership to achieve broad collaboration and establish guidelines that generate agreements among the population (Matarasso, 1997; Schuster, 2007). Likewise, for it to be affective, a continuous review and monitoring must be carried out because the continuous incidents that may arise during the implementation of the cultural development plans.

According to European Union, through its Next Generation funds, sustainability for its triple perspective, environmental, socioeconomic, and territorial, must be followed. This will generate wealth for more equitable economic development whose main aim is the territorial cohesion. This will have a positive effect on the satisfaction of the professional agents and users, contributing to the creation of significant and reliable experiences that will make the population aware of the importance of sustainability and promoting cultural practices in accordance with it (MINCOTUR, 2022).

The European Union has set two important objectives in order to achieve the territorial development through the cultural heritage:

1. Support the territories in their transformation process towards hubs of cultural or creative innovation. Being able to integrate environmental, socioeconomic, and territorial sustainability into its offer. This generates resilience strategies in front of new global challenges, such as climate change, health, or security crises.
2. Generation of greater territorial cohesion, not only relating supply and territories, but also creating synergies and connections between the territories of different regions. A balanced development of the cultural heritage potential in the whole territory must be sought, consolidating links of solidarity within the communities.

These communities must contribute to the solution of the common problems of sustainability, promoting a rational distribution of resources and burdens on the territory and consolidating management strategies that help the development processes of the territories and the generation of wealth.

To achieve these objectives, European Union through Next Generation-EU funds design four items that must be followed and they have a direct impact on the sustainability and the development of the territories. Those items are:

1. Green Transition. It is necessary to incorporate environmental limits into the design of cultural policies and the regulation of economic activity, thus stopping ecological deterioration.
2. Digital transition. The modernization of the cultural and creative sector, promoting its internationalization, the renewal of technological capital, reducing/eliminating the different digital gaps. Digitalization must be the bridge between innovation, productivity, and sustainability, as well as being the key element for territorial and social cohesion.
3. The elimination of the gaps of disadvantaged groups. The structural barriers that hamper the access of certain groups to the labour market under equal rights and conditions must be eliminated.
4. Cohesion and inclusion through impulses to employment policies. To achieve greater territorial cohesion, it is necessary to boost digitalization and teleworking to promote a greater degree of market integration.

Another of the key elements is the creation of the New European Bauhaus. This institution has marked cultural and creative character that aims to create reflection and action groups for the collective creation of prototypes, testing of new policies, solutions, and recommendations for action. The key principles of this organization are:

1. Wealth inspired by art and culture, responding to needs beyond functionality.
2. Sustainability in harmony with nature, the environment, and our planet.
3. Inclusion, promoting dialogue between cultures, disciplines, genders, and ages.

Finally, strategies in cultural heritage and creative sectors should be aimed at:

1. Recognition of cultural heritage as a multi-actor space where private and public sectors intervene. The former makes up a dynamic and central sector for the territories, the latter is made up of those responsible for the management of the territories and common goods on which a large part of the offer is built. Finally, society in general is the key actor for the strategies to be successful or not.

2. Recognition of the multilevel reality of public action in matters of culture. This translates into the leading role of the different regions and municipalities in the design of cultural policies in their territories, compatible with the role of the National Ministry of Culture of Spain. The country scale must be used to promote policies that require a joint and detailed vision to improve innovation and transformation of the territories through a sector that must be key in the country's economy and for its own promotion abroad.
3. Creation of content that generates user experiences. This can be seen in calls for plans such as the one designed by the Spanish Ministry of Tourism, aimed at creating new tourist and cultural experiences (Orden ICT/1524/2021).
4. Coordination with other Plans and Programs that affect different sectors but that have an impact on cultural heritage and creative sector, such as tourism, given its transversal nature.
5. Recognize the importance of international markets for the success of the cultural heritage and creative sectors.

DISCUSSION

Once the key elements and objectives to implement the policies to promote development through the Cultural Heritage it's necessary to take a glance to the reality of the sector in Spain.

Table 1. Size distribution of enterprises 2019

Enterprises Size	Services	Cultural Heritage, Museums, Archives and Libraries
Small	99,43%	97,27%
Medium	0,45%	2,47%
Big	0,12%	0,32%
Source: Cuenta Satélite de la Cultura en España		

Arguably one of the characteristics that separates the Cultural Heritage sector from the rest of cultural activities and services is the size structure of its enterprises. As table 1 shows the Heritage sector presents a distinctive prevalence of medium and big enterprises registered when compared with the rest of services. The reasons why there is such a significative difference can be widely discussed[1] but the main positive effects can be easily identified:

- Larger enterprises tend to pay higher wages.
- Larger companies tend to seek longer commitments and therefore offer longer and more stable contracts.

When it comes to the evolution of the enterprises in the sector the rate of growth rather different when it is compared with the rest of the services. Meanwhile medium and big enterprises are growing a steady pace in the Heritage related activities, for the rest of services the growth seems concentrated in small and micro firms.

Figure 1. Growth rate for big enterprises.
Source: Cuenta Satélite de la Cultura en España

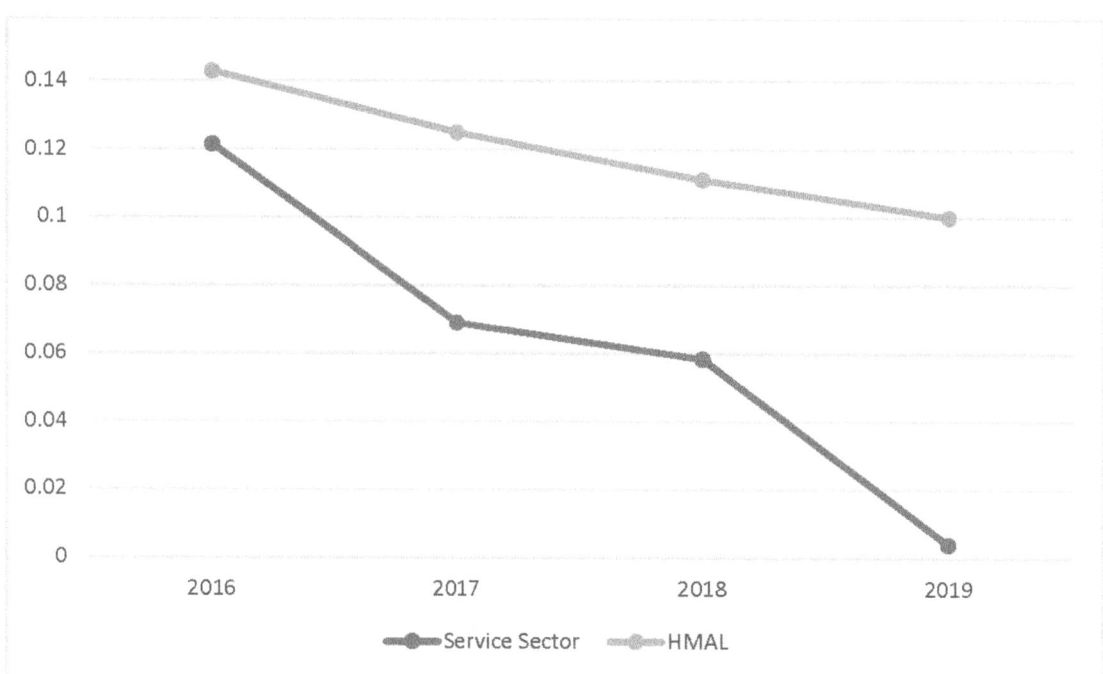

From the characteristics of the enterprises in the sector drafted earlier, table 2 helps to illustrate the impact of the differential size of the Heritage enterprises on the stability of the employment. Compared with the rest of the services and to other cultural activities, the Cultural Heritage sectors represents a greater percentage of wage-earner employees compared to its weight overall employment.

Table 2. Employment characterization for the HMAL (2019)

	Total employment (%)	Wage-earner employees (%)
Services	0,22	0,24
Cultural Sector	6,8	8,8
Source: Cuenta Satélite de la Cultura en España		

About its contribution to the national economy and the added value, the Cultural Heritage sector has been losing weight in the last five years of the available data, has presented in figure 2. This recent evolution may need some additional context to be interpreted. Once considered the stabilization of the employment in the sector and the number of enterprises, this tendency might be reflecting the different speed of the sector's growth compared with the rest of the economy. This interpretation is supported by the number of businesses active, while the Cultural Heritage has lost 5% of the enterprises in these last years the rest of the services has grown a 19,4%.

Figure 2. Evolution of the Heritage, museum, archive, and library contributions to GDP and GAV in Spain (2015-2019)
Source: Cuenta Satélite de la Cultura en España

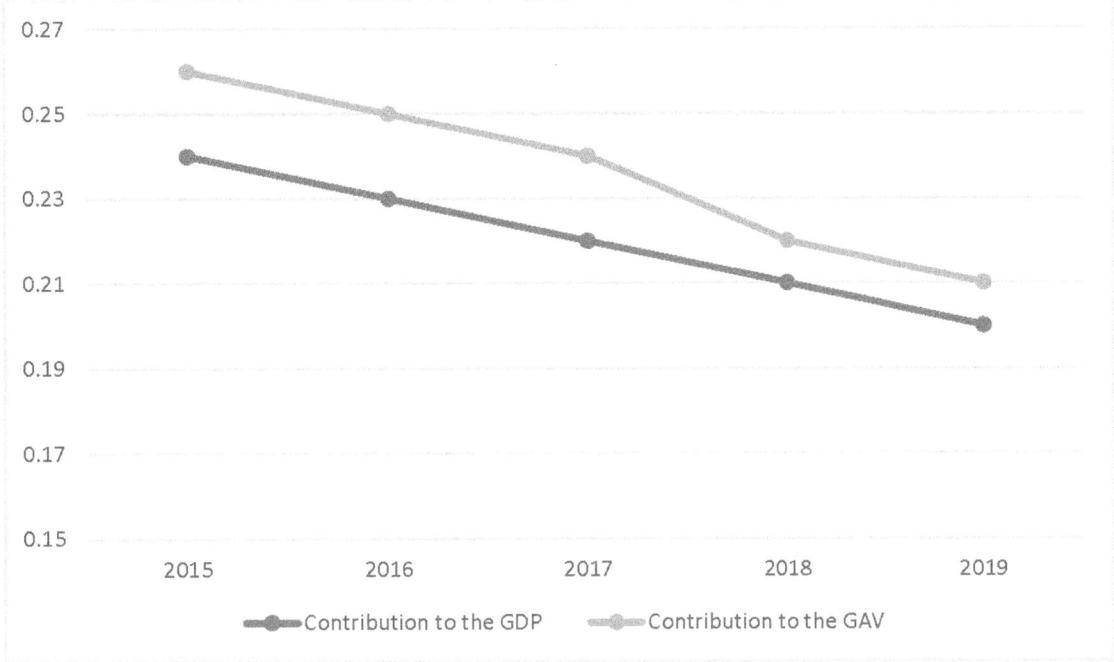

To offer a more regionalized vision of the sector the case of Andalusia represents a great opportunity, not only for its widely known diversity of Cultural Heritage sites and activities, but for the policies to develop the sector in place through the years. Originally designed with the share objectives of boosting the reconversion of the touristic sector and to support the regional Cultural Heritage as one of the defining elements of the regional identity.

In terms of highly trained career jobs the evolution of the employment in libraries and archives represent a good example of the general tendency of the sector. As figure 3 shows, 2.019 represents the peak of employment with a severe cut down in 2020 with the Covid-19 pandemic outbreak. When it comes to the profile of those working in the sector roughly 60% of the archive's personal and almost 75% when it comes to libraries has university or equivalent level of education.

The evolution of the visitors to Cultural Heritage sites reflects the key role of the Heritage as the cornerstone of the touristic policy in recent years with a steady growth and reaching its maximum by the 2.019. The sanitary and economic consequences of the Covid-19 crisis combined with the mobility and capacity restrictions represent the worse data the attendance to Cultural Heritage sites in decades. Even so, the sector seems to be recovering its vigor in 2.022 with the advanced data for the first 5 months surpassing the 70% of visitors for the year 2.021

Figure 3. Direct Employment in archives and libraries in Andalusia (2015-2020).
Source: Instituto de Estadística y Cartografía de Andalucía

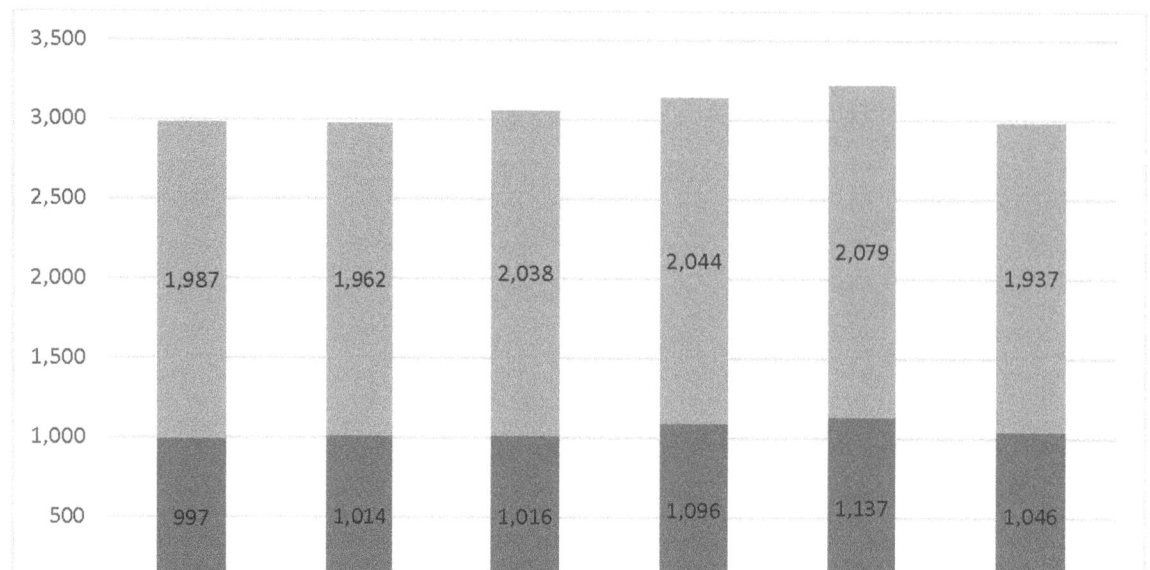

Figure 4. Visitors to Cultural Heritage sites
Source: Instituto de Estadística y Cartografía de Andalucía
* During the COVID-19 travelling and capacity restrictions
** Anticipated data January-May

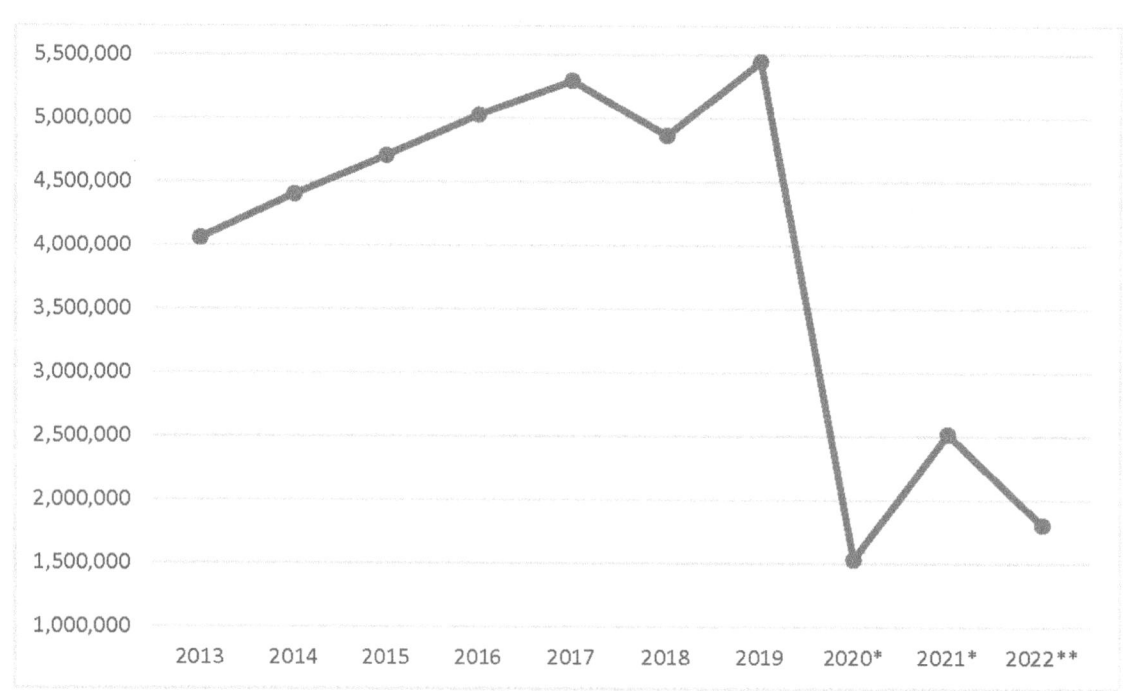

SOLUTIONS AND RECOMMENDATIONS

To success in this type of models, it is necessary to involve all agents, both creative and management. These entrepreneurial strategies must be coordinated by the managers, whether public or private, where must exist a rigorous execution and justification of each intervention that is carried out.

From the current point of view, the best instrument for complying and evaluating these models is the creation of external monitoring commissions, with the participation of both members linked to public institutions and members belonging to the involved sector. In addition, by participating members belonging to the involved sector, possible needs that arise during the implementation of the entrepreneurship strategy can be met.

FUTURE RESEARCH DIRECTIONS

Within the possible future lines of research this investigation opens the chance to track geographically the impact of the Cultural Heritage activities on a local and nuts 2 scale. This kind of research will be able to provide the data necessary not only to evaluate closely the profits derived from use of the potential that Cultural Heritage have to offer in terms of higher quality tourism and stabilization of the population; but also offers a great opportunity to study the capabilities of the Next Generation Funds to transform the local and reginal economies.

CONCLUSION

With the stabilization of the Covid-19 crisis the European economies find themselves with the grater goal of achieving the economic transition to more sustainable development frameworks. In this context a great opportunity has been created with design and set up of the Next Generation funds, specially being Spain one of the largest recipients of this program. Under these circumstances, the design of an economic policy oriented to maximizes the impact of the Cultural Heritage in the national, regional, and local economies.

The Cultural Heritage sector represents an exemptional candidate to articulate these policies and become the new engine to power up the sustainable and inclusive growth horizon due its spread through the territory and its linkage to other traditional forms of tourism, and specially its impact to the local communities where these activities are settled.

With the necessary collaboration of the different government levels, it will be possible to strengthen an institutional and entrepreneurial network to valorize the Cultural Heritage.

ACKNOWLEDGMENT

The authors disclosed receipt of the following financial support for the research, authorship, and/or publication of this article: The first author (J.H.C) received financial support from "Ayudas para la Recualificación del Sistema Universitario Español en su Modalidad Margarita Salas" granted by the

Resolución de 29 de noviembre de 2021 of Universidad de Sevilla, financed by the *European Union-NextGenerationEU.*

REFERENCES

Matarasso, F. (1997). *Use or Ornament? The Social Impact of Participation in the Arts*. Comedia.

MINCOTUR. (2022). Estrategia de Sostenibilidad Turística en Destino aprobada en la Conferencia Secotiral [Destination tourism sustainability strategy approved at the sectorial conference]. *Sede electronica.* https://sede.serviciosmin.gob.es/es-es/procedimientoselectronicos/Paginas/detalle-procedimientos.aspx?IdProcedimiento=253

Oppio, A., & Dell'Ovo, M. (2021). Cultural heritage preservation and territorial attractiveness: A spatial multidimensional evaluation approach. In *Cycling & Walking for Regional Development* (pp. 105–125). Springer.

Orden ICT. (2021). *Por la que se establecen las bases reguladoras de las ayudas para el Programa "Experiencias Turismo España" y se aprueba su convocatoria para el ejercicio 2021, en el marco del Plan de Recuperación, Transformación y Resiliencia. [establishing the regulatory bases for aid for the "Tourism Experiences Spain" Program and approving its call for the year 2021, within the framework of the Recovery, Transformation and Resilience Plan.]* BOE. https://www.boe.es/diario_boe/txt.php?id=BOE-A-2022-417

Parga-Dans, E., González, P. A., & Enríquez, R. O. (2020). The social value of heritage: Balancing the promotion-preservation relationship in the Altamira World Heritage Site, Spain. *Journal of Destination Marketing & Management, 18*, 100499.

Schuster, J. M. (2007). Participation studies and cross-national comparison: Proliferation, prudence, and possibility. *Cultural Trends, 16*(2), 99–196.

Timothy, D. J., & Boyd, S. W. (2006). Heritage tourism in the 21st century: Valued traditions and new perspectives. *Journal of Heritage Tourism, 1*(1), 1–16.

UNESCO Institute for Statistics. (2009). UNESCO Framework for Cultural Statistics: http://uis.unesco.org/en/glossary-term/cultural-heritage

KEY TERMS AND DEFINITIONS

New European Bauhaus. Is a creative and interdisciplinary initiative that connects the European Green Deal to our living spaces and experiences.

Next Generation EU: Is a more than €800 billion temporary recovery instrument to help repair the immediate economic and social damage brought about by the coronavirus pandemic. Post-COVID-19 Europe will be greener, more digital, more resilient and better fit for the current and forthcoming challenges.

UNESCO: Is a specialised agency of the United Nations (UN) aimed at promoting world peace and security through international cooperation in education, arts, sciences and culture.

ENDNOTE

[1]   Two main reasons can explain the differential size. Firstly, there's a pure production logic, the initial investments required in this line of services in terms of infrastructure and personal are relatively higher than for other cultural industries. Linked to this first there's a second reason related with the institutional framework, since most of the enterprises in this sector work through a public license or concession, which implies that during the concession process bigger enterprises will be better candidates to win the contracts.

Chapter 8
Geographical Preconditions of the International Controversies Around the Turów Mine

Artur Boháč

 https://orcid.org/0000-0001-6238-7472

Technical University of Liberec, Czech Republic

Ewa Łaźniewska

 https://orcid.org/0000-0002-2784-2190

Poznań University of Economics and Business, Poland

Joanna Kurowska-Pysz

WSB University in Dąbrowa Górnicza, Poland

ABSTRACT

The chapter examines the physical-geographical and human-geographical characteristics of the Czech-Polish-German Three-border region, particularly the Turoszów Spur in Poland and its surroundings behind the borders. These characteristics differ within the region and influence socioeconomic settings and cross-border flows. Resulting asymmetries became more visible in connection with the controversies around the Turów Mine located in the Turoszów Spur. The arguments took place mainly between the Czech Republic and Poland. However, Germany cannot be overlooked due to its importance in the region. Countries neighboring the mine are not satisfied with its long-term effects on their border areas, and their attitudes were shared by the EU. The analysis is interdisciplinary and mainly grounded in geography, specifically neo-environmental determinism, and border studies, predominantly examining the effects of market forces and cross-border flows. The text aims to illustrate the significance of geographical factors in the small region without extreme geographical barriers or differences.

DOI: 10.4018/978-1-6684-5976-8.ch008

INTRODUCTION

Asymmetries in development and cross-border flows emerge even in cross-border areas within the EU where the free movement of goods, persons, services and capital and drawing funds from various EU programs exist. These differences can have roots at the state or regional level. The chapter focuses on the specific cross-border region in Central Europe, the Czech-Polish-German Three-border region. The studied region epitomizes a socioeconomic periphery or semiperiphery for all three countries because of its marginal location and complicated modern history. The most problematic areas within this border region are territorial protrusions such as the Turoszów Spur in Poland or Frýdlant Spur in the Czech Republic. These protrusions are the furthest from the countries' economic and administrative cores. Peripheral Turoszów Spur became internationally medialized because of the Czech-Polish conflict over the non-ecological operation of the Turów Mine in Poland. Controversies around the mine have broad geographical and socioeconomic reasons in the Turoszów Spur and surrounding territories in the Czech Republic and Germany. The quarrel between Poland and the Czech Republic was more heated than with Germany, so their issues and territorial conditions are highlighted. Also, the economic level of the German part of the region is significantly different from the Czech and Polish parts.

The text emphasizes the influence of geographical preconditions on asymmetries in socioeconomic matters and cross-border contacts leading to the escalation of the dispute, despite the currently promoted narrative of the decreasing importance of space within globalization and technology modernization. Scholars and the media have not yet reported such findings.

Theoretical Background

The text is grounded predominantly in geography in its complexity, underlining the natural connection between physical and human geography. The authors assume the influence of geographical factors on socioeconomic development, e.g. the types of economy, settlements, social contacts, transport lines and border permeability, and search for proof in the specific region. Their scientific approach can be defined as neo-environmental determinism on a small scale.

The importance of spatial settings for economic development and related asymmetries is essential for new economic geography or neo-environmental determinism, represented by Paul Krugman (1999) and other economists (Gallup et al., 1998). They follow the line of environmental or geographical determinism, which was the central paradigm in the 19th century but without racial or social theories. They claim that location, terrain and climate are important factors for economic development and determine the types of economy and transport, but they focus predominantly on the global or macroregional level, unlike this chapter's authors. Jeffrey Sachs said: *If social scientists were to spend more time looking at maps, they would be reminded of the powerful geographical patterns in economic development.* (Gallup et al., 2003, p. 1) Analyzing maps is one of the methods used in this chapter. By the way, geographical preconditions can be surpassed, but the price of triumph over them is high.

An asymmetry mentioned in the text is based on specific criteria, partly according to Oleński (2016):

- Asymmetry of potentials (social, technological, economic and information) and capitals (social and institutional) of national areas of transborder economies
- Asymmetry of institutional regulations, laws and procedures

- Asymmetry of resources located in the space of transborder economy on the territories of different countries

Asymmetry in the socioeconomic development of border regions can be an opportunity for mutual compensation in various sectors. Secondly, existing asymmetry can be a barrier to developing cross-border ties, particularly in the scope of institutional cooperation known from Euroregions (Opioła & Böhm, 2022).

Peripheries are among the frequent topics studied by economic geographers. When exploring border regions, it is necessary to distinguish the effects of peripherality and the border effect. In the first case, it is essential to whom the area is peripheral. In the second case, between which units the border leads. The border effect is explained in the paragraph below, dealing with border studies. By its very nature, the borderland fulfils the characteristics of the periphery, specifically the positional peripheries, such as territorial protrusions. Border regions are often less developed economically, have a negative demographic balance and suffer from environmental issues connected with harmful industry or post-military heritage. Peripherality can be divided into several types (Pénzes & Demeter, 2021):

- Economic – based on a weak economy
- Social-cultural – based on negative socio-cultural characteristics
- Political – a periphery lacks political power and importance
- Environmental – based on the lousy state of the environment
- Geometric – based on the negative placement within economic-geographical theories of localization
- Demographic – takes into account depopulation development
- Physical-geographical – peripheries are located in the worst physical-geographical conditions

On the level of the EU, peripheries are regions with a GDP per capita less than 75% of the EU average. These regions receive finances from the structural funds. Euroregions should help the peripheries in the borderlands build cross-border trust and cooperation. The key barriers to the development of cross-border cooperation include (Kurowska-Pysz et al., 2018):

- Shortage of capital
- Differences in interests and goals between partners
- Insufficient knowledge of cross-border partnership management
- Lack of strategy for long-term cooperation between partners
- Hindered cooperation because of communication distance
- Poor understanding of the neighbouring country's language
- Different administrative procedures
- Inequality of financial potential between partners
- Cultural, religious, social, political and social differences, etc.

Specific examples of peripheries are territorial protrusions in the borderlands, such as the Turoszów Spur. A spur is a part of the territory of one state running deeply into the territory of another state. Territorial protrusions usually have traffic complications because the shortest or the most practical route connecting two places in the same country often must be taken through the neighbouring country's territory. These complications might worsen in the case of impermeable or low-permeable borders. Unfortunately, there is a lack of geographical research on territorial protrusions.

The border is an essential geographical, political and social phenomenon, a dividing line that determines the distribution and spatial arrangement of the geographical environment (Paasi, 2011). Thus, indirectly, it affects its overall socioeconomic development. It also separates functional spaces defined by administrative systems, land use, etc. The strength of a border depends mainly on its type, function, openness and permeability, and the nature of neighboring regions across the border. A lower permeability of a border means a higher border effect. A strong border effect leads to an economic orientation towards inland and the peripheralization of an area. Even intensive cross-border flows of goods and people may bypass peripheral border regions because of their isolation, distance from economic centers and low quality of transport lines. In these cases, the regions suffer from the skip effect (Capello et al., 2018).

Border studies provide another theoretical pillar of the chapter. Inherently, border studies involve some cross-border cooperation typical for the EU. Brunet-Jailly (2005) grounds border studies on the interaction of the following factors:

- The effect of market forces and flows of goods, persons and services
- The political action of different vertical levels of government on two or more sides of the border
- Specific culture of cross-border communities
- Contextual place-specific environments of individual cross-border communities

It is noteworthy that the topics of socioeconomic development and cross-border settings in the Turoszów Spur or the Turów dispute are scarce in scientific literature. Vít Pászto et al. (2019) from the Czech Republic focus on Czech-Polish cross-border continuity in various indicators and bring interesting statistical evaluations of symmetries and asymmetries. Polish authors Piotr and Paweł Żuk (2022) deal with the energy and international political context of the Turów dispute and their text contains scant information about the Turoszów Spur's socioeconomic development. Therefore, collecting fragments from many information sources, especially on the internet, was necessary.

Research Design

The text aims to determine the influence of geographical preconditions on cross-border asymmetries, which led to the escalation of the Turów dispute to the European level. The primary focus is on the Czech-Polish border (following the project *The crisis at the Turów Mine and its impact on Czech-Polish cross-border cooperation: An evaluation, conclusions and recommendations*), but relations with Germany cannot be ignored. Assessment of the effect of geographical factors on socioeconomic asymmetries and the state of cross-border flows in the region is based on different methods that make it possible to look at a more comprehensive picture of the phenomenon examined rather than single cases. The text is based on the following:

- Desk research of geographical, economic, and other social sciences secondary sources about the Three-border region and the Turów dispute
- Analyzing available economic and demographic data from the Czech Republic, Poland and Germany on various hierarchical levels – some data do not exist for the minor levels. The data come from the Czech Statistical Office (CZSO, 2022), which also covers statistics of the Euroregion

Neisse – Nisa – Nysa (ERN), Statistics Poland (Statistics Poland, 2022) and the Statistical Office of the Free State of Saxony (Sachsen.de, 2022). The data are for the year 2021 unless otherwise stated.

- Artur Boháč's non-participant observation in the municipalities of the Three-border Region (Bogatynia, Zittau, Ostritz, Hrádek nad Nisou, Chrastava, Heřmanice, Kunratice, Višňová) in 2021 and 2022
- The geographical analysis of the studied region based on the methods mentioned above and studying maps and public transport timetables related to the region
- Processing the results of surveys carried out under the project

In the first half of 2022, the surveys were conducted with Czech and Polish representatives of local governments, the Turów industrial complex and local governments representing the ERN. The analysis covered the entities operating in the ERN and involved in cross-border cooperation (15 anonymized in-depth interviews with the Czech representatives of offices, institutions, organizations and local businesses and 15 with the Polish ones) and the entities functioning in the Polish-Czech borderland in the ERN and involved in cross-border cooperation (35 questionnaires to the Czech representatives and 35 to the Polish ones), as well as the residents of the Euroregion (180 Poles and 150 Czechs). The sampling was purposeful in the case of the representatives of the entities and random in the case of the residents.

The questionnaire was prepared in Polish and Czech. It was designed in closed form using a five-point Likert scale to ensure comparability and distributed in the border areas affected by the operation of the Turów Mine, such as Bogatynia, Hrádek nad Nisou and Chrastava. Siatkowski et al. (2022) contain the details about the surveys.

Hypothesis One: Geographical factors significantly affect cross-border socioeconomic asymmetries and the intensity and type of cross-border flows.

This hypothesis is based on the theoretical background above.

Hypothesis Two: Existing cross-border socioeconomic asymmetries and the intensity and type of cross-border flows contributed significantly to the escalation of the Turów dispute.

This hypothesis works with the concept that cross-border asymmetry weakens cooperation and communication and limits cross-border flows to pragmatic ones (Böhm & Opioła, 2019; Kurowska-Pysz et al., 2018). Cross-border cooperation is integral to conflict amelioration because it develops inter-communal relations and intercultural dialogue. Limited contact leaves room for misunderstanding (Mccall, 2013).

BASIC INFORMATION ABOUT THE studied REGION AND THE TURÓW DISPUTE

The Turów lignite mine and the Turoszów Spur, with its only commune Bogatynia, lie in the loosely defined cultural-historical Three-border Region (Trojzemí/Trzy Państwa/Dreiländerregion), specifically in southwestern Poland (the Lower Silesian Voivodeship, Zgorzelec County) near the borders with the Czech Republic (the Liberec Region, Liberec District) and Germany (Saxony, Görlitz District). Three-border Region, where approximately 200 000 inhabitants live, is defined by the towns Bogatynia, Hrádek nad Nisou and Zittau and the Neisse (Nisa/Nysa) River. The region is a part of the ERN, the oldest Euroregion including postcommunist countries, which is precisely delineated.

The studied area epitomizes a socioeconomic periphery or semiperiphery for all three countries because of its marginal location and turbulent modern history of population changes, border shifts and economic transformations. The changes occur especially in Czechoslovakia, where three mils. Germans were expelled, and Poland shifted to the West on the former German territory. A new German-Polish border was created on the Oder and Neisse rivers. The displaced German population was replaced with immigrants and an industrialized area with a high migration rate occurred on both sides of the newly formed Czechoslovak-Polish border. The traditional ties in the region disappeared. After World War 2, Czechoslovakia unsuccessfully sought to obtain the Turoszów Spur, which was part of the Czech kingdom until the Thirty Years' War. The territory was assigned to Poland. Several treaties of border demarcation between Czechs and Poles were signed. Nevertheless, a small territorial debt of the Czech Republic persists.

The Turów crisis has become a dispute involving many local, regional, and state actors in the last three years. A global perspective can also be considered regarding UN climate policy violations. Czechoslovakia and Germany operated lignite mines (Olbersdorf, Berzdorf, Kristýna) in the Three-border Region but closed them until 1991 for economic and environmental reasons. The former mines were transformed into lakes with tourist facilities. The Czech Republic and Germany still operate brown coal mines, which damage the environment and endanger human settlements. The difference between these mines and the Turów Mine is they are not located so near the border. The only exception is the Jänschwalde Mine in Germany on the border with Poland, which a Czech company Czech Coal owns. Several Polish politicians used the environmental burden of this mine as a counterargument to the Turów dispute. The Jänschwalde Mine will stop operation in 2023 (Visegrád Post, 2021).

The Turów Mine has been operating in modern form since 1904. Since 1962 the Turów Power Plant has operated. Before, the mine supplied the nearby power plant in Hirschfelde in the GDR (Izidorczyk, 2022). The Turów Power Plant was a source of cross-border problems in the past because of its emissions, causing acid rain and damaging forests in the Jizera Mountains. The power plant introduced advanced desulphurization technology in the 1990s, improving the situation significantly. The problems with water loss on Czech territory came with a continuous expansion of the mine, although efforts are to mitigate dust and noise pollution from the mine by creating walls and limiting night works and promoting restoration and reforestation of post-mining areas (PGE, 2022). At present, the pit is located less than 1 km from the Czech Republic and 200 meters from Germany, causing adverse environmental effects that have exacerbated dissatisfaction among residents and activists. Czechs point out air and noise pollution, soil subsidence causing cracks in buildings, mudflows from the mine dump to Czech territory and especially drainage of underground waters by the mine. According to Czech scholars, 30 000 inhabitants in the borderland are endangered by a lack of drinking water (Datel & Hrabánková, 2020). The most affected settlements were Uhelná and Václavice, parts of Hrádek nad Nisou. A decrease in estate prices was evident from browsing Czech real estate websites. Germans point out air and noise pollution and terrain drops showing that Zittau is slowly approaching the pit. They are also afraid of water drainage (Zittau, 2022). The externalities of the mine operation are minimal on Polish territory outside Bogatynia.

Czech-Polish negotiations on various levels about the mine in the 2010s were organized but without a clear and binding effect. Civil initiatives to mitigate the effects of the dispute were relatively unknown to people on both sides of the border. Nearly half of the Czech population and 70.4% of Polish residents had heard about local social consultations regarding the resolution of the dispute over the Turów Mine. However, they only participated in these social consultations to a minimal extent and had limited knowledge of their organizers.

The discontent of the Czechs and Germans peaked in 2019 when a proposal to expand the mine and operate until 2026, respectively 2044, was introduced by the mostly state-owned consortium PGE (Polska grupa energetyczna = Polish Energy Group). The Polish authorities supported this plan without proper cross-border consultations and research. This step violated the law of the EU, EIA and SEA processes, the European Water Framework Directive and the UN's Paris Climate Accords. PGE promotes the slow transformation of the municipality of Bogatynia with the help of the EU's Just Transformation Fund concerning the energy security of Poland and the locals' jobs. About 2 500 people work in the mine, about 1 200 in the power plant and about 15 000 people work in subsidiaries cooperating with the mine (Żuk & Żuk, 2022). The power plant provides water and heat to Bogatynia.

Several pro-Turów and anti-Turów demonstrations have occurred on the Czech-Polish borders since 2019. Not many Czechs and Germans shared Polish opinions and vice versa. The differences between individual actors in one state were mainly in the level of engagement and radicality of demands. Czech municipalities affected by the mine's operation, Bílý Kostel nad Nisou, Černousy, Dětřichov, Frýdlant, Heřmanice, Hrádek nad Nisou, Chotyně, Chrastava, Kunratice and Višňová, sent a petition against the mine with 13 000 signatures to the European Parliament in cooperation with the Liberec Region and Greenpeace (Město Frýdlant, 2019). All these municipalities belong to the settlements directly affected by the mine, according to the Liberec regional government, together with Bulovka, Habartice, Mníšek, Oldřichov v Hájích and Pertoltice. These settlements lie next to the border or no more than 10 km away from the border. The petition was later found to be justified, and the European Parliament's endorsement influenced later proceedings of the European Commission and the court's decision. The Liberec Region, represented by its governor Martin Půta, was very active in the dispute. Půta tried to find a solution with the Lower Silesian governor Cezary Przybylski and the Czech government. The Czech state was represented primarily by its ministries of environment and foreign affairs and agencies such as the Czech Environmental Inspection and Czech Geological Survey. One of the most active civic groups was the Neighborhood Association Uhelná, whose leader lives in the settlement concerned, Milan Starec (2022).

Several cross-border organizations, such as the ERN or EGTC Tritium, did not actively participate in the issue and denied any conflict, probably because of their cross-border character. Also, the Small Triangle, a union of partner towns Hrádek nad Nisou, Bogatynia and Zittau, was relatively inactive because of the non-cooperation of Bogatynia's mayors who had legal issues. Organization Stop Turów consisted of Czechs, Germans, and a few Poles and opposed expansion and urged the mine's closure as early as possible.

Representatives of Zittau led by mayor Thomas Zenker were active. Zittau, together with Görlitz and members of the Saxon parliament, filed a complaint against the illegal operation of the mine to the European Commission in 2021. A complaint from Zittau is still pending (Zittau, 2022). German policy was more placatory than Czech, possibly due to the relatively functioning cooperation between Zittau and Bogatynia and the presence of lignite mines in the north of the Görlitz District.

The Polish government, Lower Silesian Voivodeship, PGE, representatives and residents of Bogatynia and trade unionists from the Solidarność (Solidarity) union of the mine were most visible on the Polish side. Their motivation was energy and socioeconomic security. Trade unionists had the main motto Ręce precz od Turówa (Hands off Turów), and they protested not only on the border but also in Luxembourg (Makarewicz, 2021). Trade unions' status is very high in Polish society and politics, making the coal phase-out difficult. The main party of the Polish government, PiS (Prawo i Sprawiedliwość = Law and Justice), prides itself on supporting the mining regions. Current Bogatynia mayor Wojciech Dobrołowicz is a member of PiS. Rozwój tak - odkrywki nie (Yes to development - no to mining) was a prominent Polish organization opposed to the mine project.

Environmental activists and the members of the Neighbourhood Association Uhelná were most radical in their statements and protests on the Czech side and trade unionists on the Polish side. Unsurprisingly, activists on the Czech side were not satisfied with the later Czech-Polish agreement (Starec, 2022). They consider it too concessive and file a constitutional complaint. The Czech and Polish parliamentary oppositions also criticized the deal.

Public discontent and the Liberec Region's pressure led to the Czech government's action. The Czech Republic sued Poland over the mine at the ECJ (European Court of Justice) and won the dispute. The court fined the Polish state 500 000 EUR for each day the mining continued. The Polish government opposed the decision but finally led the Polish side to a compromise with the Czech government (Żuk & Żuk, 2022). The final agreement between Czech prime minister Petr Fiala and Polish prime minister Mateusz Morawiecki was signed on 4 February 2022 (Ministerstvo životního prostředí ČR, 2022). Poland made a payment of 45 mils. EUR to the Czech Republic as compensation for the mining effects, predominantly for building new waterlines on the Czech side and promised cooperation in monitoring the Turów mine effects. The Polish side must build the green ground rampart on the southwestern border of the mine and the underground barrier against water drainage. A second obligation is to finance the Small Projects Fund to mitigate mining effects within cross-border cooperation. The agreement establishes a joint Czech-Polish commission consisting of regional governments and local representatives, which should monitor mining and prepare a fair regional transformation. The Czech government withdrew its charges at the ECJ after signing the agreement. Nevertheless, the situation around penalty payments accrued before 4 February 2022 is not settled. The mayor of Zittau stays afraid of his town's fate and is dissatisfied with the Saxon and German governments' passive approach to the case because they did not join the Czech lawsuit (Zittau, 2022).

ECONOMIC-GEOGRAPHICAL ANALYSIS

Economy and Society

The text deals with the town and commune (gmina) of Bogatynia on the Polish side, where the Turów Mine (26 km^2) is localized. Apart from the town of Bogatynia, the commune contains many villages: Białopole, Bratków, Działoszyn, Jasna Góra, Kopaczów, Krzewina, Lutogniewice, Opolno-Zdrój, Porajów, Posada, Sieniawka, Wolanów and Wyszków. The article also concerns the Czech municipalities near the Czech-Polish border affected by the operation of the mine, according to the Liberec Regional Government: town Hrádek nad Nisou, town Frýdlant, town Chrastava, Bílý Kostel nad Nisou, Bulovka, Černousy, Dětřichov, Habartice, Heřmanice, Chotyně, Kunratice, Mníšek, Oldřichov v Hájích, Pertoltice and Višňová. German side includes border municipalities, concretely the district commune (Kreisstadt) Zittau, with settlements town Zittau, Dittelsdorf, Drauendorf, Eichgraben, Hartau, Hirschfelde, Pethau, Schlegel, Wittgendorf, and commune (Landstadt) Ostritz, containing town Ostritz and Leuba. Polish and German municipalities (LAU/LAU2) are considerably larger than Czech ones and encompass many settlements. All three sides are similar in terms of the number of inhabitants. Still, the population density is significantly lower in the Czech part, which shows the rural character of the territory and increased urbanization in Bogatynia or Zittau. Statistics for all three sides are available in table 1 at the end of this section.

The disproportion of average wages and GDP per capita in the Czech Republic, Poland and Germany is well known. It causes the willingness of Poles to commute for work to the Czech Republic and Germany and Czechs to work in Germany. No Czech or German is employed in Bogatynia. Few Germans work on the Czech side. Poles usually work in the automotive industry in the Czech part (Böhm & Opioła, 2019). Czechs and Poles in Germany work in a variety of fields. The wage asymmetry does not fully relate to the prices of estates or food. A Czech journalist Filip Horáček (2022) conducted the model purchase of 25 identical items in the Three-border Region. It included a bakery, meat, dairy products, beverages, and drugstores. The resulting amount on the receipt was 48.01 EUR in the Czech Republic, 45.13 EUR in Germany and 34.07 EUR in Poland. Poland is a popular grocery destination, so cars with Czech license plates are visible on the parking lots near the supermarkets in Bogatynia. Czech cars are dominant in the Biedronka market in Porajów, conveniently available from the Czech Republic. Czechs also frequently visit the Kaufland supermarkets in Zittau. The project survey showed that 24.6% of Czechs often shop in Poland, while 6.52% of Poles often shop in the Czech Republic. Polish customers in the Czech Republic usually do not buy food. Germans do not necessarily aim for the lowest prices and are not usual guests in shops in Bogatynia or the Czech municipalities. They prefer their supermarkets with food of higher quality and slightly higher prices.

The most problematic subregions regarding socioeconomic development are territorial protrusions such as the Turoszów Spur in Poland or Frýdlant Spur in the Czech Republic. German Zittau Spur does not have such negative characteristics compared to the mentioned areas behind the border. Its GDP is over 75% of the EU. Though, on the German level, it belongs to the least developed regions.

The territory between Zittau and Liberec, with the towns Hrádek nad Nisou and Chrastava, represents a semiperiphery. This territory has a joint cross-border development plan created by German and Czech specialists supported by the Liberec Region and Saxony (Von Korff & Maier, 2020). It forms a settlement belt in the lowland along the Neisse between Zittau, Liberec and Jablonec nad Nisou. The agglomeration is well connected to highway D10 from Prague and has no significant geographical barrier. The belt is an attractive area for foreign investments in building factories in industrial zones. All municipalities between Zittau and Liberec experienced population growth in the last decade because of the suburbanization process. Another settlement belt without a physical-geographical barrier can be recognized in Germany between Zittau and Görlitz. However, from the view of Saxony or Germany, the location of Zittau is marginal, far from the closest German highway A4 and determines a need for cooperation with their neighbors behind the borders. Zittau and surrounding municipalities face unemployment caused by the termination of local mining and related industrial activities.

The Frýdlant Spur is isolated from the Czech mainland by the Jizera Mountains, with only one passenger railway and one narrow road of regional importance prone to snowdrifts in winter. There is a population decline in the protrusion, including its western part and municipalities affected by the Turów Mine, e.g. Frýdlant, Višňová. The average age is higher than in the area around Hrádek nad Nisou and Chrastava. The unemployment rate is also slightly higher (on average, 5% x 3.5%). Kunratice and Dětřichov, municipalities from the studied part of the protrusion, show the lowest percentages of university-educated persons (2.8 and 4.0%) from the entire Liberec Region. There are also problems with socially excluded localities formed predominantly by Roma people. Frýdlant Spur is predominantly a rural area socioeconomically dependent on Liberec. It has a protected mountain landscape area, making it appealing to tourists.

Bogatynia is one of the wealthiest communes in Poland because of the Turów Mine and nearby power plant. The total incomes of the municipality's budget per capita are around 1 500 EUR. For example, the nearby commune, with a similar number of inhabitants, Lubań, works with the amount of approximately 880 EUR. The Turów energy complex is a dominant employer in Bogatynia, where unemployment rate is only 2.2%. It represents one of Europe's largest brown coal reserves with 271 mils. tons of lignite. It supplies the power plant, which provides Poland's 7% of national energy (Izidorczyk, 2022). Despite Bogatynia's wealth, it is isolated due to the below-mentioned issues. The state of several roads, buildings, and sewerage is not indicative of wealth. A two-year-old but closed aquapark in Bogatynia is another telling example. Moreover, the municipality is damaged by mining and industrial activities. There are no viable economic transition programmes for Bogatynia offering the necessary 10 000-15 000 job opportunities and the region remains dependent on mining and heavy industry. The Czech Republic and Germany promote protecting the environment, citizens' health and peaceful cross-border relations. Poland prefers energy security and jobs in Bogatynia.

Almost no differences in the sectoral distribution of economic activities between Bogatynia and the Czech municipalities were found in the euroregional statistical data. Nevertheless, there is a significant disproportion in the number of companies and entrepreneurs. Also, the German part has a variety of small and medium-sized enterprises. Few economic subjects operate in Bogatynia, even in terms of Polish communes. The dominance of the Turów energy complex and its subcontractors is unquestionable. The situation is similar in the civil sector in Bogatynia. There is a lack of NGOs not connected to Turów.

Demographic trends in the region are diverse. The Polish and German parts suffered from emigration and ageing of the population in the last three decades. Still, the Czech part experience experienced a slight increase in population mainly due to emigration from less developed regions in the Czech Republic and suburbanization in Liberec. Nevertheless, there is a difference between the settlement belt between Hrádek nad Nisou, Chrastava and surrounding municipalities with positive demographic balance and the municipalities in the western Frýdlant Spur with slightly negative demographic balance. In the studied German part of the region, the population dropped by over 30%, due to the exodus of people after the suppression of mining and industry in the last 30 years. Population decline in Bogatynia is more gradual (Von Korff & Maier, 2020). Since the 2010s, the population decline has stopped in Zittau due to the immigration of Czechs and Poles. Especially Czechs like Zittau for its friendly estate prices, significantly lower than in Liberec, low occupancy of flats and good transport connection to Liberec. The estate prices in Bogatynia are also lower than in the Czech Republic, but Czechs do not migrate there.

More statistically evaluated information on socioeconomic indicators in the Czech-Polish borderland is provided by Pászto et al. (2019). Their findings for the Czech-Polish border within the ERN show relative continuity in population density and proportion of built-up area and discontinuity in emigration rate, ecological stability and crude mortality rate, favoring the Czech side. These findings correspond with those provided here.

Germany's economic power attracts its neighbors. However, cross-border entrepreneurship is made difficult by administrative and legal differences, despite the activities of the ERN in providing consultancy and statistics. The popularity of the German language in the Czech and Polish parts of the studied region declined, which is evident from the knowledge levels (Boháč, 2022) and the number of small cross-border language education projects within the ERN (Böhm, 2022). Even the understanding between Czechs and Poles is poor, even though they belong to the same language group. Linguistic asymmetries in the Neisse-Nysa-Nisa Euroregion identity lead to an *us and them* way of thinking and complicate cross-border cooperation or large-scale cross-border labor market. Language barriers in the region result from the preference for English, ignorance and, in the case of the Czech-Polish barrier, also from geographical preconditions. Other cross-border cooperation obstacles persist due to historical traumas and national stereotypes among Central European nations (Hřebíčková & Graf, 2014). These irrational feelings might suppress the concept of *homo economicus*.

Tourism is a globally growing economic sector, but not in Bogatynia. The commune lacks striking natural and cultural monuments except for Upper Lusatian houses and the small nature reservation Grądy on the shore of the Neisse. It contrasts with the Czech part comprising castles Frýdlant and Grabštejn, Kristýna Lake, Archeopark Curia Vítkov in Chrastava or Pagan Stones (Pohanské kameny) in Višňová and the German part containing ZOO Zittau, historic town Zittau, St. Marienthal Abbey or industrial monument of the Hirschfelde Power Plant.

Table 1. Three-border Region in selected indicators and features (2021)

	Polish part	**Czech part**	**German part**
Area (km²)	136.2	297.13	90.28
Population	21 891	30 439	26 804
Population density (/km²)	160.72	102.44	296.9
Natural population increase	-126	-99	-474
Migration balance	-43	107	109
Average salary per month (EUR)	1 098	1 366	3 316
Economic subjects	1 906	5 812	2 891
Registered unemployed people	315	803	3 016
Forest area (km²)	38.13	117.6	20
Length of tourist routes (km)	43.8	173	65
Length of cycling routes (km)	7.6	142	61
Overnight stay options	4	20	11

Source: CZSO (2022), Statistics Poland (2022), Sachsen.de (2022) and own calculations

In connection with Europe's energy problems connected with the war on Ukraine, a plan for cheap hot water transport from the Turów Power Plant to the Liberec Region through a 30 km long pipeline existing since 2010 should be mentioned. The plant director, Roman Walkowiak, met with the chairman of ERN, Petr Skokan, and discussed how to cofinance the project with EU funds. The city of Liberec, with its own heating plant, was against the proposal considering it too abstract. However, smaller towns such as Chrastava and Hrádek nad Nisou were interested in the project. A plan for heat transport from Turów to Liberec was revived in 2022. It was supported by the Energy Agency of the Three-border Region, considering that Liberec belongs to the cities with the most expensive heating. The plan can bring reasonable heating costs and lower emissions in the Liberec Region. However, Liberec declined it again with arguments of lacking deeper analysis and short-term solution regarding the end of mining in the Turów mine. The project is not worth it without Liberec (Česká televize, 2022).

Cross-border mistrust is also evident in the attempt to settle the Czech debt to Poland by returning part of the Kunratice territory. Its inhabitants are afraid that the Polish side will extend the dump to this territory and closer to the center of the village (Aktuálně.cz, 2008).

Transport

Bogatynia is 87 km from the regional capital of Saxony Dresden, where is the closest airport located, 148 km to the regional capital of the Lower Silesian Voivodeship Wrocław and 55 km to the subregional capital Jelenia Góra. The distance to the Liberec Region's capital is only 16 km. The shortest distances between the two points are given. However, due to geographical barriers, such as mountains, Turów Mine and its dump, transport lines do not always follow them. Therefore, it takes approximately 40% longer to reach the destination. The quality of the roads and traffic volume play a role too. For example, travelling from Bogatynia to Jelenia Góra by car takes 1.20 h because of the low quality of the roads. Getting to Wrocław takes 2.25 h when using a highway A4 during a 201 km long way. There is a shorter (176 km) but the longer-lasting alternative route through Jelenia Góra (3 h). The journey to the county capital Zgorzelec, which creates a twin town with German Görlitz and provides advanced services to the citizens, is completed in 45 minutes despite being 31 km long. The journey to Liberec, the closest city with over 100 000 inhabitants, takes 35 minutes.

Another big problem of Bogatynia is an insufficient connection with public transport to the neighbouring towns. There is a bus connection number 645 between Bogatynia and Liberec, passing through Frýdlant and operating 5x a weekday and 1x per Saturday and Sunday. The connection is adapted to the shifts in industrial zones in Liberec and can also be used by Polish workers employed in Frýdlant. The bus is operated by ČSAD (Československá automobilová doprava = Czechoslovak car transport) Liberec. Connections of this link are more frequent this year than in previous years, indicating the interest caused by the increase in Polish commuter workers. Unfortunately, there is no precise data on Polish commuters. However, the project survey showed that 7.09% of Poles commute to work in the Czech Republic very often and 1.1% of them often. Another link operated by ČSAD Liberec is bus number 691, connecting Zittau and Świeradów-Zdrój through Bogatynia and Frýdlant. This link is primarily intended for tourists and runs 3x a day during weekends. Bus number 831 from Bogatynia to Zittau operated by ZVON (Zweckverband Verkehrsverbund Oberlausitz-Niederschlesien = Special purpose association Upper Lusatia-Lower Silesia) provides infrequent connection (Lüer, 2021). There is practically no public transport connection between Bogatynia and Hrádek nad Nisou, although Polish employees work in the local industrial zone. The connection to Zittau is also insufficient, considering the Poles employed in industrial zones around Zittau. The crucial bus connection for the inhabitants of Bogatynia is bus link 890, running to Zgorzelec once per hour during the daytime. This connection is operated by the Polish company Bielawa Busy and is probably the best choice when going for some advanced services to a larger city.

The roads in Bogatynia belong to the district or lower level. Their quality is decreased by the intensive truck transport connected with the operation of mining and industrial facilities. Car traffic in the city is quite heavy due to the lack of public transportation. From a geographical and developmental point of view, the Turoszów Spur, represented by the municipality of Bogatynia, has the poorest position in the whole Three-border Region, which can be partly derived from its specific shape. The shape creates an appendix-like territory wedged between Germany and the Czech Republic and connected to the Polish mainland only by the 3 km wide corridor. The shape is also problematic from a physical-geographical perspective. The Neisse bounds the western part of the Turoszów Spur. The river is not wide, but there is a lack of bridges suitable for car transport in the region, probably due to the border of low permeability during the Communist era. A 22 km section of the Polish-German border, between Sienawka-Zittau and Radomierzyce-Hagenwerder border crossings, is without a suitable bridge, requiring significant overtaking on specific routes between central Turoszów spur and Germany. The southern and eastern parts of the protrusion are bounded by the foothills of the Jizera Mountains, with the highest peak Lysý vrch (643 m) and the most famous peak Výhledy (Guslarz) (569 m). The mentioned foothills are not high but, compared to the altitude of Bogatynia (250 m), epitomize natural barriers reducing socioeconomic and cultural contact with neighboring countries.

The best transport situation in the Turoszów Spur is in its southwestern lowland with well-bridged Neisse. Two critical roads and one passenger railway connect the Czech Republic and Germany through a few hundred meters of Polish territory. However, Poles cannot take a chance of this area because of the mine as a barrier between it and Bogatynia and because of general ignorance of their representatives. This ignorance is evident in the lack of concern for the railway, even though there are plans for its reconstruction and the creation of a train stop in Porajów. Currently, the three-national railway between Zittau and Liberec passes 3 km through Polish territory without stopping (Boháč, 2021). The southwestern tip containing settlements Porajów and Sienawka was a part of Zittau before World War 2. The settlements are still urbanistically its suburbs. The Czech or German parts of the region contain essential transport routes such as the passenger railways between Zittau and Liberec operated by Die Länderbahn (State Railway), Zittau and Görlitz operated by Ostdeutsche Eisenbahn (East-German Railway) and Liberec and Černousy operated by the ČD (České dráhy = Czech Railways). A similar situation is present on roads of regional importance when major roads usually run along railways in Germany and the Czech Republic. The Czech-German traffic connection in the region is flawless.

There is a substantial border effect on the Czech-Polish border between Bogatynia and Kunratice, more robust than in other border-crossings between the Liberec Region and Poland, such as Habartice-Zawidów, Nové Město pod Smrkem-Świeradów-Zdrój and Harrachov-Szklarska Poręba. On average, 558 cars per day cross the border. Several possible factors contribute to this, including the low quality and importance of transport routes, the peripheral location of the municipality of Bogatynia and the neighboring Frýdlant protrusion. The opposite transport trend is observable on the roads between Hrádek nad Nisou and Zittau, crossing through the tip of the Turoszów Spur. Their daily average is 9 609 cars (Drápela & Bašta, 2018). The difficult transport situation in Bogatynia leads to the skip effect. Bogatynia has a sparse and low-quality network of cycling routes and tourist routes compared to the German or Czech parts, with a famous Oder–Neisse route and its branches. The southern part of Bogatynia has cycling routes in the settlements of Porajów or Opolno-Zdrój, but these routes are part of standard roadways with high traffic. Polish tourist website Turystyka w gminie (2022) declares that Bogatynia has 43.8 km of tourist routes, but authors know only about one 8 km route from Bogatynia to Výhledy (Guslarz) Mountain.

Environment

The Zittau Basin forms the center of the studied region. It is a tectonic depression that runs from the territory of Germany and Poland to the depressed area between the Jizera Mountains and Ještědsko-Kozákovský Ridge in the Czech Republic. The basin's total area is 187 km², with an average altitude of 384 m. The Zittau Basin is covered in the northwestern parts by Tertiary lacustrine sediments with lignite layers and Quaternary deposits of glaciogenic, glaciolacustrine, glacifluvial, partly fluvial, eolian and gravity origin. The thicknesses of lignite, as well as the thicknesses of individual coal beds, vary considerably throughout the basin. In the Czech part, the coal seam is shrinking towards the eastern border of the basin. Thus, it is not mineable there. Tertiary volcanics emerging in the perimeter of the Zittau Basin also form locally immediate subsoil. They are represented by basalt rocks, cherts and their tuffs. The foothills of the Jizera Mountains are made of granite and gneiss (Demek, 1987). The area most affected by mine operation corresponds geologically to the southern part of the Tertiary Zittau Basin. It is defined in the southern and eastern parts by the edge of the Zittau Basin structure, the western boundary is the flow of the Neisse and the northern border is the Turów Mine or the Poludňový Fault that passes through this mine.

As a result of water flowing into the mine, there is a radical decrease in groundwater levels. The drop reaches 40 km² and extends into the Czech Republic and Saxony. It manifests itself in tertiary and quaternary collectors, where the state of the groundwater is monitored using boreholes. Nevertheless, the network of boreholes in the region is insufficient. The relatively small amount of data allows Poland to question the influence of the mine. The drop in the groundwater level affects the drainage conditions of the Oldřichovský stream, which often dries up due to the groundwater deficit in the settlements Uhelná and Václavice (Datel & Hrabánková, 2020). Czech territory in the borderlands is not only affected by cross-border water drainage but also floods on a small scale. Even though retention tanks and reinforcing walls have been in place on the Polish side since 2007, floods and mudflows containing heavy metals are still evident in Višňová, a town next to the high mine dump (over 450 meters above the surrounding landscape). Minkovický and Višňovský streams flow from the dump and they can become wild when it rains heavily. Floods and mudflows damage the properties in Višňová and landslides are also a risk (MAS Frýdlantsko, 2020).

Moreover, most of the Three-border Region is inundated by floods on the rivers Neisse, Smědá (Witka) and Oleška (Miedzanka) in case of heavy rainfalls or snow melting in the Jizera Mountains. The region experienced a massive flood in 2010. Bogatynia was cut off from help because of the lack of transport lines highlighted during the catastrophe. Operation of the mine threatens the flow of the Neisse and several times the river was close to spilling into the pit. Despite the occasional occurrence of floods, the rivers in the region have been affected by the drought in the last years. This trend works against the planned recultivation of the mine by its flooding. Under current hydrological conditions, it would last 144 years. Mine water containing sulphates, cadmium and nickel pollutes the Neisse downstream from the mine in Germany (Krupp, 2020).

Due to insufficient long-term communication with the Polish side, it is impossible to determine the exact range of emissions from the Turów energy complex, concretely dust particles, benzo(a)pyrene, NO_2 and SO_2. Bogatynia is strongly polluted by dust from the excavation site, pool hopper, coal sorting site, coal site and coal transport route in the Turów Mine (Eko-Unia, 2019). In the case of no wind, temperature inversions are manifested, during which there is a greater concentration of air pollution in the interaction of worsened scattering conditions and mostly local sources of heating and emissions from transport. German settlements near Hirschfelde are also affected by such situations. Moreover, the prevailing westerly airflow brings emissions from Bogatynia to the western part of the Frýdlant Spur, where the wind hits the massif of the Jizera mountains and where it often rains. The dump also contributes to smog and the intention to construct a large wind park on the dump scares local people (MAS Frýdlantsko, 2020). Massive overall pollution in Bogatynia might be the cause of the high crude mortality rate in the commune (Pászto et al., 2019).

Bogatynia has a similar share of forests as the Czech municipalities. However, the woods on the reclaimed mine dump are considered in the statistics. Settlements existed in the territory of the dump and pit but were destroyed because of mining. Nowadays, the mine expansion has endangered the settlement Opolno-Zdrój, known as the spa before the wars. Several houses were demolished (Maciejewska, 2021).

RESULTS

The first hypothesis set within the research design was confirmed. Specific geographical factors are significant in the socioeconomic development of various parts of the studied region and the flows between them.

Direct geographical influence is evident in the following:

- Structure of economy
- Transport
- Environmental issues

Indirect geographical influence is evident in the following:

- Socioculutural matters

From the physical-geographical and political-geographical (state borders) point of view, the position of the Turoszów Spur is very peripheral. It meets six of the seven characteristics of the periphery laid out in the theoretical background. The only exception is economic characteristics because of the existence of the Turów energy complex, which makes the protrusion economically crucial for Poland. The economic asymmetry between the Czech and Polish is not based on significant differences in economic performance or sectoral economic distribution,except for mining within the primary sector, but the number and variety of economic subjects. This finding was a bit surprising. The Turów energy complex economically controls Bogatynia.

The wealth from mining is not apparent in the general development of Bogatynia. Overall peripherality and low development of Bogatynia make a commune unattractive to live in, which is evident from the gradual population decline. The commune's ruined landscape also affects people from neighboring states who do not enter the city except for quick shopping. Several factors of cross-border cooperation defined by Brunet-Jailly (2005) are weak (flows of goods, persons and services) or do not exist (specific cross-border communities).

The second hypothesis was also confirmed. The cross-border ties between Poles and Czechs in the region are pretty weak. Identified barriers to practical Czech-Polish cross-border cooperation are differences of interests and goals, lack of strategy for long-term collaboration, poor knowledge of neighboring country's language and social and economic asymmetries (Kurowska-Pysz et al., 2018). The communication between both sides was insufficient, according to the in-depth interviews with the key representatives in the area. That is why the Turów dispute went to the level of the EU. Nevertheless, Czech representatives saw the beginning of non-communication on the Polish side and the Polish representatives vice versa. Inactivity was also evident in the ERN. Euroregions have a mission to promote cooperation and the complex Turów dispute was probably too dangerous for the ERN's positive diplomatic image. The Czech and Polish parts of the Euroregions shared the views of their national governments in the case more or less openly. The attitude of the ERN was opposite to that of the Euroregion Cieszyn Silesia, which negotiated the easing of border measures during the Covid-19 pandemic with national governments (Opioła & Böhm, 2022).

According to the project survey, the most common reasons for Czechs to cross the border are travel, specifically transit and shopping. Inhabitants on the Polish side also show minor or moderate mobility for sport and tourism, transit and work. They most frequently cross the border for sport and tourism.

Current economic weak ties and asymmetries are the product of:

- Low or average infrastructure access
- Differences in national economic development
- Differences in institutional matters
- Mutual distrust arising from the issues listed below

Current social weak ties and asymmetries are the product of:

- The existence of a border which was little permeable in the past
- Absence of historical ties with an influx of people unrelated to the region
- Poor knowledge of the neighbors' language
- The entrenchment of national stereotypes and historical traumas
- Non-existence of Czech, Polish or German minorities in the region
- Very formalized cross-border cooperation without more significant involvement of locals
- Preference of national matters over cross-border ties
- Lack of stronger common economic ties that bring people together
- Low or average infrastructure access

There are obvious economic asymmetries between the German part and its eastern neighbors in the Three-border Region. Nevertheless, they did not lead to any severe contradiction. Germany's policy concerning the region is cautious and diplomatic, except for the recent initiative of the Zittau mayor. The German part of the ERN is a primary driving force of cross-border cooperation.

FUTURE RESEARCH DIRECTIONS

Future research could focus on specific social, economic or cross-border segments in the studied region or the concrete settlements. This chapter employs a more complex way to highlight the importance of geographical factors in the region. Another direction could also work with quality of life or genius loci concepts. This is because the undevelopment of the Turoszów Spur is not fully evident from the usual data. Many topics with solid publication potential were more or less indicated in the text. Future research has a high chance of funding from national science agencies or European cross-border funds because of the apparent regional asymmetries and the continuation of mining in Turów until 2044, which might bring another cross-border controversy.

CONCLUSION

Geography plays an imperative role in regional development, which is apparent even from a small area such as the Three-border Region. Physical-geographical factors significantly determine human-geographical matters, as was shown in the economic-geographical analysis. In the case of border regions, also political-geographical phenomena of borders should be considered, although nowadays, within European integration, their importance decreases. They played a role in establishing cities, building industry and shaping national histories, geopolitical traditions and cross-border relations. Sometimes, they can determine oddly shaped border territories, such as the Turoszów Spur, with developmental issues typical for economic peripheries. Thus, it is a bit hypocritical to blame Poland for (un)development in the Turoszów Spur. Most states would approach the territory similarly, given its geographical preconditions, specifically the peripheral location and fossil fuel richness. However, valid criticism concerns the lack of communication and the absence of a viable plan for the area's development during the mining slowdown.

It was outlined in the theoretical part of the text that asymmetry can be an opportunity in border regions but only in the case of functioning cross-border flows and cooperation in various sectors. Such intensive contact can gradually mitigate the asymmetry and related geographical preconditions. Long-term sustainability of border regions can be achieved through economic, social, institutional and social cooperation. The first thing that can be done to prevent conflicts is two-way communication on various hierarchical levels. Communication is conditioned by the knowledge of languages, ideally by the knowledge of the neighbor's language. The promotion of multilingualism within cross-border projects in the region is weak. The positive mental attitude of the participants is also critical because the stereotypes still show up. The authors conclude that a lack of effective communication caused part of the Turów dispute despite of existence of the ERN or various cross-border initiatives. The absence of communication exacerbated existing socioeconomic asymmetry. Building lookout towers, organizing events for chosen specific groups and taking photos with the EU flags are not always the same as having effective communication and a proactive policy to deal with acute cross-border issues.

ACKNOWLEDGMENT

This research was supported by the Polish National Agency for Academic Exchange under the NAWA Urgency Grants Scheme program within the project within the project The Turów coal mine crisis and its impact on the Czech-Polish cross-border cooperation: assessment, lessons learned and recommendations [grant number BPN/GIN/2021/1/00069/DEC/1].

REFERENCES

Aktuálně.cz (2008). *České území Polsku? Lidi straší polský důl* [Czech territory to Poland? People are haunted by a Polish mine]. Aktuálně. https://zpravy.aktualne.cz/ceske-uzemi-polsku-lidi-strasi-polsky-dul/r~i:gallery:6906

Boháč, A. (2021). State borders and cross-border cooperation in Czechia in the post-communist era: Trends and developments. *Észak-magyarországi Stratégiai Füzetek [Northern Hungary Strategy Books]*, *18*(2), 15-23.

Boháč, A. (2022). Knowledge of the German language among geography students at the Technical University of Liberec: a case study from the Czech-German borderlands. In T. Weber & H. Böhm (Eds.), *Wissenskommunikation unter Bedingungen von Mehrsprachigkeit [Knowledge communication under the conditions of multilingualism],* (pp. 28–54). Peter Lang.

Böhm, H. (2022). Sprachliche (A-)Symmetrien in der Euroregion Neisse-Nysa-Nisa: Analyse von Projekten zur Förderung der Nachbarschaftssprachen [Linguistic (A)symmetries in the Euroregion Neisse-Nysa-Nisa: Analysis of projects to promote neighboring languages]. In Weber, T., & Böhm, H. Wissenskommunikation unter Bedingungen von Mehrsprachigkeit [Knowledge communication under the conditions of multilingualism], (pp. 55-71). Peter Lang.

Böhm, H., & Opioła, W. (2019). Czech–Polish Cross-Border (Non) Cooperation in the Field of the Labor Market: Why Does It Seem to Be Un-De-Bordered? *Sustainability, 11*(10), 2855. doi:10.3390u11102855

Brunet-Jailly, E. (2005). Theorizing Borders: An Interdisciplinary Perspective. *Geopolitics, 10*(4), 633–649. doi:10.1080/14650040500318449

Capello, R., Caragliu, A., & Fratesi, U. (2018). Measuring border effects in European cross-border regions. *Regional Studies, 52*(7), 986–996. doi:10.1080/00343404.2017.1364843

Česká Televize (2021). *Události v regionech: Liberec odmítl dodávky tepla z polské elektrárny Turów [Events in the regions: Liberec refused heat supplies from the Polish Turów power plant].* Česká Televize https://www.ceskatelevize.cz/porady/10118379000-udalosti-v-regionech-praha/212411000140416/cast/199021

CZSO. (2022). *Český statistický úřad* [Czech Statistical Office]. CZSO. https://www.czso.cz

Datel, J. V., & Hrabánková, A. (2020). *Povrchový důl Turów: Stručné shrnutí současných i potenciálních budoucích negativních dopadů na poměry povrchových a podzemních vod na území České republiky* [Turów open-pit mine: Brief summary of current and potential future negative impacts on surface and underground water conditions in the Czech Republic]. VUVTGM. https://www.kraj-lbc.cz/getFile/id:1084382/TUROW-laickeshrnuti-VUV-FINAL.pdf

Demek, J. (1987). Zeměpisný lexikon ČSR: Hory a nížiny [Geographical lexicon of Czechoslovakia: Mountains and Lowlands]. *Academia (Caracas).*

Drápela, E., & Bašta, J. (2018). Kvantifikace síly hraničního efektu na hranicích Libereckého kraje [Quantification of border effec on the borders of the Liberec Region]. *Geografické informácie, 22*(1), 51-60.

Eko-Unia. (2019). *Bogatynia, one of the most polluted cities – what's next?* Eko-Unia. https://eko-unia.org.pl/en/bogatynia-one-of-the-most-polluted-cities-whats-next

Frýdlantsko, M. A. S. (2020). *Frýdlantsko 2020: Analyzická část* [The Frýdlant Region: Analytic part]. MASIF. https://www.dataplan.info/img_upload/7bdb1584e3b8a53d337518d988763f8d/sclld_88.pdf

Gallup, J. L., Gaviria, A., & Lora, E. (2003). *Is Geography Destiny? Lessons from Latin America.* Intra-American Development Bank. doi:10.1596/0-8213-5451-5

Gallup, J. L., Sachs, J. D., & Mellinger, A. D. (1998). *Geography and economic development.* National Bureau of Economic Research. doi:10.3386/w6849

Horáček, F. (2022). *Srovnali jsme stejný nákup s Polskem a Německem. Česko nevychází příliš dobře* [We compared the same purchase with Poland and Germany. Czechia is not doing well]. https://www.seznamzpravy.cz/clanek/ekonomika-byznys-trendy-analyzy-srovnani-stejny-nakup-stoji-v-cesku-stejne-jak-v-nemecku-polsko-je-levnejsi-209620

Hřebíčková, M., & Graf, S. (2014). Accuracy of National Stereotypes in Central Europe: Outgroups Are Not Better than Ingroup in Considering Personality Traits of Real People. *European Journal of Personality*, *28*(1), 60–72. doi:10.1002/per.1904

Izidorczyk, H. (2022). *Kopalnia Węgla Brunatnego Turów 1947-2022* [The Turów lignite mine 1947-2022]. Wydawnictwo AEM Paul Huppert.

Krugman, P. (1999). The role of geography in development. *International Regional Science Review*, *22*(2), 142–161. doi:10.1177/016001799761012307

Krupp, R. E. (2020). Expert report on the cross-border effects of the continuation of lignite mining in Turów (Poland) on water in Germany. https://www.greenpeace.org/static/planet4-poland-stateless/062974b1-turow_one_pager_summary_krupp_eng.pdf

Kurowska-Pysz, J., Szczepańska-Woszczyna, K., Štverková, H., & Kašík, J. (2018). The catalysts of cross-border cooperation development in euroregions. *Polish Journal of Management Studies*, *18*(1), 180–193. doi:10.17512/pjms.2018.18.1.14

Lüer, Ch. (2021). Study on providing public transport in cross-border regions. Mapping of existing services and legal obstacles: bus line 831A Zittau (Germany) – Bogatynia (Poland): case study report. European Commission.

Maciejewska, B. (2021). *Dziura kopalnii Turów pożre sudecki kurort ze średniowiecznym DNA* [The Turów mine hole will devour the Sudetes resort with its medieval DNA]. WYBORCZA. https://wroclaw.wyborcza.pl/wroclaw/7,35771,26760522,dziura-kopalnii-turow-pozre-wielowiekowy-sudecki-kurort-maciejewska.html

Makarewicz, N. (2021). *Spór o Turów. Związkowcy: Dlaczego pan Kurtyka jest jeszcze ministrem?* [The Turów dispute. Trade unionists: Why is Mr. Kurtyka still a minister?] RMF. https://www.rmf24.pl/raporty/raport-kopalnia-turow/news-spor-o-turow-zwiazkowcy-dlaczego-pan-kurtyka-jest-jeszcze-mi,nId,5563389#crp_state=1

Mccall, C. (2013). European Union Cross-Border Cooperation and Conflict Amelioration. *Space and Polity*, *17*(2), 197–216. doi:10.1080/13562576.2013.817512

Město Frýdlant. (2019). *Zachraňte vodu v pohraničí, podepište petici* [Save the water in the border area, sign the petition]. Město Frýdlant. https://www.mesto-frydlant.cz/cs/obcan/archiv/archiv-2019/zachrante-vodu-v-pohranici-podepiste-petici.html

Ministerstvo životního prostředí ČR (2022). *Dohoda mezi vládou České republiky a vládou Polské republiky o spolupráci k řešení vlivů těžební činnosti v povrchovém hnědouhelném dole Turów v Polské republice na území České republiky* [Agreement between the Government of the Czech Republic and the Government of the Republic of Poland on cooperation to address the effects of mining activity in the surface lignite mine Turów in the Republic of Poland on the territory of the Czech Republic]. MZP. https://www.mzp.cz/web/web-news2.nsf/EB4B0E394778ED4EC12587DD006687E5/$file/Turow_CZ-PL%20dohoda.pdf

Oleński, J. (2016). Typology of Transborder Economies and the Need of Transborder Statistics in Globalized World. *International Journal on Transborder Economics. Politics and Statistics*, *1*(1), 9–32.

Opioła, W., & Böhm, H. (2022). Euroregions as political actors: Managing border policies in the time of Covid-19 in Polish borderlands. *Territory, Politics, Governance*, *10*(6), 1–21. doi:10.1080/2162267 1.2021.2017339

Paasi, A. (2011). Border theory: an unattainable dream or a realistic aim for border scholars? In Wastl-Walter, D. (Ed.)., A Research Companion to Border Studies (pp. 11-31). Ashgate.

Pászto, V., Macků, K., Burian, J., Pánek, J., & Tuček, P. (2019). Capturing cross-border continuity: The case of the Czech-Polish borderland. *Moravian Geographical Reports*, *27*(2), 122–138. doi:10.2478/mgr-2019-0010

Pénzes, J., & Demeter, G. (2021). Peripheral areas and their distinctive characteristics: The case of Hungary. *Moravian Geographical Reports*, *29*(3), 217–230. doi:10.2478/mgr-2021-0016

PGE. (2022). *Ochrona szrodowiska* [Environmental protection]. PGE. https://kwbturow.pgegiek.pl/Ochrona-srodowiska

Sachsen.de. 2022. *Statistik* [Statistics]. https://www.statistik.sachsen.de

Siatkowski, J., Olszewski, M., & Konik, J. (2022). *The Turów Mine crisis and its impact on Czech-Polish cross-border cooperation: evaluation, conclusions and recommendations*. Report available on request from the authors.

Starec, M. (2022). *Nová zjištění odhalují naprosté selhání česko-polské dohody o dolu Turów [New findings reveal the complete failure of the Czech-Polish agreement on the Turów mine]*. Denik Referendum. https://denikreferendum.cz/clanek/34158-nova-zjisteni-odhaluji-naproste-selhani-ceskopolske-dohody-o-dolu-turow

Statistics Poland. (2022). *Basic data*. Statistics Poland. https://stat.gov.pl/en/basic-data

Turystyka w gminie (2022). *Turystyka w gminie Bogatynia [Tourism in the municipality of Bogatynia]*. Turystyka w gminie. http://www.turystykawgminie.pl/bogatynia

Van Korff, J., & Maier, K. (2020). *Koncept rozvoje pro mezinárodní rozvojovou oblast Liberec – Žitava: Svazek 1 – Regionální analýza [Concept of development for the international development area Liberec – Zittau: Volume 1 – Regional analysis]*. Futour.

Visegrád Post. (2021). *Turów may be bad for the environment, but so is Jänschwalde*. Visegrad. https://visegradpost.com/en/2021/10/25/turow-may-be-bad-for-the-environment-but-so-is-janschwalde

Zittau (2022): *Tagebau Turów bedroht die Menschen in der Dreiländerregion* [Turów Mine threatens people in the Three-border Region]. Zittau. https://zittau.de/de/turow-studie

Żuk, P., & Żuk, P. (2022). The Turów Brown Coal Mine in the shadow of an international conflict: Surveying the actions of the European Union Court of Justice and the populist policies of the Polish government. *The Extractive Industries and Society*, 10.

ADDITIONAL READING

Beck, J. (Ed.). (2019). *Transdisciplinary Discourses on Cross-Border Cooperation in Europe*. Peter Lang. doi:10.3726/b15288

Dołzbłasz, S. (2015). Symmetry or asymmetry? Cross-border openness of service providers in Polish-Czech and Polish-German border towns. *Moravian Geographical Reports*, *23*(1), 2–12. doi:10.1515/mgr-2015-0001

Havlíček, T., Jeřábek, M., & Dokoupil, J. (2018). *Borders in Central Europe After the Schengen Agreement*. Springer. doi:10.1007/978-3-319-63016-8

Makkonen, T., & Williams, A. M. (2016). Border region studies: The structure of an 'offbeat' field of regional studies. *Regional Studies, Regional Science*, *3*(1), 355–367. doi:10.1080/21681376.2016.1209982

Pugh, R., & Dubois, A. (2021). Peripheries within economic geography: Four "problems" and the road ahead of us. *Journal of Rural Studies*, *87*, 267–275. doi:10.1016/j.jrurstud.2021.09.007

Scott, A. J. (2006). *Geography and Economy: Three Lectures*. Oxford University Press. doi:10.1093/oso/9780199284306.001.0001

Sohn, C. (2014). Modelling Cross-Border Integration: The Role of Borders as a Resource. *Geopolitics*, *19*(3), 587–608. doi:10.1080/14650045.2014.913029

Van Houtum, H. (2000). An Overview of European Geographical Research on Borders and Border Regions. *Journal of Borderlands Studies*, *15*(1), 57–83. doi:10.1080/08865655.2000.9695542

KEY TERMS AND DEFINITIONS

Border Effect: An effect of a border as a barrier of transport, lower intensity of cross-border flows means a more substantial border effect.

Cross-Border Cooperation: A collaboration between regions, municipalities or other subjects across borders, one of the foundations of European integration.

Geographical Periphery: A lesser socioeconomically developed locality or region with insufficient linkages to developed territories.

Neo-Environmental Determinism: An economic-geographic approach emphasizing geographical factors on an economy without imperial or racist trends of old environmental determinism.

Socioeconomic Asymmetry: A gap in socioeconomic markers between territories.

Three-Border Region: The cultural-historical region in southwestern Poland, southeastern Germany and the northern Czech Republic with towns Hrádek nad Nisou, Bogatynia and Zittau.

Territorial Protrusion: A specific example of a periphery determined by a border shape when part of the territory of one territorial unit runs deeply into the territory of another unit.

Chapter 9
Innovative Potential of Regions:
Accelerator of Sustainability and Development

Vojtech Kollár

Bratislava University of Economics and Management, Slovakia

Silvia Matúšová

https://orcid.org/0000-0002-3471-850X

Bratislava University of Economics and Management, Slovakia

ABSTRACT

The concepts of innovation and innovation potential have become crucial in the implementation of conceptual changes and strategic plans leading to changes in competitiveness. Innovation consists of the realization of new ideas projected into products, services, processes, systems, and social relations. Quantitative growth of innovations in the country and its regions as innovative capital is reflected in the innovativeness of products and the quality of services provided, affecting the behaviour of employees, the culture of companies, and the perception of the value of innovative products by consumers. The aim of the research is to compare the results of Slovakia and its regions with the results of European and V4 countries in terms of innovation potential. Based on analysis and comparison, the authors identified the strengths and weaknesses in the innovation potential of Slovakia and Slovak regions and the gaps that need to be overcome regarding the increase of the innovation potential and sustainable development.

INTRODUCTION

Innovation has become a crucial driver of the contemporary world, the global economy, and the micro-economy. The 21st century development requires new ideas and continuous progress in which entrepreneurs fulfil the roles of thinkers and creators of constantly renewing programs that respond to domestic and foreign requirements.

DOI: 10.4018/978-1-6684-5976-8.ch009

Innovations fundamentally affect the competitiveness of enterprises, production and services sectors, becoming preconditions for the economic success of countries in a strong competitive global environment (Kollár and Matúšová, 2019, pp. 7-8).

The chapter´s focus is on the innovation performance of Slovakia and Slovakia´s regions. The assessment was elaborated in accordance with the European Innovation Scoreboard 2021 and the Regional Innovation Scoreboard. The innovation performance rate of Slovakia was compared with the EU and Visegrad Group countries.

For the characteristics of Slovakia, macroeconomic indicators, including GDP, employment rate, monthly nominal wage, and FDI were applied and assessed. For development trends in research, development, and innovation potential, the indicators as human resources, public expenditure in education, R&D, the market, and the labour market were deployed.

Methods of analysis, comparison, assessment, and synthesis of data were applied. The assessment concerned the data interlinked to innovation potential in Slovakia and its regions.

The outcomes of assessment refer to strengths and weaknesses of Slovakia as a whole and its regions, including Bratislava region, Western Slovakia, Central Slovakia, and Eastern Slovakia.

The main objective was to test the assumption that the innovation policy of decision-makers at central and regional governance levels should be based on investments and promotion of innovative potential on regional and municipal levels and thus to help decrease enormous regional disparities in Slovakia.

The results presented in tables and figures should demonstrate the processing procedures.

BACKGROUND

The European Commission (2021a, 2021b) defined innovation as "the successful creation, introduction and use of innovations in the economic and social sphere or as the renewal and expansion of the range of products and services and their associated markets, the creation of new methods of production, supply, distribution, the introduction of changes in management, work organization, working conditions and workforce qualifications" (Kollár and Matúšová, 2019).

For the characteristic of Slovakia and Slovakia´s regions as the object of the research of innovation potential, we applied several macroeconomic indicators, including GDP which measures income and total expenditure in the country and follows the territorial principle (Lisý, 2016, p. 353).

Table 1. Real GDP growth in Slovakia [in %]

GDP	2014	2015	2016	2017	2018	2019	2020
in current market prices – nominal GDP	76 092,7	79 888,1	81 014,3	84 442,9	89 430,0	94 048,0	92 079,3
in constant prices – real GDP	76 239,2	80 061,4	81 431,3	83 428,6	87 647,0	91 760,0	89 948,7
Real GDP per capita	13 600,0	14 300,0	14 550,0	14 960,0	15 510,0	15 890,0	15 180,0
GDP at current prices/ per capita	14 040	14 730	14 920	15 530	16 420	17 250	16 860
real GDP growth [%]	2,6%	5,1%	1,8%	2,8%	3,6%	2,5%	-4,5%

Source: own processing due to Statistical Office SR

The real GDP growth in Slovakia from 2014 to 2020 reached the highest GDP value of 5.1% in 2015. After a drop of more than 3% from 2016, real GDP growth of less than 2% was recorded in 2017. The GDP rate in 2020 went into negative numbers for the first time since 2008 and 2009 due to the impact of the COVID-19 pandemic (Table 1).

Foreign trade recovered slowly due to the lack of production capacity, especially in industry. In some sectors, the lack of inputs and weaker imports had a dampening effect on household consumption. Exports and investment were the primary reason of the fall in GDP during the 2020 pandemic. In contrast to the recovery in exports, the recovery in investment remains negative. Household consumption is currently dampened by the rise of inflation.

Employment and labour market efficiency were worse in 2020. The number of unemployed is slowly decreasing because of the slow return of employees to sectors affected by lockdowns (Figure 1).

Figure 1. The number of working persons [in thousands] compared to the unemployment rate [in %] from 2014 to 2020
Source: own processing due to Statistical Office SR

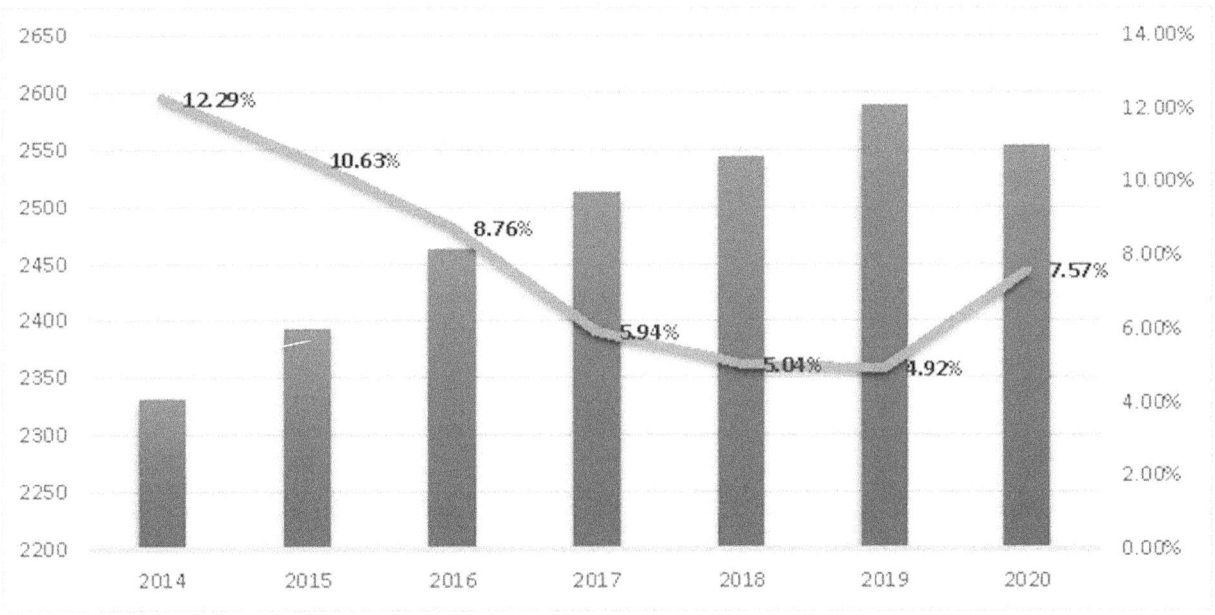

Figure 2 presents the average monthly nominal wage of an employee, which increased by an average of €45 annually, reaching its highest value in 2020 (€1,133), followed by a slowdown in the growth of the average nominal wage (by 3.8%). Compared to 2019, it fell by almost half.

As many as 12,672 job seekers applied to the labour market in January 2022, which is 5,097 more than in December 2021. More young people under the age of 29 and more long-term unemployed found new jobs.

The largest inflow of foreign direct investment (FDI) in 2014-2020 was recorded in 2017 (Figure 3). Compared to 2016, this is an almost 5-fold increase in investments.

Figure 2. Development of the average monthly nominal salary of an employee for 2014 – 2020 [in €]
Source: own processing due to Statistical Office SR

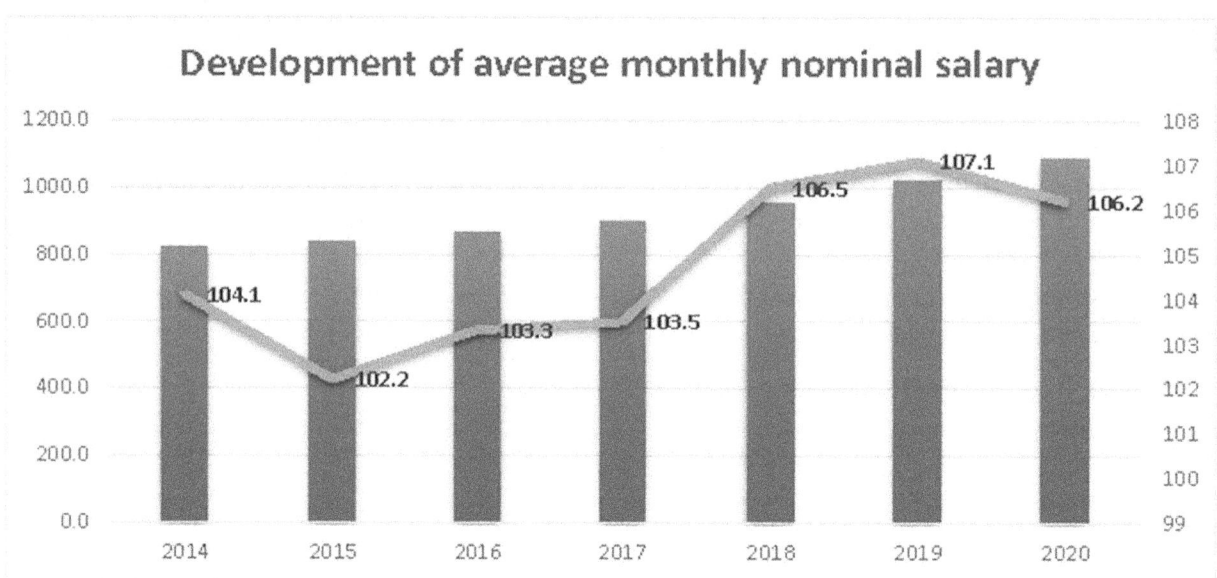

In 2020, the value of foreign investments fell due to the pandemic by 4,379 million USD which caused the weakening of the economy and the restriction of foreign trade.

Economic forecast for 2022 foresees the growth of 3.5%. The development will be accompanied by inflation, which will reduce the real income and consumption. The economy will revive at the end of 2022, when the creation of jobs will accelerate. A strong, up to 53% dependence on the import of raw materials from the Russian Federation could cause a decline in the economy. In 2023, GDP growth is expected due to higher use of EU funds.

Figure 3. Development of direct FDI in Slovakia in the period 2014 – 2020 [in millions USD]
Source: own processing according to UNCTAD

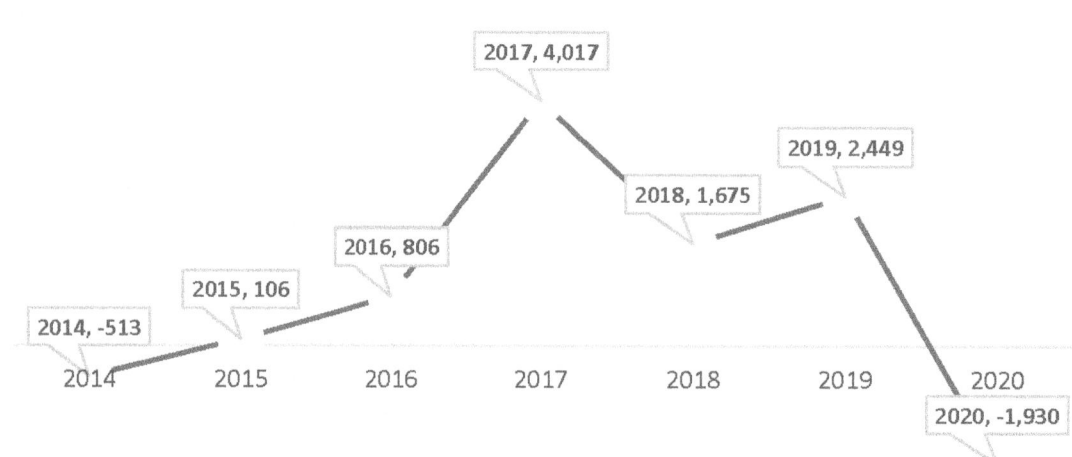

MAIN FOCUS OF THE CHAPTER

The focus of the chapter aims at the innovation performance of Slovakia and Slovakia´s regions. The innovation performance was assessed from three different aspects, due to the European Innovation Scoreboard 2021, Regional Innovation Scoreboard, and within the Visegrad Group (Slovakia, Czech Republic, Hungary, and Poland).

Slovakia´s rank in European Innovation Scoreboard 2021

The European Innovation Scoreboard differentiates four main types of activities - framework conditions, investments, innovation activities and impacts, each activity monitors three dimensions, altogether 12 dimensions, and 32 indicators in total.

Table 2. European Innovation Scoreboard (EIS)

1. Framework conditions	1. dimension Human resources 2. dimension Attractive research systems 3. dimension Digitalisation
2. Investment	1. dimension Finance and support 2. dimension Firm investment 3. dimension Use of information technologies
3. Innovation activities	1. dimension Innovators 2. dimension Linkages 3. dimension Intellectual assets
4. Impacts	1. dimension Employment impacts 2. dimension Sales impacts 3. dimension Environmental sustainability

Source: EIS 2021. Executive Summary

European Innovation Scoreboard (EIS) applies four types of activities (Table 2):

a) the framework conditions capture the main drivers of innovation performance external to the firm, and cover the three dimensions of innovation,
b) investments capture private and public investment in research and innovation,
c) innovation activities capture innovation efforts at the level of the enterprise,
d) impacts cover the effects of innovation activities of companies.

The ranking of EU countries and the classification to four performance groups (Table 3) denotes:

1. innovation leaders achieve innovation performance higher than 125% of the EU average;
2. strong innovators achieve innovation performance in the range of 100 to 125% of the EU average;
3. moderate innovators have innovation performance in the range of 70 to 100% of the EU average;
4. emerging innovators achieve innovation performance below 70% of the EU average.

Table 3 Performance of EU Member States´ innovation systems

Sweden	SE	156,5	Innovation leaders
Finland	FI	151,4	
Denmark	DK	147,5	
Belgium	BE	143,5	
Netherlands	NL	138,5	Strong innovators
Germany	DE	137,9	
Luxembourg	LU	136,5	
Austria	AT	133,6	
Estonia	EE	128,3	
France	FR	122,3	
Ireland	IE	121,3	
EU average	EU	112,5	Moderate innovators
Italy	IT	108,1	
Cyprus	CY	106,5	
Malta	MT	101,8	
Slovenia	SI	100,5	
Spain	ES	96	
Czech Republic	CZ	94,4	
Lithuania	LT	92,1	
Portugal	PT	90,3	
Greece	EL	88,5	
Croatia	HR	78,2	Emerging innovators
Hungary	HU	76,4	
Slovakia	**SK**	71	
Poland	PL	65,9	
Latvia	LV	55,9	
Bulgaria	BG	50,1	
Romania	RO	35,1	

Source: own processing according to EIS 2021

Sweden was ranked first in the group of innovation leaders, followed by Finland, Denmark, and Belgium. Slovakia ranked in the group of emerging innovators, with Croatia, Hungary, Poland, Latvia, Bulgaria and Romania. Slovakia's score according to the main types of activities is in Table 4.

Assessment of Slovakia's scores in 2020 compared to 2021 showed the following:

1. Framework conditions focus on individuals with tertiary education, most cited publications, and individuals with basic digital skills. Slovakia did not reach the EU average in any indicator. The indicators Lifelong learning and 10% of the most cited publications were worst rated. The indicator Individuals with tertiary education scored best and inclined towards the EU average, which was only less than 2% below the EU average. The new indicator Individuals with above basic digital skills scoring the rate of digitization and digital skills reached 81%.

Table 4. The score of Slovakia in the EIS according to the main types of activities

		2020		2021	
		Slovakia	EU average	Slovakia	EU average
1.1 Human resources	New doctorate graduates in science, technology, engineering, mathematics	77,0	100,0	77,0	88,5
	Percentage of population aged 25-34 with tertiary education	110,7	122,3	127,3	128,9
	Lifelong learning	34,4	107,8	30,0	110,0
1.2 Attractive research system	International scientific co-publications	94,5	122,6	101,1	131,1
	Top 10% of most cited scientific publications	37,8	98,8	41,8	98,3
	Foreign doctorate students	60,8	113,0	61,3	118,8
1.3 Digitalisation	Broadband penetration	114,0	137,8	122,5	151,7
	Individuals with above basic overall digital skills	133,3	111,1	100,0	122,2
2.1 Finance and support	R&D expenditure in the public sector	35,1	94,7	35,1	96,5
	Venture capital expenditures	18,8	155,5	25,0	168,2
	Direct government funding for business R&D	15,2	110,5	27,8	115,7
2.2 Firm investments	R&D expenditure in the business sector	31,5	110,2	31,5	111,0
	Non-R&D innovation expenditures	99,0	109,7	105,7	113,6
	Innovation expenditures per persons employed	43,4	144,5	55,6	132,0
2.3 Use of information technologies	Enterprises providing training to develop or upgrade ICT skills of their personnel	86,7	120,0	73,3	100,0
	Employed ICT specialists	100,0	128,6	123,8	133,3
3.1 Innovators	SMEs with product innovations	32,0	110,5	42,2	141,1
	SMEs with business process innovations	29,7	107,3	32,8	133,0
3.2 Linkages	Innovative SMEs collaborating with others	92,2	107,1	92,4	146,5
	Public-private co-publications	90,2	112,8	84,8	112,1
	Job-to-job mobility in Human Resources in Science and Technology	53,8	135,9	33,3	143,6
3.3 Intellectual assets	Patent applications	19,2	91,5	15,6	86,8
	Trademark applications	78,1	105,3	79,7	105,0
	Design applications	29,1	77,6	27,7	68,5
4.1 Employment impact	Employment in knowledge-intensive activities	60,0	106,7	70,7	109,3
	Employment in innovative enterprises	32,1	93,2	30,4	96,6
4.2 Sale impact	Medium and high-tech product exports	142,2	109,6	142,2	109,6
	Knowledge-intensive services export	45,5	103,8	44,1	105,9
	Sales of product innovations	161,1	94,2	83,6	86,9
4.3 Environmental sustainability impact	Resource productivity	90,6	139,8	108,9	148,1
	Air emission by fine particulates in industry	106,4	105,5	109,9	106,3
	Development of environment-related technologies	117,2	81,9	125,0	75,1

Source: own processing due to Regional Innovation Scoreboard 2021

2. Investments in innovations in the dimension Finance and support show that Slovakia achieved the worst results in all three indicators. Expenditures in R&D in the business sector and expenditures on innovation per employed person is not even half of the EU average. The best-rated indicator at the level of 94% of the EU average is expenditure not directly referring to R&D, but related to patents and licenses application.

3. Innovation activities include three innovation dimensions and eight indicators. The new indicator Job-to-job mobility in science and technology measures the exchange of knowledge between human resources in the job exchange. The Trademark Application indicator scored best at the level of approximately 76% of the EU average. Another best rated indicator is Public-private co-publications denoting research cooperation in the business and public sectors. The worst rated indicator is Patent application scoring below 80% of the EU average.

4. Impacts refer to employment, sales, and environmental sustainability. In 2021, newly introduced dimension monitored environmental sustainability, environmental protection and environment-related technologies. The technologies, and medium and high-tech product exports were rated above the EU average. In environment-related technologies, Slovakia reached 66% above the EU average, in innovative enterprises approximately 30% above the EU average.

Slovakia's score (table 5) revealed differences, strengths, and weaknesses. Indicators marked in green denote Slovakia´s score above the EU average, indicators with scores slightly above the EU average are marked in pale green, indicators with scores approaching to the EU average are marked in yellow and indicators in which Slovakia lags behind the EU average are marked in brown.

Table 5. Strengths and weaknesses of Slovakia in EIS

		2021	
		Slovakia	**EU average**
1. Framework conditions			
1.1 Human resources	New doctorate graduates in STEM	77,0	88,5
	Population aged 25-34 with tertiary education	127,3	128,9
	Lifelong learning	30,0	110,0
1.2 Attractive research system	International scientific co-publications	101,1	131,1
	Top 10% of most cited scientific publications	41,8	98,3
	Foreign doctorate students	61,3	118,8
1.3 Digitalisation	Broadband penetration	122,5	151,7
	Individuals with above basic overall digital skills	100,0	122,2
2. Investments			
2.1 Finance and support	R&D expenditure in the public sector	35,1	96,5
	Venture capital expenditures	25,0	168,2
	Direct government funding for business R&D	27,8	115,7
2.2 Firm investments	R&D expenditure in the business sector	31,5	111,0
	Non-R&D innovation expenditures	105,7	113,6
	Innovation expenditures per persons employed	55,6	132,0

continues on following page

Table 5. Continued

		2021	
		Slovakia	**EU average**
2.3 Use of information technologies	Enterprises providing training to develop or upgrade ICT skills of their personnel	73,3	100,0
	Employed ICT specialists	123,8	133,3
3. Innovation activities			
3.1 Innovators	SMEs with product innovations	42,2	141,1
	SMEs with business process innovations	32,8	133,0
3.2 Linkages	Innovative SMEs collaborating with others	92,4	146,5
	Public-private co-publications	84,8	112,1
	Job-to-job mobility in Human Resources in Science and Technology	33,3	143,6
3.3 Intellectual assets	Patent applications	15,6	86,8
	Trademark applications	79,7	105,0
	Design applications	27,7	68,5
4. Impacts			
4.1 Employment impact	Employment in knowledge-intensive activities	70,7	109,3
	Employment in innovative enterprises	30,4	96,6
4.2 Sale impact	Medium and high-tech product exports	142,2	109,6
	Knowledge-intensive services export	44,1	105,9
	Sales of product innovations	83,6	86,9
4.3 Environmental sustainability impact	Resource productivity	108,9	148,1
	Air emission by fine particulates in industry	109,9	106,3
	Development of environment-related technologies	125,0	75,1

Source: own processing due to EIS 2021

Table 6 presents that Slovakia scored a) with a below-average score (at the level of 30% of the EU average), b) approaching the EU average (at the level of 95-100% of the EU average), and c) with the highest achieved score (at a level higher than 100% of the EU average).

Slovakia achieved an above-average rating in the indicators Environment-related technologies, Air emission by fine particulates and Medium and high-tech product exports. The indicators Sales of innovative products and Individuals with tertiary education show that Slovakia came closer to the EU average. The indicators Venture capital expenditures, Direct government funding for business R&D, R&D expenditure in the business sector, Job-to-job mobility in HRST, and Patent applications did not even reach 25% of the EU average.

The results indicate to which areas the funds from the Recovery and Resilience Plan should be directed, and which aspects of innovation performance should be reflected in government policies and public and private sector measures.

Table 6. Comparison between Slovakia and EU in selected indicators

Indicators with a below-average score (up to 30% of the EU average)	• Lifelong learning • Venture capital expenditures • Direct government support for business R&D • Funding for business R&D • SMEs with product innovations • SMEs with business innovations Job-to-job mobility in HRST • Patent applications
Indicators approaching to the EU average (from 95% to 100%)	• Individuals with completed tertiary education • Sales of product innovations
Indicators with the highest achieved score (above the EU average)	• Medium and high-tech product exports • Air emission by fine particulates in industry • Environment-related technologies

Source: own processing

Slovakia and V4 Countries in European Innovation Scoreboard

In 2021, Slovakia ranked to the group of emerging innovators, not even reaching 70% of the EU average. Slovakia is frequently compared with Czech Republic, Hungary, and Poland (V4 Group since 1993). Table 7 shows the position of the V4 countries in the EIS in 2019, 2020 and 2021.

Table 7. V4 countries in EIS 2021

	2019	2020	2021
Czech Republic	14.	16.	17.
Hungary	23.	22.	22.
Poland	25.	24.	24.
Slovakia	22.	21.	23.

Source: own processing due to EIS 2021

The Czech Republic became the leader in 2021, however it fell by three ranks, compared to 2019. As the only V4 country, it was ranked among moderate innovators in the EU. Hungary was the second and maintained its position. Slovakia ranked the third and fell by one place. Poland took the fourth place. In 2021, Slovakia achieved the rating in innovation performance between 70 and 100% of the EU average. Table 8 presents the V4 countries in innovation performance in the twelve dimensions of the EIS 2021.

In Human Resources, the Czech Republic scored best, reaching 81.9% of the EU average. Slovakia took the third place, slightly ahead of Poland, which ranked last.

In Digitalisation, Hungary, Poland, and Slovakia achieved more than 80% of the EU average, while the Czech Republic was catching up. No V4 country reached the EU average in the first three dimensions.

In Finance and support, Hungary was the best rated country. Slovakia achieved the worst result, not reaching a third of Hungary's score.

In Firm investments, Slovakia achieved a negative result. Slovakia, Hungary, and Poland were ranked at approximately the same level, but compared to other EU countries, their rankings were low.

Table 8. The comparison of V4 countries in EIS dimensions

Dimensions	CZ	HU	PL	SK	EU average
1.1 Human resources	86,8	44,5	67,7	79,4	106,0
1.2 Attractive research system	83,5	76,6	44,3	63,5	112,5
1.3 Digitalisation	109,8	119,5	114,9	112,3	138,3
2.1 Finance and support	82,8	99,4	66,7	30,4	119,1
2.2 Firm investments	88,4	77,6	72,7	58,2	119,3
2.3 Use of information technologies	135,6	90,2	90,7	96,8	115,5
3.1 Innovators	122,7	48,8	20,7	37,2	136,8
3.2 Linkages	107,1	112,5	92,7	66,2	134,8
3.3 Intellectual assets	51,7	41,7	73,2	41,8	86,7
4.1 Employment impact	90,3	46,8	31,9	47,1	101,9
4.2 Sale impact	99,6	96,4	64,8	92,2	101,9
4.3 Environmental sustainability impact	99,9	75,2	64,8	114,9	104,1
Scores for 2021	94,4	76,4	65,9	71,0	

Source: own processing according to European Innovation Scoreboard 2021

In Use of information technologies, the Czech Republic ranked above the EU average. Other V4 countries ranked similarly.

Regarding Innovators, the biggest differences were observed. The Czech Republic became the leader, while Poland, as the least innovative in the V4, scored four times lower.

In Linkages, the V4 countries achieved similar scores, while Slovakia lagged. Intellectual assets were the only dimension in which Poland achieved the first place.

In Employment impact and Sales impact, the Czech Republic achieved the highest score, coming close to the EU average.

In Environmental Sustainability, related to the environment-related technologies and environmental protection, Slovakia ranked above the V4 countries, and exceeded the EU average.

Innovation Performance of Slovak Regions

The Regional Innovation Scoreboard (RIS) compares 240 regions in 22 EU member states, the UK, Switzerland, Serbia, and Norway.

As the regional division is different from the administrative division of countries, the Nomenclature of Territorial Units for Statistics (NUTS) is applied, representing a hierarchical system of division into 3 levels.

Only 210 regions in 22 EU countries were assessed. Estonia, Latvia, Luxembourg, Malta, and Cyprus are not regionalized and therefore not included. The indicators in RIS are identical to the indicators in EIS 2021, or slightly adjusted.

Slovakia's division according to NUTS 2 applies to the Bratislava Region, Western Slovakia, Central Slovakia, and Eastern Slovakia.

The assessment of Slovakia is based on five indicators in the Framework conditions.

In the dimension Human Resources, individuals with tertiary education are largely represented in the Bratislava Region, and almost twice as high as in other regions. Western Slovakia and Eastern Slovakia are approximately at the same level. Central Slovakia achieved the worst results, but the difference compared to Western Slovakia and Eastern Slovakia is minimal.

Table 9 shows that the Bratislava Region achieved in all indicators higher scores than Slovakia as a whole, and in some indicators ranked above the EU average. Other regions did not even come close to the EU average.

In the dimension Lifelong education, the Bratislava Region is a leader, achieving a higher score than Slovakia as a whole, but not above the EU average. The second region with best rating is Central Slovakia, followed by Eastern Slovakia and finally Western Slovakia

Differences can be seen between the Bratislava Region and Western Slovakia. In the dimension Attractive research system in the indicator International scientific co-publications, Western Slovakia achieved the lowest score. Eastern Slovakia achieved approximately the same score as Slovakia as a whole, Western Slovakia and Central Slovakia ranked below the country´s score. The Bratislava Region achieved the highest score than Slovakia as a whole and a higher level than the EU average.

In the indicator Top 10% most cited publications, the Bratislava Region has the lowest share (19%). The lead was achieved by Western Slovakia. Other regions did not come close to the EU average but achieved a higher score than Slovakia as a whole. The indicator Individuals with basic digital skills reached the same share in Western Slovakia and Eastern Slovakia. The Bratislava Region boasted by the first place, but the difference compared to Central Slovakia is only 2%.

New Challenges in Labour and Education Markets Associated with Innovation Potential

The current problem of innovation potential could be seen in the departure of qualified researchers abroad, the structure of the education market, labour market requirements, unsatisfactory demographic development, and the unsustainability of public finances.

Migration refers to the mobility of individuals between countries and regions, changing the number of inhabitants. Internal migration represents the mobility of individuals from the eastern regions to the western regions, especially to Bratislava. The long-term trend significantly affects the number of inhabitants in Slovakia´s regions. Aging is manifested by an increase of senior age groups. In 2011, the population aging index was 82.96%, it increased to 107.34% in 2020.

The education market is dominated by new requirements regarding the abilities and skills of employees. Up to 70% of professions will be threatened by automation of production. Slovakia ranked first in comparison with OECD (2020) countries.

A major risk is the ratio of the population in productive and post-productive age, which currently stands at 10:2, by 2060 it is forecast to be 10:6, indicating 6 persons in non-productive age for every 10 employed persons. The OECD Strategy for the Slovak Republic (2019-2020) concerns the strengthening of skills in young adults and employees in order to acquire, renew and improve the skills needed to perform tasks in current professions, and to prepare for newly emerging professions. The ability to cope with automation, digitization and dynamization dominates the selection of employees. Tertiary education at universities partly contributes to greater adaptability and resilience of graduates. In the period 2005-2015, the number of university graduates aged 25-34 doubled in Slovakia. In 2018, the share was 37%, still significantly lower compared to the OECD average of 45%.

Table 9. Regional disparities of Slovakia in EIS

		Bratislava Region	Western Slovakia	Central Slovakia	Eastern Slovakia	Slovakia	EU average
1. Framework conditions							
1.1 Human resources	Individuals with tertiary education	203,85	105,32	93,23	105,81	127,3	128,9
	Lifelong learning	70,71	26,26	40,40	31,31	30	110
1.2 Attractive research system	International scientific publications	196,92	73,68	83,51	100,33	101,1	131,1
	Top 10% of the most cited publications	35,34	52,84	50,90	46,78	41,8	98,3
1.3 Digitalisation	Individuals with above basic digital skills	105,25	101,75	96,50	101,75	100	122,2
2. Investment							
2.1 Finance and support	R&D expenditure in the public sector	107,04	19,72	36,62	30,99	35,1	96,5
2.2 Firm investments	R&D expenditure in the business sector	49,61	40,94	25,98	18,11	31,5	111
	Non-R&D innovation expenditures	89,25	130,31	157,40	131,89	105,7	113,6
	Innovation expenditures per persons employed	109,15	64,61	79,12	66,79	55,6	132
3. Innovation activities							
3.1 Innovators	SMEs with product innovations	70,37	50,41	69,99	47,00	42,2	141,1
	SMEs with business process innovations	63,83	36,83	48,27	41,61	32,8	133
3.2 Linkages	Innovative SMEs collaborating with others	146,80	75,93	82,41	75,64	92,4	146,5
	Public-private co-publications	163,71	62,45	62,28	68,23	84,8	112,1
3.3 Intellectual assets	Patent applications	39,49	37,86	37,00	37,62	15,6	86,8
	Trademark applications	106,12	49,69	54,70	50,49	79,7	105
	Design applications	59,95	55,58	52,19	38,21	27,7	68,5
4. Impact							
4.1 Employment impact	Employment in knowledge-intensive activities	177,27	175,41	113,03	93,48	70,7	109,3
	Employment in innovative enterprises	62,22	44,76	57,71	61,63	30,4	96,6
4.2 Sale impact	Sales of product innovations	91,31	58,41	87,45	97,29	83,6	86,9
4.3 Environmental sustainability	Air emission by fine particulates in industry	75,02	71,74	55,67	52,11	109,9	106,3

Source: own processing according to EIS 2021

In 2021, the Global Institute (McKinsey, 2021) in an analytical study "56 DELTA skills" focused on 56 foundational skills intended to help equip employees to function in digital environment in multiple sectors and professions. Skills are divided into cognitive, interpersonal, self-management (and entrepreneurship) and digital. The level of proficiency correlates with education. The highest correlation was achieved in digital skills, which are acquired in all types of education (formal, informal, nonformal). Digital skills should be incorporated into university education and lifelong learning as the Industry4.0 paradigm requires analytical and critical thinking, mathematical and digital skills. Attained education is the most important component of human capital, representing the driver of economic activities and the development of regions. However, the number of students at Slovak universities was decreasing since 2012-2020 (Figure 4).

Figure 4. Development of university graduates in Slovakia (1989-2019)
Source: Quantitative overviews of demographic development in Slovak tertiary education 1989-2020

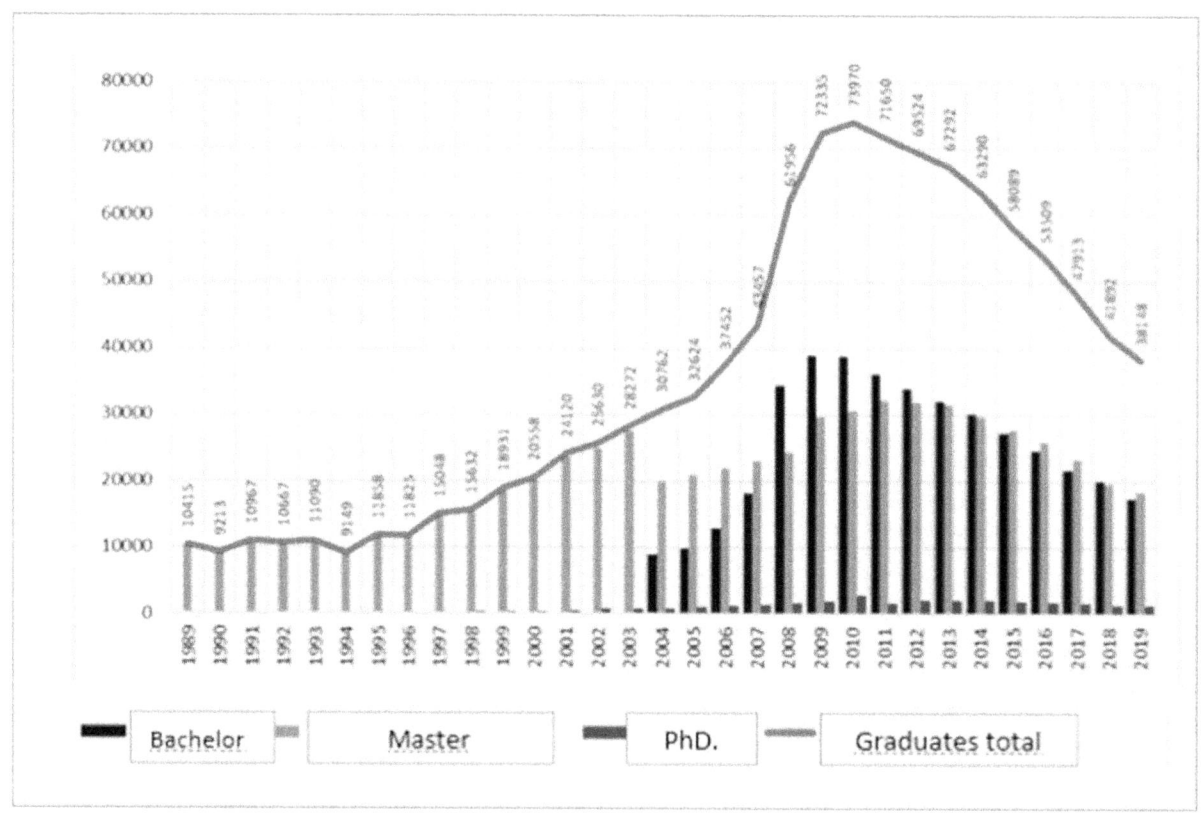

The quality of education is determined by the quality of teachers. The results of the OECD survey had shown that the average age of all teachers in Slovakia is 44 years, of which 82% are women. The share of teachers under the age of 30 is only 8.2%.

SOLUTIONS AND RECOMMENDATIONS

The links between science, research, innovation and a prosperous economy are observed worldwide. The rivalry between the US, the European Union and China in investment in R&D in relation to GDP is growing. China increases the investment and strives for leadership.

In the European Union, the ex aequo leaders in 2020 were Belgium and Sweden, each country invested 3.5% of GDP in R&D. Slovakia, Romania, Malta, Latvia, Cyprus, and Bulgaria took the lowest ranking.

The sustainability and the quality assurance of the R&D employees require suitable conditions in tertiary education. The lack of researchers in Slovakia can be attributed to the neglect of investments in education, causing the departure of smart students for abroad, who do not return after graduation.

The innovation of education can be seen in several EU countries which, along with the modernization of education, generate a large number of graduates, spend more expenditures on R&D, and establish motivating conditions for graduates and talents. Countries investing in innovation, research and development have more prosperous and competitive economies.

The quality of R&D is affected by qualified researchers and sufficient volume of investments. With insufficient funding high-quality researchers cannot be retained, and there will be no willingness to invest without high-quality human capital. Both factors are the initial impulses of the innovativeness of the country.

Table 10. Investments in research and development in Slovakia as the percent of GDP

	2014	2015	2016	2017	2018	2019	2020
R&D investments as a percent of GDP	0,88%	1,16%	0,79%	0,89%	0,84%	0,83%	0,92%

Source: own processing according to the EUROSTAT database

The ratio of investments in R&D to GDP (Table 10) shows that Slovakia will hardly achieve the projected goal. Between 2014 and 2020, investments increased by only 0.13% of GDP. In 2015, investments exceeded 1% of GDP, but because of the implementation of EU Structural and Investment funds. The largest share of investment comes from business and government sources. The EU average in government sources is around 29%, but in Slovakia up to 40%.

Figure 5 presents the regions' expenditures in research and development. The Bratislava Region, as the smallest region, spends up twice as much investment in R&D compared to Western Slovakia, which is the second in order. Compared to Eastern Slovakia, the difference is more than threefold. In 2020, expenditures in the Bratislava Region exceeded 393,853,000 euros, surpassing the expenditures in 2015. The first rank can be attributed to the concentration of researchers and research institutions in Bratislava.

In Eastern Slovakia with two large cities, Košice and Prešov, the level of investment is the worst. Eastern Slovakia is considered unattractive by foreign direct investors who prefer Western Slovakia or other countries. Insufficient infrastructure and unsuitable conditions for retaining talents could be the reasons. Search for investors in Eastern Slovakia and mitigation of regional differences in R&D is a long-term mission of all stakeholders.

Figure 5. Research and development expenditures of Slovakia´s regions (2014 – 2020) [in €]
Source: own processing according to EUROSTAT database

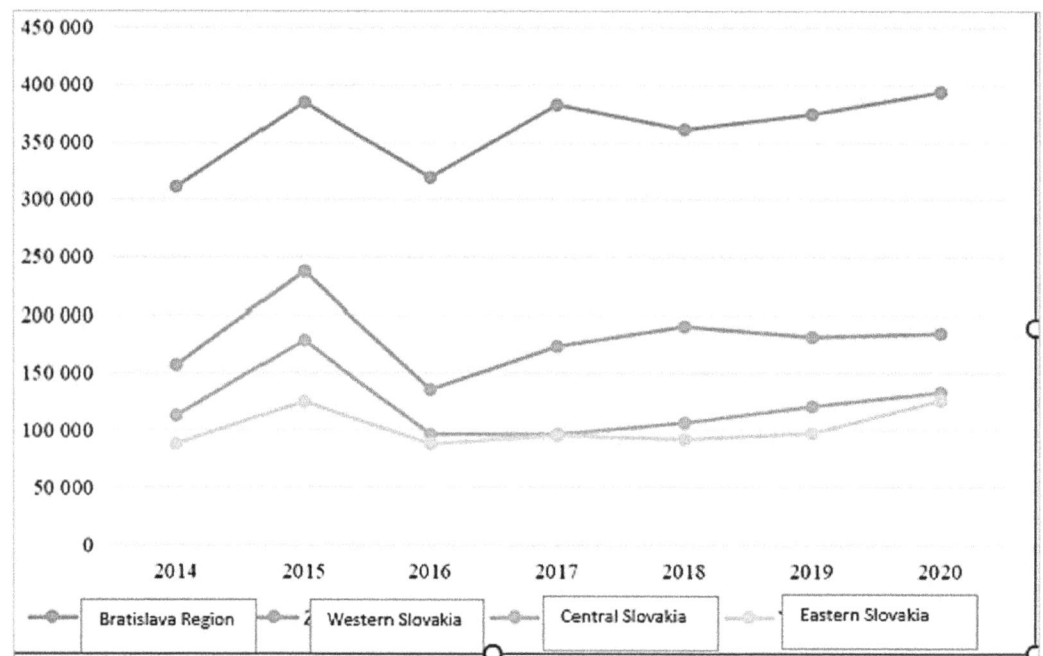

Research and development expenditures allocated to NUTS 2 regions are highly differentiated (Table 11).

Western Slovakia reports the highest number of enterprises, especially SMEs. The business sector, with more than 70%, is the largest source of investment. The smallest share comes from non-profit organizations. The government sector contributes the least compared to other regions.

In 2020, the Bratislava Region with the second highest number of SMEs and the highest share of large enterprises received the lowest financial support from the government sector (30.9%). A significant share came from foreign sources, as foreign investors consider the region to be the most attractive.

Central Slovakia has a relatively balanced ratio of investments from business and government sources, (approximately 41%). A relatively high share of investment comes from universities in the region. Non-profit organizations participate to the highest extent.

Eastern Slovakia invests the least. Funding sources come mainly from business and government. Almost 17% comes from foreign sources, which is only 1% less than in the Bratislava region.

The funding in R&D divided by research fields show that technical sciences received the largest share. Technical sciences include fields such as construction, mechanical engineering, information technologies and electrical engineering, which are the most represented sectors. Western Slovakia invested the most in technical sciences. The second most supported field was agriculture, with a key impact on the quality of life.

Sciences such as mathematics, physics, chemistry, biology, and Earth sciences received the most funding in the Bratislava Region with nine university faculties focused on science. The least supported field was agriculture. Technical sciences received a significant share of funding. Medical sciences, social sciences and humanities significantly exceed other regions.

Table 11. Research and development expenditures by NUTS 2 regions in Slovakia [in thousands €]

	2014	2015	2016	2017	2018	2019	2020
SK01_Bratislava Region	311 169	384 880	319 931	383 071	360 836	374 848	393 853
SK02_Western Slovakia	157 150	238 126	135 371	173 342	190 773	182 009	184 837
SK03_Central Slovakia	112 787	178 737	97 337	97 054	106 828	121 669	133 361
SK04_Eastern Slovakia	88 527	125 528	88 197	95 488	92 509	98 064	126 876
R&D investment by scientific field in Slovak regions [in thousands €]							
SK01_Bratislava Region	**2014**	**2015**	**2016**	**2017**	**2018**	**2019**	**2020**
Sciences	80 201	102 845	70 155	112 995	120 087	120 741	152 128
Technical sciences	122 386	145 578	162 605	194 911	166 198	167 099	139 006
Medical and pharmaceutical sciences	36 884	28 776	25 344	23 114	20 954	24 614	36 750
Agricultural sciences	0	5 513	5 718	6 369	5 946	8 349	4 505
Social sciences	51 277	84 941	38 895	26 284	26 979	29 987	34 051
Humanities	20 421	17 229	17 214	19 398	20 674	24 058	27 414
SK02_Western Slovakia	**2014**	**2015**	**2016**	**2017**	**2018**	**2019**	**2020**
Science	7 864	14 170	12 294	13 515	7 620	7 911	9 173
Technical sciences	96 379	139 205	80 808	120 048	145 328	136 365	142 511
Medical and pharmaceutical science	2 937	10 785	3 159	3 252	3 461	3 062,834	3 187
Agricultural science	33 301	50 223	26 240	22 904	20 520	18 572,541	12 868
Social sciences	6 816	17 900	6 603	6 761	6 544	6 953,040	7 497
Humanities	9 853	5 841	6 266	6 863	7 302	9 145,350	9 600
SK03_Central Slovakia	**2014**	**2015**	**2016**	**2017**	**2018**	**2019**	**2020**
Sciences	7 946	12 330	6 660	6 251	7 352	9 209	10 856
Technical science	71 633	127 281	68 814	71 102	77 556	89 428	90 136
Medical and pharmaceutical sciences	19 786	24 031	7 773	6 001	6 908	7 939,833	15 128
Agricultural science	4 689	5 605	4 506	4 468	4 800	5 504,515	6 897
Social sciences	3 993	3 903	4 321	4 453	4 814	4 897	5 451
Humanities	4 739	5 587	5 264	4 780	5 399	4 688	4 894
SK04_Eastern Slovakia	**2014**	**2015**	**2016**	**2017**	**2018**	**2019**	**2020**
Sciences	22 995	18 479	15 145	13 747	14 092	19 148	16 532
Technical sciences	36 154	33 258	45 137	49 364	52 276	58 859	88 331
Medical and pharmaceutical sciences	7 216	5 751	6 326	5 797	4 867	4 831	5 190
Agricultural science	8 488	12 548	3 824	5 401	4 841	3 784	4 430
Social sciences	7 131	52 172	13 706	16 494	10 584	5 379	6 735
Humanities	6 543	3 302	4 058	4 685	5 848	6 062	5 659

Source: EUROSTAT, online data code: RD_E_GERDTOT

Technical sciences were the most funded in Central Slovakia, which exceeded other scientific fields tenfold. Medical sciences focusing on human health, diagnosis and treatment of diseases were in second place. Humanities received the lowest support.

In Eastern Slovakia, technical sciences received the most, sciences ranked in second place, other fields were financed at approximately the same level. The region is the least subsidized region.

FUTURE RESEARCH DIRECTIONS

Investment in R&D is directly related to employees. The number of R&D employees in the EU is increasing. The number of R&D employees in Slovakia is increasing yearly (Figure 6). In 2020, this number represented 22,404.6 workers in FTE equivalent, of which 31% were males.

In 2020, the sector of higher education employed 45.6% of researchers, the business sector 35.9%, the government sector 18,4% (4,127), the non-profit sector 0.05% of all employees. The number of employees in R&D represented 0.81% of the total workforce in Slovakia. The EU average is 1.44%. Slovakia is below the EU average, and the worst among the V4 countries. The Czech Republic, with a share of 1.54% of the total labour force, was the only V4 country to exceed the EU average.

In the period 2014 - 2020, the number of R&D employees in FTE equivalent increased continuously, the highest number in 2020 was reached in the Bratislava Region (10,588.8). Western Slovakia with 4,396 employees in 2016-2017 had the second highest share of employees and employed 56 additionally by 2020. In Eastern Slovakia, the number of employees did not differ significantly, in 2020 it crossed the limit of the four thousand, approaching to the level of Western Slovakia. Central Slovakia recorded the lowest number of employees, while the highest number was in 2019 (3,255.3), followed by a decrease in 2020 (3,187.4).

Figure 6. Number of employees in R & D in Slovak regions in 2014-2020 [in FTE]
Source: own processing according to the Yearbook on Science and Technology of the Slovak Republic, 2021

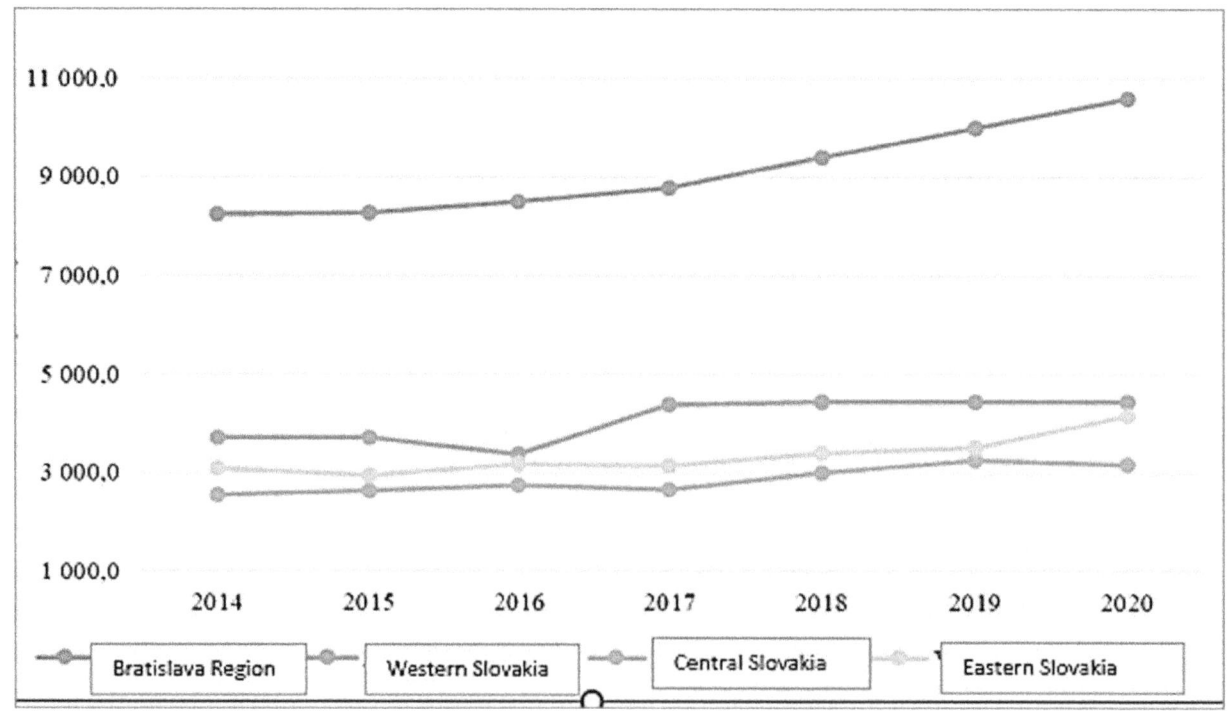

Human resources in science and technology (HRST) represent employees with the third level of university education or university graduation. Figure 7 shows the percentage of the workforce in science and technology from the total workforce in Slovakia´s regions. The leader is the Bratislava Region with a high concentration of researchers, universities, and research institutions. The second rank was taken by Eastern Slovakia, apparently with the contribution of the Technical University in Košice. In 2017, Western, Central and Eastern Slovakia reached almost the same level in this indicator. The Bratislava Region ranked above the EU average, but Slovakia as a whole took one of the lowest ranks with 17.3% of the total workforce.

Figure 7. Human resources in science and technology in Slovak regions in 2014 – 2020 [in %]
Source: own processing according to the EUROSTAT database

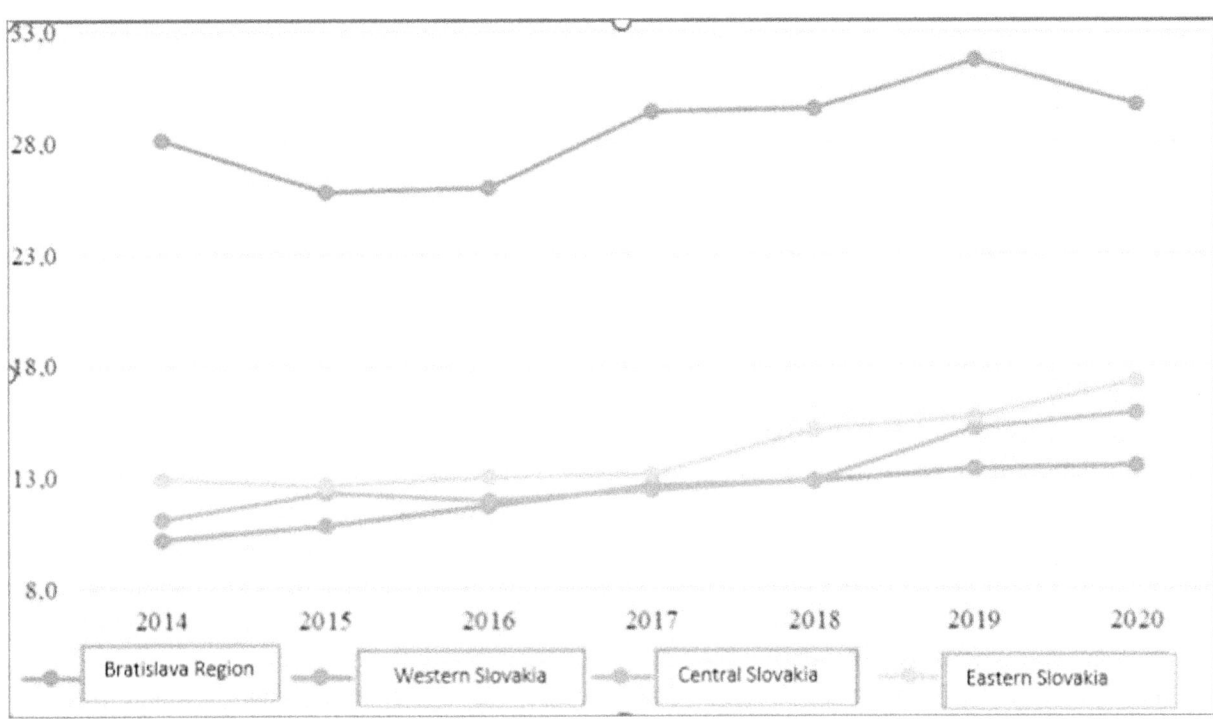

The neglect of funding in education and the imbalance between the demand and the supply of graduates on labour markets may cause a shortage of R&D employees. Some graduates do not meet the requirements of innovation activities and are not prepared for the Industry4.0 paradigm.

The reform of education becomes a necessity with the advent of the Industry4.0 paradigm focusing on digitization, up-to-date formal education and lifelong vocational development, technological knowledge, and skills.

The Recovery and Resilience Plan as the EU financial instrument is intended to help restart the economy and contribute to Slovakia´s innovativeness and competitiveness. This financial package with 6.575 billion euros can be implemented until 2026. The acquisition of funds is determined by the approved objectives.

The above analysis of innovation performance indicated that the Recovery and Resilience Plan needs to focus on science, research, and innovation. According to the Slovak Government decree, the plan will focus on selected areas (Table 12).

Table 12. Recovery and Resilience Plan: Distribution of funds

Reforms and investments	Share of investment [in mil. €]
Better health	1533
Green economy	2301
Effective public administration and digitalisation	1110
Quality education	892
Science, research, and innovations	739
Total	6575

Source: own processing due to the Recovery and Resilience Plan

CONCLUSION

The assessment of innovation potential of Slovakia and Slovak regions was carried out in accordance validated results in European Innovation Scoreboard and Regional Innovation Scoreboard. Comparisons with EU and V4 countries revealed the shortcomings, including low investment in innovation potential in Slovakia's regions, especially R&D, the insufficient number of university graduates apt for R&D, insufficient saturation of labour market requirements, inflexible education reforms in terms of digitization and the Industry4.0 paradigm.

Elimination of regional disparities is associated with economic development, job creation, R&D investments, and favourable conditions for the retention of talents and workforce. The Recovery and Resilience Plan represents an open challenge for decision-makers at central and regional levels of governance, business entities, universities, and employers' associations with the aim to support the innovative environment and innovative potential.

More effective management and funding of R&D, green and digital transformation, smart mobility, smart cities and regions, IT, cyber-security, biotechnologies, and green technologies are expected to facilitate innovations and strengthen innovative potential of Slovakia.

ACKNOWLEDGMENT

This research was funded by Bratislava University of Economics and Management, Slovak Republic, grant number 1/2021-M: Circular economy is an accelerator of the transition to a climate-neutral economy.

REFERENCES

European Commission. (2021a). *European Innovation Scoreboard 2021*. Author.

European Commission. (2021b). *Regional Innovation Scoreboard 2021*. Author.

Eurostat. (2021). *Investment in Research and Development in Slovakia*. Author.

Kollar, V., & Matusova, S. (2019). Manažment inovácií [Innovation management]. Bratislava: VŠEMVS.

Lisy, J. (2016). *Ekonómia* [Economics]. Wolters Kluver.

McKinsey Global Institute. (2021). *56 DELTA skills*. Author.

OECD. (2020). *Strategy for the Slovak Republic (2019-2020)*. OECD.

ADDITIONAL READING

Kollar, V. (2021). *Circular economy is an accelerator of the transition to a climate-neutral economy*. International research project. Bratislava University of Economics and Management. https://www.vsemba.sk/VedaAVyskum/VyskumneProjekty/MedzinarodneProjekty

Yearbook of science and technology of the Slovak Republic. (2021). Statistical Office of the Slovak Republic.

KEY TERMS AND DEFINITIONS

Education Market: Denotes institutions providing services in terms of education, personal and professional growth of employed persons due to training needs and employers´ demands.

Innovation: Denotes a human capacity to produce new ideas and solutions projected into design, production, distribution and use of products, services, processes, systems, and social relations.

Innovation Potential as Composite Indicator: Denotes the capacity of human capital to contribute with innovative ideas to innovativeness and competitiveness of countries. Innovation potential is measured by innovation scoreboard. In Europe, European Commission monitors EU members and other countries in innovation and innovation potential annually and produces ranking lists.

Labour Market: Denotes the market with the workforce supply and employers´ demands. The demands are formulated by businesses, enterprises, and producers due to demands of existing and emerging professions and jobs.

Regional Disparities: Refer to differences and inequalities among regions. They indicate gaps that need to be eliminated. The development of regions needs to be addressed by central and regional authorities with the aim to promote human resources development, high-quality education, competitiveness, and innovativeness which are the attractors for investors.

Chapter 10
Common Assessment Framework in the Czech Republic Public Sector:
Main Issues for the Czech Republic Regions and Municipalities

Jan Procházka

Czech Technical University in Prague, Czech Republic

ABSTRACT

This chapter deals with the common assessment framework (CAF) and its application in the local and regional administration in the Czech Republic before the summer of 2022. After a background about how CAF works and should be applied, there are two parts about how the quality policies and CAF are used for the public administration and public sector in the country. The discussion and the solutions and recommendations parts discuss the most important issues found for the topic and for the (future) research itself. A short part about possible future research directions follows up on these issues.

INTRODUCTION

Total quality management (TQM) has been applied in many firms and institutions, but it is complex and expensive. However, it has also advantages for improvement that can be used in the public sector.

The European Foundation for Quality Management (EFQM) adapted the TQM for the needs of institutions in Europe and the EU. Its Excellence model is an efficient way to improve any institution wanting to use this approach.

That is why the Common Assessment Framework (CAF) has been developed for helping the European institutions to have a quality management technique tailored for them. Of course, it has some advantages that are inconveniences from a certain point of view.

DOI: 10.4018/978-1-6684-5976-8.ch010

The main advantage is that it is free, compared to the business versions of quality management. That is probably the biggest advantage that makes this quality management system accessible to any institution anywhere in the world, including NGO's and public administration. That is why it is applied also outside Europe.

Institutions from around the world can ask for help. At the end of 2019, the responsible people for helping with its implementation, the so called EUPAN CAF Correspondents were from EIPA, the European Commission, and 19 EU countries, five other European countries, and other nine non-European countries were "piloting CAF" to help with it worldwide.

In 2022, EIPA, another institution, and 23 European countries had assigned experts to be contacted for assistance – of course, this includes some countries from outside the EU, too. On the website of EIPA, there are no contacts for outside Europe now.

For instance, the Dominican Republic made the CAF mandatory for all public institutions since 2010. That was presented at a conference and published by the European Institute of Public Administration (EIPA) in 2012.

In this paper, we will use the terms "public sector" and "public administration" sometimes as synonyms, although there are some differences. In reality, public administration institutions are a part of public sector. This corresponds to the definition by the Encyclopaedia Britannica. (Wegrich, 2022)

BACKGROUND

CAF and Its Application

The main definition of CAF is used in the latest manual published to help organisations to implement it (EUPAN, EIPA, 2019):

The Common Assessment Framework (CAF) is a total quality management model for self-assessment developed by the public sector for the public sector. The CAF is free of charge and available in the public domain to assist public sector organisations to improve their performance. It has been designed for use in all parts of the public sector, and it is applicable to national/federal, regional and local levels. Although the CAF has been developed in a European context, it can be used in any public organisation all around the world.

As mentioned above, the CAF is a tool to apply quality management techniques. It can be used for continuous improvement by many types of institutions. (Ministry of Information Society and Administration, OSCE, 2017)

The definition confirms it is based on the total quality management (TQM) techniques. Even if designed originally for institutions in the EU and in Europe, it can be used by any institution worldwide – and institutions from other continents using this model can be found, too. (EIPA, 2022)

An example of this worldwide use is the fact that the Dominican Republic made CAF "mandatory" in 2010 by the "Decree 211-10, that specifies that all public institutions should conduct a self-assessment using this model". (EIPA, 2012) However, it was not possible to find out how successful this was and whether it was updated with the other versions of the Common Assessment Framework.

Up to the European Institute of Public Administration (EIPA), founded in 1981 to help diverse administrations in the EC (and EU) to improve their management and public services, there were more than 3000 institutions using CAF in January 2022. (EIPA, 2022)

The first model of CAF was introduced in 2000, although its history is officially dated from 1998. Since then, several major revisions took place. (EIPA, 2021) These revisions are resulting from a long-term development process which continues.

Since 2000, the CAF has been the original European quality improvement tool for the public sector. (Vrabková, 2013) That is probably the main reason, why responsible institutions at both the EU and national levels are trying to motivate their public institutions to implement this model.

In 2020, the fifth version, called CAF2020, has been published. It has been updated, in order to help public institutions using it can better adapt to digitalisation, sustainability, innovation, and become more agile. (EIPA, 2013; Vrabková, 2013)

The main positive results an institution using CAF approach are summed up by EIPA in the following way (EUPAN, EIPA, 2019; EIPA, 2021):

- CAF will help public institutions to know TQM and find ways for improvement;
- It will guide them to use the PDCA cycle (the plan-do-check-act cycle is a tool used in several quality management approaches);
- It will help them to evaluate themselves and diagnose what they can improve, it will also help them to find the ways how;
- The institutions will find it easier to compare mutually and learn from each other,
- And if necessary, they will better understand other models of Quality management (QM).

The CAF (and its model of excellence) consists of 8 principles of excellence (in alphabetical order, EUPAN, EIPA, 2019):

- Citizen/customer focus:
- Continuous innovation and improvement
- Leadership and constancy of purpose
- Management of processes and facts
- Partnership development
- People development and involvement
- Results orientation
- Social responsibility

Other documents put these in a different order (or different orders). However, we decided to put them in alphabetical order – in order to make sure there is no other hierarchy.

Let us sum up the explanation or some comments on some of these (EUPAN, EIPA, 2019; EIPA, 2021):

- **Citizens are the main customers**, and as in other types of quality management – the main stakeholders – of public administration. The first principle is logical in this way. However, as the model can be used by other institutions of the public sector, and in theory by any institution, it is still better to use "customer" in general.

- **Continuous improvement**, accompanied by **innovation**, is something that basically all quality management models have. It is what makes them work, and public sector institutions using quality management systems, too.
- **Leadership and constancy of purpose** are also characteristics that all well working institutions should have, and public institutions for sure. This is valid for all levels of these institutions.
- **Management of processes and facts** – as for other quality management techniques, processes (and facts) are the way to improve, or more exactly what is to be improved. No institution can be easily continually improved, unless divided logically – and the most logical way are processes, sometimes added by facts.

At least, a **process in quality management** (Dudek, 2018):

- Is different from other processes,
- Has a start and an end,
- Has input(s) and output(s),
- Is a sequence of steps/activities that can be defined and separated between them,
- Can be described by words and by a diagram/chart,
- Has an owner that know the process and has ability (power) to influence it and its improvement,
- Can have goals and (key) performance indicators defined – even for a public institution (example: satisfaction of visitors, number of appeals, etc.).

For improving processes, it must be possible to know them and their parts. No process is a "black box," but is clear to the institution. (Dudek, 2018) Like all the most important quality management techniques, CAF helps its implementing organisation by improving its processes.

For quality management, it is sufficient to know and improve (at least) the important processes. Every institution defines which processes are to be included. Quality management process should be a part of it. (Dudek, 2018)

Let us mention some key processes that could be included for some examples of public institutions:

- In the case of a public school, the main processes can include teaching, food for employees and students, facility management, administration;
- For a grant distributing institution, there will be processes of accepting and dealing with the applications.
  1. **Partnership development** for public institutions can be misunderstood as including only partner cities (regions) or institutions, but it should focus on other stakeholders in general, too. For some activities, ministries must cooperate with other ministries or institutions, like the statistical office, the central government, municipalities, regions, the police, trade unions, interest groups, non-governmental organizations, the press, etc. These are partners, too. Firms that supply some services to these institutions, as well.
  2. **People development and involvement** are key notions of every quality management system. People should know and participate at it, for the system to work. On the other hand, their development is important for their participation and motivation – it includes personal development, professional one, but also their updating of the quality management and other needs and requirements.

3. **Results orientation** – when describing a process, we mentioned goals and indicators. These are following the main results of every process included in the quality management system (QMS) of the institution. This should be clear – if we can control results and compare them historically or otherwise, we can evaluate and improve.
4. **Social responsibility** is a necessity for every institution, for the public sector in particular. Their activities should have sense and some positive surplus for all stakeholders, i.e. each activity for most of them. This would depend on the relative externalities. In nowadays EU and most other European countries, social responsibility policies and activities are a necessity for most institutions that want to be active and have chances to grow.

The CAF itself is based on nine criteria: leadership, people, strategy and planning, partnerships and resources, processes, people results, citizen/customer-oriented results, social responsibility results, and key performance results. These are divided into two halves: Enablers (the first five of them) and Results (the remaining four), as it is shown on Figure 1.

Figure 1. The CAF model
Source: EIPA (2021)

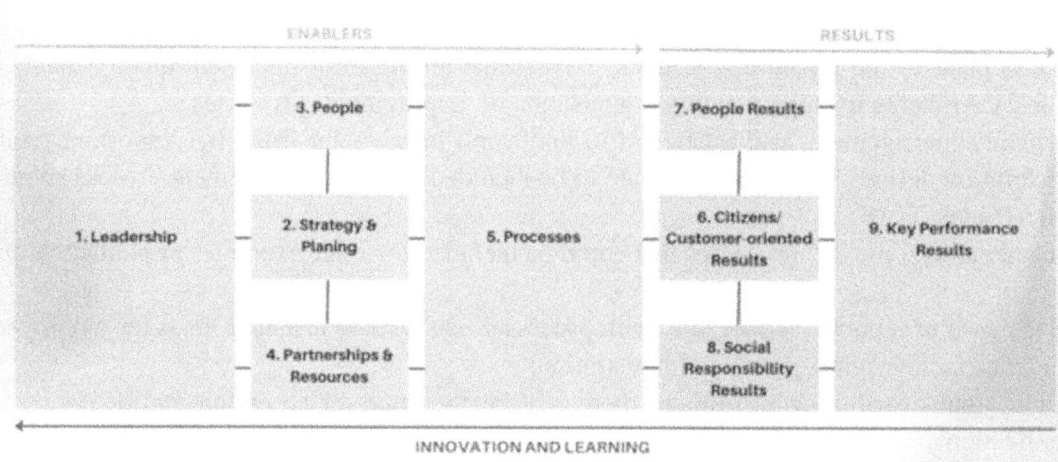

Using this model helps to see what sources (enablers) have effect on the outcomes (results), and to find what can be improved to have wished effects. (Ministry of Information Society and Administration, OSCE, 2017)

Of course, many inputs regarding possible improvements are originated from internal feedback. This comes from different ways of assessment, from the employees, etc. (Ministry of Information Society and Administration, OSCE, 2017)

As for other quality management approaches, external feedback helps to find other inputs for improvement. This can be done not only by surveys and direct asking of customers/clients, but also from other stakeholders: these include partner institutions, suppliers, etc.

External feedback can be structured, too. The CAF External Feedback Procedure is what is proposed from the CAF approach to perform it better. It proposes six major goals / objectives a good external feedback should have (EUPAN, EIPA, 2019; EIPA, 2021):

1. To support the CAF quality system of the organisation,
2. To control if the CAF (and TQM) values are well implemented,
3. Increase "enthusiasm" for continuous improvement and the CAF quality management system,
4. Promote learning between organisations and peer reviewing,
5. Reward for a good CAF quality management system (rewarding organisations),
6. Improve the CAF users' participation in the excellence models of CAF / EFQM

EIPA proposes CAF users to register, but this register is not compulsory (EIPA, 2022). That does not help to:

*   Have statistics about implementation;
*   Have better feedback about the CAF approach;
*   Promote the wished cooperation between institutions;
*   Promote learning from each other.

This is partially solved by an award system and some publications to highlight best practices, and some lists available on the EIPA website. This is completed by some lists of institutions that apply the system. (EIPA, 2022)

Some information is also findable on the websites or some responsible institutions. An example is the Ministry of Interior in the Czech Republic. It has a specialised webpage to inform about the CAF and some of its issues, including its implementation.

However, from questions sent by the researcher to EIPA and several other institutions, it is practically impossible to know (or even estimate) the number of the CAF users. This is valid even for the countries, where the central government institutions strongly support quality management in the public sector.

This is the case of the Czech Republic. There was a strong support to all public administration (and other) institutions to apply CAF, Lately, it changed into an obligation (as explained in the further text). The responsible Ministry hopes to be able to work better with it now, as a representant of the Ministry answered to the researcher.

The Czech Republic Ministry of Interior made a study in 2016 to have an overview, as a part of their strategic framework for the years 2014-2020 to support better quality in the public sector, including with the help of the CAF approach.

This strategy was even helped by official documents, including methodical guidelines – to help at least government institutions of all levels to perform it. This guideline was published in 2017, as a result of the strategic framework, too.

Besides the introduction of the PDCA cycle and self-assessment, the CAF is supposed to help the public institutions using it to cooperate and compare their results – to benchmark. This benchmarking can help them a lot: Public administration institutions should be comparable in much an easier way than for example firms.

Self-assessment was and is the main tool of CAF to control and guarantee the quality management system in the organisation. It replaces the audits that are done in other quality management approaches. Of course, self-assessment is les structured, deep, and less objective than audits, but it can be sufficient for improving the processes and the system of management of the institution.

For the business QMS approaches, internal audits prepare for external audits, and are a condition for passing the external ones, external audits help business firms to "obtain" certificates. These certificates are guarantees that the QMS of the firm(s) are working and efficient.

The main inconvenient of external audits and certificates are their costs. These costs have their reasons and motivations. However, these costs are quite high, and for many public institutions and NGO's, they would be very expensive.

On the other hand, CAF proposes a system inspired by the Total Quality Management, but for free. This is allowed only by the fact that there are no these external services and guarantees.

That is the main reason why internal assessment is the key activity of the CAF to guarantee the working and efficiency of the QMS in question, of the public sector institution.

The internal assessment is done in two main parts – that is the reason of the division of the CAF model factors to enablers and results. These parts are logically connected and structured in a way that allows the assessment to replace an (internal more than external) audit in a cheaper, but acceptable way.

First part of the criteria are enablers. The enablers criteria (Leadership, People, Strategy and planning, Partnerships and resources, Processes) are very important to see how the institution in question works and deals with its inputs. In other words, the enablers work with the inputs of the institution that are necessary for its management.

The results criteria (Citizen/Customer-oriented Results, People Results, Social Responsibility Results, Key Performance Results) on the other hand, are focused on the perception – how the respective institution is perceived by "our people, our people, citizens/customers and society".

The last criterium, Key Performance Results, is basically similar to the key performance indicators used for business processes, or in general for processes of the business QMS approaches (with certificates): These would be used for public sector institutions wishing to have a certificate of a business QMS. There are such institutions, too.

Each of the enablers has its own sub-criteria (EIPA, 2022):

1. Criterion 1 (Leadership) has 4 sub-criteria
2. Criterion 2 (People) has 4 sub-criteria
3. Criterion 3 (Strategy and planning) has 3 sub-criteria
4. Criterion 4 (Partnerships and resources) has 6 sub-criteria
5. Criterion 5 (Processes) has 3 sub-criteria
6. Criterion 6 (Citizen/Customer-oriented Results) has 2 sub-criteria
7. Criterion 7 (People Results) has 2 sub-criteria
8. Criterion 8 (Social Responsibility Results) has 2 sub-criteria
9. Criterion 9 (Key Performance Results) has 2 sub-criteria

These 28 criteria are something similar to audits of the business Quality management systems – but there are more simply defined and in a simpler structure. This makes the system more simple, cheaper to work with, but still sufficient.

This is quite logical – public institutions have a different system of management and different (key) processes than many other institutions. However, it does not say that the internal audit criteria and questions an institution having a business QMS would (in principle) always differ a lot from a public institution.

In the same way, a public institution passing from CAF to a business QMS approach, in the other direction, or combining them, can expect that the change (in its principle) between an audit and an assessment will be less important, assuming the processes are kept. This is logical, as the CAF comes from the TQM – and it should follow a similar logic. (Vrabková, 2013)

It is helpful to have a National CAF Resource Centre like in Macedonia. It serves as a contact point and a coordinator at the same time. (Ministry of Information Society and Administration, OSCE, 2017) It can help implementing and interested institutions to know more about the system.

Quality and CAF in the Czech Republic

Kadeřábková (2007, p. 17) assessed the quality of Czech Republic institutions. The biggest challenges and problems were with the enforcement of standards in general. Though, this was when CAF was in its first phases of its evolution and implementation.

Kadeřábková (2007, p. 47) show a slight improvement of institutional quality in the Czech Republic between 1995 and 2005, with worsening the relative position in the ranking between the EU and European countries by one place, up to the World Bank data. Connected to the former source, it shows an improvement, even if the quality management for public institutions was not so much standardised and comparable, too.

Hák and Janoušková (2020, p. 29) quote their source saying that qualitative regional development is to be done by intensive development. They say it happens when, in a democratic country, citizens "have the possibility to decide between individual visions and directions of development".

Hák and Janoušková (2020, p. 30) mean that qualitative development in decision-making includes not only the assessment of own development, but also comparing with other institutions, on the same level, and on other levels.

For self-assessment, the public institutions should use mainly "performance indicators" and use – besides political goals and their evaluation – also "sustainable reference values". These are derived from sustainable development principles and aligned to regional and country government strategic goals. Also, descriptive indicators and benchmarking are to be used for efficient self-assessment. (Hák and Janoušková, 2020, pp. 34-5)

Malá (2020, pp 98-99) discuss the main goals for regional development, as stated by the EU Commission for the period after 2020. One of the five goals relates to the support of "local development strategies and sustainable development". Between 65 and 85% of European Regional Development Fund (ERDF) and Cohesion Fund (CF) finances go to supporting these five goals. These are supported also by other financial sources of the European Union.

These supports are certainly influencing the goals of Czech national authorities and, via them, of regional and local administrations. That is also why the goals of development and improvement of the administrations on local and regional levels are influenced by these policies.

Effective Policy for Quality Public Administration in the Czech Republic

The Czech government tries to make all the levels of the public administration focus and improve their quality. There has been a push to the lower levels to choose and adopt at least one of several possible approaches of improvement.

Regarding quality management itself, it is exactly the CAF that the public sector should adopt and perform. The Common Assessment Framework should help all the levels.

To help this the central government approved a strategic document called Efektivní veřejná správa a přátelské veřejné služby (Effective Public Administration and Friendly Public Services). This document was approved by a decree in 2007 and is still valid.

In a similar way to the EIPA practices, there is a Czech award for public administrations applying quality management and improvement. This award should support the overall policy. If and how it supports the policy, is not published.

One of the apart categories for this year (2022) is CAF. As for other categories, only the three top winners are published. This is not much – as it is even not published how many institutions participated in this category.

In the 2020 and 2021 editions, there was no such category, up to the website on the quality policy in the Czech Republic. In those year only once, a region was rewarded – the Liberec region in the category of "Digital state".

From the websites and documents of the Czech central government (namely organised by the Ministry of the Interior of the Czech Republic), it can be seen that the public sector quality development policy is focused to the regional and municipality levels. it can be seen from the focus of the 2017 conference on the quality of the public sector.

At the same time, there are not many actual documents and information on the results. These are mainly on the level of municipalities. This is logical, as the municipalities make a strong majority of public institutions in the country.

Basically, at this central level, there is not much information about the quality management of the regions. The number of regions is much lower, so it could be easier to gather and publish such information.

In the document Systém měření a hodnocení veřejné správy za rok 2020 (System of Measurement and Assessment of Public Administration for the year 2020), which comments on the measurements of the public administration, we can only see that 100% of regions had a valid strategy development plan in 2020 – this for the region. That could be promising for the quality management and continuous improvement.

At the same time, only 14,29% of regions have a strategic development plan for the development of the administration (office). As there are 14 regions, it amounts to two regions having such a strategy. This can be understood in the way that most probably, maximum these 2 regions are implementing some quality management – hopefully. However, we cannot identify these two regions from this document, and it was not possible to find them in the public information. This is not good for the research and mainly for other institutions to learn and improve from two regions they probably cannot identify.

As an answer from a responsible employee from the Ministry of the Interior of the Czech Republic wrote answered the researcher that all public administration institutions ("service administrations") had to start applying at least some "minimal" quality measures up to the Methodical Manual by June 2022.

They had more possibilities how to apply these, including different methodologies and ways. In the proposed list, CAF was the first mentioned. Nowadays, CAF is one of the three most preferred ways, it can be combined with the other ones.

A public call was issued and (at least) 15 institutions were supported through this call to implement CAF. The deadline for this implementation is March 2023, so we have to wait for the results.

As a part of the 2022 Czech Presidency of the Council of the European Union, two actions regarding CAF were planned to take place in September and October 2022: A meeting of CAF national correspondents and a conference of CAF users. This research was concluded before it took place. Moreover, this meeting was focused on the EU level.

To questions of the researcher, EIPA answered that their database of CAF users should be updated and available again in September 2022. Of course, this register is voluntary and so not complete, but in cooperation with the 2022 Czech Presidency of the Council of the European Union plans, it can help better cooperation between and improvement of the institutions using CAF in the member states of the European Union at least.

Both answers confirmed that it is not possible to say the numbers of CAF users in the Czech Republic and in the EU, or worldwide. That makes deeper research more difficult or less efficient.

DISCUSSION

The main inputs and the core activity to guarantee the CAF quality management system is the internal assessment. It replaces internal audits, from paid and certified quality management approaches with paid external audits and certificates.

This is a big advantage for the institutions, as it allows them to have good quality continuous improvement: They can normally perform quality management, based on their needs, and it remains free at the same time.

On the other hand, this is advantage can be less "profitable" for public sector institutions that do not make part of the government and administration institutions in their pure meaning, between others:

- Public institutions that provide services for the public sector and have to take part in the tenders: In the EU, it is often required to have a quality management certificate, for which they must do other quality management approaches and pay for external audits and certificates;
- Public sector institutions and NGO's that apply for grants, subsidies, etc., which often happens via competitions and tenders: Again, if they do not have a quality management certificate, their chances to win financial or other support are diminished;
- All institutions applying only CAF – for the main reason they cannot "independently" proof the level of their quality management (lack of external certificate) to any stakeholder, with similar consequences as in the former two points, just up to the stakeholder or situation in question.

As mentioned, the CAF approach does not know external audit, a requirement for certification for business firms and institutions that need certificates. That makes the risks mentioned in the paragraph above, but it also has other risks.

Between others, there is a risk it makes the quality management activities more subjective and the goals and results done inefficiently of in "wrong directions": If all decisions are made and judged mostly internally, they can be biased.

This can have for effect lower motivation of the employees to participate in the CAF quality management system and support its activities. This can make the objectives and relative improvements less achievable.

The CAF documentation is not translated even to all EU languages, as seen from the EIPA website. It is translated only into the biggest languages. As it is not under the EU rules directly, it should not be a big issue.

However, EU Member States do not make it compulsory. As it is voluntary, there is no relevant and reliable register of the institutions using the system. Therefore, it is hard for anyone to know, how many institutions implement the CAF.

From the EIPA website, it seems there are no contacts for assistance outside the EU, which contradicts the "manual" mentioning several countries outside the EU "piloting CAF". As a result, we can find an article about the implementation in the Dominican Republic, but that is basically all a stakeholder can learn. Also, a non-European country can probably not easily get support and help in implementing the system.

From the documents available on the respective websites, the Czech award for public administration institutions applying quality management was formerly focused in a different way and changed the categories awarded. (*Quality Council*, 2022)

This award publishes only the "winners" – three first places in each category. The categories before the change did not allow to know much about the participants. (*Quality Council*, 2022)

The categories were changed, in favour of information about CAF. That makes that in one new category, the CAF one, a more than six thousand municipalities and fourteen regions can compete. That does not give a high chance to a region to be in the top three – even if we assume not all the municipalities compete for the award. (*Quality Council*, 2022)

Formerly, we mentioned that 14% of regions (so two) have a strategic development plan to develop themselves. From this, we can assume only these two probably use the CAF – it is hard to imagine a strategy of improvement without such a plan. Strategic planning is indeed a must in quality management, as mentioned in the official document Metodika zavádění řízení kvality, supporting the central policy of quality development in the Czech public administration (Ministerstvo vnitra ČR, 2017).

From the abovementioned sources, we can see that CAF used to be practised by cities a lot, and probably not much by the regions. The respective older documents from the Ministry of the Interior of the Czech Republic, it shows that CAF was not popular between regions.

SOLUTIONS AND RECOMMENDATION

In the Discussion, we have mentioned risks coming from focus on internal assessment: A free CAF approach tool that can lose objectivity. This can be solved in several ways.

As it can be seen, external feedback is a chance to prevent these setbacks and risks: If it is supported, well done, and considered as important and in a sufficient way, it can result into a good level of quality management.

Another chance to prevent the risks of "only internal assessments" is to better motivate the employees and other stakeholders in participating in the system – both to see what can be improved and find and help the solutions and continuous improvement.

For instance, this can be done by:

- Better motivation of individuals / teams, for instance by a reward system;
- Allow and ensure the anonymity of the inputs: This would probably mean ensuring discretion also to prevent "guessing the author", and probably some respective systematic ways;
- Improving information of the stakeholders about the system and its objectives, results, and so on – good information can "replace" a certificate

That is why it is good that CAF has been made obligatory for all public service institutions. It will allow better quality administration in the future.

At the same time, it will solve the register problems in some way: For public service institutions, it will be clear all are using it.

The planned conference of CAF users under the 2022 Czech Presidency of the Council of the European Union can also be a good solution for the future, if repeated regularly.

It should be analysed if such conferences are to be organised at different levels or regionally, too. This would allow better and regular pair comparison – comparison and exchange of practices with similar conditions.

So, as a main recommendation, it is to organize conferences up to diverse categories – geographic, related to size or other conditions. These conferences should be free and accessible to all institutions. Their results might also be better published.

FUTURE RESEARCH DIRECTIONS

Future research can have different levels and directions. Let us mention some of them – at least those that can be considered as the most important ones for the close future.

As mentioned in the text above, updated registers should be published by EIPA this year. That allows to make quantitative research comparing the countries or regions.

It will also allow to perform qualitative (and other quantitative) research by being able to contact different (types of) institutions applying CAF, not only from the public service sector, but also regarding all (types of) institutions that apply the Common Assessment Framework and publish this information in the EIPA register.

Regarding the research of the Czech Republic institutions, the fact that all public service institutions had to start implementing CAF since this summer, the main focus of studying them will probably be mostly qualitative.

Qualitative research regarding CAF of similar institutions can focus on different levels, for instance the different aspects of their decision making regarding the setting of their quality management system.

CONCLUSION

As we saw, the CAF seems to be a usable tool for enhancing and performing quality policy in the public sector institutions in Europe. In principle, CAF is derived from the EFQM, the European version of TQM

CAF is free and voluntary, with self-assessment instead of an audit. It makes it less deep and elaborated than even an internal audit, and less objective, but there is also no certificate. On the other hand, any organisation can implement the system with very low costs.

We saw that there are problems in the implementation by even public administration. The registers that should help them to learn from each other are not compulsory, and therefore, not sufficient.

The Czech Republic copied some techniques for the promotion from EIPA, including the register and awards. However, these seem not sufficient and do hot help other institutions to implement the system- even not to motivate them.

In the end, the Ministry of Interior in the Czech Republic has pushed the system as obligatory for all public administration institutions from 2022. The results of this move will be available only later, not before 2023.

Seeing some of the problems the Common Assessment Framework has, mainly due to its voluntary (before the new obligation) and other characteristics, compared to the business systems, we proposed some solutions and recommendations for the development of quality management of the public sector in the Czech Republic.

Also, as the research on this topic is relatively new (also due to the youth of the CAF quality management system), many possible research directions exist. Again, some of the most important ones were mentioned in this paper.

REFERENCES

Dudek, M. (2018). *Procesní přístup. Kvalita jednoduše* [Process approach. Quality simply]. Online on 25.6.2022 from https://kvalita-jednoduse.cz/procesni-pristup/

EIPA. (2012). *CAF as guiding model for the public administration management in Dominican Republic.* European Institute of Public Administration. https://www.EIPA.eu/

EIPA. (2021). *What is CAF.* European Institute of Public Administration. EIPA. https://www.EIPA.eu/

EIPA. (2022). *About us.* European Institute of Public Administration. EIPA. https://www.EIPA.eu

EUPAN. EIPA. (2019). *CAF2020. Common Assessment Framework. The European model for improving public organisations through self-assessment.* European Public Administration Network (EUPAN), European Institute of Public Administration (EIPA). www.EIPA.eu

Hák, T., & Janoušková, S. (2020). Indikátory kvality života v regionech [Quality of life indicators in regions]. In *Regiony budoucnosti – spolupráce, bezpečí, efektivity: Inspirace pro rozvoj měst a regionů s příklady dobré praxe [Regions of the future—cooperation, safte, efficiency: Inspiration for the development of cities and regions with examples of good practice.].* Grada Publishing.

Kadeřábková, A. (2007). *Růst, stabilita a konkurenceschopnost III. Česká republika v globalizované a znalostní ekonomice* [Growth, stability, and competitiveness III. The Czech Republic in a globalized and knowledge-based economy]. Linde.

Malá, L. (2020). Financování refionálního rozvoje [Financing of Regional Development]. In *Regiony budoucnosti – spolupráce, bezpečí, efektivity: Inspirace pro rozvoj měst a regionů s příklady dobré praxe [Regions of the future cooperation, safety, and efficiency: Inspiration for the development of cities and regions with examples of good practices]*. Grada Publishing.

Ministerstvo vnitra ČR. (2017). *Metodika zavádění řízení kvality ve služebních úřadech: Podpora profesionalizace a kvality státní služby a státní správy* [Methodology for Implementing Quality Management in Service Offices: Promoting Professionalization and Quality of the Civil Service and Public Administration]. Czech Ministry of Interior.

Ministry of Information Society and Administration. (2017). Improving the Quality of the Public Sector Through the Common Assessment Framework (CAF). Ministry of Information Society and Administration & OSCE.

Quality Council. (2022). *Program CAF. Oficiální portál Rady kvality ČR* [Official portal of the Quality Council of the Czech Republic]. Quality Council. https://www.narodniportal.cz

Vrabková, I. (2013). Quality Management in Public Sector: Perspectives of Common Assessment Framework Model in the European Union. *ACTA VŠFS, 7.*

Wegrich, K. (2022). *Public Sector*Encyclopaedia Britannica. https://www.britannica.com/topic/public-sector

KEY TERMS AND DEFINITIONS

CAF: Common assessment framework.
EFQM: European Foundation for Quality Management.
EIPA: European Institute of Public Administration.
MV ČR: Ministry of the Interior of the Czech Republic.
Public Sector: Institutions owned or controlled by the government.
TQM: Total quality management.

Section 4

Turkey:
The Door to Europe and Asia

Chapter 11
Regional Growth Model With Spatial Externalities

Merve Baysoy

https://orcid.org/0000-0003-1068-7507

Istanbul Bilgi University, Turkey

ABSTRACT

This chapter presents a spatially augmented growth model that includes technological interdependence among regions to consider locational and neighbourhood effects on growth. The role of space, which can be defined in several ways, plays an important role in economic growth processes. The different types of tests allow the authors to determine the spatial dependence in regional data and specify an appropriate model. The characteristics of neighbours may stimulate or hamper the economic growth rate of a country. The spillover effects of a country are a substantial issue for a regional perspective in the economic growth process. The economic growth of a country is affected by the performance of growth rate of its neighbours. The economic growth rates depend on both region and neighbouring region characteristics, the weight matrix, which shows the spatial connectivity structure of regions and the strength of spatial dependence based on model specification.

INTRODUCTION

Economic growth is a wide multidimensional topic. The literature seeks to understand the sources, patterns and dynamics of economic growth and development process. Economic theories of growth have emphasized domestic factors for understanding a country's growth performance and have ignored the interaction among different economies. But economic growth of a country should not be isolated from other countries. The aim of this chapter is to broaden the understanding of the interdependence of economic growth of countries within a region. The objective is to analyse the influence of space connections between growth rate of countries. In this context, for practical and convenient mechanism to analyse diverging growth experiences across nations, the spatial econometrics is used, which has evolved and become integrated the economic growth literature. Spatial econometrics allows to analyse the influence

DOI: 10.4018/978-1-6684-5976-8.ch011

of space connections between countries' growth rates. The importance of "space" in an economic growth is an empirical issue that has been taken into consideration recently.

The spatial econometrics is a sub-field of econometrics dealing with spatial interaction effects among geographical units. Tobler (1970) stated the First Law of Geography as: 'everything is related to everything else, but near things are more related than distant thing.' This first law can be counted as a keystone of the fundamental precepts of spatial econometrics. The cost of ignoring spatial dependence variable is relatively high since omitting one or more relevant explanatory variable from a regression will result in biased and inconsistent estimates. Disregarding the role of spatial relationships can underestimate spillover effects and externalities across countries.

The first generation of spatial models was derived for cross-sectional data. The methodologies and specifications developed are mainly related to a two-dimensional approach that refers to observations on cross-sections of regions, cities or countries over several time periods. As Elhorst (2014) notes, spatial panel models can be used in applied economic research to control for relationships over time, space and between units. Panel data are generally more informative, and they contain more variation and less collinearity among the variables. The use of panel data results in a greater availability of degrees of freedom, and hence, increases efficiency in the estimation. In spatial panel data econometric analysis, the spatial autocorrelation coefficient which captures the degree of neighbouring relationships, is defined through the spatial weighting matrices. Given these matrices, one can create and estimate spatial econometric models. A spatial weighting matrix W is a representation of the spatial structure of the data.

This chapter presents a spatially augmented growth model that includes technological interdependence among regions to consider locational and neighbourhood effects on growth. It is organized as follows. First, the derivation of growth equation is presented, and extended to allow for spatial interdependence. Then, different kind of spatial econometric models are introduced. Following that, the spatial weighting matrices and its properties are defined. The presence of spatial dependence and the specification of the econometric models are tested by using the appropriate spatial econometric tools. Lastly, the interpretation of spatial growth regressions with direct and indirect effects are reviewed.

DERIVATION OF GROWTH EQUATION AND SPATIAL EXTERNALITIES

This section starts with the derivation of growth equation that has been used in cross-country regressions to test for convergence across countries and then extend it to allow for spatial interdependence across countries. The standard neo-classical growth model is based on a constant return to scalle production technology combined with a constant saving rate and constant growth rates of technological and population growth. Following Mankiw et al. (1992) (hereinafter MRW) that interprets in terms of country-specific data, and assumes the existence of a Cobb-Douglas production function:

$$Y_{it} = A_{it} K_{it}^{\alpha} L_{it}^{1-\alpha} \quad 0 < \alpha < 1 \tag{1}$$

where Y_{it} is the level of country-specific output (Real GDP), K_{it} denotes the level of capital and L_{it} is labor employed in the country and A_{it} is the country-specific level of labor-augmenting technological progress (total factor productivity). Assume that technology and labor grow at the constant rates g_i and n_i respectively, so that

$$A_{it} = A_{i0} exp(g_i t)$$

$$L_{it} = L_{i0} exp(n_i t)$$

The evolution of the economy is determined by

$$d\tilde{k}_{it} = s_i \tilde{y}_{it} - (n_i + g_i + \delta) \qquad (2)$$

where $\tilde{k}_{it} = K_{it} / (A_{it} L_{it})$ is capital per effective worker, $\tilde{y}_{it} = Y_{it} / (A_{it} L_{it})$ is output per effective worker, assuming a common depreciation rate, δ, of existing capital across countries while using the law of motion of capital per effective worker. At the deterministic steady state, the capital stock per effective worker is given by

$$\tilde{k}_i^* \left[s_i / (n_i + g_i + \delta) \right]^{1/(1-\alpha)} \qquad (3)$$

where s_i is the constant country-specific saving rate as a fraction of output per effective worker.

Substituting this result in the production function (1) and taking the log provides us the following equation for the output per capita $y_{it} = Y_{it}/L_{it}$ at the steady state as

$$\ln(y_{it}) = \ln(A_{i0}) + g_i t + \frac{\alpha}{1-\alpha} \ln \left(\frac{s_i}{n_i + g_i + \delta} \right) \qquad (4)$$

MRW used this equation to show how differing accumulation of capital by saving and population growth can explain the differences in the current per capita incomes across countries. Then by, they suggest including the human capital into production function as another input. Because this augmentation of human capital leads more realistic estimates of α, which shows the elasticity of output with respect to capital.

Next, the endogenous growth equation developed by implementing a log-linear approximation to equation (2) around the steady state (Mankiw et al., 1992, pp. 422-423) as $d\tilde{k}_{it} / dt = \lambda_i \left[\ln(\tilde{k}_i^*) - \ln(\tilde{k}_{it}) \right]$, in turn, yields $d \ln(\tilde{y}_{it}) / dt = \lambda_i \left[\ln(\tilde{y}_i^*) - \ln(\tilde{y}_{it}) \right]$, where $\ln(\tilde{y}_i^*)$ is the steady state level of income per effective worker and $\lambda_i = (1 - \alpha)(n_i + g_i + \delta)$ is convergence rate.

This equation implies that

$$\ln(\tilde{y}_{it}) = (1 - e^{-\lambda_i t}) \ln(\tilde{y}_i^*) + e^{-\lambda_i t} \ln(\tilde{y}_{i0}) \qquad (5)$$

where $\lambda_i > 0$ shows the convergence of effective units output to its steady state and depends on other parameters of the model. Now replace the effective units of output and output per effective units at an initial date by

$$\ln(\tilde{y}_{it}) = \ln(y_{it}) - \ln(A_{i0}) - g_i t$$

$$\ln(\tilde{y}_{i0}) = \ln(y_{i0}) - \ln(A_{i0})$$

then re-write the previous equation as

$$\ln(y_{it}) = g_i t + (1 - e^{-\lambda_i t})\ln(\tilde{y}_i^*) + (1 - e^{-\lambda_i t})\ln(A_{i0}) + e^{-\lambda_i t}\ln(y_{i0}) \tag{6}$$

Define $g_{it} = [\ln(y_{it}) - \ln(y_{i0})]/t$ as the growth rate of output per worker for country i. Then by subtracting $\ln(y_{i0})$ the equation (6) can be written as (see Durlauf et al., 2005);

$$g_{it} = g_i + \beta_{i1}\left(\ln(y_{i0}) - \ln(\tilde{y}_i^*) - \ln(A_{i0})\right) \tag{7}$$

where $\beta_{i1} = -(1 - e^{-\lambda_i t})/t$. In this representation, the coefficient β_{i1} shows that in a cross-section of countries, there should be a negative relationship between average rates of growth and initial output over any time period - countries that start out below their balanced growth path must grow relatively quickly if they are to catch up with other countries that have the same levels of steady-state output per effective worker and initial efficiency. However, this negative coefficient of initial income does not imply conditional convergence, while countries might move toward their own different steady-state growth paths. It requires the development of $\ln(\tilde{y}_i^*)$, while the equation (4) for output per capita at steady state in efficiency levels; then the growth equation becomes like:

$$g_{it} = g_i - \beta_{i1}\ln(A_{i0}) + \beta_{i1}\ln(y_{i0}) - \beta_{i0}\frac{\alpha}{1-\alpha}\ln\left(\frac{s_i}{n_i + g_i + \delta}\right) \tag{8}$$

Under the usual assumption that $g_i = g$, the common growth rate of technological progress g may be interpreted as implying perfect diffusion of technological change across the regions. Also, MRW assume A_{i0} is constant across countries, while it should be interpreted as reflecting not just technology but also country-specific influences on growth such as resource endowments, climate and institutions. They assume these differences vary randomly as, $\ln(A_{i0}) = \ln A + e_i$, where e_i is a country-specific shock distributed independently from explanatory variables.

To account for spatial interactions, Ertur & Koch (2007) assume that spatial externalities are generated from technological interdependencies. The production function for country i is given by equation (1) and following Romer (1986)'s treatment of knowledge spillover from capital investment, each unit of capital investment not only increases the stock of physical capital but also increases the level of technology for all firms in the economy through knowledge spillovers. Thus, Ertur & Koch (2007) assume that the aggregate level of technology evolves as

$$A_{it} = \Omega_i k_{it}^\phi \prod_{j \neq i}^N A_{jt}^{\gamma w_{ij}} \tag{9}$$

Let $\Omega_t = \Omega_0 e^{\mu t}$ denote the component of technological progress that is exogenous and common across all countries and let $k_{it} = K_{it}/L_{it}$ represents the capital-labor ratio in country i for the knowledge spillovers generated by physical capital, while the parameter ϕ with $0<\phi<1$ measures the strength of home externalities generated by physical capital accumulation. By modelling the knowledge spillover in country i as a geometrically weighted average of the stock of knowledge of its neighbours denoted by j, this specification assumes the external effect of knowledge embodied in capital in place in one country extends across its borders but does so with diminished intensity because of friction generated by socio-economic and institutional dissimilarities, for instance. The degree of international technological interdependence generated by the level of spatial externalities is described by γ, with $0<\gamma<1$, which is assumed identical for each country.

Under the existence of technological spillovers, countries cannot be analysed in isolation of each other but must be considered as an interdependent system. In matrix form, (9) is written as $A=\Omega+\phi k+\gamma WA$, while $(I-\gamma W)^{-1}$ exists, then A can be written as

$$A = (I - \gamma W)^{-1}\Omega+\phi(I- \gamma W)^{-1}k \tag{10}$$

where A is the $n\times 1$ vector of logarithms of the level of technology, k the $N\times 1$ vector of the logarithms of the aggregate level of physical capital per worker, and W is an $n\times N$ matrix of bilateral country weights.

This implies

$$A_{it} = \Omega_i \frac{1}{1-\gamma} k_{it}^\phi \prod_{j=1}^N k_{jt}^\phi \sum_{r=1}^\infty \gamma^r w_{ij}^{(r)} \tag{11}$$

where $w_{ij}^{(r)}$ are the elements of row i and column j of the matrix W raised to the power r. Now replacing that into production function (1) and get the output per worker for country i, $y_{it}= Y_{it}/L_{it}$ as

$$y_{it} = \Omega_t \frac{1}{1-\gamma} k_{it}^{u_{ii}} \prod_{j=1}^N k_{jt}^{u_{ij}} \tag{12}$$

where $u_{it} = \alpha +\phi\left(1+\sum_{r=1}^\infty \gamma^r w_{ij}^{(r)}\right)$ and $u_{it}\phi\sum_{r=1}^\infty \gamma^r w_{ij}^{(r)}$.

This model implies spatial heterogeneity in the parameters of the production function. However, if there are no physical capital externalities, that is $\phi=0$, we have $u_{ii}=\alpha$ and $u_{ij}=0$, then the production function is written as usual. In the Appendix, the growth equation with externalities, specifically, show that $d\ln(y_{it})/dt = g - \lambda_i\left[\ln(y_{it}) - \ln(y_{it}^*)\right]$, where λ_i is defined as well.

As before, this equation may be solved as

$$\ln(y_{it}) - \ln(y_{i0}) = gt - (1-e^{-\lambda_i t})\frac{\mu}{1-\gamma}\frac{1}{\lambda_i} - (1-e^{-\lambda_i t})\ln(yi0)+(1-e^{-\lambda_i t})\ln(y_i^*)$$

Let $g_{it}= (\ln(y_{it})-\ln(y_{i0}))/t$. Taking account of the interdependence among the output of the different countries and substituting for the steady state values, we can re-write the growth equation with externalities as

$$g_{it} = \Delta_i - \beta_1 \ln(y_{i0}) + \beta_2 \ln\left(\frac{s_i}{n_i + g + \delta}\right) + \beta_3 \sum\nolimits_{j \neq i} w_{ij} \ln(y_{j0})$$

$$+ \beta_4 \sum\nolimits_{j \neq i} w_{ij} \left(\frac{s_i}{n_i + g + \delta}\right) + \beta_5 \sum\nolimits_{j \neq i} \frac{w_{ij}}{1 - e^{-\lambda_i t}} \left[\ln(y_{jt}) - \ln(y_{j0})\right]$$

(13)

In this equation, the coefficients are given by

$$\beta_1 = -\left(1 - e^{-\lambda_i t}\right) / t$$

$$\beta_2 = \frac{(\alpha + \phi)}{(1 - \alpha - \phi)} \left(1 - e^{-\lambda_i t}\right) / t$$

$$\beta_3 = \frac{\gamma(1 - \alpha)}{(1 - \alpha - \phi)} \left(1 - e^{-\lambda_i t}\right) / t$$

$$\beta_4 = \frac{\gamma\alpha}{(1 - \alpha - \phi)} \left(1 - e^{-\lambda_i t}\right) / t$$

$$\beta_5 = \frac{\gamma(1 - \alpha)}{(1 - \alpha - \phi)} \left(1 - e^{-\lambda_i t}\right) / t$$

This kind of specification as in the last equation (13), including both a spatial lag of the dependent as well other independent variables is referred to as the Spatial Durbin Model (SDM).

SPATIAL GROWTH MODELS

In this section, the standard growth equation extended to allow for spatial interdependence across countries. Following Durlauf et al. (2005), a cross-country regression model for the growth rate of real GDP per capita may defined as follows

A cross-country regression model for the growth rate of real GDP per capita may defined as

$$g_{it} = \gamma \ln(Y_{i,\tau}) + X_{i,t}^* \theta + \varepsilon_{it} = X_{i,t}\beta + \varepsilon_{it}, \quad i=1,\ldots,N; \ t=1,\ldots,T$$

(14)

The dependent variable $g_{it} = (\ln Y_{i,t} - \ln Y_{i,\tau})/(t-\tau)$ is the average growth rate of GDP per capita between time t and τ, where $Y_{i,t}$ is GDP per capita for time t and $Y_{i,\tau}$ is the initial level of GDP per capita for a given time span between t and τ. In this expression, $X_{i,t}^*$ is a vector of explanatory variables that includes a constant. This representation follows from the simple growth regression model analyzed by Barro (1991), Mankiw et al. (1992) and Barro and Sala-i Martin (1995). The panel data framework is made possible by dividing the total period into several shorter time spans. According to Islam (1995), the appropriate time span for studying growth convergence may be five-year periods.

The sum for N countries and re-write them as a matrix form then the growth equation becomes as $g_t = \alpha + X_t\beta + \varepsilon_t$. To extend this model with spatial effects, Ertur & Koch (2007)'s model consider with technological interdependencies, which leads the general form of the spatial regression denoted by the Spatial Durbin Model (SDM). Using matrix notation, this can be expressed as

$$g_t = \rho Wg_t + Xt\beta + WX_t\Gamma + \mu + \varepsilon_t \qquad (15)$$

where β and Γ are (K x 1) vector of fixed but unknown parameters. In the SDM, the exogenous spatial lags can measure whether the GDP growth rate of country i depends on the growth determinants of other countries as well. μ denotes a spatial specific effect, which is used to control for all space-specific time-invariant variables whose omission could bias the estimates in a typical cross-sectional study (Elhorst, 2014).

The spatial growth regression models produce estimates and inferences that are conditional on the set of explanatory variables employed. However, additional source of model uncertainty arises from competing spatial regression specification. Before giving full explanation of the claim that SDM model produces unbiased coefficients, First the taxonomy of linear spatial dependence models for panel data is considered. As, Elhorst (2014) mentions that there are three types of different interaction effects that may explain why an observation associated with specific location may be dependent on observations at other locations.

A General Nesting Spatial (GNS) model with all types of interaction effects takes the form as;

$$Y_t = \rho WY_t + X_t\beta + WX_t\theta + \mu + \varepsilon_t$$

$$\varepsilon_t = \lambda W\varepsilon_t + v$$

where ρ is called the spatial autoregressive coefficient, λ the spatial autocorrelation coefficient, while θ, just as β, represents a (K x 1) vector of fixed but unknown parameters to be estimated. W is a nonnegative N x N matrix describing the spatial composition of the units in the sample.

Endogenous interaction effects, WY, indicate the decision of a spatial unit to behave in some way depends on the decision taken by other spatial units. The value of the dependent variable for one agent is jointly determined with that of neighbouring agents.

Exogenous interaction effects, WX, are considered the dependent variable of a particular unit depends on independent explanatory variables of other spatial units. If the number of independent explanatory variables in a linear regression model is K, then the number of exogenous interaction effects is also K, provided that the intercept is considered as separate variable.

Interaction effects among error terms, Wϵ, do not require a theoretical model for spatial or social interaction process, but instead, are consistent with a situation where determinants of the dependent variable omitted from the model are spatially autocorrelated, or with a situation where unobserved shocks follow a spatial pattern. These correlated effects show where similar unobserved environmental characteristics result in similar behaviour.

The Figure 1 shows all the models with the restrictions, while these models contain the three-interaction effect alone or with combinations with each other, while arrows show these possible combinations of interactions.

Figure 1. Spatial Econometric Models
Source: Created by author.

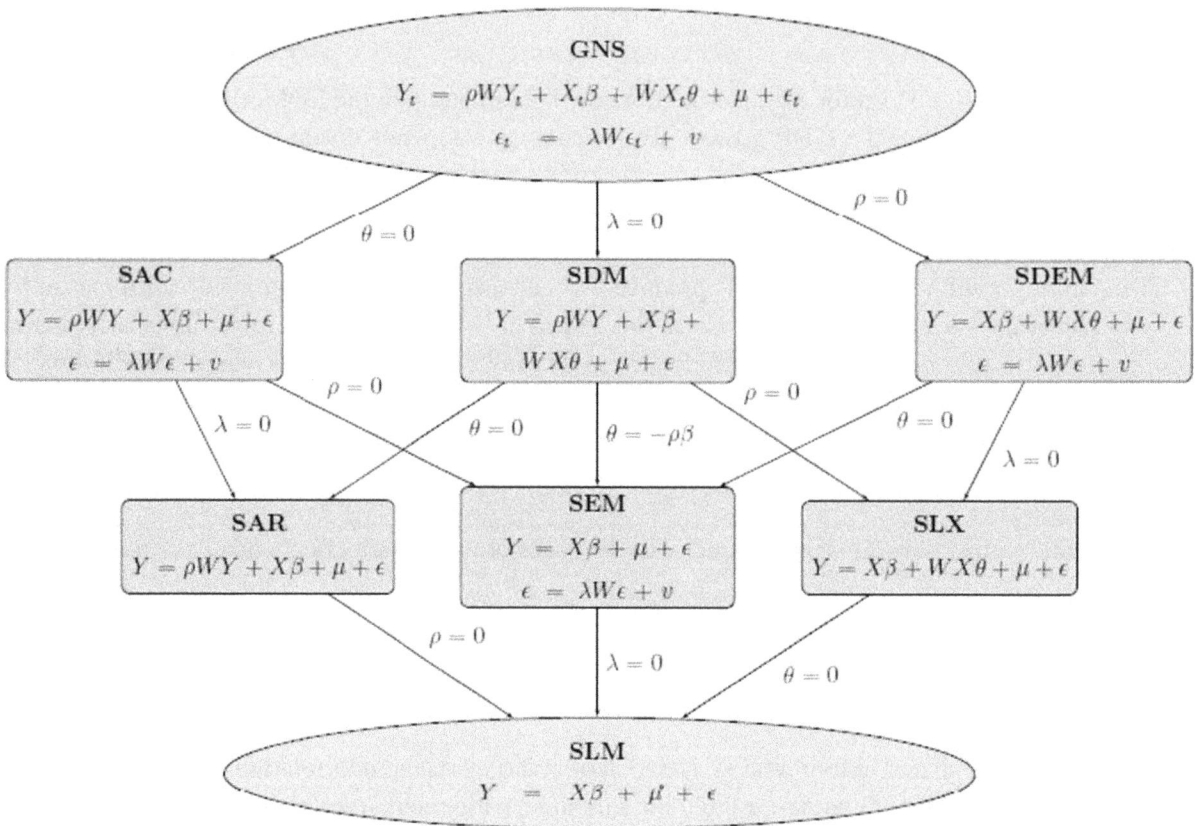

The frequently used spatial models in the growth literature show whether the spatial dependence is just in the dependent term (lag dependent variable) or in the disturbances. According to LeSage & Fisher (2008), the theoretical justification for spatial regression models rests entirely on the plausibility of a conjunction of two circumstances that seem likely to arise in applied spatial growth regression modelling of regional data samples. One of these is spatial dependence in the disturbances of an ordinary least-squares regression model. The second circumstance is the existence of an omitted explanatory variable that exhibits non-zero covariance with a variable included in the model.

Spatial dependence is a widely observed phenomenon for variables such as: per capita income levels, employment, and population variables used in the growth regression literature. Furthermore, omitted variables are also likely to characterize empirical implementations of regional growth regressions, since sample data for measuring numerous factors that may play an important role in economic growth are often limited. It is also the case that these omitted (regional) variables would likely exhibit spatial dependence as well as correlation with at least one of the included variables. (LeSage & Fisher, 2008)

The Spatial Autoregressive model (SAR) has a spatial lag structure in the dependent variable. This model is more appropriate when the growth rate of a particular country is related to that of its neighbor's growth.

$$g_t = \rho W g_t + X_t \beta + \mu + \varepsilon_t$$

$$\varepsilon_t \sim N(0, \sigma_\varepsilon^2 I_N) \text{ and } E(\varepsilon_t, \varepsilon_s) = 0_i \neq j \text{ and/or } t \neq s \quad (16)$$

where ρ is called spatial autoregressive coefficient. The SAR growth equation in each country is not only affected by its own initial per capita income and its conditioning variables, but also by the magnitudes of these variables in the whole system of countries.

The SEM model has a spatial lag structure in the error term, which implies that only an exogenous shock in a spatial unit of the model has some impact on the dependent term in all spatial units. It is more suitable to imply the SEM, if all countries share similar unobserved features. While the random shock in a country affect growth rates in that country and additionally impacts all other countries through spatial transformation. SEM equation recognises the presence of global externalities associated solely with random shock.

$$g_t = X_t \beta + \mu + \phi_t \text{ and } \phi_t = \lambda W \phi_t + \varepsilon_t$$

$$\varepsilon_t \sim N(0, \sigma_\varepsilon^2 I_N) \text{ and } E(\varepsilon_t, \varepsilon_s) = 0 \ i \neq j \text{ and/or } t \neq s \quad (17)$$

$$g_t = X_t \beta + \mu + (I - \lambda W)^{-1} \varepsilon_t$$

where ϕ_t reflects the spatially autocorrelated error term and λ is called the spatial autocorrelation coefficient.

Additionally, Ertur & Koch (2007) prefer to work with SEM and extend it to the more general form SDM to estimate technological interdependence among economies and examine the impact of spillover effects.

Spatial Weighting Matrices

One can create and estimate spatial econometric models based on spatial weighting matrices, which are the formal expression of spatial dependence between observations. They impose a structure regarding each location's neighbourhood and assign weights that measure the intensity of the relationship among pairs of spatial units.

The spatial weighting matrix, W, is a square NxN non-stochastic, and symmetric matrix, whose elements w_{ij} measure the intensity of the spatial interaction between units i and j and take on a finite and non-negative value. A typical element, w_{ij}, has a value greater than 0 if the observations i and j are connected. By convention, $w_{ii} = 0$ for the diagonal elements to rule out an own effect. To normalize the outside influence upon each unit, the spatial weighting matrix is standardized such that the elements of a row sum up to one. Row normalization is used to create proportional weights in cases where individual units have an unequal number of neighbours, and it implies that the impact on each unit by all other units is equalized. Moreover, the mutual proportions between the elements of *W* remain unchanged, and do not lose their property of symmetry because of these normalizations.

The problem of technically incorporating spatial dependence into the model is a major issue in spatial econometrics. The main assumption is that the structure of spatial dependence is known, not estimated, and that it specifies the degree of interdependence among observations. The use of physical distance between countries as a measure of proximity has the advantage in that it may unambiguously be considered as exogenous to the model. Therefore, it can avoid estimation problems due to identification. One can use several types of spatial weights matrices according to geographical neighbourhood criteria, like the contiguity, inverse distance, inverse-squared distance matrices, and inverse distance matrix with a cut-off point of say m kilometres *and* many others. Each spatial weighting matrices express different spatial relations.

The contiguity weighting matrix can be defined as a common boundary relationship between two countries. However, this structure of spatial-weighting matrices has limited dependence. It allows for an assessment of local effects of neighbourhood spillovers without considering the global context. While it does not include spatial relationship further than the first order neighbours. The only advantage of using this matrix is the ease of construction and the interpretation of results.

The use of physical distance between countries as a measure of geographical relatedness based on distances, d_{ij}, which are calculated following the great circle formula using latitudes and longitudes of the most important cities, like centroids or capitals. It is more appropriate to use the inverse distance matrix with elements of $\dfrac{1}{d_{ij}}$, because in the distance matrix, a larger value implies a greater weight.

Therefore, inverting the bilateral distances to get a larger value for the variable w_{ij} implies that country *i* is closer to country *j* in terms of the transformed weighting matrix. It just allows for testing global spatial interaction effects without considering local clusters.

Most of the studies are based on geographical spatial dependence, though none of them has proved that the use of geographical distances is optimal. Therefore, the notion of observations being nearby one another should not restricted on determining purely by physical distance, but there can be more general sense of relatedness. It is proper to use of any concept of nearness that makes theoretical sense so long as it does not violate any of the assumptions about the weighting matrices. Elhorst (2014) mentions that spatial econometric models can also be used to explain the behaviour of economic agents other than geographical units if they are related to each other through networks. It is convenient to do the estimations with a suitably well-defined non-geographic notion of distance as well. It can be much more effective by allowing for variants of interactions that go beyond geography. However, preserving the exogeneity of the weights is important to avoid identification problems, when considering such alternative specifications of weighting matrices.

There have been many studies (LeSage & Pace, 2009, Mur et al., 2013, and Debarsy & Ertur, 2019) that attempt to investigate how robust results are to different specifications of W and to *d*etermine which one best fits the data using criterions such as the log-likelihood function values and Bayesian posterior model probabilities.

TESTING FOR SPATIAL DEPENDENCE

Exploratory Analysis

In analyses that seek to uncover dependencies, the first question to consider is whether the data exhibit spatial autocorrelation or not. The general approach is to start with a non-spatial linear regression model using OLS and then test whether or not the model needs to be extended with spatial interaction effects. Among many measures of spatial relationships, Moran's I statistic is the most widely used measure to test for spatial dependence. Moran's I statistic can be used to generate data that can theoretically or statistically justify the use of spatial models and it provides a method of checking for spatial correlation in the data, within an exploratory analysis framework.

$$I = \frac{N \sum_{i=1}^{N} \sum_{j=1}^{N} w_{ij} d_i d_j}{s \sum_{i=1}^{N} d_i^2} \tag{18}$$

where N denotes the number of areas, $d_i = x_i - \overline{x}$ measures the deviations of x_i from $\overline{x}$, the mean of all the observed values and w_{ij} is the entry of the ith row and the jth column in the spatial weight matrix W and S is the sum of all the entries is W. The Moran's I statistics can be calculated for the dependent variable.

The Global Moran's I test examines whether there are any regular patterns among geographically connected units (Moran, 1950 and Cliff & Ord, 1981). If there are no regular patterns of spatial association, then the static is not significant. Otherwise, if there are significant spatial associations, the static can be positive or negative. Moran's I usually ranges between -1 and 1, with large positive values indicating neighbourhood similarity of the rates and values close to zero indicating absence of spatial autocorrelation. Haining & Li(2020) argue that the formulation of equation (18) tells us that if most pairs of neighbouring areas have the same sign regarding their deviations from the mean, then the values of I will be positive and away from 0, indicative of positive spatial autocorrelation. Otherwise, if most of the pairs of neighbours have deviations from the mean in the opposite directions, then I will be negative and away from 0. This suggest negative spatial autocorrelation is present. Statistically insignificant values of I indicates the absence of the spatial autocorrelation, it can be considered that the spatial allocation of the observations is random.

The Global Moran's I can be applied to regression residuals as well. Global spatial autocorrelation can arise in the residual from a regression model if some of the unobserved/unmeasured independent variables are themselves spatially autocorrelated. In spatial econometrics, testing for residual spatial autocorrelation is often a first step before fitting one or another spatial regression model. Now $d_i = \varepsilon_i$ where ε_i is the least square residual for the ith observation. There is no need to subtract the residual mean, as residuals have a mean of zero by construction. Second, because the sum of the residuals is zero, the residuals themselves are not independent: if you are given (N-1) residuals, knowing that the sum of the N residuals is zero, the Nth residual can be calculated. For this reason, the mean and the variance of the sampling distribution for the global Moran's I statistic under the null hypothesis of no residual spatial autocorrelation is not the same as in the case under equation (18). However, the previously described permutation test remains an option to derive an empirical p-value.

If the panel data involves a spatial dependence, then OLS may result biased and inefficient coefficient estimates due to the omitted variable. In this case, Maximum Likelihood estimation will be more appropriate; Elhorst (2014). As LeSage & Pace (2009) argue that by construction, the OLS model does not allow for spillovers since it makes the implicit assumption that outcomes for different units are independent of each other, which is restrictive especially when dealing with spatial data. One such model that allows an empirical assessment of the magnitude and significance of spillover effects is the SAR model. This is clearly an advantage compared to other widely used SEM model.

Also, in the panel data estimation, specific effects must be controlled for. These spatial specific effects may be treated as fixed effects (FE) or as random effects (RE). In the fixed effects model, a dummy variable is introduced for each spatial unit, while in the random effects model, μ_i is treated as a random variable that is independently and identically distributed with zero mean and variance σ. Furthermore, it is assumed that the random variables μ_i and ε_{it} are independent of each other. The spatial Hausman test, which has null hypothesis that the random effects model is consistent, can be used to define these specific effects. A spatial data analysis, controlling for FE to remove the effect of spatial dependence from that of spatial heterogeneity and of omitted variables, improves the performance of the models.

Models with controls for spatial fixed effects utilize the time-series component of the data, whereas models without controls for spatial fixed effects utilize the cross-sectional component of the data. As a result, some studies argue that models with controls for spatial fixed effects tend to give short-term estimates and models without controls for spatial fixed effects tend to give long-term estimates (Baltagi, 2005, pp. 200-201). A related problem of controlling for spatial fixed effects is that any variable that does not change over time or only varies a little cannot be estimated, because it is wiped out by the demeaning transformation. This is the main reason for many studies not controlling for spatial fixed effects. In spatial econometric models, time fixed effects get special attention because there can be common shocks across time that would lead to an upward bias in the interested spatial parameter estimates. Lee & Yu (2010) remark that time FEs may be specifically associated with growth theory, while FEs remove the effect of time-invariant characteristics. The methods of Elhorst (2014) and LeSage & Pace (2009) will be pursued to determine the appropriate spatial model.

Model Selection Process

There are two approaches in the spatial econometrics literature for selecting the best model. The first one is the specific-to-general approach which is developed by Florax et al. (2003) using Lagrange Multiplier tests based on the estimated non-spatial model and it is against a spatially lagged dependent variable and spatial error correlation. The second case is a general-to-specific approach, herein if the non-spatial model is rejected, then the most general model Spatial Durbin Model is estimated to test whether it can be simplified to the spatial lag or the spatial error model using both hypotheses above. As Elhorst (2014) notes, if both approaches, namely, the specific-to-general and general-to-specific, point to the same model, then it is safe to choose that model as the best model. On the contrary, if non-spatial model versions of the model such as SAR or SEM are rejected while the SDM is not, then the SDM may be selected as the preferred model.

The use of Lagrange Multiplier tests provides a good guide to decide which specification of spatial models is the most appropriate according to the specific-to-general selection criteria. Florax et al. (2003) develop model selection criteria using Lagrange Multiplier tests with LM_ρ and LM_λ for a spatially lagged dependent variable and spatial error correlation, respectively. They also present robust versions of these tests that control for local misspecification. Denote the robust version of the Lagrange multiplier test for spatial lagged dependence in the presence of spatial error autocorrelation by L*ρ and the robust version of the Lagrange multiplier test for spatial error autocorrelation in the presence of spatially lagged dependent variable by L*λ. Following Florax et al. (2003), a hybrid specification strategy that combines the classical and robust tests may be implemented as follows:

1- Estimate the initial model $g_{it} = \alpha + X_{i,t}\beta + \varepsilon_{it}$ by OLS.

2- Test the hypothesis of no spatial dependence due to an omitted spatial lag or due to spatially autoregressive errors, using LM_{ρ} and LM_{λ}. If both tests are insignificant, then I cannot reject the hypothesis of no spatial lags and no spatial error term.

3- If both tests are significant, then estimate the specification pointed to by the more significant of the *robust* tests. For example, if L*ρ > L*$_{\lambda}$, then select SAR. If L*ρ < L*$_{\lambda}$, then select SEM.

4- If LM_{ρ} is significant but LM_{λ} is not, then select SAR. Otherwise, select SEM.

Florax et al. (2003) also show how similar specification strategies may be implemented using only the classical or robust versions of the LM tests. They further compare the classical, robust and hybrid LM based strategies to a so-called Hendry strategy that uses the general-to-specific approach and show that the LM based strategies dominate with respect to detecting spatial dependence.

Secondly, the general-to-specific approach starting with the SDM also allows us to implement model selection criteria to select the most appropriate model. The hypothesis H_0: $\Gamma = 0$ can be tested to investigate whether this model can be simplified to the SAR and the hypothesis H_0: $\Gamma = -\rho$ (or equivalently, H_0: $\Gamma + \rho\beta = 0$) can be used to test whether the model can be simplified to the SEM; see (Burridge, 1981). To see this last point, substitute for $\Gamma = -\rho\beta$ in the regression equation as $g_t = \rho W g_t + X_t \beta + W X_t(-\rho\beta) + \mu + \varepsilon_i$.

Simplifying yields $(I-\rho W)g_t = (I-\rho W)X_t\beta + \mu + \varepsilon_t$ or $g_t = X_t\beta + (I-\rho W)^{-1}(\mu + \varepsilon_t)$ which is the SEM specification. Both tests follow a chi-square distribution with K degrees of freedom. If both models are estimated, then these tests can take the form of a likelihood ratio (LR) test. Otherwise, they can only take the form of Wald test. It is another advantage of estimating models by Maximum Likelihood estimation.

INTERPRETING THE SPATIAL GROWTH REGRESSIONS

Direct and Indirect Effects

The spatial growth regression models include a spatial lag of the dependent and independent variables, a change in a given explanatory variable in region i as well an indirect impact on other regions $i \neq j$. In a traditional non-spatial model, the partial derivative associated with X is simply going to be the parameter β. However, in the spatial econometric models, it is more complicated. In the spatial growth model, the partial derivative associated with a given explanatory variable X_r, $r = 1,...K$ is the derivative of the N × 1 vector of growth rates g with respect to the rth explanatory variable.

In matrix form, equation (SAR) for a single cross-section becomes $g = \rho W g + X\beta + \varepsilon$, which can be written as $(I_n - \rho W)g = X\beta + \varepsilon$ implying

$$g = (I_N - \rho W)^{-1}X\beta + (I_N - \rho W)^{-1}\varepsilon \tag{19}$$

Hence,

$$\frac{\partial g}{\partial X_r} = (I_N - \rho W)^{-1} I_N \beta_r = G I_N \beta_r,$$

where the $N \times N$ matrix G denoted as the impact matrix has the form

$$G = (I_N - \rho W)^{-1} = I_N + \rho W + \rho^2 W^2 + \rho^3 W^3 + \ldots$$

The explanatory variables have both effects while the magnitude of the change in X will not just depend on parameter beta as in the non- spatial model. This is because the change in X in country i not only has a primary effect on g in country i, but also potential effects on growth in all other countries in the sample. These secondary effects on growth can be counted as spillover effects. The magnitude of the change in X_r on the elements of g will depend on (1) the degree of friction between countries which is governed by the W matrix used in the model, (2) the parameter ρ measuring the strength of spatial dependence between countries, and (3) the estimated parameter, β_r. This is because the change in X_r in country i not only has a primary effect on the growth rate of country i, g_i, but also potential effects on g in all other countries in the sample. These secondary effects on g can be counted as spillover effects.

LeSage and Pace (2009) show how to compute the statistical measures of dispersion for these effects. These measures allow inferences regarding the statistical significance of the direct, indirect and total impacts that arise from changes in the explanatory variables. They propose an approximation to the infinite expansion of the G matrix based on trace of the powers of the weighting matrix, W, where the highest power considered in the approximation is large enough to ensure approximate convergence.

The diagonal elements of the matrix $G = (I_N - \rho W)^{-1}$ contain the direct impacts, and the off-diagonal elements represent indirect impacts. The direct effect can be used to test the hypothesis as to whether a particular variable has a significant effect on the dependent variable in and of itself. As Debarsy and Ertur (2019) note, the impact matrices G are generally full and not symmetric, regardless of the sparsity and the structure of the interaction matrix, W. They call the country in column j of this matrix as the emitting country and country in row i as the receiving country. The sum of the ith row of the G matrix represents the total impact on the dependent variable in country i due to a unit change in X in all the countries in the sample. The sum of column j gives the total impact on the dependent variable of all the countries of a unit change in X in country j. In the spatial autoregressive model (SAR), the indirect effect can be used to test whether spatial spillovers exist.

The direct effect can be used to test the hypothesis as to whether a particular variable has a significant effect on the dependent variable in itself. This direct effect would be analogous in interpretation to the single parameter β associated with the explanatory variable X in a non-spatial framework. However, the magnitude of the direct effects can slightly change across countries due to feedback effects. As Debarsy and Ertur (2019) note: "The own derivative for country i includes feedback effects, where country i affects country j and also country j also affects country i as well as longer paths which might go from country i to j to k and back to i." By contrast, the indirect effect is measured by the average of either the row sums or the column sums of the non-diagonal elements and shows the changes in the average effect that comes from all other countries. In the SAR, the indirect effect can be used to test whether spatial spillovers exist. By contrast, in SEM, only the direct effect exists. In Appendix A.2, the estimates of the direct and indirect effects of SDM is shown as well.

CONCLUSION

This chapter reviewed alternative approaches and main developments to regional growth and convergence study, focusing on the spatial econometric methodologies. The goal of this chapter is to broaden the understanding of the interdependence of economic growth of countries within a region. It is able to improve the understanding of regional growth. Analysing regional growth and convergence involve important economic and econometric issues and differs from existing literature by applying the spatial econometric models to economic convergence issues.

This chapter develops an economic growth model that includes technological interdependence among regions using externalities to consider locational and neighbourhood effects on growth and convergence. Unlike non-spatial case, the economic growth rates depend on both own region and neighbouring region characteristics, the weight matrix, which shows the spatial connectivity structure of regions, and the strength of spatial dependence based on model specification. Additionally, the significant benefit of these spatial methods is the ability to quantify the magnitude of direct and indirect (spillover) effects of changing regional characteristics on own region and neighbouring regions.

With these spatial economic growth models, one can analyse the consequences of spatial dependence on regional growth and convergence processes and interpret the spillover effect of growth rates. The impact of having a bad or good neighbour is determined for a regional perspective. These spillover effects of a country are substantial issue for a regional perspective in economic growth process. The economic growth of a country affected by the performance of growth rate of its neighbours. The appearance of the spatial autocorrelation effect indicates that growth in one country tends to have a positive impact on growth in neighbouring countries. That means, the average growth rate of a given country is positively affected by the average growth rate of neighbouring countries in the region. On the other hand, the negative spatial relations hint the dissimilarity of reactions between countries which is interpreted as a kind of competition.

The focus can be on understanding the benefits emanating them for the individual country and the region. The regional economists can apply the accurate spatial econometric models and fit these models to real data. The neighbourhood effects in a region could be an important issue for policy implications since they may create a divergence between the incentives of regional officials and those of supra-regional entities. The policy choices of the countries in a region have been a critical subject, while the results of growth spillover effects can provide support for effectiveness of the policies that were explicitly designed to promote regional growth. As a policy implication, the estimated positive spillover effect promotes the cooperation agreements among countries that would be beneficial for the economic growth of the regions. This cooperation could be in the form of improving trade relations, sharing technological knowledge and innovations, facilitating communications.

REFERENCES

Baltagi, B. H. (2005). Econometric Analysis of *Panel Data (3rd ed.)*. *John Wiley &* Sons.

Barro, R. J. (1991). Economic Growth in a Cross Section of Countries. The Quarterly Journal *of Economics, 106(2), 407–443. do*i:*10.*2307/2937943

Barro, R.J., & Sala-i, M. X. (1995). Economic Growth. M*cGraw Hill.*

Burridge, P. (1981). Testing for a Common Factor in a Spatial Autoregression Model. Environment and *Planning A. Economy and Sp*ace, *13, 795–800.*

*C*liff, A. D., & Ord, J. K. (1981). Spatial Proc*esses: Models and Applications. Pion Londo*n.

Debarsy, N., & Ertur, C. (2019). Interaction Matrix Selection in Spatial Autoregressive Models with an Application to Growth Theory. Regional *Science and Urban Economics, 75, 49*–69. doi:10.1016/j.regsciurbeco.2019.01.002

Durlauf, S. N., Johnson, P. A., & Temple, J. R. W. (2005). Growth Econometrics. In Handbo*ok of Economic Growth (vol. 1A, pp. 555–677). Nort*h-Holland.

Elhorst, J. P. (2014). Spatial Econometrics: From Cross-Sectional Data to Spatial Panels. Springer Briefs in Regional Science. Springer-Verlag. doi:10.1007/978-3-642-40340-8

Ertur, C., & Koch, W. (2007). Growth, Technological Interdependence and Spatial Externalities: Theory and Evidence. *Journal of Applied Econometrics*, *22*(6), 1033–1062. doi:10.1002/jae.963

Florax, R., Folmer, H., & Rey, S. (2003). Specification Searches in Spatial Econometrics: The Relevance of Hendry's Methodology. *Regional Science and Urban Economics*, *33*(5), 557–579. doi:10.1016/S0166-0462(03)00002-4

Haining, R. P., & Li, G. (2020). *Modelling Spatial and Spatial-Temporal Data: A Bayesian Approach.* Chapman and Hall/CRC. doi:10.1201/9780429088933

Islam, N. (1995). Growth empirics: A panel data approach. *The Quarterly Journal of Economics*, *110*(4), 1127–1170. doi:10.2307/2946651

Lee, L. F., & Yu, J. (2010). Estimation of Spatial Autoregressive Panel Data Models with Fixed Effects. *Journal of Econometrics*, *154*(2), 165–185. doi:10.1016/j.jeconom.2009.08.001

LeSage, J. P., & Fischer, M. M. (2008). Spatial growth regressions: Model Specification, Estimation, and Interpretation. *Spatial Economic Analysis*, *3*(3), 275–304. doi:10.1080/17421770802353758

LeSage, J. P., & Pace, R. (2009). *Introduction to Spatial Econometrics*. Chapman and Hall. doi:10.1201/9781420064254

Mankiw, N. G., Romer, D., & Weil, D. N. (1992). Contribution to the Empirics of Economic Growth. *The Quarterly Journal of Economics*, *107*(2), 407–437. doi:10.2307/2118477

Moran, P. A. P. (1950). Notes on Continuous Stochastic Phenomena. *Biometrika, 37*, 17-23.

Mur, J., Herrera, M., & Ruiz, M. (2012). Selecting the Most Adequate Spatial Weighting Matrix: A Study on Criteria. *MPRA Paper, 73700.*

Romer, P. (1986). Increasing Returns and Long-Run Growth. *Journal of Political Economy*, *94*(5), 1002–1037. doi:10.1086/261420

Tobler, W. (1970). A Computer Movie Simulating Urban Growth in the Detroit Region. *Economic Geography*, *46*, 234–240. doi:10.2307/143141

KEY TERMS AND DEFINITIONS

Externality: Excessive attention to external or outward features.

Growth: An increase in the size or the importance of something.

Impact: The force of impression or influence of one thing on another.

Interaction: Reciprocal action or influence, where two or more people or things communicate or react each another.

Interdependence: Mutually reliant or depending on each other.

Neighbourhood: A district where people live, the immediate environment; surroundings.

Spatial: Having a character of space, which relates to the position, area, and size of things.

Spillover: The effects of an activity have spread further.

Weighting: A level of importance given to something compared to other things.

APPENDIX

A. Convergence in the Model With TFP Spillovers

The capital-output ratio for country i is constant at the steady state value of capital as $(k_i/y_i)^* = s_i/(n_i + g + \delta)$, which implies that

$$k_{it}^* = \Omega_t^{\frac{1}{(1-\gamma)(1-u_{ii})}} \left(\frac{s_i}{(n_i + g + \delta)} \right)^{\frac{1}{1-u_{ii}} \prod_{j \neq i} (k_{jt}^*)^{\frac{u_{ij}}{1-u_{ii}}}} \tag{A.1}$$

Where the balance growth rate $g = \mu/[(1-\alpha)(1-\gamma) - \phi]$. Writing the logarithm of output per worker as $y = A + \alpha k$, replacing A by equation (10), and pre-multiplying both sides by $(I - \gamma W)$ yields $y = \Omega + (\alpha + \phi) k - \alpha \gamma W k + \gamma W y$. Re-writing this equation for country i and substituting for the steady-state capital-output ratio in logarithms implies

$$\ln(y_{it}^*) = \frac{1}{1-\alpha-\phi} \ln(\Omega_t) + \frac{(\alpha+\phi)}{1-\alpha-\phi} \ln\left(\frac{s_i}{n_i + g + \delta} \right)$$
$$+ \frac{\gamma\alpha}{1-\alpha-\phi} \sum_{j \neq i}^{N} w_{ij} \ln\left(\frac{s_i}{n_i + g + \delta} \right) + \frac{\gamma(1-\alpha)}{1-\alpha-\phi} \sum_{j \neq i} w_{ij} \ln(y_{jt}^*) \tag{A.2}$$

Consider the fundamental dynamic capital equation implied by the Solow neoclassical model as $\dot{k}_{it} = s_i y_{it} - (n_i + \delta) k_{it}$ Using the definition of output in country i given by (12);

$$\frac{\dot{k}_{it}}{k_{it}} = s_i \Omega_t^{\frac{1}{1-\gamma}} k_{it}^{-(1-u_{ii})} \prod_{j \neq i}^{N} k_{jt}^{u_{ij}} - (n_i + \delta) \tag{A.3}$$

As before, the transitional dynamics of the model may be represented using a log-linear approximation to equation (A.3) around the steady state as

$$\frac{d \ln(k_{it})}{dt} = g - (1 - u_{ii})(n_i + g + \delta) \left[\ln(k_{it}) - \ln(k_{i,t}^*) \right] + \sum_{j \neq i} u_{ij}(n_j + g + \delta) \left[\ln(k_{jt}) - \ln(k_{j,t}^*) \right] \tag{A4}$$

However, this system of differential equations does not admit an easy solution. Hence, I consider the relations showing the gaps between countries relative to their own steady states as

$$\ln(k_{it}) - \ln(k_{i,t}^*) = \Phi_j \left[\ln(k_{jt}) - \ln(k_{j,t}^*) \right] \tag{A.5}$$

$$\ln(y_{it}) - \ln(y_{i,t}^*) = \Phi_j \left[\ln(y_{jt}) - \ln(y_{j,t}^*) \right] \tag{A.6}$$

Now substitute equation (A.4) for $i = 1,\ldots,N$ into the production function by writing it as

$$\frac{d \ln(y_{it})}{dt} = \frac{1}{1-\gamma} \frac{d \ln(\Omega_t)}{dt} + u_{ii} \frac{d \ln(k_{it})}{dt} + \sum_{j \neq i} u_{ij} \frac{d \ln(k_{jt})}{dt}$$

This yields

$$\frac{d \ln(k_{it})}{dt} = \frac{\mu}{1-\gamma} + u_{ii} \left[g - (1-u_{ii})(n_i + g + \delta) \left[\ln(k_{it}) - \ln(k_{i,t}^*) \right] + \sum_{j \neq i} u_{ij}(n_j + g + \delta) \left[\ln(k_{jt}) - \ln(k_{j,t}^*) \right] \right]$$

$$+ \sum_{j \neq i} u_{ij} \left[g - (1-u_{jj})(n_j + g + \delta) \left[\ln(k_{jt}) - \ln(k_{j,t}^*) \right] + \sum_{k \neq j} u_{jk}(n_k + g + \delta) \left[\ln(k_{kt}) - \ln(k_{k,t}^*) \right] \right]$$

or

$$\frac{d \ln(y_{it})}{dt} = \frac{\mu}{1-\gamma} + g - (1-u_{ii})(n_i + g + \delta) \left[\ln(k_{it}) - \ln(k_{i,t}^*) \right] + u_{ii}^2 (n_i + g + \delta) \left[\ln(k_{it}) - \ln(k_{i,t}^*) \right]$$

$$+ u_{ii} \sum_{j \neq i} u_{ij}(n_j + g + \delta) \left[\ln(k_{jt}) - \ln(k_{j,t}^*) \right] - \sum_{n \neq j} u_{ij} u_{ii}(n_j + g + \delta) \left[\ln(k_{jt}) - \ln(k_{j,t}^*) \right]$$

$$+ u_{jj} \sum_{j \neq i} u_{ij} \left[\ln(k_{jt}) - \ln(k_{j,t}^*) \right] + \sum_{j \neq i} u_{ij} \sum_{k \neq j} u_{jk}(n_k + g + \delta) \left[\ln(k_{jt}) - \ln(k_{j,t}^*) \right]$$

Where $\sum_{j=1}^{N} u_{ij} g = g$ since $\sum_{j=1}^{N} u_{ij} = 1$.

Then

$$\frac{d \ln(y_{it})}{dt} = \frac{\mu}{1-\gamma} + g \sum_{j=1}^{N} u_{ij} - \sum_{j=1}^{N} u_{ij}(n_j + g + \delta) \left[\ln(k_{jt}) - \ln(k_{j,t}^*) \right]$$

$$+ \sum_{j=1}^{N} u_{ij} \sum_{k=1}^{N} u_{jk}(n_k + g + \delta) \left[\ln(k_{kt}) - \ln(k_{k,t}^*) \right]$$

or

$$\frac{d \ln(y_{it})}{dt} = \frac{\mu}{1-\gamma} + g - \sum_{j=1}^{N} u_{ij}(n_j + g + \delta) \left[\ln(k_{jt}) - \ln(k_{j,t}^*) \right]$$

$$+ \sum_{j=1}^{N} u_{ij} \left[\ln(k_{jt}) - \ln(k_{j,t}^*) \right] \sum_{k=1}^{N} u_{jk}(n_k + g + \delta) \frac{1}{\Phi_k}$$

or

$$\frac{d\ln(y_{it})}{dt} = \frac{\mu}{1-\gamma} + g - \left[\ln(k_{it}) - \ln(k_{i,t}^*)\right]\sum_{j=1}u_{ij}(n_i + g + \delta)\frac{1}{\Phi_i}$$

$$+ \left[u_{ii}\left[\ln(k_{it}) - \ln(k_{i,t}^*)\right]\sum_{k=1}^{N}u_{ik}(n_k + g + \delta)\frac{1}{\Phi_k}\right.$$

$$\left.+ \sum_{j\neq1}^{N}u_{ij}\left[\ln(k_{jt}) - \ln(k_{j,t}^*)\right]\sum_{k=1}^{N}u_{jk}(n_k + g + \delta)\frac{1}{\Phi_k}\right]$$

or

$$\frac{d\ln(y_{it})}{dt} = \frac{\mu}{1-\gamma}g - \left[\ln(k_{it}) - \ln(k_{i,t}^*)\right]\sum_{j=1}u_{ij}(n_j + g + \delta)\frac{1}{\Phi_j}$$

$$+ \left[\ln(y_{jt}) - \ln(y_{j,t}^*)\right]\sum_{k=1}^{N}u_{ik}(n_k + g + \delta)\frac{1}{\Phi_k}$$

But

$$\left[\ln(k_{it}) - \ln(k_{i,t}^*)\right] + \sum_{j=1}u_{ij}(n_j + g + \delta)\frac{1}{\Phi_j}$$

$$= \frac{\sum_{j=1}^{N}u_{ij}\sum_{k=1}^{N}u_{jk}(n_k + g + \delta)\left[\ln(k_{kt}) - \ln(k_{k,t}^*)\right]}{\sum_{j=1}^{N}u_{ij}\frac{1}{\Phi_j}} = \frac{\left[\ln(y_{it}) - \ln(y_{i,t}^*)\right]\sum_{k=1}u_{ik}(n_k + g + \delta)\frac{1}{\Phi_k}}{\sum_{j=1}^{N}u_{ij}\frac{1}{\Phi_j}}$$

Therefore,

$$\frac{d\ln(y_{it})}{dt} = \frac{\mu}{1-\gamma} + g - \left[\ln(y_{it}) - \ln(y_{i,t}^*)\right]\left(\sum_{j=1}u_{ij}(n_j + g + \delta)\frac{1}{\Phi_j}\right)\Big/\left(\sum_{j=1}^{N}u_{ij}\frac{1}{\Phi_k}\right)$$

$$+ \left[\ln(y_{it}) - \ln(y_{i,t}^*)\right]\sum_{k=1}^{N}u_{jk}(n_k + g + \delta)\frac{1}{\Phi_k}$$

or

$$\frac{d\ln(y_{it})}{dt} = \frac{\mu}{1-\gamma} + g - \Lambda_i\left[\ln(y_{it}) - \ln(y_{i,t}^*)\right] + \left[\ln(y_{jt}) - \ln(y_{j,t}^*)\right]\sum_{k=1}^{N}u_{jk}(n_k + g + \delta)\frac{1}{\Phi_k}$$

where

$$\Lambda_i = \left(\sum_{j=1}^{N} u_{ij} \frac{1}{\Phi_j} (n_j + g + \delta) \right) / \left(\sum_{j=1}^{N} u_{ij} \frac{1}{\Phi_j} \right)$$

Likewise, imposing (A.6) yields

$$\frac{d \ln(y_{it})}{dt} = \frac{\mu}{1-\gamma} + \lambda_i \left[\ln(y_{it}) - \ln(y_{i,t}^*) \right] \qquad (A.7)$$

where

$$\lambda_i = \Lambda_i - \sum_{j=1}^{N} u_{ij} \frac{1}{\Phi_j} (n_j + g + \delta)$$

B. Direct and Indirect Effects of SDM

The SDM has the general representation in matrix form as

$$g = \rho W g + X\beta + WX\Gamma + \mu + \varepsilon$$

which can be written as

$$(I_N - \rho W)g = (\beta + W\Gamma)X + \mu + \varepsilon$$

Defining

$$V(W) = (I_N - \rho W) - 1 = I_N + \rho W + \rho^2 W^2 + \rho^3 W^3 + \dots$$

$$S_r(W) = V(W)(I_N \beta_r + W\Gamma_r)$$

the SDM has the representation

$$g = \sum_{r=1}^{k} S_r(W) X_r + V(W)\mu + V(W)\varepsilon .$$

Thus, the impact on country *i*'s growth of a change in the explanatory variable *r* of country *j* may be computed as

$$\frac{\partial g_i}{\partial X_{jr}} = S_r(W)_{ij}, \quad i,j=1,\dots,N.$$

The terms that differentiate this from the standard non-spatial regression coefficient β are the impacts of the spatial autocorrelation parameter, ρ, which also arises in SAR model, as well as the spatial lag parameter on the explanatory variables, Γ_r.

Chapter 12
Evaluating Different Growth Strategies:
The Case of Turkey

Adem Gök
iD https://orcid.org/0000-0002-3786-2507
Kirklareli University, Turkey

Deniz Güvercin
University of Lincoln, UK

ABSTRACT

Analyzing Turkey over 2005: Q1-2017: Q4 period by ARDL approach, the study examines the growth performance of export-led, FDI-led, consumption-led, FPI-led, and investment-led strategies. The study also examines the impact of these growth strategies on various macroeconomic indicators including inflation, unemployment, and exchange rates. Results indicate that consumption-led growth strategy increases growth and unemployment without exerting statistically significant effects on any other indicators. FDI-led growth strategy positively contributes to economic growth, employment, inflation, and trade deficit. Export-led growth strategy positively contributes to economic growth, employment, external debt, and inflation. Investment-led growth strategy does not affect economic growth and employment but positively affects trade deficit and external debt. FPI-led growth strategy decreases economic growth, does not generate employment, and decreases inflation, external debt, and trade deficit.

INTRODUCTION

Main macroeconomic models, particularly economic growth models assume full employment, which basically depends on the Say's law. Supply side models do not utilize the aggregate demand as the source of the economic growth because the model does not assume lack of aggregate demand in the system that would be essential to employ all the factors of production. In these models savings drive the level

DOI: 10.4018/978-1-6684-5976-8.ch012

of economic output whereas the income per capita growth depends on the technological innovation capacity of the society.

Solow growth theory and endogenous growth theory do not consider the aggregate demand as the determining force in the long run economic growth. These theories imply that factor supplies determine the economic growth in the long run, economy is at full employment and all savings are invested. In neoclassical economic theory, nominal rigidities in the short run would be effective in determining economic output less than full employment level. However, in the long run, all nominal rigidities would be solved and all markets get cleared leaving the stage for Say's law, which ensures full employment of all resources. Later economic growth models focus on the accumulation of human capital, externalities, R&D (Romer, 1990; Lucas, 1988).

Keynesian models explain the economic growth as an aggregate demand issue, in other words, capacity utilization issue. Therefore, according to Keynesian approach to income determination, there is a scope for employing policies over the components of the aggregate expenditure. Hansen (1941) argue that full employment level achieved in 1923 and 1929 in the US resulted from the large flow of private investment, and emphasize that the income generated by private inflow is the income that fills the gap between the income at recession and income at economic boom.

Government might promote particular economic growth strategies through its control over tax, subsidies, tariffs and public investment, which would generate different economic growth experiences as we claim. Therefore, various economic growth strategies would be implemented by by focusing on different components of the aggregate demand. Therefore, Investment led growth, Consumption led growth, Foreign Direct Investment (FDI) led growth and Foreign Portfolio Investment (FPI) led growth strategies could be implemented to enable economic growth.

In the Sraffian super multiplier model, as the autonomous demand increases, economy accumulates the capital to exhaust increased demand. Therefore, significant increase in autonomous demand increases capacity utilization rate as well as capital accumulation. Investment led growth model claims that increase in investment generates economic growth due to lower capacity usage rates, which would result in rise in savings and long run economic growth.

There are direct effects of generating economic growth through increasing capacity utilization rate in the economy through effective demand management. Indirect effects of managing aggregate demand would be increasing capacity of the economy in the long run by increasing the level of the savings in the economy. In the Keynesian model, investment is exogenously determined therefore positive change in exogenous investment would lead to increase in private saving, capital accumulation and increase in economic output. Garegnani (1992, p.47) states that "... it is an independently determined level of investment that generates the corresponding amount of savings". However, policies such as increase in government expenditure (infrastructure) would increase total income through multiplier effect, which would add (private) savings into the system. Additionally, by providing (infrastructure) capital accumulation it would increase productivity of the capital and economic growth further. Therefore, there is a fiscal space to be benefitted in terms of economic growth, and there is a way to increase the tax base of the economy.

DISCUSSION

The chapter put particular emphasis on the usage of components of aggregate demand by the policy makers to induce economic growth. To this end, we compare different growth enhancing effects of different economic growth strategies for Turkiye that would be adapted by policy makers. We particularly examine the growth enhancing effects of FDI led, FPI led, Export led, Consumption led, and Investment led growth strategies. We also examine how inflation, unemployment, trade deficit, real exchange rate and debt respond to different economic growth strategies that would be adapted.

Consumption led growth theory focus on the demand side of the economic growth. Demand saturation theory that was primarily used by Rostow (1978) explains the economic growth in terms of increase in aggregate demand. Particularly, following the introduction of new commodities, demand for these commodities increases which then decreases leading to increase in economic growth rates at the initial periods which decreases over time (Aoki and Yoshikawa, 2002). Therefore, according to this theory, growth decelerates due to decrease in demand along time. Aoki and Yoshikawa (2002) argue that even there is increasing productivity in the production process of matured products as claimed by the creative destruction and quality ladder models (Grossman and Helpman, 1991; Caballero and Jaffe; 1993), high rate of economic growth can not be sustained due to demand saturation. Demand saturation theory emphasizes the linkage between demand creating efforts through producing new products into markets and economic growth.

On the other hand, consumption-led growth might result in weak economic conditions to undertake investment in future if it is financed by credit expansions followed by financial crisis and debt overhang. Therefore, consumption-led growth financed by credit expansion might result in decrease in demand in future (Lombardi et al 2017). Using data for 16 advanced economies over the 2000-2017 period, Kharrobi and Kohlsceen (2017) report that past credit to GDP growth affects positive significantly to future GDP growth for three to four years, whereas debt to GDP ratio affects negative significantly to future GDP growth rates for at least five years. Therefore, consumption led growth financed by credit expansion affects negatively to future growth rates. On the other hand, Godley (1999) argue that US economic growth and employment generation mostly depend on debt-financed consumption.

Foreign investment led growth theory might solely rest on the foreign portfolio inflows (FPI). According to Solow model, increase in the saving per capita increases the level of steady state per capita income forever. Therefore, FPI contributes directly to increase in savings, leading to higher per capita income. However, there are opposing views with regard to FPI led growth strategies. Particularly, these studies focus on its affect in future growth rates through its impact on appreciation of national currency, current account deficit, higher debt service ratio, high real interest rates, and asset bubbles. They argue that increase in capital inflows are used to finance consumption rather than investment, and leads to appreciation of national currency, resulting in the current account deficit (Singh, 1997). Then sudden capital outflows increases the interest rate, dramatically decreases the value of assets, increases debt services and interest rates, leading to dramatic drop in per capita income levels (Calvo, 1998; Rodrik and Velasco, 1999). There are studies in the literature investigating the impact of FPI on economic growth. Bekaert and Harvey (1998, 2000) argue that FPI improves macroeconomic condition in the emerging markets. Durham (2003) also argues that macroeconomic volatility, which is the one of the significant macroeconomic conditions in the Sub Saharan Africa (SSA), enhanced by FPI negatively affects economic growth.

FDI led growth implies that foreign technologies, know-how, management techniques, job training activities contribute to the technology capacity, knowledge stock and skilled labor pool of the host country, which would enhance economic growth. In particular, FDI would contribute to the economic growth via licensing agreements, joint ventures, start-up, management contracts (De Mello and Sinclair; 1995). Moreover, increase in foreign owned capital would temporarily increase the output growth under diminishing returns to scale.

Using data for 32 countries over the 1970-1990 period, De Mello (1999) argue that FDI enhances economic growth. He also argues that the extent of positive contribution of FDI on economic growth depends on the complementarity and substitution between FDI and domestic investment. On the other hand, Herzer and Klasen (2008) using data for 28 developing countries and implementing co-integration techniques country-by-country cases, argue that FDI does not exert any influence, neither short-term nor long-term, on economic growth.

The study uses data for the Turkiye to investigate the presence of the strength and weaknesses of different growth strategies on various economic indicators including economic growth, current account deficit and inflation. There are several studies examining the impact of export, FDI, portfolio investment on economic growth and some other macroeconomic indicators. Onaran (2006), argue that foreign portfolio investment led growth do not solve the problems of current account deficit and import dependency. She also argues that economic growth based on foreign investment would generate fragile patterns and over-indebtedness. On the other hand, export led growth strategy is implemented following from import substitution growth strategy. Using data for the 1992:Q1-2007:Q3 period, Temiz and Gökmen (2014) report that there is no causality running from FDI to economic growth neither in the short-run nor in the long-run. Using data for the 1992-2007 period, Alagöz et al. (2008) argue that there is no granger causality running from FDI to economic growth.

Günçavdı and Kayam (2017) argue about the structural deficiencies of the Turkish economy as import dependency, large external deficits, high dependence on foreign inflows and high current account deficits. They also argue that the export supply is not infinitely elastic and domestic demand has detrimental affect on the export expansion. Onaran and Stockhammer (2005) argue that export oriented growth strategy of Turkiye leads to low wage share, growth, investment and employment in Turkiye. Using data for the 1980-2005 period, Halicioglu (2007) argue that export enhances industrial production. Using data for the 1975-2004 period, Ozturk and Kalyoncu (2007) argue that there is bidirectional causality between FDI and economic growth.

The study examines the impact of different growth strategies on the the GDP level in Turkiye as well as its impact on macroeconomic conditions including inflation, debt, trade deficit, exchange rate, and unemployment. There are no comparative studies on economic growth strategies and its impact on macroeconomic conditions in the relevant literature. By providing findings, the study provides evidences about the macroeconomic consequences of different economic growth led strategies.

SOLUTIONS AND RECOMMENDATIONS

Data

All data are obtained from Central Bank of the Republic of Turkiye (CBRT) over the period of 2005: Q1-2017: Q4. Table 1 presents the definition and source of the data.

Table 1. Variables: definition and source

Notation	Definition	Source
gdp	Gross domestic product	CBRT(2018)
cons	Final consumption expenditure of resident households and consumption of NPISH + Government final consumption expenditure	CBRT(2018)
inv	Gross fixed capital formation + Change in stocks	CBRT(2018)
exp	Exports of goods and services	CBRT(2018)
fdi	Direct Investment: Net incurrence of liabilities	CBRT(2018)
port	Portfolio Investment: Net incurrence of liabilities	CBRT(2018)
exc	CPI Based Real Effective Exchange Rate (2003=100)	CBRT(2018)
debt	Gross External Debt of Turkiye /1000000000	CBRT(2018)
inf	Growth rate of Consumer Price Index (2003=100)	CBRT(2018)
trdef	(Imports of goods and services - Exports of goods and services) / 1000000000	CBRT(2018)
unemp	Unemployment rate (%)	CBRT(2018)
consogdp	cons/gdp	CBRT(2018)
invogdp	inv/gdp	CBRT(2018)
expogdp	exp/gdp	CBRT(2018)
fdiogdp	fdi/gdp	CBRT(2018)
portogdp	port/gdp	CBRT(2018)

Methodological Framework

The study aims to investigate the affect of different economic growth strategies on the GDP level in Turkiye as well the total debt, trade deficit, unemployment, foreign exchange rate, inflation levels. To this end, we use ARDL approach to examine the short run and long run dynamics governing the impact of different growth strategies on the macroeconomic conditions in Turkiye.

$$GDP = f(CONS, INV, EXP, FDI, PORT) \tag{1}$$

$$DEBT = f(CONSOGDP, INVOGDP, EXPOGDP, FDIOGDP, PORTOGDP) \tag{2}$$

$$EXC = f(CONSOGDP, INVOGDP, EXPOGDP, FDIOGDP, PORTOGDP) \tag{3}$$

$$INF = f(CONSOGDP, INVOGDP, EXPOGDP, FDIOGDP, PORTOGDP) \tag{4}$$

$$TRDEF = f(CONSOGDP, INVOGDP, EXPOGDP, FDIOGDP, PORTOGDP) \tag{5}$$

$$UNEMP = f(CONSOGDP, INVOGDP, EXPOGDP, FDIOGDP, PORTOGDP) \tag{6}$$

The long run relationships between the dependent and independent variables in each of six equations are investigated by ARDL Bounds testing approach, which is developed by Pesaran and Shin (1999) and Pesaran et al. (2001). The existence of a long run relationship among the variables used in the econometric model are performed, regardless of their order of integration in ARDL Bounds testing approach. ARDL bounds testing approach allows that the variables have different optimal lags. Estimation results are consistent in small sample sizes, which allow for estimating the long and short run parameters of econometric model (Cergibozan and Demir, 2017).

The ARDL Bounds tests are based on standard F and t-statistics. The asymptotic distributions of the F and t-statistics are non-standard under the null hypothesis that there exists no level relationship whether the variables are I (0) or I (1) (Cergibozan and Demir, 2017). If any variable has order of integration greater than one, then the critical bounds provided by Pesaran et al. (2001) are not valid (Cergibozan and Demir, 2017). Two sets of asymptotic critical values are provided; one assuming all variables are I(1) and the other assuming all variables are I(0). Hence, before proceeding to the estimation, the integrating properties of variables must be checked (Cergibozan and Demir, 2017).

The six models we test through ARDL procedure are as follows:

$$\Delta GDP_t = \alpha_0 + \sum_{i=1}^{p} \alpha_1 \Delta GDP_{t-i} + \sum_{i=0}^{p} \alpha_2 \Delta CONS_{t-i} + \sum_{i=0}^{p} \alpha_3 \Delta INV_{t-i} \sum_{i=0}^{p} \alpha_4 \Delta EXP_{t-i} + \sum_{i=0}^{p} \alpha_5 \Delta FDI_{t-i}$$

$$+ \sum_{i=0}^{p} \alpha_6 \Delta PORT_{t-i} + \beta_1 GDP_{t-1} + \beta_2 CONS_{t-1} + \beta_3 INV_{t-1} + \beta_4 EXP_{t-1} + \beta_5 FDI_{t-1} + \beta_6 PORT_{t-1} + \varepsilon_t$$

$$(7)$$

$$\Delta DEBT_t = \alpha_0 + \sum_{i=1}^{p} \alpha_1 \Delta DEBT_{t-i} + \sum_{i=0}^{p} \alpha_2 \Delta CONSOGDP_{t-i} + \sum_{i=0}^{p} \alpha_3 \Delta INVOGDP_{t-i}$$

$$+ \sum_{i=0}^{p} \alpha_4 \Delta EXPOGDP_{t-i} + \sum_{i=0}^{p} \alpha_5 \Delta FDIOGDP_{t-i} + \sum_{i=0}^{p} \alpha_6 \Delta PORTOGDP_{t-i} + \beta_1 DEBT_{t-1}$$

$$+ \beta_2 CONSOGDP_{t-1} + \beta_3 INVOGDP_{t-1} + \beta_4 EXPOGDP_{t-1} + \beta_5 FDIOGDP_{t-1} + \beta_6 PORTOGDP_{t-1} + \varepsilon_t$$

$$(8)$$

$$\Delta EXC_t = \alpha_0 + \sum_{i=1}^{p} \alpha_1 \Delta EXC_{t-i} + \sum_{i=0}^{p} \alpha_2 \Delta CONSOGDP_{t-i} + \sum_{i=0}^{p} \alpha_3 \Delta INVOGDP_{t-i} + \sum_{i=0}^{p} \alpha_4 \Delta EXPOGDP_{t-i}$$

$$+ \sum_{i=0}^{p} \alpha_5 \Delta FDIOGDP_{t-i} + \sum_{i=0}^{p} \alpha_6 \Delta PORTOGDP_{t-i} + \beta_1 DEBT_{t-1} + \beta_2 CONSOGDP_{t-1} + \beta_3 INVOGDP_{t-1}$$

$$+ \beta_4 EXPOGDP_{t-1} + \beta_5 FDIOGDP_{t-1} + \beta_6 PORTOGDP_{t-1} + \varepsilon_t$$

$$(9)$$

$$\Delta INF_t = \alpha_0 + \sum_{i=1}^{p} \alpha_1 \Delta INF_{t-i} + \sum_{i=0}^{p} \alpha_2 \Delta CONSOGDP_{t-i} + \sum_{i=0}^{p} \alpha_3 \Delta INVOGDP_{t-i}$$

$$+ \sum_{i=0}^{p} \alpha_4 \Delta EXPOGDP_{t-i} + \sum_{i=0}^{p} \alpha_5 \Delta FDIOGDP_{t-i} + \sum_{i=0}^{p} \alpha_6 \Delta PORTOGDP_{t-i} + \beta_1 DEBT_{t-1}$$

$$+ \beta_2 CONSOGDP_{t-1} + \beta_3 INVOGDP_{t-1} + \beta_4 EXPOGDP_{t-1} + \beta_5 DIOGDP_{t-1} + \beta_6 PORTOGDP_{t-1} + \varepsilon_t$$

$$(10)$$

$$\Delta TRDEF_t = \alpha_0 + \sum_{i=1}^{p} \alpha_1 \Delta TRDEF_{t-i} + \sum_{i=0}^{p} \alpha_2 \Delta CONSOGDP_{t-i} + \sum_{i=0}^{p} \alpha_3 \Delta INVOGDP_{t-i}$$

$$+ \sum_{i=0}^{p} \alpha_4 \Delta EXPOGDP_{t-i} + \sum_{i=0}^{p} \alpha_5 \Delta FDIOGDP_{t-i} + \sum_{i=0}^{p} \alpha_6 \Delta PORTOGDP_{t-i} + \beta_1 DEBT_{t-1}$$

$$+ \beta_2 CONSOGDP_{t-1} + \beta_3 INVOGDP_{t-1} + \beta_4 EXPOGDP_{t-1} + \beta_5 FDIOGDP_{t-1} + \beta_6 PORTOGDP_{t-1} + \varepsilon_t$$

$$(11)$$

$$\Delta UNEMP_t = \alpha_0 + \sum_{i=1}^{p} \alpha_1 \Delta UNEMP_{t-i} + \sum_{i=0}^{p} \alpha_2 \Delta CONSOGDP_{t-i} + \sum_{i=0}^{p} \alpha_3 \Delta INVOGDP_{t-i}$$

$$+ \sum_{i=0}^{p} \alpha_4 \Delta EXPOGDP_{t-i} + \sum_{i=0}^{p} \alpha_5 \Delta FDIOGDP_{t-i} + \sum_{i=0}^{p} \alpha_6 \Delta PORTOGDP_{t-i} + \beta_1 DEBT_{t-1}$$

$$+ \beta_2 CONSOGDP_{t-1} + \beta_3 INVOGDP_{t-1} + \beta_4 EXPOGDP_{t-1} + \beta_5 FDIOGDP_{t-1} + \beta_6 PORTOGDP_{t-1} + \varepsilon_t$$

$$(12)$$

where β_1 to β_6 indicate long-run relationship among the variables, while α_1 to α_6 with the signs of the sum correspond to short-run dynamics of the variables. Also, α_0 is constant term, Δ is the first-difference operator, and ε_t is the Gaussian white noise. (Cergibozan and Demir, 2017).

The results for short-run and long-run dynamics are obtained in two steps by ARDL Bounds testing approach. The first step is to estimate equation (7) to (12) with OLS method by employing an optimal lag selection criterion such as Akaike Information Criterion (AIC). We conduct F-test to test the existence of long-run relationship among the variables for each equation (Cergibozan and Demir, 2017).

The null hypothesis of no-cointegration;

H0: $\beta_1 = \beta_2 = \beta_3 = \beta_4 = \beta_5 = \beta_6 = 0$

is tested against the existence of cointegration

H1: $\beta_1 \neq \beta_2 \neq \beta_3 \neq \beta_4 \neq \beta_5 \neq \beta_6 \neq 0$

Then, the calculated F-statistic value is compared with upper and lower critical values obtained from Pesaran et al. (2001). If the calculated F-statistic value is greater than upper critical value obtained from

Pesaran et al. (2001), we reject the null hypothesis of no cointegration whether the regressors are I(0) or I(1) (Cergibozan and Demir, 2017).

Once the existence of a long-run relationship among the variables has been established, we estimate a general error correction model (ECM) as second step (Cergibozan and Demir, 2017).

The equations (7) to (12) for ECM estimation can be rewritten as follows:

$$
\Delta GDP_t = \mu_0 + \sum_{i=1}^{p}\rho_i\Delta GDP_{t-i} + \sum_{i=0}^{p}\phi_i\Delta CONS_{t-i} + \sum_{i=0}^{p}\phi_i\Delta INV_{t-i}
$$
$$
+ \sum_{i=0}^{p}\phi_i\Delta EXP_{t-i} + \sum_{i=0}^{p}\phi_i\Delta FDI_{t-i} + \sum_{i=0}^{p}\phi_i\Delta PORT_{t-i} + \psi\, ECT_{t-1} + u_t
$$

$$(13)$$

$$
\Delta DEBT_t = \mu_0 + \sum_{i=1}^{p}\rho_i\Delta DEBT_{t-i} + \sum_{i=0}^{p}\phi_i\Delta CONSOGDP_{t-i} + \sum_{i=0}^{p}\phi_i\Delta INVOGDP_{t-i}
$$
$$
+ \sum_{i=0}^{p}\phi_i\Delta EXPOGDP_{t-i} + \sum_{i=0}^{p}\phi_i\Delta FDIOGDP_{t-i} + \sum_{i=0}^{p}\phi_i\Delta PORTOGDP_{t-i} + \psi\, ECT_{t-1} + u_t
$$

$$(14)$$

$$
\Delta EXC_t = \mu_0 + \sum_{i=1}^{p}\rho_i\Delta EXC_{t-i} + \sum_{i=0}^{p}\phi_i\Delta CONSOGDP_{t-i} + \sum_{i=0}^{p}\phi_i\Delta INVOGDP_{t-i}
$$
$$
+ \sum_{i=0}^{p}\phi_i\Delta EXPOGDP_{t-i} + \sum_{i=0}^{p}\phi_i\Delta FDIOGDP_{t-i} + \sum_{i=0}^{p}\phi_i\Delta PORTOGDP_{t-i} + \psi\, ECT_{t-1} + u_t
$$

$$(15)$$

$$
\Delta INF_t = \mu_0 + \sum_{i=1}^{p}\rho_i\Delta INF_{t-i} + \sum_{i=0}^{p}\phi_i\Delta CONSOGDP_{t-i} + \sum_{i=0}^{p}\phi_i\Delta INVOGDP_{t-i}
$$
$$
+ \sum_{i=0}^{p}\phi_i\Delta EXPOGDP_{t-i} + \sum_{i=0}^{p}\phi_i\Delta FDIOGDP_{t-i} + \sum_{i=0}^{p}\phi_i\Delta PORTOGDP_{t-i} + \psi\, ECT_{t-1} + u_t
$$

$$(16)$$

$$
\Delta TRDEF_t = \mu_0 + \sum_{i=1}^{p}\rho_i\Delta TRDEF_{t-i} + \sum_{i=0}^{p}\phi_i\Delta CONSOGDP_{t-i} + \sum_{i=0}^{p}\phi_i\Delta INVOGDP_{t-i}
$$
$$
+ \sum_{i=0}^{p}\phi_i\Delta EXPOGDP_{t-i} + \sum_{i=0}^{p}\phi_i\Delta FDIOGDP_{t-i} + \sum_{i=0}^{p}\phi_i\Delta PORTOGDP_{t-i} + \psi\, ECT_{t-1} + u_t
$$

$$(17)$$

$$\Delta UNEMP_t = \mu_0 + \sum_{i=1}^{p} \rho_i \Delta UNEMP_{t-i} + \sum_{i=0}^{p} \phi_i \Delta CONSOGDP_{t-i} + \sum_{i=0}^{p} \phi_i \Delta INVOGDP_{t-i}$$

$$+ \sum_{i=0}^{p} \phi_i \Delta EXPOGDP_{t-i} + \sum_{i=0}^{p} \phi_i \Delta FDIOGDP_{t-i} + \sum_{i=0}^{p} \phi_i \Delta PORTOGDP_{t-i} + \psi\, ECT_{t-1} + u_t$$

$$(18)$$

where Δ is the first difference operator, ψ is the speed of adjustment, *ECT* is the error correction term and u_t is residual term, which is assumed to be identically, independently and normally distributed. The statistical significance of lagged error correction term ECT_{t-1} with negative sign validates the establishment of long-run relationship between variables. The coefficient of lagged error correction term ψ indicates the proportion of deviations from the long-run equilibrium in the dependent variable that are eliminated or corrected in each period (Cergibozan and Demir, 2017).

Empirical Findings

Before estimation, the stationary of the variables are checked with Phillips-Perron unit root test in order to avoid spurious regression problem. Phillips-Perron unit root test is used to evaluate the order of integration for each variable. Table 2 presents unit root tests for all variables. According to Table 2, all dependent variables in Eq. (1) to Eq. (6) are non-stationary at level, but stationary at their first differences. In other words, they are I (1). For the independent variables in Eq. (1); CONS, INV, EXP are non-stationary at level but stationary at their first differences and FDI, PORT are both stationary at level and at their first differences. Hence, CONS, INV, EXP are I (1) and FDI, PORT are I (0). The independent variables in equations (2) to (6) are both stationary at level and at their first differences. In other words, they are I (0). Hence, ARDL Bounds Testing Approach can be properly used for each model in equations (7) to (12).

The selection of optimal lag length is critical for ARDL Bounds testing approach. Akaike Information Criterion (AIC) is used for determination of optimal lag length for each equation from (7) to (12). Table 3 presents the results of ARDL co-integration test with optimal lag lengths found for each equation from (7) to (12).

There is a long-run relationship between dependent and independent variables in each equation since F-statistics for each equation are greater than the upper critical values.

Since we found the evidence for the existence of co-integration, the next step is to determine long-run and short-run relationship between dependent and independent variables for each equation from (7) to (12) with ARDL Bounds testing approach.

Tables (4) to (9) present long-run and short-run analysis for each equation from (7) to (12).

According to the estimation results in Table 4, consumption (CONS), exports (EXP) and foreign direct investment (FDI) increase gross domestic product (GDP), hence lead to growth in the long-run. Portfolio investment (PORT) decreases gross domestic product, hence leads to negative growth in the long-run. Investment has no effect on gross domestic product. This results imply that consumption led growth strategy, export led growth strategy and FDI led growth strategy increases GDP levels, however FPI led growth strategy decreases GDP levels confirming the opposing studies on the benefits of FPI led growth strategy (Krugman, 1995; Calvo, 1998; Rodrik and Velasco, 1999).

Table 2. Phillips-Perron Unit Root Test

Variable	T-Statistic (Level)	T-Statistic (First Difference)	Decision
GDP	7.104	-8.023*	I(1)
CONS	7.117	-9.412*	I(1)
INV	5.062	-7.058*	I(1)
EXP	9.392	-6.094*	I(1)
FDI	-5.510*	-13.105*	I(0)
PORT	-4.939*	-30.339*	I(0)
DEBT	3.636	-5.688*	I(1)
EXC	-3.401	-7.556*	I(1)
INF	-2.429	-6.559*	I(1)
TRDEF	-2.329	-10.949*	I(1)
UNEMP	-0.163	-14.127*	I(1)
CONSOGDP	-5.915*	-17.005*	I(0)
INVOGDP	-3.629*	-13.131*	I(0)
EXPOGDP	-4.899*	-19.830*	I(0)
FDIOGDP	-6.225*	-15.462*	I(0)
PORTOGDP	-5.154*	-24.221*	I(0)

Table 3. The results of ARDL Co-Integration Test

	Optimal Lag	F-Statistics	Critical Values % 5		Critical Values %10	
	Length		I(0)	I(1)	I(0)	I(1)
Equation (7)	(4,4,4,4,4,2)	7.57	2.39	3.38	2.08	3.00
Equation (8)	(1,4,0,4,0,4)	6.36	2.39	3.38	2.08	3.00
Equation (9)	(5,6,5,6,6,6)	7.29	2.39	3.38	2.08	3.00
Equation (10)	(4,2,2,1,1,0)	4.49	2.39	3.38	2.08	3.00
Equation (11)	(5,5,6,6,4,6)	6.31	2.39	3.38	2.08	3.00
Equation (12)	(5,1,2,3,4,4)	7.46	2.39	3.38	2.08	3.00

According to the estimation results in Table 5, investment over gross domestic product (INVOGDP) and export over gross domestic product (EXPOGDP) have positive significant effect on total debt (DEBT) in the long-run. Foreign direct investment over gross domestic product (FDIOGDP) has negative significant effect on total debt (DEBT). Consumption over gross domestic product (CONSOGDP) and portfolio investment over gross domestic product (PORTOGDP) have no significant effect on total debt (DEBT) in the long-run.

Results indicating that debt overhang issue is related to export and investment led growth strategies. This result also imply that consumption led growth strategy does not suffer from accumulation of debt that would diminish future consumption levels considerably. However, Investment led growth strategy seems to generate debt as well as no growth effect implying that external debt financed investment decreases future investment and capital accumulation levels. FDI led growth on the other hand decreases external debt level would indicate the decrease in domestic investment financed by external debt due to substitutability of domestic investment with FDI or increase in productivity through technological spillovers by FDI.

Table 4. Long and short run analysis for equation 7

Dependent Variable: GDP	Coefficients	
Variables	**Short Run Coefficients**	**Long Run Coefficients**
GDP(-1)	0.320 (2.655)**	
GDP(-2)	0.076 (0.663)	
GDP(-3)	-0.517 (-5.067)***	
CONS	0.782 (17.017)***	1.016 (11.991)***
CONS(-1)	-0.647 (-4.151)***	
CONS(-2)	-0.221 (-1.579)	
CONS(-3)	0.475 (3.939)***	
INV	0.773 (12.252)***	-0.012 (-0.070)
INV(-1)	0.334 (3.963)***	
INV(-2)	0.025 (0.259)	
INV(-3)	0.450 (4.919)***	
EXP	0.395 (6.912)***	1.202 (5.963)***
EXP(-1)	-0.674 (-5.718)***	
EXP(-2)	-0.346 (-3.197)***	
EXP(-3)	-0.154 (-1.883)*	
FDI	0.089 (0.372)	2.301 (3.033)***
FDI(-1)	-0.467 (2.438)**	
FDI(-2)	0.600 (2.613)**	
FDI(-3)	0.467 (2.438)**	
PORT	-0.281 (-3.828)***	-0.600 (-3.873)***
PORT(-1)	0.152 (1.865)*	
CONSTANT		-12.99E+9 (-2.698)**
ECT(-1)	-0.765 (-8.301)***	
Diagnostic Tests	p-value	
χ^2 (Serial Correlation)		0.2700
χ^2 (Heteroscedasticity)		0.6897
χ^2 (Normality)		0.5476
χ^2 (Functional Form)		0.4806

Table 5. Long and short run analysis for equation 8

Dependent Variable: DEBT	Coefficients	
Variables	**Short Run Coefficients**	**Long Run Coefficients**
CONSOGDP	260.461(2.701)**	-706.913 (-0.731)
CONSOGDP(-1)	276.860 (3.677)***	
CONSOGDP(-2)	145.554 (1.893*	
CONSOGDP(-3)	181.342 (2.539)**	
INVOGDP	452.790 (6.619)***	3334.239 (4.276)***
EXPOGDP	117.223 (1.512)	4213.066 (3.253)***
EXPOGDP(-1)	-287.353 (-3.640)***	
EXPOGDP(-2)	-363.806 (-4.317)***	
EXPOGDP(-3)	-316.142 (-4.593)***	
FDIOGDP	-405.627 (-4.201)***	-3751.355 (-3.699)***
PORTOGDP	83.496 (1.220)	-25.394 (-0.018)
PORTOGDP(-1)	147.579 (2.195)**	
PORTOGDP(-2)	59.683 (0.923)	
PORTOGDP(-3)	-176.975 (-2.780)***	
CONSTANT		-939.088 (-0.870)
ECT(-1)	-0.120 (-9.914)***	
Diagnostic Tests	p-value	
χ^2 (Serial Correlation)		0.7920
χ^2 (Heteroscedasticity)		0.9310
χ^2 (Normality)		0.4997
χ^2 (Functional Form)		0.4883

According to the estimation results in Table 6, investment over gross domestic product (INVOGDP) and export over gross domestic product (EXPOGDP) have positive significant effect on exchange rate (EXC), hence they lead to depreciation of currency in the long-run. Foreign direct investment over gross domestic product (FDIOGDP) and portfolio investment over gross domestic product (PORTOGDP) have negative significant effect on exchange rate (EXC), hence they lead to appreciation of currency in the long-run. Consumption over gross domestic product (CONSOGDP) has no significant effect on exchange rate (EXC) in the long-run.

Results imply that export led growth strategy as well investment led growth strategy leads to increase in currency depreciation implying rising foreign currency demands under these economic growth strategies. These results also might imply highly import dependent structure of export in Turkiye as well as the significant share of intermediate goods in total imports in Turkiye. On the other hand, it seems that both type of foreign capital flows lead to appreciation of TL whereas consumption led growth strategy does not put significant pressure on the exchange rates which coincides with the fact that small portion of total import is consumption goods.

Table 6. Long and short run analysis for equation 9

Dependent Variable: EXC	Coefficients	
Variables	Short Run Coefficients	Long Run Coefficients
EXC(-1)	0.498 (9.099)***	
EXC(-2)	0.377 (5.489)***	
EXC(-3)	0.287 (5.031)***	
EXC(-4)	0.427 (4.297)***	
CONSOGDP	192.366 (6.262)***	-14.412 (-0.105)
CONSOGDP(-1)	113.835 (3.745)***	
CONSOGDP(-2)	276.760 (7.357)***	
CONSOGDP(-3)	7.761 (0.196)	
CONSOGDP(-4)	-82-994 (-2.507)**	
CONSOGDP(-5)	-103.473 (-4.044)***	
INVOGDP	195.770 (6.251)***	340.141 (4.767)***
INVOGDP(-1)	-304.123 (-7.903)***	
INVOGDP(-2)	-28.701 (-1.312)	
INVOGDP(-3)	-101.752 (-4.437)***	
INVOGDP(-4)	-180.523 (-8.039)***	
EXPOGDP	334.366 (13.125)***	554.251 (3.173)**
EXPOGDP(-1)	-335.230 (-7.439)***	
EXPOGDP(-2)	-262.984 (-7.130)***	
EXPOGDP(-3)	-278.226 (-7.573)***	
EXPOGDP(-4)	-449.781 (-11.014)***	
EXPOGDP(-5)	-282.586 (-8.277)***	
FDIOGDP	641.858 (9.749)***	-284.584 (-2.328)*
FDIOGDP(-1)	739.216 (7.292)***	
FDIOGDP(-2)	407.066 (4.676)***	
FDIOGDP(-3)	218.526 (2.694)**	
FDIOGDP(-4)	459.682 (9.244)***	
FDIOGDP(-5)	440.173 (7.690)***	
PORTOGDP	-24.966 (-1.124)	-471.532 (-2.582)**
PORTOGDP(-1)	455.938 (9.746)***	
PORTOGDP(-2)	415.789 (13.335)***	
PORTOGDP(-3)	528.087 (13.243)***	
PORTOGDP(-4)	292.468 (6.817)***	
PORTOGDP(-5)	128.937 (4.784)***	
CONSTANT		-109.117 (-0.692)
ECT(-1)	-0.919 (-10.105)***	
Diagnostic Tests	p-value	
χ^2 (Serial Correlation)		0.1362

continues on following page

Table 6. Continued

Dependent Variable: EXC	Coefficients	
Variables	Short Run Coefficients	Long Run Coefficients
χ² (Heteroscedasticity)		0.2894
χ² (Normality)		0.9839
χ² (Functional Form)		0.4806

According to the estimation results in Table 7, export over gross domestic product (EXPOGDP) and foreign direct investment over gross domestic product (FDIOGDP) have positive significant effect on inflation rate (INF) in the long-run. Portfolio investment over gross domestic product (PORTOGDP) has negative significant effect on inflation rate (INF) in the long-run. Consumption over gross domestic product (CONSOGDP) and investment over gross domestic product (INVOGDP) have no significant effect on inflation rate (INF) in the long-run.

Results indicate that export led growth and FDI-led growth strategies increase the inflation rate. One possible explanation regarding the inflationary export led growth strategy is that decreased domestic production and depreciation of TL might lead to increase in inflation. On the other hand, FDI might contribute to inflation by raising the wage level. FPI led growth strategy through appreciation of TL, increase in import and decrease in domestic demand would result in low inflation rates.

Table 7. Long and short run analysis for equation 10

Dependent Variable: INF	Coefficients	
Variables	Short Run Coefficients	Long Run Coefficients
INF(-1)	0.592 (4.811)***	
INF(21)	0.677 (4.924)***	
INF(-3)	0.325 (2.261)**	
CONSOGDP	16.513 (2.053)**	-14.085 (-1.091)
CONSOGDP(-1)	17.676 (1.803)*	
INVOGDP	24.980 (2.050)**	-2.779 (-0.357)
INVOGDP(-1)	28.963 (2.483)**	
EXPOGDP	21.512 (1.731)*	44.759 (2.926)***
FDIOGDP	29.208 (1.547)	75.759 (4.532)***
PORTOGDP	-35.108 (-3.055)***	-29.174 (-2.362)**
CONSTANT		9.123 (0.701)
ECT(-1)	-1.258 (-6.923)***	
Diagnostic Tests	p-value	
χ² (Serial Correlation)		0.6709
χ² (Heteroscedasticity)		0.5031
χ² (Normality)		0.4465
χ² (Functional Form)		0.9633

According to the estimation results in Table 8, investment over gross domestic product (INVOGDP) and Foreign direct investment over gross domestic product (FDIOGDP) have positive significant effect on trade deficit (TRDEF), hence they lead to higher trade deficit in the long-run. Portfolio investment over gross domestic product (PORTOGDP)has negative significant effect on trade deficit (TRDEF), hence it decreases trade deficit in the long-run. Consumption over gross domestic product (CONSOGDP) and export over gross domestic product (EXPOGDP) have no significant effect on trade deficit (TRDEF) in the long-run.

As it is emphasized before, since intermediate goods are significant part of the total imports in Turkiye, investment led growth would lead to the trade deficit in Turkiye. On the other hand, FPI through its affect on appreaciton of TL might prompt the usage of the foreign intermediate goods (substitution with the local ones) leading to higher trade deficit in Turkiye.

However, it seems that FDI contributes to export more than import, leading to lower trade deficit. This result dthe results of studies on Turkiye (Onwuka and Zoral, 2009; Yalta, 2011) by claiming that FDI increases import demand.

Table 8. Long and short run analysis for equation 11

Dependent Variable: TRDEF	Coefficients	
Variables	**Short Run Coefficients**	**Long Run Coefficients**
TRDEF(-1)	2.116 (8.128)***	
TRDEF(-2)	1.585 (8.720)***	
TRDEF(-3)	1.138 (6.320)***	
TRDEF(-4)	1.110 (8.101)***	
CONSOGDP	330.541 (9.486)***	31.002 (1.158)
CONSOGDP(-1)	89.078 (1.670)	
CONSOGDP(-2)	100.440 (1.855)	
CONSOGDP(-3)	64.470 (1.125)	
CONSOGDP(-4)	-95.522 (-1.639)	
INVOGDP	362.606 (11.436)***	313.162 (18.086)***
INVOGDP(-1)	-534.881 (-7.528)***	
INVOGDP(-2)	-389.432 (-6.182)***	
INVOGDP(-3)	-287.157 (-4.617)***	
INVOGDP(-4)	-256.822 (-6.288)***	
INVOGDP(-5)	-71.406 (-3.294)**	
EXPOGDP	108.687 (3.460)***	22.141 (0.416)
EXPOGDP(-1)	93.628 (2.755)**	
EXPOGDP(-2)	184.871 (5.011)***	
EXPOGDP(-3)	241.100 (6.764)***	
EXPOGDP(-4)	297.540 (5.889)***	
EXPOGDP(-5)	121.287 (3.262)**	
FDIOGDP	-597.063 (-6.240)***	-609.759 (-16.667)***

continues on following page

Table 8. Continued

Dependent Variable: TRDEF	Coefficients	
Variables	Short Run Coefficients	Long Run Coefficients
FDIOGDP(-1)	891.142 (6.538)***	
FDIOGDP(-2)	413.490 (5.746)***	
FDIOGDP(-3)	378.872 (4.769)***	
PORTOGDP	108.489 (3.535)***	166.470 (4.542)***
PORTOGDP(-1)	-312.046 (-6.418)***	
PORTOGDP(-2)	-223.802 (-6.153)***	
PORTOGDP(-3)	-241.824 (-5.862)***	
PORTOGDP(-4)	-93.068 (-3.120)**	
PORTOGDP(-5)	51.098 (2.009)*	
CONSTANT		-95.422 (-2.832)**
ECT(-1)	-2.789 (-8.796)***	
Diagnostic Tests	p-value	
χ^2 (Serial Correlation)		0.4005
χ^2 (Heteroscedasticity)		0.2592
χ^2 (Normality)		0.7621
χ^2 (Functional Form)		0.2736

According to the estimation results in Table 9, consumption over gross domestic product (CONSOGDP), export over gross domestic product (EXPOGDP) and Foreign direct investment over gross domestic product (FDIOGDP) have negative significant effect on the unemployment rate (UNEMP), hence they lead to lower unemployment in the long-run. Investment over gross domestic product (INVOGDP) and portfolio investment over gross domestic product (PORTOGDP) have no significant effect on the unemployment rate (UNEMP) in the long-run.

Results indicate that consumption led growth, export led growth and FDI led growth strategies exert negative impact on unemployment rate indicating that these strategies reduce the level of unemployment in Turkiye. These results also comply with the estimations examining the GDP enhancing effects of various economic growth strategies. Therefore, economic growth strategies leading to higher GDP levels also generate employment opportunities different than the case of jobless economic growth.

According to the estimation results from Table (4) to (9), ECT_{t-1} always have a negative expected sign and statistically significant at %1, which suggest that there is a long-run relationship between dependent and independent variables in all equations from (7) to (12). The diagnostic tests indicate no diagnostic problem in each equation from (7) to (12).

FUTURE RESEARCH DIRECTIONS

A further research should be directed to the subject that why inward FDI-led growth strategy increase inflation level in Turkiye while it generates both income and employment without increasing debt.

Table 9. Long and short run analysis for equation 12

Dependent Variable: UNEMP	Coefficients	
Variables	**Short Run Coefficients**	**Long Run Coefficients**
UNEMP(-1)	0.222 (1.961)*	
UNEMP(-2)	0.291 (3.770)***	
UNEMP(-3)	-0.027 (-0.334)	
UNEMP(-4)	0.374 (4.018)***	
CONSOGDP	-17.103 (-3.215)***	-81.120 (-2.270)**
INVOGDP	-32.757 (-7.319)***	-21.022 (-0.965)
INVOGDP(-1)	14.701 (-2.811)**	
EXPOGDP	-17.451 (-3.278)***	-179.482 (-2.940)***
EXPOGDP(-1)	22.130 (3.391)***	
EXPOGDP(-2)	24.619 (4.497)***	
FDIOGDP	-17.665 (-1.354)	-112.172 (-3.242)***
FDIOGDP(-1)	-16.574 (-1.344)	
FDIOGDP(-2)	37.115 (-3.114)***	
FDIOGDP(-3)	-14.953 (-1.636)	
PORTOGDP	7.186 (1.489)	-7.619 (-0.202)
PORTOGDP(-1)	12.415 (2.335)**	
PORTOGDP(-2)	19.512 (3.672)***	
PORTOGDP(-3)	14.556 (2.804)**	
CONSTANT		119.513 (2.965)***
ECT(-1)	-0.333 (-8.156)***	
Diagnostic Tests	p-value	
χ^2 (Serial Correlation)		0.6359
χ^2 (Heteroscedasticity)		0.6809
χ^2 (Normality)		0.8386
χ^2 (Functional Form)		0.4551

CONCLUSION

Table 10 illustrates impact of different economic growth strategies on GDP and various macroeconomic conditions. Consumption led growth strategies seems to generate GDP as well as employment whereas it does not have statistically significant affect on inflation, trade deficit, external debt and exchange rate depreciation/appreciation.

Investment led growth strategy on the other hand generate neither income nor employment opportunities. However, as the Turkish economy is import dependent, the expansion of the capital stock and investment puts certain pressure on exchange rate and trade deficit. The results also indicate that investment is financed by (foreign) debt where the size of the debt is related to factors such as global risk appetite, liquidity conditions, relative interest rates and import dependency in the Turkish economy.

FDI-led growth seems to generate both income and employment without increasing debt. However, FDI- led growth strategy seems to increase inflation level, lower the trade deficit and lead to appreciation of TL. FDI led growth generates over valued real exchange rate that would decrease imports, resulting in decrease in trade deficit. Moreover, if the imported goods are substituted by FDI produced goods through which domestic demand channeled to domestically produced goods, this would lead to increased inflation levels.

Export led growth strategy also seems to generate income and employment with the cost of increased inflation, exchange rate, and external debt. The result confirms the dependent structure of Turkish export, and its consequences on exchange rate and external debt.

FPI led growth strategy seems to decrease GDP levels without suggesting any unemployment indications. According to the results, it decreases exchange rate, inflation and debt however it increases trade deficit. The results imply that foreign investment inflows appreciates TL, decreases inflation and increases trade deficit by decreased exports due to cheap foreign exchange.

Table 10. Comparison of economic growth strategies

Growth Strategies	GDP	Unemployment	Inflation	External Debt	Trade Deficit	Exchange Rate
Consumption Led Growth	+	-	0	0	0	0
Investment Led Growth	0	0	0	+	+	+
Export Led Growth	+	-	+	+	0	+
FDI Led Growth	+	-	+	-	-	-
FPI Led Growth	-	0	-	-	+	-

REFERENCES

Alagöz, M., Erdoğan, S., & Topallı, N. (2008). Doğrudan yabancı sermaye yatırımları ve ekonomik büyüme: Türkiye deneyimi 1992-2007 [Foreign direct investment and economic growth: Turkey's experience 1992-2007]. *Gaziantep University Journal of Social Sciences*, 7(1), 79–89.

Aoki, M., & Yoshikawa, H. (2002). Demand saturation-creation and economic growth. *Journal of Economic Behavior & Organization*, 48(2), 127–154. doi:10.1016/S0167-2681(01)00229-3

Bekaert, G., & Harvey, C. R. (1998). Capital markets: An engine for economic growth. *The Brown Journal of World Affairs*, 5(1), 33–53.

Bekaert, G., & Harvey, C. R. (2000). Foreign speculators and emerging equity markets. *The Journal of Finance*, 55(2), 565–613. doi:10.1111/0022-1082.00220

Caballero, R. J., & Jaffe, A. B. (1993). How high are the giants' shoulders: An empirical assessment of knowledge spillovers and creative destruction in a model of economic growth. *NBER Macroeconomics Annual*, 8, 15–74. doi:10.1086/654207

Calvo, G. A. (1998). *Capital flows and capital-market crises: the simple economics of sudden stops.* Academic Press.

Cergibozan, R., & Demir, C. (2017). The Determinants of Foreign Direct Investment Outflows from Turkey. In Outward Foreign Direct Investment (FDI) in Emerging Market Economies (pp. 227-243). IGI Global. doi:10.4018/978-1-5225-2345-1.ch011

De Mello, L. R. (1999). Foreign direct investment-led growth: Evidence from time series and panel data. *Oxford Economic Papers*, *51*(1), 133–151. doi:10.1093/oep/51.1.133

De Mello, L. R., & Sinclair, M. T. (1995). *Foreign direct investment, joint ventures and endogenous growth*. Department of Economics, University of Kent.

Durham, J. B. (2003). Foreign Portfolio Investment, Foreign Bank Lending, and Economic Growth. In *International Finance Discussion Papers 757*. Board of Governors of the Federal Reserve System.

Garegnani, P. (1992). Some Notes for an Analysis of Accumulation. In J. Halevi, D. Laibman, & E. J. Nell (Eds.), *Beyond the steady state: A revival of growth theory*. St. Martin's Press. doi:10.1007/978-1-349-10950-0_3

Godley, W. (1999). Money and credit in a Keynesian model of income determination. *Cambridge Journal of Economics*, *23*(4), 393–411. doi:10.1093/cje/23.4.393

Grossman, G. M., & Helpman, E. (1991). Quality ladders in the theory of growth. *The Review of Economic Studies*, *58*(1), 43–61. doi:10.2307/2298044

Günçavdı, Ö., & Kayam, S. S. (2017). Unravelling the structure of Turkish exports: Impediments and policy. *Journal of Policy Modeling*, *39*(2), 307–323. doi:10.1016/j.jpolmod.2016.09.001

Halicioglu, F. (2007). *A multivariate causality analysis of export and growth for Turkey*. Academic Press.

Hansen, A. (1941). Fiscal Policy and Business Cycles. Academic Press.

Herzer, D., Klasen, S., & Nowak-Lehmann D, F. (2008). In search of FDI-led growth in developing countries: The way forward. *Economic Modelling*, *25*(5), 793–810. doi:10.1016/j.econmod.2007.11.005

Kharroubi, E., & Kohlscheen, E. (2017). *Consumption-led expansions*. Academic Press.

Krugman, P. (1995). Increasing returns, imperfect competition and the positive theory of international trade. Handbook of international economics, 3, 1243-1277. doi:10.1016/S1573-4404(05)80004-8

Lombardi, M. J., Mohanty, M. S., & Shim, I. (2017). *The real effects of household debt in the short and long run*. Academic Press.

Lucas, R. E. Jr. (1988). On the mechanics of economic development. *Journal of Monetary Economics*, *22*(1), 3–42. doi:10.1016/0304-3932(88)90168-7

Onaran, Ö. (2006). *Speculation-led growth and fragility in Turkey: Does EU make a difference or "can it happen again"?* Academic Press.

Onaran, Ö., & Stockhammer, E. (2005). Two different export-oriented growth strategies: Accumulation and distribution in Turkey and South Korea. *Emerging Markets Finance & Trade*, *41*(1), 65–89. doi:10.1080/1540496X.2005.11052596

Ozturk, I., & Kalyoncu, H. (2007). *Foreign direct investment and growth: An empirical investigation based on cross-country comparison.* Academic Press.

Pesaran, M. H., & Shin, Y. (1999). An Autoregressive Distributed Lag Modelling Approach to Co-integration Analysis. In S. Strom (Ed.), *Econometrics and Economic Theory in 20th Century: The Ragnar Frisch Centennial Symposium.* Cambridge, UK: Cambridge University. 10.1017/CCOL521633230.011

Pesaran, M. H., Shin, Y., & Smith, R. J. (2001). Bounds testing approaches to the analysis of level relationships. *Journal of Applied Econometrics, 16*(3), 289–326. doi:10.1002/jae.616

Rodrik, D., & Velasco, A. (1999). *Short-term capital flows* (No. w7364). National Bureau of Economic Research.

Romer, P. M. (1990). Endogenous technological change. *Journal of Political Economy, 98*(5, Part 2), S71–S102. doi:10.1086/261725

Rostow, W. W. (1978). *The world economy: History and prospect* (No. 04; HC51, R6).

Singh, A. (1997). Financial liberalisation, stockmarkets and economic development. *Economic Journal (London), 107*(442), 771–782. doi:10.1111/j.1468-0297.1997.tb00042.x

Temiz, D., & Gökmen, A. (2014). FDI inflow as an international business operation by MNCs and economic growth: An empirical study on Turkey. *International Business Review, 23*(1), 145–154. doi:10.1016/j.ibusrev.2013.03.003

KEY TERMS AND DEFINITIONS

Consumption-Led Growth: An increase in aggregate consumption will ultimately cause an increase in total output in the long-run.

Export-Led Growth: An increase in total exports will ultimately cause an increase in total output in the long-run.

FDI-Led Growth: An increase in foreign direct investment inflows will ultimately cause an increase in total output in the long-run.

FPI-Led Growth: An increase in foreign portfolio investment inflows will ultimately cause an increase in total output in the long-run.

Investment-Led Growth: An increase in aggregate investment will ultimately cause an increase in total output in the long-run.

Keynesian Model: This model explains the economic growth as an aggregate demand issue, in other words, capacity utilization issue.

Solow Growth Theory: This theory implies that factor supplies determine the economic growth in the long run, economy is at full employment and all savings are invested.

Chapter 13
Analysis of System Marginal Price in the Turkish Electricity Market

Aslı Boru İpek

Kütahya Dumlupınar University, Turkey

ABSTRACT

Due to climate change, growing energy prices, and increasing energy consumption, energy efficiency has become a key topic in recent years. Most energy market traders also want to be able to foresee the energy market in the future so that they can take the appropriate actions to optimize their trading profits. As a result, energy market evaluation models are required. Energy markets, on the other hand, are location-dependent, as each market has its auctions and procedures. As a result, specific models for each energy market should be developed. The primary aim of this study is to provide a comprehensive comparison of various machine learning methods in the Turkish electricity market. A comparative analysis is provided on support vector machines (SVM)-based methods, k-nearest neighbors (KNN)-based methods, and ensemble-based method to analyze system marginal price (SMP). According to the accuracy value, the ensemble-based method gives better results.

INTRODUCTION

Today's consumers have important rights that depend on electricity, including the ability to heat their homes, light their homes, travel, and communicate (Gul, 2008). Therefore, countries must deliver electricity to end-users in a timely, reliable, and economical manner. Although it helps countries' economies thrive, the availability of energy also imposes significant financial responsibilities. Countries began allowing investors to participate in the process with a win-win strategy since they realized they could not handle these enormous loads alone. Liberalization is changing markets for energy in particular by reducing public spending and increasing private sector investments. Turkey's electrical market has adopted this pattern (Ünal, Onaygil, Acuner, & Cin, 2022). The establishment of a system similar to the stock market for the electricity market provided great convenience for the participants, and trade started

DOI: 10.4018/978-1-6684-5976-8.ch013

to be carried out in a structure similar to the pool system. Thus, countries started to create their energy markets and had the opportunity to trade in these environments (Arslan & Ertuğrul, 2022). To some extent, it behaves like a stock market price; its changes are cyclical, variable, and affected by a wide range of events (Wang & Ramsay, 1997).

In Turkey, there are three different electricity markets (EPIAS, 2022a). These include the day-ahead market, the intra-day market, and the balancing market. Balancing power market provides reserve capacity that can be online within 15 minutes at the latest to sustain real-time balancing for system operators. Frequency control and demand control services are ensured through ancillary services (EPIAS, 2022a). Real-time supply and demand balance is achieved through the balancing power market (Sirin & Yilmaz, 2021). Although the electricity markets were brought to balance one day in advance through the markets operated by EPIAŞ, the demand and supply balance may change as the real-time approaches. Because of these changes, deterioration may occur in the system that was balanced the day before. The price of the bid, which corresponds to the net volume of orders issued in the balancing power market, determines the SMP (Dursun, Eke, & Tezcan, 2020).

In the previous vertically integrated industry, lowering production and operating costs was the main objective of power system planning and management. However, since the introduction of competition in the electricity market, the objective has changed to maximize the profit or return to the market participants. Employing strategies to increase profit may become possible. The SMP is the market price that is set after taking the characteristics of the generators into account during the bidding process, given the demand and condition of the power system (Lee, Park, Shin, & Lee, 2005). SMP prediction is a significant issue for both consumers and producers of electrical power. Making SMP predictions is a difficult challenge since SMP is very volatile and dependent on a wide range of variables, including the price of oil, load demand, and even natural parameters. By offering suitable bidding strategies, a good SMP prediction can assist both the consumer and the electric power company in maximizing their profit (Yudantaka, Kim, & Song, 2019).

In the competitive energy market, SMP prediction is a significant source of information. The significance of electricity price prediction models like SMP has expanded with the development of a competitive energy market. However, compared to other traded commodities, electricity is well known for being more volatile, making it more difficult to predict the SMP. Because the price of primary energy sources is a major determinant of generation costs, the SMP is also influenced by these costs, which change over time (Jufri, Oh, & Jung, 2019).

The energy surplus or deficit is taken into account when calculating the SMP (Sahin, 2018). The SMP in the electricity market is established at the point of equilibrium between the dispatch curve and the electricity load. The SMP displays several fluctuations since the electricity load fluctuates greatly and continually for a variety of factors, including seasonal variation and business operations (Moon & Jung, 2020). In particular, realized upward/downward regulating offers are used to determine the SMP. In this regard, Market Clearing Price (MCP) is one of the key factors affecting SMP (Sirin & Yilmaz, 2021). MCP is significant in the problem of strategic bidding (Prabavathi & Gnanadass, 2018 & Boru İpek, 2021). The system operator issues Load Shedding (YAT) or Load Cycling (YAL) instructions to balance the electricity surplus or deficit if the planned supply or demand in the real-time market does not appear to match the determined in the day-ahead market. SMP is the imbalance price that displays the system direction in real-time, while MCP is the reference price that occurs at the beginning of the day. It might be stated as follows: if YAL<YAT, then SMP≤MCP; if YAL>YAT, then SMP≥MCP is anticipated (Gayretli, Yucekaya, & Bilge, 2019).

Prediction is an important aspect of many countries' energy plans. Effective prediction is required to fulfill the rising energy demand because of population growth and industrialization. Some features distinguish the electricity market from other markets. Demand elasticity is low in electricity markets. In the short term, the response of consumers to changes in electricity prices is low. Electricity demand fluctuates between seasons, months, and days throughout the year. For this reason, the formation of electricity prices, and the explanation of the volatility and uncertainty in electricity prices are also the subject of academic discussions. Today, various researchers apply models to predict the uncertainty and changes in electricity prices. In the literature, various time series methods, market equilibrium methods, boosting algorithms, and neural network-based methods are encountered in the prediction models of electricity prices. Energy planning and management necessitate accurate modeling and prediction. Better prediction implies more investments that are precise and increased customer satisfaction. Prediction, on the other hand, is not a straightforward task in the energy sector; it necessitates the consideration of numerous intricate elements.

Machine learning techniques allow you to accomplish your goals with less time and effort. For this reason, machine-learning methods will be evaluated in this paper for analysis of the SMP, which is used to calculate imbalances in the power market. SMP direction will be determined using support vector machines (SVM) methods including linear SVM, quadratic SVM, cubic SVM, fine Gaussian SVM, medium Gaussian SVM, coarse gaussian SVM, k-nearest neighbor (KNN) methods including fine KNN, medium KNN, coarse KNN, weighted KNN, and optimizable KNN, and also ensemble classifier method. The primary aim of this study is to provide a comprehensive comparison of machine learning methods in the Turkish electricity market. Thus, the performances of the proposed methods will be compared to assess the prediction results. A comparative analysis will be provided on SVM-based methods, KNN-based methods, and ensemble-based method to help academicians, economists, and statisticians select the best model for determining the SMP direction. Providing energy has emerged as one of the most difficult problems due to the rising energy demands in recent decades. Therefore, the analysis of the electricity market over the short and long term is critical in assisting power distributors in managing and conserving energy for their consumers. In this paper, three research questions are described as follows: (i) which method should be selected for SMP direction prediction; (ii) does the prediction performance vary depending on the methods, and (iii) which of the proposed method is the best for prediction in the Turkish electricity market. In this regard, the goal of this study is to evaluate the literature by analyzing the classification of SMP direction in the context of Turkey. In the electricity market, SMP direction is a critical component for market participants' optimal bidding as well as regulatory bodies' market stabilization.

BACKGROUND

Electricity is used in practically every aspect of human life, including industrial development, transportation, lighting, agriculture, residential construction, and heating. Every year, the amount of electricity consumption rises. Therefore, regulators and policymakers anticipate lower electricity prices, improved electrical supply service, and customer choice, among other things. Many mature unregulated electricity markets are regulated as day-ahead electricity markets and real-time electricity markets. The day-ahead electricity market is a forward market where the one-hour electricity price is calculated for the next operating day based on generation offers, demand offers, and scheduled bilateral transactions. The balancing power market provides the system operator with a spare capacity that can be activated within a maximum of 15 minutes for real-time balancing (Şenocak, 2018).

Most energy market traders want to be able to foresee the energy market in the future so that they can take the appropriate actions to optimize their trading profits. As a result, energy market prediction models are required. On the other hand, energy markets are location-dependent because each market has its own auctions and procedures. As a result, specific prediction models for each energy market should be developed. In addition, the prediction horizon affects the prediction results in the electricity market (Yazıcı, 2020). Therefore, various researchers have evaluated electricity price prediction modeling in the literature (Aggarwal, Saini, & Kumar, 2009). Some of them are summarized as follows.

Sütçü et al. (2022) used machine learning approaches to predict the hourly electricity consumption of a city. A novel method that discretization of regression problems was created. Neural networks and novel methods were integrated to improve the prediction results. Gul (2008) presented the financial effects of interruptions in the supply of electricity to industrial and commercial consumers in Turkey. In the study, reviewing current power quality regulations, examining poor power quality's financial effects on a sample of commercial and industrial consumers, and making suggestions for power quality improvements were all part of the assessment.

Özgüner, Tör, and Güven (2017) evaluated the prediction abilities of the proposed artificial neural network (ANN) model and the multiple linear regression models for the day-ahead hourly MCP in the Turkish electricity market. The ANN method was also created to predict the SMP using input parameters such as historical and predicted load, historical SMP, historical delta, and historical system direction data. Sahin (2018) presented how network constraints affect daily energy costs. The case studies demonstrated that taking into account network constraints in the model of the day-ahead energy market results in an optimal total cost, the suggested method is suitable for implementation in the actual Turkish day-ahead electricity energy market.

Avci, Ketter, and Heck (2018) evaluated the performance of individual and ensemble models in Turkey. Because seasonality approaches can represent some particular features of electricity pricing, they expanded the set of individual models to include them. Ocakoglu and Tolga (2018) predicted market prices to reduce volatility and improve financial performance. The suitable financial alternatives and strategies for the Turkish electricity market were also discussed in the study. Dursun, Eke, and Tezcan (2020) evaluated the MCP and SMP in Turkey, which are used in the calculation of imbalances.

Sirin and Yilmaz (2021) analyzed the effects of variable renewable technologies on the balancing market. Ordered-logistic regression and quantile regression models were used to evaluate the electricity market. Kalfa, Arslan, and Ertuğrul (2021) compared the ANN and multiple linear regression considering the factors influencing the market price. To identify the pricing zones of an electrical market, Poyrazoglu (2021) suggested clustering algorithms in a case study of the Turkish electricity system. Two approaches were used to solve the problem of zone detection: a machine learning strategy that used the k-means clustering method and a spatial and temporal-based approach that used a spatially constrained clustering method. Ünal et al. (2022) created four mixed-integer linear programming models under three alternative scenarios for the possible Turkish energy efficiency obligation system.

Yukseltan et al. (2022) examined how sensitively the electricity demand was affected by constraints, how the system reacted to changes, how the daily demand profile changed, and how much of the demand was transferred to the night. Depren et al. (2022) examined electricity prices using both time series econometric models and machine learning algorithms. Additionally, the study used both high-frequency (daily) and low-frequency (weekly) data. According to the results, machine learning algorithms outperformed time series econometric methods. Arslan and Ertuğrul (2022) evaluated the MCP formed in the day-ahead electricity market. The impact of the variables in the model created by the multiple regression method was examined. The same data were also analyzed using the ANN, and the results obtained by the multiple regression method were compared with the price estimation analysis of the models with different neuron numbers.

Although there is no clear consensus in economic research regarding the most effective method, the SMP mechanism has grown in popularity (Guerci & Rastegar, 2012). Wang and Ramsay (1997) predicted the SMP using the ANN. In the proposed method, gradient descent in weight space was implemented for a multilayer feedforward network via backpropagation. Kim, Yu, and Song (2002) predicted the SMP using the five-scaled reconstruction method, and the relationship between demand and SMP was discussed using a second-order regression polynomial. In addition, the impact of demand on SMP forecasting was properly taken into account using the conventional multiple regression method. Li and Guo (2002) integrated dynamic clustering and back propagation neural networks to predict short-term SMP. They used short-term SMP prediction as the basis for bid strategies of power plants. Short-term SMP is useful for market participants to develop bidding strategies in the power market driven by economic profits. To predict the SMP, Lee et al. (2005) considered the historical power demand and SMP for a multilayer feed-forward neural network. According to the study, integrating the time and day axis approaches can increase the accuracy of SMP prediction.

Georgilakis (2006) proposed an adaptively trained ANN to predict 24-day-ahead MCP. There are three steps in the proposed methodology for MCP prediction. The day-ahead load was predicted using the ANN in the first step. The persistence approach was used to predict the MCPs in the second step. The MCPs were predicted using the ANN approach in the third stage. A feedback process built into the adaptive training mechanism enables the ANN to learn from errors and improve output by changing its design as new data becomes available. Ceyhan (2016) presented a statistical comparison between the MCP formed in the day-ahead electricity market and the SMP formed in the balancing power market in Turkey. While the averages of both prices are expected to be the same in the long term, it had been shown that the MCP average is higher than the SMP average in 11 hours of the day and lower in 3 hours.

Guerci and Rastegar (2012) used a data-driven computational model to empirically test the proposed model in the case of SMP auction at a macro level to better replicate the real characteristics of the Italian electricity market. To evaluate the performances of the two auction systems and validate the model empirically, three simulation scenarios were also run. Chae, Kim, and Yoo (2012) presented the long- and short-term causal relationships between SMPs and Liquefied Natural Gas (LNG) fuel prices in the Korean electricity market. Several time-series approaches were employed to identify the causalities. Moon and Jung (2020) presented a long-term positive relationship between the SMP in Korea and the import price of LNG. Using time-series econometric techniques, the study evaluated the problems and difficulties associated with long-term contract auctions and looked into the relationship between electricity price changes and this auction. Papaioannou, Papaioannou, and Parliaris (2014) analyzed a relationship between the dynamics of the SMP's volatility, stability, or complexity, and the gradual formation of the Greek electricity market. It was determined that Greek electricity market exhibits the majority of the stylistic properties that other power markets do.

Kölmek and Navruz (2015) investigated a day-ahead price prediction with the ANN, and network performance was evaluated considering various topologies, input sets, and training procedures. The prediction performance of price modeling with the ANN was also compared using the Autoregressive Integrated Moving Average (ARIMA) model. It demonstrated that compared to a time-series model, the ANN model produced better outcomes. Jufri, Oh, and Jung (2019) improved the accuracy of the ANN-based model by using the k-fold cross-validation optimization procedure with both long-term and short-term historical data for day-ahead SMP prediction.

Yudantaka, Kim, and Song (2019) used both long short-term memory (LSTM) and multilayer perceptron (MLP) to improve SMP prediction. In the study, LSTM was first trained using past load and SMP data, and a prediction was then created using the trained LSTM. The finding was used to train an MLP. With the help of partial real-time data combined with historical load demand and temperature data, short-term load demand forecasting was improved, and utilizing the load forecasting result improved the SMP prediction. Noh and Cho (2020) utilized the MLP and nonlinear autoregressive exogenous (NARX) model to predict the SMP. A comparison was also made using the ARIMA. For all predictions, the forecast errors were generally small in the order of ARIMA, MLP, and NARX. Shin, Kim, Kwag, and Kim (2021) examined the financial effects of any new pricing mechanisms when they are implemented in the Korean electricity market. It was mentioned that when the market price is too low and it is necessary to increase the revenues of generation businesses, the SMP mechanism may be a good choice.

Kim et al. (2021) employed LSTM to predict the SMP in the Korean electricity market. Korea Electric Electricity Corporation sets SMP differently every hour. In other words, when the SMP is high, prosumers might profit greatly. Garcia Rendon, López-Rodríguez, and Moncada-Mesa (2021) evaluated the wholesale electricity market. Kyeong-Rok, Keon-Woo, and Kyung-Nam (2021) predicted the yearly SMP using the KNN, light gradient boost machine (LGBM), random forest, and support vector regression models. LGBM provided the most accurate results. Mohamed, Best, Liu, and Morrow (2022) presented a prediction model with four sequential stages based on the ANN to predict the SMPs and single electricity market demand. The proposed model has given reasonable accuracy but additional historical data was required to provide a more reliable model.

Energy demand increases as the industry expands, which is why it is seen as a crucial element of national policy. Additionally, the usage of energy increases along with the economy and human achievements. As a result, one of the most important challenges in today's world is the evaluation of energy usage. The contributions of this paper can be given as follows. Firstly, SVM-based methods are used to classify the SMP direction. Secondly, KNN-based methods are employed to classify the SMP direction. Thirdly, the ensemble-based method is utilized to classify the SMP direction. Finally, the proposed methods' performances are evaluated to assess the classification results using different performance metrics including accuracy, True Positive Rates (TPR), False Negative Rates (FNR), Positive Predictive Values (PPV), and False Discovery Rates (FDR).

DISCUSSION

The electricity market is regulated through bilateral agreements and/or electricity exchanges. Since electricity cannot be stored, bilateral agreements that are signed between the two parties and are known only to these two parties, where the prices are not standard, must be negotiated to maintain supply and demand in balance. The electricity exchange provides a spot market for electricity and provides a reference price (Tür, 2019). Since they make the reference price for all market participants, electricity day-ahead auctions are also essential for the long-term viability of electricity markets. Accurate prediction becomes one of the most important tools for minimizing spot price risk for market participants in emerging markets due to the limited quantity and variety of hedging tools. On the other hand, one of the primary responsibilities of policymakers is to create a market with an appropriate level of transparency so that market participants may provide reasonable predictions using public data (Avci, Ketter, & Heck, 2018). In Turkey, electricity markets are brought into balance one day in advance through the markets operated by Energy Markets Management Inc. (EPIAŞ, 2022a). However, as the real-time approaches, the demand and supply balance may change, and because of these changes, disruptions may occur in the system that was balanced the day before. Because they do not want to be exposed to real-time market pricing, market participants that trade in the day-ahead and intra-day markets aim to reduce energy imbalances. This is due to two factors: first, resistance to the high risk associated with real-time market pricing; and second, the penalty payments made in addition to this risk. In the current condition, market participants falling into imbalance are both applied the higher one in the buying direction/lower one in the selling direction of the MCP and SMP, and an additional 3% penalty is applied to these prices (Tenva, 2015). If there is no deterioration in the production and consumption balance in any time zone, SMP is equal to MCP. In case of imbalance, the load taking offers given in the balancing power market are sorted and evaluated starting from the lowest to meet the additional energy need of the system with the least cost (Özgül, 2018). Energy deficit, balance, and energy surplus can be observed in the system. Prediction of system direction is important to provide safe conditions and technical quality standards in the electricity market.

In this paper, the dataset for the electricity market has been provided by EPIAS (EPIAS, 2022b). The information from the electricity market between 29/06/2021 and 29/06/2022 (8784 observations) was used. The inputs are SMP, MCP, Positive Imbalance Price, and Negative Imbalance Price, and the output is SMP direction. SMP direction is determined using SVM methods, KNN methods, and the ensemble classifier method.

SVM is one of the machine learning techniques that were initially developed to solve the classification problem and then extended to a variety of other problems. In a high-dimensional feature space, the goal of support vector classification is to efficiently find a "good" separation hyperplane, "good" in the sense of some metric of generalization performance (Mammone, Turchi, & Cristianini, 2009). A subset of the training input is used to create the solution by SVM. SVM is a discriminant method that offers an analytical solution to the convex optimization problem. SVMs are arguably the most well-known machine learning approach for supervised learning while having a very straightforward theoretical foundation (Awad & Khanna, 2015). Details about the SVMs can be found in Mammone et al. (2009) and Awad & Khanna (2015).

One of the most fundamental classification techniques is the KNN classification. The KNN method can be one of the best options for classification when there is little or no prior knowledge about the distribution of the data (Parvin, Alizadeh, & Minati, 2010). By calculating all of the distances between the unclassified sample and the samples in the training set, the KNN algorithm searches for the k-nearest neighbors of an unknown sample. Therefore, the computational complexity may affect the algorithm's performance if the training set or the number of samples to classify is large (Mucherino, Papajorgji, & Pardalos, 2009).

Ensemble methods integrate a set of trained weak learner models and data on which these learners were trained. By integrating predictions from its weak learners, it can predict ensemble responses to new data (MathWorks, 2022a). Dietterich (2000) evaluated ensemble methods and explained why ensembles frequently outperform single classifiers. An ensemble of classifiers is a group of classifiers whose individual classification decisions are somehow merged to classify new samples. Even if a variety of ensemble methods is offered, it might be challenging to identify the best configuration for a given dataset (Kshatri et al., 2021).

Given the relevance of the research topic and the research opportunities available, it is no surprise that interest in power market analysis studies has been raised recently. In light of the previous studies, it is determined that traditional mathematical methods make it difficult to model the electricity market. At this point, machine-learning methods can be applied. They have numerous benefits that help people and businesses all around the world. Machine learning methods can learn from the provided information. The model's accuracy and efficiency in generating decisions improve with each new set of data added. Machine learning methods improve numerous decision-making tasks and contribute significantly to the progress of electricity market prediction models. Therefore, SVM methods, KNN methods, and ensemble method are employed in this paper to evaluate SMP in the Turkish electricity market. The reason for selecting these machine learning methods can be given as follows. Simplicity, robustness to noisy training data, and effectiveness with the right training data are some strengths of the KNN (Parvin, Alizadeh, & Minati, 2010). SVM methods are known for their robustness, strong generalization ability, and unique global optimum solutions (Awad & Khanna, 2015). Ensemble methods generally give a remarkable performance in prediction due to including the group of classifiers.

SOLUTIONS AND RECOMMENDATIONS

In Turkey's energy planning, the support given to reduce foreign dependency is highlighted in the policies used. Expanding the resource portfolio has become important in ensuring supply security. In this direction, increasing the use of domestic resources in electricity generation, it is aimed to significantly reduce Turkey's foreign dependency and to make it a more effective actor in the global energy market (Karagöl & Tür, 2017). In Turkey, the electricity market includes the day-ahead market, the intra-day market, and the balancing market. All three markets ensure the realization of a balanced market and trade by keeping electricity production and consumption equal. In the balancing power market, which is the market closest to real-time trading, offers are given days in advance, but their conversion into orders converges to the relevant time zone according to the real-time imbalance expectation and situation. Balancing power market, which is a more specific market, differs significantly from the other two markets. Within the scope of spot markets, the real-time cost of the final load in the system, which is also used in calculating the individual or group imbalance costs of the participants in the balancing power market, consists of the SMP (Özgül, 2018).

In this paper, three research questions are answered. Firstly, the selected methods for SMP direction prediction are SVM methods including linear SVM, quadratic SVM, cubic SVM, fine gaussian SVM, medium gaussian SVM, and coarse gaussian SVM, KNN methods including fine KNN, medium KNN, coarse KNN, weighted KNN, and optimizable KNN, and also ensemble classifier method. Secondly, prediction performance varies depending on the methods as given in Table 1-3 and Figure 1. Thirdly, the ensemble method is the best method when compared with other methods according to the accuracy value of all the proposed methods. The accuracy value of all the proposed methods is given in Figure 1. One of the most popular techniques for assessing a model's performance in a classification problem is based on the confusion matrix. The number of rows and columns is equal to the number of classes in the confusion matrix. Additionally, each cell in the confusion matrix contains a different value (Bozkurt Keser & Buruk Sahin, 2021). There are four main characteristics in the confusion matrix that are utilized in this paper. TPR, FNR, PPV, and FDR are used to evaluate the proposed methods (Table 1-3). The TPR (also referred to sensitivity or recall) measures how many observations are accurately classified per true class. The FNR measures how many observations are inaccurately classified per true class. The PPV (or precision) is the proportion of correctly classified observations per predicted class. The FDR is the proportion of incorrectly classified observations per predicted class (Mathworks, 2022b). The values of TPR, FNR, PPV, and FDR vary according to SMP direction including energy deficit (-1), balance (0), and energy surplus (+1) in Table 1-3. The results showed that when the SMP direction is -1 that means the energy deficit is better classified. According to Table 1-3 and Figure 1, it can be said that the SVM method, KNN methods, and ensemble methods can be used to classify the SMP direction in the Turkish electricity market.

Figure 1. The accuracy value of all the proposed methods.

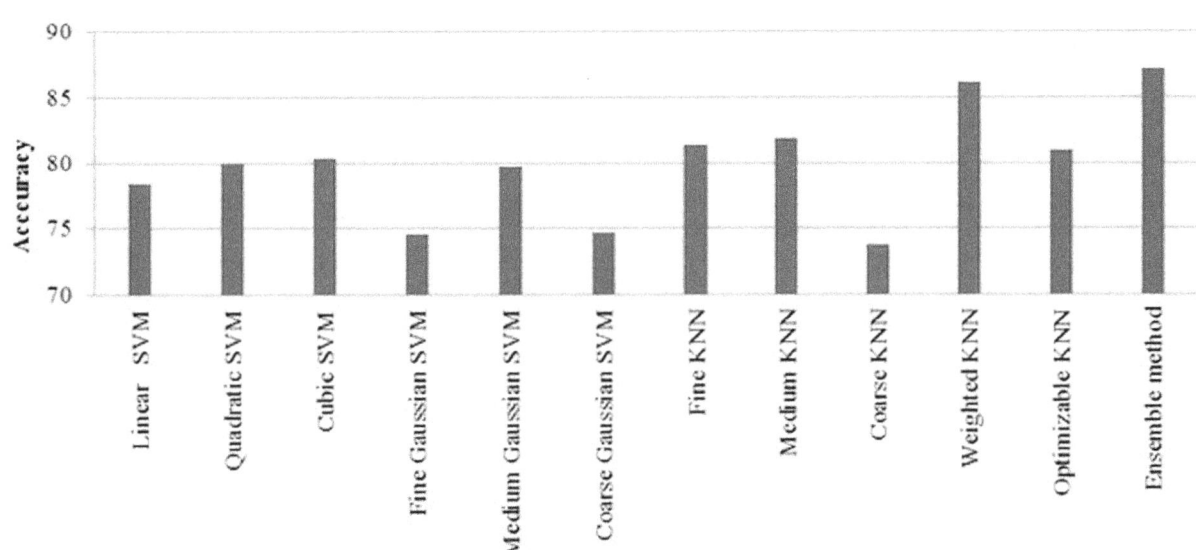

FUTURE RESEARCH DIRECTIONS

The advent of competition has led to global deregulation, privatization, and reorganization of the electric power industries. Energy price prediction is a crucial task for all market participants in this circumstance (Lee et al., 2005). Anywhere that electricity is used, including the energy sector, is significantly impacted by the price of electricity. Policymakers could also use the price as a political tool. The engineering and mathematical modeling fields are not the only ones that have something to do with the electricity price system. It is a crucial social issue that needs to be handled from a multidisciplinary perspective (Poyrazoglu, 2021). Electrical energy is one of the most significant types of energy. Electrical energy is essential to life since it is straightforward to use, and can shift into different forms as needed. In addition to being a vital component of economic development, electricity also plays a fundamental role in increasing social welfare. Electrical energy has been an effective resource needed in almost every activity of life from the past to the present. It has key roles in transportation, city lighting, and other areas of daily life. With its consumption rate, it is a highly significant measure of the levels of national development. However, electricity markets are highly volatile. Technological advances and developments have changed market structures. Because of the development of information technologies, the generation, transmission, and distribution of electricity, today can all be quantified. This provided a suitable environment for competition.

There is no single method that has been used in all electricity markets. Various methods, including different inputs, prediction horizons, and performance measures, are available for different electricity markets. Suitable selected methods can help academicians, economists, and statisticians determine the best strategy in the electricity market. Therefore, more research is needed in the Turkish electricity markets. This will make it easier to evaluate SMP and comprehend how prices have changed in the electricity market.

Table 1. The results of the SVM methods

		-1	0	+1
Linear SVM	TPR	99.3	0	25.2
	FNR	0.7	100	74.8
	PPV	77.8	0	91.7
	FDR	22.2	100	8.3
Quadratic SVM	TPR	99.1	5	31.6
	FNR	0.9	95	68.4
	PPV	79.3	18.5	92.4
	FDR	20.7	81.5	7.6
Cubic SVM	TPR	98.9	10.5	33.3
	FNR	1.1	89.5	66.7
	PPV	79.7	25.5	94.5
	FDR	20.3	74.5	5.5
Fine Gaussian SVM	TPR	99.5	3.4	9.3
	FNR	0.5	96.6	90.7
	PPV	74.7	13.1	89.7
	FDR	25.3	86.9	10.3
Medium Gaussian SVM	TPR	99.4	1.7	30.3
	FNR	0.6	98.3	69.7
	PPV	78.9	8.3	93.8
	FDR	21.1	91.7	6.2
Coarse Gaussian SVM	TPR	99.7	0	9.1
	FNR	0.3	100	90.9
	PPV	74.7	0	92
	FDR	25.3	100	8

Table 2. The results of the KNN methods

		-1	0	+1
Fine KNN	TPR	90.6	11.8	61.9
	FNR	9.4	88.2	38.1
	PPV	85.5	5.7	87.5
	FDR	14.5	94.3	12.5
Medium KNN	TPR	98.5	0	41.9
	FNR	1.5	100	58.1
	PPV	80.9	0	90.1
	FDR	19.1	100	9.9
Coarse KNN	TPR	100	0	4.8
	FNR	0	100	95.2
	PPV	73.5	0	99
	FDR	26.5	100	1
Weighted KNN	TPR	98.1	12.6	58.7
	FNR	1.9	87.4	41.3
	PPV	85.3	38	93.2
	FDR	14.7	62	6.8
Optimizable KNN	TPR	98.7	11.3	36.6
	FNR	1.3	88.7	63.4
	PPV	80	40.9	93.5
	FDR	20	59.1	6.5

Table 3. The results of the ensemble method

		-1	0	+1
Ensemble method	TPR	98.2	7.1	63
	FNR	1.8	92.9	37
	PPV	86.2	28.8	93.7
	FDR	13.8	71.2	6.3

The proposed prediction models did well in the thorough evaluations of accuracy, and the results were encouraging. However, this study can be strengthened for future research by developing a hybrid method such as ANN-based SVM, and LSTM-based SVM. Various metaheuristics such as genetic algorithms can be used to determine input variables in future studies. Future research can also use non-dominated sorting genetic algorithm II and other optimization techniques to determine the parameters of the proposed methods. Hourly, daily, and yearly predictions can be utilized to evaluate the effect of time horizon in the electricity market.

CONCLUSION

Effective modeling and prediction are necessary for energy planning and management. More accurate investments and satisfied consumers result from better predictions. However, making predictions in the energy sector is a difficult procedure that necessitates taking into account many intricate details. Additionally, accurate SMP evaluation is a crucial problem to fulfill the increasing demand for energy and serves as a basis for decision-making. SMP has distinct characteristics, such as a daily cycle, seasonal variation, temperature changes, unit maintenance, coal price fluctuations, power plant bidding strategy adjustments, and accidents. Therefore, SMP prediction is difficult and a robust and adaptable SMP prediction model is required. Accurate information related to the SMP is crucial for energy firms' decision-making and strategic planning.

By examining the classification of SMP direction on the balancing market in the context of Turkey using various machine learning techniques, this work contributes to the current literature. This paper provides which prediction method produces the most useful results in the electricity market. Future studies in this area will benefit from knowing which of the prediction method that is often utilized in the literature will produce more useful results. Furthermore, the proposed methods can be used by both producers and consumers to choose their bid strategies and increase their profits.

REFERENCES

Aggarwal, S. K., Saini, L. M., & Kumar, A. (2009). Electricity price forecasting in deregulated markets: A review and evaluation. *Electrical Power & Energy Systems*, *31*(1), 13–22. doi:10.1016/j.ijepes.2008.09.003

Arslan, B., & Ertuğrul, İ. (2022). Forecasting and analysis in Turkish electricity market with multiple regression, ARIMA and artificial neural network methods. *Journal of Management and Economics Research*, *20*(1), 331–353.

Avci, E., Ketter, W., & van Heck, E. (2018). Managing electricity price modeling risk via ensemble forecasting: The case of Turkey. *Energy Policy*, *123*, 390–403. doi:10.1016/j.enpol.2018.08.053

Awad, M., & Khanna, R. (2015). *Efficient learning machines: theories, concepts, and applications for engineers and system designers*. Springer Nature. doi:10.1007/978-1-4302-5990-9

Boru İpek, A. (2021). Prediction of market-clearing price using neural networks based methods and boosting algorithms. *International Advanced Researches and Engineering Journal*, *5*(2), 240–246. doi:10.35860/iarej.824168

Bozkurt Keser, S., & Buruk Sahin, Y. (2021). Response surface methodology to tune artificial neural network hyper-parameters. *Expert Systems: International Journal of Knowledge Engineering and Neural Networks*, *38*(8), e12792. doi:10.1111/exsy.12792

Ceyhan, G. (2016). *Türkiye'de elektrik piyasa takas fiyatı ve sistem marjinal fiyatı farkı üzerine istatistiksel bir çalışma*. Accessed on 29 June 2022. Available from: https://silo.tips/download/trkye-de-elektrk-pyasa-takas-fyati-ve-sstem-marjnal-fyati-farki-zerne-statstksel

Chae, Y., Kim, M., & Yoo, S.-H. (2012). Does natural gas fuel price cause system marginal price, vice-versa, or neither? A causality analysis. *Energy, 47*(1), 199–204. doi:10.1016/j.energy.2012.09.047

Depren, S. K., Kartal, M. T., Ertuğrul, H. M., & Depren, Ö. (2022). The role of data frequency and method selection in electricity price estimation: Comparative evidence from Turkey in pre-pandemic and pandemic periods. *Renewable Energy, 186*, 217–225. doi:10.1016/j.renene.2021.12.136

Dietterich, T. G. (2000). Ensemble methods in machine learning. In Lecture Notes in Computer Science: Vol. 1857. *Multiple Classifier Systems*. Springer. doi:10.1007/3-540-45014-9_1

Dursun, A., Eke, İ., & Tezcan, S. S. (2020). Artificial neural networks with Turkey interconnected system for day ahead market transmission lines estimated losses. *International Journal of Engineering Research and Development, 12*(2), 549–564. doi:10.29137/umagd.600962

EPIAS. (2022a). Accessed on 29 June 2022. https://www.epias.com.tr/en

EPIAS. (2022b). *MCP-SMP and Imbalance Price Listing*. Accessed on 29 June 2022. Available from: https://rapor.epias.com.tr/rapor/xhtml/ptfSmfListeleme.xhtml

Garcia Rendon, J. J., López-Rodríguez, J., & Moncada-Mesa, J. (2021). Firm location, regional weather conditions and bid pricing strategies in the Colombian wholesale electricity market. *Regional Studies, 56*(9), 1554–1570. doi:10.1080/00343404.2021.1994136

Gayretli, G., Yucekaya, A., & Bilge, A. H. (2019). An analysis of price spikes and deviations in the deregulated Turkish power market. *Energy Strategy Reviews, 26*, 100376. doi:10.1016/j.esr.2019.100376

Georgilakis, P. S. (2006). Market clearing price forecasting in deregulated electricity markets using adaptively trained neural networks. In *Hellenic Conference on Artificial Intelligence* (pp. 56-66). Springer. 10.1007/11752912_8

Guerci, E., & Rastegar, M. A. (2012). Comparing system-marginal-price versus pay-as-bid auctions in a realistic electricity market scenario. In Managing Market Complexity: The Approach of Artificial Economics, Lecture Notes in Economics and Mathematical Systems 662 (pp. 141-153). Springer. doi:10.1007/978-3-642-31301-1_12

Gul, O. (2008). An assessment of power quality and electricity consumer's rights in restructured electricity market in Turkey. *Electrical Power Quality and Utilisation Journal, 14*(2), 29–34.

Jufri, F. H., Oh, S., & Jung, J. (2019). Day-ahead system marginal price forecasting using artificial neural network and similar-days information. *Journal of Electrical Engineering & Technology, 14*(2), 561–568. doi:10.100742835-018-00058-w

Kalfa, V. R., Arslan, B., & Ertuğrul, İ. (2021). Determining the factors affecting the market clearing price by using multiple linear regression method. *Alphanumeric Journal, 9*(1), 35–48. doi:10.17093/alphanumeric.882847

Karagöl, E. T., & Tür, M. R. (2017). *Türkiye'de Elektrik Enerjisi* [Electrical Energy in Turkey]. Accessed on 29 June 2022. Available from: https://www.researchgate.net/publication/321197687_Turkiye'de_Elektrik_Enerjisi

Kim, B., Lee, D., Rusetskii, N., Shusterzon, K., Sidorov, D., Song, M., & Kim, I. (2021). A study on the effect of energy storage systems and distributed generators on reliability. *2021 24th International Conference on Electrical Machines and Systems (ICEMS)*, 802-807. 10.23919/ICEMS52562.2021.9634523

Kim, C.-I., Yu, I.-K., & Song, Y. H. (2002). Prediction of system marginal price of electricity using wavelet transform analysis. *Energy Conversion and Management*, *43*(14), 1839–1851. doi:10.1016/S0196-8904(01)00127-3

Kölmek, M. A., & Navruz, İ. (2015). Forecasting the day-ahead price in electricity balancing and settlement market of Turkey by using artificial neural networks. *Turkish Journal of Electrical Engineering and Computer Sciences*, *23*, 841–852. doi:10.3906/elk-1212-136

Kshatri, S. S., Singh, D., Narain, B., Bhatia, S., Quasim, M. T., & Sinha, G. R. (2021). An empirical analysis of machine learning algorithms for crime prediction using stacked generalization: An ensemble approach. *IEEE Access: Practical Innovations, Open Solutions*, *9*, 67488–67500. doi:10.1109/ACCESS.2021.3075140

Kyeong-Rok, M., Keon-Woo, L., & Kyung-Nam, K. (2021). Forecast of long-term trend of system marginal price with amounts of machine learning train data. *Journal of the Korean Solar Energy Society*, *41*(5), 13–24. doi:10.7836/kses.2021.41.5.013

Lee, J.-K., Park, J.-B., Shin, J.-R., & Lee, K. Y. (2005). A system marginal price forecasting method based on an artificial neural network using time and day information. *IFAC Proceedings Volumes, 38*(1), 122-127.

Li, C., & Guo, Z. (2002). Short-term system marginal price forecasting with hybrid module. *Proceedings. International Conference on Power System Technology*, 4, 2426-2430. 10.1109/ICPST.2002.1047221

Mammone, A., Turchi, M., & Cristianini, N. (2009). Support vector machines. *Wiley Interdisciplinary Reviews: Computational Statistics*, *1*(3), 283–289. doi:10.1002/wics.49

Mathworks. (2022a). *Classification ensemble*. Accessed on 29 June 2022. Available from: https://www.mathworks.com/help/stats/classreg.learning.classif.classificationensemble-class.html

Mathworks. (2022b). *Assess classifier performance in classification learner*. Accessed on 29 June 2022. Available from: https://es.mathworks.com/help/stats/assess-classifier-performance.html

Mohamed, A. A. R., Best, R. J., Liu, X., & Morrow, D. J. (2022). Single electricity market forecasting and energy arbitrage maximization framework. *IET Renewable Power Generation*, *16*(1), 105–124. doi:10.1049/rpg2.12345

Moon, J., & Jung, T. Y. (2020). A critical review of Korea's long-term contract for renewable energy auctions: The relationship between the import price of liquefied natural gas and system marginal price. *Utilities Policy*, *67*, 101132. doi:10.1016/j.jup.2020.101132

Mucherino, A., Papajorgji, P. J., & Pardalos, P. M. (2009). K-nearest neighbor classification. Data Mining in Agriculture, Springer Optimization and Its Applications, 34, 83-106. doi:10.1007/978-0-387-88615-2_4

Noh, J., & Cho, H. C. (2020). Forecasting system marginal price using multilayer perceptron and nonlinear autoregressive exogenous model. *Journal of The Korean Society of Mineral and Energy Resources Engineers, 57*(6), 585–592. doi:10.32390/ksmer.2020.57.6.585

Ocakoglu, K. O., & Tolga, A. C. (2018). Effective trading in Turkish electricity market: hedging with options. *Proceedings of the World Congress on Engineering, 1.*

Özgül, A. U. (2018). *Spot price models in electricity markets: The case of Turkey* [PhD thesis]. Pamukkale University Institute of Social Sciences.

Özgüner, E., Tör, O. B., & Güven, A. N. (2017). Probabilistic day-ahead system marginal price forecasting with ANN for the Turkish electricity market. *Turkish Journal of Electrical Engineering and Computer Sciences, 25*(6), 4923–4935. doi:10.3906/elk-1612-206

Papaioannou, G. P., Papaioannou, P. G., & Parliaris, N. (2014). *Modeling the stylized facts of wholesale system marginal price (SMP) and the impacts of regulatory reforms on the Greek Electricity Market.* arXiv preprint arXiv:1401.5452

Parvin, H., Alizadeh, H., & Minati, B. (2010). A modification on k-nearest neighbor classifier. *Global Journal of Computer Science and Technology, 10*(14), 37–41.

Poyrazoglu, G. (2021). Determination of price zones during transition from uniform to zonal electricity market: A case study for Turkey. *Energies, 14*(4), 1014. doi:10.3390/en14041014

Prabavathi, M., & Gnanadass, R. (2018). Electric power bidding model for practical utility system. *Alexandria Engineering Journal, 57*(1), 277–286. doi:10.1016/j.aej.2016.12.002

Sahin, C. (2018). Consideration of network constraints in the Turkish day ahead electricity market. *International Journal of Electrical Power & Energy Systems, 102*, 245–253. doi:10.1016/j.ijepes.2018.04.027

Şenocak, F. (2018). *Elektrik piyasa takas fiyatı ağırlıklı ortalamasının anfis ve yapay sinir ağları ile tahmini* [Forecasting of weighted average electricity market clearing price using artificial neural networks and anfis] [Master Thesis]. Karadeniz Technical University.

Shin, H., Kim, T. H., Kwag, K., & Kim, W. (2021). A comparative study of pricing mechanisms to reduce side-payments in the electricity market: A case study for South Korea. *Energies, 14*(12), 3395. doi:10.3390/en14123395

Sirin, S. M., & Yilmaz, B. N. (2021). The impact of variable renewable energy technologies on electricity markets: An analysis of the Turkish balancing market. *Energy Policy, 151*, 112093. doi:10.1016/j.enpol.2020.112093

Sütçü, M., Şahin, K. N., Koloğlu, Y., Çelikel, M. E., & Gülbahar, İ. T. (2022). Electricity load forecasting using deep learning and novel hybrid models. *Sakarya University Journal of Science, 26*(1), 91–104.

Tenva. (2015). *Gün öncesi piyasası ve gün içi piyasası karşılaştırması* [Day-ahead market vs. intraday market]. Accessed on 29 June 2022. Available from: https://www.tenva.org/gun-oncesi-piyasasi-ve-gun-ici-piyasasi-karsilastirmasi/

Tür, M. R. (2019). The scenario of price creation in the electricity market based on micro-grid systems. *Gazi University Journal of Science Part C: Design and Technology, 7*(1), 192–202.

Ünal, B. B., Onaygil, S., Acuner, E., & Cin, R. (2022). Application of energy efficiency obligation scheme for electricity distribution companies in Turkey. *Energy Policy, 163*, 112851. doi:10.1016/j. enpol.2022.112851

Wang, A., & Ramsay, B. (1997). Prediction of system marginal price in the UK Power Pool using neural networks. *Proceedings of International Conference on Neural Networks (ICNN'97)*, 4, 2116-2120. 10.1109/ICNN.1997.614232

Yazıcı, S. (2020). *Optimization of imbalance costs in electricity market by using electricity generation and price forecasting methods* [Master Thesis]. Istanbul Technical University.

Yudantaka, K., Kim, J.-S., & Song, H. (2019). Dual deep learning networks based load forecasting with partial real-time information and its application to system marginal price prediction. *Energies, 13*(1), 148. doi:10.3390/en13010148

Yukseltan, E., Kok, A., Yucekaya, A., Bilge, A., Aktunc, E. A., & Hekimoglu, M. (2022). The impact of the COVID-19 pandemic and behavioral restrictions on electricity consumption and the daily demand curve in Turkey. *Utilities Policy, 76*, 101359. doi:10.1016/j.jup.2022.101359 PMID:35250191

KEY TERMS AND DEFINITIONS

Energy Market: Energy markets are location-dependent, as each market has its auctions and procedures.

Ensemble-Based Method: Ensemble methods generally give a remarkable performance in prediction due to including the group of classifiers.

K-Nearest Neighbors: It is one of the most fundamental classification techniques.

Machine Learning: It allows you to accomplish your goals with less time and effort.

Public Policy: Efficient energy planning can reduce public spending.

Support Vector Machines: It is one of the machine learning techniques to solve the classification problems.

System Marginal Price: It is very volatile and dependent on a wide range of variables, including the price of oil, load demand, and even natural parameters.

Section 5

India:
The Potential of a Giant

Chapter 14
Territorial Planning Models in Homestays:
An Indian Context

Saumya Kapil

https://orcid.org/0000-0001-7260-985X

Christ University, India

Bindi Varghese

Christ University, India

ABSTRACT

Homestays have become a sustainable accommodation option in the tourism industry. With roots in the ancient period, the revival of homestays brings an eco-friendly alternative to visitors and the local community. The agglomeration of the fringed existence of this business will result in a more significant profit and focused policymaking opportunity for governmental and non-governmental organizations. The observations in the study indicated a need for analysis of homestay clusters. This study systematically reviews the existing literature aiming to provide specifications needed for management of homestay clusters in India. This chapter identifies guidelines and has indicated external and internal determinants for an organized homestay business. The factors in the formation of agglomeration are an integrated effort driven by local community participation and appropriate government intervention for regional sustainable growth and development.

INTRODUCTION

Homestay tourism is aligned with the Philosophy of "Sufficiency Economy," as it utilizes natural resources and the cultural wisdom of the local community (Neonatal Network, 2017). It provides an exclusive opportunity for tourists to experience the local culture and lifestyle closely; in return, homestay owners earn some extra cash other than their agricultural income. Therefore, tourism, especially agritourism, plays a significant role. Agritourism is also considered to be an essential tool to reverse outmigration. Homestay

DOI: 10.4018/978-1-6684-5976-8.ch014

can further be regarded as a vital agritourism component for the local community's economic development. The agglomeration model in homestays can thus be defined as the clustered homestay community formed by aggregating all the surrounding homestays and the supporting institutions in the vicinity (Guo, 2019). This model can be implemented and analyzed in homestay networks in India, which form the base of peer-to-peer accommodation and sharing economy. Various models can be used to understand the theories of agglomeration in homestays, such as Von Thunen's model, which deals with internal economies, and Marshall (1890) further analyzes agglomeration in economies. Additionally, Porter devises three mechanisms the pool of labor force, supplier linkages, and localization of knowledge spillover (Potter et al., 2014).

According to "a Functional and Economic Impact Analysis of Homestays in India" by the Internet and Mobile Association of India (I.A.M.A.I.), homestays contribute to Rs. 2577.4 crores in India's economy with Rs. 879.5 crore Gross Value Added (G.V.A.) and 2.04 output multiplier (Homestays in India: A Functional and Economic Impact Analysis, 2021). It reflects a backward linkage to the agriculture sector; as the homestay output increases by 1 unit, rural output increases by 0.42 units. Various case studies highlight community welfare practices evident in homestay accommodations. The rural development feature of homestay accommodation helps identify multiple Sustainable Development Goals such as No Poverty, Gender Equality, Decent Work, Economic growth, and Climate Change. Adhering to the scope of homestay cluster business in the Indian tourism market, this study aims to understand the critical factors that affect the same. This framework will provide a clear view of the essential focal points required to establish a flourishing homestay cluster business.

BACKGROUND

According to Boullón's Theory of Touristic Space (2001), the territorial distribution large surface area of a destination can be bifurcated into various components such as zones, complexes, clusters, or distribution centers. Tourism clusters are "…a tourist nucleus connected to a network of roads, a factor that changes its spatial situation. This is the phase during which the nuclei consolidate their operations by constructing a tourism business". Further, Lohmann and Netto (2016) explains that the three primary considerations for forming tourism clusters are; agglomeration, affinity, and articulation. Here, agglomeration stresses the willingness of closely located organizations to establish an alliance and facilitate the exchange of products associated with tourism activities. Affinity accommodates an umbrella for all the primary, secondary, and associated tourism organizations involved in the cluster's functioning. Later, communication between the related enterprises is required for the required channel to function. The geographical affinity of the organization can be characterized through spatial models. The consideration of network and hub, and spoke model as nodal functions in spatial patterns of tourist destinations is elaborated precisely by Hoyle and Knowles (1998), "centrality and intermediation spatial qualities [which] increase the importance and levels of traffic hubs strategically located within the transport system." This can further be understood by Lue et al.'s model (1993) regarding spatial patterns for pleasure trips. It can be considered the reference for forming homestay clusters coinciding with the existing circuits in the state.

According to Zijing and Pu (2019), clustered homestays have greater scope for agglomeration than the preliminary stage of single homestays. This phenomenon is solidified by Porter's (1991) "diamond model," which inhibits the acceleration of competitive advantage if the interconnected producers co-locate with the factor of commonality. Further, Wang et al. (2018) proposed the key dimensions based on the "diamond model," which includes four systems: Government Intervention (GI), Production Factor (PF), and related industrial and demand status. Where the PF signifies the promotional activities of homestays and the associated industries cushion the diverse functioning of homestays. The related sectors ranges from the six core elements of tourism, i.e., accommodation, transport, food and beverage, attraction, shopping, and entertainment, to the ancillary aspects such as warehousing, agriculture, hospitals, etc. Therefore, tourism agglomeration is connected with the "associated tourism element (ATE)" character-ized by institutions related to scenic areas, catering services, recreational activities, shopping areas, etc. (Zijing and Pu, 2020). According to Long et al. (2018), agglomeration of homestays have given birth to a new form of tourism product resulting from the accumulation of proficient tourism management abilities of farmers, utilization of rural idle places and surplus labor, and agriculture-related products.

Homestay Business in India

Under the Incredible India Homestay Establishment classification, the authority of owning a homestay is provided to the owner or their family physically residing in the establishment with a minimum of one and maximum of six rooms (Ministry of Tourism (Hotels and Restaurants Division), 2019). Various parts of India are well-known for agritourism and homestay accommodation (Chatterjee & Prasad, 2019). Some of the success stories are Rawla Kaneriya in central India, owned by the royal family of Jamnia, indigenous homestays called Shaam-e-Sarhad in Hodka, Gujarat, and the first fully equipped homestay of India named Adarana Farms in Southern India. In Himalayan areas of India, such as Uttarakhand, the primary economic driver is agricultural activities because of the infrastructural constraints (Shah et al., 2020). Here, Green People in Goat Village of Uttarakhand and farm stays in Silent Valley are widespread agritourism practices. Further, compared to enclave tourism (mass or resort tourism), agritourism is considered more sustainable in isolated areas such as islands or infrastructurally restrained areas such as hills, where agriculture is the only source of livelihood (Naidoo & Pearce, 2018).

The first set of guidelines by the government of India regarding homestays came in 2006 under the Incredible India Bed & Breakfast Homestay Establishment guidelines (Bhuyan, 2021). These guidelines have standardized parameters that award the homestay's gold or silver status. Traditional décor and authentic food are the necessities for the establishment. According to the Draft National Strategy for Promotion of Rural Homestays (2021), various broad themes are characterized for cluster homestays. These themes include cultural dimensions such as local cuisines and crafts, folk dance/music/theatre, rural sports/events, and tribal culture, and environmental dimensions include cluster homestays in protected areas such as national parks and wildlife sanctuaries, eco-zones in the vicinity of villages, agritourism (activities associated with that) and yoga/meditation centers. Lastly, it also comprises cluster homestays in proximity to the existing Theme-based Circuit (TC). There are 15 TCs identified under the "Swadesh Darshan" scheme of the Ministry of Tourism.

Understanding the link between agglomeration and homestays will help develop fresh insight into the growing phenomenon of cluster homestays following *Chapter 7- Developing Clusters for Rural Home-stays* in "Draft National Strategy for Promotion of Rural Homestays- An initiative towards Atmanirbhar Bharat (2021)". For instance, organizations such as R.O.S.E (Rural Opportunity for Social Elevation) emerged from a small town in Kanda, Uttarakhand, that works hand-in-hand with agritourism (Chat-terjee & Prasad, 2019). It forms a sharing economy of rural homestay owners with strong national and international networks. To identify the various geographical areas of India discussed in the study, readers can access the political map of India at https://www.surveyofindia.gov.in/pages/political-map-of-india.

HOMESTAY CLUSTERS

The determinants derived from various agglomeration theories are Government Interventions, Production Factors (Wang Meiyu et al., 2018), Associated Tourism Elements (Zijing and Pu, 2020), and Theme-based Circuits (cultural and environmental dimensions). These factors have been analyzed to be the most relevant and frequently occurring in the literature. Further, the data will be deduced for internal and external relationships to constitute determinants affecting homestay clusters. The two components of internal and external environmental factors affecting Clustered Homestays are derived from Cibinskiene, A., & Snieskiene, G.'s (2015) evaluation of city competitiveness in tourism. The effects are aligned with the two environmental factors relating to Government Intervention with the State's monetary policy, Production Factor with the status of the resort, Community Participation with Travel Agencies, and Associated Tourism Elements with theatre and zoo (Cibinskiene, A., & Snieskiene, G., 2015). Theme-based Circuits are introduced as an external factor as it is a constituent of the Draft Policy introduced for Clustered Homestays.

Government Intervention

Government Intervention plays a significant role in the agglomeration of industries that comprises local community with minimum resources. Other non-governmental organizations play an equally important role in the functioning of these agglomerations. Various researches focused on Indian states highlight the intensity of these interventions and their significant role. For instance, under the policy of the state of Uttarakhand in India, "Rose Rural Tourism" homestays are a notable example of cluster homestays (Kulshreshtha and Kulshrestha, 2019). The requirement for a group of homestays to become a cluster is defined in the policy document as "more than six homestays." They will be provided with infrastructural support such as websites and mobile apps. The state government scheme that gave way to the establishment of this homestay is the Guest Uttarakhand Homestay Scheme (2015). The homestay aspirants in the state of Arunachal Pradesh under the Northeast theme circuit are undergoing various certificate programs.

Bhuyan (2021), in his article *Employment Opportunities in Rural Homestays,* elaborated on multiple initiatives and policies by the Central and State government for rural development in the state. One is a month-long certificate program by the National Institute of Rural Development and Panchayati Raj (NIRDPR) to promote rural homestays in the Northeastern states of India. With the support of the Arunanchal State Rural Livelihood Mission (ArSRLM), 21 all-women homestay aspirants turned up for the workshop. Non-governmental organizations have taken many such initiatives in the past. For instance, in 1991, an organization called "Help Tourism" emerged from a cluster of 40 families who offered clean rural homestays equipped to host special-interest travellers such as mountaineers (Kapur, 2016). Help Tourism estimated 800 rural homestays in the district of Siliguri in Darjeeling, making it a hotspot for rural tourism in India (Kannegieser, 2015). Here, tourists prefer tiny, culturally packed houses over commercial hotels.

As Bhuyan (2021) identified, the significant difficulty in establishing government-certified homestays in the Northeastern states of India is their inability to approve the 36 parameters in the guidelines. To relax this situation, GoI has allowed States and Union Territories to customize the policies accordingly. Other states with popular tourist destinations, such as Himachal Pradesh and Uttarakhand, can fulfill these criteria. At the same time, others have customized the guidelines, such as Homestays and Tourism Society (HATS) in Kerala. However, it has raised significant concerns about waste management in popular tourist destinations such as Alappuzha, Kumarakom, and Kollam (Emilda et al., 2020). According to government officials in the study, there needs to be strict regulation and gatekeeping for the licenses issued for houseboats and homestays in these areas. The negative side of these interventions can also be seen where they relocated the local community from protected areas to build infrastructure for the accommodation of guests (DeFries et al., 2010).

Thematic Spatial Classification

Every state in India has ascribed a theme that connects them externally with other states and internally with close spatial proximity and transportation infrastructure. There can be multiple future recommendations for clustered homestays with the help of the data. Further, the proximity of the cluster homestays to these theme circuits will constitute its success. For instance, Kerala is known for its phenomenal eco-tourist destinations. These regulations can be more centralized if clusters of homestays and houseboats are formed with strict waste management regulations. DeFries et al. (2010) delve into the effect of external surroundings in the protected areas of India, such as Kanha, Ranthambore, and Nagarhole National Park. It is identified that resorts and homestays are close to these protected areas. They are situated on the park boundaries increasing the human population density to about 242 people/km^2, whereas outside the park, the population density is just 67 people/km^2. Out of the three protected areas (PAs) discussed in the study, Nagarhole National Park situated in Karnataka consists of more homestays (out of which some are in existing houses in coffee plantations). The other PAs are focussing on the construction of new infrastructure for accommodation. This has created a situation of relocating households inside PAs.

Various other states have fragmented homestay accommodations in different parts of the state delivering to the theme. There is a need for agglomeration for the respective states to understand their capabilities with a similar goal. The northeast circuit has a rich cultural heritage. It is different yet similar to the seven sisters (Arunachal Pradesh, Assam, Manipur, Meghalaya, Mizoram, Nagaland, and Tripura) and a brother (Sikkim) that connects them to the Indian subcontinent. Similarly, coastal belts have a rich marine cuisine each having a distinct cultural representation. The Spiritual, Ramayana, Buddhism, and Krishna theme binds the rich religious diversity of India of myths and tales. Moreover, under the "Bharat Gaurav" Scheme various theme-based circuit trains are launched under the name of "Bharat Gaurav Trains" to facilitate the transportation between major cities of these circuits. These theme-based circuits open a mine of opportunity and scope for home-grown community development and rural upliftment. For a diverse country like India, homestays must reflect their rich culture and heritage to the global and domestic visitors'.

Associated Tourism Elements

Associated Tourism Elements (ATE) is the secret magic potion that distinguishes homestays from other forms of accommodation. Every state of India has its cultural distinctness, which is reflected in the literature. For instance, the ATE includes the experience of authentic Kumaon cuisine from farm-to-table produce. Visitors can also participate in community development programs such as teaching English and learning Hindi in Rose Public School Sunargaon, Kanda (Kulshreshtha and Kulshrestha, 2019). ATEs involved in this establishment include craft workshops and an understanding of the cultural landscape (Jayabharathi and Vedamuthu, 2017). ATE plays a significant in this cluster of homestays as it involves the Himalayan artistic representation of the encounter of Buddhist Theatre artists, the experience of farming at high altitude, authentic Himalayan cuisine, adventure sports, yak safaris as well as interaction with the local crafts (Kapur, 2016). These can also be considered farm activities.

Farm activities can be widely associated with the local culture of that particular geographical area. Such as, in the global example of Tennessee itinerary of farm activities, there are BnB (Bed and Breakfast)/ accommodation, wedding destination on-farm, mazes of corn or hay, wagon rides, winery, and site-seeing around the pumpkin patch (Khanal, Honey, & Omobitan, 2019). The agritourism activities on working farms are a significant asset to the economic development of rural areas other than agricultural business. Farm activities can also be classified as DIY (Do-it-yourself) activities (such as making cultural toys), feeding the animals or riding them, educational tours (such as bird watching), and crop picking (Rong-Da Liang et al., 2020). The activities in which tourists involve themselves inflicted more revisit intentions than educational tours with ecological guides. Based on the value co-creation aspect of agritourism from SDL design, the activities adhere to unique characteristics and instigate collaborative relationships among tourists (Rong-Da Liang, 2017).

Farm-to-table activities contribute to the sustainable development of homestay establishments and the representation and preservation of the ethnic culinary heritage of indigenous food. Authentic cuisine adds value to the destination and opens gateways to different cultures while exploring other culinary territories. "Serving" and "environment" play a significant role in tourists' satisfaction with culinary tourism (Hendijani, 2020). Moreover, the homestay provides the perfect ethno-cultural environment with the local community preparing and serving authentic cuisine. The role of gastronomy in agriculture and tourism establishes a trinomial relationship (Di-Clemente, Hernández-Mogollón, & López-Guzmán, 2020). It has become an essential complementary activity for small-scale agricultural farms. Modern tourists have taken a "quality turn" regarding health; they prefer certified organic and authentic food over fast-food outlets. This trend has become a godsend for our nation's producers to represent the local cuisine and bring traditional tastes back to the big cities.

Guided walks are given minor importance in the homestay business. Still, they significantly impact the educational enrichment of tourists related to flora, fauna, and the natural environment of the agritourism site. They also play a pivotal role in the activities such as trekking and nature walks. There is also an innovative "Roaring Fork & Farm Map" practice launched by Rural Tourism Training Academy (CRAFT) in 2018 in Colorado, USA (Romeo et al., 2021). It is a printed pocket guide that acts as a local guide to the tourists around the village guest ranches, attractions, gardens, and other points to visit. It is marked as farm-to-table outlets, local libations (beverages), public parks (Horti-tourism), and local ranches. Walks with a physical guide are also an enriched experience, which can be experienced in Tathagata farms of West Bengal, where guided walks explain the rich cultural significance of every monument and community interaction (Shah & Dave, 2020).

Production Factors

The distinct features of the geographical and cultural location are also delivered in the production factors, also known as promotional features of the business. It can be explored in the example of experiential tourism in Gujarat, known for its rich cultural heritage. Jayabharathi and Vedamuthu (2017) highlight one such project in the earthquake-affected area called Bidada, designed by an architect named Sanjay Udamale. This housing is developed from a former rehabilitation center present in the 2001 earthquake on a 7.7 Richter scale surfacing Chobari village in Kutch. This is a significant example of the utilization of properties left idle with paramount cultural importance. There was another instance of heavy rainfall in the Southern district of Kodagu in Karnataka, which destroyed 20 villages. A surge of coffee estates and homestays became the only source of socio-economic strength for villagers affected in those areas (Varsha and Rajini, 2020).

Another example of promoting heritage and culture in Gujarat is through the vibrant festival of Uttrayan (Kite festival). Patel (2019), in her article on *Uttrayan and the Built Environment,* brought to the attention a four-bedroom homestay in Khadiya named Jagdip Mehta's Heritage House, using Uttrayan as the PF to attract international guests to their homestay. The area of Khadia represents the old city charm of Ahmedabad (Gujarat), mostly known for its vibrant festivals such as Navratri and Uttrayan.

Another such cultural encounter can be witnessed in homestays of Spiti Valley in Himachal Pradesh. This valley accommodates the highest inhabited Asian village, Komic village, at 4,400 meters above sea level (Kapur, 2016). The highlighting PF of this homestay is the whooping 8,00,000 years old species of Himalayan wolves. The southern state of India, known for its backwaters, is Kerala. It has instituted a tremendous boom in backwater tourism in India (Emilda et al., 2020). Friends of Orchha is considered to be the embodiment of a friendly neighborhood, with the involvement of foreign funders and government support (Chowdhary and Sisodia, 2013). This intervention is used as the PF for this homestay. Further, Darjeeling's abundant supply of tea estates and picturesque landscapes (Queen of the Hills) is used as a PF. In this way, it is analyzed that anything can become a production factor for homestay cluster business, from natural calamities such as drought and floods to festivals and adventure marvels. This significant quality of homestay business to utilize discarded resources (destroyed in a calamity) and create it as an important historical site for visitors to witness and experience acts as a critical production factor.

Community Participation

After studying the literature on homestay business in India, it is reflected that the local community plays a key role and acts as the backbone of this industry. Their involvement in a positive stay of tourists can make or break the entire experience. The foremost example of community-based standard homestay practices is Myanmar's four villages of Myaing. Their Hotel and Tourism Ministry handles and coordinates the homestay practices and earnings, equally sharing it with the four villages. The centralized idea is to establish an arrangement of villages to take turns to cook and entertain is the clustered approach. This is the first project in the ASEAN countries to receive a standard community-based tourism certificate becoming one of the relevant examples of agglomeration and cluster homestays. Moreover, the Philippines has a robust National Tourism Development Plan targeting 20 cluster homestays comprising 78 destinations.

Two cases are reflected as the two extreme sides of a coin in the periphery of community participation in homestays: the friendly neighbourhood of Orchha and community non-participation in Kullu. Chowdhary and Sisodia (2013) elaborates the social involvement of the local community in their Case study named "Of the People, For the People, By the People: A case study of Friends of Orchha." This is a homestay facility in Madhya Pradesh organized by an Indo-Swiss-Dutch couple, Asha D'Souza and Louk Vreeswik, who moved here from Geneva in 2006. This sociologist cum anthropologist couple helped the people of Orchha procure employment through tourism in their drought-prone area. With the help of government and foreign NGOs funded schemes, the houses were renovated for visitors. The primary concerns in the village was the lack of infrastructure for water, sanitation, and waste management. After the prolonged period of drought in the year 2003-07, homestays became the primary source of income for the local community and started generating an average of INR. 3,000 per month per family (as of

November 2011) in the peak season. Moreover, homestays are considered a significant income source for women in the community (Kannegieser, 2015). It benefitted women in Darjeeling by uplifting their social status, bridging the socioeconomic gap between their communities, and maintaining a constant income source (Rawat, 2020).

The situation opposite to the harmony discussed in the Friends of Orchha is the case of community non-participation in Kullu, Himachal Pradesh (Sood et al., 2017). It included socio-cultural, practical, and apprehensive constraints of the host community. One of the major drawbacks of homestay establishments is the requirement of uniform infrastructure which has become a practical limitations for economically deprived villagers. Kullu community requires the intervention of government and non-profit organizations. In this case, homestays work under clusters such as Spiti Ecosphere in Himachal Pradesh. Standardization of building hotel-like culture is another benchmark that needs to be flexible to welcome a large economically backward population to enter the realm of homestays and let visitors experience their natural heritage and culture. This will also reduce the apprehensions of the local community. Sensitization of tourists can create a sense of security for the local community to conduct their social traditions and cultural values. CP is missing in the protected areas of India, according to the case studies of Kanha, Ranthambore, and Nagarhole National Park (DeFries et al., 2010), as there is an increase in the number of resorts and relocation of local villagers who lives on the border of Protected Areas. However, Nagarhole National Park reported increasing number of homestays constituting in the natural theme circuit under the supervision of the government.

DISCUSSION

Clustered homestays can be based on internal elements such as the Associated Tourism Elements (ATE) (Zijing and Pu, 2020) and Community Participation or external, connected through a common theme in the respective states or interstates (i.e., Theme-based Circuits (TC)) Government Intervention (GI), and Production Factor (PF). The ATE can be, for instance, weaving in Sualkuchi and Ziro or mask-making in Majuli in the Northeastern states of India (Bhuyan and Deka, 2019). The major role of the private players such as Airbnb in peer-to-peer accommodation and to some extent homestays has made these establishments reach wider audience from domestic to international prospective visitors (Tamilmani et al., 2020). Where infrastructural development is taken care by the government and NGOs, digital platforms such as Airbnb provides marketing and promotional strategies (Joseph et al., 2020; Varghese et al., 2022). Another upcoming trend is social media influencers and familiarization tours which are acting as an important promotional strategy to reach a wider market.

Although currently the focus of the paper is to streamline the infrastructural development of these clusters and economic agglomeration of the producers. In that context, Brunei Darussalam's effective Standard Operating Procedure (SOP) which can be taken as an example of international case study of cluster-based coordination models and contribute to the Production Factor, as highlighted in Wang Meiyu et al. (2018) model. Moreover, the Philippines' local tourism council's focus on micro-segments at the cluster level is also a prominent example of successful standardization of national homestay policy requirements.

The chapter determines the constituents for forming and functioning clustered homestays in India. Figure 1 is a consolidated theory formation for Clustered Homestays deduced from the analysis of existing case studies.

Figure 1. Elements affecting Agglomeration of Homestays (Source by author)

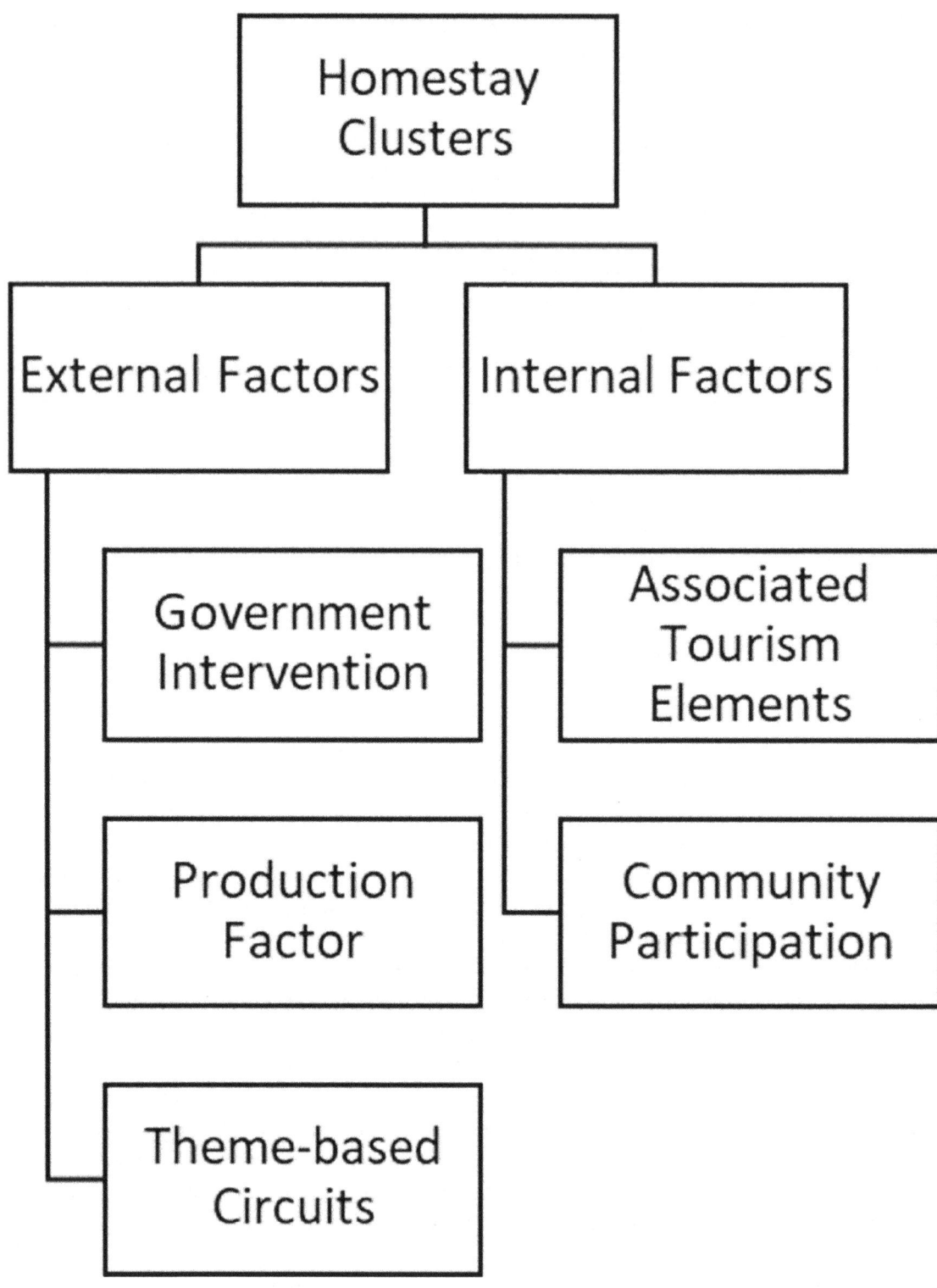

SCOPE FOR FURTHER RESEARCH

The factors studied in the research involve government interventions. However, significant scope for further research can be the comparative analysis of governmental and non-governmental organizations' role in the functioning of homestays and, to some extent, the clustered homestays. The study consists of a limited literature pan India involving eight states. Further exploration can be done in other States of India and the Union Territories, which are growing hotspots for homestay accommodation. The significant role of Theme-based circuits (TC) needs to be recognized and researched on the spatial affinity of different destinations in TCs of India. The Government of Tourism in India recently recognized clustered homestays as having great potential (Draft National Strategy for Promotion of Rural Homestays, 2021). Loopholes in the policy formation and standardization of guidelines are recognized in the study. There is a need for adjustments in the policy guidelines of homestays in India to welcome a considerable amount of the rural population who cannot align with the requirements (Bhuyan, 2021).

CONCLUSION

This study set out to determine the factors affecting Clustered Homestays in the Indian context. One of the more significant findings to emerge from this study is that Community participation is the driving factor of homestay businesses driven by governmental and non-governmental interventions. The effectiveness of government intervention is discussed in the development of Theme-based circuits and its infrastructural development. The balance between these critical internal and external factors translates into an adequate functioning of this segment of the tourism and hospitality industry. Other than the highlighting advantage of homestay accommodation i.e., providing local, personalized and affordable services. Some disadvantages also require attention of stakeholders for its smoother functioning which includes infrastructure, privacy issues of locals and behavioural issues of guests. Taken together, these findings suggest a role of the public sector in promoting Clustered homestays. The analysis of Clustered homestays undertaken here has extended our knowledge and scope of spatial conglomeration and agglomeration in alternate accommodation options. The generalisability of these results is subject to certain limitations due to the limited availability of literature.

The local community's positive attitude towards tourists plays a significant role in their revisit intention. The primary motivators of their revisit intention are accessibility and accommodation quality (Chin et al., 2018). An innovative model of Agri-tech park proposed by researchers in India involves various innovations in the farm stays, such as Artificial Intelligence safety protocols, eco-housing features, e-cart services for fresh farm produce, and interactive sessions (Rana et al., 2021). The development of homestays also contributes to the infrastructural development in the rural community (Shah & Dave, 2020). It considers proper road connectivity, drainage system, clean water availability, and electricity. Further, it contributes to the local community's development by bridging with tourism. Due to the COVID-19 pandemic, various preventive measures are proposed, such as RFID wearables and social distancing. The host community is trained for the new era of safety measures and providing an authentic experience to the guests.

REFERENCES

Bhuyan, R. (2021). Employment Opportunities in Rural Homestays. *Yojana*, (February), 50–53.

Bhuyan, R., & Deka, S. M. (2019). Homestay for Whom-Lessons of ASEAN Countries for North East India. *International Journal of Tourism and Travel*, *12*(1&2), 21.

Boullón, R. C. (2001). *Planificación del Espacio Turístico* (3rd ed.). Trillas.

Chatterjee, S., & Prasad, M. V. D. (2019). The Evolution of Agri-Tourism practices in India: Some Success Stories. *Madridge Journal of Agriculture and Environmental Sciences*, *1*(1), 19–25. doi:10.18689/mjaes-1000104

Chin, C. H., Law, F. Y., Lo, M. C., & Ramayah, T. (2018). The impact of accessibility quality and accommodation quality on tourists' satisfaction and revisit intention to rural tourism destination in Sarawak: The moderating role of local communities' attitude. *Global Business and Management Research*, *10*(2), 115–127.

Choudhury, K., Dutta, P., & Patgiri, S. (2018). Rural Tourism of North East India: Prospects and Challenges. *IOSR Journal of Humanities and Social Science*, *23*(2), 69–74.

Chowdhary, N., & Sisodia, S. (2013). Of the People, For the People, By the People: A Case Study of Friends of Orchha. In SAGE Business Cases. International CHRIE.

Cibinskiene, A., & Snieskiene, G. (2015). Evaluation of city tourism competitiveness. *Procedia: Social and Behavioral Sciences*, *213*, 105–110. doi:10.1016/j.sbspro.2015.11.411

Conference Proceedings. (2017). *Neonatal Network*, *36*(4), 261–277. doi:10.1891/0730-0832.36.4.e1

Das, P. K. (2021). Ecotourism and sustainable community development: A case study of Sillery Gaon, West Bengal. *The International Journal of Social Sciences (Islamabad)*, *10*(1), 21–28. doi:10.46852/2249-6637.01.2021.3

DeFries, R., Karanth, K. K., & Pareeth, S. (2010). Interactions between protected areas and their surroundings in human-dominated tropical landscapes. *Biological Conservation*, *143*(12), 2870–2880. doi:10.1016/j.biocon.2010.02.010

Dey, B., Mathew, J., & Chee-Hua, C. (2020). Influence of destination attractiveness factors and travel motivations on rural homestay choice: The moderating role of need for uniqueness. *International Journal of Culture, Tourism and Hospitality Research*, *14*(4), 639–666. doi:10.1108/IJCTHR-08-2019-0138

Di-Clemente, E., Hernández-Mogollón, J. M., & López-Guzmán, T. (2020). Culinary tourism as an effective strategy for a profitable cooperation between agriculture and tourism. *Social Sciences*, *9*(3), 25. doi:10.3390ocsci9030025

Hendijani, R. B. (2020). Food as a sustainable alternative tourism promotion in 3S destinations. *Journal of Environmental Management and Tourism*, *11*(02 (42)), 377–387. doi:10.14505//jemt.11.2(42).16

Hoyle, B., & Knowles, R. (Eds.). (1998). *Modern Transport Geography* (2nd ed.). Wiley.

India, I. a., & I.A.M.A.I. (2021). *Homestays in India: A Functional and Economic Impact Analysis.* Retrieved from https://ascension.org.in/wp-content/uploads/2021/08/Homestay-ecomonic-impact.pdf

Jayabharathi, P., & Vedamuthu, R. (2017). Experiential Tourism as a Response to the Sustenance of a Cultural Landscape: The Case of Banni, Kutch, Gujarat, India. In *Proceedings of the 6th International Conference of Arte-Polis* (pp. 149-166). Springer. 10.1007/978-981-10-5481-5_15

Joseph, E. K., Kallarakal, T. K., Varghese, B., & Anthony, J. K. (2020). Sustainable tourism development in the backwaters of south Kerala, India: The local government perspective. *Geo Journal of Tourism and Geosites*, *33*(4), 1532–1537. doi:10.30892/gtg.334spl13-604

Kannegieser, I. (2015). *A Home In The Hills: Examining the socioeconomic benefits of homestay tourism on rural women and their communities in the Darjeeling District.* Academic Press.

Kapur, S. (2016). Rural tourism in India: Relevance, prospects, and promotional strategies. *International Journal of Tourism and Travel*, *9*(1-2), 40–49.

Khanal, A. R., Honey, U., & Omobitan, O. (2020). Diversification through 'fun in the farm': Analyzing structural factors affecting agritourism in Tennessee. *The International Food and Agribusiness Management Review*, *23*(1), 105–120. doi:10.22434/IFAMR2019.0043

Kulshreshtha, S., & Kulshrestha, R. (2019). The emerging importance of "homestays" in the Indian hospitality sector. *Worldwide Hospitality and Tourism Themes*, *11*(4), 458–466. doi:10.1108/WHATT-04-2019-0024

Lohmann, G., & Netto, A. P. (2016). *Tourism theory: Concepts, models, and systems.* Cabi.

Long, F., Liu, J., Zhang, S., Yu, H., & Jiang, H. (2018). Development characteristics and evolution mechanism of homestay agglomeration in Mogan Mountain, China. *Sustainability*, *10*(9), 2964.

Lue, C. C., Crompton, J. L., & Fesenmaier, D. R. (1993). Conceptualization of multidimensional pleasure trips. *Annals of Tourism Research*, *20*, 289–301.

Marshall, A. (1890). Some aspects of competition." The address of the president of section F—Economic Science and Statistics—of the British Association, at the Sixtiet Meeting, held at Leeds, in September 1890. *Journal of the Royal Statistical Society*, *53*(4), 612–643. doi:10.2307/2979546

Ministry of Tourism (Hotels and Restaurants Division). (2019). Common National Standards and Guidelines for Classification of Incredible India Bed & Breakfast Establishments and Incredible India Homestay Establishments. Author.

Naidoo, P., & Pearce, P. L. (2018). Enclave tourism versus agritourism: The economic debate. *Current Issues in Tourism*, *21*(17), 1946–1965. doi:10.1080/13683500.2016.1235554

Patel, A. (2019). *Uttarayan and the Built Environment: Perspectives from a World Heritage City.* Sahapedia.

Potter, A., & Studies, H. W. (2014). *Revisiting Marshall's agglomeration economies: Technological relatedness and the evolution of the Sheffield metals cluster.* Taylor & Francis.

Rana, R., Rana, K., & Chhabra, G. (2021). Economic Development of Rural India Through Establishment of Agri-Tech Park. *Indian Journal of Economics and Finance*, *1*(2), 15–23. doi:10.35940/ijef. B2506.111221

Rawat, S. (2020). *Rural Tourism and Sustainable development in Darjeeling Hills, West Bengal: Case study of Lepchajagat.* Academic Press.

Romeo, R., Russo, L., Parisi, F., Notarianni, M., Manuelli, S., & Carvao, S. (2021). *Mountain tourism–Towards a more sustainable path.* Academic Press.

Rong-Da Liang, A. (2017). Considering the role of agritourism co-creation from a service-dominant logic perspective. *Tourism Management*, *61*, 354–367. doi:10.1016/j.tourman.2017.02.002

Rong-Da Liang, A., Hsiao, T. Y., Chen, D. J., & Lin, J. H. (2020). Agritourism: Experience design, activities, and revisit intention. *Tourism Review.*

Shah, C., Shah, S., & Shah, G. L. (2020). Agritourism as a Local Economic Development Tool for Rural Hill Regions. In *Extension Strategies for Doubling Farmer Income* (pp. 19–33). https://www.research-gate.net/publication/343569529

Shah, N., & Dave, D. (2020). The Scope and Challenges of Agro-tourism in India. GH Patel Postgraduate Institute of Business Management, 10.

Sood, J., Lynch, P., & Anastasiadou, C. (2017). Community non-participation in homestays in Kullu, Himachal Pradesh, India. *Tourism Management*, *60*, 332–347. doi:10.1016/j.tourman.2016.12.007

Tamilmani, K., Rana, N. P., Nunkoo, R., Raghavan, V., & Dwivedi, Y. K. (2020). Indian travellers' adoption of Airbnb platform. *Information Systems Frontiers*, 1–20.

Varghese, B., Chennattuserry, J. C., & Kureethara, J. V. (2022). Sinking houseboats and swaying home stays: community resilience and local impacts of COVID-19 in managing tourism crisis in Kerala. *International Journal of Tourism Cities.*

Varsha, V., & Ranjini, S. S. (2020). A Study on the Sustainability of Homestays in Kodagu District after the Disaster-August-2018. *International Journal of Psychosocial Rehabilitation*, *24*(05).

Wang, M. Y., Li, X. Y., & Hou, Y. X. (2018). Research on the transformation and upgrading of homestay industry from the perspective of supply-side reform — A case study of Yangshuo. *Journal of Guangxi Cadres College of Economic and Management*, *30*(2), 67–73.

Zijing, X., & Pu, Z. (2020). A Study on Service Quality Evaluation Model of Clustered Homestay. *Journal of Tourism and Hospitality Management*, *8*(2), 35–44. doi:10.15640/jthm.v8n2a8

KEY TERMS AND DEFINITIONS

Associated Tourism Elements: These are the supporting infrastructure and activities for the functioning of the Homestay business. For instance, farm-to-table, guided walks, and workshops.

Clustered Homestay: The agglomeration of homestays connected by spatial proximity, theme, or geographical location. They share the labor force, localize the knowledge spillover, and links supplier to their benefit.

Government Intervention: The public sector's role in uplifting the local community by introducing policies and reforms in the tourism and hospitality industry.

Hosts: They are the local community directly involved in tourist activities and constantly in contact with tourists visiting the destination, making them responsible for the overall experience.

Local Community: The people residing in tourist destinations directly or indirectly, voluntarily, or involuntarily involved in tourist activities, are known as the local community.

Production Factor: These are a destination's promotional features that set it apart from other business counterparts and connect it through a theme or spatial proximity.

Theme-Based Circuits: This kind of circuit is prevalent in the tourism and hospitality industry and is considered a production factor for promoting the connected theme (such as religion, geographical, cultural, and many more) of a country or tourist destination.

Section 6

USA:
Laying Out Smart Cities

Chapter 15
Smart City in the Global Economy:
Information and Organization Support Development

Tetiana Momot
Coggin College of Business, USA

Russell Triplett
Coggin College of Business, USA

Angelo Cristian Azueta
Coggin College of Business, USA

Olena Filonych
iD https://orcid.org/0000-0001-5428-6794
The Educational and Scientific Institute of Economics and Management, Kharkiv, Ukraine

ABSTRACT

The research is devoted to developing a smart city information and organization support model based on the most prominent international smart city ranking practices of systematization. The concepts are summarized. The smart cities in the global economy in the context of leading international rankings were analyzed. Special attention is given to the variations in measurement methodologies to capture the impact of smart cities, including the Smart City Index and the Strategy Index. The top 10 smartest cities in the global economy were analyzed in terms of international rankings. The emphasis is given to American cities. The proposed smart city information and organization support model is based on the concept of the Smart City Balanced Scorecard (SCBS), which allows systematically identifying and organizing priority areas for the development of a smart city and specify strategic directions in each priority area. An approach to calculating the ranking of the integrated indicator of sustainable development of a smart city (R-SCBS) according to the Balanced Scorecard is developed.

DOI: 10.4018/978-1-6684-5976-8.ch015

INTRODUCTION

It is worth noting that the model of "smart cities" is becoming increasingly widespread worldwide. Based on the United Nation's population forecast the world population is expected to increase by 2 billion persons in the next 30 years, from 7.8 billion currently (2020) to 9.7 billion in 2050 (68% of the world population is projected to live in the urban areas by 2050). Digitalization is a key trend in urbanization over the coming years is crucial to the implementation of the 2030 Agenda for Sustainable Development. One of the great contributions of the digitalization, particularly due to telecommunication infrastructure, is to the development of the so-called smart cities (the intelligent city is the equivalent term in languages derived from Latin), which are cities that invest in social and human capital, urban mobility, modern communication infrastructure facilities, and technology, including the sensible management of natural resources, through participatory governance.

In this regard, the European Organization "European Smart Cities" notes that globalization leads to economic changes that have a large-scale impact. In particular, urbanization is forcing cities of both developed and developing countries to look for new ways to ensure competitiveness in the globalized digital world (*2018 Revision of World Urbanization Prospects*, 2018).

The concept of smart city has been shaped in the literature that spans over 30 years, since the first references to the idea of smart cities at the end of the 1980s to the current explosion of smart city publications. This terminology referred to a "direct association towards optimal, positive, and sustainable development of a town, city, or region" (Lindskog, 2004). However, the generally accepted definition of the concept of "smart cities" has not yet been established. One of the most cited concepts was developed by the European Commission; a smart city is where traditional networks and services are made more efficient using digital solutions to benefit its inhabitants and business. The smart city is characterized by six key "smart" features: smart economy, smart mobility, smart environment, smart people, smart life, and smart management. In this context, "smart" refers to progressive, inclusive, sustainable, and forward-looking policies based on information and communication technologies, human capital, and social responsibility (Smart city. EU, 2022).

At the same time, it should be noted that the "smart cities" model provides an understanding of urban space (including both real and virtual) as an open platform for interaction between authorities, businesses, urban inhabitants, SMEs, investors, banks, and researchers. In a "smart city," technology and information and organization support become the leading resource and basis for regulating "smart" urban systems, creating projects based on open data using information and communication technologies (ICT) to manage the city.

BACKGROUND

The study systematized approaches to defining the concept of "smart cities" by isolating key areas characterizing the directions of smart urban development.

The above data analysis allows us to assert that according to the classical approach, a city is considered a "smart" city that uses information technology to create comfortable living conditions.

In addition, there are other approaches to determining smart cities that develop the essence of the category in the following areas:

- technological.
- an approach that focuses on human capital (reasonable human resources);
- an approach based on proper management.
- combined approach.

As part of the technological approach, information and communication technologies are considered a central element of the functioning of smart cities. At the same time, technologies are considered in the range of complex energy technologies (intelligent networks) to transport and traffic regulation systems. In this context, there are seven signs of a smart city, namely:

- availability of intelligent traffic management systems.
- innovative approach to street lighting.
- introduction of a citywide and accessible Wi-Fi network.
- active use of alternative energy sources.
- availability of a system for alerting citizens about emergencies via SMS.
- minimal use of cash to pay for goods and services.
- involvement of citizens in management issues (Savchuk, 2018).

As part of this approach, scientists define a smart city as a city that uses intelligent computing technologies to create the most critical components of the city's infrastructure and services, including city administration, education, healthcare, public safety, real estate, transportation, and utilities (Lee et al., 2013).

Studies focusing on innovative human resources as a central element of smart city management do not ignore the impact of information and communications technology. Thus, smart cities are considered megacities with a large proportion of the adult population with higher education (Shapiro, 2006).

In research, the concept of a smart city in this direction is mainly based on the characteristics of intelligent residents in terms of their educational level (intelligent people). This level of education is considered the dominant factor in urban growth (Shapiro, 2006, Lazaroiu and Roscia, 2012).

At the same time, J. Shapiro notes that the educated population moves to cities with a high quality of life. At the same time, Winters (2011) argues that students stay in cities after they have completed their education.

Studies based on smart management as the dominant feature of a smart city determine the interaction between different groups of stakeholders of the city. Within the framework of this concept, the attention is focused on users (residents) and other groups of stakeholders (Calderoni et al., 2012). At the same time, to ensure the development of productive interaction between stakeholder groups within a smart city, it is promising to create innovation centers (Kourtit et al., 2012, Yigitcanlar, Buys, and Kamruzzaman, 2018).

The combined approach is based on a combination of three of these elements – smart technologies, smart people, and intelligent cooperation. At the same time, as Musa (2016) notes, business development and large-scale urbanization stimulate the growth of information and communication technologies, which in turn is the driving force behind the interaction of the city administration with communities and urban infrastructure. The author emphasizes that one technology is not enough; intelligent people play no less important role. Integrating various spheres of urban functioning with ICT contributes to the development of smart cities to ensure mobility, technological elasticity, and innovation.

Thus, Hollands (2020) notes that smart cities require not only complex information technologies but also the involvement of different groups of people. In accordance with Giffinger and Pichler-Milanovic (2007) in the framework of an integrated approach, the concept of a smart city is considered based on six components that conceptually combine the components of a smart city (smart people, smart management) and what they seek to achieve (smart economy, smart mobility, smart environment, and intelligent life).

Within the framework of an integrated approach, the definition of a smart city by A. Caragliu and others, according to which the city is reasonable, deserves attention when investments in human and social capital and traditional (transport) and modern (ICT) communication infrastructure provide sustainable economic growth and high quality of life, with good management of natural resources through participatory management (Caragliu et al., 2011).

According to P. Drucker's definition, the formula for effective city management can be symbolically presented in the form of the abbreviation SMART, namely: Specific (specific), Measurable (measurable), Achievable (achievable), Realistic (realistic), and Time (defined in time). Thus, the smart city can be considered open, effective management based on the application of innovative technologies used wisely by the city's residents (Drucker, 2010).

Meijer and Bolivar (2016) consider the smartness of the city as its ability to attract human capital and mobilize it in cooperation with various (organized and individual) participants through the use of information and communication technologies.

Thus, summarizing the approaches under consideration, the concept of a "smart city" should be defined as an integrated and multifactorial municipal ecosystem based on the attraction of human capital and the full-scale use of information and communication technologies through the integration of physical, digital, and human subsystems in an artificially created environment to solve the current problems of the city, ensure its sustainable and balanced development in the economic, social, environmental and institutional sphere to ensure the improvement of safety, comfort and quality of life for citizens in the future.

Therefore, a "smart city" in the context of ensuring balanced development of a large city is considered as:

- "smart community," formed and united around a system of specialized institutions integrated into the urban space, from the point of view of an institutional approach.
- the space of life of increased comfort, created, in particular, due to the effective use of the human factor, intellectual capital as the basis for progressive institutional and economic transformations in the city, from the point of view of a social approach.
- economically capable urbanized system of generation and effective distribution of public goods, qualified for accelerated development and improvement by combining the possibilities of full-fledged financial support with technological saturation and social readiness for self-development, from the point of view of the economic approach.

In general, the functioning of "smart cities" is aimed at ensuring a synergistic combination of sustainable development goals, namely:

- economic goals: improving the productivity of resource use, saving energy, time, and financial resources in solving current problems of the city's functioning, attracting investment, and increasing local budget revenues.

- social goals: improving the quality of life of citizens, ensuring social stability and human development, life safety, inclusiveness of services, and trust in the authorities.
- environmental goals: clean energy, clean air, high-quality water, minimization of the destructive impact of citizens' vital activity and production on the environment.

Urban expert Hutchinson (2013) characterizes a smart city as "a city where doctors are called by video communication, where there is no corruption, and cars drive without drivers" and proposed the classification of smart cities according to versions 1.0, 2.0, and 3.0., namely:

- in the "smart city" version 1.0, there is no general strategy; automation affects individual, unrelated components.
- in version 2.0, the unification and interrelationship of previously independent initiatives and the most significant possible number of different sources of information are conducted.
- version 3.0 assumes that the unification of all components is complete, and the whole infrastructure is saturated with intelligent technologies.

Digital transformation leads to the emergence of new unique systems and processes (e-commerce and business infrastructure, cashless economy, etc.), which make up their new value essence and contribute to increasing the competitiveness of sectors of the smart cities economy.

Transformations in the industry take place by the concept of "Industry 4.0" and with the advent of cyber production, cyber systems, and cyber machines. Therefore, the "smart economy" is considered an economy based on high-tech industries, including ICT and those that use ICT at different stages of the production cycle.

Smart mobility involves sustainable, innovative, and secure ICT-based transport systems - infrastructures that improve urban traffic and mobility in everyday life.

The barrier to urban development based on the concept of "smart cities" is the lack of sufficient competence for citizens to work with data (digital skills), relevant education, professions, etc. Therefore, an essential feature of a smart city is "smart people" - residents with a high level of education and qualifications who actively integrate into the city's social life. It is worth noting that in the context of digital transformations, the principle of learning "know everything" changes to "know how to learn throughout life and become self-fulfilling and competitive," which makes it suitable to reform education in all areas, including secondary school and higher education institutions. In this context, Nam and Pardo (2011) emphasize that ingenious solutions put people at the center of smart cities, not technology.

Innovating gives cities a competitive advantage, so investing in human and social capital is a significant element of developing smart cities.

An essential area of smart cities is the "smart environment," which includes attractive natural conditions for life and environmental measures.

Most smart city concepts also focus on sustainability, with information and communications technology as a primary means of achieving this goal.

Some models emphasize the importance of civic participation in management and the need for fair use by residents of cities and enterprises of available resources. "Smart management" is seen as diversified management. Delegation of functions and diversification of power is the basis of social interaction of social institutions in a "smart city," since for the transition of individual and group cognitive and value attitudes to an intersubjective sphere, a common (general) social context is essential, formed by different practices of institutional and personal interaction between the state and citizens.

The transition to the concept of a smart city provides new opportunities for improving the level of law and order and citizens' comfortable and safe life. "Reasonable living" means a high level of development of various components of the quality of life (safety, health care, housing, tourism, culture, etc.). In this context, essential areas of ensuring public safety are digital projects in road safety, protecting each person's life and health through specialized web services, improving citizens' access to emergency response services, etc.

In healthcare, the quality of life in a smart city is ensured through the development of digital medicine, which allows for online interaction between patients, healthcare professionals, and institutions through digital technologies.

We agree with the opinion of Muzhanova (2017) that the priorities for the development of a "smart city" should be based on an effective territorial and spatial organization "because the use of modern digital technologies will not have such comprehensive consequences without solving the issues of territory planning, urban planning vision of the prospects for its development; organization of the street-road network, control of traffic flows and quality of road surface; increase in the number of charging stations for electric vehicles; production of software and hardware complex of traffic and public transport management". Interesting is the proposal of M. Boykova, which proposes to classify large cities heading to the "amortization" of their services by three types:

- magnet cities are large economic centers or capitals that attract residents with opportunities for employment and comfortable life.
- city strategists implementing high-tech projects develop innovative concepts, the priority of which is to increase the comfort of the life of their residents in the long term.
- innovators who survived the crisis due to the decline of traditional sectors of the economy and were able to apply an innovative approach to creating new growth points and attracting intellectual resources (Boykova, 2011).

Thus, summing up and based on an integrated approach, within the framework of this study, the "smart city" is defined as a comprehensive and multifactorial urban ecosystem, including the attraction of human capital and the full-scale use of information and communication technologies through the integration of physical, digital and human subsystems in an artificially created environment to solve the current problems of the city, ensure its balanced development in the economic, social, environmental and institutional sphere to ensure the improvement of the safety, comfort, and quality of life of citizens in the future. It is indicated that this definition is constantly expanding because the number of a wide variety of digital solutions and breakthrough technologies being implemented to solve the problems of cities in the global economy is continuously increasing.

MAIN FOCUS OF THE CHAPTER

The development of the information and organization support of smart city strategy and further understanding of its implementation is based on the world's leading smart cities' experience systematization.

According to a new Navigant Research Global Market Report, more than 250 smart city projects are from 178 cities worldwide. The majority focuses on five key areas: smart energy, smart water, smart transport, smart buildings, and smart government sectors, emphasizing government and energy initiatives, followed by transportation, facilities, and water goals (*More than 250 Smart City Projects Exist in 178 Cities Worldwide,* 2017).

Based on our previous research, the smart cities in the global economy in the context of leading international rankings were analyzed (Table 1) (Momot and Muraev, 2021).

Table 1. Comparable analysis of the Top 10 smartest cities in the global economy in terms of international rankings*

City	IESE Cities in Motion Index, 2020 (CIMI)	IMD – SUTD (SCI) Smart City Index 2020	Smart City Strategy Rating (SCSI)	PwC Cities of Opportunity 7	EasyPark Smart City Index 2019	Kearney (GCI) (GCO) 2020
London (Great Britain)	1 (0)	15 (+5)	Advanced (3)	1	50	2 (0)
New York (USA)	2 (0)	10 (+28)	None	6	23	1 (0)
Paris (France)	3 (-1)	61 (-10)	Implementation Follower (10)	4	38	3 (0)
Tokyo (Japan)	4 (-2)	79 (-17)	None	15	54	4 (0)
Reykjavik (Iceland)	5 (0)	-	None	-		-
Copenhagen (Denmark)	6 (-2)	6 (-1)	None	-	4	20 (-3)
Berlin (Germany)	7 (-2)	38 (+1)	None	12		15 (-1)
Amsterdam (Netherlands)	8(+5)	9 (+2)	None	5	3	23 (-3)
Singapore (Singapore)	9 (-2)	1 (0)	Advanced (2)	2	9	9 (-3)
Hong Kong (China)	10 (-1)	32 (+5)	None	9	87	6 (-1)
Zurich (Switzerland)	11 (-4)	3 (-1)	None	-	11	22 (-7)
Oslo (Norway)	12 (0)	5 (-2)	None	-	1	-
Chicago (USA)	13 (-4)	44 (+12)	Well progressing (5)	13		8 (0)
Stockholm (Sweden)	14 (+1)	16 (+9)	None	7	5	8 (2)
Vienna (Austria)	18(+8)	25 (-8)	Advanced (1)	-	7	22 (+3)
Helsinki (Finland)	22 (0)	2 (+6)	None	-	19	
Taipei (Taiwan)	27 (-3)	8 (-1)	None	-	25	26 (-1)
Geneva (Switzerland)	34 (+2)	7 (-3)	None	-	33	16 (-4)
Auckland (New Zealand)	35 (0)	4 (+2)	None	-	58	-
Beijing (China)	84 (+1)	82 (-22)	None	19	99	5 (+4)
Toronto (Canada)	30 (+12)	30 (-15)	None	3		19 (-2)
San Francisco (USA)	20 (-1)	27 (-15)	None	8		13 (+9)
Sydney (Australia)	17 (-2)	18 (-4)	None	10		12 (+1)
Kyiv (Ukraine)	115 (+4)	98 (-6)	None	-	-	-

(Data source: Compiled by the authors according to Berrone and Ricart, 2020; Bris et al., 2020, Cities of Opportunity, 2016; Kearney 2020)

The data show that various systematic approaches to assessing the rating of smart cities in the world's top ten "smart cities" of the same year, according to various leading compilers, entered different cities. Moreover, according to other ratings, cities occupy different positions. Only cities such as London, Singapore, and Paris are represented in the rankings reviewed.

The Center for Globalization and Strategy of the IESE Business School of the University of Navarre since, 2014, annually compiles the IESE Cities in Motion Index (CIMI), which is calculated to help the public and governments determine the effectiveness of the city. The CIMI indicator system is a research platform based on an integrated approach, which combines an innovative approach to urban management and a twenty-first-century city model based on four factors: sustainable ecosystem, innovation, equal opportunities for citizens, and well-connected territories based on nine main aspects, including human capital, social cohesion, economy, management, environment, mobility and transport, urban planning, international importance, and technology. The analytical platform is based on in-depth interviews with representatives of the city authorities, entrepreneurs, scientists, and experts whose activities are related to the development of smart cities.

According to the 2020 report (sixth edition), experts examined the degree of development in 174 cities (including 79 capitals) from 80 countries. The conceptual model of the SIMI index is based on the ranking of cities, which is considered a set of steps covering the study of the situation, the construction of a strategy, and its subsequent implementation. It is important to note that the SIMI indicator system includes not so many indicators characterizing the use of SMART technologies and ICT but the results of their service. According to the IESE Cities in Motion Index (SIMI) 2020, Europe is the most efficient geographical region, with 14 cities among the top 25 smart cities (Table 1).

According to the IESE rating for six consecutive years, London has never dropped below the second position and, since 2019, ranks first, including human capital (due to many business schools and universities) and conditions for international cooperation. Since 2017, it has remained in the top ten regarding management, mobility and transport, technology, and urban planning. In addition, more startups and programmers are concentrated in the British capital than in any other city.

Singapore is an island city-state, confidently in the world's top rankings of smart cities. The successful implementation of the Smart Nation program has already allowed Singapore residents to get high-speed Internet access in every home. And for every resident of Singapore, there are three smartphones. Along with developing high-tech ICT production in Singapore, it is actively used in the social sphere.

In the IESE ranking, New York leads the North America ranking and is also in the second position in the overall classification in the world due to the best economic performance (1st place in the world in terms of urban economy), high human capital, advanced urban planning, and good conditions for establishing international relations. New York has nearly 7,000 high-tech companies and ranks 8th in manufacturability, providing many integrated technology services, such as LinkNYC's free Wi-Fi network. Like Londoners, social cohesion (137 positions), which has improved compared to 151 posts in 2019, New Yorkers have not yet been able to achieve.

For the calculation of 2020 CIMI, in addition to New York, 15 more US cities have been included. Among them, the top -5 are New York (2nd position in the world ranking), Chicago (13th position), Washington (15th position), Los Angeles (16th position), and San Francisco (20th position) (Figure 1).

American cities took the top position in the dimension "Economics," including all aspects that promote the economic development of a territory, due mainly to their high GDP per capita and the growth shown in recent years. New York City remains top in the ranking for this dimension, thanks largely to its high GDP and the number of headquarters of publicly traded companies. Also, five US cities, namely Los

Angeles (2nd position), New York (3rd position), Boston (4th position), Washington (7th position), and Chicago (10th position) in the top 10 in the dimension "Human Capital" due to capability of attracting and retaining talent, creating plans to improve education and promoting both creativity and research.

According to the Center for Digital GoStatest, Los Angeles has been named the United States Number One Digital City for the third consecutive year. Los Angeles is a leader in innovation and uses data to improve its inhabitants' quality of life.

Relatively strong position the US cities hold in the dimension of "Urban Planning." New York City, the city with the most skyscrapers and buildings, takes first place in this dimension.

Among the cities that occupy the top ten positions in the dimension "Technology," there are also five US cities, including San Francisco (3rd position), Boston (5th position), New York (8th position), Seattle (9th position), and Denver (10th position).'

At the same time, US cities face challenges to urban functionality, such as environmental problems such as pollution, climate change, and the threat of natural disasters such as hurricanes and earthquakes.

According to 'smartest' cities in the world – SUTD (SCI) Smart City Index 2020, compiled by the Smart City Observatory of the Center for World Competitiveness of the Institute of Management Development (IMD) in cooperation with the Singapore University of Technology and Design (SUTD), the Top 10 smartest cities in the world include Singapore (Singapore), followed by Helsinki (Finland), Zurich (Switzerland), Auckland (New Zealand), Oslo (Norway), Copenhagen (Denmark), followed by Geneva (Switzerland), Taipei (Taiwan), Amsterdam (Netherlands) and New York (USA). The ranking is compiled starting from 2019 by surveying residents about the technological capabilities of their city in five key areas: health and safety, mobility, activities, opportunities, and management (Kearney, 2020). In 2020, 109 cities were surveyed. The assessment is based on how people perceive the scale and impact of efforts to make their cities "smart," combining "economic and technological aspects" with "humane dimensions." The study also assessed the availability of technology for urban inhabitants (Table 1).

The most recent STUD Smart City Index (2021) includes five American cities in the top 50 rankings. However, each of the five cities, ordered by rank: New York, Los Angeles, Washington D.C., Seattle, and Denver, showcased a drop in rankings from the previous index publication. In fact, in the top 50 rankings, American cities fell by 46 positions (-46), with Washington D.C. displaying the most significant decline of 23 positions (-23). Within the index, city inhabitants were tasked to select five from among 15 indicators that signified priority areas of most urgency for their cities. In all five American cities, city inhabitants displayed a trend in selecting *Affordable Housing* and *Road Congestion* as their precedencies. Moreover, New York, Los Angeles, and Washington D.C. all indicated an urgency in *Security,* while Seattle and Denver leaned more toward *Air Pollution.*

Singapore spent the most in the world on innovative city initiatives, far outpacing New York, London, and Tokyo, investing $1.1 billion. U.S. dollars.

R. Berger's Smart City Strategy Rating (SCSI) report found that 153 cities worldwide, including both large and small, have published the official Smart City strategy. Fifteen of them have strategic plans that demonstrate a comprehensive strategic approach. Moreover, only 8 of them are at an advanced stage of implementation. In addition, the report notes that there are about 500 cities around the world with a population of more than one million (according to UN estimates). At the same time, only 49 have an official Smart City strategy (Table 1). According to the results of 2019, the group of advanced cities included: Vienna (selected flagship projects: E – medicine, open public data, virtual office), London (selected flagship projects: open city data ecosystem, sensor infrastructure), and Singapore (selected flagship projects: digital and sensor platforms, national digital identity) (Alkandari, 2012). Regarding

American cities, R. Berger only ranks Chicago, IL. Chicago's fifth-place ranking in the categorization among *Moderate Strategies* comes in justification from the 2015 completion of the city's 2013 public-private technology plan. Summarizing the experience of the world's leading cities, R. Berger proves the need to apply a participatory approach to developing a smart city strategy.

According to the Cities of Opportunity 7 PricewaterhouseCoopers LLP rating, five cities are rated in the top ten: London, New York, Tokyo, Amsterdam, and Paris. London maintains the No. 1 ranking among 30 cities rated by three indicators: intellectual capital and innovation, technological readiness, and global openness. Intellectual capital and innovation generated by a highly experienced society are channelers of the development of the modern urban ecosystem. The leaders within this group of indicators are London, San Francisco, Paris, Amsterdam, Toronto, New York, Los Angeles, Tokyo, Sydney, Stockholm, and Chicago. Evaluation of technological readiness is carried out by considering such components as quality (or reliability of connections), speed (loading / downloading), value (cost), and digital security. The top ten for this component include Singapore, London, Amsterdam, New York, Stockholm, Hong Kong, San Francisco, Tokyo, Paris, and Toronto. The indicators of the third group allow us to assess the global connections and attractiveness of the city beyond its local borders and measure the city's international attractiveness, considering the city's social, economic, and cultural magnetism internationally. The American cities included in the ranking include, by order, New York, San Francisco, Chicago, and Los Angeles. PricewaterhouseCoopers notes that the American cities collectively showcase high indicators of *Intellectual Capital and Innovation*. In addition, the area of low ranking among American cities is predominantly *City Gateway*. New York continues its downward trend in this category as rankers point towards a decrease in global travel and tourism initiatives. London remains at the top of this group of indicators. Paris moved from 7th position in 2014 to 2nd in 2020. Among the leaders in this group of hands are Beijing, Dubai, Hong Kong, Tokyo, Singapore, and Amsterdam (Andrienko, 2018).

Swedish developer of electronic solutions for urban parking management, EasyPark, developed a Smart Cities Index consisting of 19 components. Within the framework of an integrated approach to the calculation of the index, both criteria directly related to the use of ICT and general standards reflecting the level of development of the urban economy and the quality of life in the city as a whole are proposed (Korepanov, 2018). EasyPark's Smart Cities Index heavily favors American cities, as displayed in their latest rankings published in 2021. In the categorization of cities with populations of three million inhabitants or more, in the top 10, four American cities appear, namely, New York (2nd), San Fransico (3rd), Seattle (7th), and Washington D.C. (10th).

The leading international management consulting company Kearney assesses the rankings of the world's top cities according to the Global Cities Index (GCI) (assesses global urban activity) and Global Cities Outlook (GCO) (assesses the city's ability to attract talented human capital, ensure economic growth, increase competitiveness, and ensure stability and security), which together provide a comprehensive analysis of the state and prospects of urban development. For the fourth year in a row, New York tops the ranking of world cities, followed by London, Paris, and Tokyo. The best cities rated by GCO are London, New York, and Paris. One year onward (2021), New York continues to reign superior over its competitors in the Global Cities Index (GCI).

Other American cities included in the GCI Top 10 rankings include the likes of Los Angeles and Chicago, which had previously been included in the previous year's Top 10. Notably, Los Angeles gained two positions by leaping to fifth place.

Summing up, it is worth noting that as a result of using different criteria for assessing and creating a ranking in the same year, other cities entered the top ten "smart cities" of the world according to different compilers. Thus, in the positions of the first ten "smart" cities worldwide, 22 cities occupy different ratings. Of these, three – London, Paris, and Singapore are represented in all the rankings.

Thus, the study allows us to conclude that today there is no single methodological approach to assessing the rating of a smart city. All considered methodological approaches are based on the calculation of the critical criterion that characterizes not only the use of smart technologies and ICT but how much the result of their such affects the city's state and level of development. Smart cities in dynamics and is an informative basis for positioning the city by selected components with the definition of competitive advantages for developing a strategy for creating a smart city in a global economy.

Figure 1. Smart American cities in the global economy: IESE Cities in Motion Index 2020

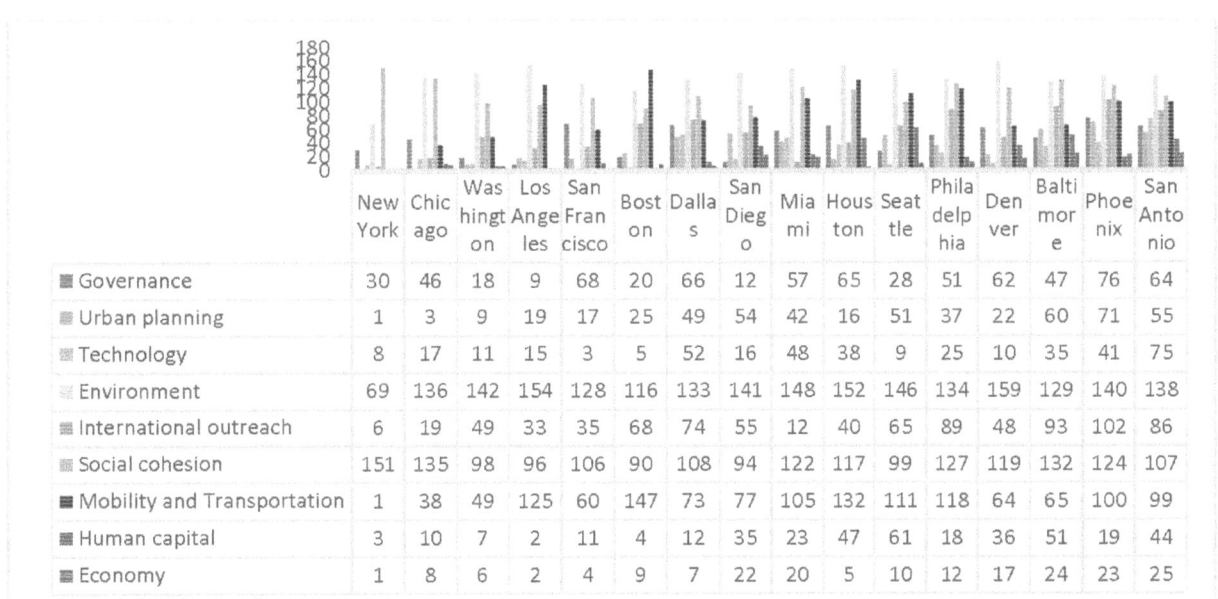

	New York	Chic ago	Was hingt on	Los Ange les	San Fran cisco	Bost on	Dalla s	San Dieg o	Mia mi	Hous ton	Seat tle	Phila delp hia	Den ver	Balti mor e	Phoe nix	San Anto nio
Governance	30	46	18	9	68	20	66	12	57	65	28	51	62	47	76	64
Urban planning	1	3	9	19	17	25	49	54	42	16	51	37	22	60	71	55
Technology	8	17	11	15	3	5	52	16	48	38	9	25	10	35	41	75
Environment	69	136	142	154	128	116	133	141	148	152	146	134	159	129	140	138
International outreach	6	19	49	33	35	68	74	55	12	40	65	89	48	93	102	86
Social cohesion	151	135	98	96	106	90	108	94	122	117	99	127	119	132	124	107
Mobility and Transportation	1	38	49	125	60	147	73	77	105	132	111	118	64	65	100	99
Human capital	3	10	7	2	11	4	12	35	23	47	61	18	36	51	19	44
Economy	1	8	6	2	4	9	7	22	20	5	10	12	17	24	23	25

Along with the advantages of rating smart cities, disadvantages should be noted. First, collecting statistical information to compile a ranking of intelligent cities is problematic. Secondly, there is a correlation between the indicators characterizing the different components of the ranking. Thirdly, the considered methodological approaches do not substantiate the choice of weighting values for creating a smart city ranking. Fourthly, when conducting surveys of experts, the level of influence of the subjective factor remains high. Fifthly, the use of not only statistical indicators in the ranking gives rise to the problem of ambiguous interpretation of the results obtained. There may even be a politicized nature in the performance of the results obtained and the interests of individual parties. In addition, the ratings state the facts of past achievements of cities in areas that are analyzed and do not consider the prospects for strategic development.

However, despite these shortcomings, the urban ranking is a sufficiently justified tool for making strategic decisions and determining priority areas of activity for developing smart cities in the global economy.

SOLUTIONS AND RECOMMENDATIONS

According to the results of the study of the process of development and implementation of the strategy of the leading smart cities in the world, it was established that the development of a smart city strategy should be carried out through the use of information and organization support with the calculation of an integrated indicator for the priority areas of smart city development (Momot and Muraev, 2021).

To end, a model of information and organization support for the development of a strategy of smart cities under a balanced system of indicators is proposed, which is considered as a complex, open, holistic, integrated into external processes model, which should be organically combined with the overall strategy of the city development and ensure the balance of long-term goals for sustainable development of the city (Figure 2).

Unlike existing ones, the proposed model is based on indicator analysis with the implementation of a critical assessment of interdependent indicators of the balanced development of a smart city. To do this, according to the results of the systematization of methodological approaches to the evaluation of smart cities according to international ratings, an information and analytical framework for assessing the level of sustainable development of smart cities was formed according to the balanced system of indicators of the smart city SCBSC (Smart City Balanced Scorecard), which allows determining priorities and measures for the development of a strategy for the development of a smart city in the global economy. The proposed information and analytical model for assessing the level of sustainable development of smart cities are based on the assessment of the integrated indicator of a smart city in the following priority areas of life support of a smart city (or SCBSC perspectives): intelligent people (human capital, digital skills, social cohesion), innovative governance (partner ecosystem, e-governance, process administration, accountability and transparency of government, urban planning), ICT and infrastructure (digital infrastructure, telecommunications, social networks), smart economy (cashless payments, financing, e-commerce, international integration, investments, innovations), quality of life and comfort in the city (transport, healthcare, security, education, environment, culture, and information policy).

It is worth noting that a smart city's strategy is considered a component of the overall local development strategy.

In general, the vision of a smart city can be defined as a modern city based on the widespread use of information and communication technologies that stimulate opportunities and innovations to improve the quality of life and comfort of people's living environments based on the intensification of their participation in solving urban development problems as a prerequisite for sustainable growth. In such conditions, the development of a strategy for a smart city requires the formation of information and organizational support.

Information support for the development of a smart city strategy is based on the formation of the city's open data portal for the creation of a transparent system of management decision-making on the principles of openness by default, efficiency and clarity, accessibility and use, comparability and interoperability, the development of e-governance and the involvement of citizens to make managerial decisions. In this context, the formation of online open data platforms in the city is a priority direction for implementing the best practices of the smartest cities in the world.

Figure 2. Conceptual model of information and organization support for the development of a smart cities strategy according to a balanced scorecard. Source: Developed by authors

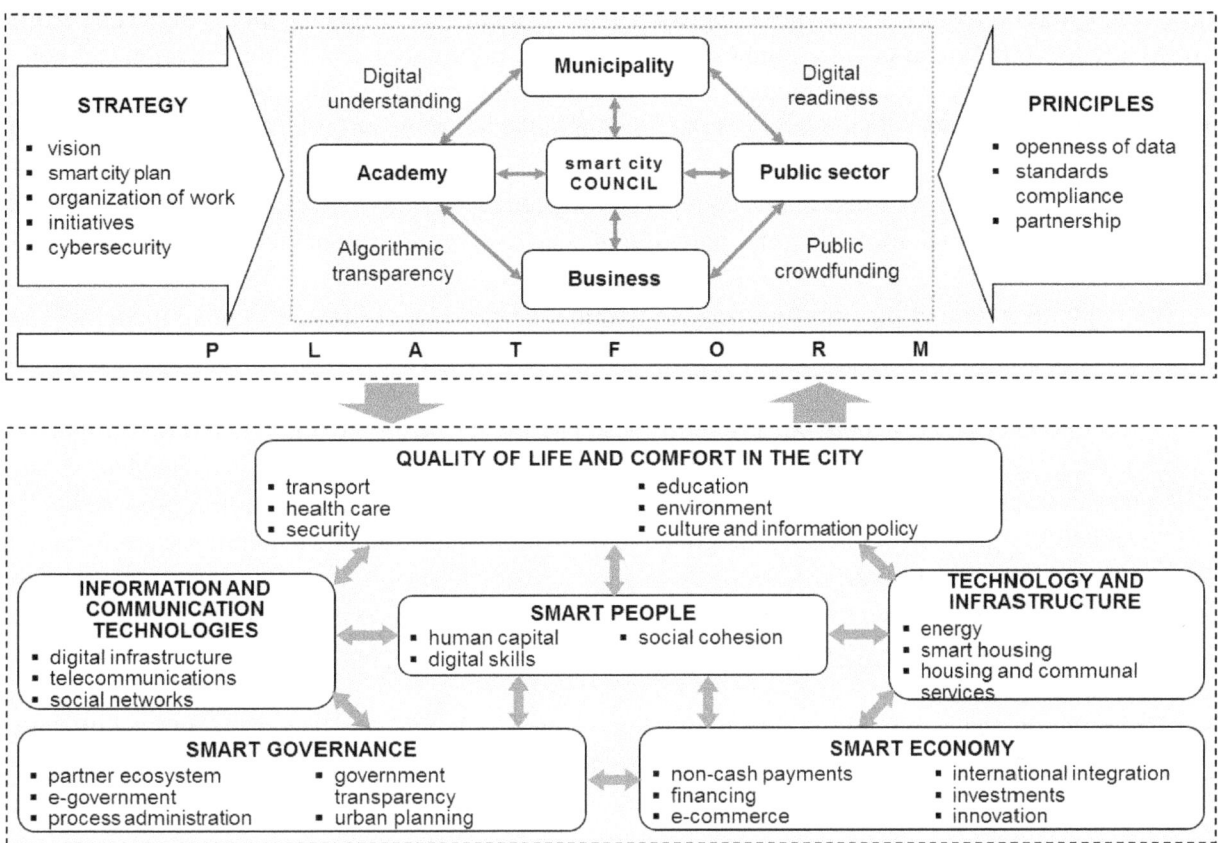

Methodological support for developing a smart city strategy should be based on the formation of modern architecture of a smart city with the definition of the main directions for the implementation of the components of a smart city. At the same time, the justification of the conditions for the formation of a smart city is carried out based on the results of analytical work on the socio-economic development of the city and the development of an integral indicator using reasonable methodological approaches to the reinforcement of smart cities.

Systematization of methodological approaches to the assessment of smart cities according to international rankings in the global economy allows substantiating the feasibility of applying information and analytical system for assessing the level of balanced development of smart cities under a balanced approach of smart city indicators (Smart City Balanced Scorecard (SCBS) as an integrated model of strategic management, which allows systematically to identify and organize priority areas for the development of a smart city and specify strategic directions in each priority area, which at the same time can serve as an evaluation system according to the developed system of key indicators (KPIs) using open data based on the results of online surveys, meetings, discussions with key groups of stakeholders, taking the public, and is a powerful tool for disseminating information in the global economy (Table 3).

A balanced smart city scorecard (SCBS) allows for transforming a defined vision of a smart city into specific goals. It forms a strategic management system using key indicators (KPIs).

The number of SCBS components is selected according to the priority areas of development of a smart city, which allows them to be hierarchically placed according to the logic based on an integrated approach, which combines an innovative approach to urban management and the model of the city of the twenty-first century. Smart people, competent management, information and communication technologies (ICT), technology and infrastructure, innovative economy, quality of life and working conditions in the city for settlements, and modeling of the integral indicator of the rating of balanced development of a smart city.

An essential element of smart cities' strategy in the global economy is the definition of the digital nature of services and the formation of a portfolio of services considering modern breakthrough technologies (Table 2).

The implementation of the priorities defined within the framework of the conceptual model will be ensured in the following areas of activity (perspectives):

1. Smart people. Smart people build smart cities. The main goal of any city should be to improve human capital. A city with innovative governance should be able to attract and retain talent, create plans to improve education and promote creativity and research. This projection is proposed to be evaluated by groups of indicators integrated into the following components: human capital, digital skills, and social cohesion.
2. Smart governance - groups of indicators are integrated into the following components: partner eco-system, quality of process administration, accountability and transparency of power, E-governance, and urban planning.
3. Information and communication technologies – groups of indicators characterizing the following integral components are used: digital infrastructure, telecommunications, and social networks.
4. Technology and infrastructure – groups of indicators that are integrated into the following components: energy, smart housing, housing, and communal services.
5. Smart economy: groups of indicators characterizing the following integral components are used: cashless payments, e-commerce, international integration, financing, investments, and innovations.
6. Quality of life and comfort in the city: groups of indicators are used that are integrated into the following components: transport, safety, environment, healthcare, education, culture, and information policy.

To assess the level of balanced development of a smart city in a digital economy, based on world practice, an integral indicator of the rating of balanced development of a smart city (R-SCBSC) has been developed – a generalized index of the level of balanced development of a smart city, which is carried out from the standpoint of combining four perspectives of a balanced system of city' key performance indicators. For each component of the R-SCBSC rating, a KPI system was formed. The KPI R-SCBSC indicator system covers the results of various studies based on both formalized parameters and the results of the survey of urban residents, namely: municipal surveys;

rating of accountability of cities within the framework of the online platform "TransparentCities" in 14 areas of activity of local self-government authorities according to 86 indicators of methodology («TransparentCities», 2021); the results of the survey of residents according to NUMBERO (*Eastern Europe: Quality of Life Index by City,* 2021); *Index of competitiveness of cities,* 2020).

To calculate the integral indicator of the rating of balanced development of a smart city, a comprehensive assessment is applied, which provides for determining the list of indicators that affect the level of balanced development of a smart city and most fully reflect digital transformations, grouping indicators by established areas of activity (perspectives); calculation of partial indices for these perspectives. The results of a comprehensive assessment of the integral indicator - the ranking of smart city balanced development allows further determination of the average indicator of integrated assessment, which can serve as a basis for assessing the degree of depressiveness of systems (when the value of the integral ranking is lower than the average), the latter, in turn, is evidence that such territorial socio-economic systems "need state support" (Kearney, 2020).

Table 2. Model of the information and analytical system for assessing the level of balanced development of smart cities according to a balanced approach of smart city indicators (Smart City Balanced Scorecard -SCBS)*

Quality of life	Quality of life and comfort in the city	Transport	Security	Environment
		Health	Education	Culture and Information Policy
Digital economy	Smart Economy	Competitiveness	E-commerce	International integration
		Financing Cashless payments	Investment	Innovation
Technological Innovation	Technology and infrastructure	Energy	Smart housing	Housing and Utilities
	ICT	Digital infrastructure	Telecommunications	Social networks
Smart people and government	Smart governance	Partner ecosystem	Quality of process administration	Accountability and transparency of government
		E-governance	Urban planning	
	Smart people	Human capital	Digital skills	Social cohesion

Source: Developed by authors

A methodical approach to calculating the integral indicator of sustainable development of a smart city (R-SCBS) according to a balanced system of indicators has been developed, which provides for the implementation of such stages (Figure 3).

- **First stage:** Formation of a system of a balanced approach of smart city indicators (SCBS). SCBS is defined as an information and analytical model for assessing the level of development of a smart city according to a Balanced Scorecard, which allows ensuring the presentation of the results of the survey of smart cities in dynamics and is an informative basis for positioning the city by selected components with the definition of competitive advantages for the development of a strategy for the smart city development in the global economy.
- **Second stage:** Formation of the KPI R-SCBS indicator system. Through the use of an indicator approach based on the results of comparative analysis, a set of indicators (KPIs) of a balanced system of indicators characterizing not only the use of intelligent technologies and ICT is selected but also the result of their use, which affects the state and level of balanced development of the city in the global economy. The KPI R-SCBS indicator system is formed by accumulating statistical

information and the results of various studies based on formalized parameters and the survey of urban residents.

- **Third stage:** Data aggregation. All indicators within the components (subindexes) have been standardized according to whether these are stimulant indicators (the higher indicator value increases the value of the resulting indicator) or whether these are destimulators (the higher indicator value corresponds to a decrease in the resulting indicator). Standardization was carried out using the following formulas (1, 2):

Figure 3. Methodical approach to calculating the rating of the integrated indicator of sustainable development of a smart city (R-SCBSC) according to a balanced scorecard

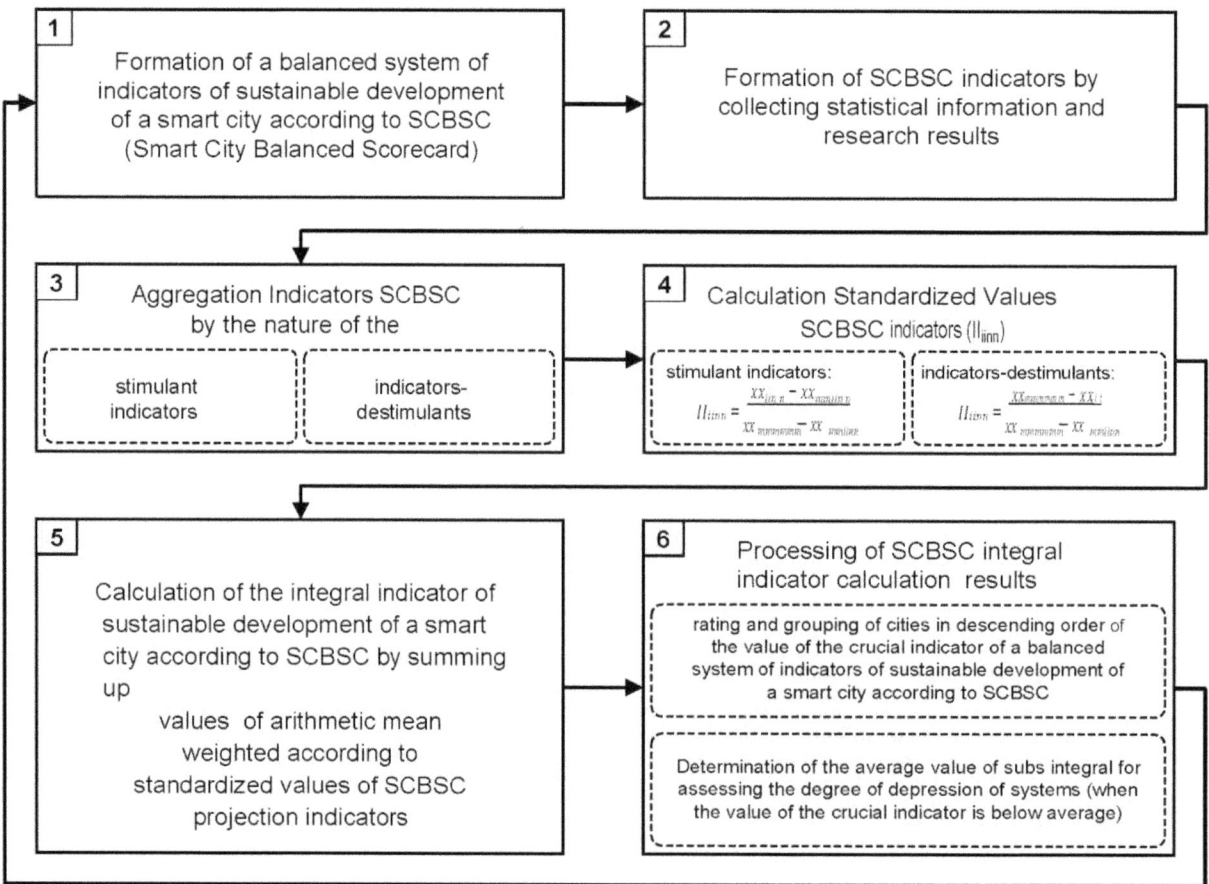

1) for stimulant indicators:

$$I_{in} = \frac{x_{in} - x_{min}}{x_{max} - x_{min}} \tag{1}$$

in – the value of the indicator *and* the city *n*.

x_{min} – the minimum indicator value among all cities.
x_{man} – the maximum indicator value among all cities.

2)   for destimulant indicators:

$$I_{in} = \frac{x_{max} - x_i}{x_{max} - x_{min}} \tag{2}$$

x_{in} – the value of the indicator *and* the city *n*.
x_{man} – the maximum indicator value among all cities.
x_{min} – the minimum indicator value among all cities.

Standardized indicator values within each component (subindex) were generalized by calculating the average arithmetic downtime and thus deriving the subindex. Similarly, data were aggregated as part of the BSC perspectives; generalized data within the measurement (BSC perspectives) were subsequently aggregated into the integrated indicator of the rating of balanced development of a smart city (R-SCBS) using the average arithmetic weighted.

The Integrated Smart City Sustainability Ranking (R-SCBS) was compiled by summing up the values of the arithmetic means of the standardized indicators of five BSC perspectives.

$$R - SCBSC = \sum_{j=1}^{5} \left(SP \bigcup_{k=1}^{3} (LK, CN, SZ) + SU \bigcup_{l=1}^{5} (PE, PPV, MP, QAP, EG) \right.$$

$$+ TI \bigcup_{m=1}^{6} (CE, SH, HCS, CI, T, CN) + SE \bigcup_{n=1}^{7} (C, F, Inv, BR, EC, MI, I)$$

$$\left. + QL \bigcup_{p=1}^{6} (T, S, Env, M, Ed, CIP) \right)$$

where *there are 5 BSC perspectives* (priority areas of life of a smart city): **SP** – smart people, **SU** – smart governance, **TI** – ICT and infrastructure, **SE** – smart economy, **QL** – quality of life and comfort in the city; *components of the perspective of smart people* **SP:** LK - human capital (consists of 3 indicators: the level of opportunities to engage in entrepreneurial activity, the level of opportunities to receive enough money for their work, personnel issues), CN - digital skills (includes the index of practical skills in the field of ICT) and SZ - social cohesion (consists of 3 indicators: the level of opportunities to freely express their own opinions; the quality of work of public organizations, social services); *components of the perspective of smart governance* **SU:** PE-partner ecosystem (contains 2 indicators: the level of opportunities to be included in the decision-making process in the city, access and participation), PPV - accountability and transparency of the authorities (consists of 2 indicators: information on the work of the local self-government body, anti-corruption policy and professional ethics), MP - urban planning (includes land use indicator and construction policy), QAP - quality of process administration (consists of 4 indicators: the number of times a person applies to the ASC, the duration of waiting for a person in the queue for a service in the ASC, the index of human satisfaction with the competence of ASC employees, the ASC satisfaction index), EG - E-governance (includes local E-democracy index), *ICT perspective* *components and* **TI:** CE – clean energy (includes indicator percentage of installed renewable energy capacity (SPP and WPP)), SH - smart housing (includes housing policy indicator), HCS – housing and communal services (includes 7 indicators: quality of water supply services, quality of sewerage services, quality of garbage collection services, percentage of waste sorting, quality of heating services in the city, utilities, communal property), CI - digital infrastructure (includes 4 indicators: speed of data loading in Vodafone network (Mbps), data transfer speed in Vodafone network (Mbps), free Wi-Fi points around the city (quantity), index of ICT development), T – telecommunications (includes 3 indicators: provision of consumers with mobile (mobile) communication per 100 inhabitants, provision of households with fixed access to the Internet per 100 households, length of the city's own optical network (km)), CN - social networks (includes 2 components: penetration of social networks Instagram (%), penetration of social networks Facebook (%)) ; *components of the perspective of smart economy* **SE:** C – competitiveness (includes competitiveness index), F – financing (includes 2 indicators: budget process, financial and material assistance, grants), Inv – investments (includes investment indicator and economic development), BR - cashless payments (includes an indicator of the percentage of non-cash transactions on the Internet), EC – e-commerce (includes the procurement indicator), MI – international integration (includes an indicator of foreign investment, USD per person, at the beginning of December 2019), I – innovations (includes an indicator of the number of innovatively active industrial enterprises); *components of the perspective of quality of life and comfort in the city* **QL:** T – transport (includes 6 indicators: traffic index, traffic index (in minutes), CO2 emission index, parking quality, lost rush hour time per year (in hours), city convenience for bicycles); S – security (includes 5 indicators: safety index, sense of security, going home alone after dark in your area, quality of police services, video surveillance system (number of street surveillance cameras), national cybersecurity index), Env – environment (includes 2 indicators: environmental quality index, pollution index), M - health care (includes 2 indicators: the level of quality of services in the field of medical institutions, the health index), Ed – education (includes 3 indicators: the quality of educational services in the city, the number of universities, the number of schools), CIP - culture and information policy (includes 6 indicators: the level of opportunities for various leisure activities, the number of theaters, the number of libraries, the number of museums, the quality of services in the field of cultural institutions, quality of work of local media).

Thus, the integrated indicator of sustainable development of a smart city (R-SCBSC) includes five perspectives *of BSC* (priority spheres of life of a smart city), 27 components, and 66 indicators.

Fourth stage: *Ranking and grouping of cities by R-SCBSC.* According to the aggregate R-SCBSC, a ranking of cities to inform of the R-SCBSC value is carried out.

Fifth stage. *Determination of the average indicator of critical evaluation.* The results of a comprehensive assessment of the crucial indicator of sustainable development of a smart city allow for further determine the average indicator of integrated assessment, which can serve as the basis for assessing the degree of depressiveness of systems (when the value of the integral index is lower than the average), the latter, in turn, is evidence that such territorial socio-economic systems "need state support."

Standardized indicator values within each component (subindex) were generalized by calculating the average arithmetic downtime and thus deriving the subindex. Similarly, data were aggregated within the measurements included in some features. The data summarized within the measurement were further aggregated into the subindex using an average arithmetic downtime.

The proposed methodical approach to calculating the ranking of the integrated indicator of sustainable development of a smart city (R-SCBS) according to the City Balanced Scorecard was tested on five Ukrainian cities: Kyiv, Kharkiv, Dnipro, Lviv, and Odessa (Murayev, 2020). Despite the time consumption impediment of the data collection process, the endeavor produced a comprehensive smart city strategy development framework. Furthermore, future research will incorporate the suggested methodological approach to American cities.

CONCLUSION

Systematization of the concepts of a smart city in the global world allows us to define the smart city as a comprehensive and multifactorial urban system based on fully incorporating information schemes and communication technologies through effectively integrating physical, digital, and human subsystems in an artificial environment. Moreover, these mechanisms are designed to solve current problems of cities and, in turn, deliver their sustainable, prosperous, and inclusive future in the economic, social, environmental, and institutional spheres via the improvement of the standards of safety, comfort, and quality of life for its citizens in the future.

The generalization of foreign experience indicates the need to introduce the ranking of smart cities in a global economy based on the proposed information and analytical model to assess the level of balanced development of smart cities using methodological approaches of leading world smart cities rankings.

A methodical approach to calculating the ranking of the integrated indicator of sustainable development of a smart city (R-SCBS) according to the Balanced Scorecard has been developed, which provides for the implementation of five stages: formation of a system of a balanced approach to smart city indicators (SCBS); formation of the KPI R-SCBS indicator system; data aggregation; ranking and grouping of cities by R-SCBS; determination of the average indicator of critical evaluation.

According to the results of the study, it was found that information and organization support for the development of a smart city strategy according to a balanced system of indicators is defined as a complex, open, integral, integrated system in external processes, which should be organically combined with the general strategy for the development of the city and ensure a balance of long-term goals for the sustainable development of the smart city in the global world.

A model of information and organization support for the development of a smart city strategy based on a Balanced Scorecard is proposed, which, in contrast to the existing ones, is based on an integrated approach that combines an innovative approach to smart city management and the Smart City Balanced Scorecard (SCBS), which allows identifying priorities and measures to develop a strategy for the development of a smart city in a global economy.

Information and analytical model for assessing the level of balanced development of smart cities are proposed, which is an informative base for positioning the city according to the selected components of the balanced indicator system, which ensures the compactness and visibility of the ratings and sub-ratings obtained for and is a good tool for presenting the results of the survey of smart cities in dynamics with determining competitive advantages for working out a strategy for the development of a smart city in a global economy.

To conclude, in our capricious society of high instability, geo-political conflicts, and natural disasters, a smart city analytical and organization support system can promote efficiency and sustainable development in cities by incorporating transparency platforms that use ICTs for stakeholder coalition.

REFERENCES

2018 *Revision of World Urbanization Prospects.* (2018). United Nations. Retrieved from https://www.un.org/development/desa/pd/sites/www.un.org.development.desa.pd/files/files/documents/2020/Jan/un_2018_wup_report.pdf

Andrienko, A. A. (2018). SMART-approaches to the development of large cities: Prospects for implementation in Ukraine. *Public Administration and Local Self-Government*, 3(38), 100–106.

Berrone, P., & Ricart, J. E. (2020). *IESE Cities in Motion Index 2020*. University of Navarra. Retrieved from https://media.iese.edu/research/pdfs/ST-0542-E.pdf

Boykova, M. V. (2011). *Buduschee gorodov Goroda as agents of globalization and innovation* [The Future of Cities: Cities as agents of globalization and innovation]. Salazkin. Retrieved from https://cyberleninka.ru/article/n/buduschee-gorodov-goroda-kak-agenty-globalizatsiii-innovatsiy

Bris, A., Cabolis, C., Lanvin, B., Caballero, J., Hediger, M., Jobin, C., . . . Zargari, M. (2020). Smart City Index 2020. A Tool for Action, an Instrument for Better Lives for All Citizens. Academic Press.

Calderoni, L., Maio, D., & Palmieri, P. (2012). Location-aware mobile services for a smart city: Design, implementation and deployment. *Journal of Theoretical and Applied Electronic Commerce Research*, 7(3), 74–87.

Caragliu, A., Del Bo, C., & Nijkamp, P. (2011). Smart Cities in Europe. *Journal of Urban Technology*, 65–82.

Cities of Opportunity. (2016). PwC. Retrieved from https://www.pwc.com/us/en/cities-of-opportunity/2016/cities-of-opportunity-7-report.pdf

Drucker, P. (2012). *The practice of management.* Routledge.

Eastern Europe: Quality of Life Index by City. (2021). NUMBEO. Retrieved from https://www.numbeo.com/quality-of-life/region_rankings.jsp?title=2021&region=151&displayColumn=0

Giffinger, R., & Pichler-Milanović, N. (2007). *Smart cities: Ranking of European medium-sized cities.* Centre of Regional Science, Vienna University of Technology.

Hollands, R. G. (2020). Will the real smart city please stand up?: Intelligent, progressive or entrepreneurial? In *The Routledge companion to smart cities* (pp. 179–199). Routledge.

Hutchinson, B. (2013 February 25). Direct speech: Bill Hutchison on smart cities and stupid Moscow A city where a doctor is called by video link, where there is no corruption, and cars drive without drivers, the chief expert in the field of smart cities told The Village about the high-tech future. *The Village.* Retrieved from https://www.the-village.ru/city/city/117185-hatchinson

Index of competitiveness of cities. (2020 September 16). Resuscitation Package of Reforms. Retrieved from https://rpr.org.ua/news/indeks-konkurentospromozhnosti-mist-ukrainy-2019-2020/

Kearney. (2020). *Global City Index 2020*. Kearney. https://www.kearney.com/global-cities/2020

Korepanov, O. S. (2018). Methodological principles of statistical support for managing the development of "smart" sustainable cities in Ukraine: a monograph. SE "Inform.-analyst. agency".

Kourtit, K., Nijkamp, P., & Arribas, D. (2012). Smart cities in perspective–a comparative European study by means of self-organizing maps. *Innovation (Abingdon)*, *25*(2), 229–246.

Lazaroiu, G. C., & Roscia, M. (2012). Definition methodology for the smart cities model. *Energy*, *47*(1), 326–332.

Lee, J. H., Phaal, R., & Lee, S. H. (2013). An integrated service-device-technology roadmap for smart city development. *Technological Forecasting and Social Change*, *80*(2), 286–306.

Lindskog, H. (2004). Smart communities initiatives. *Proceedings of the ISOneWorld Conference.* Retrieved from https://www.researchgate.net/profile/Helena_Lindskog/publication/228371789_Smart_communities_initiatives/links/549812230cf2519f5a1db56d.pdf

Meijer, A., & Bolívar, M. P. R. (2016). Governing the smart city: A review of the literature on smart urban governance. *Revue Internationale des Sciences Administratives*, *82*(2), 417–435.

Momot, T., & Muraev, Y. (2021). Model of organizational and information support of smart city strategy development in the conditions of digital economy. *Innovative Technologies and Scientific Solutions for Industries*, *1*(15), 83-90.

More than 250 Smart City Projects Exist in 178 Cities Worldwide. (2017 March 16). Guidehouse Insights. Retrieved from https://guidehouseinsights.com/news-and-views/more-than-250-smart-city-projects-exist-in-178-cities-worldwide#:~:text=Click%20to%20tweet%3A%20According%20to,%2C%20buildings%2C%20and%20water%20goals

Murayev, E.V. (2020). Development of a strategy for smart cities of Ukraine according to a balanced system of indicators in the digital economy. *Bulletin of Khmelnytsky National University*, *4*(2), 106-109.

Musa, S. (2016). *Smart City Roadmap.* https://www. academia. edu/21181336/Smart_City_Roadmap

Muzhanova, T. M. (2017). "Smart City" as an innovative management model. *Economics. Management. Business (Atlanta, Ga.)*, *2*(20), 116–122.

Nam, T., & Pardo, T. A. (2011, September). Smart city as urban innovation: Focusing on management, policy, and context. *Proceedings of the International Conference on Theory and Practice of Electronic Governance*, 5.

Savchuk, A. (2018). *Concept "Umnyi Gorod": Main provisions, Description, Device, Examples.* Retrieved from https://fb.ru/article/399297/kontseptsiya-umnyiy-gorod-osnovnyie-polojeniya-opisanie-ustroystvo-primeryi

Shapiro, J. M. (2006). Smart cities: Quality of life, productivity, and the growth effects of human capital. *The Review of Economics and Statistics*, *88*(2), 324–335.

Smart Cities. (2022). *EU Regional and Urban Development.* https://ec.europa.eu/info/es-regionu-ir-miestu-pletra/temos/miestai-ir-miestu-pletra/miestu-iniciatyvos/smart-cities_en#what-are-smart-cities

Smart City Index. (2020). https://www.imd.org/smart-city-observatory/smart-city-index/

Smart City Profiles. (n.d.). https://www.imd.org/smart-city-observatory/smart-city-profiles/

Winters, J. V. (2011). Why are smart cities growing? Who moves and who stays. *Journal of Regional Science*, *51*(2), 253–270.

Yigitcanlar, T., Buys, L., & Kamruzzaman, M. (2018, Nov. 28). Just how 'city smart' are local governments in Queensland? *The Conversation*.

KEY TERMS AND DEFINITIONS

Smart City: Is defined as a comprehensive and multifactorial urban ecosystem, including the attraction of human capital and the full-scale use of information and communication technologies through the integration of physical, digital and human subsystems in an artificially created environment to solve the current problems of the city, ensure its balanced development in the economic, social, environmental and institutional sphere to ensure the improvement of the safety, comfort, and quality of life of citizens in the future.

Smart City Balanced Scorecard (SCBS): Is an integrated model of strategic management, which allows systematically to identify and organize priority areas for the development of a smart city and specify strategic directions in each priority area, which at the same time can serve as an evaluation system according to the developed system of key indicators (KPIs).

Smart City Information and Organization Support Model: A complex, open, holistic, integrated into external processes model, which should be organically combined with the overall strategy of the city development and ensure the balance of long-term goals for sustainable development of the city. The proposed information and analytical model for assessing the level of sustainable development of smart cities are based on the assessment of the integrated indicator of a smart city.

Smart City Key Performance Indicators (KPIs): Is a system of key performance indicators (KPIs), which includes the following six areas of activity (perspectives): smart people, smart governance, information and communication technologies, technology and infrastructure, smart economy, and quality of life and comfort in the city.

Smart City Strategy: Is considered as a component of the overall local development strategy, which is based on the formation of the city's open data portal for the creation of a transparent system of management decision-making on the principles of openness by default, efficiency and clarity, accessibility and use, comparability and interoperability, the development of e-governance and the involvement of citizens to make managerial decisions.

Section 7

Latin America:
Territory and Natural Resource Abundance

Chapter 16
Analyzing the Spatial Configuration of Agriculture:
The Colombian Case

Helmuth Yesid Arias-Gomez

ⓘ https://orcid.org/0000-0003-0107-8611

Masaryk Institute of Advanced Studies (MIAS), Czech Technical University in Prague, Czech Republic

Juan Pablo Cely

Pedagogical and Technological University of Colombia, Colombia

ABSTRACT

The authors deploy a descriptive approach for recognizing recent trends in the Colombian agricultural output. They combine the production analysis and the spatial perspective, streamlining the data and the spatial positioning. Using the agricultural Census 2014, they identified the territorial trends in flourishing commodities pushed by forceful changes in the international demand, and by the pressing tightening in the international food markets. In contrast, the Colombian competing imported products were demoted by the foreign imported production. The Colombian agriculture has been influenced by subsequent frameworks of economic policy, spanning from the protectionist stage through the liberalization era, until the current predominance of bilateral trade agreements. The spatial analysis bears out a random distribution of agricultural output across the territory, demonstrating the diversity of production and a scattered spatial pattern. In spite of the disparate production diversity, the agricultural export supply shows scarce diversification.

INTRODUCTION

The food industry and agricultural production have undergone a stubborn global transformation in terms of technologies, products and organizational schemes. In microeconomic terms, the predominance of commercial agriculture exacerbated greed and profit eagerness. The irruption of big capital players into the sector disrupted the production system and the conventional model of agriculture. The global new

DOI: 10.4018/978-1-6684-5976-8.ch016

trend in the agricultural production responds to price signals moving around capitals in an international scenario. Perhaps, the differences between countries rely on the idiosyncratic production vocation and the comparative advantages. However, the agricultural exploitation model tends to follow similar trends, striving for maximizing the profits through the exploitation of intensive agriculture (Renting et al., 2003).

Figure 1. Colombia: Commodity Export Price Index, Individual Commodities Weighted by Ratio of Exports to GDP
Source: IMF

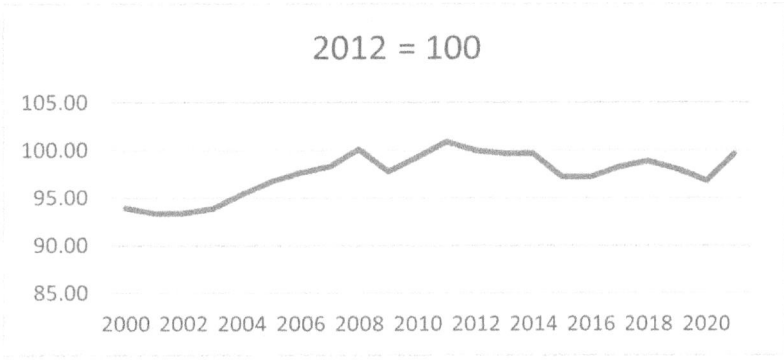

As a component of the producers' income, the prices indicate the fortunes of farmers. The National Planning Department (2015) states the evolution of relative agricultural prices using the ratio between the sectorial and overall deflectors. The trend in relative prices suffered two important drops: during the 1991-1996 and the 2011-2013 periods.

The upward agricultural cycle that producers are facing nowadays, is closely related to a global trend for pressures in the prices of the basic commodities and energy. High market prices make up a stimulus for the production of staple food, and contribute to mobilizing resources in the sector towards perennial crops. However, the cost structure in agriculture is likewise out rightly affected by the cost of energy, and the inputs that normally follow the same trend in international markets. Agriculture heavily demands energy directly (petroleum, gasoline), but also indirectly in the form of fertilizers, pesticides and lubricants. Therefore, the net effects on the sector can end up in a profit squeeze. Going further, the agro-industry also requires sizable quantities of fuels, mainly for the crushing of oilseeds and the milling of grains (FAO 2021).

Commodities markets have undergone disruptive transformations alongside the emergence of sizable players as China and India, and the recent conflict in Ukraine. The challenges for global producers of staple food and commodities pave the way for expansion and growth. However, the pervasive schemes of subsidies in Europe and the USA, threaten to extend further the harmful distorting effects on international commodities markets in the light of soaring prices. In the Latin American context, some neighbors such as Brazil, Peru and Chile harnessed the expansion in international markets, whereas Mexico leveraged the expansion of its internal market. The Latin American partners have recently upgraded their participation in some international niche markets, ending up as important players in global exports: Brazil as an exporter of orange juice (1st place) and soya (2nd place), Peru as an exporter of mango (5th place) and asparagus (1st place) and Chile as an exporter of grapes (1st place) and apples (5th place). (Reina et al. 2011)

Agriculture has played a crucial role in the Colombian economic development in terms of employment and output, mainly in terms of pushing forward international insertion and specialization and subsequently through disparate flagship commodities, namely quina (Cinchona officinalis), tobacco, coffee, flowers and a handful of other products nowadays. During the end of 19th and the early 20th centuries coffee was the flagship export commodity, strengthening the international reserve position and enabling the international reserves to underpin the investment in other economic sectors, mainly the manufacturing activity. The current boom in the international markets intensified the specialization of Colombian agriculture. However, exceptional to some new undertakings, the overall Colombian export supply is rather scarce and undiversified. This trend led to a reduction in the sectorial balance of trade due to an unusual growth of imports, growing on average by 13% per year during the period 1991-2014, whereas the exports reported an average growth by 4.4%. (National Planning Department 2015)

Recent transformations led by market forces demonstrated an important transformation in the Colombian agricultural landscape, with a flourishing expansion of perennial products induced by the price incentives of international markets. The case of palm oil, for instance, furnishes sizable profits derived from the favorable international conditions, alongside domestic tax incentives (UN-DP 2011).

Not only the Colombian agricultural sector has been shaken by the events in international markets and food sector trends, but the agricultural producers are confronting a changing panorama. The world demographic trends, the forecasts anticipating a strong demand and the convulsive scenario conveyed by the invasion of Ukraine, boosted international staple food prices, in particular wheat and sunflower seed.

The increasing world demand favored the response of gifted agriculture countries, which enhanced the crop areas and enlarged their output. In such context, the tropical countries can harness the geographical position, the luminosity condition and the idiosyncratic climate for enhancing their share in a market that looms promising at least, if the demographic trends are confirmed. In spite of the pressing problems the global economy is facing, such as the inflation rebound and the economic downturn, staple food markets demonstrate a specific tightening pushing the prices up (FAO 2021). This movement has offered to Colombian agriculture the incentive to relaunch exports of specific commodities experiencing boost in demand, but with a limited scope in terms of commodity diversification. Accordingly, in spite of the enormous productive potential, effective international insertion is rather scarce (Perfetti 2011, Ocampo 2017). In other words, Ocampo (2011) described the result of the Colombian agriculture as a scarce expansion of exports (with the role of oil palm exceling) alongside a broad diversification of imports (mainly wheat, maize and soy).

BACKGROUND

The Colombia agricultural sector has undergone a radical transformation since the implementation of free-market liberalization during the 90s until the present time, re-addressing the Colombian vocation towards more perennial and more internationally competitive commodities, edging out the traditionally highly protected and barely efficient crops as cotton, barley and wheat. In fact, the imported competing commodities showed the most acute drop, whereas the non-tradeable goods expanded, as in case of potatoes (see table 1). Perennial crops such as sugar cane and oil palm (Jaramillo 2001) demonstrated a positive behavior.

In this appraisal of a sort of 'creative destruction', the global incentives transmitted by the markets, have triggered the blossoming of prosperous activities based on extensive exploitations with the crucial role of sizable companies, heavily mechanized and mobilizing enormous amounts of capital under the agribusiness model (palm oil, sugar, banana, etc.). On the other hand, the traditional flagship Colombian commodity, coffee, has been shaken by cyclical movements in the international prices, experiencing important declining trends during the 90s and enjoying a real boom nowadays.

Now, regarding the trade policy, a set of stringent free-market measures was applied during the sectoral liberalization. Between 1990 and 1991 non-tariff barriers were dismantled. and the average tariff was planned to drop from 38.6% to 11% over a 4-year period. However, a remaining protectionist scheme of a price band based on variable tariffs was applied to cope with the volatility in international prices, specifically in 9 commodities: wheat, barley, rice, maize, sorghum, soybeans, oil palm, milk, and sugar (Jaramillo 1997).

Once the Colombian free market reforms were implemented during the 90s, the general outcome for the sector was a noticeable transversal downturn in the set of crops, but the recoil in the annual crops (cotton, wheat, barley, etc.) was more concentrated. The long-lasting protection, the absolute lack of competitiveness, the technological lag and the distortive schemes of protection in the advanced world, pushed the annual crops into a definitive decline.

Table 1. Colombia: Agricultural performance during the liberalization model. Value of Production growth (%) (Constant prices 1975)

Commodity	Growth 1990-1997	Commodity	Growth 1990-1997
Annual Crops -3.2%		Perennial Crops 1.9%	
Rice	-2.1	Coffee	-3.9
Potato	1.4	Sugarcane	4.0
Maize	-3.1	Plantain	1.4
Vegetables	0.8	Panela cane	2.2
Cotton	-15.1	Flowers	4.3
Sorghum	-12.3	Oil Palm	8.9
Soybeans	-13.5	Cassava	-2.1
Beans	0.5	Fruits	10.4
Wheat	-10.5	Banana	3.4
Barley	-23.8	Cocoa	-0.9
Sesame seeds, peanuts, light tobacco.	-5.1	Yams, jute, export plantains, coconut, dark tobacco.	1.9

Source Jaramillo (2001)

The scarce competitiveness alongside with the appreciation of Colombian currency and the drop in international agricultural prices during the 90's, all combined originated a critical drop in the production of some agricultural items (see table 1).

In the second half of 1992 a powerful set of palliative measures had to be implemented. The government announced purchases of cereals and oilseeds, changes in the price bands for maize and sorghum, export subsidies for banana, sugarcane and flowers and explicit refinancing programs for indebted farmers.

In another set of measures, the government applied minimum import prices to grains and oilseed, reduction in the tariffs for inputs, safeguarded against eventual increases in imports and focalized employment plans. For coping with the deleterious effects on cotton producers, a stabilization fund and direct subsidies to farmers were implemented (Jaramillo 2001).

In the aftermath of the liberalization process, Colombia demonstrated a relatively high competitiveness in the perennial crops, a trend reinforced by very recent behavior in new varieties exported: avocado and the strengthened role of cacao. This expansion came about alongside the notable performance of oil palm and banana. In this way, the perennial production became the predominant group in the Colombian agriculture. In fact, according to the 2014 Agricultural Census, 18.3 million out of the total 34 million of tons produced corresponded to perennial products. The fortune of annual varieties has been rather uncertain, due to more technical production implemented in developed countries such as the USA and scarce competitiveness of national production.

The recent trend in the Colombian trade policy emphasizing the bilateral agreements had clear effects on the Colombian external sector. Due to international conditions, traditional exports increased their pace of growth in value, but deepened the concentration in a scarce range of products. On the other hand, there was a soaring share of American imports in the domestic staple food sector, within the framework of the bilateral agreement signed in 2012 (see table 2).

Put in another way, Volpe and Gomez (2009) pointed out that the real positive Colombia – USA Trade agreement effects should be harnessed during the first stage of liberalization due to the sizable reduction of tariffs. The subsequent periods of marginal reduction of tariffs loom to be less meaningful for encouraging the Colombian exports. In other terms, the agreement has not been fully leveraged and the benefits for Colombia have remained unexplored so far.

Table 2. Top 10 U.S. Agricultural Exports to Colombia. (values in million USD)

Commodity	2017	2018	2019	2020	2021
Corn	785	927	682	879	1,100
Soybean meal	340	481	412	485	557
Pork and Pork Products	163	215	221	147	258
Soybean	212	256	223	192	229
Meat	173	88	137	133	193
Dairy products	65	72	144	124	145
Poultry Meat & Products	70	82	114	93	117
Feeds, Meals & Fodders	81	100	83	86	116
Ethanol (non-beverage)	56	76	116	120	89
Distillers Grains	33	46	42	46	65
All Others	606	642	608	558	544
Total Exported	2584	2985	2781	2863	3413

Source: U.S. Department of Agriculture

DISCUSSION

When tackling the spatial configuration of agriculture, the definition of two approaches is evident: the production perspective and the geographical point of view. Due to the diversity of climate conditions and the territorial extension, Colombia enjoys a disparate range of climatic conditions which allows crop and harvests cold, mild and hot climate commodities on a relatively reduced regional surface.

The combination of the coastal and mountain areas renders a motley overview of commodities, underpinning a production profile based fully on comparative advantages. In fact, the sequence of export commodities throughout the history responds to idiosyncratic determinants. The geographic conditions promote additional competition when facing the international market. The location in the equatorial zone provides continuous territory's sun exposure, and diversity in the landscape which spans the highest lands in the cordillera and coastal lowlands and natural forest in the Easter fringe (Perfetti 2011).

In comparison with Western Europe and Japan, Colombia enjoys a relative abundance of land, even more when the production potential in the southern and eastern territories is taken into account.

Figure 2 is conducive to the conclusion that geography blatantly intervenes in determining the Colombian production vocation and the comparative advantage. The country is crossed by one disruptive cordillera that keeps its continuity in the neighboring countries of Ecuador and Venezuela. Going across the cordillera in the south-north direction, it in turn diverts its structure into three Colombian systems: the western, central and eastern cordillera; furthermore, upon getting to the Colombian territory, the *Cordillera de los Andes* determines the atitude and the diversity of climates.

In particular, the valley made up between the central and eastern cordillera, clears the way for the course of Magdalena River, the main national body of water. Looking towards the west, there is another crucial basin: The Cauca River which runs in parallel and irrigates the fruitful sugarcane crops area of the department of Valle del Cauca and the coffee areas, spanning the departments of Risaralda, Valle del Cauca and Caldas (see Figure 2).

In turn, the northern lands make up the flat Caribbean coastal fringe. But the contiguous inner plain lands were suitable for cotton crops in the Departments of Córdoba and Cesar and for cattle activities.

Finally, the southern and western genuine forests emerge as the most powerful endowment in terms of biodiversity, presenting a huge challenge for the future in terms of transforming this area, nowadays fully made up by virgin forest, into a productive territory in a sustainable way. This virgin forest occupies a half of the Colombian territory spanning the departments of Putumayo, Caquetá, Amazonas, Guaviare, Vaupés, Guainía, and Vichada.

The demographic patterns out rightly altered the use of land and transformed the natural landscape. The agriculture was the flagship purpose when the inner colonization adventures were launched, having its antecedents throughout the 19th century. UN – PNUD (2011) includes a wide description of the evolution of agricultural deployment alongside the expansion of the production frontier. During the 19th century, tobacco crops proliferated across the lowlands and simultaneously, the primitive coffee production laid specifically toward the east in the territories of Norte de Santander. Afterwards, in the earlier 20th century the expansion of coffee activities reached the slope fringes of the western cordillera in the actual 'coffee axis', finding conducive conditions of altitude and land predisposition for positioning the coffee beans as a highly productive crop. Later on, coffee crops expanded towards the south in areas of the departments of Huila, Nariño, and even towards the northern mountain system in the Sierra Nevada de Santa Marta.

Figure 2. Colombia: Agricultural Output by Department. (Thousands of Tons)
Source: Own Elaboration with data DANE-Censo Agropecuario Nacional 2014 and Instituto Geográfico Agustín Codazzi.

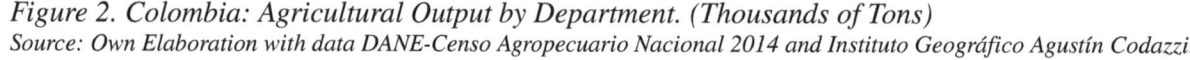

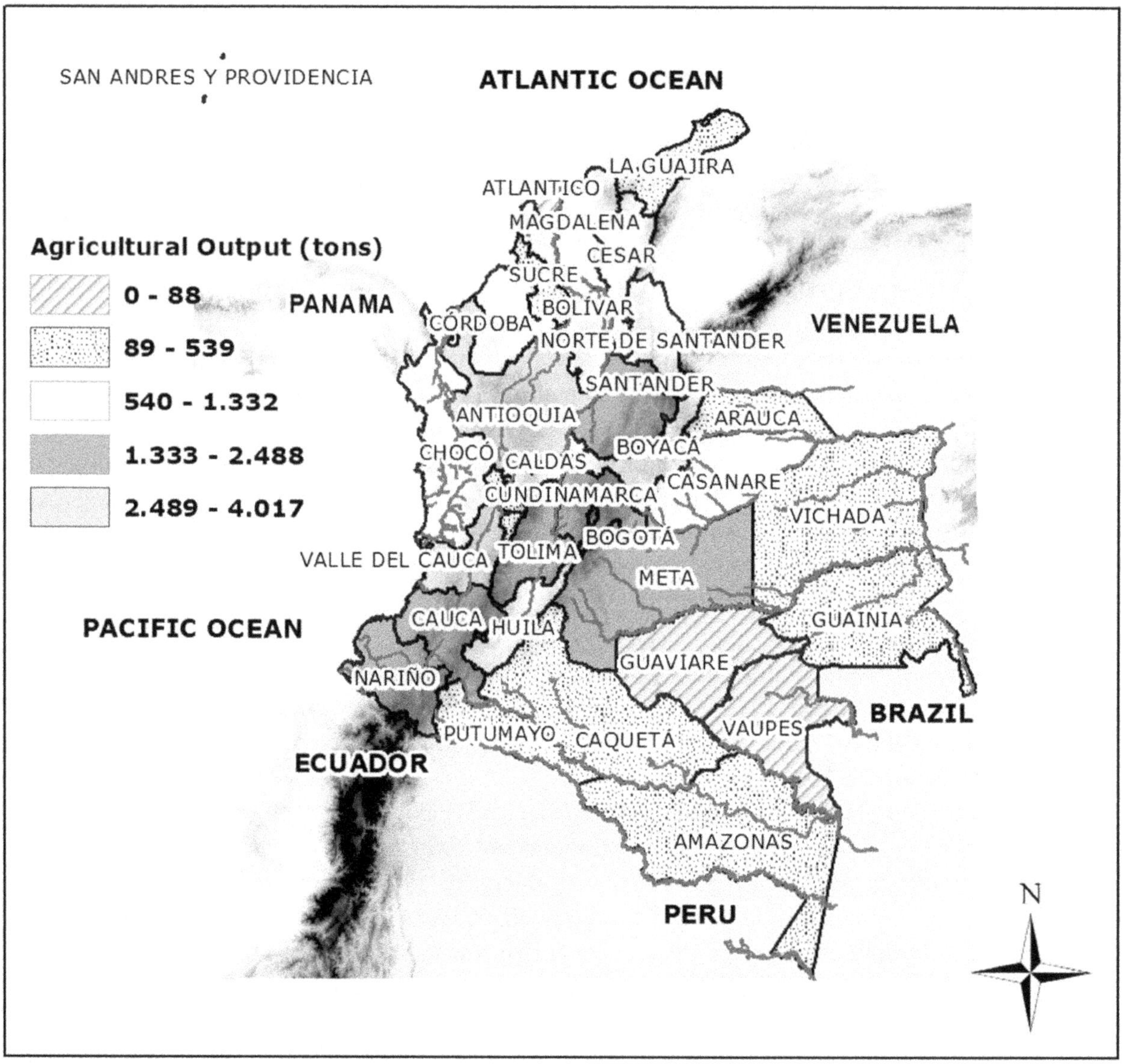

The production expansion of land potential in Colombia was made through grappling colonization processes, enhancing the production frontier towards the mild territories. This colonization process was introduced in the aftermath of the industrialization process that came about during the first half of the 20th century, and was developed by brave Colombian colonizers striving to expand the agricultural frontier in the direction to the west valleys, clearing the way for the inception of new agricultural areas to be replenished with coffee, banana and mild products. On the other hand, across the higher lands in the Cundinamarca and Boyacá Plateau, cold climate commodities are harvested, mainly potato and onion.

According to UN-PNUD (2011), the process of colonization has been prevalent since the Hispanic conquest and colony during the 16th and 17th centuries, but is even in effect nowadays. During the 20th century, forceful processes to enhance the agricultural frontier were implemented in the Orinoquía, the Amazonía, Antioquia and Chocó. The current replenishment of the existent territories forced the expansion of the productive territory beyond the productive edge; further exploitation continued legally, as well as in some cases illegally. Recent processes of colonization captured natural protected areas for production purposes, but also natural territories occupied lastingly by ethnical minorities.

The territorial tensions during the expansion of the agricultural frontier have been harnessed by huge multinational projects intended to invest heavily in immense-scale food projects, which can significantly alter the genuine natural conditions of Panamazonía and Orinoquía (UN PNUD 2011). This kind of developments took place in the departments of Meta and Vichada (from Puerto López towards Puerto Carreño), based extensively on the exploitation of soy, maize, rice, sugarcane, oil palm, and rubber.

In terms of biodiversity and environmental equilibrium, Colombia must preserve the natural forest spanning through the Amazonas River Basin, cutting across the departments of Putumayo, Caquetá, Guaviare, Vaupés and Amazonas. This natural reserve practically covers a half of the country in territories yet untouched by outsiders (see Figure 2). The intrusion of economic activities in such a virgin forest could disrupt the customs of ethnical communities located there.

In accordance with the Figure 1, the regional distribution of commodities is scattered according to the climate and geographic conditions. The production of tradeable goods such as coffee, cocoa, avocado, flowers and fruits takes place in the Andean regions, and spans as far as the Pacific region. Oil palm predominates in the Orinoquía and the Caribbean region. Banana crops lay in the Caribbean region and in the Urabá area in the department of Antioquia.

The natural conditions purported a successful process of production of oil palm in the described geographical zones, particularly demonstrating the highest productivity within the group of oleaginous crops. In fact, the productivity per hectare is 8 to 10 times higher over there. The association of producers pointed out that the oil palm crops span across 19 departments involving 107 municipalities. (UN-DP 2011). Regarding the imported competitors' commodities, maize crops span the overall national territory, and ice production predominates in the Orinoquía and the Andean region.

The non-tradeable goods category determines the specialization in some Colombian departments. Potato crops predominate in Cundinamarca, Boyacá and Nariño, whereas plantain and casaba are more ubiquitously situated across the national geography. From the 60s until the 90s in the department of Valle del Cauca, the production of soy, sorghum, maize and sesame was really relevant, although its decline coincided with the period of liberalization. Regarding rice, the privileged regions of Tolima and Huila concentrated its production during the 70s, and afterwards a meaningful expansion occurred in the department of Casanare. Another commodity badly affected by the liberalization process was cotton, that actually promoted the agricultural expansion in the areas of Cesar, Córdoba and Meta during the 70s. Turning the attention to the cordillera, Boyacá, Cundinamarca and Nariño replenished the highlands with potatoes, also applying crops rotation, alternating maize, beans and grass. In milder climates, leveraging the mountains slopes and in absence of coffee crops, the land demonstrated to be gifted for the production of sugar cane and panela.

Regarding the perennial crops, banana started in the banana zone in the Caribbean fringe during the early 20th century, but during the 60s it moved towards the Urabá region (the coastal fringe in the departments of Antioquia and Chocó) where the main production is concentrated. Oil palm moved around widely as well. The original crops started in Caquetá, the area of Tumaco, the department of Valle del

Cauca and Urabá region in Antioquia, but it is currently predominant alongside the Magdalena River and expanding its influence in flat lands of the department of Meta.

However, the Colombian land understood as a production factor, shows a regime of exploitation which proved inefficient in some cases, and on the other hand, due to land utilization, the factor has been misused for long, so the condition of the soil according to the production vocation does not correspond to the effective economic purpose. According to FEDESARROLLO (2019), based on the Agricultural Census, the land with optimal natural traits for agriculture stretches across 36.7 million of hectares, however only 7.1 million are used for agriculture purposes. This fact points out the misuse and the inefficient management of land that creates ubiquitous conflicts in the use of land.

The mismatch between the soil suitability and the effective exploitation has disparate explanations (FEDESARROLLO 2019). The predominance of the Andean demographic trend, across the valleys and slopes forced the agricultural exploitation nearby, and the crops over there harnessed the agglomerative conditions, namely: labor supply, basic connections developed and urban markets. In particular, crops as coffee, avocado and cocoa proliferate in favorable conditions laying on the slopes of mild mountains, without sizable environmental effects on soils. Coffee exploitation has conservational effects instead. This is a semi-permanent crop which normally minimizes the ploughing process and the use of herbicides, and fosters the ancillary process of planting fruits to create shade.

The comparative advantage represented by the tropical climate and the geographical position endows the country to produce a myriad of commodities, but their positioning in international markets depends on the degree of competitiveness and the unfair international system of subsidies to agricultural products, that encourage a distorted world production system. In Colombia, the broad supply of agricultural commodities is produced thanks to the diversified climate conditions, but the output is intended for three specific markets (FEDESARROLLO 2019). The FEDESARROLLO (2019) research derived several conclusions matching each commodity class and the specific requirements in terms of production factors. The interpretation corresponds to productive and territorial implications described as follows, and the table 3 points out the relevance of each group in terms of tons of output:

- Tradeable goods: intended for international markets or products demonstrating an important potential for being sold abroad, namely: coffee, oil palm, cocoa, avocado, banana, flowers, gulupa and uchuva. The production cycle is predominantly permanent, requiring frequent interventions of labor factor. Loosely speaking, banana and oil palm crops are grown more on extensive plantations and more endowed with capital and land. In addition, the requirement of facilities is also necessary to consider due to ulterior processes of transformation and packaging.
- Tradeable commodities such as flowers, gulupa and uchuva. The production regime predominantly takes place in small units amid family crops under relatively short periods of mellowing. The involvement of labor factor is fully determined by successful production conditions, with an outright effect of female labor, in particular in case of the flower crops.
- Competing imported goods: this includes items which confront the competition of imported products such as wheat, maize and soy. Other products can be produced domestically, but occasionally an imported commodity arises, namely rice.
- Non-tradeable commodities: the supply is intended for domestic consumption, namely potato, cassaba (Manihot esculenta) and plantain. They make up short-term crops with important intensity of labor and with high water requirements. In fact, the irrigation systems availability demon-

strated a positive effect on productivity. In this group of products, the modality of production is a blended regime of large extensions of land and small units.

Table 3. Colombia: Output by commodity and productivity 2013-2014 (in tons).

Commodity	Output (Ton)	Productivity (Ton/hectare)	Average World Productivity (Ton/hectare)
Tradable Commodities			
Coffee	660 284	1.0	0.8
Oil Palm	935 722	2.9	14.8
Cocoa	79 714	0.5	0.4
Avocado	344 374	5.7	9.5
Banana	1 183 398	35.6	21.1
Flowers	285 244	25.2	-
Gulupa	5 498	1.1	-
Uchuva	3 918	2.1	-
Import Competitors			
Maize	1 063 139	3.6	9.9
Rice	2 091 447	5.1	4.5
Soy	1 807	0.3	2.5
Wheat	10 913	2.7	3.3
Non-Tradable Commodities			
Plantain	4 368 410	5.7	6.9
Cassaba	4 591 511	10.9	11.4
Potato	2 383 894	15.9	20.1

Source: FEDESARROLLO (2019) with data from DANE - CNA, FAOSTAT

Triggered by the international context, the biofuel sector is pushing a change in the spatial dimension, but also involves a huge transformation in agricultural production, highlighting the role of profit incentives and introducing several challenges for the production of some varieties of staple food. Colombia compelled by the markets, is promoting several fields of biofuels production, spatially concentrated, responding to climate and geographical conditions. The eastern plains have been traditionally intended to produce rice, and to raise cattle in Meta and Casanare. But this flat fringe of territory has demonstrated to be conducive for the production of palm trees. Ethanol, a by-product of the sugar industry, is produced predominantly in the department of Valle del Cauca on the Pacific Coast, and biodiesel as a by-product of the exploitation of palms in the flat lands of the eastern plains. Other territorial undertakings lay in clear spatial placement: the east (Norte de Santander), the north and the west (UN UNDP 2011).

In such terms, several concerns are raised when considering food sufficiency. The eagerness for profits can divert the strictly considered food purpose toward the production of biofuels. Accordingly, maize, sugar and oilseeds are commonly regarded as feedstock in the production of the main biofuels: bioethanol and biodiesel. And when international energy prices soar sufficiently, the diversion towards biofuel by-products gets the producers enticed to prioritize the biofuel activity instead of staple food. (FAO 2021)

Ford (2012) discloses the threat for food security related to the diversion of food production to industrial purposes, because the close correlation between the fossil fuel prices and the oil by-products, which drives the agriculture production from feed to other purposes (namely lubricants, plastics and adhesives). Due to market incentives, the crops can be used as chemical feedstock and the diversion from feed purposes to ethanol or biodiesel, raises the threat that the future production may not be able to meet the human needs.

The government identified specific products during the implementation of strategies intended to enhance and diversify the Colombian export supply. The spatial connotation can be deduced promptly, bringing a broad availability of comparative advantages. The spatial deployment of potential products requires a broad range of conditions. These products include uchuva and exotic fruits from the Amazonía: Pineapple, coconut, sandia and papaya being suitable for lowlands. In milder climates, citrus, fruit of passion and guayaba can be produced. In cold climates: blackberry, strawberry, lulo and fruit tomato. When it comes to vegetables and tubercles, cassaba and ñame flourish in lowlands and potatoes in highlands (Perfetti 20).

SOLUTIONS AND RECOMMENDATIONS

The agricultural output is fully determined by climate and geographical conditions, and the spontaneous exploitation is closely related to the suitable sort of commodities resulting from the natural landscape and production tradition. However, the productivity of crops depends on the technology applied, the degree of mechanization and the production organization. In Colombia, the rugged territory and the disparate altitude across the regions lead to a widely variable agricultural output, providing the country with the potential for satisfying the domestic food needs. Despite the market conditions, the degree of competitiveness and the trade policy drove the Colombian agriculture to a scenario of successful international participation in a very scarce range of commodities, while the domestic market of staple food is dominated by more competitive imported stuff (US Department of Agriculture 2021).

The spatial analysis is intended to deploy and interpret the distribution of economic and social variables in space, using numerical values that in this case correspond to the agricultural output. The most remarkable municipalities exceling in the output are really scattered across the territory. Figure 3 indicates the geographical position of the main producers in terms of tons. The map imparts the idea of the extended diversity in terms of varieties, and the broad geographical dispersion of the main producers. Looking at the list of municipalities, the most outstanding producers are: Turbo (banana), Palmira (sugar cane), Apartadó (banana), Zona Bananera (banana), Carepa (banana), Tumaco and Cumaribo (oil palm), Bojacá (potato), Candelaria (sugar cane), Espinal (rice), Chogorodó (banana), Ipiales (potato), Cerrito (sugar cane), Puerto López (oil palm), Bugalagrande (plantain, casaba and banana), Tuluá (plantain), La Macarena and Cúcuta (oil palm), Inídira and El Charco (cassaba and plantain), Buga (sugar cane), inter alia.

The above list demonstrates that the external sector forced the production of valuable commodities, and contributed to enhancing the scope of local output, increasing the scales of production. The main banana exporters are located in the Antioquia´s Urabá and the department of Magdalena. The expansion of oil palm triggered the emergence of production belt spanning the municipalities of Puerto Gaitán, Puerto López and Cumaribo.

Figure 3. Colombia: Agricultural Output by Municipalities. (Thousands of Tons)
Source: DANE-Censo Agropecuario Nacional 2014 and Instituto Geográfico Agustín Codazzi.

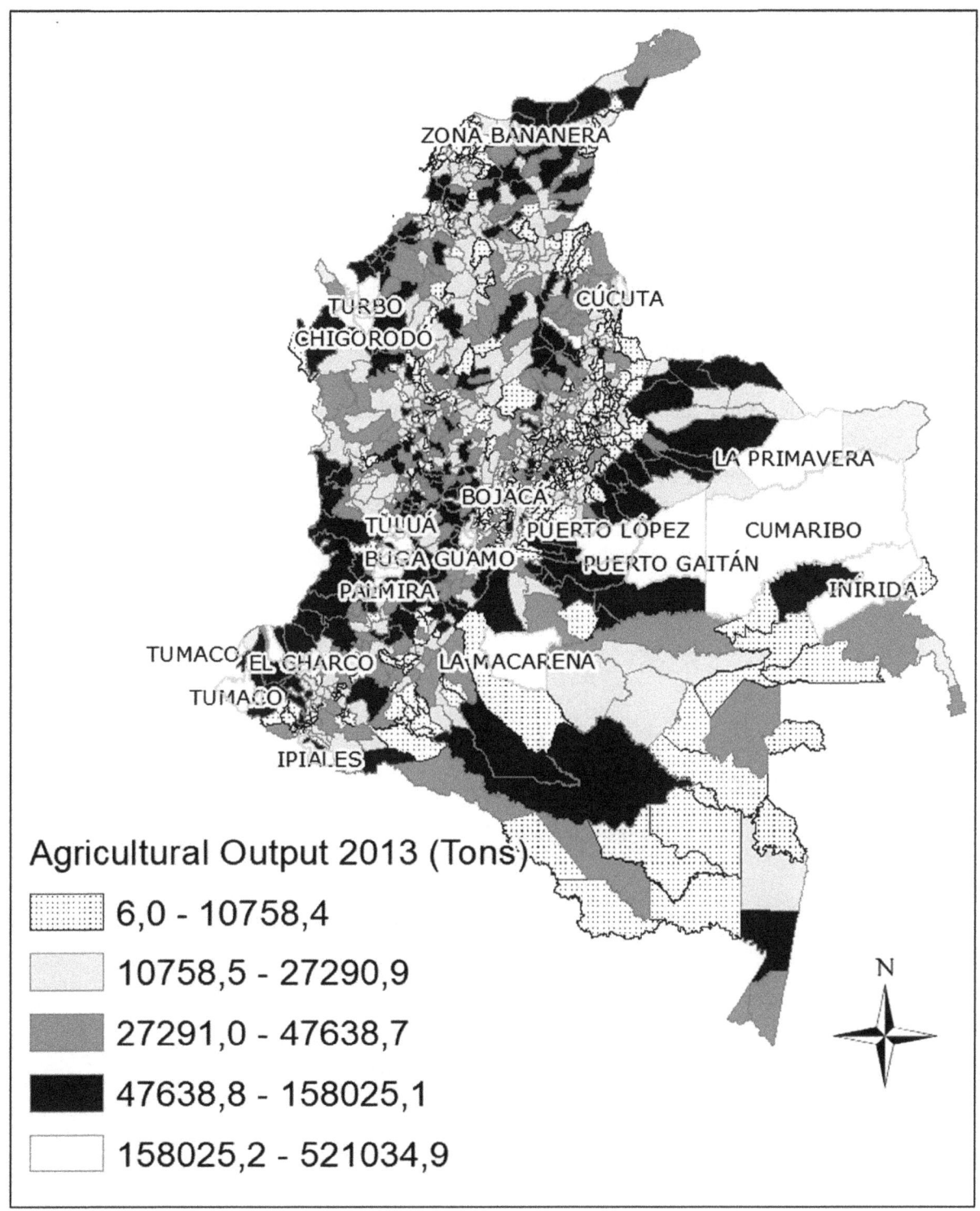

The once first export commodity, coffee, appears in a further position in terms of the municipal output size. The list of coffee producer towns spans across a diversity of regions, confirming the territorial expansion of the crop harnessing the mountains geography, suitability of soil and the willingness of farms for launch overtaking based on this being the historical flagship commodity. The diversity of outstanding local producers spans different departments and concrete municipalities such as: Pitalito, Andes, Ciudad Bolivar, El Tambo, Acevedo, Planadas, La Plata, Ataco, Piendamó, Salgar, Concordia, Garzón y Anserma, inter alia.

Emergent commodities have appeared recently, creeping up in the external sector statistics and positioning abroad, for instance: avocado. The shipments abroad have increased recently to exotic destinations, and sourced crops from across different municipalities, namely: Palmira, Fresno, Mariquita, Valledupar, San Pedro de Urabá, Falan, and El Carmen de Bolivar, inter alia.

The previous empirical observation conveys important assertions about localization determinants of production. A worthy contribution to develop an analysis of agricultural sector, is to inquire about the economic and spatial aspects related to the size of output at a local level. And one relevant conclusion points out the close association between the size of agricultural production and the external market and, in consequence, the territorial dispersion of exported crop commodities.

Next, the Moran´s Index measures the degree of spatial dependence figuring out the existence of any specific spatial pattern when analyzing the agricultural output. The information can indicate insights about the randomness or if there is a clustered distribution across the territory.

Figure 4. Report of the Moran's I Statistic.

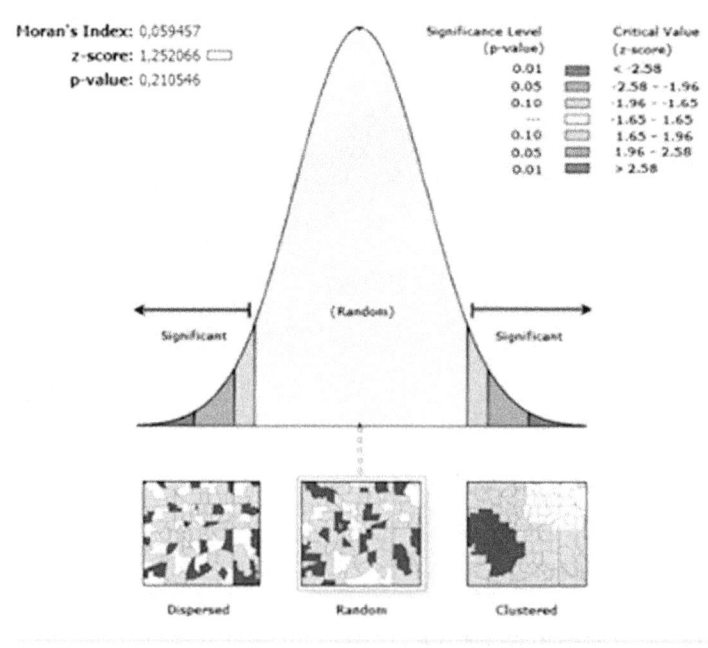

Given the z-score of 1.25, the pattern does not appear to be significantly different than random.

Table 4. Agricultural Output by Municipality 2014. Global Moran Index.

Moran´s Index	0.059457
Expected Index	-0.041667
Variance	0.006523
z-score	1.252066
p-value	0.210546

The Moran´s Index discloses the spatial autocorrelation in the values of the variable, giving insights about the spatial patterns in the agricultural output. The null hypothesis is posed in terms of absence of spatial dependence across different geographical units. In this case, the contrast is unable to reject the null hypothesis, addressing the conclusion that there is no spatial autocorrelation when analyzing the agricultural output in terms of tons.

The noticeable dispersion of the most remarkable producers reinforces the idea of a spatial distribution based on specific placements embedded in a neighborhood of municipalities with very different values of the interest variable. In some cases, the highest agricultural producers surrender to municipalities with low values of output. However, local clusters can be identified at the eastern fringe, focused on the production of oil palm.

Nevertheless, this consideration surpasses the 'Modifiable Areal Unit problem' in terms of irrelevance of the administrative boundaries when analyzing the spatial behavior of economic forces and the sectorial output. Normally, the relevant economic processes cannot be comprised of artificial administrative frontiers, emphasizing the mismatch between arbitrary spatial units and spontaneous economic forces (Arbia et al. 2008 and Espa et al. 2013)

In other cases, political division of data may have no economic significance because it doesn't reflect the economic interaction across agents. Some theorists have defined such situation in terms of an administrative split of territory with no economic relevance, as recognized by Krugman (1992) and Duranton and Overman (2005).

FUTURE RESEARCH DIRECTIONS

The sustainable exploitation of agriculture poses a huge challenge for the future, in the light of the soaring world demand and the potential territorial endowments granted to the Colombian territory.

The structure of land ownership in Colombian agriculture is strikingly dual, directly affecting productivity and efficiency. Firstly, the most productive commodities are handled under the principles of commercial agribusiness exploiting wide land extensions. In other sorts of commodities, a small-scale production and a tiny size of plots with scarce technological intensity confront harder conditions for accessing the credit markets. Coffee production deserves a special analysis because due to the production tradition, a myriad of small-scale producers is widely predominant. However, a very solid sectorial institutionalization ensures the absorption of production and supports small farmers with technical assistance and training.

The agricultural sector faces acute market failures. The technology is not being implemented adequately, and credit markets are very reluctant to lend funds without a solid collateral. This failure explains the lagging technological level, the lack of competitiveness and the strong drawback caused by crop destructions during the liberalization period. Observing the international context, the distorting scheme of subsidies in the developed world and the strongly capital endowed agriculture in the United States, make it harder for the Colombian products to be competitive. In such conditions, the domestic market has been affected by imports in basic staple food, in spite of the domestic production potential.

Colombia is confronting a definite dilemma when facing the necessity to incorporate sustainably the southern and eastern territories that amount to about a half of the national territory. Progressively, the market pressures will compel the country to engage in a process of expansion of production, incorporating new territories and making the existent production more productive. FAO (2017) recommends a strategy combining the intensification of production, the conservation of forest resources and the improvement of food security.

In spite of the Colombian-style strategic trade policy and the current reality in international commodity markets, the agricultural sector has hardly been successful in the process of diversification of the agricultural export bundle. The incorporation of new varieties into the export offer is the result of market signals coming from international markets, and the efforts of individual farmers, associations and transnational investors. The actual expansion of international markets clears the way for qualifying the export supply, creating opportunities for more added value products such as pulps and juices of fruits. However, the recent increasing role of bilateral trade agreements conveyed the effect of the expansion of imports alongside a scarce diversification of exports (Ocampo 2017). The criterion for a sustainable way to exploit natural resources is to avoid harvesting natural resources faster than they can be replenished (Ford 2012). The undue use of land makes up a risk for the sustainability as well. The tillage, the ploughing or cultivation to destroy weeds, slow down the natural cycle of soil formation. In addition, the irrigation water can deposit salt which is deleterious for the plants, and this salt content must be removed by drainage.

CONCLUSION

Loosely speaking, the agricultural production profile is a fully comparative advantage-molded activity. The emergence of specimens, tailored to the climate and particular geographical conditions, make up the bedrock for the development of a production structure.

The Colombian agricultural history has spanned a period of protection, later, a liberalization process during the 90s when the inefficient production ceased, and a recent rearrangement of exports towards perennials and fully comparative advantage-based crops. In turn, staple food and cotton have been produced on small and barely technical plots, reaching scarce scales of production and getting minimal levels of efficiency. This production is unable to cope with the competition of internationally subsidized production, and heavily technical production in advanced countries.

Global market conditions driving up staple food prices have twofold consequences on poor countries. The increasing prices are beneficial for the farmers (or in a better way, the global companies under the intensive new model of exploitation), but represent a looming danger for starving communities in poor countries (mainly in Africa). If this really regressive global trend goes on uncontrolled, it will lead to a deleterious economic stress on the poorest livelihoods (FAO 2021).

The post-liberalization stages defined a clear profile for the Colombian agriculture. The most remarkable products measured by the export dynamics were mainly perennial crops such as oil palm and banana. More recent successful growth has been seen particularly in avocado. Coffee maintained a high representation in agricultural exports. In other specimens, the case of uchuva and fruits have thrived. Non-tradeable goods relying on domestic demand remained dynamic as long as the home market grew steadily.

The forceful expansion of commercial agriculture under the modality of monocrop threatens the required diversification of agricultural supply and food safety. The successful experiences in the international market, reinforce the fully comparative advantage-based model for products tailored to the Colombian production conditions (oil palm, banana, flowers, etc.). On the other hand, the long-lasting agriculture with scarce capital endowments, is unable to compete with the powerful and fully technical first-world production. At another level, the production intended to meet the internal market, harnesses the domestic consumption pattern and the proximity to markets (potato, casaba).

The international scheme of protection of the agricultural sector in rich countries, distorts the global division of labor and stifles the potential production in developed countries. But furthermore, the overwhelming advanced US production predominates in the international market of staple food, and makes it harder for the Colombian production to compete.

The global transformation in food production models came about along the modifications in consumption patterns, mainly in developed countries in terms of the growing concerns regarding sustainability, health and animal welfare, clearing the way for potential niche markets characterized by contested quality aspects of food (Renting et al. 2003). Compliance with labor and environmental regulations determines the position of developed countries when amending trade agreements (for instance the U.S.A. trade agreement).

REFERENCES

Arbia, G., Espa, G., & Quah, D. (2008). A class of spatial econometric methods in the empirical analysis of clusters of firms in the space. *Empirical Economics*, *34*(1), 81–103. doi:10.100700181-007-0154-1

Arias-Gómez, H., & Antosová, G. (2018). Spatial Patterns of Agriculture in Boyacá. *Apuntes del Cenes*, *37*(66), 191–224.

Espa, G., Arbia, G., & Giuliani, D. (2013). Conditional versus unconditional industrial agglomeration: Disentangling spatial dependence and spatial heterogeneity in the analysis of ICT firms' distribution in Milan. *Journal of Geographical Systems, Springer.*, *15*(1), 31–50. doi:10.100710109-012-0163-2

FAO. (2017). *The future of food and agriculture – Trends and challenges*. Food and Agriculture Organization of the United Nations Rome.

FAO. (2021). *Food Outlook – Biannual Report on Global Food Markets. Food Outlook, November 2021*. Food and Agriculture Organization of the United Nations. doi:10.4060/cb7491en

FEDESARROLLO. (2019). *Uso Potencial y Efectivo de la Tierra Agrícola en Colombia: Resultados del Censo Nacional Agropecuario* [Potential And Effective Use Of Agricultural Land In Colombia: Results Of The National Agricultural Census]. Informe Final. FEDESARROLLO.

FEDESARROLLO. (2019). *Uso potencial y efectivo de la Tierra Agrícola en Colombia: Resultados del Censo Nacional Agropecuario* [Potential and effective use of agricultural land in Colombia: Results of the National Agricultural Census]. FEDESARROLLO.

FEDESARROLLO & Sociedad de Agricultores de Colombia (SAC). (2013). *Políticas para el desarrollo de la agricultura en Colombia* [Policies For The Development Of Agriculture In Colombia]. Author.

Ford, R. (2012). *Darwinian Agriculture: How Understanding Evolution Can Improve Agriculture.* Princeton University Press.

Jaramillo, C. F. (2001). Crisis, and Change: Colombian Agriculture in the 1990s. *Economic Development and Cultural Change, 49*(4), 821–846. doi:10.1086/452526 PMID:19069305

National Planning Department. (2015). *El campo colombiano: un camino hacia el bienestar y la paz. Misión para la transformación del campo* [The Colombian countryside: a path to well-being and peace. Mission for the transformation of the countryside]. Departamento Nacional de Planeación.

Ocampo, J. (2017). La política comercial agropecuaria colombiana en el contexto internacional [Colombian agricultural trade policy in the international context]. *Coyuntura Económica: Investigación Económica y Social, 47*(1-2), 49-95.

Ocampo, J., & Perry, S. (1995). *El giro de la política agropecuaria* [The Shift In Agricultural Policy]. Tercer Mundo Editores – Departamento Nacional de Planeación.

Perfetti, J. (2011). Colombia's Agricultural Potential Supply in a New Market Environment. In La política comercial del sector agrícola en Colombia (pp. 103 - 133). Cuadernos de Fedesarrollo 38.

Perfetti, J., & Cortés, S. (2013). La agricultura y el desarrollo de los territorios rurales. In *Políticas para el desarrollo de la agricultura en Colombia. FEDESARROLLO- Sociedad de Agricultores de Colombia* (pp. 1–64). SAC.

PNUD. (2011). *Colombia rural Razones para la esperanza* [Rural Colombia Reasons for hope]. Informe Nacional de Desarrollo Urbano.

Reina, M., Zuluaga, S., Bermúdez, W., & Oviedo, S. (2011). Protección e incentivos agrícolas en Colombia [Agricultural protection and incentives in Colombia]. In La Política Comercial del Sector Agrícola en Colombia. Cuadernos de Fedesarrollo 38. FEDESARROLLO.

Renting, H., Marsden, T., & Marsden, J. (2003). Understanding alternative food networks: Exploring the role of Short Food Supply Chains in Rural Development. *Environment & Planning, 35*(3), 393–411. doi:10.1068/a3510

US Congressional Research Service. (2021). *The United States-Mexico-Canada Agreement.* https://crsreports.congress.gov

US Department of Agriculture. (2021). *Colombia 2021 Export Highlights.* https://www.fas.usda.gov/colombia-2021-export-highlights

US Geological Survey. (2006). *Rates, Trends, Causes, and Consequences of Urban Land-Use Change in the United States.* Professional Paper 1726. Author.

Volpe, C., & Gómez, S.G. (2009). *Trade Policy and Export Diversification: What Should Colombia Expect from the FTA with the United States*. IDB working paper series 136.

KEY TERMS AND DEFINITIONS

Annual Crops: Specimens with a productive cycle shorter than one year. In this sort of products once finished the harvest process, one sowing process must be launched.

Concentrated Animal Feeding Operations (CAFO): The boosting international paradigm of animal production, based on the intensive exploitation of resources intended to maximize the benefits, concentrating the production in reduced extensions, and prompting the outcomes.

Department: The main regional administrative breakdown in the Colombian arrangement. It is run by a regional Governor (Gobernador), elected by popular election.

Departamento Administrativo Nacional de Estadística (DANE): The official Colombian statistical office. It is the responsible entity for producing the official statistical information and for conducting the Agricultural Census, and a more frequent annual agricultural survey (Encuesta Nacional Agropecuaria ENA).

Instituto Geográfico Agustín Codazzi (IGAC): The official Colombian geographical office. It produces the official cartographies and the basic layers as source for the spatial analysis.

Municipality: The main local administrative breakdown in the Colombian arrangement. It is run by a Major (alcalde), elected by popular election.

Perennial Crops: The agricultural varieties demanding a long run process of sowing, cropping, and harvesting spanning several years of maturity. They furnish one or several harvests by year, and once the harvest is made, it is not necessary a new sowing process.

Third National Agricultural Census 2014: Comprehensive statistical operation for gathering and processing the information about the agricultural information in Colombia. The process was conducted by the Colombian statistical office (DANE) with the participation of the Ministry of Agriculture and Rural Development. The basic unit of analysis is the Agricultural Production Unit (UPA).

Chapter 17
Economic Deglobalization, Regionalism, and Localism Processes Driven by Populism and Nationalism

José G. Vargas-Hernandez
Instituto Tecnológico Mario Molina, Mexico

Omar C. Vargas-González
https://orcid.org/0000-0002-6089-956X
Tecnológico Nacional de México, Ciudad Guzmán, Mexico

ABSTRACT

The aim of this chapter is to analyze the nationalism and populism as the driving forces of economic deglobalization processes and regionalism. The analysis departs from the assumption that the economic deglobalization processes responds to more complex dynamic forces created by the economic, financial, and the most recent health crisis that blocks the continuity of the economic globalization. Moreover, at the center of the analysis is the conceptualization that both globalization and deglobalization are two faces of the same coin, but with opposite driving forces. Nationalism and populism are the driving forces of deglobalization leading to find regional and more local solutions to economic growth and social and environmental problems.

INTRODUCTION

During the first half of the 20th century, Europe suffered a destruction induced by nationalism and militarism. Initially, globalization processes were reduced to European countries that had democratic political structures, but there was awareness of expanding the participation of other countries that were stable constitutional democracies. Since 1945, internationalism has been promoted with economic cooperation

DOI: 10.4018/978-1-6684-5976-8.ch017

systems supported by the Bretton Woods agreements and the emerging global governance institutions such as the General Agreement on Tariffs and Trade, as well as the Marshall Plan and the United Nations.

Western economic nationalism provokes tensions that lead to a trade war and that leaves the global space to the east to take the leadership of the processes of globalization that promote a new global concept. However, this connectivity becomes the medium of contagion. The impact has been reflected in the resurrection of the nationalist entrepreneurial spirit that promotes the return of companies. The growing phenomenon of nationalism is manifested in different versions with identity religions, including eurocentrism, Brexit, America First, etc., which tend to undermine multilateralism and paralyze the World Trade Organization. The health crisis reaffirms the doctrine of America First as the way for companies and thus jobs to return to the United States. Globalization is widely criticized for its negative effects and loss of valuation; it has fueled nationalist and populist movements.

The processes of globalization have had devastating effects from the 2008-09 financial crisis on the jobs of workers in various sectors of the industry. The answer has been commercialism, nationalism, and populism. Since 2010, nationalisms and populisms have resurfaced with force, trends in proximity trade are expanding, sustainability emerges as a concern for achieving an ecological balance between the exploitation of resources, productive activities, and the effects on socio-ecosystems. For some years now, nationalist, and populist governments have been promoting the reproduction of productive activities.

This paper first analyzes the implications of nationalism and populism on the economic deglobalization processes as the result of the most recent economic, financial and health crisis, leading to more regional and local alternatives to give continuity to the economic globalization. Finally, a discussion on the implications of these issues is offered.

BACKGROUND

Nationalism and Populism

The growing phenomenon of nationalism is manifested in different versions with identity religions, including eurocentrism, Brexit, America First, etc., which tend to undermine multilateralism and paralyze the World Trade Organization. The health crisis reaffirms the doctrine of America First as the way for companies and thus jobs to return to the United States.

Until now, the manifestations of the deglobalization processes are nationalist dynamics that, under the allegation of the principle of sovereignty, oppose international agreements and treaties through the construction of physical and tariff barriers to their national borders. Both populism, nationalism and commercialism can be threats. The old and emerging middle classes are those who consume the most with objectives that are different and that serve as an argument for populism, despite that egalitarianism as well as excessive inequality are obstacles.

Populism slows down the processes of globalization rather than correcting it, with a return to the areas of influence of the great economic powers. Nationalist deglobalization is regressive and not progressive that tends to continue interactions and interrelations with the international community of nations in a creative way to achieve a balanced relationship between the different local and international levels of the economy.

Not only do nationalist and populist governments oppose the deepening of globalization processes, but also other more open governments that demand that globalization be controlled without regulations. Popular discontent has turned into pressure from social movements with nationalist sentiments, the rise of ultra-nationalist and xenophobic parties.

The processes of globalization were considered as an unavoidable and irreversible phenomenon to form a community that required a reduction of nationalism to delegate powers inherent to sovereign power to give rise to the formation of international organizations capable of making mandatory, binding decisions and subject to a regime international rights and sanctions. The resurgence of nationalism is a form of reaction and rejection of the current processes of globalization, which demand the elimination of local communities, their history, local traditions and customs, and the resurgence of religious and cultural ties and values that traditionally unite groups. and communities.

The expanding economic globalization has brought also devastating negative effects on increasing levels of pollution in one part of the world that leads to extreme climate change and weather events and destruction of the eco systems and biodiversity. The negative effects of the processes of economic globalization have increased inequalities and economic and social inequality that are used as an argument to devalue globalization due to the emergence of new nationalist and populist movements.

The new globalizing institutions must face the challenges before nationalist and populist options roll back progress. If the processes of deglobalization intensify and are confined within the borders of the national states, and in the best of cases, regionally, they offer the opportunity to grow and develop with the implementation of their own model that require a revision internal competition system to accelerate internal growth.

Deglobalization

Economic and commercial history shows that intense periods of globalization are followed by periods of deglobalization based on the closing of the borders to international trade and the nationalist sentiment that is based on giving priority to the national before, to the foreign, both in economic matters, commercial, financial, tourist, etc. The global economy is in a process of deglobalization, manifested in the slowdown or reversal of the prevailing economic order since the second half of the 20th century, in such a way that communications, interactions and interdependencies have reached a level of exacerbation or rejection. The deglobalization process represents the end of the traditional forms of global economic and commercial relations.

The term deglobalization is a neologism coined to refer to the slowdown and reduction of the advance of the processes of economic globalization. The neologism deglobalization has been created to signify a step back that the processes of economic globalization are taking with their ebbs that reduce the commercial, financial, and migratory exchanges of people and labor. However, the networks that facilitate transnational financial operations remain intact while labor has always had interruptions in its flows for its global displacement.

The processes of economic globalization reached their peak to initiate a return to globalization processes with a specific location, also known as deglobalization. Walden Bello and Focus on the Global South, coined the term deglobalization with a positive connotation by setting the objective to restructure the world economic and political system to strengthen national and local economies (Bello, 2005). Deglobalization refers to the reverse process of globalization in which the economy, society, politics, and culture are regionalized. The beginning of a deglobalization phase is underpinned by a regionalization of the economies. Deglobalization is an impulse from the geopolitical situation of crisis management that intensifies economic policy and accelerates trade wars between the main powers.

Deglobalization processes involve the movement slowdown of goods, inputs, materials, premium services, as well as people, information, and ideas, as in the cases of tourism activities and higher education. Deglobalization processes present some characteristics that seem to be evident motivated more by political reasons than economic, social, or technological. Deglobalization processes are characterized by a slowdown and reduction of the functions of international and supranational institutions that oversee regulating economic, commercial, financial, political, and personal relations, ideas that are carried out between the nations. Financial deglobalization marks a recovery of the national sovereignty of the countries that had already given part of the globalization processes.

The phenomena of ralentization and economic deglobalization mark a period of reversal of globalization processes that have a high impact on economies that produce raw materials and inputs. Deglobalization is a process of weakening the economic, commercial, and financial interdependence between nations. The processes of economic deglobalization can be defined as a decrease in the economic, commercial, financial, people and ideas interdependence among all the countries of the world.

The KOF index developed by the Swiss Economic Institute in 1979 measures deglobalization with indicators of exports, investments, migration, geopolitics, and culture. The index has shown a constant increase in the processes of globalization, especially in the eighties with the connection of world stock markets, the dissolution of the USSR and the end of the Cold War, which motivated Fukuyama to declare the end of history in 1992. However, the globalization and deglobalization processes have been promoted and steered by the great economic and political powers to pursue their own local priorities and benefits. The reduction of the World Trade Organization (WTO) concerning the trade governance is one of the relevant points to bring downward pressure towards deglobalization.

The evidence suggest that globalization is giving way to a period of deglobalization in trade and foreign direct investment (FDI) began in 2007-2008, after more than two decades of integration and increasing flows in the global market, and since then the restrictions are increasing. Deglobalization is not a new phenomenon because it had already manifested itself since the economic-financial crisis of 2008 with the fall of Leman Brothers.

The evidence that suggests that a period of deglobalization has been entered is presented (Witt, 2016) by suggesting that trade globalization flows began to decline between 2007 and 2010, while the globalization of foreign direct investment flows began to decline between 2007 and 2011 (Witt, 2019). Some analyses on economic deglobalization trend are focusing on the evidence of free flows of trade, finances, and movements of people since the economic and financial crisis of 2008-2009. The trend towards the economic deglobalization of trade, financial, foreign investment and migration flows that reinforce the trend towards isolationism.

The trend of deglobalization processes that began with the financial economic crisis of 2008-09, continues with the arrival of Trump to the US government, which anticipates a change in the international economic integration processes that take shape and deepen with the coronavirus health crisis. Deglobalization as a phenomenon that was already observable before the health crisis and that is accelerating with it. The advance of a period of deglobalization intensifies with the health crisis of the pandemic having an impact and consequences in shocks to aggregate demand and supply.

In addition, this period of deglobalization is more pressured by the economic and financial crises that broke out in 2008-2009 and has deepened with the health crisis of the corona virus pandemic. The global health crisis has deepened the already existing economic, political, and social crisis that will not be able to be rescued by China like the previous financial crisis of 2008-2009.

Deglobalization is a phenomenon that has occurred several times throughout the history of the world economy, although it currently has different characteristics and since commercial and financial activities have slowed down since 2013. The term deglobalization was coined by Walden Bello in his book Deglobalization: Ideas for a New World Economy

The analysis of trends on the uncertainty of global economic development confirms an open regionalism marked by the North American Chinese tension and the traumatic Brexit and driven by deglobalization processes under the assumption that it is preferable to have close allies with more reliable and solid economies and with more stable regulatory frameworks. Some relevant deglobalization political movements are the start point Brexit referendum in 2016, the movement of Trump in the United States in 2016 and Bolsonaro in Brazil, in 2018, and other minor movements that provide evidence of confrontation between people and the globalization processes (James 2018; Inglehart and Norris, 2016). The de-globalization processes integrated to politics induces a shift in strategies, structures, and behaviors in international business (Witt, 2019).

The implications for the trade war between China and US on the WTO moves toward further deglobalization of trade. WTO demise is becoming increasingly dysfunctional a turning point for trade towards deglobalization, which brings some pressure for global growth. The United States has declared trade war on various partners and China in particular, while the UK has pulled out of the European Union after 47 years. Both events question the integration of the global economy and open the possibilities for processes of economic deglobalization. The major economies were open and integrated into the world economy. The peak of globalization processes was reached with the trade war between the United States and China to initiate a return through a process of national localization also known as deglobalization.

The strategic competition between the two great economic powers, US and China has become increasingly hostile relationship between the largest economies fostering the deglobalization tendency with further consequences in trade, finances, and technology, with implications of a trade war, as well as other additional deglobalization forces. In 2016, the United States and China launched a trade tariff war that, if it continues, could lead to the risk of a debilitating crisis of a chaotic deglobalization overreaction that can deepen the problems.

Before the emergence of the coronavirus health crisis, deglobalization was already a trend. The economic decline deepened by the health crisis is the beginning of a sustained deglobalization that slows the world economy and affects geo-economics and geopolitical changes. The uncertainty generated by the health crisis of the pandemic can lead to negative reactions to the behavior of human beings expressed in less liberal traits that can manifest themselves in the new deglobalization project (Bremmer, 2013).

The tendency towards nationalist retreat in the face of economic globalization processes has deepened with the health crisis of the pandemic and has accelerated the deglobalization processes with the consequent recovery of the regulatory functions of the State. Insourcing such as the return of factories to the country of origin and robotization are two of the trends that have been accompanying the deglobalization processes as a direct impact of the health crisis of the pandemic.

The public policies that emanate from national governments in response to the health crisis of the pandemic are very different, depending on the country in question, and they range from bailouts to large companies and banks, payment of salaries or a part of them, etc., which in many cases are dysfunctional and lead to more political and national tensions. These processes of deglobalization tend to concentrate wealth and create higher levels of poverty

This situation of deglobalization gives rise to a paradox because the risks are global, such as the increase in economic and social inequalities, demographic and migratory imbalances, climate changes, the emergence of technologies that are disruptive, while solutions are taken to local levels where social, political, and cultural activities take place. van Bergeijk (2010) analyses comprehensively the drivers and risks of deglobalization. Any excess in the deglobalization processes can generate more risks and damages than benefits to economies, especially the most advanced ones. If somebody overreacts to deglobalization processes, they can do more harm than good. However, deglobalization also poses economic risks for all countries, but more so for the more advanced ones.

The sharp drop in international credits (Financial Times, April 24, 2020) is explained as part of a long process of globalization. Credit, banking and financial deglobalization affects more the financing flows of emerging economies, which in the case of Latin America report a withdrawal of 4 percent of GDP according to Corsetti & Marin (2020) and Davis (2020).

The current global economic and financial crisis is the total sum of domestic crisis and does not offer local solutions which have to be looked for each nation, therefore the deglobalization tendency is to look for local solutions to a global crisis. Among the characteristics of the current one the globalization process indicates the increase in market volatility of financial products and currencies that increases the risk margins and uncertainty of exports and imports, the impoverishment of the middle classes due to the maintenance of competitiveness at the cost of salary reductions, and the limitations that emerging economies must sustain economic growth despite the free trade policies adopted.

The current processes of deglobalization weaken cross-border and inter-state commercial and financial relations that, if not properly reordered, will introduce new, more chaotic problems that can significantly reduce real global GDP, affecting all advanced and developing economies.

The decentralization of policies and the growing externalities result in a deglobalization of macroeconomic and financial configurations, unlike territorial approaches focused on the deglobalization of financial entities and at the universal level through a binding international treaty that stabilizes the international financial system and avoid regulatory arbitrage and deglobalization of finances.

The decrease has been shown to have secondary effects on employment, among others. Another of the dysfunctional effects of deglobalization processes is the decrease in remittances as unemployment increases. Deglobalization processes go beyond the economic and are in other areas such as higher education to be trapped in national borders.

Furthermore, it is difficult for the deglobalization processes to last due to the existing interconnections between the countries of the world and the now digital relationships created by economic, commercial, financial, scientific, technological, and educational exchanges, etc. Physical deglobalization is encouraged by digital globalization and adopts technology to accelerate the production of food, medicine, and other important commodities for regional consumption. Digital globalization encourages sectors such as business, tourism, and education. The digital economic transformation transforms spaces and times towards deglobalization.

Deglobalization processes have shown the deficiencies and risks that the economic globalization model has, such as the outsourcing of strategic production systems in a multilateral system in crisis. Defenders of globalization focus on minimizing the effects of disruption brought about by the period of deglobalization and aim to create the foundations for more sustainable processes with strategies that maintain the balance between efficiency, resilience, and greater aversion to risk.

The direct effects of deglobalization processes are manifested in a greater increase in production and distribution costs, which affect the efficiency of companies and require a strategic change. All the changes that come with the deglobalization processes are certain to occur, but what cannot be determined is how deep and in what dimensions they will be. While some analysts believe that deglobalization will increase the well-being of the population, others consider that it will reduce well-being.

Theoretical Approach

The processes of economic deglobalization for the 21st century require a conceptual theoretical framework that facilitates the analysis of variables such as cooperation and integration and dimensions of development strategies through which the international community carries out negotiations to redesign a way of globalization more closely related between the socio-ecosystem and humanity.

With the processes of deglobalization, history comes into contradiction with the centripetal integrating forces. Deglobalization processes are an inverse phenomenon to globalization, it is a return to the era of nationalisms due to the failure to develop the international community based on values, ideas and a culture that are shared by local communities. The global interaction and interdependence of the economy, society and politics become forces with a more regional or local centrifugal orientation, a return to the territory of national states. Deglobalization re-embeds the economy and the market in society and not a society that continues to be governed by the market economy.

Deglobalization is a backlash against globalism supported by mixed with nationalism and market segmentation, which has been considered a transition towards globalization 2.0 as the new kind. Globalization 2.0 promotes economic integration through infrastructure of large regions instead of the populist deglobalization driven by different nationalistic issues moving towards the nation states. Deglobalization processes are a transition between economic globalization and post-globalization whose only alternative is to decrease, slow down and retract. Findlay and O'Rourke in Power and Plenty. Trade, War, and the World Economy, argues that the world system has expansive stages of economic globalization processes followed by stages of deglobalization that are determined by geopolitics rather than geo-economics.

The nation state is receiving demands from citizens to take back control responding to the failures of the economic and financial globalization to fulfill the promises. Populist governments, from the right and from the left, have taken advantage of this discontent and providing a compelling rallying cry and to heat the deglobalization pressure. Deglobalization represents a new paradigm that presents the extreme right in a nationalist version of deglobalization that excludes immigrants and racial minorities.

Deglobalization is backed by backlashes against globalization that threaten the international order constructed in the second half of the twentieth century. The deglobalization movements around the world can be framed in the complex system theory which signals all the interdependencies among the local economies when there is a need to reduce these complex interrelationships.

Economic ideas and theories about globalizing and deglobalizing dynamics enter contradictions and conflict, as in the case of free trade, if the results achieved in economic growth are considered, while there are economies that have grown their GDP per capita, there are others that they have not grown. According to Witt (2019) the deglobalization theories from political science are liberalism and realism both of which lead to different expectations. While liberalism visions economic visions, realism sees economic blocs.

The principle of deglobalization processes based on a logic of a construct of rigorous empirical data on the limitations of globalization processes based on multinational companies operating in a global economy and market. Decisions on the location of operations must consider the patterns of survival or investment in deglobalization processes, such as political and military patterns. Direct investment has slowed down with a direct consequence of accelerating deglobalization. The economic decisions submitted to the political deliberation of the national states advance towards processes of economic and financial deglobalization.

The dynamics of the deglobalizing processes affect each of the nations in different ways as the trend is accentuated because they have very different internal challenges and commitments in relation to the exercise of global governance. The trend of economic deglobalization moves towards the regionalization or location of production, distribution, and consumption, with an emphasis on local companies and markets. Deglobalization processes are not uniform or global in the same way that globalization was because it was not fully accepted by non-governments of countries with autocratic political systems that have no affinity with the promoted values. The zero-polar world, predicted by Bremmer (2013), is the characteristic world order of deglobalization processes in which there would be no national or international power to face the challenges of world leadership.

Populist governments have had difficulty inserting themselves into globalization processes with very limited progress, which is why they are now promoting deglobalization. Many of these governments only participated nominally according to their historical-political contexts.

Deglobalization processes are the result of the globalization crisis due to cultural modifications introduced to secular values, such as, for example, intolerance expressed in norms towards certain intellectual expressions and manifestations. The excess of globalization has led to an opening of cultural values treated in normative terms such as gender.

Regionalism

Regionalization focuses on regions and are less interconnected than globalization. From the business corporation's perspective, it means to develop goods and services considering the habits of people living in these regions.

In the 1970s some national economies opened by adopting the development of free trade policies and world exports increased between the different regions of the world. The economic and ðnancial crisis of 2008 and 2009 brought negative effects to regions of developed economies contributing to some drawback in the globalization processes and connected to economic recession. The period of decline in international commercial, financial and people flows began in the years prior to 2020 after the health crisis, mainly due to the risks posed by dependence on the provision of supplies from international geographic locations. What the health crisis has done is to deepen this trend towards regional and local production.

The current situation of the global economy is only comparable in magnitude of the impact of the crisis of the thirties of the last century and there is no region that escapes this economic shock that threatens all national economies. This situation requires the generation of support mechanisms to mitigate the impact of the crisis.

Globalization can be seen as the result of regional collective action and transnational co-operations between economic regions (Balme 1996) that leads to interstate international relations system in the context of regionalism (Ibarra and Letamendia 1999). The development of economic regionalism as part of the process of economic de-globalization is based on the promotion of regional and local alliances to enhance technological and organizational capacities for the production, distribution, and consumption of satisfiers with high levels of regional content and with an orientation responsible for information management and the new challenges of sustainable development.

Globalization has benefited some countries or regions more economically than others, while it has promoted constitutional democracy and the recognition of rights and freedoms, as well as an increase in the level of education. The globalization of economic agents allows international reach and extraterritorial coverage in a process that encompasses all areas of economic competition that includes all countries and does not exclude any region (Berumen 2002: 350).

The globalization processes in the digital age are transformed and are moving towards a stage of more regional fragmentation under a new multilateral international trade model. This new multilateralism requires a profound revision or the creation of new existing institutions and regulations to build a new world order with greater capacities to regulate the new balances of power. World global cities globalization of economies play a relevant role in advanced producer and financial services increasing international interconnectedness of the corporate governance structures at the regional, national and international levels (Friedmann 1986: 70, 73 ff.; Sassen 1991: 127 ff.; Beaverstock, Smith and Taylor 2000: 125 ff.; Derudder, Taylor and Witlox et al. 2003: 876 ff.; Taylor 2004: 175 ff.; Robinson 2005: 757 ff.; Hanssens, Derudder and Taylor et al. 2010: 2 ff.; Lüthi, Thierstein and Goebel 2010: 115 ff.; Sassen 1991: 65 ff.).

Economic globalization is driving economic growth with disproportioned benefits to individuals, regions, and nations, bringing some negative non homogenous consequences such as income inequalities. Despite the multiple benefits, the ongoing economic globalization processes has brought complicated financial crisis, growth of unemployment, social unrests, and environmental sustainability problems. Still, the global economy is going into a large-scale continues transformation processes towards different type of globalization from which all the stakeholders participating may benefit.

However, the economic globalization has not fulfilled the expectations promised for all, so that, except for some, it has not delivered the expected benefits. It has been accompanied by risks, especially when the prevailing logic is to obtain the maximum benefit in economic rationality to produce in some regions of the world where cheap resources abound and then commercialize in other regions of the globe, without any sanitary controls. These effects have not been as expected and have motivated a transition towards more regional and local economic processes.

However, researchers sustain that globalization had surfaced some atypical tendencies in this wave (Karunaratne, 2012; Miskiewicz, Ausloos, 2010, Swiss Economic Institute, 2014, and Zehra2011). The world economy is immersed in a process of regression of flows of goods and services, investments and people that have the tendency to regionalize after a hectic period of growth of global interdependence and interaction.

Economic globalization has increased the transnational economic integration through changes on the mobility of economic factors that have had a high impact on regional development and territorial consequences in investment and development of regional industries and firms. These changes affect the international competition and transform the socioeconomic conditions and the political processes. This situation is giving space to regional-local public policies to design a new economic, social, political, and environmental scenario structured multilevel and polycentric form of governance to influence development without challenging the power of nation states (Hooghe 1996; Keating and Jones 1985; Le Galès and Lequesne 1998).

Intra-regional trade relative to global trade in goods has increased in the last 7 years, reflecting the increase in consumption in emerging markets. This trend is reflected in the production activities that are in neighboring countries inserted in the international flows of production, distribution, trade and consumption of goods and services.

The new global economic shift towards valorization of more local production and supply channels instead of the cost structure, centered on more personal service and sustainable values and principle, based on new disruptive technologies with regional value and new patterns of consumer behavior. The new phases of the globalization processes must converge in those constitutive elements that articulate all the economic, social, environmental, political, cultural elements at all levels: World, regional, national, local, community and individual.

Global international, regional and national financial centers are always in closed interrelated and in interconnected relationships with one another (Parr and Budd 2000: 605 ff.; Taylor 2004: 110 ff.; Harrschar-Ehrnborg 2002; Poon, Eldredge and Yeung 2004; Merki 2005; Cassis 2006). Clustering of financial services in financial centers in urban systems requires knowledge-intensive activities and economies of scale and scope at the global, international, regional, or national levels of business operations (Porteous 1999: 3 ff.; Lo and Schamp 2001: 27; Schmidt/Grote 2005: 1 ff.; Schamp 2009: 89 ff.; Parr/Budd 2000: 605 ff.; Taylor 2004: 110 ff.; Harrschar-Ehrnborg 2002; Poon, Eldredge and Yeung 2004; Merki 2005; Cassis 2006).

The processes of reconfiguration of globalization require new alternatives, initiatives and structures for world and regional integration that promote harmonious development in multiple dimensions, in such a way that national states maintain their sovereign decisions in the face of globalization without ceasing to be functional to the world system. The alternative has been the creation of regional and bilateral free trade agreements.

Economic globalization processes are required to reach global consensus to be redesigned involving the connections between the economic systems and market impacted by socioeconomic and cultural issues, regional and local specificities, collaborative networks. A more rational globalization process must be based on the formation and integration of an international community capable of sharing values, ideas, traditions, customs, etc., that is, the creation of a more global culture while respecting the differences and diversity of regional and local cultures.

DISCUSSION

The great western economic powers have played a preponderant role in the deglobalization processes to configure a new global order. However, the winners of the current globalization processes have been the countries known as the BRICS with China at the forefront, who may become the losers of the deglobalization processes or in the reversal of the globalization process. The deglobalization process represents the end of the traditional forms of global economic and commercial relations. Deglobalization represents a limited period in the integration of international economic relations and globalization. International cooperation aimed at maintaining prosperity and global peace is weakened by the effects of deglobalization with the reduction of the activities of the international commercial and financial systems.

The most recent stage of the processes of economic globalization is different from the previous stages due to the speed and scale of exchanges and interactions that entail other processes with negative effects with the spread of enormous risks such as the rapidity of the overwhelming contagion of the coronavirus pandemic that can accelerate the deglobalization processes of the world economy. The deglobalization process limits the circulation of goods, services, finances, and people that during intense globalization only had sanitary limitations.

The processes of economic globalization have been inclined towards globalization rather than deglobalization of the economy. Globalization was intended to replace the nation states in a perverse and coercive manner and what it has achieved is a response from the populist and nationalist movements that have prevented it from deepening and that have supported the processes of deglobalization. The processes of deglobalization that are so contradictory are manifestations of new configurations of a new phase of the processes of globalization with expressions that are more exclusive, brutal, and pathologically dangerous for the harmonious economic growth, inclusion, and social justice, as well as the environmental sustainability of all countries.

The deglobalization of economic processes means decrease or withdrawal, it is a transition period towards a post-global period with a strong energy component. Deglobalization processes imply a decrease in commercial and financial exchange activities, movements of people and ideas with well-determined impacts on socio-ecosystems that can degrade nature. On the contrary, deglobalization processes should contribute to improving the conditions of economic growth, social development with inclusion and social justice, and environmental sustainability, which benefit individuals and communities more than multinational and transnational organizations.

SOLUTIONS AND RECOMENDATIONS

Proponents of globalization need to be more pragmatic in managing gradual and orderly processes of partial de-globalization so that they can lay the foundations for relaunching more sustainable and inclusive globalization processes. Deglobalization processes require the redesign of a more economic, social, and environmentally sustainable development based on more rebalanced investments and re-invigorated technology, science, and innovation. The new development model that results from the deglobalization processes must adjust to the promotion of economic decisions from the spaces of the national state to factories and businesses, which are promoting equality, inclusiveness and social justice and fostering interrelationships between the economy, society, and environmental socio-ecosystems.

Finding a balance between the processes of globalization and deglobalization that allows growth and evolution, reducing the gaps of economic, social, political, cultural inequality and the recovery of local identities. Economic globalization has been identified as a generator of economic and social inequalities, which have motivated anti-globalization movements that propose the beginning of a period of economic deglobalization within the framework of the 2030 agenda to point out a period of regression in international economic interrelations. between States, and the influence exercised by multinational companies to focus on national sovereignty with the detriment of the international standards imposed by international organizations and treaties for economic cooperation and integration.

In the case of Mexico, the entry into force of the T-MEC coupled with the trend of deglobalization accelerates the processes that can encourage and benefit the development of Mexican companies. Mexico can take advantage of deglobalization trends as a partner of the T_MEC commercially integrated with the United States and Canada. The coronavirus health crisis demonstrates the relevance of proximity to the North American market to have more certainty in ensuring the provision of supplies for production.

CONCLUSION

The non-existence of a project and a model of deglobalization processes based on geopolitics that is based on institutions that are not entirely democratic, limits the scope to achieve economic growth, social development, and environmental sustainability of the nation states. In the phase change of globalization processes to deglobalization processes, the national state recovers its functions in the face of the existence of a cosmopolitan international institutional community that was going to solve the problems. The reality has reached the international organizations formed by the nation states. The national state is responsible for intensifying rather than contracting international economic relations.

The tendency towards deglobalization, the concepts of urban development and politics have been re localized shifting towards more functionalist concepts such as creative cities and integrating of diversity and social justice. The distances between the localities in a context of deglobalization acquire a determining role to influence the regions and countries transversally, where those most addicted to energy abundance are the ones that suffer the most. Deglobalization processes must face the profound changes that globalization produced in the economic, social, political, social, and cultural transformations that affect all aspects of individual and social life.

The model of the deglobalized world moves away from the other possible world of the anti-globalizers. An alternative deglobalization process must be centered on populations and nature. However, the current processes of deglobalization do not offer alternative solutions and can aggravate the imbalances and contradictions that can lead to scenarios that increase social vulnerability with more inequality and injustice. The socio-political arguments are more supportive of deglobalization processes, such as avoiding the increase in inequalities with a better distribution of benefits, promoting inclusive mechanisms in technological changes and advances. Otherwise, there will continue to be discontent movements, social upheavals, trade wars, etc.

Deglobalization processes can be presented in scenarios of their future development. A first scenario is one of soft changes that do not modify the structures of international institutions but that focus on regulating distortions to free trade, as well as the conditions imposed on developing countries.

The deconstruction of globalization processes, known as deglobalization, must be for a better reconstruction that truly integrates humanity through economic, political, and social change, and does not disintegrate. This change requires weakening the hegemony of the system of globalizing institutional powers, delegitimizing its ideology and its rules.

FUTURE RESEARCH DIRECTIONS

Future research must be to analyze and determine the tensions between the deglobalization processes and the sources of nationalism and populism at all levels, including the regional and local, confronting discriminations on racial, ethnical, geographical, economic, political, social, and environmental grounds in a never-ending process of open-close systems experiencing serious difficulties with greater competence between the actors and agents.

Further research and critical analysis are also required in the future trends of global socio-economic scenarios moving towards nationalist and populist ideologies leading to more economic neo-protectionism, regionalism, and localism in a deglobalization processes as the response to the neoliberal economic globalization processes of the three decades.

Also, future research needs to be carried out to study of the mechanisms and motives that lie behind populisms and nationalisms and their relationships with global, regional, and local economic growth, social justice, and environmental sustainability.

REFERENCES

Balme, R. (1996). *Les politiques du néo-régionalisme: action collective régionale et globalisation*. Paris Economica.

Beaverstock, J. V., Smith, R. G., & Taylor, P. J. (2000). World-City Network: A New Metageography? *Annals of the Association of American Geographers*, *90*(1), 123–134. doi:10.1111/0004-5608.00188

Bello, W. (2005). *Deglobalization: Ideas for a New World Economy*. Zed books.

Berumen, S. (2002). *Economía internacional*. Editorial Continental, Ciudad de México.

Bremmer, I. (2013). *Every Nation for Itself. What Happens When No One Leads the World*. Portfolio / Penguin.

Cassis, Y. (2006). Capitals of capital – A history of international financial centres, 1780-2005. Cambridge.

Corsetti, G., & Marin, E. A. (2020). *A Century of Arbitrage and Disaster Risk Pricing in the Foreign Exchange Market*. CEPR Discussion Paper No. 14497.

Davis, S. (2020). *Emerging-Market Economies Face COVID-19 and a 'Sudden Stop' in Capital Flows*. Federal Reserve Bank of Dallas. Retrieved from https://www.dallasfed.org/research/economics/2020/0414

Derudder, B., Taylor, P. J., Witlox, F., & Catalano, G. (2003). Hierarchical Tendencies and Regional Patterns in the World City Network: A Global Urban Analysis of 234 Cities. *Regional Studies*, *37*(9), 875–886. doi:10.1080/0034340032000143887

Financial Times. (2020, April 24). US Banks Pull Back from Lending to European Companies. *Financial Times*.

Friedmann, J. (1986). The World City Hypothesis. *Development and Change*, *17*(1), 69–83. doi:10.1111/j.1467-7660.1986.tb00231.x

Hanssens, H., Derudder, B., Taylor, P. J., Hoyler, M., Ni, P., Huang, J., Yang, X., & Witlox, F. (2010): The changing geography of globalized service provision, 2000-2008. The Service Industries Journal. doi:10.1080/02642069.2010.503887

Harrschar-Ehrnborg, S. (2002): Finanzplatzstrukturen in Europa: Die Entstehung und Entwicklung von Finanzzentren. Academic Press.

Hooghe, L. (Ed.). (1996). *Cohesion policy and European integration: building multi-level governance*. Oxford University Press.

Ibarra, P., & Letamendia, F. (1999). Los movimientos sociales. In M. Caminal (Ed.), *Manual de Ciencia Política*. Tecnos.

Inglehart, R., & Norris, P. (2016) *Trump, Brexit, and the rise of populism: economic have-nots and cultural backlash.* HKS Faculty Research Working Paper Series RWP16-026.

James, H. (2018). Deglobalization: The rise of disembedded unilateralism. *Annual Review of Financial Economics, 10*(1), 219–237. doi:10.1146/annurev-financial-110217-022625

Karunaratne, N. D. (2012). The Globalization Deglobalization Policy Conundrum. *Modern Economy., 3*(4), 373–383. doi:10.4236/me.2012.34048

Keating, M., & Jones, B. (Eds.). (1985). *Regions in the European Community.* Oxford University Press.

Le Galès, P., & Lequesne, C. (1998). *Regions in Europe.* Routledge.

Lo, V., & Schamp, E. W. (2001). Finanzplätze auf globalen Märkten – Beispiel Frankfurt/Main. *Geographische Rundschau, 53*(7/8), 26–31.

Lüthi, S., Thierstein, A., & Goebel, D. (2010). Intra-firm and extra-firm linkages in the knowledge economy: The case of the emerging mega-city region of Munich. *Global Networks, 10*(1), 114–137. doi:10.1111/j.1471-0374.2010.00277.x

Merki, C. M. (Ed.). (2005). *Europas Finanzzentren. Geschichte und Bedeutung im 20.* Jahrhundert.

Miskiewicz, J., & Ausloos, M. (2010). Has the World Economy Reached Its Globalization Limit? Physica A, 389(4), 797-806. DOI: .physa.2009.10.029 doi:10.1016/j

Parr, J. B., & Budd, L. (2000). Financial Services and the Urban System: An Exploration. *Urban Studies (Edinburgh, Scotland), 37*(3), 593–610. doi:10.1080/0042098002131

Poon, J. P. H., Eldredge, B., & Yeung, D. (2004). Rank Size Distribution of International Financial Centers. *International Regional Science Review, 27*(4), 411–430. doi:10.1177/0160017604267629

Porteous, D. J. (1999). The Development of Financial Centres: Location, Information Externalities and Path Dependence. In R. Martin (Ed.), *Money and the space economy* (pp. 95–114).

Robinson, J. (2005). Urban geography: World cities, or a world of cities. *Progress in Human Geography, 29*(6), 757–765. doi:10.1191/0309132505ph582pr

Sassen, S. (1991). *The global city.* London, Tokyo. Princeton.

Schamp, E. W. (2009). Das Finanzzentrum – ein Cluster? Ein multiskalarer Ansatz und seine Evidenz am Beispiel von Frankfurt/Rhein-Main. *Zeitschrift für Wirtschaftsgeographie, 53*(1-2), 1–2, 89–105. doi:10.1515/zfw.2009.0006

Schmidt, R. S., & Grote, M. (2005). *Was ist und was braucht ein bedeutender Finanzplatz?* Working Paper Series Finance and Accounting 150, Department of Economics, Johann Wolfgang Goethe-University Frankfurt.

Swiss Economic Institute. (2014). *Press Release, KOF Index of Globalization: Switzerland no Longer Among the Top Ten.* Available from: http://globalization.kof. ethz.ch/media/filer_public/2014/04/16/press_ release_2014_en.pdf

Taylor, P. (2004). *World City Network: A global urban analysis.* doi:10.4324/9780203634059

Van Bergeijk, P. A. G. (2010). *On the Brink of Deglobalization.* Edward Elgar. doi:10.4337/9781849805803

Witt, M. A. (2019). De-Globalization: Theories, Predictions, and Opportunities for International Business Research. *Journal of International Business Studies, 50*(7), 1053–1107. doi:10.105741267-019-00219-7

Witt, M. A., & Jackson, A. (2016). Varieties of Capitalism and institutional comparative advantage: A test and reinterpretation. *Journal of International Business Studies, 47*(7-2), 778-806.

Zehra, N. (2011). The Realist State and Deglobalization. Policy Perspectives, 2.

KEY TERMS AND DEFINITIONS

Economic Deglobalization: Decline in international flows of goods, services, capital, people.

Localism: Esteem or admiration for the culture and traditions of the locality or region.

Nationalism: Political doctrine and movement that claim the right of a nationality to reaffirm its own personality through political self-determination.

Populism: Tendency or fondness for the popular in all areas of life, especially in art.

Racism: Ideology that defends the superiority of one race over the others and the need to keep it isolated or separated from the rest within a community or a country.

Regionalism: Doctrine or political tendency that defends that the government of a State must consider the way of being and the aspirations of each region.

Compilation of References

2018 *Revision of World Urbanization Prospects*. (2018). United Nations. Retrieved from https://www.un.org/development/desa/pd/sites/www.un.org.development.desa.pd/files/files/documents/2020/Jan/un_2018_wup_report.pdf

Ad Alliance GmbH. (2020). Studie Die Corona-Pandemie und ihr Einfluss auf den Alltag – 4. [Study The corona pandemic and its impact on everyday life – 4.] *Welle*. https://www.ad-alliance.de/cms/unternehmen/presse/corona-und-ihr-einfluss.html

Adner, R. (2017, January). Ecosystem as Structure: An Actionable Construct for Strategy. *Journal of Management, 43*(1), 39–58. doi:10.1177/0149206316678451

Aggarwal, S. K., Saini, L. M., & Kumar, A. (2009). Electricity price forecasting in deregulated markets: A review and evaluation. *Electrical Power & Energy Systems, 31*(1), 13–22. doi:10.1016/j.ijepes.2008.09.003

Aitken, R., & Campelo, A. (2011). The four Rs of place branding. *Journal of Marketing Management, 27*(9-10), 913–933. doi:10.1080/0267257X.2011.560718

Aktuálně.cz (2008). *České území Polsku? Lidi straší polský důl* [Czech territory to Poland? People are haunted by a Polish mine]. Aktuálně. https://zpravy.aktualne.cz/ceske-uzemi-polsku-lidi-strasi-polsky-dul/r~i:gallery:6906

Alagöz, M., Erdoğan, S., & Topallı, N. (2008). Doğrudan yabancı sermaye yatırımları ve ekonomik büyüme: Türkiye deneyimi 1992-2007 [Foreign direct investment and economic growth: Turkey's experience 1992-2007]. *Gaziantep University Journal of Social Sciences, 7*(1), 79–89.

Allex, B., Brandenburg, B., Liebl, U., Gerersdorfer, T., & Czachs, C. (2013) Hot town, summer in the city – entwicklung von hitzerelevanten Anpassungsstrategien im Städtetourismus [Development of heat-related adaptation strategies in city tourism]. Regional Development and Information Society: 393-398.

Allport, G. (1998). Lichnost v psihologii [Personality in psychology]. KMP+; Yuventa.

Allport, G. (2002). *Stanovlenie lichnosti. Izbrannye trudy [Becoming a Personality. Selected Works]*. (L. V. Trubicynoy & D. A. Leonteva, Trans. in Eng.). Smysl.

AMSP ČR. (2020). *Online conference "Nové trendy v podnikání MSP"*. [*New trends in SME* entrepreneurship".] [Video]. Youtube.https://www.youtube.com/watch?v=TDXjfcuFvKQ&list=PLRV-VoSMvlATvlELqO0yMgGlz-wuGLSM8

Andrienko, A. A. (2018). SMART-approaches to the development of large cities: Prospects for implementation in Ukraine. *Public Administration and Local Self-Government, 3*(38), 100–106.

Andriiako, T. Yu. (2010). Pedahohichna sutnist i struktura konkurentospromozhnosti [Pedagogical essence and structure of competitiveness]. *Pedahohichna nauka: istoriia, teoriia, praktyka, tendentsii rozvytku [Pedagogical science: History, theory, Practice, development trends], 1*(3). http://intellect-invest.org.ua/pedagog_editions_e-magazine_pedagogical_science_vypuski_n3_2010_st_6/.

Antošová, G. (Ed.). (2022). *Innovative Strategic Planning and International Collaboration for the Mitigation of Global Crises.* IGI Global. doi:10.4018/978-1-7998-8339-5

Aoki, M., & Yoshikawa, H. (2002). Demand saturation-creation and economic growth. *Journal of Economic Behavior & Organization, 48*(2), 127–154. doi:10.1016/S0167-2681(01)00229-3

Arbia, G., Espa, G., & Quah, D. (2008). A class of spatial econometric methods in the empirical analysis of clusters of firms in the space. *Empirical Economics, 34*(1), 81–103. doi:10.100700181-007-0154-1

Arias-Gómez, H., & Antosová, G. (2018). Spatial Patterns of Agriculture in Boyacá. *Apuntes del Cenes, 37*(66), 191–224.

Arroyo, M. (2001). *La contraurbanización: un debate metodológico y conceptual sobre la dinámica de las áreas metropolitanas.* [*Counterurbanization: a methodological and conceptual debate on the dynamics of metropolitan areas.*] Geo Critica. https://www.ub.edu/geocrit/sn-97.htm

Arslan, B., & Ertuğrul, İ. (2022). Forecasting and analysis in Turkish electricity market with multiple regression, ARIMA and artificial neural network methods. *Journal of Management and Economics Research, 20*(1), 331–353.

Ashworth, G. J., & Voogd, H. (1990). *Selling the city: Marketing approaches in public sector urban planning.* Belhaven.

Autio, E., & Thomas, L. D. W. (2014). Innovation ecosystems: implications for innovation management. In M. Dodgson, D. M. Gann, & N. Phillips (Eds.), *The Oxford Handbook of Innovation Management.* Oxford University Press.

Avci, E., Ketter, W., & van Heck, E. (2018). Managing electricity price modeling risk via ensemble forecasting: The case of Turkey. *Energy Policy, 123*, 390–403. doi:10.1016/j.enpol.2018.08.053

Awad, M., & Khanna, R. (2015). *Efficient learning machines: theories, concepts, and applications for engineers and system designers.* Springer Nature. doi:10.1007/978-1-4302-5990-9

Babiachok, R. I., & Kulchytskyy, I. I. (2018). Main trends in the development of startups in ukraine - problems, obstacles and opportunities. EU. https://www.civic-synergy.org.ua/wp-content/uploads/2018/04/Osnovni-tendentsiyi-rozvytku-startapiv-v-Ukrayini-1-1.pdf

Bachinger, M., & Pechlaner, H. (2011). Netzwerke und regionale Kernkompetenzen: der Einfluss von Kooperationen auf die Wettbewerbsfähigkeit von Regionen [Networks and Regional Core Competencies: The Impact of Cooperations on the Competitiveness of Regions]. In M. Bachinger, H. Pechlaner, & W. Widuckel (Eds.), Regionen und Netzwerke: Kooperationsmodelle zur branchenübergreifenden Kompetenzentwicklung [Regions and Networks: Models of Cooperation for a. Intersectoral Development of Competencies] (pp. 3–28). Gabler. doi:10.1007/978-3-8349-6846-3_1

Bachinger, M., Kofler, I., & Pechlaner, H. (2020). Sustainable instead of high-growth? Entrepreneurial Ecosystems in Tourism. *Journal of Hospitality and Tourism Management, 44*, 238–244. doi:10.1016/j.jhtm.2020.07.001

Bachinger, M., Kofler, I., & Pechlaner, H. (2022). Entrepreneurial ecosystems in tourism: An analysis of characteristics from a systems perspective. *European Journal of Tourism Research, 31*, 3113. doi:10.54055/ejtr.v31i.2490

Bachinger, M., & Pechlaner, H. (2022). Entrepreneurial Destination Ecosystem. In D. Buhalis (Ed.), *Encyclopedia of Tourism Management and Marketing* (pp. 93–96). Edward Elgar.

Balme, R. (1996). *Les politiques du néo-régionalisme: action collective régionale et globalisation.* Paris Economica.

Baltagi, B. H. (2005). *Econometric Analysis of Panel Data* (3rd ed.). John Wiley & Sons.

Bandura, A. (1984). Regulation of cognitive process through perceived self efficacy. *Developmental Psychology, 25*(5), 729–735. doi:10.1037/0012-1649.25.5.729

Barro, R.J., & Sala-i, M. X. (1995). *Economic Growth*. McGraw Hill.

Barro, R. J. (1991). Economic Growth in a Cross Section of Countries. *The Quarterly Journal of Economics*, *106*(2), 407–443. doi:10.2307/2937943

Basile, G., Dominici, G., & Tani, M. (2016). Place marketing and management: A complex adaptive systems view. The strategic planning of the city of Avellino, Italy. *Systemic Practice and Action Research*, *29*(5), 469–484. doi:10.100711213-016-9372-9

Beaverstock, J. V., Smith, R. G., & Taylor, P. J. (2000). World-City Network: A New Metageography? *Annals of the Association of American Geographers*, *90*(1), 123–134. doi:10.1111/0004-5608.00188

Bekaert, G., & Harvey, C. R. (1998). Capital markets: An engine for economic growth. *The Brown Journal of World Affairs*, *5*(1), 33–53.

Bekaert, G., & Harvey, C. R. (2000). Foreign speculators and emerging equity markets. *The Journal of Finance*, *55*(2), 565–613. doi:10.1111/0022-1082.00220

Bello, W. (2005). *Deglobalization: Ideas for a New World Economy*. Zed books.

Benedikter, R. (2020). Foreword by Roland Benedikter. In H. Pechlaner, E. Innerhofer, & G. Erschbamer (Eds.), *Overtourism: Tourism Management and Solutions* (pp. xiii–xviii). Routledge.

Beránek, J. (2013). *Ekonomika cestovního ruchu [Tourism economics.]*. Mag Consulting.

Beritelli, P., Bieger, T., & Laesser, C. (2007). Destination governance: Corporate governance theories as a foundation for effective destination management. *Journal of Travel Research*, *46*(1), 96–107. doi:10.1177/0047287507302385

Berrone, P., & Ricart, J. E. (2020). *IESE Cities in Motion Index 2020*. University of Navarra. Retrieved from https://media.iese.edu/research/pdfs/ST-0542-E.pdf

Berry, B. J. L. (1976). *Urbanization and Counterurbanization*. Sage.

Berumen, S. (2002). *Economía internacional*. Editorial Continental, Ciudad de México.

Bhuyan, R. (2021). Employment Opportunities in Rural Homestays. *Yojana*, (February), 50–53.

Bhuyan, R., & Deka, S. M. (2019). Homestay for Whom-Lessons of ASEAN Countries for North East India. *International Journal of Tourism and Travel*, *12*(1&2), 21.

Bichler, B. (2018). Trends in tourism: A media analysis from 2011 – 2016. In C. Maurer & B. Neuhofer (Eds.), *Iscontour 2018: Tourism Research Perspectives* (pp. 274–285).

Bieger, T. (2001). Kompetenzorientierte kommunale Standortstrategie [Competence-oriented municipal location strategy]. In C. Lengwiler (Ed.) Luzerner Beiträge zur Betriebs- und Regionalökonomie: Vol. 8. Gemeindemanagement in Theorie und Praxis [Lucerne contributes to business and regional economy: vol. 8, Community management in theory and practice, (pp. 445-466). Rüegger.

Bieger, T. (2020) *Future of tourism in the wake of relaxing SARS-CoV-2 shutdowns Small steps to a temporary new "normal"*. AIEST. https://www.aiest.org/fileadmin/ablage/dokumente/Covid-Reports/Report_20200510_Tourism_Future.pdf

Bieger, T., & Beritelli, P. (2013). *Management von Destinationen [Management of Destinations]*. Oldenbourg. doi:10.1524/9783486721188

Bieger, T., & Klumbies, A. (2022). From destination management to integrated development of places – enabling personal networks instead of management and control. In H. Pechlaner, N. Olbrich, J. Philipp, & H. Thees (Eds.), *Towards an Ecosystem of Hospitality – Location:City:Destination* (pp. 50–59). Graffeg Publishing.

Binggeli, U., Constantin, M., & Pollack, E. (2020. *COVID-19 tourism spend recovery in numbers*. McKinsey. https://www.mckinsey.com/industries/travel-logistics-and-transport-infrastructure/our-insights/covid-19-tourism-spend-recovery-in-numbers?cid=other-eml-alt-mip-mck&hdpid=e3159b12-26b1-4f41-87c3-a48e24932630&hctky=12250927&hlkid=03ea3268d42442ca8b40146eec3c8990

Blank, S., & Dorf, B. (2013). *The Startup Owner's Manual Startup: The Founder's Handbook*. Alpina Publisher.

Blaug, M. (1990). *Economic Theory in Retrospect*. Cambridge University Press.

Block, J., & Icks, S. (2010). *Stadtmarketing [City marketing]*. Bundesvereinigung City- und Stadtmarketing Deutschland.

Boháč, A. (2021). State borders and cross-border cooperation in Czechia in the post-communist era: Trends and developments. *Észak-magyarországi Stratégiai Füzetek [Northern Hungary Strategy Books]*, *18*(2), 15-23.

Boháč, A. (2022). Knowledge of the German language among geography students at the Technical University of Liberec: a case study from the Czech-German borderlands. In T. Weber & H. Böhm (Eds.), *Wissenskommunikation unter Bedingungen von Mehrsprachigkeit [Knowledge communication under the conditions of multilingualism]*, (pp. 28–54). Peter Lang.

Böhm, H. (2022). Sprachliche (A-)Symmetrien in der Euroregion Neisse-Nysa-Nisa: Analyse von Projekten zur Förderung der Nachbarschaftssprachen [Linguistic (A)symmetries in the Euroregion Neisse-Nysa-Nisa: Analysis of projects to promote neighboring languages]. In Weber, T., & Böhm, H. Wissenskommunikation unter Bedingungen von Mehrsprachigkeit [Knowledge communication under the conditions of multilingualism], (pp. 55-71). Peter Lang.

Böhm, H., & Opioła, W. (2019). Czech–Polish Cross-Border (Non) Cooperation in the Field of the Labor Market: Why Does It Seem to Be Un-De-Bordered? *Sustainability*, *11*(10), 2855. doi:10.3390u11102855

Boru İpek, A. (2021). Prediction of market-clearing price using neural networks based methods and boosting algorithms. *International Advanced Researches and Engineering Journal*, *5*(2), 240–246. doi:10.35860/iarej.824168

Boullón, R. C. (2001). *Planificación del Espacio Turístico* (3rd ed.). Trillas.

Boykova, M. V. (2011). *Buduschee gorodov Goroda as agents of globalization and innovation* [The Future of Cities: Cities as agents of globalization and innovation]. Salazkin. Retrieved from https://cyberleninka.ru/article/n/buduschee-gorodov-goroda-kak-agenty-globalizatsiii-innovatsiy

Bozkurt Keser, S., & Buruk Sahin, Y. (2021). Response surface methodology to tune artificial neural network hyperparameters. *Expert Systems: International Journal of Knowledge Engineering and Neural Networks*, *38*(8), e12792. doi:10.1111/exsy.12792

Brakmannn, S., Garretsen, H., & van Marrewijk, Ch. (2009a). *The new Introduction to Geographical Economics* (2nd ed.). Cambridge University Press. doi:10.1017/CBO9780511818745

Brakmannn, S., Garretsen, H., & van Marrewijk, Ch. (2009b). Economic Geography Within and Between European Nations: The Role of Market Potential and Density Across Space and Time. *Journal of Regional Science*, *49*(4), 777–800. doi:10.1111/j.1467-9787.2009.00633.x

Bramwell, A., Hepburn, N., & Wolfe, D. A. (2012). *Growing innovation ecosystems: university-industry knowledge transfer and regional economic development in Canada, Final Report*, p. 62. University of Toronto.

Bremmer, I. (2013). *Every Nation for Itself. What Happens When No One Leads the World*. Portfolio / Penguin.

Bris, A., Cabolis, C., Lanvin, B., Caballero, J., Hediger, M., Jobin, C., . . . Zargari, M. (2020). Smart City Index 2020. A Tool for Action, an Instrument for Better Lives for All Citizens. Academic Press.

Brown, L. (1991). *Place, Migration and Development in the Third World*. Routledge. doi:10.4324/9780203321263

Brunet-Jailly, E. (2005). Theorizing Borders: An Interdisciplinary Perspective. *Geopolitics*, *10*(4), 633–649. doi:10.1080/14650040500318449

Budweg, S., Schaffers, H., Ruland, R., Kristensen, K., & Prinz, W. (2011). Enhancing collaboration in communities of professionals using a Living Lab approach. *Production Planning and Control*, *22*(5-6), 594–609. doi:10.1080/095372 87.2010.536630

Buhalis, D. (2000). Marketing the competitive destination of the future. *Tourism Management*, *21*(1), 97–116. doi:10.1016/S0261-5177(99)00095-3

Burgess, J. A. (1982). Selling places: Environmental images for the executive. *Regional Studies*, *16*(1), 1–17. doi:10.1080/09595238200185471

Burridge, P. (1981). Testing for a Common Factor in a Spatial Autoregression Model. *Environment and Planning A. Economy and Space*, *13*, 795–800.

Business Center. (1991). Startup development center opened in Mariupol. *Business Center*. https://cutt.ly/1kcTYx3

Butcher, J. (2017). In praise of the holiday revolution. *Spiked*. https://www.spiked-online.com/2017/10/23/in-praise-of-the-holiday-revolution/

Caballero, R. J., & Jaffe, A. B. (1993). How high are the giants' shoulders: An empirical assessment of knowledge spillovers and creative destruction in a model of economic growth. *NBER Macroeconomics Annual*, *8*, 15–74. doi:10.1086/654207

Calderoni, L., Maio, D., & Palmieri, P. (2012). Location-aware mobile services for a smart city: Design, implementation and deployment. *Journal of Theoretical and Applied Electronic Commerce Research*, *7*(3), 74–87.

Caleb, H. (2014). *Savannah's startup ecosystem*. HiimCaleb. http://www.hiimcaleb.me/savannahs-startup-ecosystem/

Calvo, G. A. (1998). *Capital flows and capital-market crises: the simple economics of sudden stops*. Academic Press.

Capello, R., Caragliu, A., & Fratesi, U. (2018). Measuring border effects in European cross-border regions. *Regional Studies*, *52*(7), 986–996. doi:10.1080/00343404.2017.1364843

Caragliu, A., Del Bo, C., & Nijkamp, P. (2011). Smart Cities in Europe. *Journal of Urban Technology*, 65–82.

Carmona, M. (2021). *Public Spaces, Urban Places: The Dimensions of Urban Design* (3rd ed.). Routledge. doi:10.4324/9781315158457

Cassis, Y. (2006). Capitals of capital – A history of international financial centres, 1780-2005. Cambridge.

Cergibozan, R., & Demir, C. (2017). The Determinants of Foreign Direct Investment Outflows from Turkey. In Outward Foreign Direct Investment (FDI) in Emerging Market Economies (pp. 227-243). IGI Global. doi:10.4018/978-1-5225-2345-1.ch011

Česká Televize (2021). *Události v regionech: Liberec odmítl dodávky tepla z polské elektrárny Turów [Events in the regions: Liberec refused heat supplies from the Polish Turów power plant]*. Česká Televize https://www.ceskatelevize.cz/porady/10118379000-udalosti-v-regionech-praha/212411000140416/cast/199021

Ceyhan, G. (2016). *Türkiye'de elektrik piyasa takas fiyatı ve sistem marjinal fiyatı farkı üzerine istatistiksel bir çalışma*. Accessed on 29 June 2022. Available from: https://blog.metu.edu.tr/e162742/files/2016/08/PTF_vs_SMF_original.pdf

Chae, Y., Kim, M., & Yoo, S.-H. (2012). Does natural gas fuel price cause system marginal price, vice-versa, or neither? A causality analysis. *Energy*, *47*(1), 199–204. doi:10.1016/j.energy.2012.09.047

Chatterjee, S., & Prasad, M. V. D. (2019). The Evolution of Agri-Tourism practices in India: Some Success Stories. *Madridge Journal of Agriculture and Environmental Sciences*, *1*(1), 19–25. doi:10.18689/mjaes-1000104

Chazov, E. (2013). Startup as a new form of business. *Scientific works of the National University of Food Technologies*, *52*, 122-128

Chica, J., Cano, R., & Chica, M. (2007). Modelo hedónico espacio-temporal y análisis variográfico del precio de la vivienda. [Spatio-temporal hedonic model and variographic analysis of house prices.]. *GeoFocus*, *7*, 56–72.

Chin, C. H., Law, F. Y., Lo, M. C., & Ramayah, T. (2018). The impact of accessibility quality and accommodation quality on tourists' satisfaction and revisit intention to rural tourism destination in Sarawak: The moderating role of local communities' attitude. *Global Business and Management Research*, *10*(2), 115–127.

Choudhury, K., Dutta, P., & Patgiri, S. (2018). Rural Tourism of North East India: Prospects and Challenges. *IOSR Journal of Humanities and Social Science*, *23*(2), 69–74.

Chowdhary, N., & Sisodia, S. (2013). Of the People, For the People, By the People: A Case Study of Friends of Orchha. In SAGE Business Cases. International CHRIE.

Christaller, W. (1933). *Die zentralen Orte in Süddeutschland. Eine ökonomisch-geographische Untersuchung der Gesetzmäßigkeit, Verbreitung, und Entwicklung der Siedlungen mit städtischen Funktionen [The central places in southern Germany: An economic-geographical study of the regularity, distribution, and development of settlements with Urban functions]*. Gustav Fischer.

Cibinskiene, A., & Snieskiene, G. (2015). Evaluation of city tourism competitiveness. *Procedia: Social and Behavioral Sciences*, *213*, 105–110. doi:10.1016/j.sbspro.2015.11.411

Cicerone, G., McCann, P., & Venhorst, V. (2020). Promoting regional growth and innovation: Relatedness, revealed comparative advantage and the product space. *Journal of Economic Geography*, (20), 293–316.

Cities of Opportunity . (2016). PwC. Retrieved from https://www.pwc.com/us/en/cities-of-opportunity/2016/cities-of-opportunity-7-report.pdf

Cliff, A. D., & Ord, J. K. (1981). *Spatial Processes: Models and Applications*. Pion London.

Cobbinah, P. B. (2017). Managing cities and resolving conflicts: Local people's attitudes towards urban planning in Kumasi, Ghana. *Land Use Policy*, *68*, 223–231. doi:10.1016/j.landusepol.2017.07.050

COM. (2011). Communication From The Commission To The European Parliament, The Council, The European Economic And Social Committee And The Committee Of The Regions. European Comission. https://eur-lex.europa.eu/LexUriServ/LexUriServ.do?uri=COM:2011:0681:FIN:EN:PDF

COM. (2016). Communication From The Commission To The European Parliament, The Council, The European Economic And Social Committee And The Committee Of The Regions: A European agenda for the collaborative economy. European Comission.https://ec.europa.eu/transparency/documents-register/detail?ref=COM(2016)356&lang=ru

Conference Proceedings. (2017). *Neonatal Network, 36*(4), 261–277. doi:10.1891/0730-0832.36.4.e1

Corsetti, G., & Marin, E. A. (2020). *A Century of Arbitrage and Disaster Risk Pricing in the Foreign Exchange Market*. CEPR Discussion Paper No. 14497.

Court, A. T. (1939). *The dynamics of automobile demand*. General Motors.

Crevoisier, O. (1996). Proximity and Territory versus space in regional science. *Environment & Planning, 28*(9), 1683–1697. doi:10.1068/a281683

ČSÚ. (2020). *Nerezidenti v HUZ v Praze v 2Q 2020. [Non-residents in HUZ in Prague in Q2 2020.]*. CSU. https://vdb.czso.cz/vdbvo2/faces/cs/index.jsf?page=vystup

ČSÚ. (2020-2021). *Satelitní účet cestovního ruchu. [Tourism Satellite Account.]*. CSU. https://www.czso.cz/csu/czso/satelitni_ucet_cestovniho_ruchu

CZSO. (2022). *Český statistický úřad* [Czech Statistical Office]. CZSO. https://www.czso.cz

Das, P. K. (2021). Ecotourism and sustainable community development: A case study of Sillery Gaon, West Bengal. *The International Journal of Social Sciences (Islamabad), 10*(1), 21–28. doi:10.46852/2249-6637.01.2021.3

Datel, J. V., & Hrabánková, A. (2020). *Povrchový důl Turów: Stručné shrnutí současných i potenciálních budoucích negativních dopadů na poměry povrchových a podzemních vod na území České republiky* [Turów open-pit mine: Brief summary of current and potential future negative impacts on surface and underground water conditions in the Czech Republic]. VUVTGM. https://www.kraj-lbc.cz/getFile/id:1084382/TUROW-laickeshrnuti-VUV-FINAL.pdf

Davis, S. (2020). *Emerging-Market Economies Face COVID-19 and a 'Sudden Stop' in Capital Flows*. Federal Reserve Bank of Dallas. Retrieved from https://www.dallasfed.org/research/economics/2020/0414

De Mello, L. R. (1999). Foreign direct investment-led growth: Evidence from time series and panel data. *Oxford Economic Papers, 51*(1), 133–151. doi:10.1093/oep/51.1.133

De Mello, L. R., & Sinclair, M. T. (1995). *Foreign direct investment, joint ventures and endogenous growth*. Department of Economics, University of Kent.

De Vries, J. (1990). Problems in the measurement, description, and analysis of historical urbanization. *Urbanization in history*, 43-60.

Debarsy, N., & Ertur, C. (2019). Interaction Matrix Selection in Spatial Autoregressive Models with an Application to Growth Theory. *Regional Science and Urban Economics, 75*, 49–69. doi:10.1016/j.regsciurbeco.2019.01.002

DeFries, R., Karanth, K. K., & Pareeth, S. (2010). Interactions between protected areas and their surroundings in human-dominated tropical landscapes. *Biological Conservation, 143*(12), 2870–2880. doi:10.1016/j.biocon.2010.02.010

Deloitte. (n.d.). *Business ecosystems come of age*. Deloitte. https://www2.deloitte.com/za/en/pages/strategy-operations/articles/business-ecosystems-come-of-age.html

Demek, J. (1987). Zeměpisný lexikon ČSR: Hory a nížiny [Geographical lexicon of Czechoslovakia: Mountains and Lowlands]. *Academia (Caracas)*.

Depren, S. K., Kartal, M. T., Ertuğrul, H. M., & Depren, Ö. (2022). The role of data frequency and method selection in electricity price estimation: Comparative evidence from Turkey in pre-pandemic and pandemic periods. *Renewable Energy, 186*, 217–225. doi:10.1016/j.renene.2021.12.136

Derudder, B., Taylor, P. J., Witlox, F., & Catalano, G. (2003). Hierarchical Tendencies and Regional Patterns in the World City Network: A Global Urban Analysis of 234 Cities. *Regional Studies, 37*(9), 875–886. doi:10.1080/0034340032000143887

Dewey, J. (1999). *Psykhologiya i pedagogika myshleniya [Psychology and pedagogics of thinking]*. (N. M. Nykolskaya, Trans. in Eng.). Labirint.

Dewey, J. (2003). Problema cheloveka [Problem of a human]. *Rekonstruktsyia v filosofii [Reconstruction in philosophy]*. (L. E. Pavlova, Trans. in Eng.). Moskva, 133–450.

Dey, B., Mathew, J., & Chee-Hua, C. (2020). Influence of destination attractiveness factors and travel motivations on rural homestay choice: The moderating role of need for uniqueness. *International Journal of Culture, Tourism and Hospitality Research*, *14*(4), 639–666. doi:10.1108/IJCTHR-08-2019-0138

Di-Clemente, E., Hernández-Mogollón, J. M., & López-Guzmán, T. (2020). Culinary tourism as an effective strategy for a profitable cooperation between agriculture and tourism. *Social Sciences*, *9*(3), 25. doi:10.3390ocsci9030025

Dietterich, T. G. (2000). Ensemble methods in machine learning. In Lecture Notes in Computer Science: Vol. 1857. *Multiple Classifier Systems*. Springer. doi:10.1007/3-540-45014-9_1

Docampo, M., & Otero, R. (2012). Territorial Transition: Theoretical Model and Contrast with the Spanish Case. *Reis*, *139*, 133–162.

Dodds, R., & Butler, R. (2019). *Overtourism: Issues, Realities, and Solutions*. De Gruyter. doi:10.1515/9783110607369

Döll-König, H., & Pechlaner, H. (2022). Foreword. In H. Pechlaner, N. Olbrich, J. Philipp, & H. Thees (Eds.), *Towards an Ecosystem of Hospitality – Location:City:Destination* (pp. 6–7). Graffeg Publishing.

Drápela, E., & Bašta, J. (2018). Kvantifikace síly hraničního efektu na hranicích Libereckého kraje [Quantification of border effec on the borders of the Liberec Region]. *Geografické informácie*, *22*(1), 51-60.

Drucker, P. (2012). *The practice of management*. Routledge.

Dudek, M. (2018). *Procesní přístup. Kvalita jednoduše* [Process approach. Quality simply]. Online on 25.6.2022 from https://kvalita-jednoduse.cz/procesni-pristup/

Durham, J. B. (2003). Foreign Portfolio Investment, Foreign Bank Lending, and Economic Growth. In *International Finance Discussion Papers 757*. Board of Governors of the Federal Reserve System.

Durlauf, S. N., Johnson, P. A., & Temple, J. R. W. (2005). Growth Econometrics. In *Handbook of Economic Growth (vol. 1A, pp. 555–677)*. North-Holland.

Dursun, A., Eke, İ., & Tezcan, S. S. (2020). Artificial neural networks with Turkey interconnected system for day ahead market transmission lines estimated losses. *International Journal of Engineering Research and Development*, *12*(2), 549–564. doi:10.29137/umagd.600962

Dymchenko O.V., Smachilo V.V., Rudachenko O.O., & Drill N.V. (2022). Modeling the processes of formation of startup ecosystems on the basis of cluster analysis: entrepreneurial aspect. *Communal management of cities, 2*(169), 71–78.

Eastern Europe: Quality of Life Index by City. (2021). NUMBEO. Retrieved from https://www.numbeo.com/quality-of-life/region_rankings.jsp?title=2021&region=151&displayColumn=0

Eckert, C., & Pechlaner, H. (2019). Alternative Product Development as Strategy Towards Sustainability in Tourism: The Case of Lanzarote. In U. Martini & F. Buffa (Eds.), *Marketing for Sustainable Tourism* (pp. 105–122). MDPI.

EESC. (2020). Entrepreneurship 2020 Action Plan. EESC. https://www.eesc.europa.eu/en/our-work/opinions-information-reports/opinions/entrepreneurship-2020-action-plan#downloads

EIPA. (2012). *CAF as guiding model for the public administration management in Dominican Republic*. European Institute of Public Administration. https://www.EIPA.eu/

EIPA. (2021). *What is CAF*. European Institute of Public Administration. EIPA. https://www.EIPA.eu/

EIPA. (2022). *About us*. European Institute of Public Administration. EIPA. https://www.EIPA.eu

Eko-Unia. (2019). *Bogatynia, one of the most polluted cities – what's next?* Eko-Unia. https://eko-unia.org.pl/en/bogatynia-one-of-the-most-polluted-cities-whats-next

Elhorst, J. P. (2014). Spatial Econometrics: From Cross-Sectional Data to Spatial Panels. Springer Briefs in Regional Science. Springer-Verlag. doi:10.1007/978-3-642-40340-8

EPIAS. (2022a). Accessed on 29 June 2022. https://www.epias.com.tr/en

EPIAS. (2022b). *MCP-SMP and Imbalance Price Listing.* Accessed on 29 June 2022. Available from: https://rapor.epias.com.tr/rapor/xhtml/ptfSmfListeleme.xhtml

Eric, R. (2011). *The Lean Startup: How Today's Entrepreneurs Use Continuous Innovation to Create Radically Successful Businesses.* Crown Books.

Erikson, E (1996). *Identichnost: yunost i krizis [Identity: youth and crisis].* (A. V. Tolstyh, Trans. in Eng.). Progress.

Ertur, C., & Koch, W. (2007). Growth, Technological Interdependence and Spatial Externalities: Theory and Evidence. *Journal of Applied Econometrics*, 22(6), 1033–1062. doi:10.1002/jae.963

Espa, G., Arbia, G., & Giuliani, D. (2013). Conditional versus unconditional industrial agglomeration: Disentangling spatial dependence and spatial heterogeneity in the analysis of ICT firms' distribution in Milan. *Journal of Geographical Systems, Springer.*, 15(1), 31–50. doi:10.100710109-012-0163-2

EUPAN. EIPA. (2019). *CAF2020. Common Assessment Framework. The European model for improving public organisations through self-assessment.* European Public Administration Network (EUPAN), European Institute of Public Administration (EIPA). www.EIPA.eu

European Comission. (2021). *Long-Term Vision for Rural Areas.* European Comission. https://knowledge4policy.ec.europa.eu/publication/communication-com2021345-long-term-vision-eus-rural-areas-towards-stronger-connected_en

European Commission. (n.d.). *Civil justice.* Europa. https://ec.europa.eu/justice/civil/commercial/insolvency/index_en.htm

European Comission. (n.d.). *Projects and studies on entrepreneurship education.* European Comission. https://ec.europa.eu/growth/smes/supporting-entrepreneurship/entrepreneurship-education/projects-and-studies-entrepreneurship-education_en

European Comission. (n.d.). *Startup Europe.* European Comission. https://digital-strategy.ec.europa.eu/en/policies/startup-europe

European Commission. (2021a). *European Innovation Scoreboard 2021.* Author.

European Commission. (2021b). *Regional Innovation Scoreboard 2021.* Author.

Eurostat. (2021). *Investment in Research and Development in Slovakia.* Author.

Evans, A. W. (1990). The assumption of equilibrium in the analysis of migration and interregional differences: A review of some recent research. *Journal of Regional Science*, 30(4), 515–531. doi:10.1111/j.1467-9787.1990.tb00119.x PMID:12316475

Fallas, Y. (2022 July 1). Opinion: EU Missions and the importance of Climate Neutral and Smart Cities: the case of Kozani. *Greenovate!* https://greenovate-europe.eu/opinion-eu-missions-and-the-importance-of-climate-neutral-and-smart-cities-the-case-of-kozani/

FAO. (2017). *The future of food and agriculture – Trends and challenges.* Food and Agriculture Organization of the United Nations Rome.

FAO. (2021). *Food Outlook – Biannual Report on Global Food Markets. Food Outlook, November 2021.* Food and Agriculture Organization of the United Nations. doi:10.4060/cb7491en

FEDESARROLLO & Sociedad de Agricultores de Colombia (SAC). (2013). *Políticas para el desarrollo de la agricultura en Colombia* [Policies For The Development Of Agriculture In Colombia]. Author.

FEDESARROLLO. (2019). *Uso potencial y efectivo de la Tierra Agrícola en Colombia: Resultados del Censo Nacional Agropecuario* [Potential and effective use of agricultural land in Colombia: Results of the National Agricultural Census]. FEDESARROLLO.

FEDESARROLLO. (2019). *Uso Potencial y Efectivo de la Tierra Agrícola en Colombia: Resultados del Censo Nacional Agropecuario* [Potential And Effective Use Of Agricultural Land In Colombia: Results Of The National Agricultural Census]. Informe Final. FEDESARROLLO.

Fedorov, R. K. (2021). The state and main directions of development of startups in Ukraine. *Electronic professional edition: Effective economy, 4.* http://www.economy.nayka.com.ua/pdf/4_2021/202.pdf

Fedulova, L. I., & Marchenko, O. S. (2015). Innovative ecosystems: essence and methodological principles of formation. *Economic theory and law, 2*(21), 21–33.

Ferguson, F. (2019). *Make City: A compendium of urban alternatives.* Jovis.

Financial Times. (2020, April 24). US Banks Pull Back from Lending to European Companies. *Financial Times.*

Florax, R., Folmer, H., & Rey, S. (2003). Specification Searches in Spatial Econometrics: The Relevance of Hendry's Methodology. *Regional Science and Urban Economics, 33*(5), 557–579. doi:10.1016/S0166-0462(03)00002-4

Ford, R. (2012). *Darwinian Agriculture: How Understanding Evolution Can Improve Agriculture.* Princeton University Press.

Freud, A. (2016). *Psihologiya YA i zashchitnye mekhanizmy [Psychology of I and defensive mechanisms].* Piter.

Friedmann, J. (1986). The World City Hypothesis. *Development and Change, 17*(1), 69–83. doi:10.1111/j.1467-7660.1986.tb00231.x

Frýdlantsko, M. A. S. (2020). *Frýdlantsko 2020: Analyzická část* [The Frýdlant Region: Analytic part]. MASIF. https://www.dataplan.info/img_upload/7bdb1584e3b8a53d337518d988763f8d/sclld_88.pdf

Fujita, M., & Krugman, P. (2004). La nueva geografía económica: pasado, presente y futuro. [The new economic geography: past, present and future.] Investigaciones Regionales, 4, Asociación Española de Ciencia Regional Madrid, 177-206

FVW. (2020). *Reiselust der Kunden bleibt ungebrochen.* [*Customers' desire to travel remains unbroken.*]. FVW. https://www.fvw.de/reisevertrieb/datenanalyse/reiseanalyse-september-umfrage-macht-hoffnung-212547

Gallup, J. L., Gaviria, A., & Lora, E. (2003). *Is Geography Destiny? Lessons from Latin America.* Intra-American Development Bank. doi:10.1596/0-8213-5451-5

Gallup, J. L., Sachs, J. D., & Mellinger, A. D. (1998). *Geography and economic development.* National Bureau of Economic Research. doi:10.3386/w6849

Garcia Rendon, J. J., López-Rodríguez, J., & Moncada-Mesa, J. (2021). Firm location, regional weather conditions and bid pricing strategies in the Colombian wholesale electricity market. *Regional Studies, 56*(9), 1554–1570. doi:10.1080/00343404.2021.1994136

García, M., & Otero, R. (2012). Transición territorial: Modelo teórico y contraste con el caso español. [Territorial transition: theoretical model and contrast with the Spanish case.]. *Reis*, *139*, 133–162.

Garegnani, P. (1992). Some Notes for an Analysis of Accumulation. In J. Halevi, D. Laibman, & E. J. Nell (Eds.), *Beyond the steady state: A revival of growth theory*. St. Martin's Press. doi:10.1007/978-1-349-10950-0_3

Gayretli, G., Yucekaya, A., & Bilge, A. H. (2019). An analysis of price spikes and deviations in the deregulated Turkish power market. *Energy Strategy Reviews*, *26*, 100376. doi:10.1016/j.esr.2019.100376

Gedik, A. (2005). *Toward a Theory of Mobility Transition: Test of Zelinsky's Theory with the Japanese and Turkish Data, 1955-2000*. Princeton.

Georgilakis, P. S. (2006). Market clearing price forecasting in deregulated electricity markets using adaptively trained neural networks. In *Hellenic Conference on Artificial Intelligence* (pp. 56-66). Springer. 10.1007/11752912_8

Giffinger, R., & Pichler-Milanović, N. (2007). *Smart cities: Ranking of European medium-sized cities*. Centre of Regional Science, Vienna University of Technology.

Giving honest businesses a second chance: Commission proposes modern insolvency rules. (2012) European Commission. https://ec.europa.eu/commission/presscorner/detail/en/IP_12_1354

Godley, W. (1999). Money and credit in a Keynesian model of income determination. *Cambridge Journal of Economics*, *23*(4), 393–411. doi:10.1093/cje/23.4.393

Graves, P. E., & Greenwood, M. J. (1987). *Two views of recent regional location patterns in the United States: competing models with noncompeting implications*. Paper presented al the International Conference on Migration and Labor Market Efficiency, Knoxville, TN.

Greenovate. (2013). *Commission sets out Entrepreneurship Action Plan*. Greenovate! https://greenovate-europe.eu/commission-sets-out-entrepreneurship-action-plan/

Greenwood, M. J. (1997). Internal Migration in developed countries. Handbook of Population and Family Economics, (vol. 1B). Netherlands.

Greison, J., & O'Dell, K. (1991). *Amerykanskiy menedzhment na poroge XXI veka [American management on the threshold of the XXI century]*. Ekonomika..

Gretzel, U., & Koo, C. (2021). Smart tourism cities: A duality of place where technology supports the convergence of touristic and residential experiences. *Asia Pacific Journal of Tourism Research*, *26*(4), 352–364. doi:10.1080/10941665.2021.1897636

Grossman, G. M., & Helpman, E. (1991). Quality ladders in the theory of growth. *The Review of Economic Studies*, *58*(1), 43–61. doi:10.2307/2298044

Guerci, E., & Rastegar, M. A. (2012). Comparing system-marginal-price versus pay-as-bid auctions in a realistic electricity market scenario. In Managing Market Complexity: The Approach of Artificial Economics, Lecture Notes in Economics and Mathematical Systems 662 (pp. 141-153). Springer. doi:10.1007/978-3-642-31301-1_12

Gul, O. (2008). An assessment of power quality and electricity consumer's rights in restructured electricity market in Turkey. *Electrical Power Quality and Utilisation Journal*, *14*(2), 29–34.

Günçavdı, Ö., & Kayam, S. S. (2017). Unravelling the structure of Turkish exports: Impediments and policy. *Journal of Policy Modeling*, *39*(2), 307–323. doi:10.1016/j.jpolmod.2016.09.001

Gurak, D. T., & Cases, (1992). Migration networks and the shaping of migration systems. en Mary Kritz, Lin Lean Lim and Hania Zlotnik (eds.), *International Migration Systems: A Global Approach.* Clarendon Press, pp.: 150-176.

Haas, H. (2008). *Migration and development A theoretical perspective. Working papers, Paper 9.* International Migration Institute. University of Oxford. Pp:57

Haas, G. C. (1922). *Sale Prices as a Basis for Farm Land Appraisal. Technical Bulletin, 9, Agricultural Experiment Station.* University of Minnesota.

Haining, R. P., & Li, G. (2020). *Modelling Spatial and Spatial-Temporal Data: A Bayesian Approach.* Chapman and Hall/CRC. doi:10.1201/9780429088933

Hák, T., & Janoušková, S. (2020). Indikátory kvality života v regionech [Quality of life indicators in regions]. In *Regiony budoucnosti – spolupráce, bezpečí, efektivity: Inspirace pro rozvoj měst a regionů s příklady dobré praxe [Regions of the future—cooperation, safte, efficiency: Inspiration for the development of cities and regions with examples of good practice.].* Grada Publishing.

Halicioglu, F. (2007). *A multivariate causality analysis of export and growth for Turkey.* Academic Press.

Hall, T. (2020). *Town planning – the basics.* Routledge.

Hamburg Marketing Gmb. (2019). *Strategischer Marketingplan für das Hamburg-Marketing 2019-2024 [Strategic Marketing plan for Hamburg marketing, 2019-2024].* Hamberg marketing. https://marketing.hamburg.de/strat-marketingplan.html

Hamin, E. M., & Marcucci, D. J. (2008). Ad Hoc Rural Regionalism. *Journal of Rural Studies*, *24*(77), 467–477. doi:10.1016/j.jrurstud.2008.03.009

Han, J. H., & Park, H. Y. (2019). Sustaining Small Exporters' Performance: Capturing Heterogeneous. *Effects of Government Export Assistance Programs on Global Value Chain Informedness. Sustainability*, *11*(8), 2380. doi:10.3390u11082380

Hansen, A. (1941). Fiscal Policy and Business Cycles. Academic Press.

Hanssens, H., Derudder, B., Taylor, P. J., Hoyler, M., Ni, P., Huang, J., Yang, X., & Witlox, F. (2010): The changing geography of globalized service provision, 2000-2008. The Service Industries Journal. doi:10.1080/02642069.2010.503887

Harrschar-Ehrnborg, S. (2002): Finanzplatzstrukturen in Europa: Die Entstehung und Entwicklung von Finanzzentren. Academic Press.

Hausmann, R., & Klinger, B. (2007). The Structure of the Product Space and the Evolution of Comparative Advantage. *CID Working Paper,* 146. Center for International Development at Harvard University.

Hayek, F. A. (2001). Individualizm i ekonomicheskiy poryadok [Individualism and economical order]. Moskva: Izograf; Nachala-Fond..

Hedorfer, P. (2022). A message from Petra Hedorfer, Chief Executive Officer of the German National Tourist Board (GNTB). In H. Pechlaner, N. Olbrich, J. Philipp, & H. Thees (Eds.), *Towards an Ecosystem of Hospitality – Location:City:Destination* (pp. 8–9). Graffeg Publishing.

Hendijani, R. B. (2020). Food as a sustainable alternative tourism promotion in 3S destinations. *Journal of Environmental Management and Tourism*, *11*(02 (42)), 377–387. doi:10.14505//jemt.11.2(42).16

Herzer, D., Klasen, S., & Nowak-Lehmann D, F. (2008). In search of FDI-led growth in developing countries: The way forward. *Economic Modelling*, *25*(5), 793–810. doi:10.1016/j.econmod.2007.11.005

Hill, A., & Prossek, A. (Eds.). (2012). *Metropolis und Region: Aktuelle Herausforderungen für Stadtforschung und Raumplanung [Metropolis and Region: Current Challenges for Urban Research and Spatial Planning]*. Verlag Dorothea Rohn.

Hollands, R. G. (2020). Will the real smart city please stand up?: Intelligent, progressive or entrepreneurial? In *The Routledge companion to smart cities* (pp. 179–199). Routledge.

Hooghe, L. (Ed.). (1996). *Cohesion policy and European integration: building multi-level governance*. Oxford University Press.

Horáček, F. (2022). *Srovnali jsme stejný nákup s Polskem a Německem. Česko nevychází příliš dobře* [We compared the same purchase with Poland and Germany. Czechia is not doing well]. https://www.seznamzpravy.cz/clanek/ekonomika-byznys-trendy-analyzy-srovnani-stejny-nakup-stoji-v-cesku-stejne-jak-v-nemecku-polsko-je-levnejsi-209620

Hoyle, B., & Knowles, R. (Eds.). (1998). *Modern Transport Geography* (2nd ed.). Wiley.

Hřebíčková, M., & Graf, S. (2014). Accuracy of National Stereotypes in Central Europe: Outgroups Are Not Better than Ingroup in Considering Personality Traits of Real People. *European Journal of Personality*, *28*(1), 60–72. doi:10.1002/per.1904

Hutchinson, B. (2013 February 25). Direct speech: Bill Hutchison on smart cities and stupid Moscow A city where a doctor is called by video link, where there is no corruption, and cars drive without drivers, the chief expert in the field of smart cities told The Village about the high-tech future. *The Village*. Retrieved from https://www.the-village.ru/city/city/117185-hatchinson

Iansiti, M., & Levien, R. (2004). *The Keystone Advantage: What the New Dynamics of Business Ecosystems Mean for Strategy, Innovation, and Sustainability*. Harvard Business School, Press.

Ibarra, P., & Letamendia, F. (1999). Los movimientos sociales. In M. Caminal (Ed.), *Manual de Ciencia Política*. Tecnos.

Ilienko, O. (2018a). Philosophical foundation of the concept of competitiveness of an individual. *Imperatives of civil society development in promoting national competitiveness: Proceedings of the 1st International Scientific and Practical Conference*, Batumi, Georgia, *1*, 270–272.

Ilienko, O. (2018b). Specific features of training competitive professionals of municipal economy. *European Humanities Studies: State and Society*, *3*, 33–45.

Index of competitiveness of cities. (2020 September 16). Resuscitation Package of Reforms. Retrieved from https://rpr.org.ua/news/indeks-konkurentospromozhnosti-mist-ukrainy-2019-2020/

India, I. a., & I.A.M.A.I. (2021). *Homestays in India: A Functional and Economic Impact Analysis*. Retrieved from https://ascension.org.in/wp-content/uploads/2021/08/Homestay-ecomonic-impact.pdf

Inglehart, R., & Norris, P. (2016) *Trump, Brexit, and the rise of populism: economic have-nots and cultural backlash*. HKS Faculty Research Working Paper Series RWP16-026.

Innerhofer, E., Pechlaner, H., & Glüher, G. (Eds.). (2016). *Orte und Räume: Perspektiven für Kunst und Kultur [Places and spaces: perspectives for art and culture]*. Athesia.

Isenberg, D. J. (2010). How to start an entrepreneurial revolution. Harvard business review, 88(6), 40-50.

Islam, N. (1995). Growth empirics: A panel data approach. *The Quarterly Journal of Economics*, *110*(4), 1127–1170. doi:10.2307/2946651

ISTAT. (1996). *Rapporto Annuale. La situazione del paese nel 1995* [Annual Report. The situation in the country in 1995.]. Istituto Nazionale di Statistica.

ISTAT. (2005) I Sistemi Locali del Lavoro. Censimento 2001. [Local Labour Systems. 2001 Census.] Dati definitivi. Istituto Nazionale di Statistica. Roma.

ISTAT. (2015). Statistiche Report. I distretti Industriali. [Statistics Report. Industrial districts.] Istituto Nazionale di Statistica. https://www.istat.it/it/files//2015/02/Distretti-industriali.pdf

Izidorczyk, H. (2022). *Kopalnia Węgla Brunatnego Turów 1947-2022* [The Turów lignite mine 1947-2022]. Wydawnictwo AEM Paul Huppert.

Jackson, D. J. (2011). *What is an innovation ecosystem?* National Science Foundation. http://erc-assoc.org/sites/default/files/topics/policy_studies/ DJackson_Innovation%20Ecosystem_03-15-11.pdf

Jacobides, M., Cennamo, C., & Gawer, A. (2018). Towards a Theory of Ecosystems. *Strategic Management Journal*, *39*(8), 2255–2276. doi:10.1002mj.2904

James, W. (1997). *Prahmatizm. Volia k vere [Pragmatism. Will to believe].* (L. V. Blinnikova, & A. P. Poliakov, Trans. in Eng.). Respublika.

James, W. (2000). *Psikhologiya lichnosti [Psychology of a personality].* Moskva: Teksty..

James, H. (2018). Deglobalization: The rise of disembedded unilateralism. *Annual Review of Financial Economics*, *10*(1), 219–237. doi:10.1146/annurev-financial-110217-022625

Jansen, D. (2006). *Einführung in die Netzwerkanalyse – Grundlagen, Methoden, Forschungsbeispiele [Introduction to network analysis—basics, methods, research examples].* Springer.

Jaramillo, C. F. (2001). Crisis, and Change: Colombian Agriculture in the 1990s. *Economic Development and Cultural Change*, *49*(4), 821–846. doi:10.1086/452526 PMID:19069305

Jayabharathi, P., & Vedamuthu, R. (2017). Experiential Tourism as a Response to the Sustenance of a Cultural Landscape: The Case of Banni, Kutch, Gujarat, India. In *Proceedings of the 6th International Conference of Arte-Polis* (pp. 149-166). Springer. 10.1007/978-981-10-5481-5_15

Jennissen, R. P. W. (2003). Economic Determinants of Net International Migration in Western Europe. *European Journal of Population*, *19*(2), 171–198. doi:10.1023/A:1023390917557

Jiricka-Pürrer, A., Brandenburg, Ch., & Probstl-Haider, U. (2020). City tourism pre- and post-covid-19 pandemic – Messages to take home for climate change adaptation and mitigation? *Journal of Outdoor Recreation and Tourism*, *31*, 31. doi:10.1016/j.jort.2020.100329

Job. Interview. *Career Studies*. Retrieved from https://www.fehb.org/Classes/AEC/AECCulArts/pdfFiles/Job%20Interviewing%20Skills%20Lesson%20Plan.pdf

Johnson, B. E., & Shultz, B. (2016). Cities of the future. In S. D. Brunn, M. Hays-Mitchell, D. J. Zeigler, & J. K. Graybill (Eds.), *Cities of the World: Regional Patterns and Urban Environment* (pp. 537–570). Rowman & Littlefield.

Joint Report under the ET 2020 strategic framework for European cooperation in education and training. (2020). Retrieved from https://www.tesguide.eu/policy-strategy/itemid/41941/

Joseph, E. K., Kallarakal, T. K., Varghese, B., & Anthony, J. K. (2020). Sustainable tourism development in the backwaters of south Kerala, India: The local government perspective. *Geo Journal of Tourism and Geosites*, *33*(4), 1532–1537. doi:10.30892/gtg.334spl13-604

Jufri, F. H., Oh, S., & Jung, J. (2019). Day-ahead system marginal price forecasting using artificial neural network and similar-days information. *Journal of Electrical Engineering & Technology*, *14*(2), 561–568. doi:10.100742835-018-00058-w

Kachniewska, M. A. (2015). Tourism development as a determinant of quality of life in rural areas. *Worldwide Hospitality and Tourism Themes*, *7*(5), 500–515. doi:10.1108/WHATT-06-2015-0028

Kadeřábková, A. (2007). *Růst, stabilita a konkurenceschopnost III. Česká republika v globalizované a znalostní ekonomice* [Growth, stability, and competitiveness III. The Czech Republic in a globalized and knowledge-based economy]. Linde.

Kalfa, V. R., Arslan, B., & Ertuğrul, İ. (2021). Determining the factors affecting the market clearing price by using multiple linear regression method. *Alphanumeric Journal*, *9*(1), 35–48. doi:10.17093/alphanumeric.882847

Kannegieser, I. (2015). *A Home In The Hills: Examining the socioeconomic benefits of homestay tourism on rural women and their communities in the Darjeeling District.* Academic Press.

Kapoor, R., & Lee, J. M. (2013). Coordinating and Competing in Ecosystems: How Organizational forms Shape New Technology Investments. *Strategic Management Journal*, *34*(3), 274–296. doi:10.1002mj.2010

Kapur, S. (2016). Rural tourism in India: Relevance, prospects, and promotional strategies. *International Journal of Tourism and Travel*, *9*(1-2), 40–49.

Karagöl, E. T., & Tür, M. R. (2017). *Türkiye'de Elektrik Enerjisi* [Electrical Energy in Turkey]. Accessed on 29 June 2022. Available from: https://www.researchgate.net/publication/321197687_Turkiye'de_Elektrik_Enerjisi

Karemera, D., Oguledo, V. I., & Davis, B. (2000). A gravity model analysis of international migration to North America. *Applied Economics*, *32*(13), 1745–1755. doi:10.1080/000368400421093

Karunaratne, N. D. (2012). The Globalization Deglobalization Policy Conundrum. *Modern Economy.*, *3*(4), 373–383. doi:10.4236/me.2012.34048

Kearney. (2020). *Global City Index 2020*. Kearney. https://www.kearney.com/global-cities/2020

Keating, M., & Jones, B. (Eds.). (1985). *Regions in the European Community*. Oxford University Press.

Kerr, G. (2005). From destination brand to location brand. *Journal of Brand Management*, *13*(4/5), 276–283.

Khalil, S., Ismail, A., & Ghalwash, S. (2021). The Rise of Sustainable Consumerism: Evidence from the Egyptian Generation Z. *Sustainability*, *13*(24), 13804. doi:10.3390u132413804

Khanal, A. R., Honey, U., & Omobitan, O. (2020). Diversification through 'fun in the farm': Analyzing structural factors affecting agritourism in Tennessee. *The International Food and Agribusiness Management Review*, *23*(1), 105–120. doi:10.22434/IFAMR2019.0043

Kharkiv. (2019 April 14). *Municipal It-Startup Center To Be Opened In Kharkiv.* Kharkiv IT Cluster. https://it-kharkiv.com/en/municipal-it-startup-center-to-be-opened-in-kharkiv-2/

Kharkiv. (n.d.). *Register of acts of the Kharkiv City Council.* Kharkiv. http://kharkiv.rocks/reestr/663864

Kharroubi, E., & Kohlscheen, E. (2017). *Consumption-led expansions.* Academic Press.

Kilper, H. (Ed.). (2009). *German annual of spatial research and policy 2009: New disparities in spatial development in Europe.* Springer-Verlag. doi:10.1007/978-3-642-03402-2

Kim, B., Lee, D., Rusetskii, N., Shusterzon, K., Sidorov, D., Song, M., & Kim, I. (2021). A study on the effect of energy storage systems and distributed generators on reliability. *2021 24th International Conference on Electrical Machines and Systems (ICEMS)*, 802-807. 10.23919/ICEMS52562.2021.9634523

Kim, C.-I., Yu, I.-K., & Song, Y. H. (2002). Prediction of system marginal price of electricity using wavelet transform analysis. *Energy Conversion and Management*, *43*(14), 1839–1851. doi:10.1016/S0196-8904(01)00127-3

Kim, H. A. (2008). *Study of the Inﬂuences of Public Support Programs on the Technology Innovation and Survival in the IT Small Enterprises*. Science and Technology Policy Institute.

Kollar, V., & Matusova, S. (2019). Manažment inovácií [Innovation management]. Bratislava: VŠEMVS.

Kölmek, M. A., & Navruz, İ. (2015). Forecasting the day-ahead price in electricity balancing and settlement market of Turkey by using artificial neural networks. *Turkish Journal of Electrical Engineering and Computer Sciences, 23*, 841–852. doi:10.3906/elk-1212-136

Korepanov, O. S. (2018). Methodological principles of statistical support for managing the development of "smart" sustainable cities in Ukraine: a monograph. SE "Inform.-analyst. agency".

Kotler, P., Haider, D. H., & Rein, I. (1993). *Marketing Places*. The Free Press.

Kourtit, K., Nijkamp, P., & Arribas, D. (2012). Smart cities in perspective–a comparative European study by means of self-organizing maps. *Innovation (Abingdon), 25*(2), 229–246.

KPMG. (2017). *A startup guide and toolkit for local government*. KPMG. https://citiespowerpartnership.org.au/wp-content/uploads/2021/02/AustraliaLocal-Government-StartupGuide.pdf

Krlev, G., Pasi, G., Wruk, D., & Bernhard, M. (2021). Reconceptualizing the Social Economy. *Stanford Social Innovation Review*.

Krugman P., (1998). Space: the final frontier. *Journal of economic perspectives, 12*(2), 161 – 174.

Krugman, P. (1993b) First nature, second nature and metropolitan location. *Journal of Regional Science, 33*(2). 129-144.

Krugman, P. (1995). Increasing returns, imperfect competition and the positive theory of international trade. Handbook of international economics, 3, 1243-1277. doi:10.1016/S1573-4404(05)80004-8

Krugman, P. (1999) Was It All In Ohlin? MIT. https://web.mit.edu/krugman/www/ohlin.html

Krugman, P. (2008). *New trade, new geography, and the troubles of manufacturing*. Nobel Price Slides Lecture. www.nobelprize.org

Krugman, P. (2008). *The increasing returns revolution in trade and geography*. Nobel Prize Lecture. Stockholm. www.nobelprize.org

Krugman, P. (1980). Scale economies, product differentiation, and the pattern of trade. *The American Economic Review, 70*(5), 950–959.

Krugman, P. (1991). *Geography and trade*. MIT Press.

Krugman, P. (1991). Increasing return and economic geography. *Journal of Political Economy, 99*(3), 483–499. doi:10.1086/261763

Krugman, P. (1993a). On the relationship between trade theory and location theory. *Review of International Economics, 1*(2), 110–122. doi:10.1111/j.1467-9396.1993.tb00009.x

Krugman, P. (1999). The role of geography in development. *International Regional Science Review, 22*(2), 142–161. doi:10.1177/016001799761012307

Krupp, R. E. (2020). Expert report on the cross-border effects of the continuation of lignite mining in Turów (Poland) on water in Germany. https://www.greenpeace.org/static/planet4-poland-stateless/062974b1-turow_one_pager_summary_krupp_eng.pdf

Kshatri, S. S., Singh, D., Narain, B., Bhatia, S., Quasim, M. T., & Sinha, G. R. (2021). An empirical analysis of machine learning algorithms for crime prediction using stacked generalization: An ensemble approach. *IEEE Access: Practical Innovations, Open Solutions*, 9, 67488–67500. doi:10.1109/ACCESS.2021.3075140

Kubanov, R. (2014). Vymohy do profesiinoi pidhotovky fakhivtsiv ekonomichnykh spetsialnostei ta yikh realizatsiia v osvitnomu protsesi vyshchoho navchalnoho zakladu [Requirements for professional training of economic specialists and their implementation in the main process of a higher educational institution]. *Naukovyi visnyk Melitopolskoho derzhavnoho pedahohichnoho universytetu [Scientific Bulletin of the Melitopol State Pedagogoical University]*, 2(13), 294–301 (in Ukr.).

Kulshreshtha, S., & Kulshrestha, R. (2019). The emerging importance of "homestays" in the Indian hospitality sector. *Worldwide Hospitality and Tourism Themes*, 11(4), 458–466. doi:10.1108/WHATT-04-2019-0024

Kurowska-Pysz, J., Szczepańska-Woszczyna, K., Štverková, H., & Kašík, J. (2018). The catalysts of cross-border cooperation development in euroregions. *Polish Journal of Management Studies*, 18(1), 180–193. doi:10.17512/pjms.2018.18.1.14

Kyeong-Rok, M., Keon-Woo, L., & Kyung-Nam, K. (2021). Forecast of long-term trend of system marginal price with amounts of machine learning train data. *Journal of the Korean Solar Energy Society*, 41(5), 13–24. doi:10.7836/kses.2021.41.5.013

Lancaster, K. J. (1966). A new approach to consumer theory. *Journal of Political Economy*, 74(2), 132–157. doi:10.1086/259131

Layard, R., Balnchard, O., Dornbusch, R., & Krugman, P. (1992). *East-West Migration. The Alternatives*. MIT Press.

Lazaroiu, G. C., & Roscia, M. (2012). Definition methodology for the smart cities model. *Energy*, 47(1), 326–332.

Le Galès, P., & Lequesne, C. (1998). *Regions in Europe*. Routledge.

Lee, J.-K., Park, J.-B., Shin, J.-R., & Lee, K. Y. (2005). A system marginal price forecasting method based on an artificial neural network using time and day information. *IFAC Proceedings Volumes, 38*(1), 122-127.

Lee, J. H., Phaal, R., & Lee, S. H. (2013). An integrated service-device-technology roadmap for smart city development. *Technological Forecasting and Social Change*, 80(2), 286–306.

Lee, L. F., & Yu, J. (2010). Estimation of Spatial Autoregressive Panel Data Models with Fixed Effects. *Journal of Econometrics*, 154(2), 165–185. doi:10.1016/j.jeconom.2009.08.001

Lee, W., & Kim, B. (2019). Business sustainability of start-ups based on government support: An empirical study of Korean start-ups. *Sustainability*, 11(18), 4851. doi:10.3390u11184851

Lee, Y. J., & Yang, Y. (2018). An impact of startup business performance by entrepreneurs' perceived importance, satisfaction, and level of meeting to expectaiion over government startup business aid programs. *Asia-Pac. J. Bus. Ventur. Entrep*, (13), 31–41.

Leminen, S., Rajahonka, M., & Westerlund, M. (2017). Towards third-generation living lab networks in cities. *Technology Innovation Management Review*, 7(11), 21–35. doi:10.22215/timreview/1118

LeSage, J. P., & Fischer, M. M. (2008). Spatial growth regressions: Model Specification, Estimation, and Interpretation. *Spatial Economic Analysis*, 3(3), 275–304. doi:10.1080/17421770802353758

LeSage, J. P., & Pace, R. (2009). *Introduction to Spatial Econometrics*. Chapman and Hall. doi:10.1201/9781420064254

Lesáková, L. (2012). The role of business incubators in supporting the SME start-up. *Acta Polytechnica Hungarica*, 9(3), 85–95.

Lewis, G. J., & Maund, D. L. (1976). The Urbanization of the Countryside: A Framework for Analysis. *Geografiska Annaler*, *58*(1), 17–27. doi:10.1080/04353684.1976.11879409

Li, C., & Guo, Z. (2002). Short-term system marginal price forecasting with hybrid module. *Proceedings. International Conference on Power System Technology*, 4, 2426-2430. 10.1109/ICPST.2002.1047221

Lindskog, H. (2004). Smart communities initiatives. *Proceedings of the ISOneWorld Conference.* Retrieved from https://www.researchgate.net/profile/Helena_Lindskog/publication/228371789_Smart_comm unities_initiatives/links/549812230cf2519f5a1db56d.pdf

Lisy, J. (2016). *Ekonómia* [Economics]. Wolters Kluver.

Lohmann, G., & Netto, A. P. (2016). *Tourism theory: Concepts, models, and systems.* Cabi.

Lombardi, M. J., Mohanty, M. S., & Shim, I. (2017). *The real effects of household debt in the short and long run.* Academic Press.

Long, F., Liu, J., Zhang, S., Yu, H., & Jiang, H. (2018). Development characteristics and evolution mechanism of homestay agglomeration in Mogan Mountain, China. *Sustainability*, *10*(9), 2964.

Lo, V., & Schamp, E. W. (2001). Finanzplätze auf globalen Märkten – Beispiel Frankfurt/Main. *Geographische Rundschau*, *53*(7/8), 26–31.

Lucas, R. (1997). Internal migration in developing countries. Handbook of Population and Family Economics, (vol. 1, pp. 721-798). Elsevier.

Lucas, R. E. Jr. (1988). On the mechanics of economic development. *Journal of Monetary Economics*, *22*(1), 3–42. doi:10.1016/0304-3932(88)90168-7

Lue, C. C., Crompton, J. L., & Fesenmaier, D. R. (1993). Conceptualization of multidimensional pleasure trips. *Annals of Tourism Research*, *20*, 289–301.

Lüer, Ch. (2021). Study on providing public transport in cross-border regions. Mapping of existing services and legal obstacles: bus line 831A Zittau (Germany) – Bogatynia (Poland): case study report. European Commission.

Lüthi, S., Thierstein, A., & Goebel, D. (2010). Intra-firm and extra-firm linkages in the knowledge economy: The case of the emerging mega-city region of Munich. *Global Networks*, *10*(1), 114–137. doi:10.1111/j.1471-0374.2010.00277.x

Maciejewska, B. (2021). *Dziura kopalni Turów pożre sudecki kurort ze średniowiecznym DNA* [The Turów mine hole will devour the Sudetes resort with its medieval DNA]. WYBORCZA. https://wroclaw.wyborcza.pl/wroclaw/7,35771,26760522,dziura-kopalnii-turow-pozre-wielowiekowy-sudecki-kurort-maciejewska.html

Mack, O. (2003). *Konfiguration und Koordination von Unternehmensnetzwerken. Ein allgemeines Netzwerkmodell [Configuration and coordination of corporate network, a General Network model].* Springer Gabler. doi:10.1007/978-3-322-81488-3

Mair, C. A., & Thivierge-Rikard, R. V. (2019). The Strength of Strong Ties for Older Rural Adults: Regional Distinctions in the Relationship Between Social Interaction and Subjective Well-Being. *International Journal of Aging & Human Development*, *70*(2), 119–143. doi:10.2190/AG.70.2.b PMID:20405586

Makarewicz, N. (2021). *Spór o Turów. Związkowcy: Dlaczego pan Kurtyka jest jeszcze ministrem?* [The Turów dispute. Trade unionists: Why is Mr. Kurtyka still a minister?] RMF. https://www.rmf24.pl/raporty/raport-kopalnia-turow/news-spor-o-turow-zwiazkowcy-dlaczego-pan-kurtyka-jest-jeszcze-mi,nId,5563389#crp_state=1

Malá, L. (2020). Financování refionálního rozvoje [Financing of Regional Development]. In *Regiony budoucnosti – spolupráce, bezpečí, efektivity: Inspirace pro rozvoj měst a regionů s příklady dobré praxe [Regions of the future cooperation, safety, and efficiency: Inspiration for the development of cities and regions with examples of good practices]*. Grada Publishing.

Mammone, A., Turchi, M., & Cristianini, N. (2009). Support vector machines. *Wiley Interdisciplinary Reviews: Computational Statistics*, *1*(3), 283–289. doi:10.1002/wics.49

Mankiw, N. G., Romer, D., & Weil, D. N. (1992). Contribution to the Empirics of Economic Growth. *The Quarterly Journal of Economics*, *107*(2), 407–437. doi:10.2307/2118477

Marcouiller, D. W. (1997). Toward Integrative Tourism Planning in Rural America. *Journal of Planning Literature*, *11*(3), 337–357. doi:10.1177/088541229701100306

Markert, P. (2018). Wirtschaftsförderung und Standortmarketing [Business promotion and location marketing]. In H. Meffert, B. Spinnen, & J. Block (Eds.), *Praxishandbuch City- und Stadtmarketing [Practical Handbook of City and Town Marketing]* (pp. 205–223). Springer Gabler.

Marshall, A. (1890). *Principles of economics* (8th ed.).

Marshall, A. (1890). Some aspects of competition." The address of the president of section F—Economic Science and Statistics—of the British Association, at the Sixtiet Meeting, held at Leeds, in September 1890. *Journal of the Royal Statistical Society*, *53*(4), 612–643. doi:10.2307/2979546

Martens, R. (1976). *Sotsialnaya psikhologiya i sport [Social psychology and sport]*. Fyzkultura y sport [Physial Education and sports].

Maruri, I., Arboleda, L., & Barrachina, M. (2004). Un modelo de gravedad ampliado para la inmigración internacional en España. [An expanded gravity model for international immigration in Spain.] *RVEH, 12*(3), 149-169

Maslow, A. (2003). Samoaktualizaciya [Self-actualization]. *Prosveshchennyy menedzhment, Organizacionnaya teoriya [Enlightened Management, Organizational Theory]* (N. Levkinoy, A. C. Hekha, Trans. in Eng.). Piter, 41-147..

Maslow, A. (2006). *Motivatsiya i lichnost [Motivation and personality]*. Piter..

Massey, D., Arango, J., Hugo, G., Kouaouci, A., Pellegrino, A., & Taylor, J. E. (1998). *Worlds in Motion. Understanding International Migration at the End of the Millenium*. Oxford University Press.

Matarasso, F. (1997). *Use or Ornament? The Social Impact of Participation in the Arts*. Comedia.

Mathworks. (2022a). *Classification ensemble*. Accessed on 29 June 2022. Available from: https://www.mathworks.com/help/stats/classreg.learning.classif.classificationensemble-class.html

Mathworks. (2022b). *Assess classifier performance in classification learner*. Accessed on 29 June 2022. Available from: https://es.mathworks.com/help/stats/assess-classifier-performance.html

Mccall, C. (2013). European Union Cross-Border Cooperation and Conflict Amelioration. *Space and Polity*, *17*(2), 197–216. doi:10.1080/13562576.2013.817512

McCann, P. (2013). *Modern urban and regional economics*. Oxford University Press.

McGowan, E. (2022 April 7). What Is a Startup Company, Anyway? *StartUps*. https://www.startups.com/library/expert-advice/what-is-a-startup-company

McKinsey Global Institute. (2021). *56 DELTA skills*. Author.

Meijer, A., & Bolívar, M. P. R. (2016). Governing the smart city: A review of the literature on smart urban governance. *Revue Internationale des Sciences Administratives, 82*(2), 417–435.

Meijers, E. (2007). From central place to network model: Theory and evidence on paradigm change. *Tijdschrift voor Economische en Sociale Geografie, 98*(2), 245–259. doi:10.1111/j.1467-9663.2007.00394.x

Merki, C. M. (Ed.). (2005). *Europas Finanzzentren. Geschichte und Bedeutung im 20.* Jahrhundert.

Město Frýdlant. (2019). *Zachraňte vodu v pohraničí, podepište petici* [Save the water in the border area, sign the petition]. Město Frýdlant. https://www.mesto-frydlant.cz/cs/obcan/archiv/archiv-2019/zachrante-vodu-v-pohranici-podepiste-petici.html

Mill, J. (1980). *Osnovy politicheskoy ekonomiki [Basics of political economy]* (Trans. in Eng.). (Vol. 1). Progress..

Millinton, J. (1994). Migration, Wages, Unenployment and the Housing Market. A Literature Review. *International Journal of Manpower, 15*(9/10), 89–133. doi:10.1108/01437729410074227

MINCOTUR. (2022). Estrategia de Sostenibilidad Turística en Destino aprobada en la Conferencia Secotiral [Destination tourism sustainability strategy approved at the sectorial conference]. *Sede electronica.* https://sede.serviciosmin.gob.es/es-es/procedimientoselectronicos/Paginas/detalle-procedimientos.aspx?IdProcedimiento=253

Ministerstvo vnitra ČR. (2017). *Metodika zavádění řízení kvality ve služebních úřadech: Podpora profesionalizace a kvality státní služby a státní správy* [Methodology for Implementing Quality Management in Service Offices: Promoting Professionalization and Quality of the Civil Service and Public Administration]. Czech Ministry of Interior.

Ministerstvo životního prostředí ČR (2022). *Dohoda mezi vládou České republiky a vládou Polské republiky o spolupráci k řešení vlivů těžební činnosti v povrchovém hnědouhelném dole Turów v Polské republice na území České republiky* [Agreement between the Government of the Czech Republic and the Government of the Republic of Poland on cooperation to address the effects of mining activity in the surface lignite mine Turów in the Republic of Poland on the territory of the Czech Republic]. MZP. https://www.mzp.cz/web/web-news2.nsf/EB4B0E394778ED4EC12587DD006687E5/$file/Turow_CZ-PL%20dohoda.pdf

Ministry of Information Society and Administration. (2017). Improving the Quality of the Public Sector Through the Common Assessment Framework (CAF). Ministry of Information Society and Administration & OSCE.

Ministry of Tourism (Hotels and Restaurants Division). (2019). Common National Standards and Guidelines for Classification of Incredible India Bed & Breakfast Establishments and Incredible India Homestay Establishments. Author.

Miskiewicz, J., & Ausloos, M. (2010). Has the World Economy Reached Its Globalization Limit? Physica A, 389(4), 797-806. DOI: .physa.2009.10.029 doi:10.1016/j

Mohamed, A. A. R., Best, R. J., Liu, X., & Morrow, D. J. (2022). Single electricity market forecasting and energy arbitrage maximization framework. *IET Renewable Power Generation, 16*(1), 105–124. doi:10.1049/rpg2.12345

Momot, T., & Muraev, Y. (2021). Model of organizational and information support of smart city strategy development in the conditions of digital economy. *Innovative Technologies and Scientific Solutions for Industries, 1*(15), 83-90.

Monzon, J. L., & Chaves, R. (2017). European Economic and Social Committee, Recent evolutions of the Social Economy in the European Union, p. 66.

Moon, J., & Jung, T. Y. (2020). A critical review of Korea's long-term contract for renewable energy auctions: The relationship between the import price of liquefied natural gas and system marginal price. *Utilities Policy, 67*, 101132. doi:10.1016/j.jup.2020.101132

Moore, J. F. (1993). Predators and prey: A new ecology of competition. *Harvard Business Review*, *71*(3), 75–86. PMID:10126156

Moran, P. A. P. (1950). Notes on Continuous Stochastic Phenomena. *Biometrika, 37,* 17-23.

More than 250 Smart City Projects Exist in 178 Cities Worldwide. (2017 March 16). Guidehouse Insights. Retrieved from https://guidehouseinsights.com/news-and-views/more-than-250-smart-city-projects-exist-in-178-cities-worldwide#:~:text=Click%20to%20tweet%3A%20According%20to,%2C%20buildings%2C%20and%20water%20goals

Morhunova, S. O., & Rezvan, O. O. (2017). *Treninh sotsialnoi vzaiemodii: navch.-metod. posibnyk [Social interaction training, educational and methodological manual].* Miskdruk.

Motoyama, Y., & Wiens, J. (2019). *Guidelines for Local and State Governments to Promote Entrepreneurship.* Ewing Marion Kauffman Foundation. https://cutt.ly/FkcTPlr

Mucherino, A., Papajorgji, P. J., & Pardalos, P. M. (2009). K-nearest neighbor classification. Data Mining in Agriculture, Springer Optimization and Its Applications, 34, 83-106. doi:10.1007/978-0-387-88615-2_4

Mur, J., Herrera, M., & Ruiz, M. (2012). Selecting the Most Adequate Spatial Weighting Matrix: A Study on Criteria. *MPRA Paper, 73700.*

Murayev, E.V. (2020). Development of a strategy for smart cities of Ukraine according to a balanced system of indicators in the digital economy. *Bulletin of Khmelnytsky National University, 4*(2), 106-109.

Musa, S. (2016). *Smart City Roadmap.* https://www. academia. edu/21181336/Smart_City_Roadmap

Muzhanova, T. M. (2017). "Smart City" as an innovative management model. *Economics. Management. Business (Atlanta, Ga.),* 2(20), 116–122.

Myrdal, G. (1957). *Rich Lands and Poor.* Harper and Row.

Nachira, F. (2002). Towards a network of digital business ecosystems fostering the local development. *European Commission Discussion Paper. Bruxelles*, p. 23.

Naidoo, P., & Pearce, P. L. (2018). Enclave tourism versus agritourism: The economic debate. *Current Issues in Tourism, 21*(17), 1946–1965. doi:10.1080/13683500.2016.1235554

Nam, T., & Pardo, T. A. (2011, September). Smart city as urban innovation: Focusing on management, policy, and context. *Proceedings of the International Conference on Theory and Practice of Electronic Governance*, 5.

National Planning Department. (2015). *El campo colombiano: un camino hacia el bienestar y la paz. Misión para la transformación del campo* [The Colombian countryside: a path to well-being and peace. Mission for the transformation of the countryside]. Departamento Nacional de Planeación.

Nie, L. (1993). *Die Bedeutung der Wirtschaftsförderungsgesellschaft für die regionale ökonomische Entwicklung im Land Nordrhein-Westfalen [The Importance of the Economic Development Agency for Regional Economic Development in the State of North Rhine-Westphalia]* [Unpublished doctoral dissertation, University of Bonn, Germany].

Noh, J., & Cho, H. C. (2020). Forecasting system marginal price using multilayer perceptron and nonlinear autoregressive exogenous model. *Journal of The Korean Society of Mineral and Energy Resources Engineers, 57*(6), 585–592. doi:10.32390/ksmer.2020.57.6.585

O'Leary, R., & Iredale, I. (1976). The marketing concept: Quo vadis? *European Journal of Marketing, 10*(3), 146–157. doi:10.1108/EUM0000000005043

Obeso, I. (2019). Definir la urbanización periférica: Conceptos y terminología. [Defining peripheral urbanization: concepts and terminology.]. *Eria*, *2*(2), 183–206. doi:10.17811/er.2.2019.183-206

Ocakoglu, K. O., & Tolga, A. C. (2018). Effective trading in Turkish electricity market: hedging with options. *Proceedings of the World Congress on Engineering*, 1.

Ocampo, J. (2017). La política comercial agropecuaria colombiana en el contexto internacional [Colombian agricultural trade policy in the international context]. *Coyuntura Económica: Investigación Económica y Social, 47*(1-2), 49-95.

Ocampo, J., & Perry, S. (1995). *El giro de la política agropecuaria* [The Shift In Agricultural Policy]. Tercer Mundo Editores – Departamento Nacional de Planeación.

OECD. (2020). *Strategy for the Slovak Republic (2019-2020).* OECD.

Oleński, J. (2016). Typology of Transborder Economies and the Need of Transborder Statistics in Globalized World. *International Journal on Transborder Economics. Politics and Statistics, 1*(1), 9–32.

Onaran, Ö. (2006). *Speculation-led growth and fragility in Turkey: Does EU make a difference or "can it happen again"?* Academic Press.

Onaran, Ö., & Stockhammer, E. (2005). Two different export-oriented growth strategies: Accumulation and distribution in Turkey and South Korea. *Emerging Markets Finance & Trade, 41*(1), 65–89. doi:10.1080/1540496X.2005.11052596

Opioła, W., & Böhm, H. (2022). Euroregions as political actors: Managing border policies in the time of Covid-19 in Polish borderlands. *Territory, Politics, Governance, 10*(6), 1–21. doi:10.1080/21622671.2021.2017339

Oppio, A., & Dell'Ovo, M. (2021). Cultural heritage preservation and territorial attractiveness: A spatial multidimensional evaluation approach. In *Cycling & Walking for Regional Development* (pp. 105–125). Springer.

Orden ICT. (2021). *Por la que se establecen las bases reguladoras de las ayudas para el Programa "Experiencias Turismo España" y se aprueba su convocatoria para el ejercicio 2021, en el marco del Plan de Recuperación, Transformación y Resiliencia. [establishing the regulatory bases for aid for the "Tourism Experiences Spain" Program and approving its call for the year 2021, within the framework of the Recovery, Transformation and Resilience Plan.]* BOE. https://www.boe.es/diario_boe/txt.php?id=BOE-A-2022-417

Ostergren, R. C., & Rice, J. G. (2004). *The Europeans. A Geography of People, Culture and Environment.* The Guilford Press.

Ottaviano, G., & Puga, D. (1997). Agglomeration in the global economy: a survey of the new economic geography. Center for Economic Performance. *Discussion Paper 356*, 1 – 32.

Özgül, A. U. (2018). *Spot price models in electricity markets: The case of Turkey* [PhD thesis]. Pamukkale University Institute of Social Sciences.

Özgüner, E., Tör, O. B., & Güven, A. N. (2017). Probabilistic day-ahead system marginal price forecasting with ANN for the Turkish electricity market. *Turkish Journal of Electrical Engineering and Computer Sciences, 25*(6), 4923–4935. doi:10.3906/elk-1612-206

Ozturk, I., & Kalyoncu, H. (2007). *Foreign direct investment and growth: An empirical investigation based on cross-country comparison.* Academic Press.

Paasi, A. (2011). Border theory: an unattainable dream or a realistic aim for border scholars? In Wastl- Walter, D. (Ed.)., A Research Companion to Border Studies (pp. 11-31). Ashgate.

Palatková, M. (2011). *Marketingový management destinací: strategický a taktický marketing destinace turismu, systém marketingového řízení destinace a jeho financování, řízení kvality v destinaci a informační systém destinace.* [*Marketing management of destinations: strategic and tactical marketing of the destination tourism, system of marketing management of the destination and its financing, quality management in the destination and information system of the destination.*] Grada.

Pancíř, T. (2020). *"K věci": Dopady koronaviru. Rozhovor s ředitelkou Středočeské centrály cestovního ruchu Zuzanou Vojtovou.* [*"To the point": The effects of the coronavirus. Interview with Zuzana Vojtová, Director of the Central Bohemian Tourist Board.*]. Podmailer. https://podmailer.com/podcast/k-v-ci/dopady-koronaviru-ve-st-ednich-echach-neotev-ely-d

Papaioannou, G. P., Papaioannou, P. G., & Parliaris, N. (2014). *Modeling the stylized facts of wholesale system marginal price (SMP) and the impacts of regulatory reforms on the Greek Electricity Market.* arXiv preprint arXiv:1401.5452

Parga-Dans, E., González, P. A., & Enríquez, R. O. (2020). The social value of heritage: Balancing the promotion-preservation relationship in the Altamira World Heritage Site, Spain. *Journal of Destination Marketing & Management*, *18*, 100499.

Parr, J. B., & Budd, L. (2000). Financial Services and the Urban System: An Exploration. *Urban Studies (Edinburgh, Scotland)*, *37*(3), 593–610. doi:10.1080/0042098002131

Parvin, H., Alizadeh, H., & Minati, B. (2010). A modification on k-nearest neighbor classifier. *Global Journal of Computer Science and Technology*, *10*(14), 37–41.

Paskaleva-Shapira, K. A. (2007). New paradigms in city tourism management: Redefining destination promotion. *Journal of Travel Research*, *46*(1), 108–114. doi:10.1177/0047287507302394

Pászto, V., Macků, K., Burian, J., Pánek, J., & Tuček, P. (2019). Capturing cross-border continuity: The case of the Czech-Polish borderland. *Moravian Geographical Reports*, *27*(2), 122–138. doi:10.2478/mgr-2019-0010

Patel, A. (2019). *Uttarayan and the Built Environment: Perspectives from a World Heritage City.* Sahapedia.

Pearce, D. G. (2015). Destination management in New Zealand: Structures and functions. *Journal of Destination Marketing & Management*, *4*(1), 1–12. doi:10.1016/j.jdmm.2014.12.001

Pechlaner, H. & Philipp, J. (2022). *Moving from Traditional Destination Understanding Towards a Holistic 'Ecosystem of Hospitality* [Paper presentation]. Rethinking Tourism, Hospitality and Events for a Better Future, Ukulhas, Maledives.

Pechlaner, H., & Fischer, E. (Eds.). (2009). Strategische Produktentwicklung im Standortmanagement: Wettbewerbsvorteile für den Tourismus [Strategic Product Development in Location Management: Competitive Advantages for the Tourism Industry]. Erich Schmidt Verlag.

Pechlaner, H., Philipp, J., & Bachinger, M. (2022). *The Entrepreneurial Destination Ecosystem – On the pathway to resilient destinations* [Paper presentation]. 5th Advances in Destination Management Forum, Kalmar, Sweden.

Pechlaner, H., Philipp, J., & Olbrich, N. (2022). Destination Governance: The New Role of Destination Management, Stakeholder Networks and Sustainability. In J. Saarinen & C.M. Hall (Eds.) The Handbook of Tourism Governance. Edward Elgar.

Pechlaner, H., Thees, H., Eckert, C., & Zacher, D. (2018). Vom Entrepreneurship Ecosystem zur Entrepreneurial Destination – Perspektiven einer Standortentwicklung am Beispiel der Freizeitszene München [From entrepreneurship ecosystem to entrepreneurial destination- Perspectives of location development using the example of the leisure scene in Munich]. In M. Bruhn & K. Hartwig (Eds.), Service Business Development, Band 2: Methoden – Erlösmodelle, Marketinginstrumente [Methods—revenue models, marketing instruments], (pp. 477-508). Springer.

Pechlaner, H. (Ed.). (2019). *Destination und Lebensraum: Perspektiven touristischer Entwicklung [Destination and living space: Prospects for tourism development].* Springer Gabler. doi:10.1007/978-3-658-28110-6

Pechlaner, H., Bieger, T., & Weiermair, K. (Eds.). (2006). *Attraktionsmanagement: Führung und Steuerung von Attraktionspunkten [Attraction Management: Management and Control of Attraction Points].* Linde.

Pechlaner, H., Hamann, E.-M., & Fischer, E. (Eds.). (2008). *Industrie und Tourismus: Innovatives Standortmanagement für Produkte und Dienstleistungen [Industry and tourism: Innovative location management for products and services].* Erich Schmidt Verlag.

Pechlaner, H., Olbrich, N., Philipp, J., & Thees, H. (Eds.). (2022). *Towards an Ecosystem of Hospitality – Location:City:Destination.* Graffeg Publishing.

Pechlaner, H., & Raich, F. (2005). Vom Destination Management zur Destination Governance [From destination management to destination governance]. In T. Bieger, C. Laesser, & P. Beritelli (Eds.), *Jahrbuch der Schweizerischen Tourismuswissenschaft 2004/2005 [Yearbook of Swiss Tourism Studies]* (pp. 221–234). IDT-HSG Institut für Öffentliche Dienstleistungen und Tourismus.

Pechlaner, H., Raich, F., & Kofink, L. (2011). Elements of Corporate Governance in Tourism Organizations. *Tourismos: An International Multidisciplinary Journal of Tourism, 6*(3), 57–76.

Pechlaner, H., & Schön, S. (Eds.). (2010). *Regionale Baukultur als Erfolgsfaktor im Tourismus: Nachhaltige Vermarktung von Destinationen [Regional building culture as a success factor in tourism: Sustainable marketing of destinations].* Erich Schmidt Verlag.

Pechlaner, H., Volgger, M., & Nordhorn, C. (2017). Hospitality Management ist mehr als Service Management: Skizzen eines umfassenden Qualitätsansatzes [Hospitality management is more than a service management: outlines of a comprehensive approach to quality]. In H. Pechlaner & M. Volgger (Eds.), *Die Gesellschaft auf Reisen – Eine Reise in die Gesellschaft [Traveling Society—A Journey into Society],* (pp. 139–162). Springer Fachmedien. doi:10.1007/978-3-658-14114-1_8

Pecqueur, B. (2001). Qualité et développement territorial: L'hypothèse du panier de biens et de services territorialisés. [Quality and territorial development: the hypothesis of the basket of territorialized goods and services.]. *Économie Rurale (Paris), 261*(1), 37–49. doi:10.3406/ecoru.2001.5217

Pellegrini, P.A. & Fotheringham, A.S., (2002). Modelling Spatial Choice: A Review and Synthesis in a Migration Context. *Progress in Human Geography, 26* (4), 487-510.

Pénzes, J., & Demeter, G. (2021). Peripheral areas and their distinctive characteristics: The case of Hungary. *Moravian Geographical Reports, 29*(3), 217–230. doi:10.2478/mgr-2021-0016

Perfetti, J. (2011). Colombia's Agricultural Potential Supply in a New Market Environment. In La política comercial del sector agrícola en Colombia (pp. 103 - 133). Cuadernos de Fedesarrollo 38.

Perfetti, J., & Cortés, S. (2013). La agricultura y el desarrollo de los territorios rurales. In *Políticas para el desarrollo de la agricultura en Colombia. FEDESARROLLO- Sociedad de Agricultores de Colombia* (pp. 1–64). SAC.

Persic, M., & Magas, D. (2005). *Integrated Destination Management* [Paper presentation]. *4th International Scientific Conference on Kinesiology,* Optija, Croatia.

Pesaran, M. H., & Shin, Y. (1999). An Autoregressive Distributed Lag Modelling Approach to Co-integration Analysis. In S. Strom (Ed.), *Econometrics and Economic Theory in 20th Century: The Ragnar Frisch Centennial Symposium.* Cambridge, UK: Cambridge University. 10.1017/CCOL521633230.011

Pesaran, M. H., Shin, Y., & Smith, R. J. (2001). Bounds testing approaches to the analysis of level relationships. *Journal of Applied Econometrics*, *16*(3), 289–326. doi:10.1002/jae.616

Petersen, T. (2022). Demographic change, decarbonization and digitalization – megatrends changing the outlook for tourism. In H. Pechlaner, N. Olbrich, J. Philipp, & H. Thees (Eds.), *Towards an Ecosystem of Hospitality – Location:City:Destination* (pp. 24–31). Graffeg Publishing.

Peters, M., & Eichelberger, S. (2022). Framework conditions of entrepreneurial ecosystems in destinations. In H. Pechlaner, N. Olbrich, J. Philipp, & H. Thees (Eds.), *Towards an Ecosystem of Hospitality – Location:City:Destination* (pp. 60–67). Graffeg Publishing.

Pflüger, M., & Tabuchi, T. (2016) Comparative advantage and agglomeration of economic activity. Institute for the Study of Labor. *Discussion Paper 10273*. Bonn.

PGE. (2022). *Ochrona szrodowiska* [Environmental protection]. PGE. https://kwbturow.pgegiek.pl/Ochrona-srodowiska

Philipp, J., Thees, H., & Olbrich, N. (2022). Towards common ground: Integrating destination, location and living space. In H. Pechlaner, N. Olbrich, J. Philipp, & H. Thees (Eds.), *Towards an Ecosystem of Hospitality – Location:City:Destination* (pp. 32–41). Graffeg Publishing.

Philipp, J., Thees, H., Olbrich, N., & Pechlaner, H. (2022). Towards an Ecosystem of Hospitality: The Dynamic Future of Destinations. *Sustainability*, *14*(2), 821. doi:10.3390u14020821

Pike, A., Rodríguez-Pose, A., & Tomaney, J. (2007). What kind of local and regional development and for whom? *Regional Studies*, *41*(9), 1253–1269. doi:10.1080/00343400701543355

Pike, S. (2012). *Destination Marketing. An Integrated Marketing Communication Approach*. Elsevier.

Pinilla, V., & Sáez, L. A. (2020). La despoblación rural en España: génesis de un problema y políticas innovadoras. [Rural depopulation in Spain: genesis of a problem and innovative policies.] SSPA. http://sspa-network.eu/wp-content/uploads/Informe-CEDDAR-def-logo.pdf

Piore, M. J. (1979). *Birds of Passage: Migrant Labor in Industrial Societies*. Cambridge University Press. doi:10.1017/CBO9780511572210

Pissarides, C. A., & Wadsworth, J. (1989). Unemployment and the inter-regional mobility of labour. *Economic Journal (London)*, *99*(397), 739–755. doi:10.2307/2233768

PNUD. (2011). *Colombia rural Razones para la esperanza* [Rural Colombia Reasons for hope]. Informe Nacional de Desarrollo Urbano.

Poon, J. P. H., Eldredge, B., & Yeung, D. (2004). Rank Size Distribution of International Financial Centers. *International Regional Science Review*, *27*(4), 411–430. doi:10.1177/0160017604267629

Porteous, D. J. (1999). The Development of Financial Centres: Location, Information Externalities and Path Dependence. In R. Martin (Ed.), *Money and the space economy* (pp. 95–114).

Porter, M. (1980). *Competitive strategy: techniques for analyzing industries and competitors*. The Free Press.

Postma, A., Buda, D.-M., & Gugerell, K. (2017). The future of city tourism. *Journal of Tourism Futures*, *3*(2), 95–101. doi:10.1108/JTF-09-2017-067

Posylkina, O. V., & Bratishko, Yu. S. (2016). Doslidzhennia vymoh robotodavtsiv do kandydativ na posadu menedzhera iz sotsialnoi vidpovidalnosti suchasnykh farmatsevtychnykh pidpryiemstv [Study of employers' requirements for candidates for the position of social responsibility manager of modern pharmaceutical enterprises]. *Upravlinnia, ekonomika ta zabezpechennia yakosti v farmatsii [Management, economics, and quality assurance in pharmacy]*, *3*(47), 38-44 (in Ukr.).

Potter, A., & Studies, H. W. (2014). *Revisiting Marshall's agglomeration economies: Technological relatedness and the evolution of the Sheffield metals cluster*. Taylor & Francis.

Poulain, M. (1981). Contribution à l'analyse spatiale dúne matrice de migratin interne. [Contribution to the spatial analysis of the internal migration matrix.] Louvaine-La-Neuve, ed. Cabay.

Poyrazoglu, G. (2021). Determination of price zones during transition from uniform to zonal electricity market: A case study for Turkey. *Energies*, *14*(4), 1014. doi:10.3390/en14041014

Prabavathi, M., & Gnanadass, R. (2018). Electric power bidding model for practical utility system. *Alexandria Engineering Journal*, *57*(1), 277–286. doi:10.1016/j.aej.2016.12.002

Presenza, A., Sheehan, L., & Ritchie, J. B. (2005). Towards a model of the roles and activities of destination management organizations. *Journal of Hospitality. Tourism and Leisure Science*, *3*(1), 1–16.

Quality Council. (2022). *Program CAF. Oficiální portál Rady kvality ČR* [Official portal of the Quality Council of the Czech Republic]. Quality Council. https://www.narodniportal.cz

Raeymaeckers, P., & Kenis, P. (2015). The influence of shared participant governance on the integration of service networks: A comparative social network analysis. *International Public Management Journal*, *19*(3), 397–426. doi:10.1080/10967494.2015.1062443

Rana, R., Rana, K., & Chhabra, G. (2021). Economic Development of Rural India Through Establishment of Agri-Tech Park. *Indian Journal of Economics and Finance*, *1*(2), 15–23. doi:10.35940/ijef.B2506.111221

Ravenstein, E. G. (1885). *The laws of migration*. Royal Statistical Society. doi:10.2307/2979181

Rawat, S. (2020). *Rural Tourism and Sustainable development in Darjeeling Hills, West Bengal: Case study of Lepchajagat*. Academic Press.

Ray, C. (2006). Neo-endogenous rural development in the EU. In P. Cloke, T. Marsden, & P. Mooney (Eds.), *Handbook of Rural Studies*. Sage. doi:10.4135/9781848608016.n19

Reddel, T. (2002). Beyond participation, hierarchies, management and markets: 'New' governance and place policies. *Australian Journal of Place Administration*, *61*(1), 50–63. doi:10.1111/1467-8500.00258

Reina, M., Zuluaga, S., Bermúdez, W., & Oviedo, S. (2011). Protección e incentivos agrícolas en Colombia [Agricultural protection and incentives in Colombia]. In La Política Comercial del Sector Agrícola en Colombia. Cuadernos de Fedesarrollo 38. FEDESARROLLO.

Reinhold, S., Beritelli, P., & Grünig, R. (2019). A business model typology for destination management organizations. *Tourism Review*, *74*(6), 1135–1152. doi:10.1108/TR-03-2017-0065

Renting, H., Marsden, T., & Marsden, J. (2003). Understanding alternative food networks: Exploring the role of Short Food Supply Chains in Rural Development. *Environment & Planning*, *35*(3), 393–411. doi:10.1068/a3510

Renz, T. (1998). *Management in internationalen Unternehmensnetzwerken [Management in international corporate networks]*. Springer Gabler. doi:10.1007/978-3-322-89492-2

Rezvan, O. O. (2014). *Formuvannia profesiino-refleksyvnoi pozytsii maibutnikh fakhivtsiv avtomobilno-dorozhnoi haluzi [Formation of a professional and reflexive position of future specialists in the automobile and road industry].* Tochka.

Ricardo, D. (2001). *The principles of political economy and taxation.* EconLib. https://www.econlib.org/library/Ricardo/ricPCover.html

Ricci, L. (1997). A Ricardian Model of New Trade and Location Theory. *Journal of Economic Integration, 12*(1), 47–61. doi:10.11130/jei.1997.12.1.47

Ricci, L. (1999). Economic geography and comparative advantage: Agglomeration versus specialization. *European Economic Review, 43*(2), 357–377. doi:10.1016/S0014-2921(98)00065-8

Roback, J. (1988). Wages, rents, and amenities: Differences among workers and regions. *Economic Inquiry, 26*(1), 23–41. doi:10.1111/j.1465-7295.1988.tb01667.x

Robinson, J. (2005). Urban geography: World cities, or a world of cities. *Progress in Human Geography, 29*(6), 757–765. doi:10.1191/0309132505ph582pr

Rodrik, D., & Velasco, A. (1999). *Short-term capital flows* (No. w7364). National Bureau of Economic Research.

Rogers, K. R. (1984). *Empatiya. Psihologiya emociy [Empathy. Psychology of emotions]* (Trans. in Eng.). MGU.

Rogers, K. R. (2000). *Stanovlenie lichnosti: vzglyad na psihoterapiyu [Becoming a personality: a look at the psychotherapy]* (Trans. in Eng.). EKSMO-Press..

Romanovskiy, A. G., Mihaylichenko, V. E., & Gren, L. N. (2018). *Pedagogika liderstva: monografiya [Pedagogics of Leadership: a monography].* FLP Brovin A. V.

Romanovskyi, O. H., Ponomarov, O. S., & Reznik, S. M. (2014). *Otsinka konkurentospromozhnosti fakhivtsia i yakosti yoho profesiinoi pidhotovky: navch.-metod. posib [Evaluation of the competitiveness of a specialist and the quality of his professional training: educational and methodological manual].* NTU, KhPI.

Romao, J., Kourtit, K., Neuts, B., & Nijkamp, P. (2018). The smart city as a common place for tourists and residents: A structural analysis of the determinants of urban attractiveness. *Cities (London, England), 78*, 67–75. doi:10.1016/j.cities.2017.11.007

Romeo, R., Russo, L., Parisi, F., Notarianni, M., Manuelli, S., & Carvao, S. (2021). *Mountain tourism–Towards a more sustainable path.* Academic Press.

Romer, P. (1986). Increasing Returns and Long-Run Growth. *Journal of Political Economy, 94*(5), 1002–1037. doi:10.1086/261420

Romer, P. M. (1990). Endogenous technological change. *Journal of Political Economy, 98*(5, Part 2), S71–S102. doi:10.1086/261725

Rong-Da Liang, A. (2017). Considering the role of agritourism co-creation from a service-dominant logic perspective. *Tourism Management, 61*, 354–367. doi:10.1016/j.tourman.2017.02.002

Rong-Da Liang, A., Hsiao, T. Y., Chen, D. J., & Lin, J. H. (2020). Agritourism: Experience design, activities, and revisit intention. *Tourism Review.*

Rosen, S. (1974). Hedonic prices and implicit markets: Product differentiation in pure competition. *Journal of Political Economy, 82*(1), 34–55. doi:10.1086/260169

Rostow, W. W. (1978). *The world economy: History and prospect* (No. 04; HC51, R6).

Sachsen.de. 2022. *Statistik* [Statistics]. https://www.statistik.sachsen.de

Sahin, C. (2018). Consideration of network constraints in the Turkish day ahead electricity market. *International Journal of Electrical Power & Energy Systems, 102*, 245–253. doi:10.1016/j.ijepes.2018.04.027

Sainaghi, R. (2006). From contents to processes: Versus a dynamic destination management model (DDMM). *Tourism Management, 27*(5), 1053–1063. doi:10.1016/j.tourman.2005.09.010

Samuelson, P. (1983) Thünen at two hundred. [Thünen at two hundred.] *Journal of Economic Literature, 21*(4), 1468-1488

Sassen, S. (1991). *The global city*. London, Tokyo. Princeton.

Savchuk, A. (2018). *Concept "Umnyi Gorod": Main provisions, Description, Device, Examples*. Retrieved from https://fb.ru/article/399297/kontseptsiya-umnyiy-gorod-osnovnyie-polojeniya-opisanie-ustroystvo-primeryi

Schamp, E. W. (2009). Das Finanzzentrum – ein Cluster? Ein multiskalarer Ansatz und seine Evidenz am Beispiel von Frankfurt/Rhein-Main. *Zeitschrift für Wirtschaftsgeographie, 53*(1-2), 1–2, 89–105. doi:10.1515/zfw.2009.0006

Schmidt, R. S., & Grote, M. (2005). *Was ist und was braucht ein bedeutender Finanzplatz?* Working Paper Series Finance and Accounting 150, Department of Economics, Johann Wolfgang Goethe-University Frankfurt.

Schmied, M., Götz, K., Kreilkamp, E., Buchert, M., Hellwig, T., & Otten, S. (2009). *Traumziel Nachhaltigkeit: Innovative Vermarktungskonzepte nachhaltiger Tourismuskonzepte für den Massenmarkt [Dream goal of sustainabiltity: Innovative marketing concepts for sustainable tourism concepts for the mass market]*. Physica-Verlag.

Schneider-Sliwa, R., Erismann, C., & Saalfrank, C. (2009). *Das Image von Basel: Wohnort, Arbeitsort, Touristendestination und Unternehmensstandort [The image of Basel: place of residence, place of work, tourist destination, and business location]*. Schwabe Verlag.

Schuster, J. M. (2007). Participation studies and cross-national comparison: Proliferation, prudence, and possibility. *Cultural Trends, 16*(2), 99–196.

Scotchmer, S., & Thisee, J. (1992). Space and competition a puzzle. *The Annals of Regional Science, 26*, 269–286.

Selod, H., & Shilpi, F. (2021). Rural-urban migration in developing countries: Lessons from the literatura. *Regional Science and Urban Economics, 91*.

Semichenko, V. A. (2004). *Problemy motivacii povedeniya i deyatelnosti cheloveka. Modulnyy kurs psihologii. Modul,, Napravlenost": lekcii, prakticheskie zanyatiya, zadaniya dlya samostoyatelnoy raboty [Problems of motivation of behavior and human activity. Modular psychology course. "Direction" module: lectures, practical exercises, tasks for independent work]*. Millenium.

Şenocak, F. (2018). *Elektrik piyasa takas fiyatı ağırlıklı ortalamasının anfıs ve yapay sinir ağları ile tahmini [Forecasting of weighted average electricity market clearing price using artificial neural networks and anfis] [Master Thesis]*. Karadeniz Technical University.

Seo, J. H., Perry, V. G., Tomczyk, D., & Solomon, G. T. (2014). Who benefits most? *The effects of managerial assistance on high-versus low-performing small businesses. Journal of Business Research, 67*(1), 2845–2852. doi:10.1016/j.jbusres.2012.07.003

Sforzi, F. (2007). Il contributo dei distretti industriali al cambiamento dell'economia italiana. [The contribution of industrial districts to the change of the Italian economy.] *Economía italiana, 1*, 79-104.

Shah, C., Shah, S., & Shah, G. L. (2020). Agritourism as a Local Economic Development Tool for Rural Hill Regions. In *Extension Strategies for Doubling Farmer Income* (pp. 19–33). https://www.researchgate.net/publication/343569529

Shah, N., & Dave, D. (2020). The Scope and Challenges of Agro-tourism in India. GH Patel Postgraduate Institute of Business Management, 10.

Shapiro, J. M. (2006). Smart cities: Quality of life, productivity, and the growth effects of human capital. *The Review of Economics and Statistics*, *88*(2), 324–335.

Shapovalov, V. I. (2017). *Konkurentosposobnost lichnosti v paradigme innovacionnogo pedagogicheskogo menedzhmenta [Competitiveness of the individual in the paradigm of innovative pedagogical management]*. Uchil. http://uchil.net/?cm=83719...

Shin, H., Kim, T. H., Kwag, K., & Kim, W. (2021). A comparative study of pricing mechanisms to reduce side-payments in the electricity market: A case study for South Korea. *Energies*, *14*(12), 3395. doi:10.3390/en14123395

Siatkowski, J., Olszewski, M., & Konik, J. (2022). *The Turów Mine crisis and its impact on Czech-Polish cross-border cooperation: evaluation, conclusions and recommendations*. Report available on request from the authors.

Silvestre Rodríguez, J. (2000). Aproximaciones teóricas a los movimientos migratorios contemporáneos: Un estado de la cuestión. [Theoretical approaches to contemporary migratory movements: A state of the art.]

Singh, A. (1997). Financial liberalisation, stockmarkets and economic development. *Economic Journal (London)*, *107*(442), 771–782. doi:10.1111/j.1468-0297.1997.tb00042.x

Sinning, H. (2011). Europäische Stadt und Stadtmanagement: 29 Korrelationen, Widersprüche, Perspektiven [European city and urban management: 29 correlations, contradictions, perspectives]. In O. Frey & F. Koch (Eds.), *Die Zukunft der Europäischen Stadt: Stadtpolitik, Stadtplanung und Stadtgesellschaft im Wandel [The future of the European city: urban politics, urban planning, and urban society in transition]* (pp. 208–228). VS Verlag für Sozialwissenschaften. doi:10.1007/978-3-531-92653-7_13

Sirin, S. M., & Yilmaz, B. N. (2021). The impact of variable renewable energy technologies on electricity markets: An analysis of the Turkish balancing market. *Energy Policy*, *151*, 112093. doi:10.1016/j.enpol.2020.112093

Smachilo, V., Halina, V., & Chaika, D. (2021). Formation of a local startup ecosystem. *Economy and Society*, *2021*(23). doi:10.32782/2524-0072/2021-23-9

Smart Cities. (2022). *EU Regional and Urban Development*. https://ec.europa.eu/info/es-regionu-ir-miestu-pletra/temos/miestai-ir-miestu-pletra/miestu-iniciatyvos/smart-cities_en#what-are-smart-cities

Smart City Index. (2020). https://www.imd.org/smart-city-observatory/smart-city-index/

Smart City Profiles. (n.d.). https://www.imd.org/smart-city-observatory/smart-city-profiles/

Smith, A. (1997). *Teoriya nravstvennyh chuvstv [Moral sentiment theory]*. Respublika..

Smith, A. (2007). *Issledovanie o prirode i prichinah bogatstva narodov [Research on the nature and causes of the wealth of nations]*. Eksmo..

Smith, J. M. C. (2018). Transforming Places. In J. Smith (Ed.), *Transforming Travel: Realising the Potential of Sustinable Tourism* (pp. 63–78). CABI. doi:10.1079/9781786394194.0063

SOCR ČR. (2020). *Dopady na cestovní ruch způsobené pandemií koronaviru. [Impacts on tourism caused by the coronavirus pandemic.]*. SOCR CR. http://www.socr.cz/clanek/dopady-na-cestovni-ruch-zpusobene-pandemii-koronaviru/

Söderbaum, F., & Shaw, T. M. (2004). *Theories of New Regionalism*. Palgrave Macmillan.

Solomon, G. T., Bryant, A., May, K., & Perry, V. (2013). Survival of the fittest: Technical assistance, survival and growth of small businesses and implications for public policy. *Technovation*, *33*(8-9), 292–301. doi:10.1016/j.technovation.2013.06.002

Sood, J., Lynch, P., & Anastasiadou, C. (2017). Community non-participation in homestays in Kullu, Himachal Pradesh, India. *Tourism Management*, *60*, 332–347. doi:10.1016/j.tourman.2016.12.007

Stam, E., & Spigel, B. (2017). Entrepreneural Ecosystems. In R. Blackburn, D. De Clercq, J. Heinonen, & Z. Wang (Eds.), *Handbook of Entrepreneurship and Small Business*. SAGE.

Starec, M. (2022). *Nová zjištění odhalují naprosté selhání česko-polské dohody o dolu Turów [New findings reveal the complete failure of the Czech-Polish agreement on the Turów mine]*. Denik Referendum. https://denikreferendum.cz/clanek/34158-nova-zjisteni-odhaluji-naproste-selhani-ceskopolske-dohody-o-dolu-turow

Startup Blink. (2021). *StartupBlink: Global Startup Ecosystem Index*. Startup Blink. https://www.startupblink.com/startupecosystemreport202

Startup Commons. (n.d.). *What Is Startup Ecosystem?* Startup Commons. www.startupcommons.org/what-is-startup-ecosystem

Statistics Poland. (2022). *Basic data*. Statistics Poland. https://stat.gov.pl/en/basic-data

Stead, D., & Meijers, E. (2009). Spatial Planning and Policy Integration: Concepts, Facilitators and Inhibitors. *Planning Theory & Practice*, *10*(3), 317–332. doi:10.1080/14649350903229752

Stoffelen, A., Ioannides, D., & Vanneste, D. (2017). Obstacles to achieving cross-border tourism governance: A multi-scalar approach focusing on the German-Czech borderlands. *Annals of Tourism Research*, *64*, 126–138. doi:10.1016/j.annals.2017.03.003

Storey, D. J. (1994). *Understanding the Small Business Sector. The Birth of Firms. London*. International Thomson Business Press.

Sütçü, M., Şahin, K. N., Koloğlu, Y., Çelikel, M. E., & Gülbahar, İ. T. (2022). Electricity load forecasting using deep learning and novel hybrid models. *Sakarya University Journal of Science*, *26*(1), 91–104.

SWD. (2021). *Annual Single Market Report 2021*. European Union. https://eur-lex.europa.eu/legal-content/en/TXT/?uri=CELEX%3A52021SC0351

Swiss Economic Institute. (2014). *Press Release, KOF Index of Globalization: Switzerland no Longer Among the Top Ten*. Available from: http://globalization.kof. ethz.ch/media/filer_public/2014/04/16/press_ release_2014_en.pdf

Sycheva, I. N., Chernyshova, O. V., Panteleeva, T. A., Moiseeva, O. A., Chernyavskaya, S. A., & Khout, S. Y. (2019). Human capital as a base for regional development: A case study. *International Journal of Economics & Business Administration*, *7*(1), 595–606. doi:10.35808/ijeba/304

Tamilmani, K., Rana, N. P., Nunkoo, R., Raghavan, V., & Dwivedi, Y. K. (2020). Indian travellers' adoption of Airbnb platform. *Information Systems Frontiers*, 1–20.

Tansley, A. G. (1935). The use and abuse of vegetational concepts and terms. *Ecology*, *16*(3), 284–307. doi:10.2307/1930070

Taylor, P. (2004). *World City Network: A global urban analysis*. doi:10.4324/9780203634059

Temiz, D., & Gökmen, A. (2014). FDI inflow as an international business operation by MNCs and economic growth: An empirical study on Turkey. *International Business Review*, *23*(1), 145–154. doi:10.1016/j.ibusrev.2013.03.003

Tenva. (2015). *Gün öncesi piyasası ve gün içi piyasası karşılaştırması* [Day-ahead market vs. intraday market]. Accessed on 29 June 2022. Available from: https://www.tenva.org/gun-oncesi-piyasasi-ve-gun-ici-piyasasi-karsilastirmasi/

The Entrepreneurial School. (n.d.). *The Entrepreneurial School.* TES Guide. https://www.tesguide.eu/

Thees, H., Pechlaner, H., Olbrich, N., & Schuhbert, A. (2020). The Living Lab as a Tool to Promote Residents' Participation in Destination Governance. *Sustainability, 12*(3), 1120. doi:10.3390u12031120

Thees, H., Zacher, D., & Eckert, C. (2020). Work, life and leisure in an urban ecosystem – co-creating Munich as an Entrepreneurial Destination. *Journal of Hospitality and Tourism Management, 44,* 171–183. doi:10.1016/j.jhtm.2020.06.010

Thierstein, A. (1999). Standortmanagement – Alter Wein in neuen Schläuchen oder wie macht man aus einem Gürtel einen Hosenträger? [Site management—old wine in new bottles or how do you turn a belt into braces?] *Anforderungen an ein zeitgemässes Standortmanagement [Requirements for a modern site management].* https://www.alexandria.unisg.ch/13651/1/idt-stmg.pdf

Thierstein, A. (2002). Von der Raumordnung zur Raumentwicklung [From spatial planning to spatial development]. *disP – The Planning Review, 38*(148), 10-18.

Thorns, D. C. (2002). *The Transformation of Cities: Urban Theory and Urban Life.* Palgrave Macmillan. doi:10.1007/978-1-4039-9031-0

Timothy, D. J., & Boyd, S. W. (2006). Heritage tourism in the 21st century: Valued traditions and new perspectives. *Journal of Heritage Tourism, 1*(1), 1–16.

Tobler, W. (1970). A Computer Movie Simulating Urban Growth in the Detroit Region. *Economic Geography, 46,* 234–240. doi:10.2307/143141

Travel Consul. (2020) *The Impact and Outlook of The COVID-19 Outbreak to Travel Distribution Partners.* Travel Consul. https://rsvp.theworldsbest.events/o7npp.

Treyz, G. I., Rickman, D. S., Hunt, G. L., & Greenwood, M. J. (1993). The dynamics of US internal migration. *The Review of Economics and Statistics, 75*(2), 209–214. doi:10.2307/2109425

Trimble, S.J., Ferran, K., & McDermott, H. (2020). *COVID-19: Pandemic impacts on European city tourism.* https://s3.amazonaws.com/tourism-economics/craft/Latest-Research-Docs/Summary-GCT_corona_regional_RB_EUR-final-TE-PDF.pdf

Tür, M. R. (2019). The scenario of price creation in the electricity market based on micro-grid systems. *Gazi University Journal of Science Part C: Design and Technology, 7*(1), 192–202.

Turystyka w gminie (2022). *Turystyka w gminie Bogatynia [Tourism in the municipality of Bogatynia].* Turystyka w gminie. http://www.turystykawgminie.pl/bogatynia

UA Gov. (n.d.). *Verkhovna Rada of Ukraine.* Government portal. https://zakon.rada.gov.ua/

UA Government. (n.d.). *Ministry of Health and Protection of Ukraine.* Covid19.gov. https://covid19.gov.ua/prohramy-pidtrymky-biznesu

UKR Stat. (n.d.). *State Statistics Service of Ukraine.* UKR Stat. https://www.ukrstat.gov.ua/

Ünal, B. B., Onaygil, S., Acuner, E., & Cin, R. (2022). Application of energy efficiency obligation scheme for electricity distribution companies in Turkey. *Energy Policy, 163,* 112851. doi:10.1016/j.enpol.2022.112851

UNESCO Institute for Statistics. (2009). UNESCO Framework for Cultural Statistics: http://uis.unesco.org/en/glossary-term/cultural-heritage

United Nations. (2022). The 17 Goals – Sustainable Development Goals. UN. https://sdgs.un.org/goals

UNWTO. (2020). *Global guidelines to restart tourism.* UNWTO reports. https://webunwto.s3.eu-west-1.amazonaws.com/s3fs-public/2020-05/UNWTO-Global-Guidelines-to-Restart-Tourism.pdf

UNWTO. (2020). *International tourist numbers down 65% in first half of 2020.* UNWTO reports. https://www.unwto.org/news/international-tourist-numbers-down-65-in-first-half-of-2020-unwto-reports

US Congressional Research Service. (2021). *The United States-Mexico-Canada Agreement.* https://crsreports.congress.gov

US Department of Agriculture. (2021). *Colombia 2021 Export Highlights.* https://www.fas.usda.gov/colombia-2021-export-highlights

US Geological Survey. (2006). *Rates, Trends, Causes, and Consequences of Urban Land-Use Change in the United States.* Professional Paper 1726. Author.

Vachevskyi, M. V., Madzihon, V. M., & Prymachenko, N. M. (2007). *Osnovy ekonomiky: navch. posibnyk [Basics of economy: a tutorial].* Ped. dumka.

Van Bergeijk, P. A. G. (2010). *On the Brink of Deglobalization.* Edward Elgar. doi:10.4337/9781849805803

Van Korff, J., & Maier, K. (2020). *Koncept rozvoje pro mezinárodní rozvojovou oblast Liberec – Žitava: Svazek 1 – Regionální analýza [Concept of development for the international development area Liberec – Zittau: Volume 1 – Regional analysis].* Futour.

Varghese, B., Chennattuserry, J. C., & Kureethara, J. V. (2022). Sinking houseboats and swaying home stays: community resilience and local impacts of COVID-19 in managing tourism crisis in Kerala. *International Journal of Tourism Cities.*

Varsha, V., & Ranjini, S. S. (2020). A Study on the Sustainability of Homestays in Kodagu District after the Disaster-August-2018. *International Journal of Psychosocial Rehabilitation, 24*(05).

Visegrád Post. (2021). *Turów may be bad for the environment, but so is Jänschwalde.* Visegrad. https://visegradpost.com/en/2021/10/25/turow-may-be-bad-for-the-environment-but-so-is-janschwalde

Viter, S. (2012) Vymohy do maibutnikh fakhivtsiv ekonomichnoho profiliu u konteksti pidhotovky dlia ahrarnoi sfery [Requirements for future specialists of the economic profile in the context of training for the agrarian sphere]. *Molod i rynok, 6 (89),*140-145.

Vogelgesang, M., & Stember, J. (2021). Netzwerke, Ebenen und Organisationen der Wirtschaftsförderung [Networks, levels, and organizations of economic development]. In Stember, J., Vogelgesang, M., Pongratz, P. & Fink. A. (Eds.), Handbuch Innovative Wirtschaftsförderung [Handbook for Innovative Business Development] (pp. 97-119). Springer Gabler.

Volgger, M., Pechlaner, H., & Pichler, S. (2017). The practice of destination governance: A comparative analysis of key dimensions and underlying concepts. *Journal of Tourism. Heritage and Services Marketing, 3*(1), 18–24.

Volgger, M., & Pfister, D. (Eds.). (2020). *Atmospheric Turn in Culture and Tourism: Place, Design and Process Impacts on Customer Behaviour, Marketing and Branding.* Emerald Publishing.

Volpe, C., & Gómez, S.G. (2009). *Trade Policy and Export Diversification: What Should Colombia Expect from the FTA with the United States.* IDB working paper series 136.

Vrabková, I. (2013). Quality Management in Public Sector: Perspectives of Common Assessment Framework Model in the European Union. *ACTA VŠFS, 7.*

Walsh, P. (2001). Improving Governments' Response to Local Communities – is Place Management an Answer? *Australian Journal of Public Administration, 60*(2), 3–12. doi:10.1111/1467-8500.00204

Wang, M. Y., Li, X. Y., & Hou, Y. X. (2018). Research on the transformation and upgrading of homestay industry from the perspective of supply-side reform — A case study of Yangshuo. *Journal of Guangxi Cadres College of Economic and Management, 30*(2), 67–73.

Wang, A., & Ramsay, B. (1997). Prediction of system marginal price in the UK Power Pool using neural networks. *Proceedings of International Conference on Neural Networks (ICNN'97)*, 4, 2116-2120. 10.1109/ICNN.1997.614232

Wardwell, J. M. (1977). Equilibrium and Change in Nonmetropolitan Growth. *Rural Sociology, 42*(2), 156–178.

Wegrich, K. (2022). *Public Sector* Encyclopaedia Britannica. https://www.britannica.com/topic/public-sector

Weigl, M., & Zöhrer, M. (2005). Regionale Selbstverständnisse und gegenseitige Wahrnehmung von Deutschen und Tschechen. [Regional self-conceptions and mutual perception of Germans and Czechs.]. CAP.

Wiesner, K. A. (2021). *Professionelles Standort- und Destinationsmanagement: Instrumentarien und Praxisbeispiele für erfolgreiches Place-Management und –Marketing [Professional location and destination management: instruments and practical examples for successful place management and marketing]*. Erich Schmidt Verlag.

Winters, J. V. (2011). Why are smart cities growing? Who moves and who stays. *Journal of Regional Science, 51*(2), 253–270.

Witt, M. A., & Jackson, A. (2016). Varieties of Capitalism and institutional comparative advantage: A test and reinterpretation. *Journal of International Business Studies, 47*(7-2), 778-806.

Witt, M. A. (2019). De-Globalization: Theories, Predictions, and Opportunities for International Business Research. *Journal of International Business Studies, 50*(7), 1053–1107. doi:10.105741267-019-00219-7

World Health Organisation. (2020). *Coronavirus*. WHO. https://www.who.int/health-topics/coronavirus#tab=tab_1

Yazıcı, S. (2020). *Optimization of imbalance costs in electricity market by using electricity generation and price forecasting methods* [Master Thesis]. Istanbul Technical University.

Yigitcanlar, T., Buys, L., & Kamruzzaman, M. (2018, Nov. 28). Just how 'city smart' are local governments in Queensland? *The Conversation.*

Yudantaka, K., Kim, J.-S., & Song, H. (2019). Dual deep learning networks based load forecasting with partial real-time information and its application to system marginal price prediction. *Energies, 13*(1), 148. doi:10.3390/en13010148

Yukseltan, E., Kok, A., Yucekaya, A., Bilge, A., Aktunc, E. A., & Hekimoglu, M. (2022). The impact of the COVID-19 pandemic and behavioral restrictions on electricity consumption and the daily demand curve in Turkey. *Utilities Policy, 76*, 101359. doi:10.1016/j.jup.2022.101359 PMID:35250191

Zadorozhna, N. V. (2013). Formuvannia komunikatyvnoi kompetentnosti u profesiinii pidhotovtsi ekonomistiv [Formation of communicative competence in professional training of economists]. *Neperervna profesiina osvita: teoriia i praktyka [Continuous Professional Education: Theory and Practice], 3-4,* 75-78. http://nbuv.gov.ua/UJRN/NPO_2013_3-4_13 (in Ukr.).

Zakharova, M. A., Mezynov, V. N., & Karpacheva, Y. A. (2017). *Teoriya i praktika formirovaniya konkurentosposobnosti uchitelya v vuze: monografiya [Theory and practice of the teacher competitiveness formation at the university: a monograph]*. EHU ym. Y. A. Bunyna.

Zavalevskyi, Yu. I. (2014) *Teoretyko-metodychni zasady formuvannia vchytelia yak konkurentospromozhnoho fakhivtsia: monohrafiia [Theoretical and methodological principles of the formation of a teacher as a competitive professional: a monograph]*. Bukrek.

Zehra, N. (2011). The Realist State and Deglobalization. Policy Perspectives, 2.

Zijing, X., & Pu, Z. (2020). A Study on Service Quality Evaluation Model of Clustered Homestay. *Journal of Tourism and Hospitality Management*, 8(2), 35–44. doi:10.15640/jthm.v8n2a8

Zimmerbauer, K., & Paasi, A. (2013). When old and new regionalism collide: Deinstitutionalization of regions and resistance identity in municipality amalgamations. *Journal of Rural Studies*, (30), 31–40.

Zittau (2022): *Tagebau Turów bedroht die Menschen in der Dreiländerregion* [Turów Mine threatens people in the Three-border Region]. Zittau. https://zittau.de/de/turow-studie

Żuk, P., & Żuk, P. (2022). The Turów Brown Coal Mine in the shadow of an international conflict: Surveying the actions of the European Union Court of Justice and the populist policies of the Polish government. *The Extractive Industries and Society*, 10.

About the Contributors

Helmuth Yesid Arias Gomez is a lecturer at Masaryk Institute of Advanced Studies of the Czech Technical University in Prague (MUVS-CVUT). He enjoys with the redaction of scientific articles on economic theory, New Economic Geography, Trade Theory, localization of manufacturing activities, industrial economics, theory of firm, Location Theory, Regional and Local development and Regional Science. He has published in Journals of Europe and Latin America. His research procedure combines the GIS techniques and visualizations with econometric tools and statistical computational packages. He is enticed by econometrics and the specialized software. He has experience in handling packages as R, STATA, Rats and E Views. In terms of visualizations and geo-processing he has handled spatial software as Arc MAP, Arc PRO, Arc Scene, R, and has acquired basic skills in the programming of Python. He often visits european universities for teaching, in the framework of ERASMUS program.

Gabriela Antošová, Ph.D., is a member of the Institute of Education and Communication, Czech University of Life Sciences in Prague. Her work has attracted the best research paper awards in the Second International Congress of Innovation and Sustainability in Latin America. She is a research member of the CITUR and Academia Europa Nostra. Research interests: strategic planning, management and tourism development, social innovation process, innovation of internationalization, sustainability.

* * *

Angelo Azueta is a Belizean scholar who received his AA in Business Administration from the University of Belize in 2021. In August 2021, he moved to Jacksonville, Florida, to enroll in a BBA in Finance program at the Coggin College of Business at the University of North Florida (UNF). In August 2022, Azueta was hired as a Supplemental Instructor for Principles of Microeconomics under the Student Academic Success Services at UNF. In collaboration with Dr. Tetiana Momot, his academic mentor, he pursues an interest in fin-tech, researches the integration of smart technology in economies, and is a co-author of Smart City in the Global Economy: Information and Organization Support Development (2022).

Merve Baysoy received her MS in Economics from London School of Economics University in 2014, after that she got her PhD from Koc University in 2020. She was working as teaching assistant and also as a part time instructor at Koc University and Bahcesehir University for international economics and international finance courses. She writes and presents widely on issues of economic growth with spatial concentration using spatial econometrics. She becomes a faculty member in Economics department at Istanbul Bilgi University.

Artur Boháč is an assistant professor at the Department of Geography at the Technical University of Liberec. He holds a PhD in geography from the University of Ostrava and specializes in cultural and political geography. The regions of Central Europe and the Middle East, with a focus on border regions and minorities, are his main interests. Artur Boháč is a member of the European Non-Territorial Autonomy Network and the Borders and Migration Research Group. Numerous Czech geographical magazines have invited him to serve on their editorial boards.

Asli Boru İpek is currently an Assistant Professor in the Department of Management Information System at the Kütahya Dumlupınar University. She holds a MSc degree from Adana Science and Technology University and Çukurova University (Joint Master of Science Program). She received her PhD in Industrial Engineering from Çukurova University. She has studied simulation optimization, metaheuristics, and supply chain management.

Juan Sebastian Castillo-Valero is an associate professor of Economy, Sociology and Agricultural Policy, University of Castilla-La Mancha. He graduated in Economy en University of Valencia and has a PhD (European Doctor) in Agricultural Economics (1997) from University of Castilla-La Mancha. He focuses his research on Management and Performance of Agri-Food Systems, Wine Sector and Social Economy, Agricultural Policy and Rural and Territorial Development.

Juan Pablo Cely Acero is a researcher at the Pedagogical and Technological University of Colombia, CREPIB group, Tunja, Colombia.

Nataliia Dril is a senior lecturer at Department of Entrepreneurship and Business Administration, O.M. Beketov National University of Urban Economy in Kharkiv.

Olena Dymchenko is head of the Department of Entrepreneurship and Business Administration, O.M. Beketov National University of Urban Economy in Kharkiv.

Olena Filonych has a PhD (Economics Sciences), O. M. Beketov National University of Urban Economy in Kharkiv, Doctoral Student of the the Finance, Accounting & Business Security Department of O.M. Beketov National University of Urban Economy, The Educational & Scientific Institute of Economics & Management in Kharkiv, Ukraine. Her research is mainly focused on issues within the areas of economics of construction and urban planning.

María Carmen García Cortijo s a contracted researcher at the Regional Development Institute, University of Castilla-La Mancha. She graduated in Economics Sciences (University of Castilla La Mancha, 2000) and PhD in Computer Engineering (National Distance Education University, 2007). She focuses his research at econometric methods and their application to Agri-Food systems and Rural and Territorial Development.

Adem Gök is currently employed in Department of Economics at Kırklareli University, Turkey as an associate professor. He received his bachelor degree in economics from Boğaziçi University in 2008 and master degree in economics (English) from Marmara University in 2012. He holds a Ph.D in economics (English) from Marmara University since 2016. His research area includes foreign direct investment, growth and development, economics of governance, environmental economics, economics of education and financial economics.

Deniz Güvercin is currently employed in Lincoln International Business School at University of Lincoln, UK as an assistant professor. He received his bachelor degree in economics from Dokuz Eylül University in 2004, master degree in economics from Istanbul Technical University in 2007, master degree in economics from Iowa State University in 2010. He holds a Ph.D in Economics from Istanbul Bilgi University since 2015. His research area includes political economy, development economics and labor economics.

Jesús Heredia-Carroza, PhD., investigates and manages in the cultural economics & leisure and tourism sectors. Nowadays, he is Posdoctoral Researcher of Universidad de Sevilla through the competitive: "Ayudas para la Recualificación del Sistema Universitario Español en su Modalidad Margarita Salas" granted by the Resolución de 29 de noviembre de 2021 of Universidad de Sevilla, financed by the European Union-NextGenerationEU. He is co-founder of the Workshop on Popular Culture Economics and Management, Director of the Social Theory, Politics and, the Arts Conference and, Vicepresident of Fundación. He has published in prestigious journals on cultural participation, copyright and appreciation of intangible cultural heritage.

Olena L. Ilienko has a PhD in Philology, a Doctor of Science in Pedagogy, Full Professor, Head of the Department of Foreign Linguistics and Translation of O.M. Beketov National University of Urban Economy in Kharkiv, Ukraine. Ilienko has 40 years of experience teaching EFL, ESP, Academic English to undergraduate and PhD students. Her interests include methodology of EFL and ESP teaching, pedagogy of higher education, intercultural communication, English as a media of instruction. She is a co-author of two books and developer of tutorials and other teaching materials; organized and presented at many professional trainings of the English teachers' association TESOL-Ukraine. .

Saumya Kapil is a research scholar in Tourism Department of Christ University, Bangalore, India. Her Ph.D. thesis is along the lines of environmental sustainability and tourism. She is an avid reader and a keen participant in various international conferences. She holds a Master's Degree in Travel and Tourism Management from Amity School of Hospitality and a Bachelor's in Arts with a specialization in English Literature and Psychology. Before her current role, she worked as an academic writer. She has a deep interest in water sustainability and community well-being.

Vojtech Kollár, PhD. graduated from Faculty of Chemistry of the Slovak University of Technology in 1973; 1973-1974 Slovak Academy of Science-Applied Chemistry Institute, Bratislava, study stay; 1974-1983 Research Institute of Preventive Medicine, Bratislava, researcher;1983-2019 Faculty of Commerce, University of Economics in Bratislava; 2007-2012 University of Central Europe in Skalica; since 2012 School of Economics and Management in Public Administration in Bratislava. Functions: Head of Department in the Faculty of Commerce of the University of Economics in Bratislava 1989-1993; Vice-Rector for social work of the University of Economics in Bratislava 1991-1992; Vice-Rector for EU Education in Bratislava 1994-2000; Rector of the University of Economics in Bratislava in 2000-2007; Rector of University of Central Europe in Skalica in 2007-2012; Vice-Rector of Bratislava University of Economics and Management in Bratislava since 2013, presently in charge of internal control system.

Researcher and co-researcher of international and national research projects. Scientific activities focus on product management, product policy, quality management, commerce and marketing. He is the author of textbooks and monographs, the author and co-author of more than four hundred scientific articles and papers. As a supervisor of doctoral studies, he trained 15 doctoral students in the field of Branch and Cross-Sectional Economics. He served in the Economic Council of the Government of the Slovak Republic, served as a chairman and member of the Scientific Board of Universities and Colleges in the Slovak Republic and abroad, Chairman of the Board of the CERTIWELD Quality Systems Certification Body, Vice-Chairman of the Slovak Environmental Society in Bratislava, Member of the Commission for Voluntary Environmental Policy Instruments at the Ministry of the Environment of the Slovak Republic.

Joanna Kurowska-Pysz is an associate professor at the WSB University in Dabrowa Gornicza (Poland) and also works there in the position of the Director of the Research Institute on Territorial and Inter-Organizational Cooperation. She is a doctor of economic sciences with a habilitation. Key research topics: public governance, inter-organizational cooperation and territorial cooperation, including the involvement of minorities in cross-border cooperation. She is the author or co-author of more than 150 papers, chapters and monographs. She participates in many international research projects funded mainly by INTERREG, Erasmus Plus, and Horizon 2020. She is a member of ERSA, AMA, Polish Academy of Sciences and international research groups: ARAM (Spain), VALORIZA (Portugal) and LABOTER (Brazil). She was an expert in the EC REGIO (2019-2021). Since 2022 she has been an expert in the EC REGGIO program: b-Solutions.

Ewa Łaźniewska is a senior lecturer at the University of Economics in Poznań (Poland). She deals with issues connected with regional development, innovation, cross-border cooperation and energy. She conducts numerous research projects related, inter alia, to the labor market. She is a member of the RSA Association and an expert evaluator of applications involving the use of digital technologies.

Ignacio Martínez Fernandez, PhD(C)., is Professor in the Department of Economics and Economic History in the University of Seville. During his PhD has been invited researcher in the University Alexandru Ioan Cuza (Iasi, Romania) and the University of Coimbra (Portugal) Has published a variety of papers and chapters of books focusing in the fields of Applied Economics and Economic Analysis.

Silvia Matúšová has a PhD. and graduated in 1974 from Comenius University, Faculty of Arts, major Educational Psychology, minor English language. In 1974-1978 Institute of Experimental Pedagogy, Bratislava; 1978-1991 National Institute for In-service Education of Teachers, Bratislava; 1991-1993 Central Methodical Centre, Bratislava, director, 1994-1996 National Institute of Education, Bratislava, director; 1997-2006 Government Office of the Slovak Republic, Bratislava, director of department and director general of the European Affairs Section; 2006 - 2010 Ministry of Finance of the Slovak Republic, director of the Central Financing and Coordinating Unit; 2010-2017 Catholic University in Ružomberok, university teacher, teaching general psychology, developmental psychology, communication skills, European values in education, researching in international and national projects (focus on knowledge-based society, key competences of teachers, values in teaching profession). Since 2010-present university teacher at Bratislava University of Economics and Management. The supervisor of the Supplementary Pedagogical Study (2013-2019). In bachelor's and master's studies she lectures on integration processes in Europe, public administration, international trade, intercultural management. She lectures in English in the Erasmus + program and the English program. Research activities focus on adult education, online education, human resources development, public administration, regional development. Author and co-author of study texts, monographs, conference papers and articles published in Slovakia and abroad. Member of the Accreditation Council for Continuing Education of Educational and Non-educational Employees at the Ministry of Education, Science, Research and Sports of the Slovak Republic (2011-2016). Since 2019 member of Editorial Board of the Central European Journal of Educational Research, Debrecen (Hungary).

Tetiana Momot is a professor of Economics (Doktor Nauk/DoE) and Chair of the Finance, Accounting & Business Security Department of O.M. Beketov National University of Urban Economy, The Educational & Scientific Institute of Economics & Management in Kharkiv, Ukraine. Since August 2021 she has been appointed as Visiting Professor of Microeconomics in the Department of Economics and Geography in the Coggin College of Business at the University of North Florida (UNF). She researches and presents widely on the amalgamation of economic development, value-creation strategies, microeconomics, corporate governance and the application of the information and analytic methodology in urban economies.

Karel Němejc is the director of the Institute of Education and Communication, Czech University of Life Sciences Prague, and the head of the Department of Pedagogy. His research and lectures are focused mainly on evaluation in education, school management and leadership.

Luis Antonio Palma-Martos, PhD., has researched or taught at 20 foreign universities such as Northwestern University, Goettingen, Poitiers, Firenze, Jagellonian or Iasi. Now, he is Chairman of Competition Policy at the Universidad de Sevilla and Director of the Doctoral Program of Economics, Management and Social Sciences in Universidad de Sevilla. His essays have appeared in the Journal of Cultural Economics, the International Journal of Arts Management or the European Management Review. He has led cultural projects as Estudio de impacto económico de las fiestas de primavera en la ciudad de Sevilla or Estudio de demanda y plan de gestión del proyecto Santa Clara: los espíritus de Sevilla.

Harald Pechlaner is professor and holds the Chair of Tourism / Center for Entrepreneurship at the Catholic University Eichstätt-Ingolstadt, Germany. He is also Head of the Center for Advanced Studies at EURAC Research, Italy. Furthermore, he is Adjunct Research Professor at the School of Management and Marketing, Curtin Business School, Perth, Western Australia. He has been President of AIEST (International Association of Scientific Experts in Tourism) since 2014 and President of the German Association of Tourism Research (Deutsche Gesellschaft für Tourismuswissenschaft e.V.) from 2002 to 2010. His research foci are destination governance and development, regional development and networks, stakeholder management and entrepreneurship.

Julian Philipp is a research associate and PhD Candidate at the Chair of Tourism / Center for Entrepreneurship at the Catholic University of Eichstätt-Ingolstadt, Germany. He holds a master's degree in International Hospitality, Events and Tourism Management from Oxford Brookes University, United Kingdom. Prior to his current role, he worked in different areas such as marketing, event management, consulting and teaching. His research and publications focus on destination governance, destination development, integrated location and destination management, entrepreneurship and entrepreneurial ecosystems, with a particular focus on the role of local identity and identification in the governance of spatial ecosystems and ecosystems of hospitality.

Jan Procházka studied in the Czech Republic, France, and Italy, and graduated in Economics, with his main focus on public policies, transition and development economics, and European Integration, at the Charles University in Prague. At the same University, he completed his Ph.D. in Sports Economics. During his academic life, he has been active as a lecturer in the Czech Republic and the Netherlands, as a guest lecturer or conference participant in several European countries, and at a University in the USA (guest lecturer). Following professional business positions, he added marketing and quality management to his specializations. He can work and teach in seven languages.

Oksana O. Rezvan, Doctor of Science in Pedagogy, Full Professor, Head of the Department of Psyhology, Pedagogy, Language Training of O.M. Beketov National University of Urban Economy in Kharkiv, Ukraine. Has 30 years of experience teaching Pedagogy and Psychology to the students majoring in Philology, Management as well as PhD students. She is interested in pedagogy of higher education, psychological and pedagogical reflection, methods of teaching psychology for PhD, psychology of manipulations in texts and with the consciousness of people; organized and presented at many professional trainings.

Olha Rudachenko has a PhD, and is an assistant professor at Department of Entrepreneurship and Business Administration, O.M. Beketov National University of Urban Economy in Kharkiv

Valentyna Smachylo is an assistant professor at Department of Entrepreneurship and Business Administration, O.M. Beketov National University of Urban Economy in Kharkiv

Russell Triplett is an Associate Professor and Chair of the Department of Economics and Geography at the University of North Florida. He holds a Ph.D. in Economics from the University of North Carolina at Chapel Hill, and he taught previously at Stetson University and Elon University. His primary teaching and research interests are in the areas of international economics, economic development, microeconomic theory, and applied econometrics.

Omar Vargas-González is professor and head of Systems and Computing Department at Tecnologico Nacional de Mexico Campus Ciudad Guzman, professor at Telematic Engineering at Centro Universitario del Sur Universidad de Guadalajara with a master degree in Computer Systems. Has been trained in Innovation and Multidisciplinary Entrepreneurship at Arizona State University (2018) and a Generation of Ecosystems of Innovation, Entrepreneurship and Sustainability for Jalisco course by Harvard University T.H. Chan School of Health. At present conduct research on diverse fields such as Entrepreneurship, Economy, Statistics, Mathematics and Information and Computer Sciences. Has colaborated in the publication of over 20 scientific articles and conducted diverse Innovation and Technological Development projects.

José G. Vargas-Hernández has an M.B.A. and a Ph.D. ORC ID 0000-0003-0938-4197; ResearcherID A-8344-2016 G6347-2017 Research professor at Instituto Tecnológico Mario Molina Unidad Zapopan, before at University Center for Economic and Managerial Sciences, University of Guadalajara. Member of the National System of Researchers of Mexico. Professor Vargas-Hernández has a Ph. D. in Public Administration and a Ph.D. in Organizational Economics. He has been visiting scholar at Carleton University Canada, University of California Berkeley and Laurentian University, Canada. He holds a Ph.D. in Economic, Keele University; Ph.D. in Public Administration, Columbia University; studies in Organizational Behavior at Lancaster University and has a Master of Business Administration; published nine books and more than 300 papers in international journals and reviews (some translated to English, French, German, Portuguese, Farsi, Chinese, etc.) and more than 300 essays in national journals and reviews. He has obtained several international Awards and recognitions. He has also experience in consultancy. His main research is in organizational economics and strategic management. He teaches for several doctoral programs.

Bindi Varghese is a Doctorate in commerce, specializing in tourism. As an academician and tourism professional, she has over 20 years of Academic experience. Currently, she is affiliated with Christ University, as an Associate Professor and is the Research Coordinator at School of Business Studies and Social Sciences. She has served many educational institutions in South India and has served as a national and international expert, for a decade among the educational institutions of India. Currently, she is actively associated with Indian Tourism Congress (ITC) and Honorary Director at Kerala Development Society (KDS), New Delhi. The active researches undertaken include Impact Assessment Studies, Medical Tourism, Destination Management Organization and Ecological Studies. Dr. Bindi completed a major research project on the title "Strategic Intervention of Destination Management Organizations to Enhance Competitiveness of Tourism Destinations– A Model for Karnataka" funded by Christ University. Along with her academic expertise, she is also an Section editor for 'ATNA- Journal of Tourism Studies', published by Christ University, Bengaluru. She has authored one book; on Medical Tourism in India: by an international publisher in Germany, and has also contributed chapters to edited books and has published several articles in areas of Destination Management, Governance, Medical Tourism, E-Tourism etc. To her credit, she has edited a book on "Evolving Paradigms in Tourism and Hospitality in Developing Countries: A Case Study of India". The book is published by CRC Press, Taylor and Francis group - international publisher in US and released in 2018.

Index

A

Agglomeration 1, 5-6, 8-9, 11, 13-15, 109, 134, 242-246, 248-251, 253, 255, 295
Agriculture 2-3, 29, 81, 162, 227, 238, 243-244, 247, 252, 280-282, 284-285, 288, 290, 293-297
Agritourism 242-244, 247, 253-254
Annual Crops 283, 297
ARDL 205, 209-211, 213-214
Associated Tourism Elements 245-246, 249, 254
Asymmetry 127-128, 130, 134, 140, 142, 146

B

Balancing Power Market 226, 228-229, 231-232
Border Effect 128-129, 138, 146

C

CAF 168-181
Career Centers 47
Central or Main Town 111
City Development 75, 268, 271, 277-278
City Management 70, 75, 259-260, 275
Cluster Analysis 19-20, 36, 42-43
Clustered Homestay 242-243, 254-255
Clustering 11, 18, 20, 228-229, 307
Commuters 16, 137
Competitive Professional 47, 50, 54-57, 62-65, 67-68
Competitiveness 27, 47-51, 54-68, 77, 86, 147-148, 165, 167, 181, 245, 252, 258, 261, 265-266, 270, 274, 276, 283-284, 288, 290, 294, 303
Components of Competitiveness 47, 54-55
Concentrated Animal Feeding Operations (CAFO) 297
Connectivity 83, 183, 197, 251, 299
Consumption-Led Growth 205, 207, 224
Coronavirus Crisis 94, 105
Covid-19 79, 94-102, 104-105, 107, 121-123, 141, 145, 149, 240, 251, 254, 310

Cross

Cross-Border Cooperation 128-130, 133, 136, 140-142, 144-146
Cultural Heritage 96, 116-124, 246-247
Czech Republic 1, 41, 94-95, 97-103, 105, 126-127, 129-131, 133-135, 137-139, 143-144, 146, 151, 156-157, 164, 168, 173, 175-181, 280

D

Departamento Administrativo Nacional de Estadística (DANE) 297
Destination Development 70
Destination Management 70-74, 76, 78, 81, 84, 86, 89-92, 96, 99
Determinism 126-127, 146
Digitization and Tourism Sustainability 105

E

Economic Deglobalization 298-299, 301-302, 304-305, 308, 312
Ecosystem of Hospitality 70, 83-84, 86-87, 89-90
Education Market 158, 167
EFQM 168, 173, 180-181
EIPA 169-170, 172-174, 176-181
Energy Market 225-226, 228, 232, 240
Ensemble-Based Method 225, 227, 230, 240
Entrepreneurship 18, 20-21, 23-24, 26-31, 33-35, 42-45, 74, 81-82, 84, 90-92, 103, 123, 135, 160
Export-Led Growth 205, 224
Externality 199

F

FDI-Led Growth 205, 218, 220, 222-224
FPI-Led Growth 205, 224

G

Geographic Information Systems 14, 280
Geographical Periphery 146
German Interest in Travelling 101, 105
Global Startup Ecosystem Index 18-20, 36, 46
Government Intervention 242-243, 245, 249, 251, 255
Growth Spillovers 183
GRP 34, 46

H

Hedonic Models 107
Hedonic Population Model 108, 115
Homestay Business 242, 244, 247-248, 254
Hosts 74, 255

I

Important Resource Market 95, 105
Inbound Tourism 94-95, 97-103, 105
Increasing returns 2-3, 9-10, 12-16, 113, 198, 223
Industrial Agglomeration 9, 242, 295
Innovation Potential 147-148, 158, 166-167
Innovation Potential as Composite Indicator 167
Innovation Scoreboard 147-148, 151, 153, 156-157, 166-167
Instituto Geográfico Agustín Codazzi (IGAC) 297
Interdependence 22, 77, 183-184, 187-188, 191-192, 197-199, 301, 304, 306
Intra-Rural Dynamic 107
Intra-Rural Movement 115
Investment-Led Growth 205, 223-224
ISTAT 10-11, 15-16, 111-112, 115

J

Job Requirements 47

K

Keynesian Model 206, 223-224
K-Nearest Neighbors 225, 231, 240

L

Labour Market 48, 118, 148-149, 158, 166-167
Living Space 61, 70-76, 78, 80-81, 83, 85, 89-90, 93
Local Community 85, 242-243, 245-249, 251, 255
Localism 298, 309, 312
Location Development 77, 90

Location Management 71-72, 75, 89
Location Theory 1-2, 8, 15

M

Machine Learning 225, 227-228, 231-232, 236-238, 240
Main Town 107, 111, 115
Market Clearing Price 226, 237, 239
Marshallian Externalities 1, 6, 14
Marshallian Industrial Districts 16
Municipality 11, 110-111, 115, 132, 135, 137-138, 145, 168, 176, 293, 297
MV ČR 181

N

Nationalism 298-300, 304, 309, 312
Neighbourhood Effects 183-184, 197
Neo-Environmental Determinism 126-127, 146
New Economic Geography (NEG) 1, 8, 12-16, 109, 127
New Tourism Segments 105
New Trade Theory (NTT) 12, 16
Next Generation EU 124

P

Pecuniary Externalities 1-2, 14, 16
Perennial Crops 281-282, 284, 287, 295, 297
Periphery 8-9, 12, 107, 109-110, 115, 126-128, 131, 140, 146, 248
Place Management 70, 74-75, 79-81, 84-85, 92-93
Population Movements 107-110, 112, 115
Populism 298-299, 309, 311-312
Principle of Complementarity 55, 68
Process of Competitiveness Development 68
Production Factor 5, 242-243, 245, 248-249, 255, 288
Professional Competences 54, 58, 64-65
Professional Requirements by the Employers in Modern Urban Economy 68
Project Management 53, 94
Public Policy 11, 45, 112, 240
Public Sector 85, 168-174, 176-177, 180-181, 251, 255
Public Service 53, 168, 179
Pure Externalities 16

R

Racism 312
Regional Development 13, 75-77, 81, 90-93, 97, 102-103, 124, 142, 175, 181, 306

Regional Disparities 147-148, 159, 166-167
Regional Economy 73, 86, 116
Regional Growth 14, 183, 190, 197
Regionalism 109, 113, 115, 298, 302, 305, 309, 312
Renewal of Tourism 100, 106
Rural Areas 28, 44, 88, 107-109, 247
Rural District 108-110, 112, 115

S

Scientific and Methodical System 47-48, 62, 64
Self-Assessment 55-57, 64, 168-169, 174-175, 180
Smart City 79, 91, 257-263, 265-278
Smart City Balanced Scorecard (SCBS) 257, 269, 275, 278
Smart City Information and Organization Support Model 257, 278
Smart City Key Performance Indicators (KPIs) 278
Smart City Strategy 262, 265-266, 268-269, 275, 277-278
Socioeconomic Asymmetry 142, 146
Solow Growth Theory 206, 224
Spatial Econometrics 14, 183-184, 192-194, 198
Spatial Weighting Matrices 184, 191-192
Specialization 1-3, 9, 11-16, 51, 282, 287
Spillover 183-184, 186-187, 191, 194, 196-197, 199, 243, 255
Startup Ecosystem by Levels 24
Startup Ecosystems 18-20, 36, 42-43
Support of Changes 94

Support of German Inbound Tourism 105
Support Vector Machines 225, 227, 238, 240
System Marginal Price 225, 237-240

T

Technological Interdependencies 183, 186, 189
Technology of Competitiveness 68
Territorial Protrusion 146
The Sensitivity of German Consumers 101, 106
Theme-Based Circuits 245-246, 249, 251, 255
Third National Agricultural Census 2014 297
Three-Border Region 126-127, 129-131, 134, 136-137, 139, 141-142, 145-146
TQM 169-170, 173, 175, 180-181
Training Program 47, 55
Turoszów Spur 126-131, 134, 137-138, 140-142

U

UNESCO 116-117, 124-125
Urban Economy 5, 18, 20, 24-25, 47-48, 51-58, 60-65, 68, 264, 266

W

Weighting 184, 191-192, 196, 198-199, 267

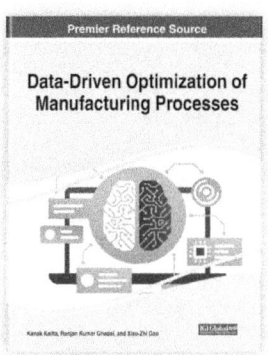

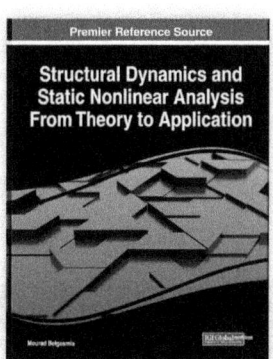

Ensure Quality Research is Introduced to the Academic Community

Become an Evaluator for IGI Global Authored Book Projects

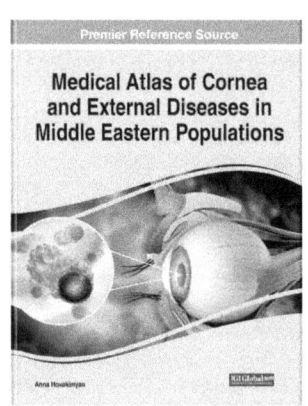

The overall success of an authored book project is dependent on quality and timely manuscript evaluations.

Applications and Inquiries may be sent to:
development@igi-global.com

Applicants must have a doctorate (or equivalent degree) as well as publishing, research, and reviewing experience. Authored Book Evaluators are appointed for one-year terms and are expected to complete at least three evaluations per term. Upon successful completion of this term, evaluators can be considered for an additional term.

If you have a colleague that may be interested in this opportunity, we encourage you to share this information with them.